www.wadsworth.com

wadsworth.com is the World Wide Web site for Wadsworth and is your direct source to dozens of online resources.

At *wadsworth.com* you can find out about supplements, demonstration software, and student resources. You can also send email to many of our authors and preview new publications and exciting new technologies.

wadsworth.com
Changing the way the world learns®

Learning and Memory

Second Edition

JESSE E. PURDY
Southwestern University

MICHAEL R. MARKHAM
Florida International University

BENNETT L. SCHWARTZ
Florida International University

WILLIAM C. GORDON
University of New Mexico

Australia • Canada • Mexico • Singapore • Spain • United Kingdom • United States

Executive Editor: *Vicki Knight*
Senior Editor: *Marianne Taflinger*
Assistant Editor: *Jennifer Wilkinson*
Signing Representative: *Miguel Ortiz*
Project Editor: *Pam Suwinsky*
Print Buyer: *Mary Noel*
Permissions Editor: *Bob Kauser*

Production Service: *Proof Positive/Farrowlyne Associates, Inc.*
Art Editor: *Roberta Broyer*
Cover Designer: *Jennifer Dunn*
Cover Images: *PhotoDisc*
Cover Printer: *R. R. Donnelley & Sons*
Compositor: *Black Dot Group*
Printer: *R. R. Donnelley & Sons*

For permission to use material from this text, contact us by Web: *http://www.thomsonrights.com*
Fax: 1-800-730-2215
Phone: 1-800-730-2214

Library of Congress Cataloging-in-Publication Data
Learning and memory.—2nd ed. / Jesse E. Purdy . . . [et al.].
    p. cm.
  Rev. ed. of: Learning and memory / William C. Gordon, c1989.
  Includes bibliographical references (p.) and indexes.
  ISBN 0-534-16914-7
  1. Learning, Psychology of. 2. Memory. 3. Conditioned response. I. Purdy, Jesse E. II. Gordon, William C. Learning and memory.

BF318.G67 2000
153.1—dc21   00-034043

  ISBN (pbk.) 0-534-63354-4

For more information, contact:
Wadsworth/Thomson Learning
10 Davis Drive
Belmont, CA 94002-3098
USA
http://www.wadsworth.com

International Headquarters
Thomson Learning
International Division
290 Harbor Drive, 2nd Floor
Stamford, CT 06902-7477
USA

UK/Europe/Middle East/South Africa
Thomson Learning
Berkshire House
168-173 High Holborn
London WC1V 7AA
United Kingdom

Asia
Thomson Learning
60 Albert Street, #15-01
Albert Complex
Singapore 189969

Canada
Nelson Thomson Learning
1120 Birchmont Road
Toronto, Ontario M1K 5G4
Canada

To Dr. Henry A. Cross, Jr.,
mentor and friend
—Jesse E. Purdy

To my wife, Leslie D. Frazer
—Bennett L. Schwartz

Contents

Preface

We live in an age of information overload. We have driven the information highway, and it is clear that the accumulation of information is growing exponentially. As a consequence it is becoming more and more difficult to keep current. The days of the Renaissance person may be ending; it may no longer be possible to be an expert and excel in multiple fields of investigation. Psychology is no exception. Indeed, the U.S. Congress declared the 1990s to be the "Decade of the Brain," and it appears that the first decade of the new millennium will be named the "Decade of Behavior." These designations have had and will have an enormous impact on psychological science. The result will be an even greater increase in the number of psychological journals and the number of published papers in psychology. As the amount of information increases, our ability to access, then filter this information becomes critical. There are now ways to access information that were not available 10 years ago. We have instant access to vast sources of information through the Internet, but easy access to information is causing problems. How are we to discriminate between good information and bad? How do we sift through vast amounts of information and make sense of what we see? The answers lie in our ability to critically read and make informed decisions about the quality of the evidence and the methods by which that evidence was obtained.

CRITICAL READING, CRITICAL THINKING

This text is designed to help the student critically read and understand theoretical positions and to assess and interpret data in light of their theoretical implications. My colleagues and I have taken a subtle approach. We will present both sides of an issue, and we will consider the evidence for each position. We will approach issues from a historical perspective, and we will examine how the evidence has changed the questions that are asked and how theoretical positions are changed in light of new evidence. Often in this book the students may express concern because we will spend a fair amount of time considering a position only to conclude that a new theory is needed or that a new theory needs to be tested more thoroughly. Students may ask or demand that they simply be given the answer. The problem, of course, is that there may not be simple answers. Science moves forward, but its progress is not always evident. Thus, it is important for students to know that the study of learning and memory in psychological science is a work in progress. We have learned much, but we have much to learn. This text is designed to inform students about what we know and how we know it. But the text is also written with the goal that the student finishes the course knowing that it is only through the continued application of the scientific method that further progress can be made.

HOW BIOLOGY CONSTRAINS LEARNING

It would have been possible for my colleagues and I to write a book of this length with no reference earlier than 1990, but that would have been a mistake. Many of the important discoveries concerning the role of reinforcement in determining behavior were made 40 or more years ago, and much of the current literature builds on the foundation of those earlier studies. Indeed, many of today's theories rest on earlier theoretical positions, and these theories are often best understood in historical light. For example, to understand the current emphasis on biological constraints on learning and the adaptive role that learning plays in the life of an organism, it is important to remember that in the 1940s and 1950s learning was studied more or less as an end in and of itself. Most researchers in the 1940s and 1950s were not concerned with the role of evolutionary history in what an organism learned or remembered. Many of the apparatuses and most of the stimuli used in the study of learning and memory were designed to reduce the influence of evolutionary and ecological variables. This made sense because the current theme at the time was the belief that the general laws of learning transcended evolutionary history. As a result of this perception, working with a large number of species and worrying about the effects of the animal's evolutionary history and its ecological niche was viewed as nonproductive. However, with the finding that some animals can associate certain stimuli more easily than others and that in other species the opposite is true, there was renewed interest in understanding learned behavior in the context of the organism's evolutionary and ecological background.

COMPREHENSIVE AND APPLIED

In writing this book, my colleagues and I faced difficult problems. We wanted the book to be comprehensive. We wanted to present discoveries and theoretical positions in a historical light and show how they changed as a result of more and better data. We wanted to provide students with a solid foundation of terminology and theory upon which they could begin to appreciate the depth of understanding already achieved, as well as an appreciation for the direction of future research. Finally, we wanted to provide a foundation for students to continue their study of learning and memory and to enhance their appreciation for the role that learning and memory play in all aspects of psychology. This latter goal was critical: Knowledge of learning and memory can help practicing clinicians devise effective therapy strategies. It also can inform educational psychologists of the means by which material is acquired and retained and provide insight into the best ways to present material. Knowledge of learning and memory can help the social psychologist understand how changes in attraction, prejudice, and attitude can occur, and it can help human factors engineers understand how to build safer and more efficient machines.

BLENDS ANIMAL AND HUMAN RESEARCH IN A WAY THAT'S BASIC AND APPLIED

In light of these emphases, this edition of *Learning and Memory* is a comprehensive text that combines current with classic research and includes a unique chapter 7 that bridges learning and memory by discussing the roles that stimulus generalization and discrimination learning play in concept formation in human and nonhuman animals. The text offers also an innovative blend of animal and human research that is both basic and applied. For example, basic research with animals includes comprehensive discussion of the observing response literature and sign tracking as well as extensive treatment of recent theories of classical conditioning by Wagner and others. Basic research with humans is considered in the discussions on concept formation as well as discussion of short-term and long-term memory. Applications of basic research in learning are considered in discussions of the role of classical conditioning in drug abuse and aversion therapies as well as the role of operant techniques in treating autism. Applications of basic research in memory are considered in discussions of false and repressed memories, amnesia, eyewitness memory, and memory practice and mnemonic improvement. My colleagues and I also made the text student friendly by providing examples and stories that introduce topics in ways that are easy to grasp and that are relevant and appropriate for students. Chapter 7 opens with a scenario in which a researcher, having been awarded a federal grant to observe vervet monkeys in the wild, discovers the communication abilities of vervets as they encounter different predatory threats. In addition, the text includes many examples and figures, which not only serve as visual counterpoint but also help make the text easier to read and comprehend.

RESOURCES FOR TEACHERS AND STUDENTS

Wadsworth Publishing Company has made available several resources for the instructor and the student. These resources supplement the text, bring the material to life for the student, assist the student in the course, and reduce the instructor's teaching load by providing a test bank that contains numerous questions of varying formats. In addition, the test bank provides a description of Wadsworth's popular software package "Sniffy, the Virtual Rat." This interactive software program allows students enrolled in institutions with or without operant conditioning labs to learn in a hands-on manner how to shape an animal to perform an operant task and the basics of classical conditioning. Depending on the package you choose, the program supports 16 to 40 separate exercises that teach the student the basics of operant and classical conditioning. Students learn to shape a virtual rat to press a bar for virtual cheese. They learn about cumulative records, schedules of reinforcement, and more complex behavioral phenomena including generalization and discrimination learning, extinction, and spontaneous recovery. In the exercises on classical conditioning, students learn about basic acquisition and extinction of a conditioned response, the effects of varying the strength of the CS and US, pre-exposure effects, blocking and overshadowing, and others.

Students enjoy training Sniffy to perform in an operant and classical conditioning setting, and they learn from the various exercises. We do not propose that Sniffy should be substituted for actual experience with live animals. However, in many institutions there is no other option. For these schools, Sniffy is a must to bring to life the material in this book. For programs that have an animal laboratory component associated with this course, Sniffy provides a good starting place for teaching students about conditioning animals. The instructor's manual that accompanies this text outlines the various exercises available from the Sniffy programs and shows where the material is covered in the text. Through Sniffy, students are able to see and experience what they have read, and they obtain a better sense of what life in a learning laboratory might be like. For more ideas about how to use Sniffy in courses, call the Wadsworth Marketing Department at 1-877-999-2350 to request a six-minute video.

Another resource offered by Wadsworth is Info Trac College Edition. Info Trac is a fully searchable online university library that includes the full text of articles from hundreds of scholarly and popular publications. Hot linked, expertly indexed, and ready to use, Info Trac College Edition is updated daily with articles going back as far as four years. You can give your students four months' access—24 hours a day, 7 days a week—to this online library if you choose to package Info Trac College Edition with this book. Included among the large number of journals available to the student and that would be of interest to students enrolled in a course in learning and memory are the *American Journal of Psychology, American Scientist, Annual Review of Psychology, British Journal of Psychology, Ecological Monographs, Ecology, Journal of Cognitive Neuroscience, Journal of Experimental Education, Journal of General Psychology, Journal of Neuroscience, Journal of Social Psychology, Psychological Record, Quarterly Review of Biology*, and *Science*.

ACKNOWLEDGMENTS

We deeply appreciate the following colleagues, who reviewed the manuscript at various stages and whose comments and suggestions were extremely helpful: Paul Amrhein, University of New Mexico; Barbara Basden, California State University-Fresno; Richard Block, Montana State University; Joshua Blustein, Beaver College; James Brennan, Loyola University-Chicago; Marion Cohn, Ohio Dominican College; Stephen Coleman, Cleveland State University; Thomas Cunningham, Seattle University; Charles Grah, Austin Peay State University; David Hogberg, Albion College; David Pittenger, Marietta College; Randolph A. Smith, Ouachita Baptist University; Dale Swartzentruber, Ohio Wesleyan University; Cedric Williams, University of Virginia; and Thomas Zentall, University of Kentucky.

SUMMARY STATEMENTS

The second edition of *Learning and Memory* was written by authors who are experts in the areas of learning and memory and whose experience teaching undergraduate courses in learning and memory total more than 50 years. The text has been updated and expanded. It offers many more references and new topics including a section on punishment and behavioral systems theory. The text also includes a new chapter on the interaction of classical and operant conditioning and the chapter on verbal learning has been omitted. Finally, the text is much more biologically oriented and attempts to couch the topics of learning and memory within the total ecological and evolutionary history of the animal. In this vein we include sections that address which areas of the brain underlie the various components of learning and memory.

We have enjoyed writing this book, and we believe students will enjoy reading it.

About the Authors

Dr. Jesse E. Purdy received his B.S. in psychology in 1974, his M.S. in general-experimental psychology in 1976, and his Ph.D. in 1978 from Colorado State University. He graduated with an emphasis in comparative psychology. He currently holds the title Brown Distinguished Research Professor and chairs the Department of Psychology at Southwestern University, where he has been since 1978.

Dr. Purdy has an active research program that extensively involves undergraduate students. With his students he has authored and co-authored more than 30 articles and made more than 40 conference presentations. His work is primarily carried out at Southwestern University's Aquatic Animal Research Laboratory, a facility that houses both fresh water and salt water organisms. The focus of his work is on basic animal learning processes in aquatic animals, where he continues to explore the mechanisms of learning involved in sign tracking in goldfish and cuttlefish. He is also interested in questions relating to optimal foraging, defensive behaviors, and predator-prey interactions in aquatic animals. His work with cuttlefish has been highlighted on the Discovery Channel's *World of Wonder*.

Dr. Purdy has been active in several professional organizations, including the Southwestern Comparative Psychology Association, the Southwestern Psychological Association, and Psi Chi. He served on the board of directors for SCPA and he served as president of SWPA. He is currently president-elect of Psi Chi, the national honor society in psychology.

Dr. Michael R. Markham is Assistant Professor of Psychology at Florida International University. He received his B.A. from the University of New Mexico in 1990 and his Ph.D. in psychology from the University of New Mexico in 1994. His courses include Introduction to the Experimental Analysis of Behavior, Biological Psychology, and Theories of Learning. His research interests focus on interactions of Pavlovian conditioning and stimulus classes in humans and nonhuman animals.

Bennett L. Schwartz is an Associate Professor of Psychology at Florida International University in Miami, Florida. He received his Ph.D. in psychology from Dartmouth College in 1993. He has published papers on memory, metacognition, and the tip-of-the-tongue phenomenon in journals such as *Journal of Experimental Psychology: Learning, Memory, and Cognition, Memory & Cognition,* and *Memory.* He has taught Memory and Cognitive Psychology at FIU since 1993. He recently became the proud father of an infant daughter, Sarina.

1

An Introduction to Learning and Memory

CHAPTER OVERVIEW

For most living organisms, learning and remembering are integral to the organism's survival. For animals, this means the ability to remember where food is located and learn where predators may be lurking. For humans, it also means the ability to learn to talk, read, write, drive a car, and operate a computer. Even if we humans did somehow survive until now without the ability to learn or remember, our lives would be empty movements from one moment to the next without any past or future, and we would be doomed to repeat the same behaviors, whether or not those behaviors were useful. Learning and memory are processes that are critically important for living organisms, and, for us as humans, learning and memory also are at the core of our experience of life.

Beyond the sheer necessity of learning and memory for our survival lies the fact that learning and memory are fascinating processes; they are interesting areas of study in their own right. For example, did you know that certain responses of your immune system may be learned (Ader & Cohen, 1993)? Have you ever wondered just how accurate your memory is? For instance, some researchers study the formation and retrieval of "flashbulb memories" (Brown & Kulik, 1977). Flashbulb memories refer to extremely confident personal memories that are triggered by their association with important news events, such as the sudden death of a well-known person. These memories sometimes are not as accurate as the person may think. In addition, people's expanding knowledge of learning and memory has resulted in the development of ways to improve everyday life. For example, increased knowledge of learning processes has produced effective treatments for anxiety, and memory psychologists frequently testify in court concerning the reliability of eyewitness memory.

The purpose of this chapter is to provide a broad introduction to the study of learning and memory. Not only do we plan to demonstrate how interesting this area of study is and show that learning and memory are important processes, we will also introduce four themes that will help organize and integrate the many different topics covered in this text. We begin by looking at the broad scope of learning and memory.

VARIETIES OF LEARNING AND MEMORY

When some people think about learning, they picture themselves in a classroom studying new concepts or trying new skills, such as computer programming. Learning in other species may involve simply teaching our pets to perform new tricks. Similarly, when some people think of memory, they think of remembering the capital of Ecuador for a geography exam or a friend's phone number. These certainly are situations that involve learning and memory. However, these examples do not begin to capture the numerous varieties of learning and memory situations or the pervasive roles that learning and memory play in the lives of most species.

Learning and memory occur in a wide variety of situations and can have a wide variety of effects, some that are not immediately apparent. Learning and memory occur in many species and many situations: For example, honeybees must remember the location of blossoming flowers, chimpanzees must remember which are members of the same group, human infants must learn to walk, and eventually may learn to drive a car, use a computer, and write essays. In this section, we will look at the learning situations that have received the most attention from psychologists. These by no means exhaust the types of situations in which learning may occur; rather they are the categories that have been studied most extensively. Learning and memory probably result from a variety of processes.

Within the area of learning, we will first offer for consideration simpler forms of learning, such as habituation and sensitization. We will then add two more learning situations: classical conditioning and instrumental conditioning. We will then discuss the most-studied systems of memory and the processes that serve them, namely, short-term and long-term memory and the processes of encoding, storage, representation and retrieval. In the face of this variety, however, we will find that there are features common to all these instances of learning and memory.

The goals in the study of learning have been to determine the variables that affect the learning process, to formulate laws of learning based on these effects, to devise theories of learning that can accommodate these laws, and to suggest applications. This has been a monumental task, given that learning occurs in so many species and in so many different situations. For this reason, researchers have found it helpful to categorize learning situations into different types and to study each type of situation separately. One of the major goals of memory research has been to identify whether certain variables affect different processes of memory differently. When there are many variables that affect each process differently, researchers often categorize them as different memory systems.

Habituation and Sensitization

Although people are often aware of learning something new or remembering what they have already learned, learning and remembering can also occur without awareness. For example, when was the last time you heard the sound of your refrigerator? Household refrigerators normally turn on and off several times each day, yet who notices the sound of the refrigerator? This is not because the sound is too soft, because if you are listening, you can easily hear it. People usually don't notice the sound of refrigerators because of a process called habituation. Habituation is a decrease in responding to a stimulus that is presented repeatedly and that is not associated with events of biological significance to the animal. For the moment, we will define a stimulus as any object or event that might affect behavior. Habituation occurs quite frequently, and it is often described as "getting used to," or "learning to ignore," certain odors, sounds, or other sensations. An interesting feature of habituation is that humans learn through habituation every day, although we are rarely aware of this learning.

Another learning process that sometimes goes unnoticed is sensitization, which occurs when organisms become overresponsive to mild stimuli after presentation of an intense stimulus. Imagine that you are driving along the interstate. Traffic is heavy, although it is moving at a good pace. Suddenly, a large semitrailer coming from the other direction crosses the median and heads directly toward your car. You watch in amazement as the truck hits a sharp embankment and catapults end over end over your car. Once you have recovered and continue down the interstate, you notice things you have not observed in a long time. You are more aware than you have ever been of cars that pull up close behind you, the sounds of traffic, and the feel of the wheel. As in the case of habituation, sensitization sometimes occurs without awareness.

Habituation and sensitization work hand in hand. Groves and Thompson (1970) proposed that habituation and sensitization are two processes that are responsible for decreasing or increasing responsiveness to stimuli. Sometimes the habituation process predominates and the organism's responses to a stimulus declines. At other times, the sensitization process predominates and the organism's responses to a stimulus increases. The system, then, is designed to maintain a balanced response to stimuli.

Classical Conditioning

Certain events in the environment reliably precede other more significant events. Lightning regularly precedes thunder, and a growling dog often precedes a painful bite. Through the process of classical conditioning, organisms learn to react in particular ways to events that reliably precede other significant events. Organisms also learn that certain stimuli predict other stimuli of biological significance to them. Classical conditioning demonstrates how changes in the environment affect an organism's behavior.

In classical conditioning, organisms learn to make reflexive or involuntary responses to stimuli that do not naturally produce such responses. It is known, for example, that painful stimuli naturally elicit a range of internal reactions that collectively are called fear responses. We also know

that direct physical stimulation of a certain type will naturally produce sexual arousal. Still, it is obvious that fear and sexual arousal can be elicited by any number of stimuli that do not produce these responses reflexively. For some people, fear reactions occur whenever they enter a physician's office. Others exhibit fear in elevators, on airplanes, or in classrooms. The same is true for sexual arousal; it can occur in response to a photograph or to the smell of perfume. It can be elicited by words, thoughts, or sometimes, even by articles of clothing.

The importance of classical conditioning should be evident: Through this type of learning organisms are able to make appropriate responses to important stimuli, even though the stimuli do not produce these responses naturally. This learning can affect immune systems, allergies, emotional reactions, and may even contribute to drug tolerance. Through classical conditioning humans may also come to respond in a maladaptive fashion if their reflexive responses become attached to inappropriate stimuli, as is the case in certain anxiety disorders. Research into classical conditioning has focused on the conditions necessary for this type of learning to occur. It has also centered on the variables that affect the rate and strength of conditioning.

Instrumental Conditioning

Instrumental conditioning is the process by which the consequences of behavior determine how organisms behave in the future. Organisms tend to repeat activities that are followed by certain events (for example, a cat conceals itself in the underbrush so that it can strike at birds without being seen), and organisms tend to refrain from activities that have unpleasant results.

Examples of instrumental conditioning occur every day. Children learn appropriate social behaviors through trial and error. When they behave correctly they are often praised; inappropriate behaviors are often punished. As a result of the consequences of their behavior, children begin to exhibit more and more responses that adults deem appropriate. Humans learn to perform a variety of motor skills in the same way. Whether learning to swing a golf club, to ride a bicycle, or to write in cursive, humans begin by making responses that are altered depending on the consequences, and, in turn provide consequences to modify the behaviors of others. Instrumental conditioning research examines how consequences of certain kinds alter behavior. It is also concerned with how these consequences can best be arranged to promote efficient learning.

Short-Term Memory

The term *memory* concerns with how items that have been learned are stored and later retrieved. Most researchers make a basic distinction between two kinds of memory—short-term and long-term. Short-term memory allows humans to maintain information over a short period of time; whereas long-term memory allows information to be maintained over very long periods of time. Each system works by a set of processes that allow learning, storage, and retrieval to take place. Let us consider short-term memory first.

You may recently have looked up a phone number in the Yellow Pages and, having found it, read it once and closed the book. Then you dialed the number. If asked for the phone number several minutes later, it is unlikely that you would remember it. The storage and retrieval of information over these very short delays is called short-term memory. According to many theorists, short-term memory operates according to different principles than does long-term memory. Short-term memory appears to serve several functions for the organism. First, it allows the retention of information that will be needed in the next few seconds. Second, it may serve as a "workspace" for thinking (Baddeley, 1986). In this workspace, people not only retain information but also solve problems, think, and make decisions. For example, when cooking, short-term memory may hold the knowledge that you have added salt, but not pepper, to your soup. When people do mental arithmetic, the problem and any partial solution to the problem is stored in short-term memory until it is completed. The active contents of thought are also hypothesized to reside in short-term memory.

Short-term memory is a technical term that has entered popular usage. However, it is important to distinguish its popular usage from its technical usage. In technical terms, short-term memory is a hypothetical system that holds a limited amount of information for a very short period of time, usually no longer than 60 seconds (some researchers argue that the actual span of short-term memory is much less, as low as 15 seconds). Almost all memory theorists would agree that if you remember a phone number five minutes after you learned it and you have not been rehearsing that number, you have retrieved it from long-term memory.

Long-Term Memory

In contrast to short-term memory, long-term memory is thought of as a system or set of systems that stores memories with retention intervals up to an entire lifetime of 70 or 80 years. If, during a test, you remember information you studied the night before, you can be confident that the material was stored in long-term memory even if you forget it just a few days later. Moreover, the stories your grandmother tells you of her childhood may be based in long-term memory. These memories may have been formed 65 years ago, and perhaps, if no one else has ever asked her about these events, they may have never been retrieved before.

One of the other defining features of long-term memory is its seemingly limitless ability to form and store new memories. Indeed, some research suggests that as more information is stored in long-term memory, more memory is opened up for new learning (Bjork & Bjork, 1992). Knowledge of a given area makes it easier to accumulate more knowledge in that area. Remember how difficult it was to learn about experiments when you took Introductory Psychology and were unfamiliar with psychological experimentation? Contrast that with how you attend to the experiments described in this text. This feature of long-term memory also helps distinguish it from short-term memory that appears to be limited in the number of items that it can maintain at any one time.

Long-term memory is an important aspect of normal human functioning. We use our long-term memories all the time, to store new information or to retrieve old information. For example, consider the ordinary task of shopping for groceries. First, you need to remember which store is the best or most convenient. Then you have to remember where your car is parked. You must also remember the directions to the store. Once you arrive at the market, if you do not have a shopping list, you must remember the items that you came to the store to buy, you need to remember which brands you prefer. Then, once you have paid for your groceries, you need to find your car and the way home.

Long-term memory covers an enormous range of interesting phenomena. Why do we remember some aspects of our past so vividly, but forget others almost immediately? Do we remember the past accurately, or are there sometimes distortions? Another area of long-term memory that has been studied is called prospective memory (Kvavilashvili, 1987). Prospective memory refers to "memory for the future." How do people remember what they have to do later in the day, or in a week from now? How do people remember to take the roast out of the oven after an hour of cooking? There are many interesting aspects of long-term memory.

Encoding, Storage, Representation, and Retrieval

Four processes have interested many memory researchers. *Encoding* means acquiring new information. Encoding is not simply a synonym for learning. Encoding typically refers to the learning of events that can be represented internally, such as the memory for events, words, or faces. Moreover, it derives from specific models in psychology that stress the role of the organism as an information processor. Therefore, encoding has come to generally refer to human learning of information that can be represented internally.

Storage refers to the processes that maintain memories when they are not being either encoded or retrieved. Consequently, storage is a highly controversial topic, as a "stored" memory cannot be observed. However, most researchers agree that the nature of storage can be inferred from the way memories are encoded and retrieved. Nonetheless, stored memories have never been "seen." *Representation* refers to how those memories are stored. Humans and other organisms clearly store information in systematic ways. The term representation refers to the mental arrangement of items in memory. For example, many language researchers think that the meanings of words are arranged in memory as a network of associated meanings.

There are a number of questions that come up with respect to storage and representation. If you were to draw a picture of a memory, what would it look like? First of all, what are the elements contained in a memory? Does a memory include a representation of every stimulus that is noticed during an experience, or does it contain only a subset? Regardless of how many elements there are, how are the elements represented? Are visual or imaginal representations stored as veridical pictures, or are they auditory, or symbolic in some form? Aside from these questions about memory content, researchers have dealt with the way these elements are structured. They have inquired whether all related elements appear to be linked together or whether elements seem to be arranged in some logical hierarchy. Obviously, the answers to such questions are difficult to uncover with any confidence, because memories cannot be seen directly. Still, the research techniques used in this area have suggested a number of interesting speculations concerning what memories consist of and how they are organized.

Retrieval refers to how memories are remembered, brought to awareness, or used in behavior. Retrieval is the process whereby the correct and appropriate memory is called upon at just the right time. While commonplace, the complexity of retrieval is enormous. How do you "search" for the memory of your last birthday amidst all of your other memories? How do you search your memory for just the right word to end a paragraph? Researchers concerned with memory retrieval are interested in questions like these.

Six different varieties of learning and memory have now been outlined. Certainly, all of these kinds of learning and memory appear essential. Without any one of these processes, human beings would find life extremely difficult. Second, all of these phenomena share the feature that the organism interacts with its environment and changes as a consequence. However, there are also marked differences between the varieties of learning and memory. For example, the habituation to refrigerator noise requires neither attention nor awareness, whereas the acquisition of vocabulary in a new language requires both attention and awareness.

Learning and memory come in many different forms, from habituation to autobiographical memory, from classical to instrumental conditioning, and from short-term to long-term memory. Do these different processes have anything in common? Endel Tulving, a prominent memory researcher, provided an interesting answer. He compared the study of memory to the study of locomotion in animals (Tulving, 1983). Locomotion in animals is extremely varied; some crawl, some fly, some swim, and some walk. He points out that the way a human walks, the way a cat runs, the way a snake slithers, the way a shark swims, and the way a moth flies have only one thing in common: a biological system has evolved to allow the organism to move from one location to another. Similarly, different forms of learning and memory may be accomplished by very different kinds of processes (equivalent to walking or flying). The mechanism that allows instrumental conditioning may be very different from the mechanism that allows people to retrieve childhood memories. Similarly, a dog learning to salivate in response to a bell may have only one thing in common with your learning the rudiments of Russian grammar; that is, both reflect a change in the organism that results in new behavioral responses. Tulving speculates that there may be considerable overlap in how different learning and remembering mechanisms work, because they all accomplish similar tasks, but it is important to realize that the mechanisms and processes may differ.

Tulving's analogy illustrates our first organizing theme. Although learning and memory are presumed to be basic processes, they result in an enormous variety of outcomes.

THEME 1: LEARNING AND MEMORY ARE BASIC PROCESSES THAT RESULT IN DIVERSE PHENOMENA.

DEFINING *LEARNING* AND *MEMORY*

Is there a single definition of learning or just one definition of memory? Up to this point, we have discussed learning and memory without specifically defining these terms. However, at this point, it is important to explain their essential natures so that the concepts of learning and memory can be refined further.

Defining *Learning*

Learning is a word that humans often use in daily conversation, and when it is, everyone seems to know what it means. Still, *learning* is one of those common terms that most people would have difficulty defining precisely. Part of this difficulty arises because the term is essentially used to describe several different types of activity. The unfortunate truth is that not all psychologists would agree upon a precise definition of learning. It is not possible to offer a single definition that would include all the instances meant by *learning* and exclude all those instances that are not considered learning. A working definition of learning, however, will provide a point of departure for discussion.

According to most psychologists, learning is primarily a process by which the behavior of organisms changes as a result of their experience with the environment. In other words, by interacting with the environment and encountering changes in the environment, organisms adapt to the changing environment through changes in behavior. It is this process of behavior change that we call learning.

As behavior changes through experience, the effects of certain stimuli will also change. What is really changing during learning is the relationship between the environment and behavior. Stimuli that originally may have had little significance now acquire meaning because they are related to other meaningful events. For example, when a person learns the definition of an unfamiliar word, this imparts to the novel word a new meaning or significance. This means that the person now responds differently to that word. The relationship of that word and the person's behavior has changed. In a like manner, a cat may discover that the sound of a can opener reliably precedes a dish full of tender, delicious Yummy Kat morsels. By learning from experiencing these events, the meaning of the sound changes for the cat. These examples are related to the formal characterization used by many experimenters that **learning** *is a lasting change in an organism's behavior that results from experience.*

By defining learning in this way, it becomes possible to study the variables that affect the way organisms learn. In using this definition, however, at least three points must be kept in mind. First, according to this definition, learning is reflected by a change in behavior. In this regard, it is important to understand that this change in behavior may not be observed immediately. Learning can cause changes in future behavior. This phrase is important because it recognizes that learning does not always result in an immediate change of responding. Learning changes the probability that a particular response will occur when the circumstances are appropriate. For example, a cat that has learned that a sound is associated with food is more likely to approach the sound when it is hungry. This is true because, in the past, approaching the sound has resulted in obtaining food. However, the mere fact that the cat has learned about the sound does not guarantee an approach response if the circumstances are not appropriate.

Second, this definition states that for a change in responding to be accepted as evidence for learning, the tendency to perform the new response must be long lasting. This provision is included to separate learned response changes from temporary behavior changes that are due to other factors. Psychologists know, for example, that once a response has been learned, the performance of that response can vary depending on an organism's degree of fatigue, or its tendency to emit other responses. These variations in responding are, however, only temporary. A fatigued organism may stop making a learned response, but it will usually resume responding as soon as it is rested. Researchers differentiate between such short-term changes in responding and the more durable changes that result from learning.

The third point to note is that not all behavior changes are assumed to reflect learning. Drugs and injury are two factors that can produce long-lasting changes in an organism's behavior, but psychologists do not refer to these changes as learning. Maturation is another way in which behavior can change permanently without learning. Chickens, for example, if kept in a box for 48 hours and hand-fed powdered grain, will be better at pecking than chickens that are 24-hours old. Pecking accuracy improved because of further development of the nervous system and cannot be attributed to practice or learning. As a result of these alternative means of long-lasting behavioral changes, researchers attempt to make certain that only behavior changes that result from appropriate experiences are taken as evidence that learning has occurred.

Defining *Memory*

People seldom give their memories much thought until they misplace one; most take their memory systems for granted. It is interesting that the most common and current definitions for the term *memory* differ very little from the definition used by the earliest philosophers. To Plato, for example, who conceptualized the mind as being similar to a wax tablet, memory was like an etching or picture drawn on this tablet by experience. Although present-day psychologists might be more comfortable substituting *brain* for *mind* in this characterization, most would adhere at least generally to this view. Today, **memory** is most often defined as *an internal record or representation of some prior event or experience.*

Although such definitions of memory are common, they can be misleading in one respect. Implied in this definition is the idea that the brain functions like a camera, taking snapshots of events and then filing away the finished pictures. Almost certainly, this is not the case. As we will see in later chapters, memories are seldom faithful replicas of experience. In some cases, memories are composed of less detail, or at least less vivid detail, than actually are included in the actual experiences. In other cases, memories may contain more or different details than the original experiences. In effect, memories are probably best conceptualized as constructions that are based on real events, not as actual pictures of the events as they happened.

From the definitions discussed so far, it should be obvious that the process of learning and the entity of memory are closely related. One way to conceptualize this relationship is to think of learning as a process that results in memory formation. Clearly, we form memories from what we have learned, so in this sense, we can think of a memory as being dependent on learning. At the same time, however, it is possible to think of learning as being dependent on memory. When we learn, we often associate events that are separated in time. Such associations could not be formed unless a representation of one event could be retained until the other occurred. If organisms had no memory for events, each event would be viewed in isolation, and relationships among events would not be recognizable. Thus, it is fair to say that without learning organisms would have little to remember, and without memory organisms would be unable to learn.

Even though learning and memory are closely related, it is important not to equate the terms *learning* and *memory formation*. Doing so courts the erroneous suggestion that the content of a memory and the ease with which a memory can be recalled depend entirely on factors present at the time of learning. Clearly, learning factors often influence both memory content and recall. However, this is not the entire story. Substantial evidence suggests that there are factors that affect learning but have little or no influence on the ability to remember. One variable that clearly fits this description is the meaningfulness of verbal materials. Likewise, researchers know that numerous treatments and variables can affect recall of a memory even though those treatments and variables occur after learning has ended. For example, even if two individuals have learned a task in the same way and are tested under identical circumstances, their recall still may vary considerably, depending on their experiences between the times of learning and testing.

Not only do different variables sometimes control learning and remembering, there is evidence that the content of a memory may be influenced by factors other than those present during learning. For example, some studies suggest that the content of memory may be altered at the time of recall, as well as at the time of original memory formation (see, for example, Loftus, 1979, 1993). Such studies suggest that even though we may understand the learning process that triggers memory formation, it still is probably impossible to predict what the content of a memory may be or how easily a memory will be recalled.

Learning has been defined as the process of changing behavior as a result of experience, whereas memory has been conceptualized in terms of an internal representation of that prior experience. Although the two terms have different meanings, in the natural world it is a fact that one cannot occur without the other. However, scientists can separate them experimentally by manipulating variables that affect only one. Therefore, although one cannot learn without forming a memory, and one cannot have formed a memory without engaging in learning, the two terms are not synonymous.

THEME 2: LEARNING AND MEMORY ARE INTERRELATED BUT SEPARABLE DOMAINS.

The environment around you is constantly changing, as is the environment inside you. This means that you (and all other organisms) are continually encountering changes that require some adjustment or adaptation. Some of these adjustments are necessary simply to remain comfortable as the world around you changes. In other cases, your life or health may depend on reacting appropriately to change.

THEME 3: LEARNING AND MEMORY ARE ADAPTIVE PROCESSES.

Learning and memory are adaptations that enable organisms to survive and prosper in a constantly changing world. Psychologists assume that the capacity to learn and remember is a result of natural selection, which means that organisms learn and remember because the ability to learn and remember facilitated the survival of their ancestors. How is it possible, then, for organisms to react in an adaptive manner when so many different changes occur?

Fortunately, all animal species have evolved certain mechanisms for reacting appropriately to environmental events. One such mechanism is the simple reflex that involves making a specific automatic reaction to a particular stimulus. A number of these reflexive reactions occur in humans' behavioral repertoires. When food touches your tongue, you automatically salivate. When your fingers touch a hot object, you immediately pull your hand away. Your eyelids snap shut whenever a foreign object approaches your eye. When a moving object appears at the "corner" of your eye, you turn your head toward that object. Even the changes in heart rate and glandular secretion that occur when you experience pain are reflexive responses.

Reactions like these are automatic, relatively rigid responses that allow organisms to deal with a specific set of important stimuli. Such responses are genetically programmed and do not depend upon prior experience. Reflexive behaviors are advantageous in certain situations like this because they can occur rapidly without an organism having to consider what response it should make.

Aside from reflexes, many species have at their disposal a second set of adaptive responses called instinctive, or species-typical, behaviors. Such behaviors are commonly more complex. In his influential writings concerning instinctive behaviors, Tinbergen (1951) argued that instinctive behaviors consist of a stereotyped sequence of responses that is characteristic of a particular species. Tinbergen also presumed that instinctive behaviors, like reflexes, were capable of being triggered automatically by specific stimuli. Finally, he argued that instinctive behaviors should arise from an organism's genetic makeup, not from the individual's environmental experiences.

It appears that many species exhibit species-typical behavior. Such behaviors are often stereotyped (Ardrey, 1966; Lorenz, 1965; Tinbergen 1952). It is also apparent that many of these behaviors seem to be triggered by specific stimuli. What is not clear is the degree to which such behaviors depend on genetic programming, as opposed to being shaped by environmental experiences. For example, certain male swallows (*Zonotrichia leucophrys*) invariably produce adult song patterns when they are approximately 8 months old. Since all these birds develop this capacity at the same stage of maturation, it had been widely assumed that the capacity itself was genetically preset to appear at a given age. This does not, however, appear to be the entire story. Researchers studying these birds have found that unless they are exposed to the adult songs of other birds during a critical period of development (10–90 days of age), they never develop the capacity for producing adult song (Marler & Mundinger, 1971).

Thus, the occurrence of adult singing patterns in these male swallows appears to depend on both genetics and experience. Similarly, many other behaviors once thought to be genetically determined are now known to depend at least partially on environmental stimulation. For this reason, the current thinking is that many instinctive behaviors probably arise through a combination of genetic and environmental influences.

Most organisms are born with a set of prewired reflexive reactions that allow them to adjust to particular kinds of environmental changes. It is also reasonable to conclude that at least some species possess more complex, instinct-like behaviors that arise from some interaction of genetic and environmental factors. These behaviors also qualify as mechanisms for adapting to environmental change. Still, for most organisms, these inborn tendencies to react in certain ways are inadequate for coping with a constantly changing environment. If organisms were limited solely to reflexive and instinct-like behaviors, many would simply fail to survive.

Phylogenetic behaviors are often inadequate adaptations to a changing environment for at least two reasons. First, most such behaviors are relatively stereotyped or inflexible. Once they have been triggered by some environmental event, they tend to run to completion even when the environmental requirements change. One example of this inflexibility can be seen in the behavior of the female greylag goose when she is incubating her eggs. If an egg appears outside her nest, the goose leaves the nest and approaches the egg. She then begins to roll the egg toward her nest with an up-and-down movement of her bill. Finally, she guides the maverick egg back into the nest and retakes her position over her brood.

This behavior is clearly an adaptive response because it allows the female to retrieve any eggs that inadvertently roll from the nest. However, this egg-rolling response is so inflexible that it is sometimes maladaptive. Once the egg-rolling response has begun, the goose will continue to move its bill in an up-and-down manner even if the egg is removed. In other words, if the egg falls in a hole, the goose will continue to roll a "phantom" egg back toward the nest (Hess, 1965). This means that while the goose persists in trying to retrieve an egg that is no longer there, she is leaving the other eggs unguarded. There are numerous examples of this kind of rigidity in a variety of species. In effect, once phylogenetic behaviors have been initiated, they tend not to change even when the environmental requirements do.

A second reason that reflexive and instinct-like behaviors are inadequate in coping with change is that such behaviors occur in response to only a limited number of stimuli. Certainly, the reflexive eye-blink response is an adequate mechanism for adjusting to foreign objects that approach the eye. However, there are numerous important stimuli in the environment that require some adjustment but do not naturally elicit any response. The following is one example.

Assume that you are on a transcontinental airliner. About an hour into the flight you hear the pilot's voice over the intercom. Speaking calmly, the pilot informs the passengers that one of the engines has malfunctioned, and he is attempting to return to the airport. In such a situation, your response and the responses of the other passengers would be reasonably predictable. Most probably you would experience a rush of adrenaline. Your heart would begin to race, and your palms would begin to sweat. You might well look around for the nearest emergency exit and might even begin to read the emergency instructions that you had earlier ignored. Almost certainly you would become quiet and would begin to listen carefully to the sounds of the aircraft.

Now, consider these reactions to the pilot's message. Not one of these responses is a natural or automatic reaction to hearing someone speak in a calm voice. None of these responses occurs reflexively when someone's voice is heard over an intercom. There is nothing in the stimulus input received that would automatically trigger any of the above reactions. Yet, all of the reactions are clearly attempts to adjust to the changing of the environment.

Examples of response adjustments of these kinds are numerous. If you are driving a car and you see a stop sign, you apply the brakes. You do this even though your nervous system is not prewired to move your leg in response to visual inputs from a stop sign. If you hear a question in a classroom, you may raise your hand in the air. Yet, there is no arm-raising reflex that is produced by the sound of a question. Organisms make important adjustments to environmental changes that naturally elicit no adjustment responses; response comes, appropriately, as a result of prior experience. In other words, many of the most important behavioral adjustments are not innate or prewired—they are learned through experience.

In a very real sense, learning is the ultimate mechanism that organisms have evolved for coping with environmental change. Our ability to learn, first and foremost, allows us to react in a flexible manner. We are not necessarily caught, as the goose is caught, in a series of automatic, rigid behavior patterns. Through its experiences an organism can learn that retrieving a lost egg may be worthwhile. However, it also might learn to respond differently if the egg falls in a hole. Through learning, we can react adaptively and flexibly even when the world around us changes rapidly.

Aside from giving flexibility, learning also provides organisms with a way of reacting to all those stimuli that do not naturally elicit adaptive responses. Through learning we are able to react appropriately to spoken words, to written symbols, and even to facial expressions. Everything from a road sign to a change in temperature requires some response, and learning provides the mechanism for making these responses in an adaptive manner. Clearly, the ability to learn has evolved in all organisms because it enables an organism to survive and prosper as the world around it changes.

Learning alone, however, is not an adequate adaptation to environmental change. Learning requires that an organism's experiences often produce lasting changes in behavior. For this change in behavior to persist over time, there must be some lasting change in the organism that maintains this change in behavior. This property is commonly referred to as memory. Memory can be thought of as the storage of that change that allows the organism to respond in a flexible manner. There are two important aspects of memory that distinguish it from learning. First, memory itself is the unobserved "storage" of learning. Second, for memories to be acted upon, they must be remembered or retrieved in an appropriate way. In essence, for the effects of learning to be beneficial for the organism, lasting change must occur in the organism, so that the organism can later make the appropriate responses.

These kinds of evolutionary considerations can be updated into modern times and contemporary culture. Think about your hometown or a place you used to live. Most likely, you would probably be able to describe the geography and roads of the area. You could probably direct someone to the movie theater even if you have not been to that theater for 5, 10, or more years.

In an evolutionary context, good memory for spatial layout may have been extremely important for human ancestors. Remembering where the good places for shelter were or where edible plants grew may have had strong adaptive value. Similarly, remembering where productive pasture land was and where bordering groups of people lived may have had considerable adaptive value for later humans. Spatial representation is equally important today when people may have to negotiate through streets and cities.

LEARNING AND MEMORY IN BIOLOGICAL ORGANISMS

One important consideration of the adaptive role of learning and memory is that learning and memory are processes that occur in biological organ-

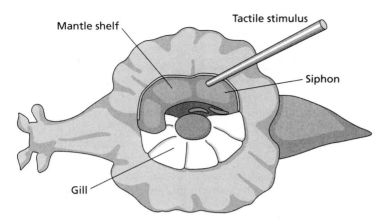

Mantle shelf

Tactile stimulus

Siphon

Gill

FIGURE 1.1(A) Withdrawal Response. Touch stimulation of an *Aplysia's* mantle, siphon, or gill causes a withdrawal response. Reprinted with permission from *Science*, 1970, *167*, March 1970, 1740–1742. ©1970 by AAAS Science.

isms. More specifically, learning and memory depend on changes that occur in the nervous systems of living organisms. This means that it should be possible to discover the biological changes that accompany learning and memory. It should also be possible to determine the areas of the nervous system that are responsible for various aspects of learning and memory. In recent decades, researchers in the area of behavioral neuroscience have made enormous progress in discovering the biological bases of learning and memory.

Issues in **neuroscience** and psychology can be studied at many different levels. It is possible to consider what happens during learning at a microscopic or cellular level, and indeed many neuroscientists are engaged in this area. Indeed, many researchers study learning at the subcellular level; what happens inside the neuron. However, it is also possible to study neuroscience at more molar or global levels of analysis. This approach aims to determine the roles of various brain structures. Many neuroscientists study this organization of the human brain. These researchers, often called cognitive neuroscientists or human neuropsychologists, study the relationship of brain regions to cognitive or behavioral function. This growing area combines a traditional area of neuropsychological research and the study of brain-damaged patients with recent trends in technology that allow scientists to make pictures and maps of intact, normal, and living brains.

The following discussion will consider analysis at both the cellular and structural level.

A Biological Basis of Learning and Memory

As already mentioned, the biological basis of memory raises two issues. One issue is what are the changes that occur at the cellular level. The second is how is the nervous system as a whole organized to learn and remember.

Learning and Memory Result in Changes in Neural Activity. One strategy in looking at the neuroscience of learning and memory is to study the processes in animals that have more simple nervous systems than a human being does and with very basic learning processes. This allows researchers to study the learning process in a rather complete way. One such animal is the sea slug, or *Aplysia*, a marine animal that is related to the common slug. It has become widely used in studies of the cellular physiology of learning in part because *Aplysia* has relatively few neurons, and some of its neurons are very large, which makes them easy to study. Researchers have determined the changes that occur at the cellular level during habituation in *Aplysia*. When the mantle, gill, or siphon of *Aplysia* is touched, the animal withdraws that structure (see Figure 1.1a). Habituation occurs in an *Aplysia* when the gill is repeatedly stimulated with a jet of seawater. The

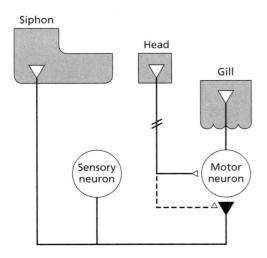

FIGURE 1.1(B) Habituation. Habituation of the gill-withdrawal reflex in *Aplysia* apparently depends on decreased transmission at the synapse between the sensory neuron and the motor neuron. Reprinted with permission from *Science*, 1970, *167*, March 1970, 1745–1748. ©by AAAS Science.

Aplysia initially withdraws its gill when it is stimulated, but eventually stops responding after repeated stimulation of its gill.

Researchers have determined the neural pathway that is responsible for sensing the touch and controlling the withdrawal response. This neural path consists of a sensory neuron, which is excited by stimulation of the gill, and a motor neuron, which controls the gill retraction response (see Figure 1.1a). When the gill is stimulated, the sensory neuron is activated and releases a neurotransmitter at its synapse with the motor neuron. The neurotransmitter excites the motor neuron, which causes the gill withdrawal.

Through a series of experiments, several researchers determined the changes that occur in this neural path during habituation. In order to do this, several possible mechanisms of habituation had to be eliminated. First, habituation does not result from fatigue of the muscle that withdraws the gill. After habituation has occurred, direct stimulation of the motor neuron still causes withdrawal of the gill (Kupfermann, Castellucci, Pinsker, & Kandel, 1970). Second, habituation does not result from a decrease in the activity of the sensory neuron, because after habituation occurs, the sensory neuron's response is still as strong as before (Kupfermann, et al., 1970). If habituation does not result from a decrease in the ability of the motor neuron to cause the response or a decrease in the response of the sensory neuron, then habituation must result from a change in the synapse between the sensory and motor neurons (see Figure 1.1b). Castellucci and Kandel (1974) confirmed this by showing that habituation results from a decrease in the amount of excitatory neurotransmitter released by the sensory neuron, resulting in decreased activity in the motor neuron.

This case shows a clear example of how learning depends on changes in the cells of the nervous system. As other learning situations are considered in later chapters, this issue will again arise. Recent research has begun to uncover the cellular changes that result from classical conditioning, instrumental/operant conditioning, and even long-term memory. Although these mechanisms are not as well understood as habituation in *Aplysia*, neuroscientists will continue to make progress toward determining the cellular mechanisms of learning and memory.

Learning and Memory Depend on the Organization of the Nervous System. In addition to depending on cellular mechanisms, learning and memory also depend on the organization of the nervous system. Because cellular mechanisms may vary from brain region to brain region, analyzing the cellular level alone may not elucidate these functional relationships. Moreover, in considering functional relationships between brain and behavior or cognition, it is necessary to consider the brain as a whole. The cells of the brain are organized into hundreds of distinct structures and areas. Many of these areas of the brain are crucial for learning and memory (see

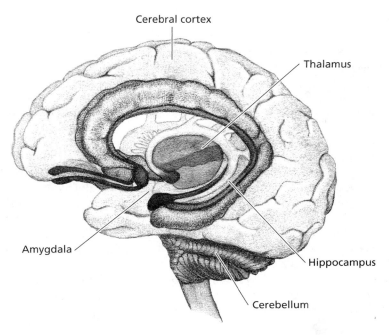

Cerebral cortex

Thalamus

Amygdala

Hippocampus

Cerebellum

FIGURE 1.2 The Anatomy of Memory. All of the brain structures identified here have been implicated in efforts to discover the anatomical structures involved in memory. Although researchers have made some exciting discoveries, the physiological bases of memory are extremely complex and are not yet well understood.

Figure 1.2), and recent research has provided a greater understanding of the roles of many of these structures. Much of this research has focused on the role of the **hippocampus** and closely related structures in the medial temporal lobe. These areas have attracted the most attention in learning and memory largely because of the memory loss suffered by individuals who have suffered damage in these areas. By far the best known of these case histories is an individual known only by his initials, H.M. (Scoville & Milner, 1957).

In 1953, H.M. underwent brain surgery to relieve untreatable epileptic seizures that had become so frequent and incapacitating that, as a last resort, surgeons removed the areas of his brain where the seizures originated. Neurosurgeons removed a structure known as the hippocampus from both sides of his brain. The surgeons also removed some other nearby areas of H.M.'s brain. Although no one knew what to expect after the operation, H.M.'s condition had deteriorated so badly that the surgeons felt that the benefits of

the surgery would outweigh any harm it caused. Unfortunately, this was not the case. (Nowadays, surgeons remove only one of the hippocampi. This procedure reduces the seizures with minimal memory impairment.)

The surgery did relieve the epileptic seizures, and H.M. appeared to remain normal in many respects. However, there were several drastic consequences of the surgery. Following the surgery, H.M. suffered a moderate inability to remember events that occurred before the surgery (a condition known as **retrograde amnesia**). He had some trouble remembering information from one to three years before the operation, but little trouble remembering older events. What was more striking was the fact that H.M. suffered an almost complete inability to learn and remember new information (a condition known as **anterograde amnesia**). He could briefly remember new information, but could not remember it after any distraction. This anterograde amnesia had a devastating effect on his life.

The difficulties encountered by H.M. are well documented. He would read the same magazine repeatedly without any loss of interest. He lived with his parents after the operation, and when they moved to a new house, H.M. could not locate anything in the house and he could not find his way home from only a few blocks away. It took him eight years to learn and remember the floor plan of the new house so that he could find his way from one room to another (Milner, Corkin, & Teuber, 1968).

H.M. has retained some ability to learn and remember. He has enormous difficulty learning new facts and remembering new events, but he has little difficulty learning new skills. He can learn to solve puzzles, and he readily learned new skills, such as reading words written in mirror-writing. Although H.M. learned new skills like these, he says that he cannot remember previously seeing any of these tasks (Cohen, Eichenbaum, Deacedo, & Corkin, 1985).

Largely because of the memory deficits caused by removal of H.M.'s hippocampus, an enormous amount of research has investigated the role of the hippocampus in learning and memory. Research has shown that the hippocampus is crucial for certain types of learning to occur but that it is not the only brain region involved in memory. Indeed, it may be necessary for some kinds of learning but not others. At this point, however, there is not widespread agreement about exactly what types of learning depend on the hippocampus (O'Keefe, 1983; Rudy & Sutherland, 1989; Squire, 1992).

A second region that has implications for learning and memory consists of the frontal lobes (see Figure 1.2). However, the amnesia associated with frontal lobe damage is quite different from H.M.'s amnesia. Patients who suffer damage to their frontal lobes, usually the left frontal lobe, often have difficulties with memory "management" (see Moscovitch, 1994). This damage, usually as a result of stroke or accident, sometimes results in memory deficits. However, the deficit does not appear to arise from people's difficulties to acquire or retrieve memories but rather their abilities to "plan" memory strategies or monitor and control retrieval. Therefore, one characteristic of "frontal" patients is an inability to successfully use mnemonic strategies. As young children we acquire knowledge about the use of rehearsal, studying habits, etc. Patients with frontal damage lose this ability. In addition, frontal patients have difficulties screening their memories. Consequently, one of the hallmarks of frontal damage is confabulation, or honest lying. Patients may make up fantastic stories that could not possibly be true, but because they lack the ability to screen their memories, they actually believe their fantasies. Despite their inability to discriminate fact from fiction, their learning is more similar to normal people than to those amnesiacs with hippocampal damage.

Numerous other areas of the brain also appear to be involved in learning and memory. Thompson (1990) presented evidence that the dentate-interpositus nucleus within the cerebellum plays a role in classical conditioning in the rabbit. Gazzaniga, Ivry, and Manjun (1998) report that short-term memory can be disrupted by lesions to the supramarginal gyrus (phonological short-term memory) and to the parieto-occipital region (visuospatial short-term memory). As we present different learning and memory processes later in this text, we will return often to the role of the brain in learning and memory.

Biological Constraints on Learning and Memory

As the preceding discussion illustrates, learning and memory occur in biological systems, and learning and memory depend on biological changes and the organization of the nervous system. If learning and memory occur in a biological system (in particular, the nervous system), then it also seems likely that the biological system is going to limit what and how certain species learn and remember. Another way of saying this is that learning and memory are constrained by their biological context. There are two notable effects of biological constraints on learning. First, certain species will learn more easily about events that are biologically relevant for members of that species. For example, Wilcoxon, Dragoin, and Kral (1971) conducted a study using rats and quail. These researchers reasoned that rats, which are nocturnal and possess strong senses of smell and taste, might be able to associate taste with illness more quickly than they could associate a visual stimulus with illness. On the other hand the quail is diurnal and is much more attuned to visual stimuli. Wilcoxon et al. reasoned that the quail should associate visual stimuli with illness more readily than taste stimuli.

In the Wilcoxon study, groups of rats and quail ingested water that was both blue in color and tasted sour. After drinking the blue/sour water, the animals were then made ill through an injection of cyclophosphamide. Test trials determined that the rats had associated the sour taste with the illness and would drink water that was blue but not water that tasted sour. Quail, on the other hand, had associated the color of the water with the illness and avoided blue, but not sour, water. The results supported the authors' assertion that animals may have evolved mechanisms to associate certain stimuli with certain other stimuli.

A second example of biological constraints on learning occurs when instinctive behaviors interfere with the learning of a new response. For example, Bolles (1970) documents that rats can learn to jump over a barrier to avoid electric shock much faster than they can learn to press a bar to avoid shock. This makes sense in light of the fact that running away from a dangerous stimulus is one of their species' typical defense responses. On the other hand, it is the rare rat that had ever had to press a bar to avoid a predator. In subsequent chapters, you will encounter numerous examples of biological constraints on learning and memory. This discussion of the biological basis and the biological constraints of learning and memory highlights the last of our organizing themes.

THEME 4: LEARNING AND MEMORY OCCUR IN A BIOLOGICAL CONTEXT.

DIFFERENCES AND SIMILARITIES IN THE STUDY OF LEARNING AND MEMORY

When students begin their first study of learning and memory, they are often surprised by how divergent the work on these two topics is. As previously pointed out, learning and memory are about as closely related as any two topics can be. Yet, the research on these topics appears to be guided by different philosophies, the language used to describe the topics is often very different, and the research in the two fields is often published in different kinds of scientific journals. What is even more disquieting is the apparent lack of communication between researchers interested in learning and those who concentrate on aspects of memory. It is legitimate to ask how the differences developed and how these developments have affected our knowledge of these two areas.

The answer to these questions may be started by saying that the study of learning and the study of memory developed out of different philosophical traditions. First, learning as a research enterprise grew mainly out of the behavioristic tradition in psychology. Without presenting the behavioral view in depth, a few points are worth noting. According to this view, the goal of research in psychology was to discover the lawful relationships between environmental events and an organism's behavior. Following this tradition, early learning researchers set out to find the variables that would produce enduring behavior changes. The term *learning* was used primarily as a label to describe these stimulus-response relationships. Few of the early learning researchers talked about the nature of the learning process as it actually occurred inside the organism. Thus, the emphasis was clearly on observable events and how they are related, not on describing processes taking place within an organism.

Another characteristic of learning research that developed from the behavioristic tradition was the frequent use of animals as experimental subjects. The early behaviorists viewed living organisms from a Darwinian perspective, seeing humans as part of a continuum of species, not as a species somehow separate from all others. From this perspective the use of animal subjects became natural. The basic idea was that the rules of learning that governed the behaviors of animals should be similar in many respects to the rules governing learned behaviors in humans. An added advantage to using animals in experiments was that researchers could control the histories and current environments of their subjects. This made it easier to look at how novel experiences resulted in enduring behavioral changes.

While behaviorism promulgated research in learning, interest in memory grew primarily from what is now called the "cognitive orientation." This general view had many early adherents in psychology, but its impact has been heaviest in the past two decades. The term *cognition* refers to the act of knowing, or acquiring knowledge. This is an important point. This knowledge is represented within the organism itself. Thus, the study of cognition is, by definition, a study of the internal processes that result in knowledge and a study of how this knowledge is structured. For this reason, researchers working within the cognitive tradition have emphasized the study of attentional, perceptual, and memory processes, as well as the organization of the memory itself. Whereas early behaviorists believed that the subject matter of psychology should be behavior and its relationship to observable events, the cognitive tradition also emphasized behavior, but not as the primary subject to be studied. Within the cognitive tradition, behavior usually has been viewed as an index or indicator for what goes on inside the organism. In other words, the cognitive psychologist does not study behavior in and of itself but instead uses behavior as a tool for

studying internal processes. For example, the cognitive researcher may use the speed with which a person recognizes a word as an indication of whether the word is represented in the person's memory. Here, speed of responding itself is not being studied. Instead, this variable is being used to help illuminate a memory the experimenter cannot see directly.

One final point about the cognitive orientation is worth making. The vast majority of studies on cognitive processes such as memory have been done with human subjects. Most probably this strategy developed for a number of reasons. First, many philosophers and psychologists have viewed humans as differing from other organisms primarily on the basis of their cognitive abilities. This is not to say that other organisms have no cognitive abilities, but simply that these abilities are more refined, more complex, and more numerous in humans than in other species. It follows naturally from this view that if humans are to study cognitive processes, the subject of choice would be the human.

A related reason for studying memory in humans rather than other organisms is the virtual absence of verbal behavior among nonhuman species. Work with Kanzi, the bonobos chimpanzee, has documented quite sophisticated language use (Savage-Rumbaugh, Sevcik, Brakke, & Rumbaugh, 1990), but only humans are able to report with some clarity what they recall. Nonhuman animals must be trained to make a response that will indicate what they recall. Humans are also able to speculate about how they may have processed some bit of information (speculations that may lead to testable hypotheses). Animals cannot make such suggestions.

Obviously, the behavioral and cognitive approaches are of great historical significance because of their impacts on early learning and memory research. Just as clearly, these approaches remain important today. Numerous learning experiments are still conducted within a behavioral framework, and the cognitive approach forms the basis for the great majority of contemporary memory experiments. Still, in recent years there has been an increasing tendency for aspects of these two approaches to merge.

For example, one of the most active research areas recently has been the field of memory and cognitive processes in animals. This is a clear step away from the notion that cognitive processes may be studied only in human subjects. Likewise, recently there has been an increase in the application of basic learning principles to humans in applied medical, psychotherapeutic, and educational settings. Such applications have been successful even though the principles were originally developed through laboratory experiments using animal subjects. Finally, as will be seen, contemporary theories of learning are often theories based on how cognitive processes bridge the gap between stimulus events and an organism's behavior. In effect, many learning researchers have now begun to "look inside" the organisms they are studying.

These examples of cross-fertilization between the areas of learning and memory are healthy signs. In many cases they have opened up avenues of research that might otherwise have gone unexplored. Just as importantly, this trend suggests that researchers have finally realized what most beginning students have suspected all along: namely, that it makes little sense to talk about either learning or memory in isolation.

SUMMARY STATEMENTS

This chapter covered a lot of ground. Discussion began with a number of learning and memory situations, and concluded that learning and memory encompass a wide variety of phenomena and often occur without an organism's awareness. After surveying the range of learning and memory phenomena, the discussion pursued definitions of learning and memory.

While illustrating the importance of learning and memory for survival, another important point emerged: that learning and memory are adaptive processes that promote the survival of organisms in a changing environment. An important correlate of the fact that learning and memory are adaptive processes is the fact that learning and memory occur in a biological context. As a result, learning and memory have a biological basis that depends upon changes at the cellular level and depends upon the organization of the nervous system. Furthermore, the biological context of learning and memory sometimes limits how learning and memory occur in a given situation.

Although psychologists routinely separate the act of learning from the act of memory, it has been shown that learning and memory cannot be easily separated. In fact, one cannot occur without the other. Four themes were also introduced that will help to organize and integrate the numerous topics that will be covered in the remainder of the book. These four themes are the following:

Theme 1: Learning and memory are basic processes that result in diverse phenomena.

Theme 2: Learning and memory are interrelated but separable domains.

Theme 3: Learning and memory are adaptive processes.

Theme 4: Learning and memory occur in a biological context.

2

Classical Conditioning:
Basic Principles

CHAPTER OVERVIEW

Sometimes, for no apparent reason, you are suddenly reminded of a lost love or a moment from your childhood. Afterward, you may realize that it was the scent of a particular cologne or perfume that reminded you of that lost love. Or perhaps it was the smell of freshly cut grass or the smell of cookies baking in the oven that reminded you of that moment from your childhood. Have you ever heard a song on the radio that suddenly made you feel like you were back in middle school again?

Consider a more extreme example. A chronic heroin user has injected the same amount of heroin every day for several months. Today, in his new apartment, he prepares to shoot up another dose. He uses the same heroin he has used for the past three days in his usual dosage. He mixes it, cooks it, then injects it. A few minutes later, he dies from an overdose. How is this possible if the amount and potency of the heroin were the same? The answer is that, because he was in a new setting, cues that normally caused his body to prepare for the heroin were not present. As a result, his body simply was not ready for the heroin. In this new setting his normal dose was deadly.

All of these examples have a common theme. In each case, certain events have come to signal other important events. These scenarios illustrate the effects of classical or Pavlovian conditioning. Classical conditioning is a learning process that explains many important and interesting aspects of our lives.

Classical conditioning fits our characterization of learning almost perfectly. In classical conditioning, the behavior of organisms changes when they encounter stimuli that reliably precede biologically significant events. These biologically significant events are capable of naturally producing reflexive or involuntary reactions. In other words, the stimuli **elicit** the reactions. Stimuli that naturally elicit physiological changes (muscle reflexes, glandular secretions), and emotional reactions all qualify as biologically significant events because they automatically produce these adaptive responses. Through classical conditioning, organisms can be prepared when these significant events occur because other less significant stimuli have come to predict their presence.

Because of classical conditioning, an organism comes to respond differently to the signaling stimulus. Usually the original stimulus produces little or no response. However, with repeated pairings, the stimulus begins to produce a reflexive or involuntary reaction much like the one produced naturally by the response-eliciting stimulus. In effect, an organism begins to react to these two stimuli in similar ways because one stimulus has reliably preceded the other.

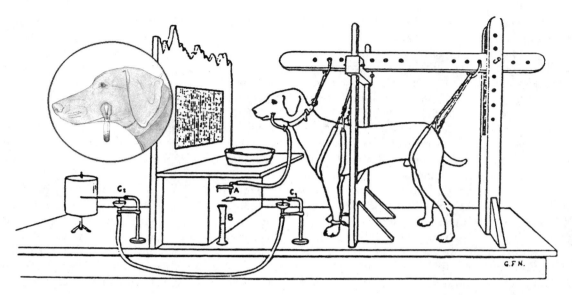

FIGURE 2.1 Classical Conditioning Apparatus. An experimental arrangement similar to the one depicted here (taken from Yerkes & Morgulis, 1909) typically has been used in demonstrations of classical conditioning, although Pavlov's original setup (see inset) was quite a bit simpler. The dog is restrained in a harness. A tone is used as the conditioned stimulus (CS), and the presentation of meat powder is used as the unconditioned stimulus (US). The tube inserted into the dog's salivary gland allows precise measurement of its salivation response. The pen and rotating drum of paper on the left are used to maintain a continuous record of salivary flow. (Inset) The less elaborate setup that Pavlov originally used to collect saliva on each trial is shown here (Goodwin, 1991).

PAVLOV'S ORIGINAL EXPERIMENTS

The discovery of classical conditioning is usually credited to Russian physiologist Ivan Pavlov. Interestingly, Pavlov was not studying learning at the time. Instead, he was investigating the physiology of the digestive system. Pavlov ultimately received the Nobel Prize in 1904 for his contributions to our understanding of how the digestive system functions. In the process, Pavlov also made a lasting contribution to the study of learning.

One aspect of Pavlov's research on digestion concerned the role of the salivary glands in digestion. To study salivation Pavlov placed dogs in a harness-like apparatus similar to that pictured in Figure 2.1. He then inserted small glass tubes into the dogs' salivary gland ducts. Thus, when the dogs salivated for any reason, the saliva would run through the tubes instead of into their mouths. This allowed Pavlov to collect and measure the amount of saliva that was produced under various conditions.

In one of the classical conditioning experiments, Pavlov attempted to measure salivary response to meat powder placed in a dog's mouth. After a few sessions, however, precise measurements became impossible because the dogs began to salivate as soon as the experimenters entered the room with the meat powder in hand. By the time the meat powder had been placed in their mouths, the dogs had already produced significant amounts of saliva.

Pavlov hypothesized that this premature salivation was occurring in response to stimuli that preceded the presentation of the meat powder. To test this idea, he began to present discrete stimuli before each presentation of food. He used stimuli such as clicking sounds or tones, which did not naturally produce the salivation response. After Pavlov presented the clicking sound before the meat powder several times, the dogs began to salivate to the sound itself. These tests were among the first experimental demonstrations of what we now call classical conditioning (Pavlov, 1927).

There were other researchers who studied classical conditioning prior to Pavlov's 1927 report. For example, Edwin Twitmyer at the University of Pennsylvania, reported demonstrations of classical conditioning before Pavlov (Twitmyer, 1905). Twitmyer sounded a bell 0.5 seconds before hitting the patellar tendon in humans. He successfully conditioned a knee-jerk response to the sound of the bell. Twitmyer's reports attracted little interest and did not lead to further research. Pavlov's work is considered the founding demonstration of classical conditioning.

Aside from providing an initial analysis of the conditioning process, Pavlov gave us a terminology we still use today to describe the elements of the conditioning situation. He chose the term **unconditioned stimulus** (US) to denote the stimulus that naturally elicits some reflexive reaction. In Pavlov's experiments, the meat powder served as the US because the presentation of the meat naturally produced salivation. Such stimuli are called unconditioned because they produce the reflexive response without the aid of any conditioning or learning experience.

The reflexive response that is naturally elicited by the US is called the **unconditioned response** (UR). In Pavlov's situation the UR was the salivation, as produced initially by the exposure to the meat powder. Like the US, the response is termed unconditioned because it occurs when the US is presented without prior conditioning or learning.

The stimulus Pavlov presented before the meat powder (for example, the clicking sound) was labeled the **conditioned stimulus** (CS). The term indicates that this stimulus becomes capable of producing the reflexive reaction only after it has been presented together with the meat powder several times (known as **pairing** the CS

and US). For this reason the CSs chosen for most classical conditioning experiments are often described as being relatively neutral. This means that before the conditioning procedure this stimulus produces no reflexive reaction of the kind that is naturally elicited by the US.

The final element of conditioning is the new response that is produced by the CS. Pavlov called this response the **conditioned response** (CR), as it is a response that can be produced by the CS only after some conditioning has occurred. In Pavlov's experiment, the salivation produced by the clicking sound is the conditioned response. Although the conditioned and unconditioned responses may be identical or at least similar, the response is labeled an unconditioned response when it is elicited by the US and a conditioned response when it is elicited by the CS after conditioning.

These four terms are used throughout the research literature on classical conditioning. Interestingly, all four are the result of a mistranslation of Pavlov's original writings in Russian. Pavlov actually used the words *conditional* and *unconditional* rather than *conditioned* and *unconditioned* (Gantt, 1966). We will use the terms *conditioned* and *unconditioned* in this text. To facilitate your familiarity with these terms, Figure 2.2 illustrates the stages of the conditioning process as they occurred in Pavlov's experiment.

EXAMPLES OF CLASSICAL CONDITIONING

Imagine for a moment that a mail carrier has started delivering mail in a new neighborhood. At one of the houses on her route, 1217 Glade Road, a small dog (a poodle) is in the yard. As the mail carrier walks through the gate to deliver the mail, the poodle crouches, growls, then runs toward her and bites her ankle. Being bitten by a dog naturally elicits a number of responses, especially fear. A few days later, the mail carrier walks through the gate at 1217 Glade Road, and the same poodle runs toward her and bites her ankle. After a few such experiences, the mail carrier

Before Conditioning

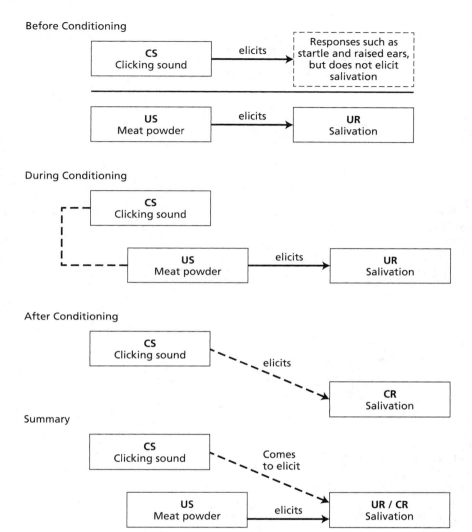

FIGURE 2.2 Stages of the Conditioning Process.

During Conditioning

After Conditioning

Summary

notices a change in her behavior. She begins to feel afraid as she approaches 1217 Glade Road. The sight of this house, which originally produced little or no response, now elicits fear.

Because of her experiences with the dog-bite stimuli, the mail carrier learned that simply seeing the house at 1217 Glade Road reliably preceded a dog bite. As a result, the sight of this *house* began to instill fear in her. Figure 2.3 illustrates the elements of this classical conditioning episode.

There are examples of classical conditioning, of course, in many situations. Certainly you salivate naturally when food is in your mouth, but you may also salivate in response to hearing or reading about the foods you enjoy. Although fear may be a natural reaction to physical pain, fear may also occur when you speak to an audience, when you take an exam, or even when you contemplate riding a crowded elevator. Even sexual arousal, which is elicited naturally by certain kinds of physical contact, can occur

Before Conditioning

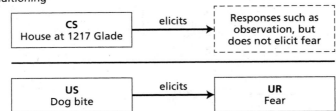

FIGURE 2.3 Classical Conditioning Episode.

During Conditioning

After Conditioning

Summary

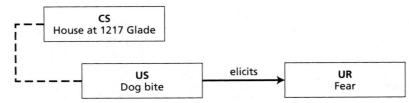

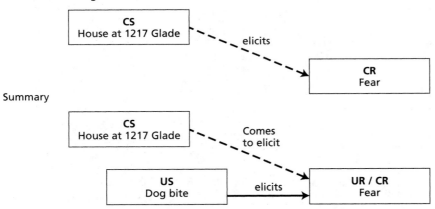

in response to a photograph, a particular aroma, or even a spoken phrase. In all these cases we make reflexive or emotional responses to stimuli that do not naturally produce them. In each case we respond to such stimuli because they are reliable signals for other soon-to-come stimuli that naturally produce such responses. Such conditioned responses, and numerous others we make every day, arise through the process of classical conditioning.

As already mentioned, classical conditioning is responsible for many of our emotional responses. In extreme cases, classical conditioning can contribute to the development of phobias and other anxiety disorders when conditioned stimuli come to elicit extreme fear (for a discussion, see Edelmann, 1992). If this is the case, then our knowledge of classical conditioning should also suggest effective ways of treating phobias. In fact, some very effective treatments for phobias, such as systematic desensitization (Wolpe, 1958; 1990) are based on principles of classical conditioning. We will look at these procedures in more detail later.

Earlier, we suggested that classical conditioning could play a role in drug tolerance and drug overdose. Although it may seem unlikely, this possibility has been supported by the research of Shepard Siegel and his colleagues (Siegel, 1984, 1989; Siegel, Hinson, Krank, & McCully, 1982). Stimuli that reliably precede the administration of drugs can become CSs that elicit conditioned responses. When administration of a drug serves as the US, the conditioned responses are sometimes the opposite of the unconditioned responses caused by the drug. These responses compensate for some of the effects of the drug. Such compensatory CRs can occur following conditioning with alcohol, narcotics, and other drugs as the US.

As in the earlier example, drug tolerance may result, in part, from such compensatory CRs. In many cases, because of the routines or rituals of drug users, certain stimuli reliably precede drug administration. Through classical conditioning, these stimuli can become CSs that elicit compensatory CRs that offset the effects of the drug. These compensatory CRs can thus produce tolerance—a decrease in the user's response to the drug. However, when the drug is taken in a new situation, or some of the CSs are not present, the compensatory CR may not occur. As a result, the drug's effects on the user are increased and, in some cases, could lead to overdose.

Siegel, Hinson, Krank, and McCully (1982) conducted an experiment to test whether classical conditioning might help to account for accidental heroin overdose. In this experiment, male rats were injected with heroin every other day for 30 days. On the days when the rats did not receive heroin injections they received injections of a dextrose (sugar) solution. The injections were administered in one of two distinctive rooms, either the rats' home room, or in a different room. Half of the rats received heroin only in their home room and dextrose only in the other

room. The other group received dextrose only in their home room and heroin only in the other room. The amount of heroin administered each day was slowly increased to a dose that produced tolerance to the heroin. A third group of rats served as a control group and received no heroin injections but received dextrose injections in both rooms.

At the end of this procedure, the experimenters injected the animals with twice their normal dose of heroin. Half of the experimental animals received this double dose in the room where heroin was normally administered. The other experimental animals received the larger dose in the room where dextrose was normally administered. The control group also received the same increased dose of heroin.

The results of this procedure are shown in Figure 2.4. The large dose killed almost all the control-group animals (96% deaths). Most importantly, there were twice as many deaths in the different-room group (64% deaths) than in the same-room group (32% deaths). Siegel and his colleagues (1982) contend that this difference occurred because features of the room where the animals received heroin became CSs that caused compensatory CRs that offset the effects of the drug. As a result the animals in this condition were not affected as severely by the increased dose. For those animals that received the increased dose in the room where they normally received dextrose, there were no CSs to cause the compensatory CRs. More of the rats in this group died from the increased dose.

Classical conditioning can affect other important physiological processes. For example, through classical conditioning, conditioned stimuli can come to cause allergic reactions (Gauci, Husband, Saxarra, & King, 1994) and asthma (Miller & Kotses, 1995). Recent studies have shown that classical conditioning can affect the immune system suppression, either suppressing it (Ader & Cohen, 1993) or activating it (Jenkins, Chadwick, & Nevin, 1993). These studies all suggest that classical conditioning can have important effects on our health.

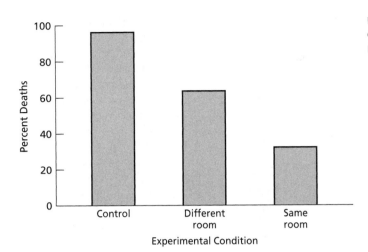

FIGURE 2.4 The Consequence of Compensatory CRs in Rat-Heroin Experiment.

THE CONCEPT OF CONTINGENCY

We have encountered the idea that classical conditioning occurs when one stimulus becomes a signal for another. Through classical conditioning, stimuli that are reliable signals for important events begin to produce new responses. At this point, however, we have not addressed how a stimulus becomes a reliable signal. This is a very important issue, because the degree of conditioning depends on how effective a signal the CS is.

If a CS is a signal for a US, these stimuli must have a contingent relationship. Very simply this means that the occurrence or nonoccurrence of the US must be contingent on the prior occurrence of the stimulus. Stated another way, the occurrence of the CS and the occurrence of the US must be **correlated** in some fashion.

When a CS is consistently followed by a US, we say that a **positive contingency** exists between them. This means that the two stimuli tend to occur together and that neither tends to occur when the other is absent. Lightning reliably precedes thunder and thunder rarely occurs without lightning, so there is a positive contingency between lightning and thunder. Where there is a positive contingency in effect, one of the events is a reliable predictor or signal for the occurrence of the other.

In a classical conditioning situation, when there is a positive contingency between a conditioned stimulus and an unconditioned stimulus, the particular type of learning that occurs is called **classical excitatory conditioning.** "Excitatory" refers to the fact that the CS acquires the capability of eliciting a response like the one that is naturally produced by the US. Our example of classical conditioning involving the house at 1217 Glade Road and the mail carrier is really an example of excitatory conditioning. In this example a positive contingency existed between the house at 1217 Glade and an imminent dog bite. As a result, the house began to produce the same fear response in the mail carrier that originally had been produced only by the dog bite.

A second type of contingent relationship is a **negative contingency.** This refers to the situation in which one stimulus regularly precedes the absence of another stimulus that is present at other times. For example, a sunny day regularly accompanies the absence of thunder. In this case there is a negative contingency between sunny days and thunder.

The effect of a negative contingency in classical conditioning can be seen when the CS is regularly accompanied by the absence of some response-eliciting stimulus. Such negative contingencies result in what psychologists call a

classical inhibitory conditioning. When this occurs, the CS begins to produce a response just as in excitatory conditioning. However, unlike what is found in excitatory conditioning, the response produced by the CS bears little similarity to the response produced naturally by a particular US. In fact, in some cases, the inhibitory CS begins to produce a response that is the opposite of the response that is elicited by the US.

With a simple addition, the example referenced earlier, in which a positive contingency existed between the house at 1217 Glade Road and a painful bite, illustrates inhibitory conditioning. Assume now that there is no dog at the next house on the street, 1219 Glade Road. When the mail carrier walks into the yard of this house, there is never a dog there so she is never bitten. In this case, the house at 1219 Glade Road would come to signal the absence of a vicious dog, and the mail carrier would feel calm or relieved upon her approach.

It is also possible to have situations where there is *no* correlation or contingency between two stimuli. This is the sort of relationship that exists between sunny days and wind. Sometimes sunny days are windy and sometimes they are calm and mild. Sometimes wind occurs on cloudy days. What happens if there is no contingency between a CS and a US—when the CS isn't a reliable signal for the occurrence or the absence of a US? Generally, the absence of a contingency between a CS and a US results in virtually no classical conditioning.

METHODS FOR STUDYING CLASSICAL EXCITATORY CONDITIONING

All the examples in the chapter thus far underscore the importance of classical conditioning. However, it is often impossible (and in some cases unethical) to study classical conditioning by creating such situations in the laboratory. Therefore, researchers use methods of studying classical conditioning appropriate for experimental research. However, this type of research should reveal laws of conditioning that help to explain real-life events.

Since Pavlov's original studies, several experimental situations have been developed to study the nature and the laws of the conditioning process. These situations, called paradigms, have evolved because they represent efficient procedures for studying conditioning in a given species. The following is a brief description of some of the paradigms researchers have used.

Human Conditioning Paradigms

Among the more common responses studied in human conditioning experiments are the eye-blink reflex, and the skin conductance response. Methods of measuring these responses are shown in Figure 2.5. In human eye-blink conditioning, a subject is usually seated in a quiet dimly lit room wearing a pair of modified goggles. The goggles contain a nozzle pointed toward the corner of the subject's eye and an apparatus to detect movements of the eyelid. Normally, eyelid movements are detected by an infrared light source and an infrared sensor positioned in front of the eye. Infrared light is reflected by the eye and detected by the infrared sensor. Movement of the eyelid causes the amount of infrared light reflected from the eye to change, thus changing the flow of electric current through the infrared sensor. These changes in electrical current can be recorded by a computer or by a paper strip recorder and used as a measure of eyelid movement. Typically, subjects are presented a light or tone as the CS. The US is normally a puff of air directed toward the outside corner of the eye via the nozzle in the headband. The air puff produces an immediate blinking response (the UR). After several pairings of the light or tone and the air puff, the subject begins to blink whenever the light or tone is presented.

One point concerning the conditioned eye-blink response is worth noting, as it is also true of most other conditioned responses we are going to discuss. The eye blink that occurs to the CS in this situation does not appear to be a voluntary reaction made to prevent the air puff from

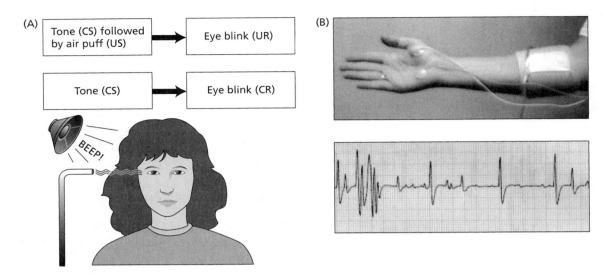

FIGURE 2.5 Human Conditioning Paradigms. Apparatus used in studying classical excitatory conditioning in humans. (A) apparatus for detecting eye blinks with a sample record showing eye blinks. (B) Preparation for measuring skin conductance. Note the two skin conductance sensors on the palm and the cuff on the forearm for delivery of mild electric shock. Bottom—skin conductance record showing skin conductance responses.

reaching the eye. As it happens, the form of the blinking response, as well as the rapidity of the response, differ when a blink is voluntary and when it occurs in response to a CS (Spence & Ross, 1959). Thus, conditioned responses to a CS are more like reflexive than voluntary reactions.

A second paradigm involving human subjects is conditioning of changes in skin conductance. When we experience some form of aversive stimulation or emotional arousal, one reaction is that certain sweat glands in our skin open. An extreme example of this process is when your palms become sweaty if you are extremely nervous. As a result, the electrical resistance of the skin decreases markedly, and the skin becomes more conductive to electricity. Some researchers have used this naturally occurring increase in skin conductance to study the conditioning process (Lachnit & Kimmel, 1993). In these experiments, electrodes are placed on the fingers or palms of the hands to measure changes in the skin's conductance (see Figure 2.5). These changes are recorded by a computer or on a paper chart recorder. Typically, a visual or auditory CS is pre-

sented just prior to an aversive stimulus such as a mild electric shock or a loud buzzer. On the first trial, an increase in skin conductance is seen only after the aversive stimulation. As the trials progress, however, the change in resistance tends to occur with greater and greater frequency as a response to the visual or auditory CS.

These, of course, are not the only responses that have been conditioned in human subjects. Changes in heart rate, changes in blood pressure, withdrawal of a finger from painful stimulation, and leg flexion are but a few of the other responses that have been studied (Beecroft, 1966). In addition to these various response systems, several types of CSs have been used in human conditioning studies. For example, some experimenters have investigated how conditioning progresses when words, visual forms, or numbers are used as CSs (Grant, 1973). From the mid-1960s through the late 1980s, there was a general decline in the number of conditioning studies employing human subjects. Coleman and Webster (1990) discuss several reasons for this decline. During the 1990s, however, there was a resurgence in classical condition-

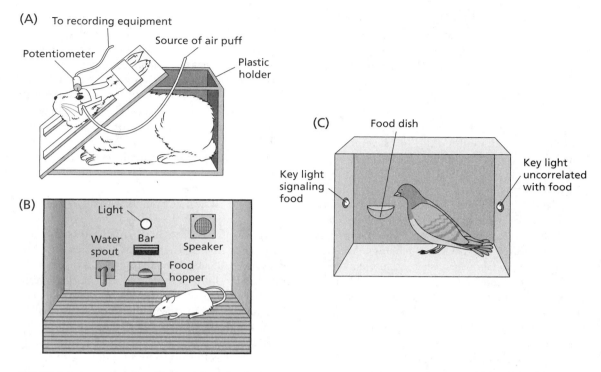

FIGURE 2.6 Apparatus Used in Studying Classical Excitatory Conditioning in Animals. (A) Rabbit nictitating membrane conditioning apparatus. (B) Operant chamber for assessing CER in rats. (C) Pigeon operant chamber showing response keys and food hopper.

ing research using human subjects. Most of the classical conditioning studies in the past 10 to 15 years, however, have examined classical conditioning in nonhuman species.

Conditioning Paradigms Used with Animals

Most contemporary studies of classical conditioning have been done with animal subjects in paradigms specifically suited to the particular species. Some of the most commonly used procedures are the nictitating membrane paradigm utilizing rabbits, the startle reflex and conditioned emotional response procedures using rats, and the autoshaping paradigm involving pigeons. Figure 2.6 illustrates the apparatuses used in these paradigms. It should be noted that these procedures have not been chosen because they involve responses that are particularly relevant to human behavior. They

have been selected because they are efficient procedures for studying the laws of conditioning.

The first of these procedures, the conditioning of the nictitating membrane in the rabbit, is a direct analog of the human eye-blink conditioning paradigm. Besides having an outer eyelid similar to that of humans, rabbits and some other rodents have an inner eyelid called a nictitating membrane. This membrane closes or blinks naturally in response to air movements or other forms of stimulation around the eye. Using procedures similar to those used for eyelid conditioning, Gormezano (1966) demonstrated that this membrane closes in response to a CS that regularly precedes the presentation of a puff of air. In recent years, this procedure has been invaluable in the study of brain mechanisms involved in conditioning (see, for example, Clark & Lavond, 1993; Krupa, Thompson, & Thompson, 1993).

The second procedure involves pigeons. They, like many other birds, make a natural pecking response when food is presented. In this case food can be considered to be a US that naturally elicits the response of pecking. It is now also known that pigeons tend to peck other objects when these objects regularly precede the presentation of food (Brown & Jenkins, 1968). For example, if a pigeon is presented with a lighted disk on several occasions and on each occasion the disk is followed by a food presentation, the pigeon will begin to peck the disk just as it had previously pecked at the food. In this case the disk represents a CS; it is not a stimulus that naturally elicits pecking. Pecking at the disk is a CR, since it is a response that occurs only because of the disk-food pairings. We will have more to say about autoshaping in Chapter 6.

Finally, a conditioning procedure widely used with rats is called the **conditioned emotional response** (CER) paradigm. This procedure involves conditioning rats to fear a previously neutral stimulus (Estes & Skinner, 1941). The conditioning procedure itself is very simple. Rats are usually presented with an auditory or visual stimulus as the CS, followed by the presentation of an aversive stimulus such as a mild shock or a loud noise. The shock or noise, which serves as the US, naturally produces a number of responses such as increased heart rate, elevated blood pressure, and the release of certain hormones. In addition, rats react to such aversive stimuli with two responses: a brief startle response (a sudden jerk) followed by freezing or halting whatever responses they were making when the aversive stimulus appeared. Several conditioned responses can be measured here. The response that is measured in the CER procedure is the freezing reaction. This response is used to determine whether the CS effectively elicits the conditioned response. After the CS-US pairings, the question of interest is whether the CS becomes capable of producing a startle or a freezing reaction on its own.

Unfortunately, measuring a freezing response is difficult. Determining whether a rat freezes when a stimulus is presented sounds simple enough. In reality, however, it is difficult because an animal's natural level of activity may be low even before any conditioning has occurred. If this is the case, it is difficult to assess when an animal is freezing and when it is simply not doing much. Most researchers in fact *train* rats to perform some active response before giving them the CS-US pairings. The rats may be trained, for example, to press a lever to receive food, or they may be taught to lick a drinking spout for water. After such training, rats tend to make these responses frequently. The researcher allows the animal to begin making the active response and then presents the CS that had been paired with the unpleasant US. If conditioning has in fact occurred, the presentation of the CS will cause the rats to freeze. This freezing in turn disrupts the bar pressing or licking the animals were engaged in before the CS. By measuring this disruption in the ongoing behavior, researchers can determine whether the CS caused the freezing response.

Table 2.1 summarizes the stages of the CER paradigm. Note that in stage 1 rats are trained to perform some active response, so that during testing a high level of responding will be assured. In stage 2 the rats receive conditioning trials involving pairings of a neutral CS with an aversive US. In stage 3, the animal begins to respond at preshock levels. Once responding has stabilized, the CS from conditioning is presented and any change in the active responding is measured. Decreases in the rate of the ongoing responding are interpreted as evidence that the CS has become capable of producing a freezing reaction.

An important point concerning the CER paradigm is that the measure of conditioning used is quite different from the measures of conditioning used in other paradigms. The measure of conditioning in the CER paradigm, called the suppression ratio, involves comparing the rate of responding before the CS presentation to the rate of responding during the CS presentation. The suppression ratio is calculated by dividing the number of responses made during the CS presentation by the number of responses the rat makes both before and during the CS.

For example, let's assume that an experimenter allows a rat to begin pressing a bar for several minutes, then presents a CS for 30 sec-

Table 2.1 Stages of Training in the Conditioned Emotional Response (CER) Paradigm

Stage	Procedure	Example
1	Train the animal to perform a voluntary response at a high rate.	Train the animal to press a bar for a food or water reward.
2	Expose the animal to a series of fear conditioning trials.	Give the animal a series of tone (CS)–shock (US) pairings.
3	Allow the animal to resume the previously learned voluntary response. Then present the CS used in fear conditioning.	Allow the animal to resume bar pressing. While it is pressing, present the tone used in fear conditioning.
4	Compare the rate of voluntary responding with and without the CS.	Compare the rate of pressing before the tone presentation to the rate of pressing during the tone.

onds. To measure suppression related to the CS, the experimenter records the number of responses the rat makes in the 30 seconds before the CS presentation, as well as the number of responses made during the CS. The suppression ratio would then be calculated as follows:

$$\frac{\text{responses during the CS}}{\text{responses before CS} + \text{responses during CS}}$$

At the outset of the experiment the onset of the CS will not affect the animal's rate of response. Let's suppose that the animal makes 25 responses before the CS, then continues responding at the same rate during the CS. The suppression ratio would be calculated as

$$\frac{25}{25 + 25} = 0.50$$

A suppression ratio of 0.50 means that no conditioning has taken place. Later on, after the animal has received several conditioning trials, it might show a response to the CS. Imagine that the rat now makes 25 bar presses in the 30 seconds before the CS, then freezes completely during the CS and makes no responses. According to the above formula, the suppression ratio would be calculated as

$$\frac{0}{25 + 0} = 0$$

Now we can see that the CS is having an effect on responding. Thus suppression ratios of zero indicate very strong conditioning. Overall then, higher suppression ratios (up to the maximum of 0.5) reflect little conditioning, while lower ratios reflect stronger conditioning.

We raise this point because in our other conditioning paradigms, higher measures indicate stronger conditioning, while lower measures indicate little conditioning. In the CER paradigm, successful conditioning is indicated by lower suppression ratios. Higher suppression ratios indicate little or no conditioning.

VARIABLES THAT AFFECT EXCITATORY CONDITIONING

From our description of conditioning paradigms, it may seem that pairings of a CS and a US inevitably produce conditioned responding. This is an oversimplification at best. As was mentioned earlier, classical conditioning is a complex learning process. A variety of factors influence the degree to which excitatory conditioning occurs.

The Relationship Between CS and US

In this context, *relationship* refers to the way occurrences of the CS and the US are arranged in time. In this section the effect of changing the

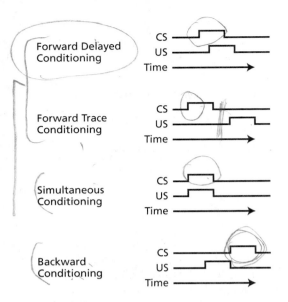

FIGURE 2.7 Common CS-US Arrangements Used in Classical Conditioning Experiments.

temporal order of CS and US occurrence and the temporal distance between these stimuli will be examined. There will also be discussion of the effects of the CS-US correlation and the effects of the number of CS-US pairings.

The Temporal Order of the CS and US

In the natural environment, potential CSs and USs can occur at any time and in any number of arrangements. For example, a potential US may occur quite some time after a potential CS has appeared. In some cases, a potential CS may not occur until after a US has already disappeared. Sometimes such stimuli may even occur at precisely the same time. What degree of conditioning should be expected when these different arrangements occur? To answer this question, researchers have analyzed a variety of CS-US configurations. The four most commonly studied arrangements are depicted in Figure 2.7.

The first two arrangements are the delayed and trace conditioning configurations. Both arrangements are examples of what is termed forward conditioning, since the beginning (onset)

of the CS precedes the onset of the US in both cases. The difference between the forward delayed and forward trace situations lies with when the end (offset) of the CS occurs relative to the beginning of the US. In **delayed conditioning,** the CS begins before the US, and it does not end until sometime after US onset. In other words, the CS and the US overlap to some degree. This is the sort of conditioning that occurs when you receive injections at your doctor's office. The hypodermic needle (the CS) appears first, then you feel the pain of the injection while the needle is still present. Finally, both the needle and the pain stop at about the same time.

In the **trace conditioning** situation the CS begins and ends before US onset. Thus, time elapses between the end of one stimulus and the onset of the other. An example of trace conditioning is found in the relationship between thunder and lightning. First, the flash of lightning begins and ends. Then, some time later, you hear the loud thunder clap. This conditioning probably accounts for why many of us are startled by a nearby lightning flash.

At times a CS can come to elicit a conditioned response when either of these forward conditioning arrangements occurs (Ellison, 1964). Most studies, however, have shown that the conditioning produced by the delayed procedure is far superior to that which occurs when a trace conditioning arrangement is used. For example, Schneiderman (1966) compared these two procedures in an attempt to condition the rabbit's nictitating membrane. He found that the delayed procedure produced much faster conditioning of the response than did the trace arrangement. This superiority was particularly evident when the trace procedure involved longer intervals between CS offset and US onset. Kamin (1965), who studied the effect of these arrangements in a CER paradigm, reported similar results.

A third type of CS-US arrangement is termed **simultaneous conditioning,** because the CS and US begin at the same time. In comparing the delayed and trace conditioning procedures, we saw that some degree of overlap between the CS and US appeared to aid conditioning. From this, one might assume that simultaneous conditioning would be very effective, as it involves total CS–US contiguity. This, however, is not the case. Although the simultaneous procedure has been studied only sparingly, most experiments have shown it to be almost totally ineffective as a conditioning procedure (Bitterman, 1964; Smith, Coleman, & Gormezano, 1969). Although simultaneous conditioning has occasionally been shown to produce small amounts of conditioned responding (see, for example, Burkhardt & Ayres, 1978), this arrangement is clearly not as effective as the forward conditioning configurations.

The final arrangement outlined in Figure 2.7 is called **backward conditioning.** This occurs whenever the onset of the US precedes the onset of the CS. After giving an injection to a young child, doctors sometimes give the child a piece of candy. This is an example of a backward conditioning arrangement, because the US (the painful injection) begins before the CS (the candy). In this situation, will the child begin to fear candy? Typically the child will not. In general, backward conditioning is inferior to the forward conditioning arrangements and produces little or no conditioned responding (see, for example, Mackintosh, 1974). However, a variety of factors influence the amount and type of response obtained with this procedure.

Some researchers have found that backward conditioning produces no evidence of excitatory conditioned responding (Terrace, 1973). Others have found that the procedure can result in classical inhibitory conditioning, especially when a large number of backward pairings are used (Hall, 1984; Moscovitch & LoLordo, 1968; Siegal & Domjan, 1971). A few studies have reported that backward conditioning can produce excitatory CRs if special conditions exist (Heth & Rescorla, 1973; Mahoney & Ayres, 1976; Spetch, Wilkie, & Pinel, 1981; Wagner & Terry, 1975). Basically, this procedure appears to result in excitatory CRs in only two types of circumstances. First, excitatory conditioning is most likely to occur when only a few conditioning trials are used. Second, excitatory CRs may result when the occurrence

of the US on each trial is particularly surprising or unpredictable.

Finally, it is important to mention the timing of the CRs. In general, early in the conditioning trials the peak CR is given early in the interval. For example, if the CS duration is five seconds and the US duration is two seconds there are three seconds between offset of the CS and onset of the US. Early in training CRs will be given just after CS offset. With extended training however, the animal will begin to produce CRs that correspond more closely with the onset of the US. Occasionally, animals will produce two CRs that correspond to CS onset and US onset. Note that the shift of timing is adaptive. If the animal produces a CR closer in time to the actual presentation of the US it will likely be more prepared for US onset.

The CS–US Interval

Even in forward conditioning arrangements, the effectiveness of conditioning depends to a large degree on the CS–US interval—that is, the time between the onset of the CS and the beginning of the US. The importance of the CS–US interval can be seen in Figure 2.8, which represents the results of an experiment by Smith, Coleman, and Gormezano (1969). In this experiment the rabbit's nictitating membrane response was studied. The experiment exposed the rabbits to a 50 millisecond (mS) tone CS and a 50-millisecond shock US. The rabbits differed in terms of the number of milliseconds that separated the CS and US onsets. As you can see, when backward (50-milliseconds) and simultaneous (0-milliseconds) arrangements were used, the percentage of conditioned responses produced was negligible. Animals that received forward conditioning configurations in which the CS–US interval was very short (50 milliseconds) also showed little evidence of conditioning. Maximal conditioning was obtained when animals were exposed to a CS–US interval of approximately 200 milliseconds. Longer CS–US intervals tended to be less effective in producing CRs.

Although the specific time intervals that result in maximal conditioning do vary from one

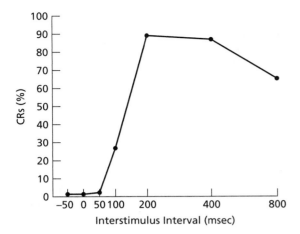

FIGURE 2.8 The Percentage of Trials on which a CR Occurs as a Function of the Length of the CS-US interval. Note that conditioning is poor when either backward (−50 msec) or simultaneous (0 msec) pairings occur. Maximal conditioning results when the CS-US interval is approximately 200 msec. After Smith, et al., 1969. ©1969 by the American Psychological Assn. Reprinted with permission.

paradigm to another, studies done with virtually all paradigms have shown that the same pattern of effects occurs. Extremely short CS-US intervals seldom result in conditioning. Maximal conditioning usually occurs when the CS-US interval is between 200 milliseconds and 2 seconds. As the CS-US interval is gradually increased beyond this optimal interval, less and less conditioned responding usually results.

Again, just as we noted when we discussed the order of stimulus occurrence, the best conditioning occurs when the CS precedes the US by some period of time. However, with extremely long CS-US intervals, it becomes less likely that the CS will signal some discrete future event. When CS-US intervals are long, the CS tends to signal a period of US absence rather than the impending onset of the US (Akins, Domjan, & Gutierrez, 1994).

There is one striking exception to the rule that long CS-US intervals fail to promote conditioning. This exception occurs in a situation that is usually termed the taste aversion paradigm (see, for example, Garcia, Ervin, & Koelling, 1966). In this paradigm, an animal is allowed to drink a liquid or consume food that has a distinctive odor or flavor. The animal is subsequently injected with a chemical that produces nausea, such as lithium chloride. When tested later, the animals usually show a clear avoidance of the odor or taste they experienced before they became ill. In this paradigm the odor or taste functions as the CS, while the US is the chemical that produces nausea. The avoidance of the odor or taste is the conditioned response (see Figure 2.9).

One of the unusual features of this paradigm is that several hours may elapse between the time the taste or odor is experienced and the time the chemical begins to produce nausea. This means that the CS-US interval in this situation often lasts for several hours. Despite this lengthy interval, conditioning obviously occurs, and the strength of the conditioning is often remarkable. Anyone who has ever eaten spoiled food or who has had too much of one substance to drink and has later become ill can attest to how aversive the taste of a particular food or drink can become. This issue takes on much more importance for those individuals undergoing chemotherapy. It is not at all clear how this particular form of conditioning can occur when such long CS-US intervals are involved. As we will see, however, the taste-aversion paradigm presents an entire range of problems for theorists in the field of classical conditioning.

In the Western United states, farmers and ranchers sometimes must kill coyotes because these animals attack and kill domesticated livestock, such as young sheep and calves. Using principles of classical conditioning, Gustafson, Garcia, Hankins, and Rusiniak (1974) baited coyotes with lamb meat laced with lithium chloride. As you may have guessed, after eating the lamb and becoming ill, the coyotes were less inclined to attack lambs. Thus, classical conditioning provided a more humane and efficient way to control the predatory behavior of coyotes.

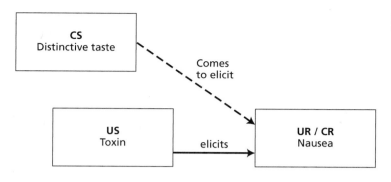

FIGURE 2.9 Avoidance of Odor or Taste as a Conditioned Response.

Another application of taste-aversion learning is **aversion therapies.** Aversion therapies are sometimes used to help individuals stop smoking cigarettes or stop drinking alcohol. In these procedures, the taste of cigarettes or alcohol (a CS) is paired with an unpleasant stimulus (the US). As a result, the taste of cigarettes or alcohol should elicit aversive conditioned responses, thus decreasing the person's use of cigarettes or alcohol. In one such procedure, termed **rapid smoking,** smokers are required to smoke very rapidly (inhaling 10 times per minute) until they become nauseous (Smith, 1991). As a result, cigarette smoke becomes a CS that elicits nausea and other unpleasant sensations, resulting in decreased smoking. Of course, this procedure is not highly recommended and should never be used for individuals with certain health problems, such as cardiovascular or pulmonary conditions.

In one type of treatment for alcohol abuse, the taste of alcohol (the CS) is paired with drugs that cause nausea and vomiting (the US). Through classical conditioning, the smell and taste of alcohol will come to elicit nausea, thus decreasing or eliminating the individual's consumption of alcohol.

The Correlation of CS and US Occurrence

We have noted that classical conditioning occurs when the CS regularly precedes the occurrence of the US. From this, you might predict that the degree of conditioning would also depend on the degree to which the CS and the US are positively correlated. This prediction is clearly supported by data from a variety of conditioning experiments.

To illustrate the importance of the CS–US correlation, consider this extreme example: Assume that you are studying conditioning in two groups of organisms. Both groups receive the same number of exposures to the CS and the US. However, one group receives a +11.0 correlation between the CS and the US. In other words, in this group the US is always preceded by the CS. The second group receives a 0.0 correlation between the two stimuli—that is, the presentations of CS and US occur totally at random. This means that for the second group sometimes two CSs might occur in sequence. At other times two USs might occur together. And, at still other times, a CS might precede a US presentation by chance. How would you expect these two groups to compare in terms of conditioned responding to the CS?

Several researchers have made this kind of comparison and the results are clear (see, for example, Gamzu & Williams, 1971; Rescorla, 1966, 1968, 1969a; Weisman & Litner, 1969). A strong positive correlation between a CS and a US usually produces substantial conditioning. However, a zero correlation produces virtually no evidence of excitatory conditioning even when some CS-US pairings do occur by chance. At first glance, these findings appear to be convincing evidence that a positive CS-US correlation is necessary for conditioning. There is, however, another way to interpret this. The

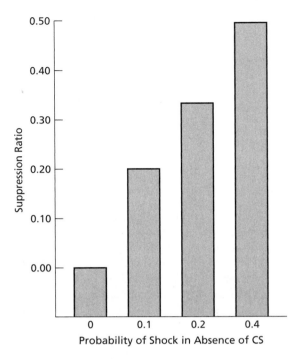

FIGURE 2.10 US-CS Correlations. Amount of conditioning as a function of the probability that the US will occur alone (From Rescorla, 1968, Exp. 2).

group that receives the positive correlation is exposed to a greater number of CS–US pairings than the zero-correlation group receives. Thus, the superior performance of the positive correlation group may be due simply to its having received more pairings, rather than the greater CS–US correlation in this group.

To choose between these alternative interpretations, it is necessary to conduct an experiment in which two groups receive the same number of CS–US pairings but are exposed to different CS–US correlations. Rescorla (1968, 1969) has carried out several experiments like this. In one of these studies (Rescorla, 1968, experiment 2), rats were trained in a CER paradigm using a tone as the CS and a mild shock as the US. Four groups of rats received the same number of tone-shock pairings. However, these groups differed in terms of the probability that shock would also occur

when the tone was absent. Since the CS–US correlation depends on how consistently the CS precedes the US, groups that received large numbers of US-alone presentations actually experienced low CS–US correlations.

The results of this experiment are plotted in Figure 2.10. Recall that better conditioning is reflected by lower suppression ratios in the CER paradigm. As you can see, the group that received no shocks in the absence of the CS exhibited substantial conditioning. However, the amount of conditioning decreased in the groups with more US-alone presentations. It is important to note that this result occurred despite the fact that all four groups received the same number of CS–US pairings in this experiment. This result illustrates that conditioning depends to a large degree on the CS-US correlation, or on how reliably the CS signals a US occurrence. As the positive correlation between a CS and a US increases, so does the amount of conditioned responding.

The Number of CS-US Pairings

If there is a strong correlation between the CS and the US and all other factors that affect conditioning are optimal, the amount of conditioned responding depends directly on the number of CS–US pairings. In general, the more CS–US pairings an organism experiences, the greater the probability that a CR will occur. There is, however, a limit to this effect. After a substantial number of CS–US pairings have occurred, this increase in conditioned responding will level off or reach asymptote, the maximal amount of responding that can be obtained with a particular set of conditioning circumstances.

In some cases asymptote is determined by the response measurement used. For example, if the measure of response is the percentage of times the CS produces a CR, this measure must obviously level off at 100 percent. In other cases, however, asymptote will depend either on the physical limitations of an organism or on the physical characteristics of the CS and US. Figure 2.11 illustrates the relationship between conditioned responding and the number of CS–US pairings in three of

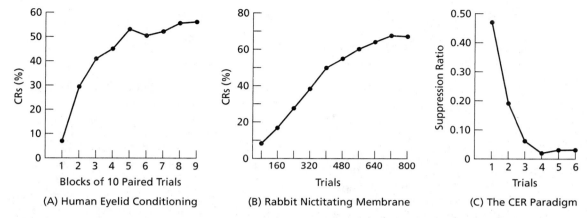

FIGURE 2.11 Amount of Conditioning as a Function of the Number of CS-US Pairings. After (A) Trapold and Spence, 1960; (B) Gormezano, 1965, from *Classical Conditioning: A Symposium* © 1965 Appleton & Lange; and (C) Lovibond, Preston, and Mackintosh, 1984, from "Context Specificity of Conditioning, Extinction, and Latent Inhibition." © 1984 by the American Psychological Assn. Reprinted by permission of the publisher and N. J. Mackintosh.

the paradigms we have discussed thus far. These graphic representations are usually called learning or acquisition curves, since they reflect the degree to which a CR is learned or acquired as a function of CS-US experiences.

CHARACTERISTICS OF THE CS AND THE US

We have seen that the relationship between CS and US can determine the degree to which conditioning occurs. In addition, it is also the case that conditioned responding depends on specific characteristics of the CS and US. In this section we will look at the effects of certain CS and US characteristics on the conditioning process. Specifically, we will examine three factors: the intensity of these stimuli, the organism's prior experience with these stimuli, and, the relationship between the CS and US characteristics.

CS and US Intensity

The intensity of a stimulus, generally speaking, is the strength of that stimulus. For example, visual stimuli vary in brightness just as auditory stimuli differ in loudness. Tactile stimuli vary in

terms of the pressures they can exert on the skin, whereas foods may differ in terms of amount of sourness or sweetness. Brighter visual stimuli are more intense than dim ones, and louder auditory stimuli are more intense than soft ones. Another aspect of intensity of a stimulus is salience. Salience is how noticeable the give stimulus is to an organism. Intense stimuli are often more salient than other stimuli. However, as we will see, some salient stimuli are less intense.

The effects of CS and US intensity on conditioning are reasonably straightforward. Conditioning normally improves as the intensity of either the CS or the US increases. In the case of the CS, it appears that the absolute intensity of the stimulus is relatively unimportant. In other words, the use of a very loud tone as a CS does not necessarily ensure better conditioning than would be obtained if a moderately loud tone were used. What is more important is the *salience* of the CS relative to the background stimuli that are present when the CS occurs. Better conditioning usually results when the CS is very salient in a situation (Logan, 1954).

A study conducted by Kamin (1965) in which he used a CER paradigm illustrates this difference between absolute intensity and salience. In this study the CS was not the presentation of a discrete stimulus. Rather, the CS was a decrease in the level of background noise that normally existed in the experimental chamber. All rats were exposed to white noise in the chamber at the level of 80 decibels. Then different groups were given varying decreases in this background noise level as their CS. The noise decrease was always followed by shock. Kamin found that the groups that experienced the largest noise decreases as a CS showed the greatest evidence of conditioning. This occurred even though the groups with large noise decreases actually were being exposed to less intense noise levels just before the time of shock delivery. Kamin's findings show that conditioning does not depend to any great extent on the intensity of the stimulus that precedes the US. What is important is that the presentation of a CS constitutes a clear change from the other stimuli present in the environment.

Prior Experience with CS or US

It is not unusual in a laboratory experiment for the CS and US to be novel. How many times, for example, are rats exposed to a particular tone or shock before they take part in a conditioning experiment? In our daily lives, however, the potential conditioning situations we encounter often involve CSs or USs with which we are already familiar. How does our prior experience with a CS or a US affect the degree to which these stimuli will promote conditioning?

Pre-exposures to a CS alone can hinder later conditioning involving that CS. This phenomenon is called latent inhibition (Lubow & Moore, 1959). Prior experience with a US also appears to interfere with the conditioning process. Several studies have demonstrated that, when an organism is exposed to a series of US-alone presentations, later conditioning involving that US tends to be slowed (Randich & LoLordo, 1979). This phenomenon is termed the US pre-exposure effect.

CS-US Relevance

For a number of years, researchers viewed classical conditioning as a relatively automatic, invariant process. They assumed that any CS could be paired with any US to produce conditioning. It was assumed, for example, that if the US were an air puff to the eye, tones, lights, tastes, odors, and tactile stimuli would all be equally effective as CSs. We now know that the rules of conditioning are not so simple. In recent years, there has been much discussion of what is termed CS-US relevance. Informally speaking, this term refers to whether a CS and a US are typically related in the natural environment (and particularly in the evolutionary history of a species). In other words, is a particular CS a relevant signal for occurrence of the US? Research in this area shows that some combinations of CSs and USs appear to promote effective conditioning while others do not.

The classic example of this principle is contained in a study conducted by Garcia and Koelling (1966). A diagram of their experimental procedures is shown in Figure 2.12. These researchers trained rats to drink a solution from a tube. As the animals drank, they were exposed to two types of stimuli. First, the solution had a distinctive flavor. Second, as the animals drank, a light and a clicking sound were presented. Thus, both taste and audiovisual stimuli occurred as CSs. Shortly after drinking, half the rats were exposed to a shock US while the other half received an injection of lithium chloride. As explained earlier, lithium chloride can serve as a US on a delayed basis because it naturally produces nausea some time after its injection.

To measure conditioned responding to the CSs in this study, Garcia and Koelling gave the rats from these two groups access to the drinking tubes once again after conditioning. Half the shocked rats and half the poisoned rats were allowed to drink a solution having the original taste. The other half of each group was allowed to drink a tasteless solution but was confronted with the audiovisual stimulus while they were drinking. The question of interest was the degree

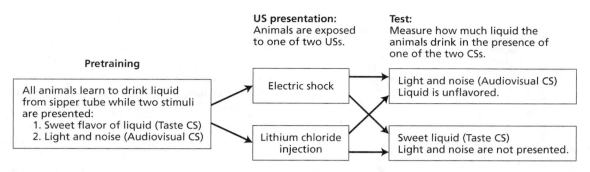

FIGURE 2.12 Schematic Flow Chart. Procedures in Garcia and Koelling (1966).

to which the rats would show an aversion to the taste or the audiovisual CSs.

From the partial results of this study shown in Figure 2.13, it is clear that rats that had been shocked drank very little when drinking was accompanied by the audiovisual stimulus. They drank a great deal, however, when the distinctive taste was the only CS present during testing. Rats that had been poisoned exhibited exactly the opposite behavior. They tended to avoid drinking when it involved contacting the distinctive taste, but they readily drank a tasteless solution that was accompanied by lights and clicks. These results indicate that certain combinations of CSs and USs (for example, a visual stimulus paired with shock or a taste paired with poison) result in effective conditioning. However, other CS-US combinations (for example, a taste paired with shock) produce little evidence of conditioned responding (for a counterexample, see Krane & Wagner, 1975).

The finding that conditioned responding depends on particular CS-US combinations has now been well established (see Domjan, 1983). However, the question of why only certain combinations of stimuli result in conditioning remains unanswered. According to some theorists, organisms come genetically prepared to make certain kinds of associations and not others (see, for example, Bolles, 1970; Seligman, 1970). Given what we know about evolutionary processes,

such an interpretation is appealing. Most genetic predispositions seem to have evolved because they contribute in some way to an organism's survival. Obviously an organism that associates sounds with illness is not as likely to avoid toxic foods as is an organism that associates tastes with illness. Thus, the rats in Garcia and Koelling's experiment conditioned more readily when the CS was a taste and the US was lithium chloride. Similarly, in natural settings, painful external stimuli (such as a bite by a dog) are most often preceded by auditory and visual stimuli. This may explain why an audiovisual stimulus became an effective CS when shock was the US, while little conditioning occurred when the CS was a taste.

The findings of Garcia and Koelling (1966) provide a good example of biological constraints on learning. One of the organizing themes of this text is that learning and memory occur within a biological context. One consequence of this fact is that the biological nature of learning sometimes sets limits on what can be learned. Specifically, in this case it appears that classical conditioning does not readily occur for certain CS-US combinations. Furthermore, other CS-US combinations appear to produce better classical conditioning. If the idea of genetic preparedness has merit, then these constraints on classical conditioning are likely the result of biological factors.

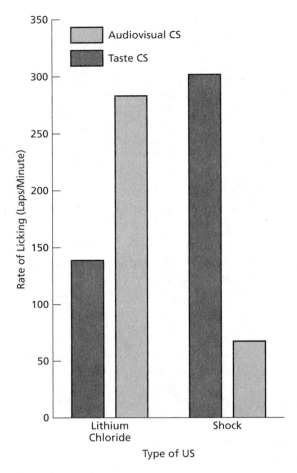

FIGURE 2.13 CS-US Relevance. Avoidance of either taste or audiovisual CSs by animals receiving either lithium chloride or shock as a US. From Garcia and Koelling, 1966. From *Psychonomic Science,* 1966, *4,* 123–124. Reprinted by permission of the publisher.

Seligman (1970) has proposed that genetic preparedness might explain why certain phobias are more common than others. Although people often are injured with knives, pins, or hot objects, these experiences rarely lead to phobias. Similarly, many people experience painful sunburns after a day at the beach, but beach phobias also are quite rare. On the other hand, phobias of snakes and spiders are relatively common despite the fact that the incidence of snake and spider bites is low. According to Seligman, phobias of stimuli such as

snakes and spiders are more common because fear of snakes and spiders likely contributed to our ancestors' survival. Thus, he proposes that humans are genetically prepared to develop conditioned fears of stimuli such as snakes and spiders.

Still, the notion of genetic preparedness as an explanation of why only particular combinations of CS and US result in conditioning is problematic. The major problem is that in advance of conditioning no one has been able to determine, based solely on what we know about an organism's nervous system, which stimuli should lead to conditioning and which should not. As a result, the preparedness hypothesis gives us no way to predict when conditioning should be successful and when it should not be. The tendency has been to try conditioning with certain stimuli, and when it is successful, to assume that an organism was prepared to associate those particular stimuli. This does not mean, of course, that the notion of genetic preparedness is necessarily incorrect. For it to be a useful explanation, however, experimenters must determine in advance of conditioning which stimuli are likely to be associable and which are not, based on foreknowledge of the organism's genetic makeup.

In summary, it is clear that not all CSs are interchangeable in the conditioning process. Certain CSs may come to produce one response when paired with a US, while other CSs paired with the same US may produce an entirely different CR. It is also clear that using a given set of conditioning parameters, some CS-US combinations result in evidence of conditioning while others may not. A complete understanding of conditioning requires an understanding of why these phenomena occur. Current research is aimed at investigating these issues.

The Presence of Other Stimuli During Conditioning

To this point we have discussed conditioning situations in which a single CS is paired with a single US. In the natural environment, however, CSs rarely if ever occur by themselves. In fact, even in laboratory settings it is impossible to present a CS in isolation from other stimuli. When people talk about a particular CS, they usually are referring to one stimulus out of a large array of stimuli that are present in a given situation. In an earlier example of conditioning, we mentioned the conditioning that occurs when a child receives a painful injection from a doctor. Although there are hundreds of stimuli present, such as chairs, calendars, notepads, pencils, etc., most people are not afraid of these stimuli. Instead, they are afraid of only hypodermic needles.

Consider another example of conditioning. You arrive home one evening and find that your puppy has gnawed a gigantic hole in the living room couch. In an effort to modify the puppy's behavior (and probably to vent your own anger), you roll up a newspaper, hold the puppy's nose against the gnawed upholstery, and proceed to spank the puppy with the paper. The next evening you come home, sit on the damaged couch, and begin to read the newspaper. As you read, you notice that the puppy is not in its accustomed place next to your feet but is instead cowering in a corner of the room.

Clearly, the spanking episode has resulted in a conditioned fear reaction. The dog exhibits fear to some stimulus that has not before elicited such a response. But, what stimulus in particular is producing the fear CR? Is it the sight of the menacing newspaper? Is it you? If it is you, then what specific aspect of you does the dog fear? It could be your facial expression, your odor, your physical build, or your shoes. All these stimuli were present when the dog was spanked, and any one or any combination of them could have become effective CSs.

The degree to which conditioning to one stimulus occurs often depends on what other stimuli are present at the time of conditioning. We will refer to the stimuli present at the time of conditioning as a stimulus compound, where *compound* refers to a set of two or more stimuli. Conditioning to one stimulus in a CS compound usually is affected by the nature of the other stimuli in that same compound. We will concentrate on three conditioning phenomena.

In the first, overshadowing, one stimulus in a compound is more salient than the others. In the second phenomenon, called blocking, one component of a compound has already undergone some conditioning to the US. In the third, we will consider situations in which conditioning to one stimulus component depends on how well other stimuli in the compound are correlated with the US.

Overshadowing. Some stimuli in a compound are more salient to an organism simply because they are more intense than other stimuli. For example, some stimuli simply may be brighter, louder, or more odorous than others. How does the differential salience of stimuli in a CS compound affect the degree to which the elements in that compound come to produce conditioned responding? As you may have guessed, the more salient stimulus will become an effective CS, and prevent or reduce conditioning to other stimuli in the CS compound.

Several experimenters have supported this conclusion through studies of how the salience of one stimulus affects conditioning to other stimuli in a compound (Kamin, 1969; Kasprow, Cacheiro, Balaz, & Miller, 1982; Mackintosh, 1971; Pavlov, 1927). In one of these experiments, Kamin (1969) trained rats in a CER paradigm using either single or compound stimuli to signal shock. Three groups of rats were given pairings of a single CS with shock. For one group the CS was a light, for another it was a loud noise (80 decibels), and for the final group it was a less intense noise (50 decibels). All three groups developed fear responses to their respective CSs, indicating that all three stimuli were effective CSs when presented alone.

The groups of primary interest were the two groups given compound CSs paired with shock. One group received the light in compound with the loud noise. Half of this group was later tested with the light alone and the other half with the loud noise alone. Kamin found that the animals exhibited a strong fear response to the light but only a mild fear response to the loud noise. This indicated that the light had somehow lessened

	Stage 1	Stage 2	Stage 3
Group 1	(No pre-exposure)	Noise + Light } Shock	**Test:** Light
Group 2	Noise-shock	Noise + Light } Shock	**Test:** Light
Group 3	(No pre-exposure)	Noise + Light } Shock	**Test:** Noise
Group 4	Light-shock	Noise + Light } Shock	**Test:** Noise

FIGURE 2.14 The Main Conditions in Kamin's Blocking Experiment. (From Kamin, 1968, 1969.)

conditioning to the noise when the two stimuli had occurred in compound as a signal for shock. In the other group, the compound CS consisted of the light and the less intense noise. Here the effect of the light was even stronger. Animals tested with the light alone again showed strong conditioning to the light. However, those rats tested with the low-intensity noise showed almost no evidence of conditioning to this stimulus.

Since the 50-decibel noise used in this study was shown to be an effective CS when it was paired alone with shock, the failure for it to condition when presented in compound must have been due to the presence of the light at the time of conditioning. Pavlov (1927) originally labeled this phenomenon *overshadowing* to indicate that more salient stimuli in a CS compound can diminish the effectiveness of less salient stimuli.

Blocking. When one stimulus in a CS compound is more salient than the other, the more salient stimulus may prevent the other from developing a conditioned response. The same is true when one element of a compound has undergone conditioning alone before it was part of the stimulus compound. The previously conditioned stimulus prevents the novel stimulus from becoming an effective CS. This form of overshadowing is given the specific label of *blocking*.

The initial demonstration of blocking came from a series of studies by Kamin (1968, 1969) in which, again, rats were trained in a CER paradigm. The treatments for the most critical groups in these experiments are outlined in Figure 2.14. The first two groups were exposed to pairings of a compound CS (noise–light) with shock. However, group 2 was given several pairings of the noise and the shock before the compound trials began. After the compound CS–shock pairings, both groups were tested to assess the fear response to light. Only group 1 showed substantial fear in the presence of the light. In group 2 the prior conditioning to the noise caused the noise to overshadow the light when the two stimuli were placed in compound.

Table 2.2 The Main Conditions Used in the Conditioning Experiment of Wagner, Logan, Haberlandt, and Price: T$_1$ = Tone 1, T$_2$ = Tone 2, and L = Light

CORRELATED CONDITION	
50% of trials	T$_1$L: US
50% of trials	T$_2$L: no US
UNCORRELATED CONDITION	
25% of trials	T$_1$L: US
25% of trials	T$_1$L: no US
25% of trials	T$_2$L: US
25% of trials	T$_2$L: no US

The last two groups were treated comparably to the first two groups in that both groups received a series of compound CS-shock pairings. In this case, however, group 4 received prior conditioning to the light. Furthermore, after compound conditioning, both these groups were tested to assess their fear of the noise. In this instance, group 3 showed evidence of fear at the noise while group 4 did not.

These findings indicate that if one stimulus is already a reliable signal for the US by virtue of prior conditioning, it will block conditioning to other stimuli with which it is compounded. We might conceptualize this effect by saying that during compound conditioning, if one stimulus already reliably signals the US, an organism will simply view other stimuli as redundant. It may be that organisms have no need to learn about new signals if a reliable signal for the US is already present.

Correlation of the Compound Elements with the US. Blocking is only one example of how conditioning to one stimulus may be affected by other stimuli present during conditioning. In most cases, the degree of conditioning to one element of a compound is inversely related to the degree to which other elements in that compound already signal US occurrence. In other words, on a given conditioning trial, a CS element is likely to increase its capacity to produce a CR as long as other elements in the compound are poor signals for the US. On the other hand, an element is likely to gain little capacity for producing a CR when other elements in the compound are good signals for US occurrence.

This principle is illustrated quite well by the results of a set of experiments by Wagner, Logan, Haberlandt, and Price (1968). The experiment used a nictitating membrane–conditioning procedure on rabbits, and involved two primary conditions outlined in Table 2.2. In the correlated condition, animals were exposed to two different compound CSs. In half the trials the animals received a compound consisting of a particular tone (T1) and a light. This compound was designated T1L. For this group T1L was always followed by the US. On the other half of their trials, the correlated group received a CS compound consisting of the same light with a different tone. We will designate this compound as T2L. The compound T2L was never followed by the US.

In the uncorrelated condition, animals were exposed to the same two CS compounds. On half the trials T1L occurred and on the other half T2L was presented. The only difference between the correlated and uncorrelated conditions was in terms of the degree to which each compound was correlated with US occurrence. Whereas the correlated animals always received a US following T1L, the uncorrelated animals received a US following only half of the T1L presentations. And, whereas the correlated animals never received a US after T2L, the uncorrelated animals again received a US on half of the T2L trials.

In effect, then, both conditions involved US presentations on half of the conditioning trials. This means that in both conditions the light was followed by the US 50% of the time. However, in the correlated condition T1 always preceded the occurrence of the US, while T2 always preceded US absence. In the uncorrelated condition, neither T1 nor T2 served as a reliable signal for the occurrence of the US. Both T1 and T2 sometimes preceded US occurrence and

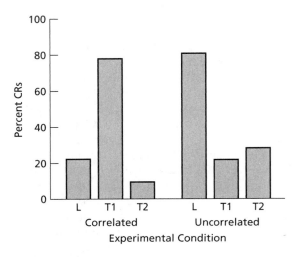

FIGURE 2.15 Correlation of Compound Elements.

sometimes preceded the omission of the US. The question of interest was the degree to which the light would develop a CR in these two conditions.

The results of these experiments were clear. As Figure 2.15 shows, the light acquired the capacity to produce a CR in the uncorrelated condition but not in the correlated condition. This difference occurred even though the light had preceded the US 50% of the time in both conditions. The difference in the conditions was in terms of whether the different tones could be used as reliable signals for US occurrence. In the correlated condition the different tones served as effective signals making the light redundant. Thus, there was little conditioning to the light. However, light did acquire the capacity to elicit a CR in the uncorrelated condition, where the tones did not function as reliable signals.

Similar results have been found in a variety of experimental situations (see, for example, Rescorla & Wagner, 1972; Ross & Holland, 1981). From such findings it is clear that the amount of conditioning to a given stimulus cannot be predicted solely on the basis of the correlation between that

stimulus and the US. It also is necessary to know how well the other elements of a compound are correlated with US occurrence.

People experienced this difficulty very often. For example, people who live on the East Coast must sometimes board up their homes and vacate in view of an approaching hurricane. The difficulty in predicting the weather lies partially in the fact that certain stimuli are better correlated with storms than others. People do not always board up their houses or cover their cars when dark clouds roll in. However, when dark clouds roll in and there is a noticeable drop in both temperature and barometric pressure, then they begin to get a little more nervous; but although certain stimuli are better predictors than others in the compound they are still not perfectly correlated. As a result we often make erroneous predictions.

CONDITIONING WITHOUT AN EXPLICIT US

Now that we have completed our discussion of factors that influence excitatory conditioning, we are ready to discover that conditioning can take place in some cases even when no explicit US appears to be present. Our discussion will concentrate on two phenomena: higher order conditioning and sensory preconditioning. These phenomena are important because they demonstrate how pervasive the conditioning process can be in the natural environment.

Higher Order Conditioning

To serve as an effective US, a given stimulus must reliably produce some reflexive response (the UR). Normally, the only stimuli that meet this requirement are those that naturally elicit reflexive responses. However, once a stimulus has served as a CS in a conditioning situation, that stimulus elicits a reflexive response. The only difference is that the CS produces its reaction because of its prior conditioning history, whereas

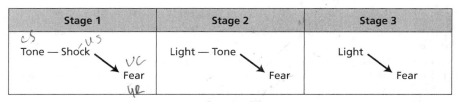

(A) Higher Order Conditioning

(B) Sensory Preconditioning

FIGURE 2.16 Conditioning Orders. Stages in (A) the higher order conditioning procedure, and (B) the sensory preconditioning paradigm.

the US produces a response because of its natural characteristics.

This similarity between a US and a previously conditioned CS is important, because once a CS begins to produce a CR, the CS can serve in place of a US in a subsequent conditioning situation. For example, if a light has been paired regularly with shock, the light begins to produce a fear response on its own. At this point, a second CS that reliably precedes the occurrence of the light will begin to produce that fear response.

When conditioning results from the pairing of a novel CS with a previously conditioned CS, we call the process second-order conditioning which is a form of higher order conditioning (see Figure 2.16a for a description of the stages involved in this form of conditioning). The occurrence of higher order conditioning is well documented (see, for example, Rescorla, 1980) and has important implications for human behavior.

We know that a child who has been bitten by a dog may begin to show fear reactions whenever the dog comes into view. This reaction occurs because the dog was present when the painful bite occurred. However, once the sight of the

dog has become capable of producing a fear response, other stimuli associated with the sight of the dog may also begin to arouse fear. The child may begin to fear venturing into the backyard if that is where the dog is normally kept. Likewise, barking sounds may begin to elicit fear. In effect, one CS that has been paired with an effective US may then help to condition a variety of additional stimuli.

Sensory Preconditioning

Conditioning also appears to occur without a US in the sensory preconditioning paradigm. This situation often is confused with higher order conditioning. The procedures for the two forms of conditioning are compared in Figure 2.16. As the figure indicates, sensory preconditioning first involves the pairing of two CSs. In other words, two stimuli that do not naturally elicit a reflexive reaction are paired in the same manner as a CS and a US normally would be. For example, a tone might be used to signal the occurrence of a light.

In stage 2 of this procedure, the signaled stimulus from stage 1 (the light) is used to signal the occurrence of a regular US such as a shock. After several conditioning trials, the light begins to produce a conditioned fear response. This result is not surprising since the light has become a reliable signal for the shock. What *is* surprising is that once the light and shock have been paired, the tone from stage 1 also becomes capable of producing a fear response. This happens despite the fact that the tone and shock have never been paired (see, for example, Brogden, 1939; Wynne & Brogden, 1962).

The usual interpretation of this result is that during stage 1 the two CSs that are paired become associated. In effect, an organism learns to react to these two stimuli as if they were equivalent. Later, when one of the stimuli is paired with a US and becomes capable of producing a CR, the organism reacts to the other CS as if it, too, had been paired with the US.

This phenomenon raises the possibility that excitatory conditioning may not really depend on a CS acting as a signal for a stimulus that elicits a response. It suggests that organisms might learn a relationship between any two stimuli that are paired such that one reliably precedes the other. It may simply be that unless a true US is involved in conditioning, no measurable response is produced by the CS. In general, the occurrence of sensory preconditioning emphasizes that learning may occur without any immediate change in an organism's behavior.

One additional point concerning this phenomenon should be made clear. Sensory preconditioning effects, and the effects of higher order conditioning, are relatively weak and short-lived. Several studies have shown, for example, that sensory preconditioning is strongest when the number of previous pairings of the two conditioned stimuli (CS2-CS) is small. Large numbers of CS2-CS pairings often result in little conditioned responding to CS2 (see, for example, Hoffeld, Kendall, Thompson, & Brogden, 1960). Thus, regardless of what sensory preconditioning may tell us about what is necessary for conditioning to occur, it is clear that conditioning is strongest when a CS signals the occurrence of a biologically significant US.

THE BIOLOGICAL BASIS OF CLASSICAL CONDITIONING

In Chapter 1, one of the organizing themes we presented was that learning and memory occur in a biological context. This is certainly true of classical conditioning. Researchers have made impressive progress in discovering the neural structures and processes that are involved in classical conditioning. An impressive example of such research is the work of Richard Thompson and his colleagues, who conducted numerous experiments to locate the precise areas of the brain that are necessary for classical conditioning of the rabbits' nictitating membrane (Clark & Lavond, 1993; Krupa, Thompson, & Thompson, 1993).

These researchers have focused on a structure in the brain known as the cerebellum, and more specifically on a region of the cerebellum known as the lateral interpositus nucleus (see Figure 2.17a). They suppressed activity in rabbits' lateral interpositus nucleus (either by cooling or injecting drugs into the area) while the rabbits received conditioning trials in several sessions. The conditioned responses did not occur during these sessions (see Figure 2.17c). They then allowed the lateral interpositus nucleus to recover and continued conditioning trials. At this point, the rabbits showed classical conditioning, but at the same rate as animals who had no previous conditioning trials (see Figure 2.17d). These animals behaved as if they had not received the previous conditioning trials.

At this point, however, we cannot be sure that the lateral interpositus nucleus is where eye-blink conditioning occurs. It is possible that suppressing activity in the lateral interpositus nucleus simply suppresses the response itself and thus prevents learning that normally occurs during the conditioning trials. To test this possibility, the researchers suppressed activity in a motor area of the brain called the red nucleus (see Figure 2.17a). The red nucleus controls the nictitating membrane response. Thus, if suppression of only the response prevents learning, then suppression

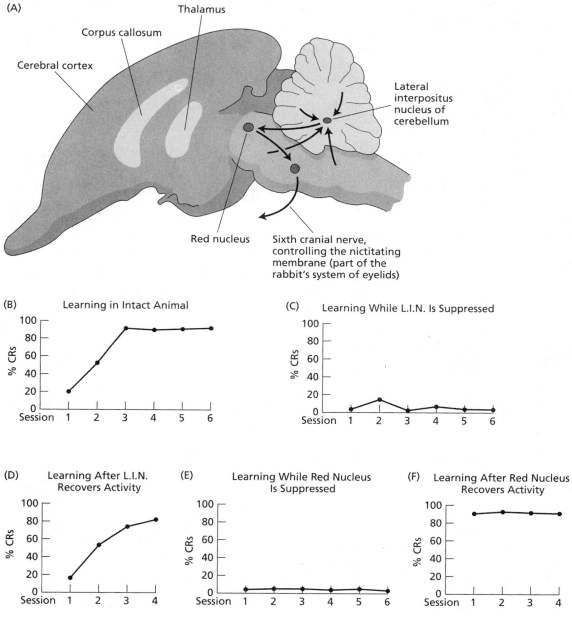

FIGURE 2.17 Summary of Experiments Localizing the Engram for a Conditioned Eyelid Response in Rabbits. Temporary suppression of activity in the lateral interpositus nucleus of a rabbit blocks all indications of learning, both during the suppression and afterward. Temporary suppression of activity in the red nucleus blocks the response during the period of suppression, but does not prevent learning itself; the learned response appears as soon as the red nucleus recovers from the suppression. Based on the experiments of Clark & Lavond (1993) and Krupa, Thompson, & Thompson (1993).

of the red nucleus should prevent conditioning of the nictitating membrane response.

While the red nucleus was suppressed, the rabbits showed no CRs during conditioning trials (Figure 2.17e). However, after the red nucleus was allowed to recover, the rabbits immediately showed high levels of conditioning to the tone (Figure 2.17f). Thus, suppressing the nictitating membrane response did not prevent classical conditioning from occurring (Clark & Lavond, 1993; Krupa, Thompson, & Thompson, 1993). From these experiments, we can conclude that the red nucleus is necessary for the motor control of the nictitating membrane response, but the lateral interpositus nucleus is where the changes necessary for the classical conditioning take place.

In addition to searching for the areas of the brain necessary for classical conditioning, many researchers are investigating the cellular changes that occur during classical conditioning. This rapidly growing area of research has already resulted in great progress toward understanding the cellular processes necessary for classical conditioning. As we will discover in Chapter 3, research on the cellular bases of classical conditioning has played an important role in developing and evaluating theories of classical conditioning.

CLASSICAL INHIBITORY CONDITIONING

Imagine that you are enrolled in a learning and memory class where you must take a quiz every Monday afternoon. As a result, Monday afternoon becomes a CS that elicits anxiety because Monday afternoon reliably precedes taking a quiz (the US). Thus, when Monday afternoon arrives, you begin to feel anxious and tense (the CR). Your anxiety and tension grow as the time for class approaches. However, when you arrive at your classroom, another CS is on the door. It is a sign that says "PSY 321: Learning and Memory—canceled today." As past experience has shown, this CS reliably precedes the absence of a

quiz. What happens when you encounter this stimulus? Your response is very likely to be the opposite of the response the US normally elicits. You feel relieved, relaxed, and happy. This is an inhibitory CR.

From an adaptive viewpoint, it is easy to see why the occurrence of inhibitory conditioning is important. In many instances, it is just as critical to learn when some significant event will be absent as it is to learn when it will occur. In recent years, interest in inhibitory conditioning has increased markedly (see, for example, Miller & Spear, 1985; Holland, 1989). Much of this interest has arisen because several contemporary theories have begun to treat excitatory and inhibitory conditioning as equally important processes (see, for example, Rescorla & Wagner, 1972). For the purposes of this text, however, discussion of inhibitory conditioning must be somewhat limited, given the relative scarcity of experimental evidence.

Problems in Measuring the Inhibitory CR

The assessment of excitatory conditioned responding is relatively simple. Following CS-US pairings, all one need do is measure changes in the overt responses that are made to the CS. The measurement of inhibitory conditioned responding has not proved to be this easy. The problem that arises has to do with the nature of the inhibitory response that is learned. In most cases, the response is one of *not* doing something. Thus, when an inhibitory CS is presented to an organism, the organism normally exhibits no discernible reaction. This makes it difficult to know when the CS has become a signal for US absence and when it has simply failed to become a reliable signal for anything.

Assume that a particular stimulus has become a signal for the availability of food. Most organisms begin to react to that stimulus with salivation and approach responses. Now assume that a second stimulus has become a signal indicating that food will *not* be presented. When this stimulus occurs, most organisms will not salivate and will not approach the stimulus. This failure to approach and salivate is similar to the reaction that would occur if we presented a novel stimulus that had never come to signal anything concerning food. How, then, is it possible to distinguish between an inhibitory CS and a stimulus that has no relation whatsoever with the US?

To make such a distinction, researchers have begun to use two tests to determine when a stimulus has become an inhibitory CS. These instruments usually are termed the retardation test and the summation test for conditioned inhibition. To determine conclusively that a stimulus has become an inhibitory CS, the stimulus must meet the requirements of both these tests.

The Retardation Test. Once a single response to a given stimulus has been learned, it is usually difficult to train the organism to make an opposing or conflicting response to that same stimulus. For example, it is relatively easy for a child to associate the sight of candy with something that tastes good. It is much more difficult for the same child to learn later that candy has negative ramifications, such as tooth decay. Whenever two responses conflict or are incompatible, it is always difficult to learn to perform both responses in the same stimulus situation.

The retardation test for conditioned inhibition takes advantage of this difficulty. It is presumed that during inhibitory conditioning a CS comes to produce withholding or suppression of some reflexive reaction. This results because the CS has become a signal for the absence of a US that normally produces that reaction. If the same CS is now paired with that US (so that it now becomes a signal for US occurrence), normal excitatory conditioning should be slowed. It should take the CS longer to begin to produce the reflexive reaction, if previously the CS had come to produce withholding of that same response.

Thus, one way to determine whether a CS has become a reliable signal for US absence is to assess how long it takes the CS to become a reliable signal for US occurrence. Inhibitory conditioning is said to have occurred if the prior inhibitory conditioning experience interferes with subsequent excitatory conditioning of the CS. This test for conditioned inhibition has been used in a variety of experiments (see, for example, Hammond, 1968; Siegel & Domjan, 1971). It is clear from such studies that prior training in which a CS signals US absence does retard later excitatory conditioning in which that same CS signals the occurrence of the US. As we will see, however, the difficulty in relying on this test alone is that several manipulations can retard excitatory conditioning. Only a few of these manipulations appear to produce inhibitory conditioning.

The Summation Test. The summation test for conditioned inhibition is also based on the idea that excitatory and inhibitory CRs are incompatible. In this case the test involves presenting a supposed inhibitory CS at the same time that a different excitatory CS is being presented. The rationale here is that if a CS has become a true response inhibitor, its presentation should decrease conditioned responding to the excitatory CS. In effect, the organism is presented with one stimulus that says "respond" at the same time another stimulus says "don't respond." This technique was first developed by Pavlov (1927); however, it has been used in numerous more recent experiments (see, for example, Hinson & Siegel, 1980; Rescorla & Holland, 1977). It is now common to accept a CS as a conditioned inhibitor if it is shown to be capable of reducing the excitatory CR produced by another CS.

Conditions That Promote Inhibitory Conditioning

By using the retardation and summation tests, it is possible to determine the degree to which inhibitory conditioning occurs in various experimental settings. Two factors are necessary for the production of inhibitory CRs. First, there must be a situation where a US might occur. Second, some stimulus must become a reliable signal for the absence of that US in that

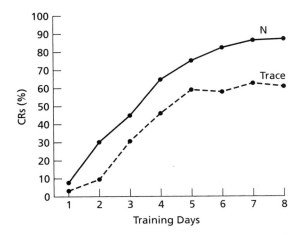

FIGURE 2.18 Conditioning with Either a Novel (N) or a Previously Trace-Conditioned (Trace) CS. From Hinson and Siegel, 1980, Exp. 1. From *Animal Learning and Behavior*, 1980, *6*, 60–66. © 1980 by the Psychonomic Society, Inc. Reprinted by permission.

situation. Experimental settings in which both these requirements are met normally promote inhibitory conditioned responding.

CS Discriminations. One way to produce inhibitory conditioning is to expose an organism to two different CSs in the same stimulus situation. If CS+ is always followed by a US and CS− is never followed by a US, CS− will begin to evoke an inhibitory CR. Evidence that the CS− becomes a conditioned inhibitor comes from studies using both retardation (Hammond, 1968) and summation tests (Grossen & Bolles, 1968; Hammond, 1967). Apparently, in this kind of paradigm, organisms come to expect the US because it has occurred in the experimental context previously. The CS− becomes an inhibitor because it signals that the US will not occur in that context for some period of time.

Long CS-US Intervals. We have seen that in both trace and delayed conditioning procedures, long CS-US intervals produce only weak excitatory conditioning effects. There is even some evidence that long CS-US intervals can result in

inhibitory conditioning to the CS. One example of such an effect comes from a pair of experiments conducted by Hinson and Siegel (1980). Both of these experiments looked at the effects of trace conditioning on the rabbit's conditioned eye-blink response. In describing these results, we will concentrate on two of the treatment conditions used in these studies.

In the first experiment, one group of animals received a number of trace conditioning trials, while a second group received no conditioning experience. The trace conditioning trials involved a brief presentation of a light or tone CS, followed 10 seconds later by a mild shock to the cheekbone. The mild shock served as the US because it naturally produced eyelid closure. Animals that received the trace conditioning showed no evidence of excitatory conditioning during this training.

In the second phase of the study, both the trace-conditioned group and the group given no training were exposed to eight days of delayed conditioning trials. The CS and the US were the same as those the trace-conditioned animals had previously experienced. In this case, however, the beginning of the US overlapped the end of the CS. From Figure 2.18, which shows the results of this training, you can see that the animals that received no prior training rapidly acquired a conditioned response to the CS. However, the animals given prior trace conditioning showed retarded acquisition of the CR. This finding indicates that a long trace interval can result in a CS becoming inhibitory and can retard later excitatory conditioning involving that CS.

The second experiment confirmed this conclusion by using a summation test of conditioned inhibition. As in the first study, one group of rabbits received trace conditioning with CS1 and the shock US. The other group received no conditioning. In stage 2 of the experiment, both groups received delayed conditioning trials involving a new CS (CS2) and a shock US. During this training both groups showed substantial excitatory conditioning to CS2. Finally, both

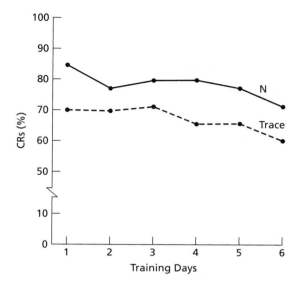

FIGURE 2.19 Summation Testing. An excitatory CS is placed in compound with either a novel (N) or a previously trace-conditioned (Trace) CS. From Hinson and Siegel, 1980, Exp. 2. From *Animal Learning and Behavior*, 1980, *6*, 60–66. © 1980 by the Psychonomic Society, Inc. Reprinted by permission.

groups received six days of tests in which CS1 and CS2 were presented in compound. The conditioned responding to the compound CS for both groups is shown in Figure 2.19. Clearly, the group given prior trace conditioning with CS1 made fewer responses to the compound than did the animals that had no experience with CS1. Since both groups had shown substantial conditioning to CS2, this result indicates that trace conditioning had promoted inhibitory conditioning to CS1. In other words, prior trace conditioning made CS1 capable of interfering with the excitatory CR produced by CS2.

Although the evidence is not as strong, some studies have suggested that inhibitory conditioning may even occur in delayed conditioning paradigms when extremely long CS-US intervals are used (Rescorla, 1967a). This means that a CS may even acquire inhibitory properties when the CS and US overlap, as long as the CS onset substantially precedes the US onset.

How is it that inhibitory conditioning can result from trace and delayed conditioning procedures when in these paradigms the CS precedes the US? In such paradigms it would appear that the CS is a signal for US occurrence, not its nonoccurrence. The key factor here appears to be the length of the CS-US interval. When CS onset reliably precedes US onset by several seconds or even minutes, the CS onset actually signals a period of time during which the US will not occur. Apparently, when this is the case, the CS becomes capable of producing an inhibitory response rather than an excitatory CR.

Other CS-US Arrangements. One way to present CSs and USs to an organism is to make sure that the two stimuli never occur together in a paired manner. This procedure normally involves presenting the stimuli in such a way that both CS-US and US-CS intervals are very long. Neither stimulus becomes a reliable signal for the occurrence of the other. As you might imagine, explicitly unpaired presentations often promote inhibitory conditioning to the CS (see, for example, Baker, 1977).

Results are not so clear in backward conditioning trials. Some studies using backward conditioning trials have found evidence of inhibitory CRs using a retardation test (see, for example, Hall, 1984; Moscovitch & LoLordo, 1968; Siegel & Domjan, 1971). Others, however, have found that under certain circumstances such trials produce excitatory CRs (for example, Mahoney & Ayres, 1976). There is little or no evidence that backward pairings produce inhibition coming from studies using summation tests. The particular type of conditioning found when backward pairings are used appears to depend on a whole variety of factors such as the number of conditioning trials and the specific characteristics of the US. A complete understanding of backward conditioning effects awaits additional research (see, for example, Gordon, McGinnis, & Weaver, 1985; Hall, 1984).

One final CS-US arrangement we have discussed is the random presentation of CSs and USs. In this procedure CSs and USs occur randomly so that there is a zero correlation between CS and US occurrence. In other words, the CS should not become a signal for US occurrence, nor should it come to signal US absence (Rescorla, 1967b). Nevertheless, some studies have shown that prior random presentations of a CS and a US can retard later excitatory conditioning involving these stimuli (see, for example, Baker & Mackintosh, 1977). It is notable, however, that studies using summation tests have failed to support such findings (see, for example, Hinson & Siegel, 1980; Siegel & Domjan, 1971). Currently, it seems doubtful that random CS and US presentations produce inhibitory conditioned responding.

Latent Inhibition Procedures. When we talked about an organism's experience with a CS, we noted that pre-exposures to a CS alone can retard later excitatory conditioning involving that CS. This latent inhibition phenomenon raises the question of whether CS-alone presentations result in inhibitory conditioned responding to the CS. The answer to this question is almost certainly "no." Several studies have shown that a CS that has been presented alone is not capable of interfering with excitatory CRs produced by another CS. In other words, a preexposed CS does not pass the summation test for conditioned inhibition (see, for example, Reiss & Wagner, 1972).

That CS preexposure does not produce inhibitory conditioning should not be surprising. In a latent inhibition paradigm, when the CS is being preexposed no USs have ever occurred. Without such a history, the CS cannot become a signal for US absence and, thus, should not become an inhibitory CS.

Why, then, does CS preexposure retard excitatory conditioning involving the preexposed CS? One suggestion is that during the preexposure an organism learns that the CS is irrelevant or that it signals nothing of significance. That is, through habituation to the CS (as discussed in Chapter 1), an organism may come to ignore the CS, and this may be what makes subsequent conditioning so difficult. It is worth noting that CS

preexposure retards both excitatory and inhibitory conditioning involving the preexposed CS (Baker & Mackintosh, 1977).

EXTINCTION

Conditioning is an adaptive process that favors an organism's adjustment and survival. When new relationships among stimuli occur, an organism's behavior changes accordingly. As we have seen, once a CS has begun to reliably signal something of biological significance, that CS begins to elicit a new response.

Even so, relationships among stimuli seldom remain static throughout an organism's lifetime. A CS that has signaled a US for some period of time may cease being a reliable signal for US occurrence. When this happens, it may no longer be adaptive to respond to the CS in the same manner. That is, the conditioned response learned when the CS was a signal may no longer be appropriate when the CS has lost its signal value. How do organisms adjust to these changing stimulus relationships?

One mechanism that allows organisms to adapt to such changes is called extinction. In this context, the term refers to the decrease and ultimate disappearance of a conditioned response once a CS has ceased to be a reliable signal for a US. This means that once a CS has come to produce a CR, that response will diminish to the extent that the CS occurs alone. One way to conceptualize extinction is to think of it as a decrease in the CR as an organism learns that the CS is no longer a reliable signal.

To clarify how extinction works, consider once again the example of the mail carrier and the vicious poodle. One particular house on her route had become a signal for an impending dog bite. Now, suppose that the owners of the poodle move to another town, taking their poodle with them. Over the next few days, when the mail carrier enters the yard of 1217 Glade Road, there is no bloodthirsty poodle in the yard. Her fear of that particular house begins to decrease as the days go by. Finally, after several days of entering the yard safely, our mail carrier is no longer afraid of the house. At this point we would say that the fear response had been extinguished.

Although extinction is well documented, for years researchers have argued about the precise mechanisms that control this phenomenon. Why do responses diminish when CS–alone presentations occur? Is the conditioned response forgotten? Does the learned association that led to the response become broken? Might it be that extinction simply results from the suppression of the learned response? We can answer some of these questions at least tentatively.

First, it is clear that extinction does not result from forgetting. As we will see later, forgetting is a decrease in the performance of a learned response that occurs with the passage of time. Forgetting does not depend on CS–alone presentations, which are necessary for extinction. Although extinction and forgetting both involve a reduction in CR performance, the variables that control these phenomena appear to be different.

Second, it seems clear that extinction does not involve a loss of the association formed during conditioning. At least two facts suggest that the learned association remains intact even after extinction of a response has occurred. First, once a CR has been extinguished, the original CS can usually be reconditioned faster than a novel CS can be conditioned (Konorski & Szwejkowska, 1950). This suggests that even after extinction, some association involving the original CS remains intact. In addition, Bouton and his colleagues have shown that the effects of extinction can be eliminated by changing the context in which extinction trials took place. In essence Bouton showed that extinguishing an animal in one context and then placing the animal in a different context reinstated the conditioned response (Bouton, 1991, 1993, 1994).

Spontaneous Recovery

Another fact that leads to the same conclusion is that, after extinction, spontaneous recovery of the response often occurs. That is, if time is al-lowed to pass after extinction, the conditioned response to the CS returns to some degree. In most cases, the degree of responding that occurs is less than that which the CS produced before extinction. Recovery of the response is not complete. Furthermore, spontaneous recovery usually can be eliminated by extinguishing the CR several times. Still, the occurrence of spontaneous recovery does suggest that extinction does not abolish the learned association responsible for the CR. If it did, we would not expect an extinguished CR to return in the absence of additional conditioning trials. Readers interested in reading further about the spontaneous recovery of an extinguished response are referred to Brooks & Bouton (1993), Pavlov (1927), and Robbins (1990).

One other point is worth noting. CS–alone presentations after conditioning do not cause the CS to become a conditioned inhibitor. Even after several extinction sessions, a CS will not pass either a summation or a retardation test for conditioned inhibition (see Rescorla & Wagner, 1972).

Variables That Affect Rate of Extinction

The rate of extinction for a given CR is affected by several factors. Rate of extinction typically is measured as the number of CS–alone presentations required for the strength of the CR to decrease to a predetermined level. One variable that affects the rate of extinction is the number of CS–US conditioning trials presented during the actual conditioning. As you might expect, the rate of extinction is slower for larger numbers of CS–US conditioning trials (Prokasy, 1958).

Another factor that affects the rate of extinction is partial reinforcement during the conditioning procedures. The term partial reinforcement describes conditioning procedures where the US does not follow the CS on every conditioning trial. By contrast, continuous reinforcement refers to conditioning procedures where the US follows the CS on every trial. In general, continuous reinforcement procedures lead to stronger conditioning than partial reinforcement procedures (Ross, 1959). In this light, the effects of partial reinforcement on extinction might surprise you. Extinction of a CR is faster following continuous reinforcement procedures and slower following partial reinforcement procedures (Hartman & Grant, 1960). Thus, a CR that is conditioned by intermittent CS–US conditioning trials will be more resistant to extinction, other factors being equal.

Treating Phobias Through Extinction

Extinction procedures have been very effective in treating some phobias. A phobia is an excessive and irrational fear of some object or situation that adversely affects one's life. Some common phobias are acrophobia (heights), claustrophobia (enclosed spaces), ophidiophobia (snakes), and arachnophobia (spiders). Many authors have argued that phobias often result from classical conditioning where the phobic stimulus is paired with a fearful event (Edelmann, 1992) which results in the phobic stimulus becoming a CS that elicits powerful fear responses. If a phobia is a result of classical conditioning where the phobic stimulus became a CS for a fear response, then extinction should be one way of eliminating the phobic response.

The first question is why phobias don't disappear over time due to extinction. For example, if someone is afraid of spiders, it would seem that over many months or years, that person would encounter enough spiders without being bitten that the fear would subside through extinction. This is not typically the case, however, because most individuals with phobias actively avoid the situations they fear. As a result, there is very little opportunity for extinction of the phobic response. To effectively treat phobias through extinction procedures, the treatment somehow must expose the client to the phobic stimulus in ways that allow extinction to occur. Two well-known treatments for phobias are based on this principle.

The first procedure, called **flooding,** involves exposing the individual to the phobic stimulus for an extended period of time, until the fear response is extinguished (Wolpe, 1990). For example, someone with a phobia of snakes might be forced to handle live snakes until the fear of snakes receded. Flooding is an effective way of treating phobias but confronting one's worst fear directly for a long period of time can be a very stressful experience. Although flooding has been shown to reduce the phobic response fairly rapidly, many clients are unwilling to experience this type of treatment. It is not recommended for clients with certain health problems, such as heart conditions.

A better alternative might be to expose the client to the fearful situation gradually. In this method the client's stress and discomfort are reduced, which allows extinction to occur. Joseph Wolpe (1958) developed a treatment based on gradually exposing the client to the fearful situation. Called **systematic desensitization,** Wolpe's treatment has since become one of the most widely used procedures in behavior therapy for phobias and is remarkably effective in treating phobias (Paul, 1969).

There are three phases of systematic desensitization: the creation of a fear hierarchy, relaxation training, and then gradual exposure to the items on the fear hierarchy. The fear hierarchy is a list of fearful situations organized from the least fearful to the most fearful. The first item on the list is a situation that elicits only mild fear, and the last item on the hierarchy is the situation that the client fears most. These fear hierarchies usually consist of 10 to 20 items. For example, most of us fear taking final exams. In this case, the least fearful situation might be reading the course syllabus at the beginning of the term and taking note of the exam date. The most fearful situation is sitting in the classroom with the final exam in front of you. A sample fear hierarchy based on this example is shown in Table 2.3.

The second phase of systematic desensitization is relaxation training. Wolpe developed a technique called deep muscle relaxation, which involves alternately tensing and relaxing major muscle groups. This procedure induces a very calm relaxed state for the client. After practicing

Table 2.3 A Sample Fear Hierarchy for Taking a Final Exam

1. Sight of the exam listed in my syllabus on the first day of class
2. Thinking about the exam one month before the exam
3. Two weeks before the exam
4. Professor announces that the final exam is in one week
5. Studying for the exam three days before the exam
6. Studying the night before the exam
7. Driving to school on the day of the exam
8. Entering the classroom to take the exam
9. Sitting down in the classroom
10. Professor enters and begins distributing the exam
11. Reading the instructions for the exam
12. Answering the first question

deep muscle relaxation for two or three sessions, the therapist begins presenting items on the fear hierarchy.

These sessions begin with 10 to 20 minutes of relaxation. Then, when the client is relaxed, the therapist describes the first item in the hierarchy and asks the client to imagine that situation. This step is repeated until the client reports feeling no fear. The treatment then moves on to the second item on the fear hierarchy and the process is repeated: relaxation followed by imagining the fearful situation. Over the course of this treatment, which can take several sessions, the therapist and client work their way up the fear hierarchy. At each step, the therapist ensures that fear of the particular situation is extinguished before moving on. This procedure continues until the client is able to experience the most fearful situation on the hierarchy without feeling afraid. Thus, systematic desensitization uses the principles of classical conditioning and extinction, along with other clinical techniques, to provide an effective treatment for phobias.

SUMMARY STATEMENTS

We have seen in this chapter that a stimulus that signals either the occurrence or the nonoccurrence of a biologically significant event becomes capable of producing a new response. When a positive contingent relationship exists between a CS and a US, the result is called classical excitatory conditioning. When a negative contingent relationship holds for these stimuli, inhibitory conditioning develops.

In the case of excitatory conditioning, we found that the development of a CR depends on a variety of factors. Among these factors are the temporal arrangement of the CS and US, the specific characteristics of these stimuli, and the presence of stimuli other than the CS and US during conditioning. We also found that in some instances excitatory conditioning seems to occur even when no explicit US is present. Finally, we considered research investigating the biological basis of excitatory conditioning.

With respect to inhibitory conditioning, we noted two factors that appear to be critical for a CS to become an inhibitory stimulus. First, there must be an expectation of US occurrence, and second, the CS must signal the absence of the US. Most situations in which these conditions are met produce CSs that pass both retardation and summation tests for conditioned inhibition.

We completed our discussion by noting that conditioned responses extinguish or decrease when a previously conditioned stimulus is presented alone. We saw that the rate of extinction is affected by the CS–US correlation during acquisition and noted that spontaneous recovery of extinguished responses does occur, however, when time passes after extinction. We concluded our discussion of extinction by considering two treatments for phobias that rely on principles of classical conditioning.

In this chapter we also encountered three of our organizing themes. We saw that classical conditioning can be an adaptive process. We also demonstrated that classical conditioning occurs in biological organisms when we considered possible biological constraints on classical conditioning. In addition, we briefly discussed the physiological basis of classical conditioning. Finally, through our descriptions and examples of classical conditioning, we found that it is a basic process that produces a wide variety of outcomes.

3

Classical Conditioning: Theoretical Issues

Chapter Overview

CHAPTER OVERVIEW

Let's begin this chapter with a simple puzzle. Suppose we give you a series of numbers, and you must guess the rule that determined our choices. The first series of numbers we present to you is 2, 4, and 6. The explanation for this series probably seems simple to you—it is a series of even numbers. This seems like a good explanation, but can you be sure it is correct? In one sense, it is a good explanation because it accounts for all the numbers you have seen so far. However, your explanation does more than just account for the numbers you have seen, it also allows you to predict what numbers will come next. In the present case, your explanation predicts that the next numbers will be 8, 10, and 12. Thus, a powerful way to gain confidence in your explanation would be to find out what the next numbers are. If the next numbers in the series follow the predictions of your explanation, then it would seem that your explanation is correct. If the next numbers do not follow your predictions, then your explanation is probably not correct. We will now tell you that the next numbers in the series are 8, 10, and 12, so it appears you have solved this first number series.

Essentially, in this exercise, we have asked you to develop a theory to explain a series of numbers, and we evaluated this theory in two ways. First, we asked whether your theory explained the available evidence. Second, we asked how well your theory predicted new evidence. Fortunately, in this first example, you easily discovered a useful and seemingly accurate theory.

Now, let's take a more difficult problem. Once again, your task is to develop a theory to explain how a series of numbers is produced. The first three numbers in this series are 1, 2, and 3. Given this series you might offer an initial theory that we are simply counting by ones. This theory accounts for all the evidence that is currently available. It also predicts that the next numbers in the series should be 4, 5, and 6. Unfortunately the next number is 5, so the series now consists of 1, 2, 3, and 5. Your initial theory cannot be correct, because there is now evidence that is inconsistent with your theory. In a case like this, you will need to revise your theory. Your next theory may be that this is a series of prime numbers. This theory accounts for the available evidence, because 1, 2, 3, and 5 are all prime numbers. In addition, your prime number theory also predicts that the next numbers in the series should be 7 and 11 because these are the next prime numbers after 5. The next numbers, however, are 8, 13, and 21. Since 8 and 21 are not prime numbers, your prime number theory doesn't seem to be correct. Now that the series consists of 1, 2, 3, 5, 8,

13, and 21, we will leave you to find a better theory to explain this series of numbers (hint: it is generated by adding numbers from the list).

These number games help to illustrate the process of developing, testing, and refining theories in science. In the case of scientific theories, researchers are faced with a set of facts about some phenomenon (like the numbers you were given). Scientists then attempt to develop a theory to explain these facts. This theory should account for the existing data and it should also predict outcomes that have not yet been tested (like predicting which number comes next in a series). Researchers then test the predictions made by the theory to discover if its predictions are accurate. The theory then gains support as the predictions made by the theory are confirmed, or the theory loses support when its predictions are not confirmed. If the theory's predictions are not confirmed or if new data arise that the theory cannot explain, it then becomes necessary to revise the theory or develop a new theory, and the process of evaluating the theory begins again.

Chapter 2 explained many facts about classical conditioning from the point of view of the factors that influence development of the conditioned response (CR). Now, the discussion will turn toward the interpretations or explanations of these facts through analyzing theories of classical conditioning.

Historically, classical-conditioning researchers have been concerned with two dominant theoretical questions. The first one is rather straightforward and has two parts: When does classical conditioning occur and when does it not occur? Stated more formally, what are the necessary and sufficient conditions for the development of a conditioned response? **Necessary conditions** are the minimum conditions required for an event to occur, and in the absence of necessary conditions, the event will not occur. As an example, bread and peanut butter are necessary for making a peanut butter sandwich because, without these ingredients, it is impossible to make a peanut butter sandwich. However the mere presence of bread and peanut butter does not produce a peanut butter sandwich, so we have not yet identified the sufficient conditions for the sandwich. **Sufficient conditions** are those conditions that should always produce a particular outcome. The sufficient conditions for a peanut butter sandwich involve spreading peanut butter on one slice of bread and covering it with another slice of bread. Every time these conditions are met, the result will be a peanut butter sandwich.

This example also helps to illustrate other important points about necessary and sufficient conditions. Note that when the necessary conditions are not present, we should never end up with a peanut butter sandwich. Note also that when the necessary and sufficient conditions are present, the result will always be a peanut butter sandwich. Similarly, when a theory postulates the necessary and sufficient conditions for classical conditioning to occur, conditioning should not occur when these conditions are not present, and conditioning should always occur when these conditions are present.

The second theoretical question researchers consider is, What is learned during classical conditioning? Essentially this is a question of whether classical conditioning results in an organism learning a relation between the conditioned stimulus and the unconditioned stimulus or a relation between the conditioned stimulus and the unconditioned response.

Recall that, through classical conditioning, a conditioned stimulus (CS) paired with an unconditioned stimulus (US) will come to elicit a conditioned response (CR) that is usually similar to the unconditioned response (UR) (see Figure 3.1a). Beyond this basic description of conditioning are two possibilities for how the CS ultimately elicits this response. First, the organism might learn a relation between the CS and the US (Figure 3.1.b). In this case, the CS activates the US, and the US in turn elicits the response. In computer jargon, you may think of the association between the CS and US as software or learned, whereas the bond between the US and the UR is hard-wired or innate. The second possibility is that the organism learns a relation between the CS and the unconditioned response (Figure 3.1.c) such that the CS directly elicits the response. In essence, Figure 3.1b predicts that the nature of the bond in classical conditioning is a stimulus-stimulus (S-S) bond. Figure 3.1c predicts that the bond is between a stimulus and a response (S-R).

In the remainder of this chapter, we will examine theories that attempt to answer these two basic questions. First, we will consider the necessary and sufficient conditions for classical conditioning. Second, we will attempt to explain what is learned during classical conditioning. As we examine each theory, we will be considering several related points. We must consider how well a theory accounts for existing evidence and how well it predicts new facts. We will also ask if there are any facts the theory cannot explain. These questions will help us to evaluate each theory and help us to understand the evolution of classical-conditioning theories during the past 50 years.

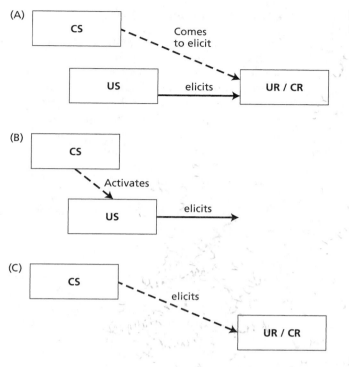

FIGURE 3.1 Possible Pathways for Classical Conditioning.

THE NECESSARY AND SUFFICIENT CONDITIONS FOR CR DEVELOPMENT

Any theory that attempts to provide a general explanation of the conditioning process must begin by stating when conditioning will occur and when it will not. Such a theory must specify the minimum conditions that are necessary for a CR to develop. This section will discuss two types of theory that have attempted to specify these conditions. The first, which we will call **contiguity theory,** proposes that the temporal arrangements of a CS and US constitute the necessary and sufficient conditions for CR development. The second type of theory, which is sometimes labeled **contingency theory,** proposes that conditioning depends on how adequately a CS serves as a predictor for US occurrence. In the contingency theory, time itself is not important. What matters is

the overall pattern of events in the organism's environment. The final theory we will examine is the **Rescorla–Wagner model of classical conditioning,** which is best described as a modified contiguity theory. The best way to begin is by looking at the basic elements of the contiguity position, then evaluate this position by considering how well it accounts for the available evidence.

Contiguity Theory: Basic Assumptions

The contiguity view of conditioning was first proposed by Pavlov in an effort to explain the results of his early studies. Pavlov proposed that excitatory conditioning occurs to the extent that neural activity provoked by the CS overlaps with neural activity produced by the US. This rather simple statement implies that two conditions are necessary and sufficient for conditioning to occur. First, excitatory conditioning depends on the occurrence of an effective CS and US, because there must be neural activity caused by the CS and the US. Pavlov defined an effective CS as any stimulus that could be sensed by an organism, and an effective US as a stimulus that reliably produced a UR. Second, this theory requires that the neural activity provoked by the CS must overlap with the neural activity provoked by the US. Pavlov assumed that such an overlap depends on the CS and US occurring in a **temporally** contiguous manner, meaning that they must occur close together in time, with the CS preceding the US.

Based on the Chapter 2 discussion, it should be clear that excitatory conditioning usually results when these two assumptions are met. The experiments reviewed in that chapter also show that when either of these assumptions is not met, conditioning becomes much less likely. For example, excitatory conditioning normally results when forward CS-US arrangements (such as delayed and trace conditioning procedures) are used. Simultaneous and backward arrangements of the CS and US are relatively ineffective in promoting CR development. Likewise, conditioning tends to be most effective with short CS-US intervals. In other words, temporally contiguous CS-US occurrences produce better excitatory conditioning (in most cases) than do noncontiguous occurrences. These basic facts about conditioning are clearly consistent with the contiguity theory.

Remember, however, that according to contiguity theory, these assumptions constitute the necessary and sufficient conditions for CR occurrence. This means that when these assumptions are met, conditioning should always occur. It also means that if either of these conditions is not met, conditioning should be relatively ineffective. Thus, to truly test this theory two questions must be asked. First, does excitatory conditioning ever fail to occur when these assumptions are met? Second, are there cases where excitatory conditioning does occur when these conditions are not met? The next section explores the answers to these questions.

Contiguity Theory: The Evidence

Since contiguity theory is consistent with some of the most basic findings from conditioning studies, it is a good idea to concentrate on findings that appear to be inconsistent with this view. Among these are situations in which conditioning fails to occur, although the assumptions of the theory have been met, and situations in which conditioning differs in two groups even though the assumptions of contiguity theory are met equally in both. Also worth exploring are findings that indicate that conditioning can occur when these assumptions of contiguity theory are not met.

Conditioning Deficits Not Predicted by Contiguity Theory. Given that a CS and a US are properly arranged in time, contiguity theory proposes that conditioning should depend on whether the two stimuli are effective. Conditioning should result as long as the CS is sensed and the US reliably produces a reflexive reaction. This prediction appears not to hold true in all cases. Several studies have shown that conditioning may not occur, even when clearly effective stimuli are used.

One example of such conditioning failures comes from Colavita's (1965) study of salivary conditioning in dogs. Colavita used a tone as the CS, but instead of using food as the US, he used a mildly acidic solution. When the acidic solution was injected into a dog's mouth, salivation reliably occurred. Thus, the acidic solution was an effective US. Still, even though both CS and US were effective, the CS failed to produce a salivary CR. Only when the solution was injected into both the mouth and the stomach of a dog did salivary conditioning occur.

This finding is not unusual. Several stimuli that reliably elicit a UR fail to serve as effective USs in a conditioning situation (see, for example, Bruner, 1965; Gerall & Obrist, 1962). This occurs even when the CS being employed is one that is effective when paired with USs of other types. For example, recall the results of Garcia and Koelling's 1966 experiment described in Chapter 2. Their results showed that pairing an audiovisual CS with shock produced better conditioning than pairing an audiovisual CS with lithium chloride, whereas pairing a taste CS with lithium chloride resulted in better conditioning than pairing a taste CS with shock. Thus, pairing effective CSs and USs does not always result in conditioning as predicted by contiguity theory.

Even when a given CS and US are known to promote conditioning, researchers have found that the amount of conditioning cannot be determined solely on the basis of CS–US arrangement and temporal contiguity. As previously discussed, when two groups of organisms receive the same number of CS–US pairings, but one also receives several US-alone presentations, conditioning in the two groups will differ (Rescorla, 1968). The group with the presentations of US-alone will show less conditioning than the group without these experiences. This finding is clearly inconsistent with contiguity theory, since according to this position, presentations US-alone should have no effect on conditioning. And, since both groups have the same number of CS–US pairings, they should show equivalent CR development.

Another finding that is inconsistent with the contiguity view is the blocking phenomenon (Kamin, 1968, 1969). As you may recall, blocking is the failure of one element of a compound CS to become conditioned when the other element of the compound already has been conditioned. Specifically, Kamin demonstrated that when a CS compound such as a light and a tone is paired with shock, both elements of the compound normally begin to produce a conditioned fear response. However, if one of the elements has been paired with shock before the compound was established, conditioning to the novel element is blocked. This shows that the amount of conditioning to a given CS cannot be predicted solely by looking at the number of times the CS has occurred in a temporally contiguous manner with the US. Conditioning may also depend on the learning history associated with other stimuli

that are present at the time of conditioning. The same conclusion can be drawn from other experiments we have discussed (see, for example, Wagner, Logan, Haberlandt, & Price, 1968).

These findings indicate that even when the assumptions of contiguity theory are met, conditioning may not occur. Furthermore, even when two groups of organisms have equal numbers of CS-US pairings, conditioning may differ. One may conclude, then, that the conditions suggested by contiguity theory are not sufficient to predict when conditioning will occur. Obviously, other assumptions are needed. However, the question remains whether these conditions are necessary for CR development, or in other words, if conditioning ever occurs when these conditions are not met.

Conditioning in the Absence of Contiguity Assumptions. As shown in Chapter 2, an initial example of a situation where the assumptions of contiguity did not appear to be met came from the work of Garcia and his colleagues on taste aversion learning (Garcia & Koelling, 1966). These researchers showed that when a taste CS was followed by the administration of an illness-producing toxin, organisms later avoided the taste as if it were an illness producer itself. Since the toxin or US did not become effective until several hours after the taste had been experienced, it appeared that in some situations conditioning could develop without temporal contiguity between the CS and US.

However, a more sophisticated form of contiguity theory proposes that what constitutes a short interval of time may depend on the response system employed. Krane and Wagner (1975) demonstrated excitatory conditioning using a taste stimulus and electric shock when 30 or 210 seconds separated presentations of the CS and US. They did not get conditioning when 5 seconds separated the CS and US. When Krane and Wagner used an audio/visual stimulus, they demonstrated conditioning when the CS–US interval was 5 seconds, but not when it was 30 or 210 seconds.

Krane and Wagner argued that taste stimuli may have a longer stimulus duration than audio/visual stimuli and that this could account for the results of the Garcia and Koelling study. In addition, it has been shown that shorter intervals in taste aversion studies generally lead to stronger conditioning than longer intervals. This finding supports the contiguity position. Thus, whereas it appeared initially that the taste aversion literature appeared at odds with contiguity theory, later studies found the results not quite so damaging. Still, to obtain conditioning when the CS and US were separated by hours as opposed to minutes, called into question the assumptions of contiguity theory.

Another example of conditioning that occurs when these assumptions are not met comes from some studies of backward conditioning. Certainly, the more typical finding is that backward arrangements of a CS and US produce no evidence of conditioning (see, for example, Mackintosh, 1974). However, it is equally clear that certain backward-conditioning situations do promote excitatory CRs. Ayres and his associates, for example, have found evidence of excitatory conditioning when only a few backward trials are presented (see Mahoney & Ayres, 1976). Likewise, other researchers have shown that backward CS-US presentations can result in excitatory CRs when each occurrence of the US is surprising to an organism (Heth & Rescorla, 1973; Wagner & Terry, 1975). It is clear that contiguity theory cannot account for these findings; according to the contiguity approach, only forward CS-US pairings should ever result in the acquisition of a conditioned response.

Finally, one of the major difficulties with the contiguity approach is that none of its assumptions deals with the occurrence of inhibitory conditioning. It has been revealed that when a CS reliably signals the absence of an expected US, the CS begins to produce an inhibitory CR. For a CS to become such a signal, CS and US must occur in an unpaired manner. According to contiguity theory, such unpaired CS-US presentations should produce no evidence of conditioning. The theory is partially correct in that such presentations produce no excitatory conditioned responding. However, there is obviously a big difference between a prediction of no conditioning and the observation that conditioning of an inhibitory nature does take place. This is a clear example of conditioning that occurs despite failure to meet the assumptions of contiguity theory.

Contingency Theory: Basic Assumptions

In the 1960s, the above-mentioned problems with the assumptions of contiguity theory led to the development of a different perspective—of the contingency view of classical conditioning. Rescorla and LoLordo (1965) and Rescorla (1966; 1968) proposed various aspects of the contingency approach. According to contingency theory, conditioning depends on the probability of the US in the presence of the CS and the probability of the US in the absence of the CS. To simplify the discussion, we will represent the probability of the US in the presence of the CS as p(US/CS) and the probability of the US in the absence of the CS as p(US/[no]CS). Contingency theory consists of the rather simple proposition that conditioning will occur to the extent that p(US/CS) is different from p(US/[no]CS) (Rescorla, 1968).

Recall from Chapter 2 that if the US reliably occurs when the CS occurs, but rarely occurs when the CS is absent there is a positive contingency between the US and CS. In terms of probabilities, p(US/CS) is greater than p(US/[no]CS), so conditioning should occur because these probabilities are quite different. This situation should lead to the formation of an excitatory CR. Conditioning should also occur when there is a negative CS-US contingency, such that US rarely occurs when the CS occurs, but the US frequently occurs in the absence of the CS. In this case, p(US/CS) is less than p(US/[no]CS), so conditioning should occur in this situation also, but the result will be an inhibitory CR. If the probability of the US occurring is approximately the same in the presence and absence of the CS, no conditioning should occur.

Contingency Theory: The Evidence

Much like contiguity theory, contingency theory is consistent with some of the most basic findings from conditioning studies. In most cases, conditioning does occur when the assumptions of contingency theory are met. More importantly, contingency theory accounts for several findings that contiguity theory cannot explain. For instance, contingency theory predicts the occurrence of inhibitory conditioning, which is not predicted or explained by contiguity theory. Perhaps the strongest and most direct support for contingency theory, however, comes from experiments by Rescorla (1966, 1968). The findings of these experiments were not predicted and could not be explained by contiguity theory, but they were perfectly consistent with contingency theory. As an example, we will briefly analyze again Rescorla's 1968 experiment, while focusing on its relevance for contingency theory.

Rescorla exposed four groups of rats to different CS-US contingencies in a CER paradigm. All four groups received the same number of CS-US pairings and the CS was always followed by the US (shock) so p(US/CS) was 1.0 for all groups. The four groups differed in the number of US-alone presentations, p(US/[no]CS). For the four groups, which we will call the high-contingency, medium-contingency, low-contingency, and no-contingency groups, p(US/[no]CS) was 0, 0.1, 0.2, or 0.4, respectively. According to contingency theory, conditioning should be greatest for the high-contingency group because the difference between p(US/CS) and p(US/[no]CS) is largest for this group. The no-contingency group should show little or no conditioning because of the small difference between p(US/CS) and p(US/[no]CS), while the medium- and low-contingency groups should show intermediate levels of conditioning. The findings of this experiment appeared to support contingency theory perfectly. Rescorla found that conditioning was a direct function of the CS-US contingency, the higher the contingency, the better the conditioning. Similar findings have been found in a number of other experiments (see, for example, Gamzu & Williams, 1971; Rescorla, 1966, 1969a; Weisman & Litner, 1969).

As with all theories of classical conditioning, there are findings that cannot be explained by contingency theory and there are cases in which the predictions of contingency theory were not supported. The following discussion will look at situations in which conditioning fails despite a strong CS-US contingency and examine some findings that indicate that conditioning can occur when there is no CS-US contingency. Finally, we will offer alternative interpretations of Rescorla's 1968 experiment that provided the greatest support for contingency theory.

Conditioning Deficits Not Predicted by Contingency Theory. In some cases, stimuli that reliably elicit a UR fail to serve as effective USs in a conditioning situation, even when there is a strong CS-US contingency (e.g., Bruner, 1965; Garcia & Koelling, 1966; Gerall & Obrist, 1962). This occurs even when the CS being employed is effective when paired with USs of other types.

The blocking phenomenon (Kamin, 1968, 1969) also poses difficulty for contingency theory. When a CS compound such as a light and a tone is paired with shock, both elements of the compound normally begin to produce a conditioned fear response. However, Kamin showed that if one of the elements has been paired with shock before the compound was established, conditioning to the novel element is blocked, despite the positive contingency between the novel element and the US. Thus, the amount of conditioning to a given CS cannot depend only on the contingency between the CS and a US (see also Wagner, Logan, Haberlandt, & Price, 1968).

Conditioning in the Absence of CS-US Contingency. A more direct challenge to contingency theory comes from experiments that demonstrate classical conditioning when no contingent relationship exists between the CS and US. In these experiments, the CS-US contingency is manipulated by the addition of US-alone presentations (for example, Rescorla, 1968). As the number of US-alone presentations increases, the CS-US contingency decreases accordingly, and contingency theory predicts that conditioning should be impaired or prevented entirely as the CS-US contingency approaches zero.

This prediction was tested by Durlach (1983; Experiment 2), who found evidence for conditioning in an autoshaping procedure even when the CS-US contingency was zero. You may recall from Chapter 2 that autoshaping entails the procedure where a localized cue (keylight in this instance) is illuminated inside a chamber and is followed by food. Durlach used three groups of pigeons, and, for each group, 25% of the CS presentations were followed by the US. One group (Group 25) received no US-alone presentations. The other groups (Group Signalled and Group Unsignaled) received 17 US-alone presentations during the experiment. For Group Signaled, these US-alone presentations were signaled by a tone, while the US-alone presentations were not signaled by any discrete stimulus.

Thus, in this experiment, Group 25 experienced a positive CS-US contingency, while there was no CS-US contingency for groups Signaled and Unsignaled. According to contingency theory, Group 25 should show evidence of conditioning while neither Group Signaled nor Group Unsignaled should show evidence of conditioning. The results of this experiment shown in Figure 3.2 do not support this prediction. Although the Unsignaled group showed no conditioning, there was strong evidence of conditioning in the Signaled group. These results show successful conditioning in the absence of CS-US contingency and suggest that CS-US contingency may not be necessary for conditioning to occur (see also Goddard & Jenkins, 1987).

Other Interpretations of Rescorla's 1968 Experiment. A final challenge to contingency theory comes from reconsideration of Rescorla's 1968 findings. Although these experiments appear to provide direct support for contingency

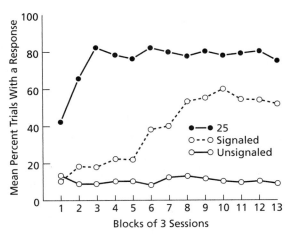

FIGURE 3.2 Durlach's Experiment. Mean percentage of target conditioned stimulus trials with a response in Experiment 2. Group 25 (solid circles) received no intertrial interval unconditioned stimulus (ITI USs). Group Unsignaled (open circles, solid lines) received unsignaled ITI USs, and Group Signaled (open circles, dotted lines) received ITI USs signaled by a tone. From *Journal of Experimental Psychology: Animal Behavior Processes, 9,* 374–389. ©1989 by the American Psychological Assn. Reprinted by permission of the publisher and P. J. Durlach.

theory, several authors have offered other interpretations of Rescorla's findings and argued that these findings may not prove that conditioning is a function of the CS-US contingency (see, for example, Estes, 1969; Papini & Bitterman, 1990). These authors suggest that the poor conditioning observed in Rescorla's no-contingency and low-contingency groups was a result of the blocking phenomenon and not due to the lack of CS-US contingency.

Recall that Rescorla manipulated the CS-US contingency by varying the number of US-alone presentations across the experimental groups. The no-contingency group and the low-contingency group received many such US-alone presentations. Notice, though, that it is not possible to actually present a US with no other stimuli present. In any experiment, there are many stimuli present in addition to the CS and US.

Other stimuli such as the experimental apparatus, odors present in the room, temperature, lighting, and extraneous noises are normally present during conditioning. These background stimuli that are present throughout a conditioning experience are known as **contextual stimuli.** In short, any stimulus that remains relatively constant during conditioning and does not vary along with the CS or US presentation can be considered a contextual stimulus.

Thus, in Rescorla's experiment, the US-alone presentations were actually Context-US presentations. In such an arrangement, contextual stimuli may have served as CSs, and conditioning to these contextual CSs might occur as a result of the Context-US presentations. Substantial evidence supports the conclusion that conditioning does occur to contextual stimuli during conditioning. One example of such evidence comes from a study by Bouton and King (1983). These researchers gave rats CS-shock pairings in a distinctive chamber (Context A). Later, they placed the same rats in Context A but allowed the animals to have access to a novel chamber (Context B). They found that these rats now showed a distinct preference for Context B over Context A, where they had been conditioned. No such preference was found in animals that had not been conditioned in Context A. This finding indicates that after receiving CS-shock pairings in Context A, the rats were fearful not only of the CS, but also of the contextual stimuli present at the time of conditioning. These experiments, together with many others, demonstrate clearly that contextual stimuli can serve as CSs during conditioning.

Let us now return to Rescorla's experiment and consider the possible role of contextual stimuli. To facilitate this discussion, we will represent the discrete Tone CS as CS_{TONE}, and the potential contextual CSs as $CS_{CONTEXT}$. We can view the US-alone presentations in Rescorla's study as instances of $CS_{CONTEXT}$-US presentations. In a similar manner the contextual stimuli were also present during CS_{TONE}-US presentations. These trials can be represented as $CS_{CONTEXT}$ + CS_{TONE}-US. As evidenced from the blocking phenomenon, when $CS_{CONTEXT}$ becomes an effective CS, it should block any conditioning to CS_{TONE}. In Rescorla's procedures, the no-contingency and low-contingency groups received the greatest number of $CS_{CONTEXT}$-US pairings, so one would expect the most conditioning to $CS_{CONTEXT}$ in these groups. Accordingly, it is in these groups where the greatest blocking to CS_{TONE} should occur. Thus, the poor conditioning observed in the low-contingency and no-contingency groups could be a result of blocking by contextual CSs and not due to the lack of CS-US contingency. Several subsequent experiments support this conclusion (see, for example, Durlach, 1989; Rescorla, 1984). Based on this evidence, it seems that Rescorla's 1968 findings do not provide conclusive support for contingency theory (Papini & Bitterman, 1990).

Conclusions About Contingency in Conditioning

Although contingency theory is still widely cited as a current theory of classical conditioning, the preponderance of recent evidence does not support contingency theory as an explanation of classical conditioning (Papini and Bitterman, 1990). At this point, this discussion of contingency theory may seem to contradict the discussion of classical conditioning in Chapter 2. In Chapter 2 the discussion relied on the notion of CS-US contingency in describing classical conditioning, yet we have just presented much evidence to suggest that contingency theory does not help to explain classical conditioning. This is understandably a confusing situation.

Another source of confusion is the fact that Rescorla, who has had an enormous impact on classical-conditioning research and theory, has at different times supported both the contingency and contiguity views of classical conditioning. Rescorla (1988) explains this apparent contradiction by noting that arrangements that promote conditioning are, in general, best described as involving CS-US contingency, but for an explanation of classical conditioning he favors, "a more complex version of contiguity" (pp. 342–343; see also Papini & Bitterman, 1990). Similarly, we have described classical conditioning in terms of CS-US contingencies throughout Chapter 2. However, as we present explanations of classical conditioning in this chapter, we shall also look to a different version of contiguity to best explain the facts of classical conditioning.

The "more complex version of contiguity" that Rescorla describes was put forward in 1972 by Rescorla and Wagner. They proposed a model of classical conditioning that included many of contiguity theory's assumptions, but went well beyond it. Their model, which has become widely known as the Rescorla-Wagner model, is perhaps best described as a modified contiguity theory. Although simple in its approach, the model is able to account for a wide variety of conditioning effects. In this vein it supports Theme 1 of this book, which is to account for a diverse set of findings with a small set of basic concepts.

MODIFIED CONTIGUITY THEORY: THE RESCORLA-WAGNER MODEL

Although the Rescorla-Wagner model is quite simple, it can seem very intimidating at first. To better understand the Rescorla-Wagner model, it is helpful to begin with an intuitive view of the model before considering the computations and terms of the equation that define the model. The following are three main assumptions of the Rescorla-Wagner model.

Assumption 1: Conditioning occurs only to the extent that the occurrence or absence of a US was not signaled. To begin to understand the Rescorla-Wagner model, think of conditioning as a mechanism by which organisms come to anticipate important events such as USs. In effect, the model assumes that it is adaptive in some manner for an organism to anticipate or predict when a US is likely to occur or not occur. Thus, conditioning will occur when an organism is exposed to an "unexpected" or "surprising" US or when it is surprised by the nonoccurrence of an expected US.

Assumption 2: A CS gains ability to elicit an excitatory CR if it precedes a US, and a CS gains ability to elicit an inhibitory CR if it precedes the absence of a US. The model also assumes that organisms learn about the occurrence or nonoccurrence of a US based on stimuli that preceded the surprising US. Only stimuli that precede an event are useful predictors of that event. Thus the Rescorla-Wagner model assumes that conditioning occurs only for stimuli that precede a surprising event. Thus, a given CS acquires the capacity for producing a CR to the extent that it precedes the presence or absence of a US. If a CS precedes a US, the CS can acquire the capacity for producing an excitatory CR. If a CS precedes the nonoccurrence of a US, it can become capable of producing an inhibitory CR.

Assumption 3: A given CS loses capacity for producing a CR when it no longer precedes US occurrence or nonoccurrence. A related assumption concerns the effect of situations in which a CS that has previously preceded the occurrence or nonoccurrence of a US suddenly stops appearing. If the CS has ceased to precede the US, then excitatory conditioning will be weakened. If an inhibitory CS is suddenly followed by a US, its capacity to act as an inhibitory CS will weaken. This behavior change is similar to the process of extinction discussed in Chapter 2.

These assumptions show that the Rescorla-Wagner model retains many of the basic ideas found in contiguity theory. It is still assumed, for example, that conditioning will not occur in the absence of an effective CS-US pair. It is further assumed that the temporal contiguity of CS and US is a critical factor in conditioning. The assumptions of the Rescorla-Wagner model, however, also represent a significant expansion or modification of the contiguity position because it includes important assumptions not made by contiguity theory. First, the Rescorla-Wagner model assumes that conditioning depends on the occurrence of a US that is surprising. The Rescorla-Wagner model also assumes that conditioned inhibition and excitation are complementary processes that can result from conditioning procedures. Finally, the model assumes that the conditioning of a particular CS is affected by the presence of other stimuli in the conditioning situation.

The Formal Expression of the Rescorla-Wagner Model

One advantage of the Rescorla-Wagner model is that its assumptions have been incorporated into a formal, mathematical expression. By substituting numbers for the symbols in this mathematical equation, it is possible to predict with great clarity the degree to which conditioning should occur in a given situation. Understanding the basic rules in the mathematical formulation is critical to understanding the model.

The purpose of the mathematical model is to predict the change in associative strength of a particular CS on any given conditioning trial. The following is the formula used to determine this change:

$$\Delta V_a = \alpha\beta(\lambda - V_{ax})$$

The first symbol in the formula is ΔV_a, which stands for the change in conditioning to stimulus A (or CS) on a given trial. This change in conditioning to a given CS can be either positive or negative. That is, the capacity a CS has for producing a CR may either increase or decrease on a given trial, depending on the circumstances.

What are these circumstances that determine the change in associative strength of a particular CS? Three factors are built into the formula. First, conditioning to CS_a depends on the salience of that CS. (Note: CS_a refers to the particular CS being conditioned.) Second, conditioning varies depending on the intensity of the US. Third, and most important, conditioning will vary as a function of how surprising a US is on a particular trial. In the formula itself, CS salience is represented by the symbol α (alpha), while US intensity is represented by the symbol β (beta). Here the symbol λ (lambda) stands for

the total amount of conditioning a given US can promote—that is, the total associative strength a US can support. The symbol V_{ax} stands for the combined associative strength of all stimuli in the situation. (Think of this as the degree of conditioning that has already occurred to all stimuli in the situation.) If λ represents the associative strength a particular US can support and V_{ax} represents the total associative strength for all stimuli in the situation, then $(\lambda - V_{ax})$ represents the difference between the maximum associative strength a US can support and the current total associative strength for all stimuli in the situation. It may help if you think of $(\lambda - V_{ax})$ as representing the difference between how much the US can be predicted and how much it is already being predicted or signaled. Thus $(\lambda - V_{ax})$ could be interpreted as representing how surprising the US is on a given trial. These symbols and their definitions are summarized as follows:

Δ	=	change
V	=	associative strength of a stimulus
V_a	=	associative strength of CS_a
V_x	=	associative strength of all other stimuli in the conditioning situation
V_{ax}	=	combined associative strength for all stimuli in the conditioning situation
α	=	salience of the CS
β	=	intensity of the US
λ	=	amount of conditioning the US can support (available associative strength)
$\lambda - V_{ax}$	=	degree to which the US is surprising on a particular trial

As we have already discussed, the associative strength of CS_a changes on any given conditioning trial according to the formula:

$$\Delta V_a = \alpha\beta(\lambda - V_{ax})$$

This formula, as proposed by Rescorla and Wagner, is simple to use. It states that the change in conditioning to a CS on a given trial (ΔV_a) is equal to the CS salience (α) multiplied by the US intensity (β), multiplied by the degree to which the US is surprising ($\lambda - V_{ax}$). As we noted, surprise is quantified as the amount of associative strength a US can support (λ) minus the amount it is already signaled by stimuli present in the conditioning situation (V_{ax}).

To use this formula for making predictions, it is necessary to keep two rules in mind. First, it is assumed that the value of $\alpha\beta$ will always be a number between 0 and 1; $\alpha\beta$ will not be 0 unless no CS occurs on a given trial. Second, λ has a value of 0 whenever a US is absent on a conditioning trial. In all other cases λ has a positive value greater than 0.

To illustrate, consider a few examples. Assume that a CS is paired with a US for the first time, and that no other stimuli present are reliable predictors for US occurrence. How will the ability of the CS to produce a CR change as a result of this first pairing? Since we are not specifying the real nature of the CS and US, we will choose arbitrary numbers to insert in the formula. For purposes of illustration, we select 0.5 as the value for $\alpha\beta$ and 100 as the value of λ. Since no stimuli in the conditioning situation already signal the US, $V_{ax} = 0$. According to the formula, then,

$$\Delta V_a = 0.5 \ (100 - 0)$$
$$\Delta V_a = 0.5 \ (100)$$
$$\Delta V_a = 50$$

This means that the capacity of the CS to produce a CR will increase by 50 units.

This number is, of course, relatively meaningless until compared to what happens in other situations. Thus, assume that several CS-US pairings have occurred, so that the CS (in combination with other stimuli in the environment) has become a completely reliable predictor for US occurrence. What would happen if one additional trial were given? In this case, the value of $\alpha\beta$ would still be 0.5 and the value of λ would remain at 100. However, because of all the prior conditioning, V_{ax} would now have a value of 100. This means that the CS and other stimuli present already fully predict the US. The occurrence of the US is no longer surprising. According to the formula, the result of this additional conditioning trial would be as follows:

$$\Delta V_a = 0.5 \ (100 - 100)$$
$$\Delta V_a = 0.5 \ (0)$$
$$\Delta V_a = 0$$

In effect, the additional CS-US pairing would lead to no change in the capacity of the CS, since the US was already fully predicted by the stimuli available. This contrasts sharply with the large increase in conditioning (+50 units) that occurred on the initial conditioning trial.

By using this formula it is possible to say how much a CS will become conditioned on any given trial, based on how much conditioning has occurred in the past. In addition, however, the formula makes it possible to predict what will happen to a CS when it occurs alone, without a US. Recall that when a US is omitted, the value of λ becomes 0. Assume that a CS has been paired with a US several times so that the value of the CS is 80 units. This means, of course, that the value of V_{ax} will also be 80 units. What happens if the CS is presented alone? The values in the formula would be as follows:

$$\Delta V_a = 0.5 \ (0 - 80)$$
$$\Delta V_a = 0.5 \ (-80)$$
$$\Delta V_a = -40$$

In other terms, the capacity of the CS to produce a CR would decrease. Before the trial began, the CS had a value of 80, but its value decreased by 40 owing to the CS-alone presentation. This, of course, is what happens to the value of a CS when it is extinguished.

One final example is worth noting. According to this model, a CS produces an excitatory CR to the extent that the CS has a positive value. When the value of the CS is negative, however, the CS becomes capable of producing an inhibitory CR. Under what circumstances does the model predict that a CS will become inhibitory? As previously discussed, a CS becomes an inhibitory stimulus when it reliably signals the absence of an otherwise expected US. This means, first of all, that there must be some stimuli present that signal US occurrence. Otherwise, there would be no expectation of the US. Second, some CS must then occur as a signal that the US will be absent. This means that the CS must occur alone. If these conditions are translated into numbers in the formula, λ is 0, since no US occurs. Also, V_{ax} has a positive value because some stimuli in the environment already signal US occurrence (for present purposes assume that V_{ax} = 50). What would happen then if a novel CS (with a value of 0) were presented without the US?

$$\Delta V_a = 0.5 (0 - 50)$$
$$\Delta V_a = 0.5 (-50)$$
$$\Delta V_a = -25$$

inhibitory

On such a trial, the CS value decreases by some amount. Since before the trial the CS had a value of 0, this decrease means that the CS takes on a negative value or becomes inhibitory.

These examples may help you to form some idea of how the formal model works to make predictions. As long as you understand the basic assumptions of the Rescorla–Wagner model, it will be possible to assess how well such a model accounts for classical conditioning phenomena.

Rescorla-Wagner Model: The Evidence

Most of the basic conditioning phenomena discussed so far are handled rather easily by the Rescorla–Wagner model. For example, we have shown that conditioning is most effective when salient CSs and intense USs are employed. In the Rescorla–Wagner model, increased CS salience results in a higher value for α, whereas increased US intensity leads to increased β values. According to this model, when either α or β values are higher, conditioning will occur to a greater degree on any given trial.

Likewise, this model predicts that long CS–US intervals should produce less effective conditioning than shorter intervals, because longer intervals reduce the contiguity between a CS and a US. As we have explained, in most cases, this prediction is upheld by the experimental data.

Finally, we have shown that forward conditioning arrangements produce better CR developments than either simultaneous or backward configurations. This finding is clearly consistent with the Rescorla–Wagner model, which states that a CS must be a reliable signal for US occurrence in order for conditioning to occur. The CS can be a reliable signal only if it precedes the US in time.

Thus, the Rescorla–Wagner model is able to account for the same basic findings that the contiguity theory was developed to explain. The major appeal of this model, however, is its ability to account for a variety of phenomena that cannot be explained by contiguity theory or contingency theory. Let us briefly describe three such phenomena.

Effects of Stimuli Other Than the CS. Earlier we reviewed a number of studies showing that conditioning to a given CS often depends on other stimuli present at the time of conditioning. One example of this finding comes from Kamin's studies (1968, 1969) of the blocking phenomenon, which showed that conditioning to one element of a compound CS depends on whether the other element has already been paired with the US in question. If one element of a compound has been associated with the US, subsequent conditioning to the other element is blocked or impeded.

Again, findings such as this can be accounted for by the Rescorla–Wagner model. One of these assumptions is that conditioning to a given CS will occur only if the US occurrence is surprising. A novel CS paired with a US will not develop the capacity to produce a CR if, at the time of the pairing, the US is already predicted by other stimuli in the environment. The blocking paradigm is, of course, a clear example of just such a situation. As a result of prior pairings with the US, one CS becomes a reliable signal for US occurrence. When that CS is later compounded with a novel CS in a conditioning situation, the occurrence of the US is not surprising, because it is being signaled by the previously conditioned CS. Since the US is not surprising, no conditioning will occur to the novel CS, even though it is paired with the US on a regular basis.

It is notable that the same logic allows the Rescorla-Wagner model to account for a variety of other conditioning phenomena. For example, this "lack of surprise" explanation has been used to explain the occurrence of the US preexposure effect. Recall that if an organism is exposed to a US several times before that US is used in a conditioning situation, conditioning to the CS is usually ineffective (Randich & LoLordo, 1979). According to the Rescorla-Wagner model, this occurs because during US preexposures the stimuli in the preexposure room (contextual stimuli) come to signal the occurrence of the US. In other words, contextual stimuli gain associative strength during the US preexposures. Later, if a novel CS is paired with the US in the same environment, the occurrence of the US is not surprising. For this reason, the novel CS will not become capable of producing a CR (see, for example, Tomie, 1976). This explanation is supported by studies indicating that US preexposure will have little effect on subsequent conditioning as long as preexposure and conditioning occur in different environments (see, for example, Hinson, 1982).

In a similar manner, the Rescorla-Wagner model also accounts for the apparent role of contingency in classical conditioning in experiments such as Rescorla (1968). In these experiments, US-alone presentations impede conditioning to the target CS. The Rescorla-Wagner model explains these findings as a case where, condition-ing to the training context leads to the contextual CS blocking CR development by the target CS. Interestingly, the Rescorla-Wagner model predicts that conditioning to the target CS will occur if the US-alone presentations are signaled by a novel stimulus. This prediction was supported in a number of experiments (see, for example, Durlach, 1983; 1989).

The Occurrence of Inhibitory Conditioning. One of the major difficulties associated with the contiguity approach was its failure to account for inhibitory conditioning. According to the contiguity position, whenever a CS signals the absence of a US, no conditioning should result. However, as we have shown, this does not appear to be the case. A CS that signals the absence of an expected US does not become capable of producing an excitatory CR. It does, however, gain the capacity to produce an inhibitory CR. The development of inhibitory responding under these conditions is clearly predicted by the Rescorla-Wagner model. Thus, one major advantage of the Rescorla-Wagner model over contiguity theory is that it predicts the occurrence of inhibitory conditioning in certain situations.

Problems Associated with the Rescorla-Wagner Model. The Rescorla-Wagner model has contributed a great deal to the study and explanation of the conditioning process. Clearly, the Rescorla-Wagner model remains an influential theory of classical conditioning and has had a widespread impact on other theories in psychology and many other disciplines (Miller, Barnet, & Grahame, 1995; Siegel & Allan, 1996). Still, this model is not without problems. For example, the Rescorla-Wagner model, as originally stated, fails to account for certain details of the blocking phenomenon. For this reason, some of the assumptions of the model have been modified in more contemporary versions of the Rescorla-Wagner model (e.g., Pearce & Hall, 1980).

More importantly, the Rescorla-Wagner formulation fails to deal with some of the apparent anomalies that occur in certain conditioning situations. It does not, for example, account for the excitatory conditioning that sometimes occurs when backward conditioning trials are used. It also fails to explain the unusual findings that have been reported in experiments featuring the taste aversion paradigm. For example, the Rescorla-Wagner model is silent when it comes to explaining how conditioning can occur in the taste aversion paradigm when such long CS-US intervals are used. It also offers no explanation of why aversions are formed only to stimuli such as tastes and odors, not to stimuli such as lights and tones. Such difficulties have led to the development of new theories. Despite the appearance of new theories of classical conditioning and problems with the Rescorla-Wagner model, this model remains a very influential theory of classical conditioning (Miller, Barnet, & Grahame, 1995). Although it is unnecessary to consider recent theoretical models in detail, it is useful to look briefly at the directions they have taken.

RECENT THEORIES OF CLASSICAL CONDITIONING

In response to the failures of the Rescorla-Wagner model, several recent theories of classical conditioning attempt to explain phenomena that the Rescorla-Wagner model cannot. Each of these theories offers explanations for one or more conditioning effects that have proven difficult for other theories. However, these theories are also faced with shortcomings, and there is currently not enough evidence to enable conclusive assessments of these theories. Nonetheless, it will be useful to look briefly at three of these recent theories of classical conditioning.

Wagner's Priming Theory

Several variations of a new classical conditioning theory have been proposed by Wagner (Wagner, 1981; Wagner & Brandon, 1989; Wagner, Rudy, & Whitlow, 1973). Although these various pro-

posals have differed to some degree, a few important themes have emerged. The basic notion common to all these hypotheses is that once a stimulus has ceased to exist in the environment, it may continue to be processed in an organism's short-term or primary memory. In other words, even though a stimulus itself may no longer be present in the outside world, a representation of that stimulus may persist in an organism's short-term memory for some finite period of time. We will discuss the concept of short-term memory in some detail in a later chapter. For present purposes, short-term memory can be characterized as the aspect of memory that is active at any particular moment. Items in short-term memory are the items an organism is currently rehearsing.

The critical assumption in Wagner's position is that conditioning involves associations that are formed between stimuli that are represented in short-term memory. According to Wagner, conditioning occurs whenever a CS and a US are represented and rehearsed jointly in short-term memory. In effect, the development of an excitatory CR depends on the degree to which the CS and US are rehearsed in memory at the same time. Alternatively, excitatory associations are broken down and inhibitory associations may be formed to the extent that a CS and US are rehearsed separately. Thus, extinction of an excitatory CR or the formulation of an inhibitory CR can occur when CS and US are represented in memory at different times.

By focusing on an organism's memory for stimuli rather than on just the occurrence of the stimuli themselves, Wagner introduces an important principle. According to this view, it is not possible to predict when a certain type of conditioning will occur solely on the basis of how stimuli are temporally arranged in the environment. To make such predictions, it is necessary to understand the factors that influence the rehearsal or processing of a stimulus in short-term memory. Only then will we be able to predict when two stimuli are and are not likely to be rehearsed jointly in memory. To illustrate the importance of this principle, let us look briefly at a few of the factors that might determine the degree to which a stimulus is rehearsed in memory.

First, Wagner has proposed that whether any stimulus is rehearsed will depend on how surprising the stimulus is. If a stimulus such as a US is surprising to an organism, the organism will tend to rehearse the stimulus in short-term memory for a substantial period of time. However, a stimulus that is expected will be represented in short-term memory only briefly. Nonsurprising stimuli are thus rehearsed for a shorter time than surprising ones, and this means that nonsurprising stimuli have less chance to be rehearsed jointly with other events. Several studies conducted by Wagner and his colleagues seem to support this notion that surprising stimuli are rehearsed longer than nonsurprising stimuli (see, for example, Terry & Wagner, 1975; Wagner, Rudy, & Whitlow, 1973).

But if this is the case, how does such knowledge improve our ability to explain conditioning phenomena? One example of the application of this view is found in the area of backward-conditioning research. As we have shown, backward-conditioning trials sometimes result in excitatory CRs when only a few trials are presented (Mahoney & Ayres, 1976). However, when several backward presentations occur, the typical finding is either no evidence of excitatory conditioning or, in some cases, the development of an inhibitory CR (see, for example, Moscovitch & LoLordo, 1968; Siegel & Domjan, 1971). Wagner attempts to explain these divergent findings by suggesting that in backward-conditioning situations, the probability of joint CS–US rehearsal changes as more conditioning trials occur.

Specifically, Wagner hypothesizes that on the first few backward-conditioning trials, the occurrence of the US is surprising to an organism and it is thus rehearsed for a long period of time. Therefore, even though the CS occurs after the US, the rehearsal of the US is still going on when the CS is presented. In other words, joint rehearsal of the two stimuli will indeed occur, and some evidence of excitatory conditioning should be found. As more and more backward presenta-

tions occur, however, the US will become less and less surprising in that situation. The organism comes to expect the US because the US has occurred previously in the presence of the contextual stimuli. As the US becomes less surprising, it is rehearsed for shorter and shorter periods of time. This means that after several backward presentations there is an increased likelihood that US rehearsal will be ended by the time CS rehearsal begins. Because the stimuli are rehearsed separately in memory, any excitatory associations formed on the initial trials will begin to break down. If enough trials of this type occur, inhibitory CRs may even begin to develop.

To test this interpretation, Wagner and Terry (1975) conducted a backward-conditioning experiment in which they attempted to maintain the surprising value of the US over several conditioning trials. Their rationale was that if the US remains surprising throughout backward conditioning, the US will continue to be rehearsed long enough to overlap with CS rehearsal. This should result in better excitatory conditioning than that which is usually found when backward presentations occur.

In brief, this experiment consisted of two phases. In Phase 1, rabbits were exposed to two different auditory stimuli we will call CS1 and CS2. Presentations of CS1 were always followed by a mild shock delivered to the skin near the orbit of the eye, whereas CS2 was never followed by a shock. As a result, CS1 began to produce a conditioned eye-blink response and CS2 did not. The purpose of the first phase was to establish CS1 as a signal for shock occurrence and to assure that CS2 became a signal for the absence of shock.

Once these CSs had been established as signals for shock occurrence or nonoccurrence, the experimenters began Phase 2, which consisted of a series of backward-conditioning trials. In Phase 2 each backward conditioning trial was preceded by the previously conditioned signal indicating whether the US would or would not occur. On half the trials the signal for shock occurrence preceded the pairing of shock and a novel CS (CS3).

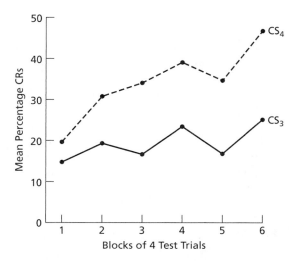

FIGURE 3.3 Wagner & Terry's Results. Conditioned responding to two CSs used in backward conditioning arrangements. CS4 is preceded by a surprising US, and CS3 is preceded by an expected US. From *Animal Learning & Behavior*, 1975, *3*, 370–374. Reprinted by permission of Psychonomic Society, Inc.

Thus, the sequence of events on these trials was (a) the presentation of the signal for shock, (b) the presentation of the shock, and (c) the presentation of the novel CS3. On these trials the occurrence of the shock would be expected because it was being signaled by the previously conditioned cue. Therefore, CS3 should show minimal excitatory conditioning.

On the other half of the trials, the experimenters presented the signal for shock absence (CS2), which was then followed by shock and then the other novel CS (CS4). Thus, the stimulus sequence on these trials was (a) the presentation of the signal for shock absence, (b) the presentation of the shock, and (c) the presentation of the novel CS4. The experimenters assumed that on these trials, the occurrence of the shock would be surprising. Thus, they predicted that CS4 would develop a substantial ability to produce an eyeblink response.

As indicated in Figure 3.3, which summarizes the results of this study, the prediction made by

Wagner and Terry was confirmed. Both CS3 and CS4 occurred after the shock US. However, CS4 developed a strong capacity to produce an excitatory CR, while CS3 did not. The main difference between the CSs was that CS4 was always preceded by a surprising shock, whereas CS3 always followed an expected shock. This result is consistent with Wagner's notion that backward-conditioning trials can produce excitatory CRs if the US is rehearsed long enough to overlap with CS rehearsal.

It is notable that this view of conditioning has also been applied to other phenomena that have been difficult to explain by means of contiguity theory, contingency theories, or the Rescorla-Wagner model. In the taste-aversion situation, for example, Wagner has tentatively attributed the puzzling results from these experiments to the rehearsal of different CSs for different periods of time (see, for example, Whitlow, 1976). Specifically, he has proposed that externally based stimuli such as lights and tones may be rehearsed in short-term memory only briefly. However, other stimuli such as odors or tastes may remain in short-term memory for much more extended periods. If it is acceptable to suggest that different CSs may be rehearsed differentially, it becomes possible to explain some of the more perplexing phenomena found in taste-aversion research.

For instance, the hypothesis of different rehearsal times would help to explain why flavors become associated with events that occur long after exposure to the flavor. According to Wagner, the memory of a flavor lasts long enough to be rehearsed jointly with, for example, illness-producing toxins. This joint rehearsal then results in the development of an excitatory CR to the flavor. The same reasoning has been used to explain why stimuli such as flavors do not appear to become associated with shock and why stimuli such as tones do not appear to become associated with illness (Garcia & Koelling, 1966).

Wagner explains this apparent lack of associability between certain stimuli by pointing out that researchers do not know exactly how these stimuli are rehearsed. He believes that tones do not become associated with illness-provoking toxins because tones are rehearsed only briefly and the toxins do not produce any effects until long after they have been administered. This means that the tone and the toxic effects are never jointly rehearsed in short-term memory. Similarly, when experimenters have attempted to induce associations between flavors and shock, they have normally presented the shock shortly after the flavor. This means that the two stimuli undergo joint rehearsal. However, if the flavor continues to be rehearsed for long periods after shock presentation, there is significant rehearsal of the CS in the absence of US rehearsal. This separate rehearsal is thought to result in the breakdown of any of the excitatory CRs that form during joint rehearsal. The rehearsal of the flavor CS, which continues to occur after rehearsal of the shock US, makes this situation similar to a backward-conditioning arrangement.

These models clearly offer explanations for some of the most puzzling findings in classical-conditioning research, but these gains come at the price of including complex assumptions about processes that are difficult to observe and measure. As a result, direct experimental tests of these models are difficult to develop. However, as shown earlier, Krane and Wagner (1975) offered support for such explanations. Still, it is not possible to directly control how long an organism rehearses a particular stimulus, and it is difficult to determine in advance of conditioning which stimuli should lead to longer rehearsal and which should not. As a result, the predictive successes of Wagner's models require the addition of complex assumptions concerning the process of conditioning.

Since its inception in the early 1970s, Wagner has continued to extend his theoretical formulation. In 1981 he introduced his "SOP" Model of classical conditioning. SOP stood for "Standard Operating Procedures" of memory or "Sometimes Opponent Process." In this model Wagner theorizes that any stimulus CS or US has a primary (A1) state and a secondary (A2) state. These states are similar to the primary and oppo-

nent states of the opponent process theory of motivation. It is assumed in this model that when a stimulus first impinges on the senses, the A1 state predominates. With time, the A2 state gradually takes over followed by its own decay.

An excitatory association between a CS and a US develops if the A1 state of the CS overlaps with the A1 state of the US. Once this occurs and the two stimuli have been jointly rehearsed, presentation of the CS will elicit the A1 state of the CS and the A2 state of the US. The SOP model predicts that in a backward-conditioning procedure, excitatory backward conditioning will result if the CS follows the US a short time later (the A1 states overlap). Inhibitory conditioning will result if the A1 state of CS overlaps with the A2 state of the US (long US–CS interval). This prediction has been confirmed (Wagner & Larew, 1985).

For the moment, it is too early to draw conclusions about the validity of Wagner's theoretical formulations. Many of the assumptions and prediction of his model have not been tested systematically enough to warrant final conclusions. It is evident, however, that these models are influencing the study of classical conditioning, and the results of several experiments support these models (see, for example, Canli, Detmer, & Donegan, 1992).

Behavior Systems Theory

All of the theoretical positions discussed so far could be characterized as associative theories of classical conditioning because these theories focus on the learning of associations among stimuli, especially the CS and US. Although the theories we have discussed are quite different from each other, they share the common perspective that classical conditioning involves learning a relation between a CS and US or a relation between a CS and a particular response.

Interesting and unique alternatives to such associative theories of conditioning are adaptive-evolutionary theories of classical conditioning. These ecological theories emphasize the role of evolution and current adaptation in the learning process. In addition they help emphasize the third theme of this book—that learning is an adaptive process that functions to ensure an animal's reproductive success. As an example of how classical conditioning might play an adaptive role, imagine the following. You are four years old and you are out playing ball with your friends. As you are pondering an ant pile you hear your friend shout "Look out!" just before you feel the ball bounce off your head. After a few days recovery time you are back out on the playing field. Again you hear the call to look out, but now your reaction is different. Now you quickly scan the environment, find the object that is rushing toward you and you duck in time to avoid being hit again. For the rest of your life the phrase "look out" will cause this reaction and more often will result in your not getting hit in the head.

This example serves to emphasize the fact that conditioned responses could serve an adaptive function. Hollis (1982) argued that classical conditioning is an innate learning mechanism whose function is to assist organisms to adapt to their environments. This is accomplished in her view by preparing animals to interact optimally and appropriately to events of biological significance. To support her position Hollis, Martin, Cadieus, and Colbert (1984) showed that the aggressive behavior of blue gourami fish could be classically conditioned. In essence, blue gourami males were shown to be more aggressive and hence better able to defend a territory if they were signaled that another male fish was about to enter their territory. Similarly, Hollis, Cadieu, and Colbert (1989) showed that males were less aggressive toward females if they received a signal announcing their arrival. As a result of this reduced aggressiveness, males were able to interact with females quicker than males who were not signaled.

Recently, Hollis, Pharr, Dumas, Britton, and Field (1997) were able to show that a classically conditioned response can directly increase the reproductive success of a male. Hollis, et al.,

demonstrated that classically conditioned male blue gouramis had a reproductive advantage over control subjects. Male blue gouramis were conditioned with a 10-second light CS followed immediately with a visual presentation of a live female blue gourami. Conditioned male subjects showed less aggression toward the female, directed significantly more courtship behaviors to the females, and mated with their female counterparts more. The end result was that conditioned males produced more offspring than the unconditioned males. Clearly the conditioned response that resulted from classical conditioning had an adaptive advantage for the fish. Similar findings have been shown in Japanese quail (Domjan, Blesbois, & Williams, 1998).

Other theorists have also attempted to couch classical conditioning within the evolutionary history of the organism. One of the adaptive-evolutionary theories that is the best developed is the behavior-systems theory developed by Timberlake and his colleagues (see, for example, Timberlake, 1994; Timberlake & Lucas, 1989). Although we cannot examine this theory in great detail, we will survey some of its most important and interesting features.

Behavior-systems theory proposes that evolutionary processes have endowed organisms with preorganized systems of behavior that include not only several behaviors but also sensitivity to certain stimuli, timing of particular behaviors, and many other features. Each behavior system serves a particular function that is important for survival, so, for example, an organism may have a system of mating behaviors, a system of feeding behaviors, a system of defensive behaviors, and so on. These behavior systems are often species-specific—the pigeon's feeding system obviously would include different behaviors and stimulus sensitivities than the rat's feeding system.

According to behavior-systems theory, a particular conditioning situation will engage a particular behavior system and the features of that behavior system will affect the type of learning that occurs. In the case of classical conditioning, the particular CS-US combinations and the

CS-US interval will affect which behavior within the system is elicited as the CR. Consider, for example, a hypothesized feeding system in the rat (from Timberlake, 1994). The system includes behaviors related to the widespread search for food (traveling, sniffing, etc.), a focused search for food (chasing, grabbing, pouncing, etc.), and consumption of food (wiping, chewing, swallowing, etc.). These modes of behavior in the rat's feeding system are termed general-search, focal-search, and handle/consume behaviors.

A conditioning situation that involves food should engage the feeding system because it is presumably sensitive to food as a stimulus. In addition, the behavior-systems approach hypothesizes that the different behaviors within this system will show other stimulus sensitivities. For example, general-search behaviors like scanning the environment might be sensitive to a distant moving stimulus, while focal-search behaviors like grabbing might be sensitive to a nearby moving stimulus, and consumption behaviors like gnawing and chewing might be sensitive to the presence of food.

Finally, the behavior-systems approach assumes that the behaviors in the system are sensitive to the intervals between stimuli. A stimulus that reliably occurs long before the delivery of food should be more likely to engage general-search behaviors, while a stimulus that occurs just prior to food delivery should engage consumption behaviors. This assumption is quite a departure from other theories of classical conditioning. Other approaches to classical conditioning assume that the conditioned response should be similar to the unconditioned response elicited by the US. Behavior-systems theory assumes that the conditioned response is not necessarily related to the unconditioned response, but instead can be one of many behaviors within a particular behavior system.

Based on these assumptions, behavior-systems theory makes the interesting prediction that, in a classical-conditioning situation, the nature of conditioning and the form of the conditioned response will depend on the particular CS that is used and on the CS-US interval. This prediction

has received support in several experiments (see, for example, Akins, Domjan, & Gutierrez, 1994; Timberlake, 1983).

In one such experiment, Timberlake, Wahl, and King (1982) demonstrated the effect of different CS-US intervals when they presented rats with a rolling ball followed by food. The CS-US interval was 2.6 seconds for one group and 7.6 seconds for the other group. When the CS-US interval was 2.6 seconds, the rats began to respond to the rolling ball by digging and burrowing in the food tray, but when the CS-US interval was 7.6 seconds, the rats began to chase and pounce on the ball. Timberlake et al. (1982) suggest that the short CS-US interval led to a CR of consumption behavior, whereas the longer interval led to a CR that included focal-search behaviors. Thus, the difference in CS-US interval seemed to cause conditioning of different behaviors within the hypothesized feeding system.

More recently Timberlake and his colleagues have further elaborated the behavior-systems approach for feeding behavior. F. Silva, Timberlake, and Gont (1998) proposed that the search modes within the feeding system of a rat can be thought of as lying along a time continuum. At the beginning of a search for food the rat is in general-search mode. It is assumed that the strength of the general-search mode is high relative to focal-search and handle/consume mode. If the rat encounters a stimulus that has been associated with food, the focal-search mode will acquire strength and the general-search-mode strategy will decrease. Once a prey item has been encountered, pursued, and captured, the rat will engage in handling and consumption. At this point, the strength of the general search is very low and the strength of the focal-search mode decreases. This continuum can be seen in Figure 3.4.

K. Silva and Timberlake (1998) attempted to test more directly the contention that, depending on where the rat is temporally in the interval between CS and US, one type of conditioned response might be favored over another. As before, the researchers predicted that if there is a long interval between CS and US, general-search behav-

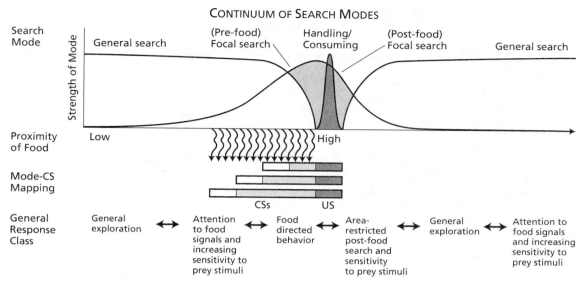

FIGURE 3.4 Continuum of Search Modes Proposed by F. Silva, Timberlake, and Gont. This figure is a representation of the sequence of search modes related to procuring and ingesting food, the associated general response classes, and the mapping between the search modes and stimuli in the environment. Note that, with a serial conditioned stimulus (CS), the first serial element (represented as the light gray rectangle in the figure) is mapped to earlier aspects of the focal search mode than is the second element (the dark gray rectangle), which is mapped to later aspects of the focal search mode. Increasing the duration of the second element causes its mapping to shift from late to early focal search/late general search. From *Animal Learning and Behavior, 26,* 299–312. Reprinted by permission of Psychonomic Society, Inc.

iors are more likely to be conditioned, and if the interval between CS and US is short, focal-search behavior should be evident. In Experiment 1 rats were trained in a large box that had a feeder, a light stimulus, and a bar at one end. On a side wall they positioned a door that could open and close, and opposite this wall there was a track channel on the floor, down which a ball bearing could be rolled. The apparatus is depicted in Figure 3.5.

In Phase 1, Silva and Timberlake gave their rats 20 trials a day for 16 days. For each trial, a series of four CSs were presented, with the fourth CS followed by food dispensed at the feeder. The four CSs were lights that differed in rate of flash from constant to fast. Each light stimulus had a duration of 12 seconds. Thus, rats received the sequence S1, S2, S3, and S4, followed by food. The rats were divided into two groups termed Group BB and Group Door. Following Phase 1

training for subjects in Group BB, Silva and Timberlake rolled a ball bearing down the channel during each of the four stimulus conditions. Thus, on 2 trials out of 20 trials, during the S1 stimulus, a ball bearing was rolled down the path. The ball bearing was also rolled down the path during the S2, S3, and S4 stimulus presentations. For subjects in Group Door, the same events occurred, except for these rats the door was opened and no ball bearing was rolled down the channel.

The results supported behavior systems theory. Rats in Group BB and Group Door responded to the feeder by putting their noses in it more during S3 stimulus presentations than during S1 and S2 stimulus presentations. In addition, they responded more to the feeder during S4 stimulus presentations than during S3 presentations. This is consistent with the idea that the conditioned responses for stimuli close to US

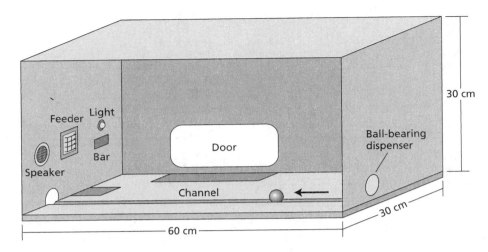

FIGURE 3.5 A Schematic of the Apparatus. From *Animal Learning and Behavior, 26,* 313–325. Reprinted by permission of Psychonomic Society, Inc.

presentation should be consummatory in nature. For Group BB, rats responded significantly more to the ball bearing stimulus during S2 than during S1, S3, or S4 stimulus presentations. This result is consistent with the contention that general-search behaviors should be conditioned with long CS-US intervals. Subjects in Group Door did not respond differentially to the door during any of the four stimulus conditions. This result also supports the behavior-systems approach in that in feeding systems, stimuli relevant to the response system examined should gain more control than less relevant stimuli.

Timberlake has shown that it is important to examine learning in light of the animal's evolutionary history and its adaptive value to the organism. By thinking about learning as an adaptive process, Timberlake's approach highlights one of the themes of this text, namely, that learning is an adaptive process. In addition, by attempting to understand learning in this context, Timberlake is able to make unique predictions that are testable and that are receiving support.

Behavior-systems theory can also help to explain some of the findings from classical-conditioning research that have been difficult to explain from other theoretical perspectives. One example is the phenomenon of CS-US relevance that was discussed in Chapter 2. As a quick re-minder, CS-US relevance refers to the fact that certain combinations of CS and US promote conditioning better than other combinations. As an example, when an illness-producing toxin was the US, the rats in Garcia and Koelling's (1966) experiment conditioned more readily with a taste CS than with an audiovisual CS. When the US was foot shock, rats conditioned more readily with an audiovisual CS and a shock US than with a taste CS. What might explain such differences? Findings such as these could be rather easily incorporated by behavior-systems theory if we make the sensible assumption that the feeding system is more sensitive to taste stimuli, while the defensive system is more sensitive to audiovisual stimuli.

Furthermore, as explained in Chapter 2, the form of the conditioned response sometimes depends on the type of CS that precedes the US. For example, Holland (1977) found that when rats were conditioned with a tone as the CS and food delivery as the US, the conditioned response was an increase in motor activity and head-jerk behaviors, whereas the conditioned response was freezing and rearing on the hind legs if a light was the CS. The behavior-systems approach might suggest that these different CRs are because certain behaviors in the feeding system are more sensitive to sound, whereas others are more sensitive to light.

As with the other recent theories that we have examined, it is still too early to draw any firm conclusions about behavior-systems theory. Although behavior-systems theory offers quite plausible explanations for several puzzling classical-conditioning phenomena, it is worth noting that such explanations are relatively easy to offer after the fact. It would be quite a different task to predict in advance that a light that precedes food presentation would cause a rat to freeze and rear up, while a tone that precedes food presentation would cause increased activity or head-jerks as the CR.

Behavior-systems theory is intended as a general theory of adaptive behavior rather than a theory of classical conditioning per se. Furthermore, behavior-systems theory does make several testable predictions, particularly concerning variations in the particular CR that will be established with a conditioning situation using a single US. A growing body of experimental evidence offers strong support for these predictions, but a final evaluation of behavior-systems theory awaits further research and development of the theory. More will be said about the work of Timberlake in Chapter 5.

WHAT IS ASSOCIATED IN CLASSICAL CONDITIONING?

Thus far, much of our discussion has been devoted to the question of the conditions necessary for CR development. Now we turn to a second theoretical issue that has been debated throughout the history of classical-conditioning research. It is widely assumed that a CS acquires the capacity to produce a CR because during conditioning the CS becomes associated with some other element of the learning situation. Historically, however, there has been disagreement over what that association entails. Specifically, theorists have disagreed about what sort of relation the organism learns in a conditioning situation. There have been two primary points of view on this matter. One viewpoint is that organisms learn a relation between the CS and the UR; the other viewpoint is that organisms learn a relation between the CS and the US.

Stimulus-Response or Stimulus-Stimulus Learning?

Stimulus–Response Learning. One way to conceptualize conditioning is to assume that the CS comes to elicit the same reflexive response produced by the US (see, for example, Hull, 1943). According to this position, a CS and a US must normally occur close together in time, because it is the contiguity of the CS and the UR that is important for learning. Once this association has been formed, presentations of the CS automatically lead to the same reflexive reaction that originally was produced by the US alone. Thus, in this view, the CS simply becomes a second stimulus (in addition to the US), which is linked to and is capable of producing the reflexive response.

Stimulus–Stimulus Learning. A somewhat different interpretation is that during conditioning the organism learns a relation between the CS and the US. This means that once conditioning has occurred, the presentation of a CS stimulates an experience of the US (this is usually understood to be a mental representation of the US). It is this US representation that then provokes the appropriate conditioned response. Thus, instead of the CS actually coming to produce a response directly, the CS triggers an experience of the US, and the response occurs as a reaction to this US experience (see, for example, King, 1979; Wagner, 1981).

Evidence Concerning the Elements in an Association

It is difficult to resolve the question of which elements become associated in classical conditioning. Speculations about the nature of what an organism has learned are easier to state than they are to test. Still, as we will find, much of the available evidence does appear to favor the view that conditioned responding depends on stimulus-stimulus learning.

Effects of Blocking the UR. The stimulus-response view of conditioning clearly assumes that for a CR to develop, both a CS and a UR must occur at the time of learning. Thus, one way to approach this issue is to determine whether conditioning can occur in the absence of a UR. Light and Gantt (1936) conducted one of the earliest studies of this type. The authors studied conditioned leg flexion in the dog. The US in this case was a shock to the dog's paw and the normal UR involved lifting the leg. In one of their groups, Light and Gantt exerted pressure on the motor nerves involved in the leg-lifting response, such that the dogs temporarily lost motor function in the legs they were being conditioned to lift. Thus, when the CS was followed by shock, no leg withdrawal (the UR) could occur. Later, however, when the dogs recovered the use of their legs, presentation of the CS led to a pronounced leg-withdrawal CR. Apparently, conditioning had occurred even though no UR was present during conditioning.

Similar results have been reported when URs have been blocked with certain drugs (see Finch, 1938; Solomon & Turner, 1962) and when apparatus arrangements have prevented URs during conditioning (see Hearst, 1978; Moore, 1973). In all these cases, a CR clearly develops even when overt URs are absent at the time of conditioning. At first glance, this evidence appears to argue strongly against a stimulus-response version of conditioning. However, researchers holding this position have argued otherwise, suggesting that the blocking of a peripheral, overt UR does not necessarily block all the internal responses an organism makes that are related to that UR. For example, a dog that is prevented from moving its leg is not necessarily unable to make internal responses that normally produce leg-lifting. Thus, conditioning may occur in these situations because of an association between the CS and some internal

response that is produced by the US (see Rescorla & Solomon, 1967, for one version of this argument).

Sensory Preconditioning. Aside from situations in which the UR is blocked, there appear to be instances of conditioning in which no overt UR can be observed. One example comes from the sensory preconditioning paradigm. Recall that in this paradigm two neutral stimuli such as a tone and a light are first paired. Then, one of the stimuli (for example, the tone) is paired with a US. In this case, not only does the tone begin to produce a CR, but also the light, which has never been paired with the US, becomes capable of producing a conditioned response (see, for example, Wynne & Brogden, 1962).

The usual interpretation of this phenomenon is that the two neutral stimuli become associated during Stage 1 of training. Later, when one stimulus acquires the capacity to produce a CR, the other stimulus that is linked to it acquires the same capacity. If this interpretation is correct, the occurrence of sensory preconditioning would constitute strong evidence that stimuli can become associated without a reflexive response occurring. Still, this interpretation is not without detractors. Some theorists have argued that when the two neutral stimuli are paired, an organism is bound to make at least some reaction to the stimuli. For example, if a light occurs followed by a tone, the organism may orient its ears toward the tone. Thus, the light may become associated with the orienting response rather than to the tone itself (see, for example, Kimble, 1961).

In effect, this argument is similar to the one advanced by stimulus-response theorists to explain how conditioning occurs when the UR is blocked. In other words, it is suggested that stimulus-response associations are actually occurring in these situations, but the responses in question are difficult to observe.

The Occurrence of Different CRs, Depending on the Nature of the CS. A third phenomenon that brings the stimulus-response position into question has to do with variations in conditioned responding as a function of CS characteristics. It is well known that the specific nature of a CR does not depend on the US alone. When different CSs are paired with the same US, the CRs may differ dramatically. One example of this phenomenon can be seen in the activity conditioning paradigm. In this situation rats are presented with food as the US. The normal reaction to the food is increased motor activity as the animal approaches the food. Holland (1977) has demonstrated that if a tone is used to signal the delivery of food, the tone becomes capable of producing increased activity as a CR. However, if a light is used to signal food availability, the CR that develops to the light is one of decreased activity. Specifically, when the light is presented, animals tend to rear on their hind legs and then remain still.

This finding, which occurs with some regularity in other paradigms (see, for example, Rescorla, 1980) presents problems for a stimulus-response interpretation of conditioning. According to this view, the CR should closely approximate the UR, since conditioning involves the association between a CS and that UR. To explain this finding using a stimulus-response view would require two assumptions. The first assumption is that the US produces multiple URs. This assumption is almost certainly the case. The second, however, is that because of their varying natures, some CSs are more likely to become associated with one UR, whereas others tend to become associated with other URs. The second assumption may be correct. However, if this is the case, the stimulus-response position must delineate the conditions under which these different associations will occur.

Postconditioning Changes in the US. According to the stimulus-response view of conditioning, the US is important only because it produces the response with which the CS becomes associated. The stimulus-stimulus view, however, suggests that the US is part of the association itself. One set of experiments that tends

to differentiate these views involves changing the nature of the US after conditioning. For example, let us assume that a tone has been paired regularly with a medium-intensity shock so that the tone begins to produce moderate fear responses. After conditioning has occurred, the shock alone is presented to the organism, but the intensity of the stimulus is either substantially stronger or weaker than it was during conditioning. Will this change in the intensity of the shock alter the fear response that is later produced by the tone?

The two views of conditioning just discussed would appear to make different predictions in answer to this question. The stimulus-response view would say that during conditioning the tone becomes associated with the moderate fear response produced by the medium-intensity shock. Since later presentations of the altered shock occur without the CS present, the CS should not become associated with any new UR. Thus, responding to the tone should be unchanged. According to the stimulus-stimulus position, however, it is the internal representations of the CS and the US that become associated. In other words, an organism's memories of the two events become linked. Responses to the CS depend on an organism's memory for what the US was like. If it is correct to assume that presenting different intensity USs to an organism alters its memory of the US, then such presentations would be expected to alter responding to the CS.

Although all the evidence pertaining to this question does not fall on the same side, the great majority of results tend to favor the stimulus-stimulus prediction. In other words, postconditioning alterations in a US often result in changes in responding to a CS. Rescorla (1974: Experiment 2) provides an excellent example of this effect. In this experiment rats were given pairings of a tone and a 0.5 mA shock. After the pairings, the rats were divided into four groups. Animals in three of these groups received eight shock-alone presentations. For one group the shocks were of the same intensity as those used during conditioning (0.5 mA). In the other two groups, shocks of either 1.0 or 3.0 mA were presented. The final group received no shocks after conditioning. Rescorla then determined the degree to which the tone from the conditioning phase would lead to suppression of a bar-pressing response.

Figure 3.6 summarizes the results of this experiment. Keep in mind that better-conditioned responding to the CS is reflected by low-suppression ratios in the CER paradigm. At least two findings evident in this graph are worth noting. First, the rats that received shock-alone presentations of the same intensity they received during conditioning (0.5 mA) responded less than rats that received no additional shocks. Rescorla interprets this finding as an example of habituation to that shock intensity. In other words, when animals are exposed to the same stimulus several times, they tend to become less and less responsive to it.

The second finding of interest in Figure 3.6 is directly related to this discussion. Rats that were exposed to shocks of greater intensity than they had experienced during conditioning showed enhanced CRs to the tone CS. According to Rescorla, this enhanced responding is probably the result of a change in the rats' memory of the shock. After the high-intensity shock presentations, the animals' memory of shock changes from that of a low-intensity shock to a recollection of a high-intensity shock. Since the CS is associated with that memory (according to the stimulus-stimulus view), responding to the CS increases. This finding, then, clearly favors the idea that the CS and US representations become associated during a conditioning experience.

Conclusions from the Evidence. The questions of whether CS-US or CS-UR associations are formed during conditioning or not cannot be answered with great confidence. The evidence we have reviewed clearly favors the stimulus-stimulus position over the stimulus-response interpretation. It is notable, however, that the stimulus-response interpretation can be stretched to account for most of the individual bits of evidence we have discussed.

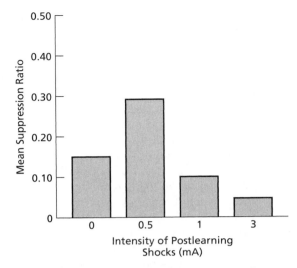

FIGURE 3.6 Conditioned Responding to a CS After Varying Intensity of Exposures to US-Alone Presentations. (From Rescorla, 1974.) Adapted by permission of Dr. Robert A. Rescorla.

This fact illustrates an important point. Seldom are complex theoretical issues resolved by a single experiment or by a single set of experiments. In many cases, researchers must make an educated judgment about the relative merits of two theoretical positions by considering all the evidence that is available. This is why researchers often conduct experiments of several different kinds, which converge on the same theoretical question. In the present case, all that can really be said is that a stimulus-stimulus conception of conditioning accounts for the majority of evidence more easily than does a stimulus-response view.

Biological Evidence. The simplest way to discover what elements of the conditioning situation become associated during conditioning is to look at the brain to find out whether the "CS center" becomes connected with the "US center" or the "UR center." Certainly, most conditioning researchers agree that discovering the changes that occur in the brain during classical conditioning would substantially enhance under-

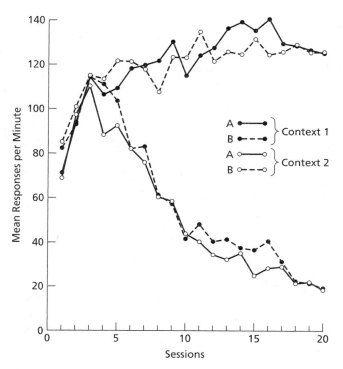

FIGURE 3.7 The Results of Training. Differential responding to two CSs that were trained differently in Contexts 1 and 2. (From Rescorla, Durlach, & Grau, 1985 in P. Balsam and A. Tomie (eds.), *Context and Learning,* © 1985 by Laurence Erlbaum & Assoc., Inc. Reprinted by permission.

standing of classical conditioning. Further, as discussed in Chapter 2, researchers have made great progress in discovering the brain mechanisms of classical conditioning. Unfortunately, this body of research clearly shows that the physiology of classical conditioning can be quite complex (see, for example, Thompson, 1986). More research is needed on both the behavioral aspects of learning and its underlying physiological mechanisms before it is possible to fully answer the question of what is learned in classical conditioning.

The Role of Context in Conditioning

It is clear from the evidence already presented that contextual stimuli in a conditioning situation can serve as CSs much like any other discrete stimulus. A large body of research, however, suggests that the role of the conditioning context is much more complex. For example, if a discrete CS comes to elicit a CR in one stimulus context,

that CR occurs most readily when the CS reoccurs in that same context. The tendency for an organism to make a conditioned response is often diminished when a CS occurs in a context that is substantially different from that used for conditioning.

The importance of contextual stimuli in controlling learned behaviors can be appreciated by looking at any number of everyday situations. For example, many people have come to fear the sight of a hypodermic needle because of their experiences with injections. These conditioned fear responses occur most readily, however, when individuals are confronted with a hypodermic needle in a physician's office or a hospital. They tend not to exhibit fear when they see a hypodermic needle for sale in a drug store or when they see a needle in a veterinarian's office. Clearly, the fear response to the needle is greatest when the object appears in the same context in which the original injections took place.

This kind of contextual control is evident from the results of numerous conditioning experiments. Some of the best examples of contextual influence come from studies that are often called "switching experiments" (see, for example, Asratyan, 1965). In one such experiment, Rescorla and his colleagues used an autoshaping paradigm with pigeons (Rescorla, Durlach, & Grau, 1985). On some occasions the pigeons were trained in one experimental chamber (Context 1) and at other times the training occurred in another chamber (Context 2). In Context 1 the pigeons received exposures to two different CSs (CS_A and CS_B), CS_A was always followed by food and CS_B was never followed by food. In Context 2 the reverse was true. Food never followed CS_A but always followed CS_B. The results of this training are shown in Figure 3.7. As you can see, the pigeons responded to CS_A when in Context 1 and to CS_B in Context 2. Although the same discrete conditioned stimuli were presented in both contexts, the pigeons obviously learned to use the contexts as cues for responding to the respective CSs.

The strength of the control that contextual stimuli exert over conditioned responding indicates that at the time of conditioning, organisms learn something about the context they are in. What is not clear, however, is what organisms actually learn about contextual stimuli. In the present section we will discuss two points of view concerning the role of the conditioning context. The first view is that contextual stimuli function only as CSs. That is, contextual stimuli are capable of becoming associated with the US in the conditioning situation. The second view suggests that contextual stimuli may control when certain CS-US relationships hold and when they do not. The implication is in essence, that contextual stimuli may act like modulators.

Contextual Stimuli as CSs

Many contemporary theories of conditioning view contextual stimuli in the same way as they view the CS in a conditioning situation (see, for example, Frey & Sears, 1978; Rescorla & Wag-

ner, 1972; Wagner, 1978). According to these theories, contextual stimuli, along with the CS, actually constitute a compound CS that comes to signal US occurrence. Because contextual stimuli are part of the CS compound, these stimuli can become associated with the US and can become capable of producing a conditioned response on their own. In most cases, it is assumed that contextual stimuli are not as effective as the CS in producing a CR. The reason is that the CS reliably signals US occurrence, whereas the context is present even when the US is unlikely to occur. Still, in many cases contextual stimuli retain some capacity for producing conditioned responding because they are at least partially reliable in signaling US occurrence.

By viewing contextual stimuli in this manner, these theories have been able to explain why conditioned responding is better in the conditioning context than it is in a novel context. After conditioning, if the CS reoccurs in the conditioning context, there are several stimuli present that are capable of producing a CR (the CS plus all the original contextual stimuli). Thus, the likelihood of a CR occurring in this situation is very great. If, however, the CS occurs in a novel context, only the CS is present to produce a CR. The contextual stimuli that had become capable of producing a CR are no longer present. Thus, in a novel environment, conditioned responding to the CS will be less likely. In effect, the more stimuli in a situation that are capable of producing a CR, the more likely the CR is to occur.

Evidence for Contextual Stimuli as CSs

Earlier in this chapter we examined evidence that shows that contextual stimuli can function as CSs in a conditioning situation. These and similar experiments leave little doubt that contextual stimuli can begin to elicit a CR if they are present at the time of conditioning. According to some theorists, this alone is enough to explain why CRs are more probable in the conditioning context than in totally novel contexts. The CR-eliciting capacity of the conditioning context simply combines with that of the CS to enhance conditioned responding. Some theorists, however, do not agree that this is the entire explanation for contextual control over conditioned responding.

Contextual Stimuli as Cues for the CS-US Relationship

Few theorists question that contextual stimuli can come to elicit CRs. Recently, however, a number of theorists have suggested that this may not be the main mechanism by which context controls learned responding. According to these theorists, during conditioning, contextual stimuli may become more than signals for US occurrence; they may become cues or signals for a particular CS-US relationship. In effect, contextual stimuli may become capable of signaling to an organism when a CS is likely to be followed by a US and when it is not. Thus, these stimuli might serve as cues to determine when an organism should respond to a CS and when it will not (see, for example, Estes, 1973; Medin, 1975; Nadel & Willner, 1980; Spear, 1973; also see Rescorla, Durlach, & Grau, 1985, for a similar view).

If context can act as a cue for a specific CS-US relationship, then over and above any CRs produced by contextual stimuli, these stimuli should aid responding by signaling when a CS-US relationship is in effect. For this reason, much of the evidence in support of this position comes from studies showing that contextual stimuli affect responding even when they do not produce observable CRs. Several studies of this type have been conducted by Miller and his associates (see, for example, Miller & Schachtman, 1985). The rationale for these experiments was to use procedures that would minimize or eliminate the contextual production of CRs during conditioning. The question of interest was whether under these circumstances the conditioning context would continue to affect conditioned responding to the CS.

In one of these experiments, for example, rats were given CS-shock pairings in a distinctive context (Balaz, Capra, Kasprow, & Miller, 1982). However, before conditioning, some rats were given extensive exposures to the conditioning context alone. We know from our previous discussions that prior exposures to a CS alone usually result in retarded conditioning to that CS (latent inhibition). The purpose of the contextual exposures in this study was to retard the subsequent development of CRs to the conditioning context. These experimenters found that animals given these prior exposures developed little or no conditioned responding to the context. Still, when responding to the CS was measured, responding was best when the CS occurred in the conditioning context. Responding to the CS was diminished when the CS was presented in a novel context. This suggests that the conditioning context aids responding to the CS even when the context itself produces no observable conditioned responding.

In a similar vein, Balaz, Capra, Hartl, and Miller (1981) gave rats CS-shock pairings in one context and then attempted to extinguish any CRs that might have developed to the contextual stimuli. They did this by exposing animals to the contextual stimuli alone after the conditioning session. As in the previous experiment, they found that extinction virtually abolished CRs to the conditioning context. Still, responding to the CS was better when the CS was presented in the conditioning context than when it occurred in a novel situation. Again, this finding suggests that contextual stimuli need not produce CRs themselves to facilitate responding to the CS. It is notable that several recent experiments in other laboratories appear to agree with this conclusion concerning contextual effects on responding (see, for example, Swartzentruber, 1995).

Conclusions About Contextual Stimuli

At the present time there is some disagreement with respect to the precise role of contextual stimuli in the conditioning process (see Balsam & Tomie, 1985). On the one hand, it appears clear that at the time of conditioning, contextual stimuli often acquire the capacity to produce CRs on their own. It seems equally evident, however, that contextual stimuli can affect responding to a CS even when these stimuli produce little in the way of conditioned responding. This latter conclusion is consistent with the notion that contextual stimuli may function to signal when a certain CS-US relationship is in effect.

In this regard, it is interesting that several recent experiments have demonstrated that non-contextual stimuli can sometimes act as signals for particular CS-US relationships (see, for example, Holland, 1983, 1985; Rescorla, 1985, 1986). These discrete stimuli appear to acquire a capacity to produce CRs themselves and also to influence responding to a second CS-US relation. Such stimuli have been termed *occasion setters* because they identify points at which a particular CS is likely to be followed by a US. This line of research on discrete stimulus signals may help to clarify the mechanism by which contextual stimuli influence conditioned responding.

SUMMARY STATEMENTS

In this chapter we have considered a number of theoretical issues in the study of classical conditioning. The first major issue concerned the necessary and sufficient conditions for development of a CR. Early theories that cited CS-US contiguity as the most important factor in conditioning were not quite correct, but neither were theories that emphasized the contingent relationship between the CS and US. Instead, a modified contiguity theory in the form of the Rescorla-Wagner model remains the most successful theory of classical conditioning to date. Despite the success of the Rescorla-Wagner model, there are findings that it cannot explain. Several recent theoretical positions have attempted to account for data that fell beyond the scope of the Rescorla-Wagner model. Two of these recent theories were examined, Wagner's priming theories and comparator and behavior-systems theory. Each of these theoretical positions offers certain strengths and shortcomings. In all cases, further research and theory development will be necessary to assess the value of each theory.

Our second concern was to show what elements of the conditioning situation become associated during classical conditioning. The preponderance of evidence favors the view that CS-US associations, not CS-UR associations, underlie the conditioning process. Through considering the role of contextual stimuli in the conditioning process, the evidence was found to be somewhat mixed. It appears that contextual stimuli sometimes act like CSs in that they become capable of producing CRs, but contextual stimuli appear to affect responding to a CS even when the context produces no observable CRs. Thus, the precise mechanism for contextual effects remains unclear.

It is clear from the discussion of theories in this chapter that research and theory are intimately related. Research produces data and scientists develop theories to explain that data. Good theories account for a majority of the available data and make additional predictions that can be subjected to experimental tests. This additional research often leads to continued theory development and suggests new theoretical questions. The process of explanation in science is ongoing.

4

Instrumental/Operant Conditioning: Learning from the Consequences of Behavior

(continued)

CHAPTER OVERVIEW

The last two chapters have contained much information about classical conditioning, a phenomenon that plays an important role in many aspects of behavior such as emotions, certain psychological disorders, drug tolerance, and even immune-system function. While discussing different theories of classical conditioning we also discovered that classical conditioning is a complex form of learning that researchers are still working to understand.

Despite the importance and complexity of classical conditioning, when most people become interested in psychology, they are more interested in behaviors that are not easily explained by classical conditioning. They are interested in how they might stop procrastinating, how they can get their children to clean their rooms, and such mysteries as why some people are better at math. These instances of behavior cannot be easily explained in terms of classical conditioning. There is no stimulus in the environment that naturally **elicits** solving calculus problems, procrastinating, or room cleaning because these behaviors are not elicited by stimuli in the environment the way that an eye blink is elicited by an air puff to the eye. Instead, these behaviors are **emitted** by an organism. To answer questions about behaviors like these, one must look at another type of learning situation. This learning situation is usually called instrumental or operant conditioning. In this type of situation, organisms learn because of the consequences that follow behaviors. By way of emphasis, note that this chapter is primarily concerned with behavior that is emitted by the organism and not with behavior that is elicited by certain stimuli.

The basic principle of instrumental and operant conditioning is fairly easy to appreciate. Organisms interact with the environment and the results of those interactions change how they behave in the future. More precisely, when an organism emits a behavior, the consequences of that behavior change the future probability of the behavior. For example, most students will agree that they have enrolled in college courses that were extremely enjoyable and they will also note that they have experienced courses that were boring and miserable. After taking the enjoyable course, the student will probably be more likely to enroll in a future course taught by the same instructor. On the other hand, after taking a course that is boring and difficult, the student will be less likely to take another course offered by that instructor. In both cases, the consequences of the student's behavior affected his future behavior. As evidenced in the above example, there are many variables that affect instrumental and operant conditioning.

Most common human behaviors result from instrumental and operant conditioning. For example, the skills of star athletes, the performances of skilled musicians, and one's ability to drive a car or ride a bicycle are all due, at least in part, to instrumental and operant conditioning. This type of learning also can produce problem behaviors. Many bad habits are also a result of instrumental and operant conditioning. Examples include smoking cigarettes or deciding to go to a movie rather than study for an exam.

This chapter will discuss instrumental and operant conditioning in some detail. It will look at different types of conditioning situations and examine the variables that affect instrumental and operant conditioning, beginning with a look at the early experiments of two pioneers who greatly influenced the study of instrumental and operant conditioning.

EARLY EXPERIMENTS: THORNDIKE AND SKINNER

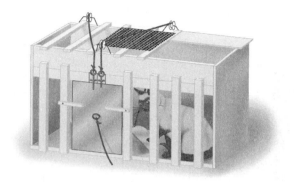

FIGURE 4.1 One of Thorndike's Puzzle Boxes. A cat could escape from this box by pulling a string, stepping on the platform, and turning one of the two latches on the front of the door. (From Thorndike, 1898.)

Thorndike's Puzzle Box. Edward Thorndike (1898; 1911) conducted early research on how behavior changes as a result of its consequences. While Pavlov was studying classical conditioning in dogs, Thorndike pioneered the systematic study of instrumental conditioning in cats. Thorndike's experiments used what he called a puzzle box (Figure 4.1). A hungry animal (usually a cat) was placed inside the box, and the door of the box opened only after the animal performed an appropriate response (pressing a lever, tugging on a rope, stepping on a floor pedal, etc.). Once the door opened, the animal could leave the box and eat a small amount of food that was available outside the door.

The first time an animal was placed in the puzzle box, it usually took quite some time before the animal made the appropriate response (usually quite by accident) and escaped from the box. What interested Thorndike, however, was how the animal would respond when it was returned to the box several times. More specifically, Thorndike was interested in how long it took an animal to escape from the box on each trial, a measure he called escape latency. Figure 4.2 shows how one cat performed over repeated trials in a puzzle box. This cat required more than 150 seconds to escape on the first trial. By the 40th trial the cat's escape latency decreased consistently to only seven seconds.

For Thorndike's cats, the behaviors that opened the door were followed by certain consequences: escape from the box and a chance to eat. As a result of these consequences, the cat became more likely to repeat the effective escape behaviors, which ultimately decreased the animal's escape latency. This situation fits the definition of instrumental conditioning almost perfectly—an organism's behavior changes because of the consequences that follow the behavior.

Skinner's Operant Chamber. Following the work of Thorndike, B. F. Skinner made many contributions to the study of operant conditioning and was primarily responsible for an enormous increase of interest in operant conditioning in the 1940s and 1950s. As a result of his work and his many accomplishments, Skinner is considered one of the most influential psychologists of the twentieth century.

Skinner's methods were different from Thorndike's in simple but important ways. In Thorndikes' research, the animal could make only one response each time it was placed in the puzzle box, and Thorndike measured the response latency as the primary dependent variable. The experimenter then had to return the animal to the puzzle box to begin the next trial. This discrete-trial procedure was time consuming and inefficient because it limited the number of trials that could be run each day.

Skinner devised methods that allowed animals to repeat a response many times in the conditioning situation. This important change meant that the experimenter did not need to intervene after each response. Some examples of these methods are studying the lever-press using rats or key pecking in pigeons. These procedures are called free operant procedures because, while the animal is in the conditioning situation, it can

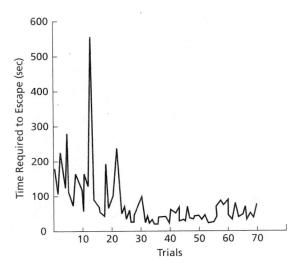

FIGURE 4.2 Escape Latency. The number of seconds required by one cat to escape from a simple puzzle box on 70 consecutive trials. (From Thorndike, 1898.)

respond at any time and the response can be repeated. It is not unusual for animals to make hundreds and sometimes thousands of responses during a single session. Skinner's new method also led to a change in the dependent variable used to measure learning. Instead of measuring response latency as Thorndike had, Skinner measured response rate (how rapidly the animal repeated the response).

The work of Thorndike and Skinner led to extensive research on instrumental and operant conditioning. This research has revealed much about the ways in which behavior changes as a result of its consequences and the many factors that affect operant conditioning. In the remainder of this chapter we will discuss instrumental and operant conditioning in some detail. We begin by looking at the kinds of consequences that follow responses and the kinds of contingencies that can exist between our behaviors and these outcomes. Then we will discuss the experimental paradigms that have been developed to study instrumental and operant conditioning. Finally, we will catalog the range of variables that influence this learning process.

BEHAVIOR, CONSEQUENCES, AND CONTINGENCIES

A consequence of behavior is any event that is contingent upon that behavior. This means that the consequence occurs after the behavior and the consequence rarely occurs in the absence of the behavior. As has already been mentioned, the contingent relationship between a behavior and its consequences changes the future probability of that behavior. This arrangement of a behavior and its consequence is known as an instrumental or operant contingency. The following discussion will cover four types of instrumental and operant contingencies: positive reinforcement, negative reinforcement, positive punishment, and negative punishment. Organisms (including human beings) encounter these contingencies every day.

Reinforcement and Punishment

The first distinction to make is between reinforcement and punishment. Both are operant contingencies, but they have very different effects on behavior. When the consequence of a behavior causes the future probability of that behavior to increase, the operant contingency is known as **reinforcement** and the consequence is called a **reinforcer.** On the other hand, if the consequence of a behavior causes the future rate of the behavior to decrease, then the contingency is known as **punishment** and the consequence is a **punisher.** Let us study some examples that will help to illustrate these definitions.

Imagine that, on the first day of a new class, a student raises her hand to ask a question. The course instructor looks up, smiles warmly, and says, "Well, I'm glad to see that you already have a question for me." In most cases, the result of this interaction will be that the student will be more likely to ask questions in the future. In this example, the instructor's statement reinforced the behavior because it increased the probability that the student will ask questions in the future. Thus, this situation is a reinforcement contingency, and the instructor's statement was a reinforcer for the student's behavior.

On the other hand, suppose that the student raises her hand to ask a question on the first day of a different class, and the instructor replies by scowling and growling, "Congratulations, you have just asked the dumbest question I have heard in 10 years of teaching!" How likely is it that the student will ask another question in this class? As a result of this action, the student will probably avoid asking questions for the rest of the term. This example illustrates a punishment contingency because the instructor's reaction reduced the future probability of the student asking questions. The instructor's statement was a punisher for the student's behavior.

In both of these examples, a statement from the course instructor followed the question. The consequence for the behavior of asking a question in class was the presentation of a stimulus (the instructor's reaction) although in one case the stimulus was a reinforcer and, in the other case, the stimulus was a punisher. When reinforcement involves the presentation of a stimulus, it is called **positive reinforcement.** When punishment involves the presentation of a stimulus, it is called **positive punishment.** In the preceding classroom examples then, the first case was really an example of positive reinforcement, and the second case was an instance of positive punishment.

The idea of positive punishment may seem strange at first. You are probably wondering how punishment can be positive. Normally, we think of *positive* as meaning that something is good or pleasant. In describing reinforcement and punishment, however, *positive* does not mean pleasant or good. Instead, *positive* is used to indicate the addition or presentation of a stimulus to the situation. Thus, when we present food pellets to reinforce a rat's bar presses, this is a positive reinforcement contingency because the food is presented and it causes bar pressing to increase.

Reinforcement and punishment can also involve the removal of a stimulus. Contingencies that involve the removal of a stimulus are called negative contingencies. In conditioning situa-

tions, *negative* does not mean "bad" or "unpleasant." Instead, the term means that in a particular contingency the consequence was the removal (or subtraction) of a stimulus from the situation. If the consequence in a reinforcement contingency is the removal of a stimulus, it is a **negative reinforcement** contingency. When punishment occurs because the consequence of a behavior is the removal of a stimulus, the contingency is called **negative punishment.** It should be emphasized that in both positive reinforcement and positive punishment the outcome or consequence is dependent on some specified response. The outcome is response dependent. This contrasts with classical conditioning in which the outcome is stimulus dependent.

When the alarm clock goes off in the morning, most people immediately press the snooze bar. The consequence of this behavior is that the aversive noise stops. The usual result is an increase in the probability that the person will press the snooze bar in the future, so this would be a case of reinforcement. The consequence of the behavior is the removal of a stimulus (stopping the annoying alarm sound), so this is a negative-reinforcement contingency.

Negative punishment occurs when the consequence of a behavior is the removal of a stimulus and the frequency of the behavior decreases. Parents often take away certain privileges, such as driving or talking on the phone after an adolescent misbehaves. If these consequences are successful in decreasing the problem behavior in the future, then these are effective examples of negative punishment.

The examples we have discussed illustrate all four types of contingency: positive reinforcement, positive punishment, negative reinforcement, and negative punishment. Figure 4.3 summarizes the four types of contingency. At first, determining what type of contingency is occurring in a situation can be difficult. This task is simplified by asking these four questions:

1. What is the behavior?
2. What is the consequence of that behavior?

Quality of Consequential Event

FIGURE 4.3 The Four Types of Contingency.

	Appetitive	Aversive
Positive (Event is produced)	Frequency of behavior increases. **Positive Reinforcement**	Frequency of behavior decreases. **Positive Punishment**
Negative (Event is prevented)	Frequency of behavior decreases. **Negative Punishment** or **Omission**	Frequency of behavior increases. **Negative Reinforcement**

TYPE OF CONTINGENCY

3. Does the response produce or prevent an event that is either appetitive or aversive?

   a. If an event is produced, this is a positive contingency.

   b. If an event is prevented, this is a negative contingency.

4. Does the rate or probability of the behavior increase or decrease?

   a. If the behavior increases, this is a reinforcement contingency, and the consequence is a reinforcer.

   b. If the behavior decreases, this is a punishment contingency, and the consequence is a punisher.

By following these guidelines, you easily can identify the type of consequence that is used in a particular learning situation.

It is especially important to remember that we define consequences and contingencies by their effects on behavior, not by what we expect their effects to be. For example, sometimes when a teacher yells at a student who is disrupting class, the student will begin to act out even more. In this situation, one might be tempted to say that yelling at the student is a case of punishment. However, this is actually an instance of positive reinforcement because the teacher's yelling increased the disruptive behavior.

Another example will be familiar to parents of teenagers. Parents are sometimes surprised to find that their approval and praise punishes their adolescent's behavior. Countless mothers and fathers have complimented how their teenager is dressed only to discover that, as a result, their son or daughter runs back to the bedroom to change clothes. Although praise from parents is a reinforcer, in this example the parents' praise has served to punish the adolescent's behavior of wearing a particular outfit.

When discussing examples of instrumental and operant conditioning, it is also important to remember that contingencies reinforce or punish *behavior;* they do not reinforce or punish *organisms.* A common parental error is to claim to have reinforced a child for cleaning her room, or punished the dog for barking at night. If looked at closely, statements like these are misleading. In fact, they are incorrect. If behavior is followed with a reinforcer, it is the *behavior* that increases in the future, not the organism itself. In the same way, punishment reduces behavior, it does not reduce the organism.

The contingent relation between behavior and outcomes can lead to behaviors that at first glance do not appear to make much sense. Take, for example, a baseball player stepping up to home plate and going through an entire series of behaviors before settling in and readying for the pitch. The player might spit three times on the ground, adjust his batting glove, adjust his hat, adjust his pants, and do any number of bizarre behaviors. These behaviors are a result of contingencies between responses and outcomes and were termed by Skinner "superstitious behaviors." Skinner was able to provide an animal model of these rituals by simply placing a pigeon in a Skinner box and programming reinforcements to be delivered regardless of response. After a period of time he would look in the box and observe pigeons twirling around with heads bobbing, approaching the wall, or any number of behaviors unrelated to receiving the reward.

It is important to mention that reinforcers and punishers serve an adaptive role in behavior. In general, responses that acquire for organisms reinforcers are adaptive. When animals respond for food, water, and mates, they are behaving in a manner that increases the probability of getting their genes into the next generation. When animals respond in such a way to terminate or avoid noxious stimuli they also are behaving adaptively. Thus when a rat learns to avoid a dangerous situation it too is behaving in such a way as to increase the probability of getting its genes into the next generation. Instrumental and operant conditioning are mechanisms that underlie behavior that has adaptive significance.

Operant Conditioning in the Treatment of Alcohol Abuse

In addition to playing a role in common or everyday behaviors, instrumental- and operant-conditioning procedures effectively can be used to treat many problem behaviors. For example, alcohol and drug abuse, though widespread, have very few effective treatments. One effective treatment for alcohol abuse is the community reinforcement approach (CRA) (Azrin, Sisson,

Meyers, & Godley, 1982; Hunt & Azrin, 1973), which is a treatment program based on operant conditioning procedures. The CRA treatment involves arranging community and social consequences such as social activities, family relations, recreational activities, and employment to reinforce maintenance of sobriety. These reinforcers are delivered reliably and often, but only as long as the client does not use alcohol. One aspect of CRA treatment, then, is to use positive reinforcement to increase and support behaviors other than alcohol use. In effect, the goal of this approach is to make sobriety more rewarding than drinking.

In addition to positive reinforcement of sober behavior, the CRA treatment also uses negative-punishment procedures to reduce or prevent drinking. If a client begins to use alcohol again, he or she will immediately lose access to community and social reinforcers. Thus, by arranging the program so that drinking is followed by the removal of these pleasant events, the CRA treatment assures that drinking will be punished. The community and social reinforcers are made available once again only after the client stops drinking.

Beyond arranging community consequences to reinforce sobriety and punish substance use, the CRA treatment includes several other components that use conditioning principles. For example, instrumental and operant procedures are used to teach drink refusal and social skills to clients. In some cases, reinforcement-based marital therapy is available for married clients. To learn more about this approach to substance-abuse treatment, see Meyers and Smith (1995).

Any discussion of instrumental and operant conditioning would be incomplete without some awareness of the fact that the effects of reinforcers and punishers depend on a variety of factors. Much of this chapter concerns the factors that influence instrumental and operant conditioning. Before commenting on these factors, however, it will be useful to examine some of the experimental paradigms that have been used to study instrumental and operant conditioning.

PARADIGMS FOR STUDYING INSTRUMENTAL AND OPERANT CONDITIONING

The Instrumental-Operant Distinction

In both instrumental- and operant-conditioning situations, an organism's behavior changes as a result of the consequences that follow the behavior. However, many researchers draw subtle distinctions between instrumental and operant conditioning. The fundamental difference between instrumental and operant situations involves the degree to which an organism is free to make a response at any given point in time.

In an instrumental-conditioning situation, there are environmental constraints on the organism's opportunities to respond. In these situations organisms can emit a behavior only at a particular time. Thorndike's puzzle-box experiments are excellent examples of instrumental conditioning, because the animals could make the appropriate response only once during each trial.

In operant-conditioning situations, an organism can emit a given response repeatedly while in that situation. In other words, no constraints are placed on when or how often a response can be emitted as long as the organism is in the appropriate situation. For example, instructors often subtly reinforce students' attention during a lecture. They do this by joking, varying their tone of voice, moving, and making eye contact when students appear to be paying attention. During the lecture, the students are free to attend to the speaker as often as they want. They are not constrained to make attentive responses at a particular time. Consequently the opportunity for responding and reinforcement of behavior is virtually unlimited during the lecture period.

People encounter both instrumental and operant situations every day. Is there really a difference between the type of learning that occurs in instrumental situations and operant situations? Probably not. What really defines the difference between instrumental and operant learning is not how organisms learn, but the type of task that the organism encounters. As mentioned earlier, in instrumental-conditioning paradigms, organisms are given discrete limited opportunities to respond, so researchers usually study the latency, probability, speed, or accuracy of an organism's responses. In operant-conditioning paradigms, organisms are placed in a situation and are given unlimited opportunities to emit a response. The primary measure of learning in paradigms like these is an organism's rate of responding. The experimenter measures how often an organism responds correctly in a given period of time. It is important to remember that in both situations, researchers are interested in how behavior changes as a result of the consequences that follow behavior.

Instrumental-Conditioning Paradigms

The Straight Runway for Rats. One of the simplest paradigms for studying instrumental learning in the rat is the straight runway procedure. The experimenter places a rat in a small chamber called a start box. When the door to the start box is opened, the rat has the opportunity to enter a straight runway several feet long. At the end of the runway is a goal box, in which the experimenter usually places a reward such as food. When the rat reaches the goal box and consumes the food, it is removed from the apparatus to await subsequent trials.

Typically, when rats begin runway training they remain in the start box for a time after the door is opened. They also spend a great deal of time exploring the runway itself. However, as more trials occur, the rats begin to traverse the runway at a faster and faster pace. This increase in speed apparently results from learning that running or moving is correlated with receiving food. Thus, learning is measured by assessing changes in a rat's speed as more and more learning trials are given. In most cases the rat's speed in leaving the start box (start speed), its speed in traversing the runway (running speed), and its speed in the terminal portion of the runway (goal speed) are all recorded.

Maze Learning Tasks. In a maze learning task an organism must choose one response rather than another to receive some desirable outcome. One of the simplest maze tasks utilizes an apparatus called a T maze (Figure 4.4). Typically a rat or other small animal is placed in a start box that opens onto a straight runway. This runway terminates in a dead-end choice point. Instead of continuing forward, the rat must choose to turn right or left. Each of the short runways ends in a goal box. In most cases a reinforcer such as food is present in the goal box of one direction but not in the other. The rat must learn to enter the correct arm of the maze. The usual measures of learning are the time to reach the appropriate goal box and the number of errors made in reaching that goal. Normally, as the number of learning trials increases, both the time and the number of errors decrease substantially.

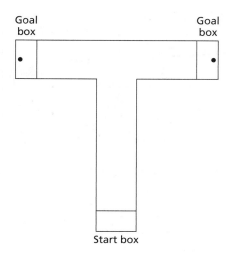

FIGURE 4.4 Diagram of the T maze. (From Brennan and Gordon, 1977.)

Escape and Avoidance Paradigms

The straight runway and the maze learning tasks usually are employed to study the effects of positive reinforcement on behavior. Researchers study the effects of negative reinforcement in escape- or avoidance-learning paradigms. In an escape-learning paradigm the experimenter exposes an organism to some form of aversive stimulation such as a loud noise, a bright light, or a mild shock. The organism must then learn to perform a specific response that results in termination or removal of the aversive stimulus. One simple apparatus often used to study escape learning (Figure 4.5, p. 102) has two chambers, which are separated by a door. In a typical study the experimenter places a rat in one chamber and exposes it to shock. When the shock is initiated, the door to the other chamber opens, and to terminate the shock, the rat must move into the other chamber. The usual measure of learning in this paradigm is the response latency with which the animal moves into the "safe" chamber after the door opens.

Whereas in escape learning the organism must learn a response to terminate an already present aversive stimulus, in avoidance-learning paradigms the organism learns to perform a response that prevents the aversive stimulus from ever being presented. Many avoidance-learning paradigms involve the use of a stimulus that signals the impending presentation of the aversive stimulus. For example, an experimenter may place a rat in a chamber and present a tone that signals the impending administration of shock. In most cases the signal will precede the shock by several seconds. To avoid shock, the animal must learn to perform some response in the presence of the signal. If the desired response does not occur, the shock is administered as scheduled.

As you might imagine, most animals fail to avoid the shock on the first few learning trials. The shock comes on and the animal simply emits various responses until one enables it to escape from the shock. However, after several trials, most animals begin to respond in the presence of the signal alone, thereby avoiding the shock altogether. The usual measure of learning in this paradigm is the time it takes for an animal to respond once the signal has begun. Times that are shorter than the signal-shock interval reflect the performance of an avoidance response.

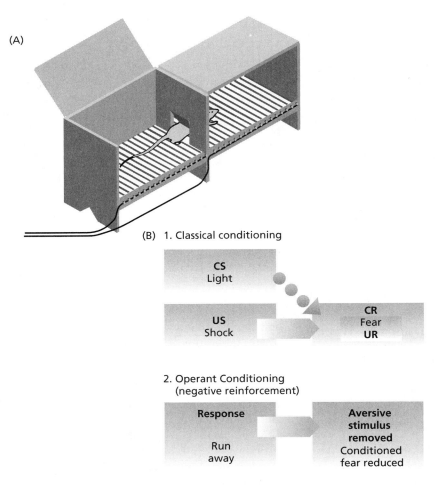

(A)

(B) 1. Classical conditioning

2. Operant Conditioning
(negative reinforcement)

FIGURE 4.5 Escape and Avoidance Learning.
(A) Escape and avoidance learning are often studied with a shuttle box like that shown here. Warning signals, shock, and the animals' ability to flee from one compartment to another can be controlled by the experimenter.
(B) Avoidance behavior involves both classical and operant conditioning. Avoidance begins because classical conditioning creates a conditioned fear that is elicited by the warning signal (panel 1). Avoidance continues because it is maintained by operant conditioning (panel 2). Specifically, the avoidance response is strengthened through negative reinforcement, since it leads to removal of the conditioned fear.

Finally, it is possible to study avoidance learning in situations that do not require an organism to leave its environment to avoid an aversive stimulus. For example, the experimenter may confront an animal with an aversive stimulus that cannot be avoided until the animal has pressed a bar or pokes its nose into a hole in the wall (see, for example, Spear, Gordon, & Martin, 1973). In some such paradigms no explicit signal precedes the aversive stimulus. Instead, organisms receive aversive stimulation on some set schedule unless they make an appropriate response. In these unsignaled avoidance situations, animals must use the passage of time as the signal for determining

when the aversive stimulus is likely to occur (see Sidman, 1962).

We should make explicit one important point regarding all these avoidance paradigms. Although each paradigm requires that an organism learn an instrumental-avoidance response, there is also the potential for classical fear conditioning in virtually all avoidance situations. In these paradigms the warning stimulus and other contextual stimuli regularly precede the occurrence of a fear-eliciting event. Thus, these stimuli can, themselves, become capable of producing conditioned fear reactions. We will discuss in chapter 6 how important this fear conditioning may be in

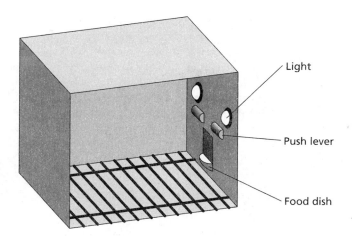

Light

Push lever

Food dish

FIGURE 4.6 An Operant Chamber for a Rat. The chamber is a small box that has a lever that the animal can press. There is a light above the lever that can be turned on or off. A food magazine or cup is connected to an electronically activated feeder. The feeder delivers a small 45-mg food pellet to the cup. In this situation the food pellet serves as reinforcement for lever pressing.

helping an organism learn an avoidance response. It is clear, however, that in most avoidance paradigms such conditioning does occur.

The study of avoidance learning has taken on special significance in recent years as many researchers have discovered parallels between how animals learn avoidance responses and how humans acquire neurotic behaviors such as phobic reactions (see, for example, Peterson & Levis, 1985). As a matter of fact, many contemporary therapies used to treat phobic responses are based directly on research into how avoidance responses are eliminated in the laboratory. As we will see, there has been some controversy concerning what is involved in the learning and extinction of avoidance responses.

OPERANT PROCEDURES

In each of the instrumental-learning paradigms discussed above, an organism receives single, discrete opportunities to emit some response. Once one of these opportunities has passed, the organism cannot respond again until another trial commences. In contrast, operant-conditioning paradigms involve placing organisms in a particular setting where there are no restrictions on how often they make a particular response. The most common operant-conditioning paradigms involve training rats to press a bar and training pigeons to peck a key.

The Bar-Press Response in Rats

Rats normally learn the bar-press response in an apparatus called an operant chamber or a Skinner box (Figure 4.6), so named because it was conceived originally by B. F. Skinner. Skinner used this apparatus extensively to investigate the variables that control operant responding (see, for example, Ferster & Skinner, 1957).

In most Skinner boxes, one wall of the chamber contains a bar or a lever that can be depressed by the rat. Depression of the bar usually results in the delivery of food or water through a hole in the wall next to the bar. Once the experimenter has placed the rat in the box, the animal is free to press the bar at any time. It is not unusual for a well-trained rat to position itself with one paw on the bar and its head near the opening in the wall. In this way it can respond repeatedly and consume the food or water as soon as it appears. The principal measure of responding in this paradigm is the rate at which the bar is depressed. The rate is derived by dividing the number of bar depressions by some unit of time. As we will see, the rate of bar pressing depends greatly on how reinforcement is scheduled by the experimenter.

The Key-Peck Response in Pigeons

As we mentioned while discussing the autoshaping paradigm in chapter 2, pigeons are ground feeders and consequently peck for their food. It is possible to modify this tendency by following each pecking response with some consequence. The apparatus used to assess key pecking is similar to the Skinner box. There is an opening in one of the chamber walls through which reinforcers can be delivered. However, instead of a bar or lever, a round disk called a key is mounted on the chamber wall. When the pigeon pecks the key, the response usually is followed by delivery of food. Placing the key on a vertical surface increases the difficulty in training the pigeon to peck the key. Still it is a popular procedure in the operant-conditioning literature. As with the bar press, the rate of key pecking is the usual measure of operant responding in this situation.

Operant Responses in Humans

As with classical conditioning, much of the research on instrumental and operant learning has been conducted with animals. Paradigms have been developed to study instrumental and operant conditioning directly in humans. For example, humans have been used in studies of operant responding for different schedules of reinforcement. Typically, subjects are seated in front of a keyboard and allowed to press one of two keys. It may take only a few presses of one key to receive a reinforcer, while several presses of the other key

may be required. Normally, human subjects adjust their key pressing behavior to maximize the rate of reinforcement (see, for example, Bradshaw, Szabadi, & Bevan, 1976; Dougher, Crossen, & Garland, 1986). Humans have also pressed levers for monetary rewards (Perone & Baron, 1980; Case, Fantino, & Wixted, 1985) and humans have played modified video games where shooting down alien spaceships constitutes the operant response (Case, Ploog, & Fantino, 1990).

Measuring the Operant Response

As we mentioned previously, the rate at which organisms emit responses is the dependent variable in most operant-conditioning studies. In most operant-conditioning research, response rate is measured using a device known as a cumulative recorder. The cumulative recorder creates a record of responses and reinforcers delivered as a function of time (see Figure 4.7). Skinner's model of the cumulative recorder consisted of a continuous roll of paper that moved slowly to the left and a moveable pen that marked on the paper as it moved. The pen moved upward a small distance each time the organism made one response. The pen also made a small slash mark each time the reinforcer was delivered.

The printed record that was created by this process was called a cumulative record. Learning to read a cumulative record takes some practice. Imagine a period of time when the organism does not respond at all. The cumulative record would be a straight horizontal line because the pen would not move upward at all, but the paper would continue moving to the left. On the other hand, if the organism responded very rapidly, the line would become almost vertical, because the pen would move rapidly upward. Thus, the slope of the line indicates the rate of responding. Steep slopes indicate rapid responding, while shallow slopes indicate slow response rates. Figure 4.8 (p. 106) illustrates these features cumulatively. Today, the cumulative recorder is still used a great deal in research, though the actual device has been replaced in most instances by a computer.

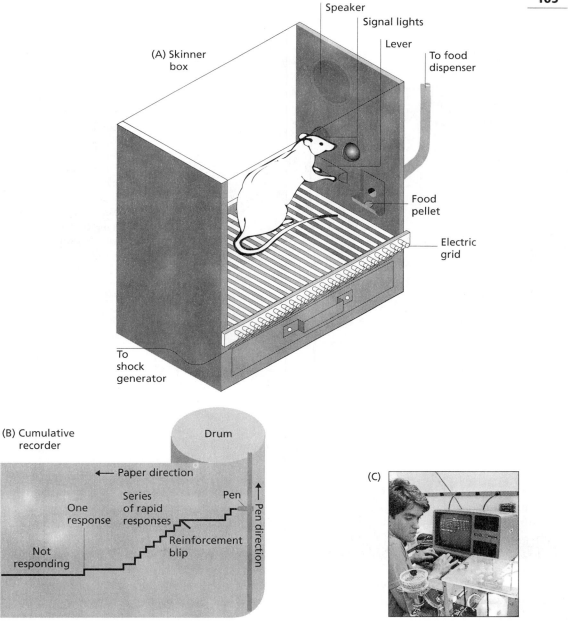

FIGURE 4.7 Skinner Box and Cumulative Recorder. (A) This diagram highlights some of the key features of a Skinner box. In this apparatus designed for rats, the response under study is lever pressing. Food pellets, which may serve as reinforcers, are delivered into the food cup on the right. The speaker and the light permit manipulations of visual and auditory stimuli, and the electric grid gives the experimenter control over aversive consequences (shock) in the box. (B) A cumulative recorder connected to the box keeps a continuous record of responses and reinforcements. Each lever press moves the pen up a step, and each reinforcement is marked with a slash. (C) This photo shows the real thing—a rat being conditioned in a Skinner box. Note the food dispenser on the left, which was omitted from the top diagram.

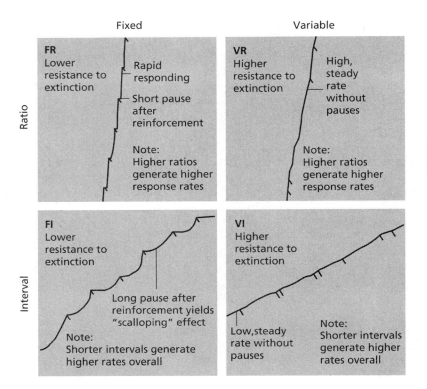

FIGURE 4.8 Schedules of Reinforcement and Patterns of Response. Each type of reinforcement schedule tends to generate a characteristic pattern of responding. In general, ratio schedules tend to produce more rapid responding than interval schedules (note the steep slopes of the FR and VR curves). In comparison to fixed schedules, variable schedules tend to yield steadier responding (note the smoother lines for the VR and VI schedules on the right) and greater resistance to extinction.

The Shaping Procedure

In our discussions of instrumental- and operant-conditioning paradigms, we have made the learning of these behaviors sound very simple. Organisms emit a particular behavior, which is followed by some consequence, and the consequence changes the future probability of the behavior. The only problem with this description is that it assumes an organism will emit the appropriate response, which then can be either reinforced or punished. In fact, seldom can we actually make this assumption.

When a rat is first placed in a Skinner box it normally explores, pokes its nose into the food-delivery opening, and grooms itself. The likelihood that it will spontaneously press the bar is very low. Just as in toilet training a child, if the parent simply waits for a correct response to occur, that parent will be in for a long wait. The problem with many emitted behaviors that we wish to increase is that they often do not occur spontaneously so that they can be reinforced.

For this reason the training of instrumental and operant responses usually requires a procedure called shaping. Shaping refers to reinforcement of behaviors that are closer and closer approximations of the target response. To exemplify the shaping procedure, let's look at how we might shape the rat's bar-press response. In the beginning, we deliver a food pellet each time the rat moves to the side of the chamber that contains the bar. After several reinforcements, the rat usually remains on the bar side of the chamber. We then stop delivering food pellets until the rat emits a behavior that is closer to the bar-press response. We may, for example, only reinforce standing next to the bar. Once the rat is consistently standing next to the bar, we deliver food pellets only when the animal touches the bar itself. Finally, we deliver food pellets only when the rat depresses the bar.

By using shaping procedures, we can train an organism to perform even very complex, low-probability behaviors. A dolphin that jumps through a hoop held high above the water or the gold-medal performance of an Olympic gymnast is an indication that extensive shaping has preceded the response. The key to shaping any behavior is selecting an appropriate sequence of behaviors that are closer and closer approximations of the target behavior. Then it is possible to reinforce, in sequence, each individual component that brings the organism closer to the desired response.

Using Shaping to Help Autistic Children Learn Language. Autism is a severe psychological disorder that begins in early childhood and can have devastating effects on the child and the family. The symptoms of autism include a lack of emotional attachment to the parents, extreme social withdrawal, aggressive behavior, repetitive ritualistic behaviors, and violent self-injury. These children sometimes spend hours repeating the same behavior, especially rocking back and forth, and often they pound their fists against their faces or strike their heads against hard or sharp surfaces. Another common feature of autism is that most of these children do not speak at all or they exhibit echolalia, which is a robot-like repetition of anything that is said to them.

The chances for improvement without treatment are quite poor. Without effective treatment, these individuals often spend their entire lives in hospitals or psychiatric institutions. Unfortunately, most therapies, including psychiatric and medical treatments, are not effective in treating autism (Lovaas, 1987). One exception is the behavioral treatment program developed by Lovaas in the 1960s. Lovaas's treatment program used operant-conditioning principles to eliminate the problem behaviors like self-injury and to train appropriate behaviors such as social behaviors and normal language (Lovaas, 1967).

We will focus on Lovaas's method for teaching language to autistic children, because it is a good example of how shaping can be used to solve certain psychological problems. At first many of the children did not speak at all (although their ages ranged from four to seven years old), so the therapists began by first saying a target word for the child to imitate (usually the child's name) and reinforcing any sound the child made. This was usually done by immediately putting a small piece of candy or food in the child's mouth. After the child's rate of making audible sounds increased sufficiently, the therapist began to reinforce any sound that remotely resembled the target word. Through many stages, the therapist would successively require the child's utterances to more closely match the target word until the child reliably and successfully said the target word.

The therapist would then begin teaching the child to say a new target word, and the process would be repeated until the child had learned to say a large number of words. Training then progressed to teaching children to name objects, respond to questions, and master abstract words such as *over, under, same,* and *different.* As you probably suspect, this type of training is very time consuming and progress can be slow. The training sessions sometimes lasted several hours, and learning the first target word could take four or more days. However, progress becomes more rapid as the child learns more words. With extended training, the child can often learn more than one word in a single day. Usually, it took several months before the children were able to answer questions and tell stories about their activities.

Despite the demanding nature of this treatment, Lovaas's method typically produces significant improvement in these children. It is important to remember that autistic children typically show little or no improvement with any other type of treatment. In addition, the long-term benefits of this treatment program are quite impressive. Lovaas (1987) found that, among a sample of 19 children who had undergone this type of treatment before entering first grade,

9 children (47% of the group) showed normal intelligence and academic performance when they entered first grade. By comparison, among a group of 40 children who did not receive Lovaas's intensive treatment program, only one child (less than 3% of the group) showed normal intelligence and academic performance upon entering the first grade. Results like these demonstrate the role of operant conditioning and shaping in a remarkably effective treatment for this very difficult disorder.

Variables That Affect Instrumental and Operant Responding

Now we will look at the variety of factors that influence responding in instrumental- and operant-conditioning paradigms, moving from variables that affect responding in positive reinforcement situations to certain negative-reinforcement and punishment paradigms.

POSITIVE REINFORCEMENT SITUATIONS

In conditioning situations that involve positive reinforcement, responding is influenced most strongly by the characteristics of the reinforcer. Of particular importance are the amount (or magnitude) of reinforcement, the quality of the reinforcer, and the time that elapses between a response and the presentation of the reinforcer.

Amount or Magnitude of Reinforcement

In most cases, responding occurs faster and becomes more accurate as we increase the amount of a reinforcer delivered after each response. This principle has been illustrated by any number of studies that have varied the magnitude of reinforcement in instrumental-learning paradigms.

In one such experiment, Crespi (1942) trained five groups of rats to run down a straight runway for food reinforcement. The groups differed in terms of the number of small food pel-

lets they received in the goal box on each trial (1, 4, 16, 64, or 256 pellets for each correct response). Crespi found that after 20 trials, the running speeds of the groups corresponded directly to the number of pellets received. The fastest running occurred in the group receiving the largest amount of food, and the speeds of the other groups decreased in direct proportion to the size of the food reinforcement. In addition, Crespi found that the animals that received the largest amounts of food improved their performance more quickly than did the other animals.

Although such findings have been replicated numerous times, there is one complicating factor in the results of reinforcement magnitude studies. Some experimenters have disagreed as to the definition of *reinforcer magnitude*. Is it the absolute size of the reinforcer, the amount of time it takes to consume it, or the number of objects the organism receives? Several studies have shown that if an experimenter gives two groups the same amount of food for each response, but for one group the food is simply broken into more pieces, the group receiving the most pieces will respond faster (see, for example, Campbell, Batsche, & Batsche, 1972). While such findings do not detract from the basic principle that larger reinforcers lead to better performance, they do suggest that organisms may not always perceive the amount of reinforcement as the experimenter intended.

Size or amount of reinforcement notwithstanding, organisms also perform better when the quality of the reinforcer is higher. We can define *quality* by assessing how vigorously an organism consumes a reward when it is presented. High-quality reinforcers are consumed quickly by organisms, whereas low-quality reinforcers are consumed less quickly. For example, it is well known that when rats are allowed to drink solutions that vary in sweetness, they drink sweeter solutions faster. Likewise, when presentation of sweet solutions is used to reinforce rats' responses, groups that receive the sweetest solutions perform best (see, for example, Flaherty & Caprio, 1976).

Delay of Reinforcement

Just as reinforcer magnitude and quality affect instrumental responding, so does the delay of any reinforcer that follows a response. The longer that reinforcement is delayed after a response, the poorer the performance of that response. This conclusion is illustrated clearly by the results of a runway experiment conducted by E. J. Capaldi, 1978). Two groups of rats received the same amount and quality of food reinforcement on each trial. However, one group received the reinforcer immediately upon entering the goal box while the other group experienced a 10-second delay. The results of this study are shown in Figure 4.9, which plots the start speed in the runway or a function of learning trials as well as delay conditions. At the end of training, the speed of the immediate-reinforcement group is substantially higher than the speed of the delayed-reinforcement group.

There are probably a number of reasons for why delay of reinforcement adversely affects instrumental responding. One reason is that, when long delays occur, an organism normally engages in a number of different behaviors during the delay between the target response and the delivery of the reinforcer. This means that the reinforcer will likely increase the frequency of these behaviors rather than the target response.

Contrast Effects

In general, the effects of quantity, quality, and delay of reinforcement on instrumental responding appear to be rather simple. However, these effects can vary depending on an organism's past experiences with a particular reinforcer. For example, a given magnitude of reinforcement may influence responding differently, depending on the magnitude of reinforcement an organism has received in the past. Crespi (1942) first demonstrated this phenomenon.

In Crespi's experiment one group of rats was trained to traverse a runway for a large amount of food, while a second group received a small

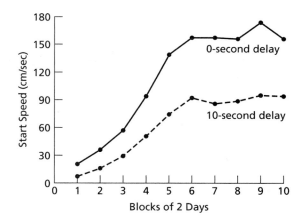

FIGURE 4.9 Acquisition of a running response as a function of the length of time reward is delayed on each trial. From E. J. Capaldi, 1978 in *Animal Learning & Behavior, 6*, 330–334. Reprinted by permission of Psychonomic Society, Inc.

amount of food for the same response. After several trials the rats receiving the large reinforcer were running consistently faster than the small-reinforcement group. Crespi then switched half of the large-reinforcement animals to the small reinforcer being given the other rats (large-small group). He also switched half the small-reinforcer rats to the large-reinforcer magnitude (small-large group). The results of this switch in reinforcer magnitude were surprising.

The animals that were switched from the large to the small reinforcer slowed their running speeds to such a degree that they ran more slowly than the rats that had received the small reinforcer all along. This phenomenon has been labeled successive negative-contrast. Likewise, animals that were shifted from the small to the large reinforcer began to run faster than the animals that had been receiving the large reinforcer since the very first trial. This phenomenon is called successive positive-contrast. Figure 4.10 illustrates the kind of reinforcer shift effects that were found by Crespi. Note that the positive- and negative-contrast effects are temporary. With training the shifted animals returned to the level of the animals that were not shifted.

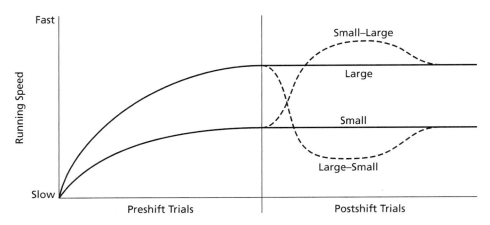

FIGURE 4.10 Contrast Effects of the Type Found by Crespi (1942). Rats shifted from a large to a small reward (Large-Small) ran more slowly than rats given a small reward (Small) throughout training. Rats shifted from a small to a large reward (Small-Large) ran faster than rats receiving a large reward (Large) throughout.

The kind of paradigm employed by Crespi has been termed a successive-contrast paradigm to denote that one reinforcer magnitude succeeds or follows another. Contrast effects have also been found in simultaneous contrast paradigms. In these paradigms, one group consistently receives one reinforcer magnitude. The other group receives the same reinforcer magnitude as the first group on some trials but either a larger or a smaller reinforcer on other trials. For example, one group may receive five food pellets on all its trials. A second group may receive five food pellets on half its trials and ten food pellets on the remainder. In a comparison of the running speeds of the two groups on the five-pellet trials only, typically the group that receives ten pellets on some trials runs more slowly than the group that receives five pellets on all trials (see, for example, Bower, 1961).

The occurrence of contrast effects is not limited to different experiences with reinforcement magnitude. Contrast effects have been obtained with shifts in reinforcer quality (Elliot, 1928), as well as when reinforcer quality is varied in simultaneous contrast paradigms (see, for example, Fla-herty, Riley, & Spear, 1973). Likewise, there is some evidence that contrast effects may occur when organisms experience different reinforcement delays (see, for example, Beery, 1968; McHose & Tauber, 1972).

Intermittent Reinforcement

In real-life settings we seldom receive reinforcement each time we emit an appropriate response. For example, it may be our plan to praise a child each time she picks up her toys. However, once this plan has been initiated, the child is likely to begin to pick up her toys even when we are not around to give praise. What is the effect of such reinforcement inconsistency on behavior?

To answer this question, several researchers have compared the performance of organisms given continuous reinforcement (reinforcement following each correct response) to that of organisms given partial reinforcement (reinforcement delivered after only a percentage of the correct responses). One might expect that in such comparisons continuously reinforced organisms would outperform organisms given partial reinforcement. Somewhat surprisingly, this has not always been the case.

Some studies have found that as long as a substantial percentage of responses is reinforced, partially reinforced responses develop almost as fast as continuously reinforced responses (see, for example, Brown & Wagner, 1964; Mikulka & Pavlik, 1966). In still other experiments, partial reinforcement actually produced a higher level of responding than reinforcement after each response (Goodrich, 1959; Wagner, 1961). This rather mixed pattern of findings does not allow us to draw any firm conclusions. However, it is clear that instrumental learning is not dependent on continuous reinforcement. In most species, instrumental responding develops quite efficiently even when reinforcement occurs only intermittently.

Schedules of Reinforcement

In operant-conditioning paradigms, researchers primarily have been interested in how different schedules of intermittent reinforcement influence the rate of a particular behavior. In other words, once a rat has learned to press a bar, how will the rate of bar pressing be affected by the schedule of partial reinforcement? Thus, researchers investigating in operant-conditioning paradigms usually are interested in the variables that affect the rate of a particular behavior.

This emphasis on well-learned responses that are intermittently reinforced may sound arbitrary until one considers the practical significance of such work. Most of our important operant behaviors (for example, working, studying, and talking) are behaviors we have already learned. As most real-world behaviors are reinforced only on certain occasions, it becomes particularly important to look at the effects of partial reinforcement schedules on operant performance.

We begin this discussion with a focus on two major types—ratio and interval schedules. These types of schedules differ in terms of the rules used to determine which responses should be reinforced.

Ratio Schedules. In a ratio schedule of reinforcement, the reinforcer is delivered only after the organism emits a certain number of responses. Thus, reinforcement does not follow every response but instead follows some number of responses. Two types of ratio schedules have been studied in detail. The first, the **fixed ratio** (FR) schedule, is so named because the reinforcer is always delivered after the same number of responses. For example, a rat may be required to press a bar 10 times for the delivery of the first reinforcer. Then it must press the bar 10 more times before the second reinforcer is delivered. In this example, the schedule of reinforcement would be termed an FR-10 schedule.

Examples of fixed-ratio reinforcement schedules are common throughout society. A political campaign worker may be paid a certain sum for each 100 flyers mailed out to prospective voters. Some reading programs for children give out a gold star or a certificate for each 10 books that a child has read. The critical feature of the fixed-ratio schedule is that an organism must make the same number of responses to acquire each reinforcer.

Figure 4.8 depicts a cumulative record of the kind normally found when organisms respond on a fixed-ratio schedule. The small diagonal slashes on the response line show when reinforcers were delivered. As you can see, fixed ratio schedules produce a fairly high, constant rate of responding. Typically, however, organisms on FR schedules do pause in their responding, usually just after a reinforcer is delivered. The duration of these postreinforcement pauses is dependent on the number of responses required for delivery of the reinforcer. The pauses tend to be short when only a few responses are necessary, but they can be relatively long when many responses are required for each reinforcer. The same pattern of responding tends to occur whenever an organism, regardless of species, is placed on a fixed ratio schedule.

Researchers have learned that this **pause after reinforcement** (PAR) may be aversive. Gentry (1968) trained pigeons to peck for a grain

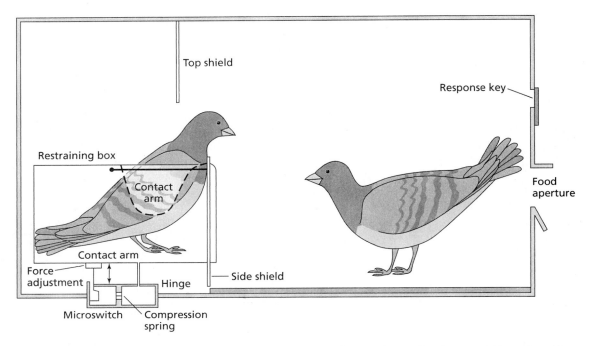

FIGURE 4.11 Schematic of the Apparatus for Measuring Attack. The experiment chamber was 25 by 11 by 14 in. high. Plexiglas shields at the top and on the sides of the restraining box prevented the experimental pigeon from getting behind the target pigeon. From W. D. Gentry (1968), *Journal of the Experimental Analysis of Behavior, 11,* 813–817. © 1968 by the Society for the Experimental Analysis of Behavior. Reprinted by permission.

reward in a modified Skinner box. The apparatus is depicted in Figure 4.11. As you can see, Gentry had the usual response key and food aperture, but he also had a second pigeon constrained in the box. This pigeon was held in a smaller enclosure, which had a microswitch and compression spring located underneath the second pigeon. This apparatus allowed the experimenter to measure both the rate of key pecking by the subject and the amount of aggression it exhibited toward the second animal. In essence, each time the pigeon pecked the constrained bird it would register both the frequency and the strength of the peck.

The experiment proper consisted of four phases. First Gentry determined a baseline level of attack behavior. It turned out to be low; very little aggressive behavior was shown toward the pigeon. Then Gentry trained the pigeon to peck the key.

He eventually brought its behavior up to an FR-50 schedule. The pigeon had to peck the key 50 times to receive brief access to the grain. Interestingly, during the PAR the level of attack rose significantly. In the third phase, Gentry removed the key and reinforcement and the level of attack behavior declined to baseline levels. In the fourth phase, Gentry once again established responding on the FR-50 schedule and the level of attack behavior again rose significantly during the pause after reinforcement. It is well known that aversive stimuli can lead to aggressive behavior and it appeared that Gentry had shown that at least under certain conditions responding on schedules of reinforcement can be aversive. This finding is not unique. Monkeys have also been shown to attack another monkey while responding on an FR schedule (Huchinson, Azrin, and Hunt, 1968).

The second major type of ratio schedule is called the **variable ratio** (VR) schedule because the number of responses required for each reinforcer changes from one series of responses to the next. In a variable ratio, the first response after an average number of responses has occurred is reinforced. Reinforcement is varied around that mean. For example, in a VR-10 schedule, the first reinforcer may be delivered after a pigeon pecks a key twice, while the second reinforcer is delivered after 18 pecks, and the third reinforcer is delivered after 10 pecks.

Figure 4.8 is an example of a cumulative record that might be found using a variable-ratio schedule. As you can see, such schedules produce a high and constant rate of responding. The rate of responding on a VR schedule is often higher than that found with FR schedules. As with FR schedules, organisms on VR schedules pause occasionally. However, these pauses do not appear to occur in any set relation to the time of reinforcement. Further, the VR schedule produces fewer and shorter pauses than are often found with FR schedules (see, for example, Ferster & Skinner, 1957). Again, it is notable that virtually all species show this typical pattern of VR responding. Humans, for example, respond this way when they are playing slot machines. Most slot machines are programmed to give payoffs on a variable-ratio schedule. Some payoffs require hundreds of lever pulls, whereas others may occur after only a few such responses. When confronted with such a payoff schedule, humans tend to pull slot machine levers at a high rate, pausing only very occasionally. Obviously, casino owners are aware of the strong control reinforcement schedules exert over operant responses.

Interval Schedules. As we have noted, partial reinforcement is assured in ratio schedules by reinforcing only a certain fraction of the responses made. Interval schedules accomplish the same end by requiring that reinforcers are delivered only for the first response that occurs after a period of time has elapsed. In the typical interval schedule, once a reinforcer has been delivered, a period of preset duration goes into effect. During this period no response is reinforced. However, the first response that occurs after the interval has elapsed is reinforced and the time period is started again. It is important to note that in an interval schedule, reinforcement is not programmed to occur as soon as the interval ends. Just as in ratio schedules, interval schedules require a correct response before reinforcement is given. However, in the interval schedule it is the first response following the time-out period that leads to reinforcement.

The first type of interval schedule we will describe is a **fixed interval** (FI) schedule, in which the length of the interval that follows each reinforcer is the same. For example, in an FI-30 sec schedule, after the first reinforcer, a rat receives a 30-second period during which no bar presses are reinforced. When the 30 seconds has elapsed, the rat's first bar press is reinforced. Then another 30-second time-out period begins. When this type of schedule is used, it becomes at least theoretically possible for an organism to learn to wait for exactly the time-out duration before emitting another response. The optimal strategy would of course involve receiving one reinforcer and then waiting to respond again until just after the time-out period has elapsed. In most cases, this is not quite what organisms do under an FI schedule.

Figure 4.8 represents the kind of cumulative record normally obtained in an FI schedule. This record shows that organisms tend to respond very little soon after receiving a reinforcer. However, responding gradually increases as the end of the time-out period approaches. Finally, responding reaches a high point at the end of the time-out period. This well-known pattern of responding is known as the FI scallop, as the cumulative record obtained with the FI schedule resembles a series of arcs or scallops.

Fixed-interval schedules occur widely in our everyday life. For example, paychecks are ready at the same time each pay period. It is interesting to note that in the FI schedule one sees the same type of pause after reinforcement that one sees in the FR schedule. One may wonder whether the higher levels of drinking and aggression one sees on a Friday night, may partially be explained by the fact that the workers just got paid and there is no possibility for another paycheck for a week or more. The pause after reinforcement and the higher incidence of aggression seen in pigeons may be operating in humans as well.

The second type of interval schedule that is commonly studied is the **variable interval** (VI) schedule. In this schedule, the organism is reinforced for the first response that occurs after an average interval of time. Again, the length of the interval is varied around some mean. For example, in a VI-2 minute schedule, a pigeon may receive a reinforcer for the first response after a 20-second period of time and may not receive a second reward until the first response after 100 seconds has elapsed. In this type of schedule it is not possible for an organism to learn when the interval period will time out.

Figure 4.8 shows the kind of cumulative record usually obtained with a VI schedule. Note that the pattern of responding is not scalloped like the FI pattern. Instead there is a moderate, fairly consistent rate of response throughout the course of each time-out period. This is the same response pattern you show when you are trying to reach someone on the telephone but continue to receive a busy signal. After some period of time, the other party will get off the phone. However, the duration of this time-out period varies from one situation to the next. Faced with this dilemma, most of us continue dialing at regular intervals until we get an answer.

More Complex Schedules of Reinforcement

DRL and DRH Schedules of Reinforcement. We turn now to a brief discussion of more complex schedules. Operant-conditioning theorists conducted a great number of studies to determine the influence of other schedules on behavior. The first schedule we will consider is known as the DRL schedule, or **differential reinforcement of low rates of response.** In this schedule an organism is reinforced if it responds at a slow rate. For example, in an experiment with a DRL 20-schedule the animal is reinforced if at least 20 seconds has elapsed since the preceding reinforcement. If a rat has just received reinforcement it must wait at least 20 seconds before responding again. If the animal waits the predetermined time it will be reinforced. If it responds before the interval has timed out, the clock is reset and the animal has to wait an additional 20 seconds before receiving the reward. This schedule, as you might have guessed, has the effect of slowing responses down. The schedule often is used with hyperactive children because it provides a way of slowing down their activity levels while still using positive reinforcement. A second complex schedule is the DRH or **differential reinforcement of high rates of response.** This schedule provides the experimenter with a way to produce very high rates of response. An example of such a schedule might be the DRH 70 per minute schedule. In this schedule, to receive reinforcement, the animal is required to produce 70 responses before a one-minute period of time has elapsed.

Multiple and Mixed Schedules of Reinforcement. In a **multiple schedule** of reinforcement, researchers present two or more schedules of reinforcement successively, each in the presence of a different exteroceptive stimulus. The exteroceptive stimulus is any stimulus that is external to the animal. The stimulus signals the schedule of reinforcement that is currently in effect. For example, in a Mult VI-2 min ext schedule a red light might be turned on in the pigeon's operant chamber for three minutes. During this period of time the pigeon receives reinforcement according to a VI-2 min schedule. Following the red light a green light might be presented on the key for three minutes and during this interval the pigeon is not reinforced. Multiple schedules of reinforcement are commonly used to teach animals to discriminate.

The **mixed schedule** of reinforcement is the same as the multiple schedule, except that there is no stimulus used to indicate which schedule the animal is under. For example, in the mix VI-2 min ext schedule, in the presence of a white light the animal operates sometimes under the VI schedule and sometimes under the extinction schedule. Mixed schedules often are used in operant-conditioning experiments as control conditions for the multiple schedule. In the example above, if the animal under the Mult VI-2 min ext schedule learns to respond in the presence of the red light and not in the presence of the green light, we could argue that the animal has learned to discriminate between the two colors. However, the animal could be using the presence or absence of food to make the discrimination. We can use another group trained on the mixed schedule to rule out this interpretation.

Multiple and mixed schedules of reinforcement are used a great deal in operant research and in applied situations. Using multiple schedules it is possible to teach dogs to distinguish the presence or absence of explosives or drugs. It is also possible to determine if children have any kind of sensory disorders related to hearing or vision. In chapter 6 we will see that the use of multiple and mixed schedules can help us to answer questions about evolution of intelligence and the mechanisms that underlie certain behaviors, such as foraging or observing.

Concurrent Schedules. In real-life settings we are seldom confronted with single-reinforcement schedules. More typically, we face more than one reinforcement schedule at the same time. In such situations, we say that **concurrent schedules of reinforcement** are in effect. For example, if you are engaged in a conversation involving several people, some individuals will listen to what you say (that is, they will reinforce your verbal responses) more intently than others. In effect, you will be differentially reinforced for your verbal output depending on the person in the group to whom you speak. When we are faced with such choices between different schedules of reinforcement, how do we respond?

To answer this question experimentally, several researchers have studied concurrent schedules of reinforcement. In such situations organisms are allowed free access to two separate processes (for example, bars to press or keys to peck). Each bar or key is associated with a different schedule of reinforcement. Pressing one bar may be reinforced on a VI 1-min schedule and responses on the other bar may be reinforced on a VI 5-min schedule. The question of how organisms allocate their responses when given such a choice was answered by a series of experiments conducted by Herrnstein (1961).

Herrnstein measured the rate at which pigeons pecked keys that were associated with different reinforcement schedules. Surprisingly, he found that pigeons did not simply choose the key having the most favorable schedule of reinforcement. That is, they did not make the vast majority of their responses to the key that provided the most reinforcement in the shortest period of time. Instead, pigeons divided their responses between the keys, and the rate of responding on each key was directly related to the rate of reinforcement on that key. For example, if responding on key number 1 was reinforced five times as often as responding on key number 2, the pigeons responded on key number 1 five times more than on key number 2.

From these data, Herrnstein proposed what is called the **matching law,** which states that when an organism has free access to two different schedules of reinforcement, it will allocate its responses in proportion to the rate of reinforcement on each schedule. The matching law is expressed as this formula:

$$\frac{B1}{B1 + B2} = \frac{R1}{R1 + R2}$$

Here, B1 is the number of type-1 responses, and B2 is the number of type-2 responses. R1 is the number of reinforcers delivered after B1, and R2 is the number of reinforcers delivered after B2.

To see how the matching law is applied, consider a pigeon pecking keys associated with two different FI schedules of reinforcement. Pecking the red key (B1) is reinforced on a variable interval of 20 seconds while pecking the green key (B2) is reinforced on a variable interval of 60 seconds. This means that for any given time period, B1 would be followed by three times more reinforcers than B2. In a one-minute period, for example, the pigeon could receive three reinforcers for B1 but only one reinforcer for B2. Thus, in this case, R1 = 3 while R2 = 1. Substituting these values in the formula yields

$$\frac{B1}{B1 + B2} = \frac{3}{3 + 1}$$

From the matching formula we see that B1 = 3 and that B2 = 1. This means that the matching law predicts the pigeon will peck the red key (B1) three times for each time that it pecks the green key (B2). Stated another way, the pigeon will spend three-fourths of the time pecking key 1 and one-fourth of the time pecking key 2.

The matching law has been shown to hold in a wide variety of experimental settings involving human subjects (McDowell, 1981, 1982) as well as other species (see, for example, deVilliers, 1974). In recent years, there has been great interest in understanding the mechanisms by which organisms match responding to reinforcement schedules (Commons, Herrnstein, & Rachlin, 1982) and in discovering how extensively this law may be applied to instances of choice behavior (see, for example, Davison & McCarthy, 1988; McSweeney, Melville, Buck, & Whipple, 1983). Regardless of the final outcome of such research, however, the occurrence of matching provides one more example of how strongly reinforcement schedules control the rate of operant responding in humans and other organisms.

Imagine a hawk who is out searching for food. Assume that the hawk can see an area that is 100 meters square. If it sits on top of a telephone pole in one patch it will search for mice in a field that has 100 mice in it. On the other hand, if the hawk sits on a different pole, it can search a comparable area with 500 mice. If Herrnstein's matching law operates in the wild, we would expect to find our hawk spending five times as much time searching in the field where the mouse density is high.

NEGATIVE REINFORCEMENT SITUATIONS: ESCAPE LEARNING AND AVOIDANCE

Amount of Reinforcement

Just as the magnitude of reinforcement affects performance in positive-reinforcement situations, so does the amount of reinforcement influence escape-learning performance. In escape learning, the amount of reinforcement corresponds to the degree to which the aversive stimulation is reduced after a successful response.

In one study conducted by Trapold and Fowler (1960), rats escaped shock by running from an alleyway into a safe box where no shock was present. Different groups of rats were exposed to different shock intensities in the alleyway. The results of this study showed that the speed of the escape response was directly related to the shock intensity in the alleyway. Rats that received the highest shock intensity ran the fastest, whereas lower shock intensities led to slower speeds.

This finding can be interpreted in two ways. One is that animals exposed to high shock intensities received the highest reduction of shock when they entered the safe box. According to this interpretation, escape speed depends on the amount of negative reinforcement. Another view is simply that escape speed depends on the intensity of the aversive stimulation. In this view it does not matter how much the stimulation is reduced upon completion of the escape response. Which of these interpretations is correct?

The answer appears to be provided in another experiment by Campbell and Kraeling (1953), who exposed all rats to the same shock intensity in the runway and reduced this shock by varying degrees in the safe box. That is, all animals received shock reduction after responding, but

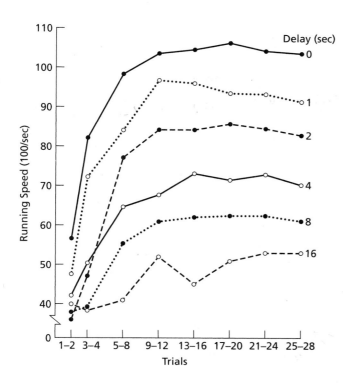

FIGURE 4.12 Acquisition of an Escape Response. Here, the rate at which the escape response is acquired is a function of the delay of shock termination on each trial. (From Fowler and Trapold, 1962.)

most animals still received some shock in the safe box. Campbell and Kraeling found that rats would learn the escape response under these conditions. Furthermore, the speed of the escape response was a direct function of the degree to which shock was reduced. It appears, therefore, that escape learning depends more on the amount of negative reinforcement than on the intensity of the aversive stimulus per se.

Delay of Reinforcement

If all organisms receive the same degree of negative reinforcement for an escape response, performance then depends strongly on the delay of reinforcement. Here, *delay of reinforcement* refers to the time between the escape response and the reduction of the aversive stimulation. The effect of this variable is clearly illustrated by the results of a study conducted by Fowler and Trapold (1962).

These experimenters exposed rats to shock in an alleyway and required the animals to run to a safe box to escape the shock. Once in the safe box, however, the groups differed in terms of the time it took for the shock to go off. The delay in shock offset varied between 0 and 16 seconds. The results, shown in Figure 4.12, indicate that escape speeds decreased as the delay of shock offset increased. Thus, the effects of delay of negative reinforcement are similar to those of delay of reinforcement in positive reinforcement situations.

Negative Reinforcement Situations: Avoidance Learning

In our original description of avoidance learning, we said that in most such situations a stimulus signals the impending presentation of the aversive event. To avoid the aversive event, the organism must respond in the presence of the signal. In effect, avoidance learning usually involves two stimuli—the signal and the aversive stimulus—that are critical for correct responding. As you might expect, then, the characteristics of both these stimuli are important determinants of avoidance learning.

The Intensity of the Aversive Stimulus. The rate at which avoidance responses are learned does appear to vary with the intensity of the aversive stimulus used. However, the manner in which intensity affects the rate of learning depends on the type of avoidance paradigm being considered. For example, earlier we discussed the one-way avoidance paradigm in which the same start chamber is used for each trial. In this situation, the more intense the aversive stimulus, the sooner the avoidance response is learned (see, for example, Dieter, 1976).

On the other hand, we also discussed the two-way avoidance procedure, where each of the boxes of a two-chamber apparatus serves as the start box on some trials and the safe box on others. In this paradigm, as we increase the intensity of the aversive stimulus, we actually retard or slow the rate of learning (see, for example, McAllister, McAllister, & Dieter, 1976). The same is true of avoidance situations that require responses such as a bar press to avoid the aversive stimulus. The higher the intensity of the aversive stimulus, the more slowly the avoidance response is acquired (see, for example, D'Amato & Fazzaro, 1966).

The Signal-Aversive Stimulus Interval. Avoidance responding clearly is related to the temporal relationship between the signal and the aversive stimulus. In our discussion of classical conditioning we spoke of trace-conditioning procedures in which the signaling CS terminates before the onset of the US. In avoidance learning, if the signal terminates before the aversive stimulus begins, the development of avoidance responding is considerably retarded (Kamin, 1954; Warner, 1932). Avoidance learning appears to occur most efficiently when the signal and the aversive stimulus overlap, as is the case in a delayed-conditioning procedure.

When the signal and the aversive stimulus do overlap, the rate of learning depends on the duration of the signal before the onset of the aversive event. In general, signals of longer duration tend to facilitate the learning of the avoidance response (see, for example, Low & Low, 1962). The reason for this effect seems fairly simple. Very short signal-aversive stimulus intervals do not allow an organism ample time to respond before the aversive stimulus occurs. Longer intervals afford the opportunity for an avoidance response.

The Termination of the Signal. Even when the organism's response results in avoidance of the aversive stimulus, the rate of learning depends on whether the response also leads to the termination of the signal. For example, Kamin (1957a) conducted a two-way avoidance experiment using rats as subjects. In this study all rats were able to avoid shock by moving to the safe chamber during the signal-shock interval. For one group of animals the signal terminated as soon as the avoidance response occurred (0-second delay). In the remaining three groups the signal ended either 2.5, 5, or 10 seconds after the avoidance response. It is clear from the results of this study in Figure 4.13 that avoidance responding suffers rather dramatically when the response does not result in immediate termination of the signal. This suggests that for organisms in avoidance situations, elimination of the aversive stimulus is not the only important response consequence. It also is important that the response terminate the stimuli that signal the aversive stimulus.

Punishment Situations

It is important to understand the variables that control instrumental and operant responding when either positive or negative reinforcement is used. The reason is that we constantly utilize positive and negative reinforcement procedures to modify the behaviors of ourselves and others. Still, no form of behavior control is chosen more often than the punishment procedure. When an

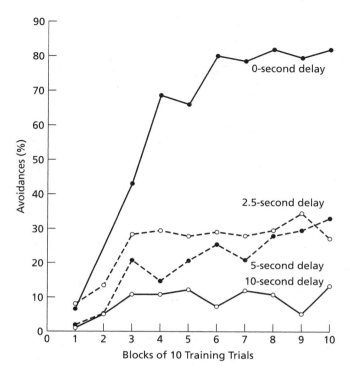

FIGURE 4.13 Acquisition of a Signaled Avoidance Response. Here, the rate at which the signaled avoidance response is acquired is a function of how long termination of the signal is delayed following each response. (From Kamin, 1957.)

organism behaves in a manner we deem inappropriate, our first inclination often is to follow that response with some form of punishment.

Although punishment procedures are used with great frequency, we often find that attempts to punish behavior actually reinforce the behaviors we wish to eliminate. For example, a teacher may find that scolding a child for being disruptive in class results in an increase in the disruptive behavior. Likewise, a dog's habit of defecating in the house is seldom modified by spanking the animal whenever the owner discovers the deed. Does this mean that punishment is ineffective in eliminating behaviors? No; it only means that in most cases our attempts at punishment fail because we do not fully understand how punishment works and how to apply it correctly.

The Intensity and Duration of Punishment. As the intensity of the punishing stimulus increases, punishment becomes more effective in

suppressing a target response. Although this finding has been reported in several experiments, it is illustrated most clearly in a study by Church, Raymond, and Beauchamp (1967). These experimenters first trained rats to press a bar for food reinforcement. Once this response had been well established, they punished a certain percentage of the bar depressions with shocks of low, medium, or high intensity. They found that bar pressing was only slightly affected by the low-intensity shock. However, rats that received the higher intensity shocks showed substantial suppression of bar pressing, and the amount of suppression was directly related to the shock intensity.

In the same experiment, Church and his colleagues also demonstrated the importance of punishment duration on response suppression. For each of the shock intensities used, different groups of rats were exposed to shocks lasting 0.25, 0.3, 0.5, 1, or 3 minutes. The suppressing effects of each shock intensity increased significantly as the duration of the shock was increased. Thus, punishing stimuli become more effective in suppressing target responses as either the intensity or duration of the stimulus increases.

These findings concerning the intensity and duration of punishment are hardly surprising. However, it is clear that in applying punishment procedures people often fail to take these effects into account. Mild punishers such as minor scoldings or looks of dissatisfaction are often used by adults attempting to punish aggressive or disruptive behaviors in children. As noted earlier, such punishers sometimes increase rather than decrease the target behaviors. One reason is that these adult reactions are not intense enough to reduce the undesirable responses. Furthermore, they involve attending to the child, which may actually function to reinforce the undesirable behavior. Obviously, most people avoid using punishers that are too severe or debilitating. Still, it's important to keep in mind that the use of very low-intensity punishers may sometimes reinforce rather than punish a target response.

Delay and Noncontingent Delivery of Punishment. Several studies have shown that punishment is most effective in reducing a target behavior if it occurs immediately after the behavior occurs (see, for example, Baron, 1965; Camp, Raymond, & Church, 1967; Kamin, 1959). The results of one such experiment conducted by Randall and Riccio (1969) are shown in Figure 4.14.

In this study albino rats were allowed access to a dark box. Since these rats normally seek out dark environments, movement into the dark chamber was a highly probable response. Once each rat had entered the dark box, it was shocked either immediately or 5, 10, 30, or 60 seconds later. Then the animals were returned to the original environment, and the experimenters measured the latency to "cross through" (that is, to move back into the dark box) on a subsequent trial. As you can see, rats that received the immediate shock suppressed moving into the dark chamber. Animals showed less avoidance of the dark chamber, however, when the original shock

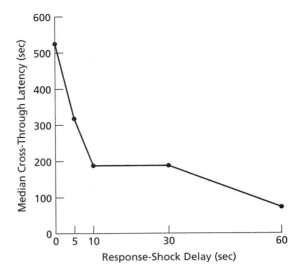

FIGURE 4.14 Latency. The latency to perform a previously punished response as a function of how long after responding the punishment occurred. From Randall and Riccio, 1969. From the *Journal of Comparative and Physiological Psychology,* 1969, *69,* 550–553. ©1969 by the American Psychological Assn. Reprinted by permission of the publisher and David Ricco.

had been delayed. Animals that had experienced the longest delay in punishment reentered the dark chamber readily.

One reason why delayed punishments are less effective than those given immediately is that substantial delays reduce the contingent relationship between the target response and the punishment. Since with long delays organisms can make numerous responses between the time of the target response and the punisher, the delivery of an aversive stimulus may affect these behaviors more than the behavior that produced the punisher. The clearest contingency exists between the punishment and the last response the organism emits before the punishing stimulus. Contingencies between the punisher and other responses are less clear, the further these responses are removed in time from the punisher.

This raises the question of what happens to responses that occur before the punishing stimulus when those responses do not produce the punishing stimulus. In other words, when punishing stimuli occur, what happens to the behaviors that have no clear contingent relationship to the punishment? In some cases behaviors that are uncorrelated with punishment do not seem to be affected. For example, in one study by Boe and Church (1967) rats were trained to press a bar. Then separate groups either were shocked for bar pressing or were given noncontingent shocks every 30 seconds regardless of what responses they were making. Rats given the shocks contingent on bar pressing showed a long-lasting reduction in responding even after the punishments ceased. On the other hand, rats given noncontingent shocks resumed the normal rate of bar pressing once the shocks had stopped.

In other cases, behaviors that do not lead to punishment may increase when some other response is punished. Dunham (1971), for example, gave gerbils the behavioral option to either drink, eat, or shred paper. All these behaviors are highly probable for gerbils. The experimenter shocked some gerbils when they approached food, others when they approached water, and still others when they began shredding paper. In each case he found that the punished behavior decreased in probability. However, if animals were shocked for eating, they tended to increase drinking and paper shredding. In other words, nonpunished behaviors increased to take the place of the punished response.

Finally, organisms that receive unavoidable intense aversive stimuli that are not contingent on any response often exhibit what has been termed **learned helplessness.** In effect, organisms exposed to such stimulation often appear to give up making responses of any type. This occurs even when the investigator changes the conditions of the experiment such that some of the organism's responses would enable it to avoid or escape from the aversive stimulus. This phenomenon was first demonstrated by Overmeir and Seligman (1967), using dogs as subjects.

In this experiment the dogs were administered unavoidable and inescapable shocks that were not contingent on any particular response. Then the dogs were placed in an avoidance apparatus in which shock could be avoided by crossing from one box into another. Overmeir and Seligman found that these animals showed significant deficits in learning to avoid. The typical response was to simply sit in the shock box and submit to the aversive stimulation. This behavior has often been compared to depressed behavior in humans who feel that they are being punished regardless of what they do and regardless of their attempts to avoid unpleasantness (see, for example, Seligman, 1975). In any event, the occurrence of learned helplessness has prompted numerous studies into the effects of uncontrollable aversive stimulation on the behavior of humans and other organisms (see, for example, Maier & Jackson, 1979; Maier & Seligman, 1976).

The practical implications of the findings discussed above should be clear. First of all, punishments will be most effective in reducing a specific target behavior when the punishing stimulus is clearly contingent on the performance of the target response. Punishments that occur in a noncontingent manner can be ineffective, or they can decrease activity in general.

Second, punishers are most effective when they follow a target response immediately. Most people who own dogs have, on several occasions, come home to find that their loyal pet has rummaged through the garbage in the kitchen and strewn trash all over the floor. The typical inclination on the part of the owner is to punish this behavior by scolding the animal, swatting it with a rolled newspaper, and putting it outside. In most cases, these consequences do not occur until well after the inappropriate behavior has occurred. Such arrangements are rarely effective in punishing the undesirable behavior. In fact, the behavior that is actually punished could be your pet's excitement over your arrival, which is the response it is probably making just before the administration of the aversive consequence.

Responses Produced by the Punishing Stimulus. A punishing stimulus is more than simply a consequence of some prior emitted behavior. Punishers usually elicit or automatically produce behaviors themselves. For example, speaking harshly to a friend may automatically produce a negative emotional response. Spanking a child may produce fear and crying. Physically punishing a dog may produce natural aggressive reactions in the animal. As it happens, the particular responses produced by a punisher often help to determine whether the punisher will reduce a prior emitted behavior.

In most cases, if a person wishes to reduce a specific target response, he should select a punisher that produces responses that interfere with that target response. If the punisher produces the same behavior the person is trying to eliminate, it is likely to be ineffective.

This general principle is illustrated by an experiment conducted by Fowler and Miller (1963). These experimenters trained rats to run down a straight runway to a goal box to receive food. Once this response had been established, the experimenters began to punish it by shocking the rats in the goal box. One group received a shock on their front paws when they stopped running. The shock caused these animals to jump backward away from the food locations. This response was incompatible with moving toward the goal box. The second group received a shock to the hind paws as they entered the goal box. This shock caused the animals to jump forward toward the food location. Obviously, this response was similar to the running response the animals were making at the time the shock was delivered. Fowler and Miller found that the running response was reduced much more in the rats that received shock on the front paws. In effect, the punisher was more effective when it produced a response that was incompatible with the target behavior.

Such findings suggest that punishment selection should be based on the particular behaviors to be eliminated. Slapping a child's hand when the child reaches out toward a hot stove may be effective because the punishment produces hand withdrawal and fear. These responses are incompatible with reaching out and exploring. How-

ever, if a child who is already fearful is crying or clinging to a parent, slapping the hand may be an ineffective punisher. In these cases the punisher produces fear and crying, the same responses the parent is trying to reduce.

THE BIOLOGICAL BASIS OF INSTRUMENTAL/OPERANT CONDITIONING

Chapter 2 discussed the idea that biological context can sometimes constrain classical conditioning. The chapter looked at examples of research investigating the neural structures and processes involved in classical conditioning. Instrumental and operant conditioning provide yet another example of the biological context of learning and memory. Researchers often have encountered biological constraints on operant conditioning, and substantial research has been directed toward discovering the neural structures and changes that serve instrumental and operant conditioning. We begin by examining examples of biological constraints on instrumental and operant conditioning.

Biological Constraints on Conditioning

In chapter 2 we discovered that sometimes animals are capable of associating certain stimuli more readily than others. Rats for example appear to be able to associate taste with illness more readily than they can associate taste with electric shock. The question of interest here is whether animals might also be genetically programmed to associate certain responses with certain outcomes more readily than other responses and outcomes. There is evidence to suggest that what was true for associating two stimuli may also be true for associating responses with reinforcers.

Bolles (1969) shows that rats are capable of quickly learning a one-way shuttle response. In this apparatus the rat is placed on one side of a barrier. A light is presented and is followed by mild electric shock. If the rat jumps over the barrier before the light stimulus is terminated, it can avoid the shock. Rats learn this task quite readily. In fact, they might learn to avoid the shock in as few as five to ten trials. However, if a two-way shuttle box is used, it takes the rat longer to acquire the task. In the two-way shuttle the rat is presented the light on one side of the barrier and must cross the barrier before the light terminates. Once it has crossed the barrier the light is turned on the side to which it just jumped, at which point the rat is required to jump back to the place where it had previously been shocked. Thus, to avoid shock the rat is required to jump from one side to the other and back. Unlike the one-way shuttle apparatus, the animal is forced to enter a place where previously it has received shock.

Even more difficult for the rat is learning to run in a wheel to avoid shock. In this apparatus the rat is placed in a running wheel. In the presence of a light stimulus if the animal runs it will avoid shock. If it freezes it will not. This is a more difficult task for the rat presumably because it is not able to escape the stimulus conditions associated with shock. More difficult still is teaching the rat to avoid shock by pressing a bar. The most difficult task is to teach a rat to rear up on its hind legs to avoid shock. Bolles argues that these findings are understandable because they reflect the animal's typical responses to danger. For rats, running and freezing are two likely behaviors in the presence of danger. The one-way shuttle apparatus takes advantage of the escape response of the rat and is quickly learned. On the other hand, running in a wheel should be more difficult to learn. Not because the rat might not naturally run in the presence of danger, but because its response does not allow it to escape the dangerous conditions. Worst of all for a rat would be to stand up in the presence or a dangerous situation. Birds or cats or other predators would be at a decided advantage if in response to their presence the rat's behavioral response was to stand up.

Bolles developed his notions about avoidance learning in 1970. In a scientific paper, Bolles argued that animals come into the world prepared to make certain responses in the presence of dangerous situations. For example, if a rat encounters a predator it might flee, freeze, or fight depending on the circumstances. If there is a perceived means of escape the rat will flee. If there is no escape path it will freeze and it will fight if the predator is too close. Bolles claimed that these behaviors were innate responses to dangerous situations and that there was little or no learning going on in these encounters. In fact, Bolles argued that if an animal had to learn to avoid a predator it would not survive very long. Bolles termed these innate responses to dangerous situations species-specific defense reactions (SSDR) (Bolles, 1970).

The phenomenon of **instinctive drift** provides another example of biological constraints on learning. Instinctive drift describes situations where instinctive behaviors interfere with the learning of a new response. We encountered one example of this phemomenon in chapter 1 (Breland & Breland, 1961). The Brelands were attempting to train a raccoon to pick up coins and deposit the coins in a cup. The raccoon learned to pick up one coin, carry it to the container, and drop the coin in the container to receive food. However, when the Brelands began teaching the raccoon to perform the same behaviors with two coins, the raccoon could not learn to drop the coins in the cup. Instead, the raccoon would rub the coins together, and dip them in the cup only to pull them back out. The persistence of this behavior made it impossible for the Brelands to continue teaching the raccoon this new trick (Breland & Breland, 1961). Thus, the raccoon's instinctive behavior of washing food before eating it interfered with the learning of a different response despite persistent efforts to reinforce the new response. The Brelands also reported cases of instinctive drift in several other species.

Does this intrusion of instinctive behavior invalidate learning principles discovered through instrumental and operant conditioning? Some authors argue that biological constraints such as instinctive drift represent critical failures of general learning principles such as operant conditioning. Other theorists acknowledge that behavior often is a result of both hereditary (phylogenetic) influences and current learning (ontogenetic influences). Even B. F. Skinner, who emphasized operant conditioning as a cause of behavior, frequently acknowledged that heredity has important effects on behavior (Skinner, 1966). For another treatment of these issues, see Seligman and Hager (1972). Although heredity clearly influences behavior, we have seen in this chapter that instrumental and operant conditioning are very effective procedures for changing behavior. Those who are interested in the ways in which the evolutionary history of the animal affects its behavior in classical and instrumental conditioning will find an excellent review on the subject by Domjan (1983).

Reinforcement Centers in the Brain

In the 1950s James Olds and Peter Milner discovered that electrical stimulation of certain brain areas could be used to reinforce the behavior of rats (Olds & Milner, 1954). In a series of experiments, these researchers implanted electrodes in various areas of rats' brains, then placed the rats in an operant chamber where each press of the lever resulted in a brief period of electrical stimulation from the electrodes. They found that electrical stimulation to several areas of the brain would reinforce the rats' behavior (Olds, 1958). Stimulation of some of these areas was a very potent reinforcer. In some cases, rats and monkeys would press the lever thousands of times per hour and continue for hours on end (Olds, 1962).

One area where electrical stimulation has reliable and powerful reinforcing effects is known as the **medial forebrain bundle,** a large bundle of nerve fibers that extends through many of the brain areas where electrical stimulation has reinforcing effects.

Research with a small number of human subjects demonstrates that electric brain stimulation can also act as a reinforcer with humans. In the 1960s, a few neurosurgeons attempted to treat epilepsy, depression, and severe pain by electrical stimulation of various brain areas. This might sound like a scene from a horror movie, but the procedures were not as severe as they might seem. The procedure is not especially dangerous and it was used only as a treatment for disorders like epilepsy. Because the brain has no pain receptors, surgeons could implant fine electrodes into areas of the patient's brain without causing discomfort. Doctors then administer very mild electric stimulation through these electrodes in an attempt to relieve the patient's symptoms. In some cases, the patients reported that the brain stimulation produced very pleasant sensations (see, for example, Delgado, 1969). Some patients requested additional brain stimulation (Delgado & Hamlin, 1960).

Operant Conditioning of Single Brain Cells. It is clear that certain brain areas are associated with the effects of reinforcement. Researchers have also investigated the possibility that reinforcement may occur at the level of individual brain cells. In a series of experiments, Stein and his colleagues have discovered evidence that the activity of individual neurons can be changed through a process similar to operant conditioning. In one of these experiments (Stein, Xue, & Belluzzi, 1993), small samples of tissue were taken from a rat's brain. These tissue samples were then kept alive in a circulating nutrient solution and placed in the experimental apparatus. This apparatus allowed the researchers to monitor the neural impulses (known as action potentials) emitted by a single neuron and to deliver minute amounts of a drug solution on to the neuron. Thus, the behavior of interest in this case was action potentials emitted by the cell, and the consequence was the delivery of the drug solution.

The particular cells used in this experiment spontaneously emit action potentials at varying intervals. At times, these cells emit bursts of several action potentials within a short period of time (for example, four action potentials within 10 milliseconds). In this particular experiment, these researchers attempted to reinforce by delivering the chemical dopamine on to the neuron

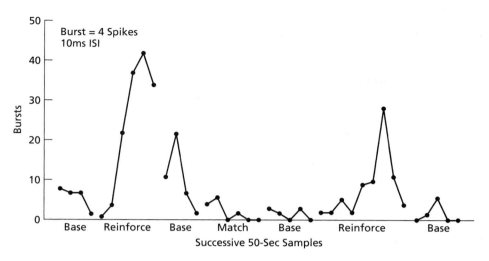

FIGURE 4.15 Operant Conditioning of a CA1 Pyramidal Cell. Operant conditioning of the activity of a CA1 pyramidal cell in a slice of dorsal hippocampus with local injections of dopamine used as reinforcement. The activity of the unit throughout seven phases of a complete experiment is shown. Each point shows the number of bursts in successive 50-s samples. Prior to the first baseline phase, a burst criterion of four or more spikes was selected. This criterion gave a burst rate for this unit that never exceeded eight per 50 s in the initial baseline period (BASE). In the reinforcement period (REINF), dopamine HC1 (1mM in 165 mM saline) was applied for 50 ms immediately after each burst; the burst rate increased to a maximum of 42 per 50 s. Following a second baseline period, the same number of dopamine injections was delivered independently of the unit's behavior as a control for possible general stimulant effects (MATCH). The number of injections was matched to that earned during the last six 50-s periods of the reinforcement phase. Bursting rates were increased by contingent dopamine injections during the reinforcement periods but were not increased when the same injections were administered noncontingently in the matched-injection period. From "A cellular analogue of operant conditioning," by L. Stein, et al., *Journal of the Experimental Analysis of Behavior,* 1993, *60,* 41–53. ©1993 by the Society for the Experimental Analysis of Behavior. Reprinted by permission.

when it emitted a burst of action potentials. Dopamine is one of several chemicals, known as neurotransmitters, that are used for communication between neurons.

The experiment consisted of several phases. During baseline phases the rate of bursts was measured, but no consequence was delivered. In reinforcement phases, each burst was followed by the delivery of dopamine. Finally, in matching phases, dopamine was delivered at various times regardless of the cell's activity. The matching phases were necessary to make sure that any increase in burst frequency was a result of reinforcement by the

dopamine and not due to the dopamine simply increasing the overall activity level of the cell. Figure 4.15 shows representative results of this experiment for one cell. These data clearly show that the rate of bursts increased during reinforcement phases, but remained at low levels during baseline and matching phases. Data from experiments such as this support the interesting possibility that an analog of operant conditioning may even occur at the level of the single cell. At this time, however, only a small number of experiments have investigated this possibility, so it is important to view the results with caution.

THE DISCRIMINATIVE STIMULUS

A familiar event during summer months is the appearance of the ice-cream truck driving down the street playing distorted children's music through a loudspeaker. Shortly after the ice-cream truck appears in the neighborhood, every child (and an occasional adult) within earshot of the music runs to the curbside where the truck has stopped. Their behavior of running to the truck is soon followed by a very potent reinforcer—ice cream.

If running to the curbside is reliably reinforced with ice cream, then the effect of this contingency should be that the children will spend much of their time running to the curbside. This is clearly not the case. Children only run to the curbside in a particular situation—when the ice-cream truck is present. When we look at examples of instrumental and operant conditioning, we usually find that particular behaviors are reinforced only when a certain stimulus is present.

A stimulus that is reliably present when a particular behavior is reinforced is called a **discriminative stimulus.** Running to the curb is followed by ice cream only when the ice-cream truck is there, and answering the phone is followed by speaking with someone only after the phone has rung. The ice-cream truck and the sound of the phone ringing are both discriminative stimuli.

After instrumental conditioning in the presence of a discriminative stimulus, the presentation of that discriminative stimulus will increase the probability of behaviors that have been reinforced in its presence. The ice-cream truck is a discriminative stimulus that evokes running to the curb; a ringing telephone is a discriminative stimulus that evokes answering the phone. The discriminative stimulus evokes the behavior, or makes a behavior more likely to occur.

It is important to note at this point that a discriminative stimulus is not the same as a conditioned or unconditioned stimulus in classical conditioning. In the case of classical conditioning, the stimuli elicit a particular response in the sense that the stimuli force the response to occur. Discriminative stimuli, in contrast, do not elicit behaviors. Discriminative stimuli make a behavior more probable, but ultimately they do not *cause* behavior to occur. It is the reinforcement contingency that controls the rate of behavior.

Due to its association with a reward, the discriminative stimulus can also be used to reward behavior. As such it is known as a secondary reinforcer. This is true for any stimulus that has been associated with a primary reinforcer. A stimulus that has been associated with a punisher can become a secondary punisher. Thus a light that has been paired with food can become a secondary reinforcer (unless it is really bad food), and a light that has been paired with electric shock can become a secondary punisher. There will be further discussion of secondary reinforcers and their impact on behavior in chapter 6.

EXTINCTION

In our discussion of classical conditioning we found that a well-learned conditioned response can be eliminated or reduced by presenting the CS regularly without the US. This decrease in the performance of the conditioned response is called extinction. In a like manner, well-learned instrumental and operant responses may be extinguished. In this case extinction occurs when an organism performs a response and no reinforcement follows. For example, if a rat has learned to press a bar or run through a maze for food, these responses can be reduced by eliminating the food that normally follows responding. When a person tries to start the car but nothing happens, the person's behavior is under extinction. In both cases, the behavior (pressing a bar or turning a key) will decrease in frequency.

We also noted while discussing classical conditioning that when some period of time is allowed to elapse after a CR has been extinguished, the conditioned response tends to reoccur. We termed this phenomenon spontaneous recovery. Spontaneous recovery also tends to occur in instrumental- and operant-conditioning paradigms. Once an instrumental response has been reduced by elimination of the reinforcement, the response tends to recover over time. As in classical conditioning, the spontaneous recovery of instrumental and operant responses can be eliminated with a series of extinction treatments.

Although extinction occurs readily in most instrumental- or operant-conditioning paradigms, the rate of extinction can vary dramatically depending on a number of variables. How resistant a response is to extinction can be influenced by the conditions that were present when the response was learned. Similarly, resistance to extinction is affected by the conditions present when extinction itself occurs.

Variables That Affect Extinction of Positively Reinforced Responses

Conditions Present During Learning. How quickly a response extinguishes depends in large part on the conditions under which it was learned. Common sense would lead us to predict that any condition that promotes rapid or strong learning should result in slower extinction. We make this prediction because it would seem that the stronger a learned response, the more difficult it should be to eliminate. Although this prediction appears logical, it is wrong. As we will see, virtually any condition that slows learning or makes learning more difficult also makes a response more difficult to extinguish. Although this general rule seems counterintuitive, it clearly holds in many cases.

As we have seen, animals learn instrumental responses faster when large reinforcer magnitudes are used. Smaller reinforcers produce slower rates of learning. Still, several experiments have shown that responses learned with small reinforcement amounts are more difficult to extinguish than responses learned for large amounts of reinforcement (see, for example, Armus, 1959; Hulse, 1958; Wagner, 1961). This type of finding is illustrated clearly in a study conducted by Roberts

(1969). Roberts trained rats to traverse a runway for reinforcers ranging from one to 25 food pellets. He then proceeded to extinguish the running response. The results of this experiment are shown in Figure 4.16, which plots the extinction performance of each reinforcement magnitude group in terms of both starting and running speeds. As indicated, the group that received one pellet for each run during learning extinguished very slowly. Groups that had received greater reinforcement amounts during acquisition extinguished progressively faster.

Another condition that tends to slow learning but makes extinction more difficult is delay of reinforcement. Here the data are in many cases conflicting. For example, some studies have shown that longer delays of reinforcement during learning slow extinction of the learned response (Capaldi & Bowen, 1964; Fehrer, 1956; Tombaugh, 1966). However, other experimenters have failed to replicate this effect (Renner, 1963; Tombaugh, 1970). In one situation, however, delay of reinforcement in learning clearly slows extinction: namely, when animals are exposed to delay of reinforcement on some, but not all, learning trials. The data consistently show that intermittent reinforcement delays during learning make extinction of the learned response more difficult (Knouse & Campbell, 1971; Tombaugh, 1970; Wike, Mellgren, & Wike, 1968).

Although both magnitude and delay of reinforcement can affect extinction, probably the most powerful influence is the schedule of reinforcement during learning. At least in mammals, in almost every case, organisms that experience intermittent reinforcement during learning show slower extinction rates than organisms that have experienced continuous reinforcement. This well-known finding is termed the partial reinforcement extinction effect (PREE).

PREE can be seen in the data from an early study by Hulse (1958). Hulse trained rats to run in a straight runway. In one group, running was reinforced with food on 100% of the trials. For a second group reinforcement occurred on only 46%

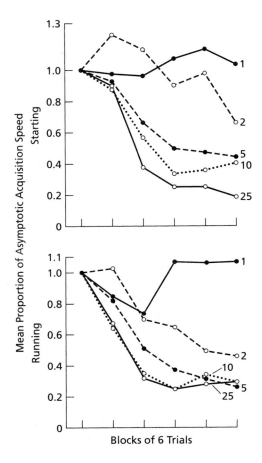

FIGURE 4.16 Extinction of the Running Response.
Rate of extinction for a running response as a function of amount of reward during learning, where 1, 2, 5, 10, and 25 refer to the number of food pellets given during learning for each response. From Roberts, 1969. From the *Journal of Comparative and Physiological Psychology*, 1969, *67*, 395–400. ©1969 by the American Psychological Assn. Reprinted by permission of the publisher and William Roberts.

In recent years it has become clear that the partial reinforcement extinction effect is not a simple phenomenon. For example, it is now known that it depends on the particular arrangement of reinforced and nonreinforced trials during learning (see, for example, Capaldi & Kassover, 1970; Spivey & Hess, 1968).

A final learning variable that appears to affect extinction is the number of learning trials an organism receives before extinction. In the case of this variable, however, the conclusions suggested by the data differ depending on the specific type of response that is studied. Several researchers have found that when rats are trained to traverse a runway, the more learning trials they receive, the more rapidly extinction occurs (Ison, 1962; Madison, 1964; North & Stimmel, 1960). On the other hand, in studies of the bar-press response, researchers typically have found that increasing the number of trials either slows extinction (Perin, 1942; S. B. Williams, 1938) or has no effect on the extinction process (D'Amato, Schiff, & Jagoda, 1962; Dyal & Holland, 1963; Uhl & Young, 1967).

For some time this conflict in evidence was attributed to the larger reinforcement amounts usually involved for runway paradigms as opposed to bar-press paradigms. Presently, however, it appears that the different effects in the two paradigms do not result simply from differences in reinforcer magnitude (see, for example, Likely & Schnitzer, 1968). As yet, there is no clear explanation of why different levels of learning affect extinction differently depending on the type of response that is studied.

Conditions Present During Extinction

The extinction of an instrumental response depends not only on how the response was learned, but also on how the response is extinguished. One of the most important variables during extinction is the intertrial interval, the period separating the extinction trials. In general, extinction is faster when extinction trials occur close together in time. Long intertrial intervals normally

of the trials. Hulse then extinguished the running in both groups. The results of the extinction treatment are presented in Figure 4.17. It is clear from these data that continuous reinforcement led to rapid extinction. However, rats that were trained on a partial-reinforcement schedule exhibited high resistance to the extinction treatment.

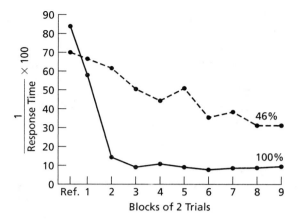

FIGURE 4.17 Continuous and Partial Reinforcement. Rates of extinction for rats given continuous and partial reinforcement during learning. (From Hulse, 1958.)

slow the extinction process significantly (see, for example, Birch, 1965; Hill & Spear, 1962; Krane & Ison, 1971).

Although this rule holds in most cases, there is an important exception. If the intertrial interval used during extinction varies widely from the intertrial interval used during learning, extinction tends to be faster. This occurs even when long intertrial intervals are used during extinction. One example of this effect comes from a study by Teichner (1952) in which rats were trained to perform an instrumental response using a 45-second intertrial interval. During the phase that measured extinction, the animals had an intertrial interval of 60, 45, or 30 seconds. Both the 30- and 60-second intertrial interval groups extinguished faster than animals exposed to a 45-second intertrial interval.

Variables That Affect Extinction of Negatively Reinforced Responses

Technically, extinction of a negatively reinforced response should involve allowing an organism to make the response and then not removing the aversive stimulus the organism has learned to es-

cape or avoid. In effect, once the organism has made the learned response, it should continue to receive aversive stimulation. Although this procedure is clearly analogous to elimination of reinforcement in positive reinforcement situations, few experimenters have utilized this approach to study extinction of negatively reinforced responses. The reason is obvious. If an organism responds and the response is accompanied by continued aversive stimulation, the response is actually being punished. Thus, it is impossible to determine whether the response is decreasing because it is being extinguished or because it is being punished.

Researchers have used other approaches to study the extinction of negatively reinforced responses. In one such procedure the contingent relationship has been removed between an organism's response and the elimination of the aversive stimulus (see, for example, Reynierse & Rizley, 1970). In this type of procedure the termination of the aversive stimulus no longer regularly accompanies the learned response. The termination of the aversive stimulus can occur before, during, or after the response. Such procedures typically result in a rapid decrease in the performance of the learned behavior and show that behavior learned through negative reinforcement will also extinguish under appropriate circumstances.

SUMMARY STATEMENTS

We have seen that the emitted behaviors of organisms are changed by the consequences of those behaviors. Emitted behaviors are increased when they are followed by either appetitive events or the prevention or termination of aversive events, and they decrease to the extent that they are followed by aversive events or the prevention of appetitive events. We also discussed some applications of instrumental and operant learning in treating psychological disorders.

We discovered that the effectiveness of reinforcement depends on a number of variables. In positive-reinforcement situations, the magnitude or quality of reinforcement was shown to increase the rate of response when these variables were increased. If reinforcement was delayed, there was a decrease in the rate of response. Finally we showed how different schedules of reinforcement affected operant behavior. In negative-reinforcement situations, amount and delay of the reinforcement, as well as characteristics of any warning stimuli, similarly affect emitted responses. In punishment paradigms, we found that the effectiveness of punishment depended primarily on the intensity and delay of the punishing stimulus, as well as the response that is produced by the punisher. In general, intense aversive stimuli suppress behavior more than less intense stimuli and immediate punishment is more effective than delayed punishment in suppressing behavior.

We also looked briefly at the biological context of instrumental and operant conditioning, including biological constraints on conditioning, brain areas involved in reinforcement, and cellular processes that may be related to reinforcement. Finally, we noted that instrumental and operant responses can be reduced by extinction procedures. Specifically, we found that extinction occurs when emitted responses no longer are followed by either positive or negative reinforcement.

5

Instrumental and Operant Conditioning: Theoretical Issues

CHAPTER OVERVIEW

The preceding chapter offered a look at a number of variables that influence instrumental and operant conditioning. Instrumental and operant conditioning play an important role in our everyday lives. They can be used to solve behavioral problems. The current chapter will delve more deeply into this issue.

Suppose you are teaching a second-grade class and you would like to use operant reinforcement to help your students spend more time on their assignments. How can you select consequences that will reinforce this behavior? Perhaps you should not use operant reinforcement at all. Can you be sure that reinforcement is really necessary for learning instead of simply giving your students a reason to perform behaviors they have already learned?

On the other hand, if one of your students is constantly throwing paper and crayons at other students, should you use punishment to reduce this problem behavior, or is there a way to reduce the behavior without using punishment? Is it wrong to use punishment? If you do use punishment, how will you select a consequence to punish the behavior and how can you ensure that the punishment will be effective?

The answers to questions such as these are critical for the effective use of instrumental and operant conditioning. Equally important is the fact that these questions are central to a more complete understanding of instrumental and operant conditioning in general. This chapter will attempt to answer these questions. To do so, it must look at theories of instrumental and operant conditioning. Theories of instrumental and operant conditioning should accomplish two aims. They must account for existing evidence and accurately predict new findings. We will also ask if there are any facts that each theory cannot explain. As we did in chapter 3, we will use these questions to help us evaluate each theory and to understand the evolution of instrumental- and operant-conditioning theories.

The present chapter deals with some of the major theoretical issues that have arisen in the study of instrumental and operant conditioning. In considering theoretical issues with classical conditioning, we found that those theories focused on a small number of important questions concerning classical conditioning. The same is true for theoretical issues surrounding instrumental and operant conditioning. Theoretical analyses of instrumental and operant conditioning also are focused on a small number of theoretical issues that are critical for our understanding of instrumental learning situations.

When it comes to theories of instrumental and operant conditioning, the theoretical issue that receives the most attention is a seemingly simple question: What makes a reinforcer reinforcing? One might be tempted to reply that pleasant events reinforce behavior, or that relieving a basic need such as hunger or thirst is reinforcing. As we look more closely at research addressing this question, we will find that the answer is not at all simple. Sometimes unpleasant events can be used as reinforcers. Sometimes seemingly uninteresting events are reinforcing. The theories that have attempted to answer this question are fascinating, and the experiments conducted to evaluate the theories are equally interesting.

A second theoretical question in instrumental conditioning can also be stated quite simply: What does the reinforcer do? Is reinforcement necessary for an organism to learn, or does reinforcement instead provide a reason for organisms to perform what they have learned already?

Third, we will examine the major theories that deal with the extinction of operant responses. Basically, these theories attempt to explain why the elimination of reinforcement results in the decrease of a previously learned behavior. Once again, this issue has important theoretical implications, but it also has important implications for dealing with operant-learning situations in our everyday lives. For example, imagine that a dog has been consistently begging for food while its owner eats dinner. Presumably, this behavior has resulted from the fact that the behavior of begging at the dinner table has previously been reinforced with scraps of food from the owner's plate. To implement an extinction procedure to reduce or eliminate the dog's begging, the owner does not give in and feed him scraps of food. If the owner is consistent in the extinction of this behavior, the dog's begging will eventually subside. But why?

In this case, the answer to another theoretical question about the process of extinction might help. Perhaps the dog stops begging because he is engaging in other behaviors instead, such as grooming, scratching his owner's leg, or sleeping. On the other hand, maybe the dog stops begging because the present situation (begging = no food!) is so different from the good times when table scraps were readily available that behaviors learned during those good times do not generalize to this new situation.

Finally, this chapter will look at theoretical issues concerning punishment. It will analyze whether punishment is the opposite of reinforcement by directly reducing the rate of behavior, or if punishment functions in some other way, such as causing an organism to temporarily suppress a particular behavior. That is, does punishment cause direct reduction of a behavior, or does it only cause the organism to suppress temporarily behavior that would occur in the absence of punishment? If the first possibility is correct, then punishment could be a useful way to reduce problem behaviors. However, if the second possibility is correct, then punishment may not be a good way to reduce behavior because the problem behavior simply will reappear later on after punishment is no longer being delivered. This chapter will also consider whether the effects of punishment are specific to the punished behavior or if punishment causes a reduction in all behaviors.

THE NATURE OF REINFORCEMENT

Primary and Secondary Reinforcers

Chapter 4 defined a *reinforcer* as "any event that causes preceding behaviors to increase in frequency." This definition is fine in a textbook, but when people attempt to reinforce behavior in natural settings such as the classroom, the problem becomes one of determining ahead of time what events should function as reinforcers.

There are two general classes of reinforcers. The first consists of all those events that can serve as reinforcers simply by virtue of their natural characteristics. These events, called **primary reinforcers,** include food, water, sexual stimulation, the reduction of pain, and many others. These events increase the occurrence of emitted responses, and they work the same way in virtually all species. In other words, primary reinforcers are like unconditioned stimuli. Both are capable of producing behavior changes naturally without the benefit of any prior learning.

The preceding chapter looked at how variations in primary reinforcement can influence operant behaviors. Still, many of our everyday emitted behaviors appear to be reinforced by a different kind of event. For example, we perform certain work duties because these responses are followed with receiving money. Likewise, children may learn table manners because their parents give verbal approval for appropriate behavior. In the same way, a dog may learn to retrieve a ball just because the response is followed by a word of praise. In all these cases emitted responses are repeated and learned, but the reinforcers used do not qualify as primary reinforcers. There is nothing about a green piece of paper or a spoken word that is inherently reinforcing. None of these consequences have an inherent or natural capacity to reinforce behavior.

Instead, these consequences are examples of what we call **secondary or conditioned reinforcers.** Secondary reinforcers are events that function as reinforcers because of their consistent association with one or more primary reinforcers. Money is a good example of a conditioned reinforcer. There is nothing about a piece of green and white paper engraved with the image of a former president that is inherently reinforcing. To convince yourself that money is not a natural reinforcer, try to imagine reinforcing a rat's bar-press response by dropping a dollar bill into its food cup. Similarly, consider how effective money would be as a reinforcer for an infant's smile. Money, praise, and verbal approval are not naturally reinforcing events. They serve as reinforcers only when they have been associated in some way with primary reinforcers. In other words, these events called conditioned reinforcers acquire the capacity to reinforce behavior only through their prior associations with primary reinforcing events. Through conditioned reinforcement, a wide variety of stimuli can come to serve as reinforcers.

To see how a stimulus becomes a conditioned reinforcer, consider some examples from the laboratory. In one well-known experiment Saltzman (1949) used food reinforcement to train rats to run down a straight runway. The goal box in which the food was delivered was white for some animals and black for others. After this training, Saltzman placed the rats in a maze that contained two goal boxes. One goal box was identical to the one used in the runway; the other was a neutral color. Although no primary reward was ever delivered, the rats learned to navigate through the maze to reach the goal box that was like the one previously used in the runway. That is, during the maze-learning phase of this experiment, the goal boxes alone served to reinforce the choice response. These stimuli acquired their reinforcing capacity because of their prior association with a food reward.

Bugelski (1938) obtained a similar result. This experimenter trained rats to press a bar for a food reward that was always accompanied by a clicking sound. Later he attempted to extinguish the bar-press response by eliminating the food. During these extinction trials, some animals continued to receive the clicking sound after every response while others did not. Bugelski found that the presentation of the clicking sound continued to reinforce bar-pressing even though food was no longer available. Apparently the clicking sound had acquired the capacity to reinforce responding through its prior association with food.

Thus, as we have illustrated, both primary reinforcers and conditioned reinforcers will function to increase and maintain operant behavior.

Theories of Primary Reinforcement

To examine various theories of primary reinforcement, it is helpful to look at two broad types of theories that attempt to explain why a particular event is or is not reinforcing. The first type of theory proposes that it is something about a particular stimulus event that makes it reinforcing. We will call these theories stimulus-based theories of reinforcement. The second type of theory proposes that a reinforcing event provides an organism with an opportunity to engage in a particular behavior and it is that behavior that functions as a reinforcer. We will call these theories response-based theories of reinforcement. This distinction may not seem clear at first. An example of food reinforcement will help to clarify the distinction.

In a simple case, an animal presses a lever because in the past that behavior has been followed by the delivery of food. There are two possibilities that might explain why food is reinforcing in this instance. According to stimulus-property theories of reinforcement, it is something about the food itself that makes this stimulus a reinforcer. Perhaps it is because food tastes good, or because the food reduces hunger, but in any event, stimulus-property theories propose that there is some quality of the food itself that results in its reinforcing function. On the other hand, response-property theories propose that the delivery of food allows the rat to engage in the behavior of eating and it is the response of eating that is reinforcing.

Stimulus-Based Theories of Reinforcement

Hull's Drive-Reduction Hypothesis. Clark Hull (1943), in his classic book *Principles of Behavior,* developed one of the earliest and most influential views of primary reinforcement. Hull conceived of learning as an adaptive process that allows organisms to cope with the biological need states that threaten survival. According to this view, biological needs develop whenever an organism's body becomes depleted in terms of any life-supporting substance (for example, fluids or nutrients). Need states also arise when an organism encounters physical stimuli that are capable of producing tissue damage (for example, painful stimuli). Hull believed that biological needs caused states of tension called drives. For example, the biological need for nutrients leads to the state we call hunger. Likewise, the need for fluids results in the drive state we know as thirst.

Hull viewed these drives as motivational states that are capable of energizing, increasing, or driving behavior. For example, organisms that have been deprived of food or water or that are in pain become more active because of these events. Their enhanced activity increases the likelihood that they will encounter stimuli or situations that will provide food, water, or relief from pain. An active organism is simply more likely than an inactive organism to contact food, water, or safety. When an organism encounters a stimulus that satisfies one of these biological needs, the associated drive state is reduced and the organism's motivation to respond decreases. By emphasizing reinforcement as reducing biological needs, Hull's theory reflects two of our organizing themes. First, this theory assumes that operant reinforcement is an adaptive process that promotes survival. Second, Hull's theory also emphasizes the biological nature of learning.

For present purposes, the most important point in Hull's analysis is that organisms do not respond in a random manner each time a drive state arises. Instead they learn to repeat the behaviors that previously have produced stimuli that relieved that particular drive state. If an organism is in a particular drive state and a response leads to a reduction in that drive state, the organism will tend to repeat that response whenever the same drive state arises. Thus, according to Hull, stimuli that reduce drives are capable of reinforcing emitted behaviors. In this sense, Hull defined a primary reinforcer as a drive-reducing stimulus.

By equating primary reinforcement with drive reduction, Hull gave us one of the first testable hypotheses concerning the nature of reinforcement. Furthermore, this hypothesis appears to be a powerful one, as it seems to describe so many of the primary reinforcers we commonly encounter. Obviously, food reinforces behavior when we are hungry just as water will reinforce behavior when we are thirsty. In certain circumstances, food and water qualify as drive-reducing stimuli, because both are capable of reducing certain drive states. Clearly, a number of reinforcing events fall into the category of drive-reducing stimuli. Thus, Hull's theory accounts for a number of known facts about reinforcers. However, this theory also predicts that any event that reduces a drive state will function as a reinforcer. Thus, to test Hull's theory further, the question is whether all reinforcers reduce drives and whether all stimuli that reduce drives function as reinforcers.

One of the first complications with the drive-reduction hypothesis was noted by Miller and Kessen (1952), who trained hungry rats to go to one goal box of a T-maze. They rewarded one group for this response by allowing them to drink milk in the goal box. Two other groups were fitted with tubes that allowed the experimenters to pump fluids directly into the animals' stomachs. One group received milk in their stomachs for entering the correct goal box, while the other received a saline-and-water solution. Miller and Kessen found that the task was learned best by the rats that actually drank milk in the goal box. Rats that received milk through the fistulas learned faster than those receiving saline, but not as fast as those that had been allowed to consume the milk.

Miller and Kessen found that the milk was a more effective reinforcer when the rats were allowed to taste it than when it was simply pumped into the stomach. This result suggests that there may be more to reinforcement than the reduction of drives.

Other problems associated with the drive-reduction idea have been pointed out in a series of studies conducted by Sheffield and his colleagues. In one such set of studies, Sheffield and Roby (1950) demonstrated that rats would learn emitted responses followed by delivery of a saccharine solution. This finding does not fit well with the drive-reduction hypothesis, since saccharine is a nonnutritive substance that fills no biological need. This means that a substance that is incapable of reducing a hunger drive also is still capable of reinforcing the responses of a hungry animal. To explain this finding within a drive-reduction framework, saccharine is a *conditioned* reinforcer but not a *primary* reinforcer. For example, one might argue that sweet-tasting substances are rewarding because the taste has been present when the animals have ingested substances (sugars) that are drive reducers. Such a mechanism is possible, but it appears unlikely in this case. Sheffield and Roby showed that saccharine continued to reinforce responding even when numerous learning trials were used. They argued convincingly that ample experiences were given to allow the rats to learn that the taste of saccharine was not associated with hunger reduction. Still, saccharine remained an effective reinforcer (see, also, Sheffield, Roby, & Campbell, 1954).

Another experiment argues against the drive-reduction view of reinforcement. Sheffield, Wulff, and Backer (1951) trained male rats to traverse a runway and enter a goal box. To reinforce this behavior they allowed the males to mount female rats in the goal box and to begin copulation. They did not, however, allow the males to ejaculate. Rather, the copulating males were removed from the females before ejaculation could occur. These experimenters found that the males rapidly learned the response that led to this so-called reinforcer. Clearly, the opportunity to begin copulation was reinforcing, even though the opportunity for orgasm was blocked.

Sheffield and his colleagues argued that the reinforcer in this case was not drive or tension reducing at all. On the contrary, this form of reinforcement appears to involve an increase in the drive or tension state. One might of course argue that the rats in this study continued to respond because they anticipated that copulation would ultimately lead to drive reduction, but this argument is not correct. None of the male rats in this study had ever copulated before the experiment. Thus, there was no prior experience upon which such an anticipation could have been based. It appears clear that the behavior of these animals was being reinforced by the pleasant sensations of copulation, which could only have served to increase their sexual tension states.

A final group of studies that presents problems for the drive-reduction hypothesis concerns the tendency of organisms to seek out additional sources of stimulation. We all know that some individuals ride roller coasters, jump out of airplanes, and drive at high speeds simply because of the excitement these activities generate. It is clear that such activities are reinforcing in many cases because these individuals tend to repeat the behaviors that lead to these forms of stimulation. This phenomenon has been demonstrated numerous times in laboratory experiments. For example, some studies have shown that rats would learn to press a bar if the only reward for doing so was the onset of a light (Kish, 1966). Similarly, Moon and Lodahl (1956) found that monkeys would learn a bar-press response in order to have a room light turned off. The same kinds of findings have been reported when the onsets and offsets of auditory stimuli have been used (see, for example, Kish & Antonitis, 1956).

Probably one of the best-known studies of this type was conducted by Butler (1954), who trained monkeys to push open the door to their cage enclosures. The consequence of this behavior was the opportunity to view another cage in the laboratory. In some cases the other cage was empty, while in other cases it contained either a food arrangement, a moving toy train, or another monkey. Each of these stimulus arrangements reinforced the door-opening behavior. However, response frequency was highest when another monkey or the toy train was used.

These studies and many others suggest that increases in stimulation can reinforce behavior (see Eisenberger, 1972, for a review of these studies). Such findings are inconsistent with the drive-reduction hypothesis for two reasons. First, we know of no identifiable biological need for increases in stimulation, except in young, developing organisms (see Wiesel & Hubel, 1965). In general, a lack of stimulation has little negative impact on an organism's functioning unless the stimulus deprivation is severe (see Bexton, Heron, & Scott, 1954). This makes it difficult to argue that the opportunity to increase visual or auditory stimulation satisfies any primary biological need. Second, like the sexual reinforcement findings of Sheffield, these studies indicate that increases in an organism's overall level of tension may be just as reinforcing as reductions in such tension. This conclusion is clearly at odds with the drive-reduction hypothesis.

To account for these anomalous findings, some drive-reduction proponents have hypothesized the existence of additional drive states such as the "drive to explore" (see, for example, Fowler, 1965). Obviously, if such a drive existed, we could say that exploring or seeking out stimulation was reinforcing because it reduced the exploratory drive. Most researchers, however, have been unconvinced by these explanations. The most common conclusion is that Hull identified a condition that is sufficient for reinforcement, but not one that is necessary. In other words, all events that reduce drives will act as reinforcers, but an event need not reduce a drive in order to function as a reinforcing event.

Optimal Arousal Hypotheses. From the discussion thus far, it would appear that events of at least two kinds qualify as reinforcers. First, organisms that experience high drive states tend to repeat the responses that lead to the reduction of those drive states. In other cases, organisms appear to respond for the sake of increasing their tension or drive states. Given this diversity of reinforcing events, we might question whether it is possible to find a common mechanism for all primary reinforcers. One proposal featuring the existence of such a common mechanism has been termed the **optimal arousal hypothesis.**

Several variations of the optimal arousal position have been proposed (see, for example, Berlyne, 1963; Fiske & Maddi, 1961; Hebb, 1955; Leuba, 1955). Most of these hypotheses share a common theme: namely, that organisms function optimally under an intermediate (or optimal) level of environmental stimulation. Just as important, these hypotheses propose that, under conditions of less-than-optimal arousal, certain stimuli can restore an optimal level of stimulation. Furthermore, organisms are motivated to achieve a certain amount of arousal that can occur only under intermediate levels of stimulation. These hypotheses suggest that either increases or decreases in stimulation can serve as reinforcers, as long as the changes help the organism to maintain an intermediate amount of stimulation and, thus, an optimal level of arousal.

For example, if an organism is hungry, the hunger produces a high level of internal stimulation. Food serves as a reinforcer in this case because it satisfies the hunger and reduces the amount of internal stimulation to an intermediate level. On the other hand, organisms that are bored experience low levels of stimulation. Thus, for these organisms stimulus changes and opportunities for exploration are reinforcing because such events increase stimulation to an intermediate level. Obviously, such hypotheses appear, on the surface at least, to be capable of explaining almost any reinforcing effect. If an increase in stimulation is reinforcing, we need only assume that the organism's original level of stimulation was too low. If a response is reinforced by a decrease in stimulation, we simply assume that the level of stimulation was too high. In effect, such hypotheses appear to provide a ready explanation for the apparent reinforcing effects of any event.

Despite its seeming advantages, the optimal-arousal notion has never had a major impact on the thinking of most learning researchers. This lack of interest most probably results from two factors. First, although it is suggested that reinforcement depends on changes in an organism's state of arousal, these hypotheses have never explained clearly how an organism's arousal level should be measured or what events will consistently change the level of arousal. There has even been some disagreement among proponents of this view concerning what the term *arousal* really means. Obviously, this confusion over the concept and the measurement of arousal presents a real problem. If we are unable to measure an organism's arousal level before a learning trial, how can we predict whether an increase or a decrease in stimulation is likely to be reinforcing? In effect, these hypotheses fail to provide us with a means of predicting when a certain event will be reinforcing and when it will not. Instead they offer a way of accounting for effects that have already been observed.

The second problem associated with these hypotheses is that they appear to make incorrect predictions in certain situations. For example, these hypotheses state that hunger produces a high level of internal stimulation. Thus, this view must predict that a hungry organism always should seek to reduce its level of stimulation to attain an optimal level of arousal. Furthermore, a hungry organism should be reinforced only by events that reduce stimulation. Neither of these predictions is upheld by the data. Several studies have shown, for instance, that hungry animals explore novel stimuli to a greater extent than satiated animals (see, for example, Fowler, Blond, & Dember, 1959; Glickman & Jensen, 1961). That is, animals that supposedly are already over stimulated seek out additional stimulation. Also, it has been shown that the opportunity to explore is a more effective reinforcer for hungry rats than for those that are satiated (Richards & Leslie, 1961). Such a result is inconsistent with the optimal-arousal view. It indicates that the opportunity to explore can serve as a reinforcer even when organisms are already highly stimulated.

Response-Based Theories of Reinforcement

Both the drive-reduction and optimal-arousal hypotheses represented attempts to define reinforcement in terms of stimulus characteristics. By focusing on the nature of the stimulus an organism experiences following some response, both attempt to specify the characteristics that enable a stimulus to serve as a reinforcer. As we have seen, such attempts have had only partial success at best. For this reason, some theorists have proposed that we should focus on the nature of the response a consequence allows an organism to make following an operant response, rather than the consequential stimulus the organism experiences. For example, instead of regarding food as being an inherently reinforcing stimulus, these theories contend that it is the behavior of eating that is the reinforcing event. Organisms are seen as learning a behavior because that behavior produces an opportunity to eat, not because the behavior leads to a particular stimulus such as food.

In one of the first hypotheses that dealt with responses as reinforcers (Sheffield, Roby, & Campbell, 1954; Sheffield, 1966), Sheffield proposed that reinforcement depends on the vigor or persistence of a **consummatory** response. According to Sheffield, when any behavior is followed by a vigorous or persistent consummatory response, reinforcement of the behavior is strong. The less vigorous or persistent the consummatory response, the less well it can serve as a reinforcer. In one sense, this hypothesis is not very different from the theories of reinforcement that concentrated on the characteristics of a "reinforcing stimulus." Sheffield himself notes that the vigor of a consummatory response often depends on the characteristics of the stimulus being consumed. For example, very palatable foods elicit stronger eating responses than do less tasty foods. Still, this hypothesis emphasizes the dependence of reinforcement on the response made possible by some reinforcer, not on what the reinforcing stimulus does for the organism's state of motivation or arousal. If the stimulus plays any role in reinforcement, it influences the consummatory response, which itself serves as the reinforcer.

Obviously, such a view has the advantage of making it unnecessary to look for some common effect that all rewarding stimuli have on an organism's internal state. According to this view, it makes no difference that saccharine fails to reduce hunger, while sugar does reduce hunger. It also makes little difference that novel stimuli and sexual stimulation appear to enhance rather than decrease states of tension. What is important is that each of these stimuli elicits a consummatory behavior—each, in other words, is capable of producing a reinforcing event.

To bolster his view, Sheffield published results from studies in which stimuli of several types were presented to rats after they ran down a straight runway. Some of the stimuli were nutritive substances; others were not. Some of the substances were novel, and others were familiar. Sheffield and his colleagues found that none of these characteristics influenced the degree to which the running response was reinforced by these stimuli. Rather, these researchers found a direct relationship between the speed of the running response and the vigor with which the animals consumed the presented stimulus (Sheffield, Roby, & Campbell, 1954).

Clearly, Sheffield's consummatory response hypothesis seems to have substantial power in identifying reinforcing events. There are, however, two problems with this notion. First, several researchers have failed to find a direct correspondence between the vigor of consummatory responding and the degree of instrumental behavior preceding that responding (Collier, Knarr, & Marx, 1961; Goodrich, 1960; Snyder & Hulse, 1961). This failure suggests that the vigor of consummatory responding may not be related directly to the reinforcement in an instrumental conditioning situation. Even more problematic are some data we discussed earlier. Recall that Miller and Kessen (1952) found that allowing animals to drink milk was more reinforcing than simply pumping milk into the rats' stomachs, although loading milk directly into the stomach still served as a reinforcer. Such a finding is difficult to explain if we assume that reinforcement depends on consummatory responding, since the rats which received milk loaded directly into their stomachs never made a consummatory response (see also Hull, Livingston, Rouse, & Barker, 1951). Thus, even the proposition that reinforcement depends on consummatory behavior apparently does not account for all the stimuli that function as reinforcers.

The Premack Principle. The next step in the evolution of theories of reinforcement is the reinforcement theory proposed by Premack (1965, 1971). Premack's view is similar to Sheffield's in that reinforcement is defined in terms of response, not stimulus, characteristics. A major difference, however, is that Premack proposed that any kind of emitted response (not just a consummatory response) can serve to reinforce operant behavior. Basically, Premack suggested that any response that is preferred by an organism can serve to reinforce the performance of a less preferred response. For example, if a child prefers eating over studying, the opportunity to eat can be used to reinforce studying. By the same token, if the child prefers studying to washing dishes, the opportunity to study will reinforce dishwashing. This hypothesis views reinforcement as a relative matter. There are no responses (or stimuli) that will always serve as reinforcers or nonreinforcers. Whether a given behavior can act as a reinforcer depends on an organism's preference for that behavior relative to other behaviors.

To test this kind of hypothesis, one must determine an organism's preference for different behaviors. Premack suggests that the most reliable measure of preference is simply the percentage of time an organism spends engaged in different behaviors. For example, we might place a rat in a cage that contains a bar and a running wheel. Then, for the next hour we could measure the amount of time spent running and the amount of time spent bar-pressing. If the rat spends much more time running on the wheel than pressing

the bar, we can presume that wheel-running is preferred over bar-pressing.

Over time, Premack and others have conducted numerous experiments that demonstrate the utility of this theory of reinforcement. Laboratory experiments have demonstrated the value of the Premack principle in studies involving manipulatory behaviors in monkeys (Premack, 1963), consummatory behaviors in rats (Bauermeister & Schaeffer, 1974), and social behaviors in nursery-school children (Homme, DeBaca, Devine, Steinhorst, & Rickert, 1963). In all these cases, the opportunity to engage in a preferred behavior has been used to reinforce less probable or less preferred responses.

The Premack principle is also effective in real-life situations. In one such experiment, Premack (1959) allowed first-graders free access to a pinball machine and a candy dispenser. To determine each child's preferences, he recorded the time they spent operating each machine. Several days after the preference test, the children were returned to the experimental setting. Premack found that he could increase the children's performance of their less-preferred behavior by following it with the opportunity to engage in the response that was more preferred. For example, if a child preferred the operation of the candy machine, he was able to increase pinball playing by following this behavior with an opportunity to operate the candy machine. Importantly, he also demonstrated that opportunities to perform the less-preferred response would not function to reinforce the preferred behavior.

The Premack principle also has been used to improve the job performance of employees working at a Burger King restaurant. Welsh, Bernstein, and Luthans (1992) first had the restaurant employees identify the criteria of good job performance at each of the restaurant's workstations and also asked each employee to choose his or her favorite workstation. For seven weeks, the experimenters then recorded the employees' performance under normal working conditions at each of these workstations to determine their normal (baseline) levels of performance. After this baseline period, the researchers implemented an intervention wherein five of the employees (the experimental subjects) were allowed the opportunity to work at their favorite workstation whenever their performance exceeded baseline performance at one of the other workstations. Other employees who worked under normal conditions during the study served as control subjects. The results of this study showed that the intervention produced substantial improvement in the experimental subjects' performance at all workstations compared to the control subjects. Thus, this experiment provides another example of the broad applicability of the Premack principle.

Premack's theory represents a clear break from attempts to define reinforcement in terms of stimulus characteristics. It has resulted in successful real-world applications, and it has encouraged the performance of numerous experiments testing this theory. Still, as with any theory, some experiments have produced findings that are inconsistent with the Premack principle. Interestingly, these findings were also difficult to reconcile with Sheffield's view. For example, in a study such as Miller and Kessen's (1952), how does reinforcement occur when the organism makes no overt consummatory response after an operant behavior, but instead simply receives a milk injection into the stomach? In fairness, we should note that these findings have proven difficult to explain even by very recent theories of reinforcement that explain reinforcement in terms of responses (e.g., Allison, 1993; Timberlake & Allison, 1974).

Much more important are findings that, under some conditions, low-probability responses can reinforce responses having a higher probability of occurrence (For example, see Eisenberger, Karpman, & Trattner, 1967; Mazur, 1975). These experiments present significant difficulties for the Premack principle because a fundamental assumption of Premack's theory is that a high-probability response should always function as a reinforcer for a lower-probability response.

To be fair, Premack recognized that preferences for different behaviors do not remain static. First he suggested that **response deprivation** (depriving an organism of the opportunity to make a response) tends to increase an organism's preference for that response. This increase in preference is particularly evident if an organism is unable to respond at the level at which it normally would choose to respond. Second, Premack has indicated that **response satiation** can also occur. In this case an organism's preference for a particular response can decrease when the performance of a response has been allowed to occur. Thus, it is possible that response A can reinforce response B for a period of time, but at some point response A may become less preferred simply because it has been performed so often (satiation of response A has occurred). When this occurs, not only will response A cease being a reinforcer, but it will become possible for response B to reinforce response A. Premack recognized that response preferences can shift over time as a function of how much a response has been performed.

Although Premack recognized the effects of response deprivation and response satiation on the reinforcing capacity of a particular response, these effects are not included in the formal statement of the Premack principle. The effects of response deprivation and satiation were later included by other theorists (Allison, 1976, 1983; Timberlake, 1980; Timberlake & Allison, 1974) who proposed the **response disequilibrium** hypothesis as a refinement and extension of the Premack principle (see also Staddon, 1979; Timberlake, 1984). We will now turn our attention to examining this theory of reinforcement.

The Response-Disequilibrium Hypothesis

Timberlake and Allison (1974) proposed the first formal statement of the response disequilibrium hypothesis. Like Sheffield's theory and the Premack principle, the response-disequilibrium hypothesis proposes that reinforcement results from the opportunity to engage in a particular behavior, rather than the nature of the stimulus that is presumed to function as a reinforcer. Despite this similarity, the response-disequilibrium hypothesis represents a significant departure from previous theories of reinforcement, primarily because this theory proposes that reinforcement is not **transituational.** That is, the same stimulus or response may or may not serve as a reinforcer in all situations. Second, this theory also provides an account of punishment by specifying the situations in which requiring a certain behavior can function as a punisher. We will discuss the application of the response-disequilibrium hypothesis to punishment situations later in this chapter. Most importantly, a clear implication of this theory is that the reinforcing or punishing function of an event can change from one situation to another, and can even change within the course of a single conditioning session.

Much like the Premack principle, the response-disequilibrium hypothesis requires observation of an organism's baseline preference for different behaviors and arrangement of a situation wherein access to one behavior can be used to reinforce performance of another behavior. Although the theories are similar in this respect, several critical differences exist between them. To discover how the response-disequilibrium hypothesis specifies the necessary and sufficient conditions for reinforcement, we will consider a common example.

Suppose that you are a second-grade teacher and you want to increase the amount of time that your students spend reading. To clearly examine the response-disequilibrium hypothesis, let us focus on the behavior of a single student. According to the Premack principle and the response-disequilibrium hypothesis, you should first determine the baseline rate of each behavior by allowing your students free access to playing and reading while recording the amount of time spent on each activity. To do this, you allow your students free access to playing and reading for one hour. Imagine that the student we are considering spends 10 minutes reading and 50 minutes playing during this one-hour baseline. You now

have an estimate of the baseline rates of each behavior for this student.

Note that the Premack principle simply states that, under these circumstances, you can reinforce this student's reading (the less preferred response) by making access to play time (the more preferred response) contingent on reading. The response-disequilibrium hypothesis makes the same prediction in this case, but this theory allows for many additional predictions that the Premack principle cannot accommodate. To further examine this theory, we must now introduce the formal expression of the response-disequilibrium hypothesis. To explain this theory more clearly, we are using notation that is somewhat different from the original statement of this theory (see Timberlake & Farmer-Dougan, 1991).

In the following inequality, we include four terms. The first is RT, target response, or the behavior that we wish to reinforce. The second term is RC, the consequence response, the behavior that will be used as the reinforcing consequence by allowing access to this behavior contingent upon occurrence of the target behavior. The other two terms are BT and BC, which represent the baseline rates of the target behavior and the consequence behavior, respectively. The response-disequilibrium hypothesis specifies that reinforcement of the target response will occur when we create a situation wherein access to the two behaviors RT and RC is controlled according to the following inequality:

$$Rt/Rc > Bt/Bc \quad \text{Inequality 5.1}$$

This inequality specifies that reinforcement of the target response RT will occur when we create a situation such that the required ratio of the target response (Rt) to the consequence response (Rc) is greater than the baseline ratio of the target behavior (Bt) to the consequence behavior (Bc).

In the case of the second-grade student, Bt (the baseline rate of reading) was 10 minutes in a one-hour period compared to Bc (the baseline rate of playing), which was 50 minutes in the same one-hour period. By substituting these values into the inequality from Inequality 5.2, the result is

$$Rt/Rc > 10/50 \quad \text{Inequality 5.2}$$

and we can simplify these values to

$$Rt/Rc > 1/5 \quad \text{Inequality 5.3}$$

In this case, then, the response-disequilibrium hypothesis predicts that reinforcement of reading RT will occur when we create a situation that requires a ratio of RT to RC (reading to playing) that is greater than 1:5.

To put this theory to work, suppose that you implement a program where this student must read for 20 minutes in order to earn the opportunity to play for 40 minutes. When we substitute these values in our equation, we get

$$20/40 > 1/5 \quad \text{Inequality 5.4}$$

which simplifies to

$$1/2 > 1/5 \quad \text{Inequality 5.5}$$

In this case, 1/2 is greater than 1/3 so response-disequilibrium hypothesis predicts that reading would be reinforced for this student.

This theory assumes that an organism's behavior under baseline conditions represents an equilibrium of dividing effort between the available responses. When some conditioning procedure does not allow the organism to maintain this equilibrium, the procedure creates a condition of disequilibrium and reinforcement (or punishment) will result.

In the present example, the student's equilibrium was to spend 1 minute reading for each 5 minutes spent playing. This student is then required to spend two minutes reading to gain 4 minutes of access to playing. Under these conditions, if the student continued to read at the same rate of 10 minutes per hour, he would be allowed to read for only 20 minutes per hour. The predicted result is that the student's rate of reading would increase, which is to say that access to playing would reinforce reading. A number of experiments in the laboratory and in real-life settings support this prediction (for example, see

Donnelan, et al., 1988; Lattal, 1969; Kazdin, 1980; Sulzer-Azaroff & Mayer, 1977).

The response-disequilibrium hypothesis makes the same prediction as Premack's theory in this situation. That is, access to a preferred response will reinforce a less-preferred response. The critical difference between these theories lies in the fact that the response disequilibrium hypothesis predicts that access to the less-preferred response can be used to reinforce the preferred response if we create the right conditions. This prediction is clearly a departure from Premack's theory and represents a major advance in theories of reinforcement. A prediction like this also has significant applications for using instrumental and operant conditioning in everyday situations. To understand this prediction of response-disequilibrium theory, let us reconsider our example of instrumental conditioning in second-grade students by imagining that we instead wanted to reinforce the rate of playing by allowing access to reading.

Recall that our observed ratio of reading to playing was 1/5 (10 minutes of reading for every 50 minutes of playing). However, playing is now our target behavior (RT) and reading is now the response we will use as the reinforcing consequence (RC). Our baseline rates are also different now. The baseline rate of our target behavior (BT) is 50 minutes per hour, while the baseline rate of our consequence behavior (BC) is 10 minutes per hour. Substituting these values into the response disequilibrium inequality we see that, in order to reinforce playing with access to reading, we must meet the following conditions

$$Rt/Rc > 5/1 \quad \text{Inequality 5.6}$$

and these values reduce to

$$Rt/Rc > 5 \quad \text{Inequality 5.7}$$

which means that to reinforce playing with reading, we must set up a situation where we require a ratio of playing to reading that is greater than 5.

To accomplish this goal, you implement a program where the student must spend 10 minutes playing (Rt) for every one minute spent reading (Rc). When we substitute these values into our inequality the result is

$$10/1 > 5 \quad \text{Inequality 5.8}$$

and these values reduce to

$$10 > 5 \quad \text{Inequality 5.9}$$

Now, your program requires a ratio of playing to reading that is 10/1 and this is indeed greater than the baseline ratio of playing to reading, which is 5/1. In this case, the response-disequilibrium hypothesis predicts that access to reading actually will reinforce playing so the rate of playing will increase. This prediction of the response-disequilibrium hypothesis is clearly contrary to Premack's theory because we have predicted that access to a less-preferred behavior will reinforce a more-preferred behavior.

One way to understand how a less-preferred behavior can reinforce a more-preferred behavior is to consider that our contingency which now requires 10 minutes of playing for access to one minute of reading creates a situation where the student cannot read as much as during baseline conditions. This situation would result in approximately six minutes of reading per hour which is below the student's baseline reading rate of 10 minutes per hour. As a result, this student is deprived of reading below baseline levels and this deprivation makes access to reading function as a reinforcer. For this reason, the response-disequilibrium hypothesis sometimes is also referred to as the response deprivation/satiation hypothesis (Dougher, 1983), or the molar-equilibrium theory (Timberlake, 1980). Today, these theories are referenced under the term *behavioral regulation theories* (Timberlake, 1984, 1993).

Although the prediction of a less-preferred response reinforcing a more-preferred response may seem unexpected, a large number of studies have supported this prediction in many situations. These experiments include laboratory experiments with rats (Eisenberger, Karpmann, & Trattner, 1967; Mazur, 1975) and applications of the response disequilibrium hypothesis in several real-world settings. For example, Konarski (1980) first observed that grade-school children preferred coloring pictures to solving arithmetic problems. This observation is probably not surprising to any of us. What might seem surprising, however, is that Konarski supported the response-disequilibrium hypothesis by showing that, under the proper circumstances, the opportunity to perform the less-preferred behavior (arithmetic) actually reinforced the more preferred behavior (coloring).

The response-disequilibrium hypothesis has also been used effectively and creatively to produce positive behavior changes in several populations and situations. In one such study, Dougher (1983) controlled access to coffee drinking for hospitalized schizophrenics to control the rates of other disruptive or inappropriate behaviors. Other investigators have used this theory to increase school attendance in high school truants (MacDonald, Gallimore, & MacDonald, 1970). In both cases, the disequilibrium-response hypothesis provided a nonintrusive way to correct problem behavior and increase appropriate behaviors.

Despite the clear predictive power and utility of the response-disequilibrium hypothesis, there are findings that are not easily explained by this theory. For example, in chapter 4, we considered experiments that showed that electrical stimulation to certain areas of the brain functioned as a powerful reinforcer for rats (Olds & Milner, 1954). This evidence of the biological basis of reinforcement has played an important role in understanding instrumental and operant conditioning.

In addition, recall the study by Miller and Kessen (1952), that demonstrated that reinforcement occurs when the organism simply receives a milk injection into the stomach. In both cases, it is quite difficult to specify a particular response that serves as the reinforcing event. Findings such as these are difficult to explain within the response-disequilibrium hypothesis. Still, the preponderance of experimental evidence suggests that the response-disequilibrium hypothesis offers the best account of the necessary and sufficient conditions for reinforcement. In addition, we will see later in this chapter that this theory also provides a convincing account of the conditions that will result in punishment.

Table 5.1   Summary of Five Theories of Reinforcement.

STIMULUS-BASED THEORIES	Nature of Reinforcement
Drive-reduction hypothesis (Hull, 1943)	Reinforcers are stimuli that reduce biological drives.
Optimal-arousal hypothesis (Hebb, 1955)	Reinforcers are stimuli that lead to an optimal level of stimulation for the organism.
RESPONSE-BASED THEORIES	
Consummatory response hypothesis (Sheffield, 1966)	Reinforcement occurs to the extent that the organism vigorously consumes the reinforcing stimulus.
Premack principle (Premack, 1965)	Access to a preferred behavior will reinforce a less-preferred behavior.
Response-disequilibrium hypothesis (Timberlake & Allison, 1974)	If an organism is not allowed to maintain its baseline rate of a behavior, access to that behavior will reinforce other behaviors.

Conclusions About Primary Reinforcement Theories

This chapter has examined several theories concerning the nature of events that function as reinforcers. Table 5.1 summarizes the major theme of each theory. All the theoretical views described in this section attempt to characterize the nature of primary reinforcing events and each of these theories has successfully explained certain facts about instrumental and operant conditioning. On the other hand, we have identified shortcomings in each of the theories we have examined. Theories of reinforcement that attempt to define reinforcement in terms of stimulus properties were successful in some situations, but overall these theories were unable to specify the necessary and sufficient conditions for reinforcement. The evolution of response-based theories of reinforcement has resulted in several theories of reinforcement that successfully specify the necessary and sufficient conditions for reinforcement in most cases.

Thus no single theory provides a perfectly adequate account of reinforcement, but we have observed that the response–disequilibrium theory is currently the most reliable predictor of what events will function as reinforcers. We have also seen that the response disequilibrium theory has proven extremely useful when using operant reinforcement in real-world settings.

THE ROLE OF REINFORCEMENT IN INSTRUMENTAL AND OPERANT CONDITIONING

We have just discussed the nature of reinforcement as we tried to identify the kinds of events that will function as reinforcers in operant learning situations. Now we turn to a different question: What role does the reinforcer play in an instrumental and operant conditioning paradigm? We will examine three possible answers. The first is the proposal that reinforcers increase the probability that a particular stimulus will cause a particular response to occur. The second possibility is that learning occurs any time a response occurs in the presence of a stimulus, and reinforcers only motivate an organism to perform behaviors that have already been learned. A third possibility is that organisms learn that certain behaviors are followed by certain reinforcers, such that instrumental and operant conditioning involves learning about the relationship between responses and reinforcers.

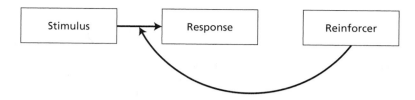

FIGURE 5.1 The Reinforcer Strengthens Stimulus-Response Associations.

The Thorndike-Hull Hypothesis

In one of the earliest views, instrumental conditioning was thought to involve the formation of associations between environmental stimuli and operant responses. For example, these theories proposed that, when a rat learned to press a bar in a Skinner box, it had learned a relation between stimuli, such as the sight of the bar, with a pressing response. The basic idea was that correct responding gradually will increase as the stimuli in a learning situation become more effective in evoking the appropriate behavior.

This view, first proposed by Thorndike (1913) and later expanded upon by Hull (1943), contained an interesting idea concerning the role of reinforcement. According to this view, which is illustrated in Figure 5.1, reinforcers are events that strengthen the associations between prior stimuli and subsequent behaviors. In other words, stimulus-response associations are formed only when an emitted response occurs in a particular stimulus situation and only when the response is followed by reinforcement. Thus, according to this view, reinforcement is a necessary condition for the formation of a stimulus-response association.

As support for this notion, Hull cited numerous experiments that indicated a strong relationship between reinforcement and the performance of operant behaviors. Organisms tend to increase operant responding as more and more reinforced trials occur. The performance of such behaviors decreases when reinforcement is eliminated. It is also clear that the degree to which operant responding occurs depends on such factors as the amount, the delay, and the quality of the reinforcer. In all these cases, Hull proposed that variations in reinforcement produce changes in performance of the operant behavior, because different experiences with reinforcement produce more or less association between stimuli and responses.

Although this position remained influential for a number of years, several findings suggest that reinforcement is not necessary for the formation and strengthening of stimulus-response associations. For instance, some experimenters have conducted studies that are usually labeled latent learning experiments (see, for example, Blodgett, 1929; MacCorquodale & Meehl, 1951; Seward, 1949; Tolman & Honzik, 1930). Tolman and Honzik (1930) trained three groups of rats to run through a 14-unit maze. One group (the rewarded control group) received food in the goal box of the maze on each of the daily trials. A second group (the unrewarded control group) never received food in the goal box. The third group (the nonreward/reward group) received no reward on the first 10 daily trials but did receive a reward on each subsequent trial. The results of these treatments can be seen in Figure 5.2, p.148.

As this figure indicates, the rewarded control group steadily improved its performance (decreased its errors) as it received more and more reinforced trials. The unrewarded control group showed only a slight decrease in errors over the course of its trials. The nonreward/reward group performed like the unrewarded animals for the first 11 trials. However, on the trial after reward was introduced, these rats improved their performance to the level of the rats that had been rewarded from the start. In effect, the nonreward/reward rats performed just as well after one reward as the other group performed after twelve rewards.

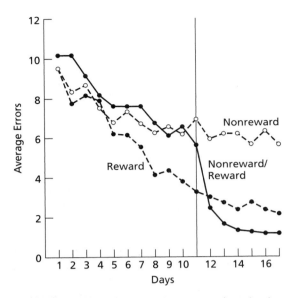

FIGURE 5.2 The Effects of Rewards. Maze learning in groups given reward on all trials, no reward on any trials, and no reward on first 10 trials but reward on trials 11–17. (From Tolman and Honzik, 1930.)

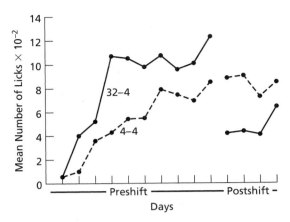

FIGURE 5.3 A Contrast Effect Experiment. Lick rates for rats consistently given 4% sucrose and for rats shifted from 32% to 4% sucrose. From Bulletin of the Psychonomic Society, 1973, 1 (1a), 25–27. Reprinted by permission of the Psychonomic Society, Inc.

Such a finding is totally unexpected if we assume that learning (and, thus, performance) depends on the number of reinforced trials an organism receives. Tolman and Honzik suggested that the rats in the nonreward/reward condition had learned how to navigate through the maze during their nonrewarded trials. However, they did not perform what they had learned until a reinforcer was provided. These latent learning studies indicate that reinforcement may not be necessary for learning an operant response, although it seems to be necessary to cause the performance of a learned response.

Making the same point are the contrast-effect experiments described in chapter 4. Recall that in this kind of experiment organisms learn some response that is followed by a given amount or quality of reinforcement. Then the quality or amount of the reinforcer is changed, whereupon organisms usually exhibit a swift change in performance. Figure 5.3 illustrates a typical set of results from a contrast effect experiment in which rats were trained to lick a drinking spout to obtain a sucrose solution (Gordon, Flaherty, & Riley, 1973). For one group the solution was very sweet (32% sucrose) and for the other group the solution was much less sweet (4% sucrose). As is typical, the licking response rate was much higher in the rats receiving the 32% solution.

On day 11 of this experiment, the rats that had been receiving the sweeter solution were shifted down to a 4% concentration. These rats exhibited an immediate decrease in licking such that their rate of responding was lower than that of the rats that had received the 4% solution all along. This phenomenon is, of course, what we have previously called a negative-contrast effect.

When the amount or quality of reward is shifted, animals immediately shift to a new level of performance. If the amount or quality of reinforcement had affected the level of learning, one would expect such changes in performance to be gradual, not immediate. We would expect a gradual change because learned changes in performance normally occur gradually. The fact that shifts in reward result in an immediate change suggests that the characteristics of reinforcement influence the momentary performance of a response, not the rate of learning. This rationale becomes even clearer when we see animals shifted from a low- to a high-quality reward. In such cases, animals immediately begin responding as well as animals that have received the high-quality reward all along. If the high-quality reward were simply strengthening the stimulus-response association, we would expect responding to have increased gradually as the association became stronger. Instead, performance increases immediately.

Recall that according to the Thorndike-Hull hypothesis, a reinforcer should always strengthen the association between a prior stimulus and response. Thus, the occurrence of a reinforcer should always strengthen an organism's tendency to perform an operant response in the appropriate stimulus situation. The contrast-effect experiments demonstrate that this assumption is not always valid. If an organism makes a response and it is followed by a 4% sucrose solution, subsequent responding will depend on whether the organism has been rewarded for the same response before. The 4% solution usually will strengthen the tendency to respond the first time a given response is rewarded. However, an organism that has been receiving a 32% solution for making the response and now is given a 4% solution will tend to decrease its response instead of increasing it. The observation that a presumed reinforcer can sometimes decrease responding is very damaging to the Thorndike-Hull notion of how reinforcers function.

The existence of positive- and negative-contrast effects suggests that an animal's performance depends on more than the current level of reinforcement. Performance also depends on an organism's previous experiences with reinforcement. Obviously, contrast effects depend on the difference between an early magnitude of reinforcement and the magnitude of reinforcement currently in effect. If this is true, it means that operant learning must depend on more than just strengthening associations between stimuli and particular responses. In other words, based on the contrast-effect data, it appears that when organisms learn an operant response, the learning depends on the particular type or amount of reinforcer that is delivered. This suggests that the reinforcer itself may be a critical element in operant learning. This proposal, of course, is different from the Thorndike-Hull position, which views the role of the reinforcer only as a strengthener of stimulus-response associations.

The Spence-Hull Hypothesis

The studies reviewed in the preceding section emphasize the distinction between learning and performance. For example, the latent learning studies indicate that organisms do not always perform in accord with what they have learned. Contrast-effect experiments suggest the same conclusion. In both cases, the data indicate that the characteristics of reinforcement may influence the performance of a response rather than the degree to which a response is learned.

Based on such findings, Spence (1956; see also Hull, 1952) proposed a change in the prevailing view of reinforcement. Spence retained the notion that instrumental conditioning involves associations between stimuli and emitted behaviors. However, he suggested that such associations result simply from the temporal contiguity of these events. In effect, stimuli and responses that occur close together in time automatically become associated even in the absence of a reinforcing event. According to this view, the function of the reinforcer is to help motivate an organism to respond; responses can then occur contiguously with situational stimuli. Reinforcement *aids* learning, but it is not *necessary* for learning (see Figure 5.4, p. 150).

Spence proposed that the characteristics of a reinforcer provide incentive motivation, a motivational state that is aroused by the characteristics of external stimuli. For example, we eat certain foods partially because we are hungry. Hunger is a motivational state produced by periodic

(A)

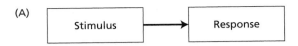

FIGURE 5.4 The Spence-Hull Hypothesis.

(B)

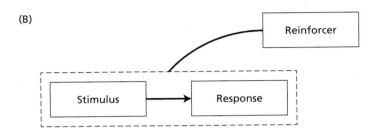

changes in our biological condition. We are also motivated to eat by the odor, the taste, and the sight of certain foods. When it is the characteristics of some food that lead us to seek out that food, we are experiencing incentive motivation. Thus, Spence viewed a reinforcer as a stimulus that arouses incentive motivation and helps to promote emitted behaviors that lead to that reinforcer.

The proposed mechanism by which reinforcers motivate responses was elucidated in some detail by Spence. Basically, he viewed a reinforcer as functioning as a US in a classical conditioning situation. When an organism encounters a reinforcer, that stimulus naturally elicits a given reaction Spence called a goal response (R_g). The goal response is analogous to an unconditioned response made to a US. For example, if the reward is food, the goal response may involve approach behaviors, salivation, or chewing movements. Since these goal responses occur in the presence of goal box stimuli (S_g), these goal stimuli, like CSs, become capable of eliciting goal responses on their own. Thus, stimuli in the goal box become capable of producing responses that are normally elicited only by the reward itself. Figure 5.5a illustrates how this classical conditioning of the goal response was presumed to occur.

According to Spence, once this conditioning has occurred, the conditioned goal response can help to elicit the responses that normally lead to the goal. To see how this happens, let's assume that we are training a rat to run down a runway for a food reward. On trial 1 the rat explores the runway and finally encounters food in the goal box. The food elicits a goal response (R_g) and the stimuli in the goal box (S_g) become capable of producing the same response via classical conditioning. On trial 2 the rat is placed in the start box of the runway (see Figure 5.5b). The stimuli in the start box (S_{sb}) are similar to those in the goal box (S_g). Thus, the start box stimuli elicit a partial goal response (r_g) because of stimulus generalization, the tendency of an organism to respond in the same way in the presence of similar stimuli. Spence called the partial goal response produced by start box stimuli a fractional anticipatory goal response. Keep in mind that the fractional anticipatory goal response (r_g) occurs only because the start box stimuli are usually similar to the goal box stimuli and the goal box stimuli have come to elicit a goal response through prior conditioning.

Spence hypothesized that these partial goal responses are important because they result in stimulus aftereffects (s_g). For example, when an animal begins to salivate in the start box, it can feel its mouth becoming wet. Such stimulus aftereffects are important because they can become associated with the running or movement responses the organism is making in the runway. And, once the stimulus aftereffects have become

(A) **Trial 1:**

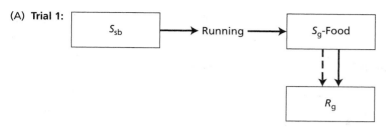

FIGURE 5.5 Influence of Rewards.
Spence's conceptualization of how reward influences performance in instrumental conditioning: (A) trial 1 and (B) trial 2.

Animal leaves start box stimuli (S_{sb}) and runs to goal box, where it encounters goal box stimuli (S_g) and food. The food naturally produces goal responses (R_g) such as salivation. Goal stimuli come to produce goal responses through classical conditioning.

(B) **Trial 2:**

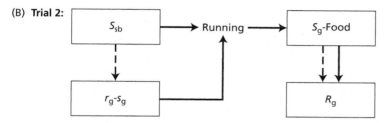

Since the start box stimuli (S_{sb}) are similar to the goal box stimuli, S_{sb} produces a fractional or partial goal response (r_g). This fractional goal response leaves stimulus aftereffects (s_g), which can become attached to running. Thus, the occurrence of r_g in the start box provides an additional set of stimuli that can aid in the production of running.

associated with the emitted response, they can help to evoke that response on subsequent occasions. In effect, the start box stimuli set off a chain of responses and stimuli that can aid in promoting the operant behavior. Start box stimuli (S_{sb}) elicit fractional goal responses (r_g), which produce stimulus aftereffects (s_g) that can become associated with operant responding.

Many researchers, as well as many beginning students, have viewed this analysis as needlessly complex. The hypothesis, however, is logically consistent and is totally in keeping with a stimulus–response interpretation of learning. According to such an interpretation, complex emitted behaviors always consist of chains of stimulus–response associations in which each stimulus elicits a response and each response also serves as a stimulus that can then elicit other

responses. Spence's hypothesis clearly reflects this explanatory tradition.

Until the mid-1960s, the Spence view of reinforcement enjoyed wide popularity among learning researchers. This conceptually elegant theory appeared to account for a substantial number of reinforcement effects and had the clear advantage of viewing reinforcement as an influence on learned performance, not as a necessary condition for learning. Thus, the theory was able to accommodate data such as those found in the latent learning and contrast effect experiments.

In latent learning the theory states that organisms learn stimulus–response associations in the absence of reinforcement. However, when reinforcement is introduced and fractional anticipatory goal responses begin, the operant response will be elicited strongly enough to occur with regularity. In contrast-effect experiments, reinforcement shifts are presumed to affect the strength of classical conditioning in the goal box. According to this view, reinforcer shifts affect the strength of the fractional anticipatory goal response and lead to changes in how strongly an operant response is elicited. Reinforcer shifts do not directly affect the association between stimuli and the operant response; they affect the degree to which the incentive for responding is present.

In addition to providing an explanation for latent learning and contrast effects, this theory suggested a mechanism that would account for a variety of other reinforcement phenomena. For example, we know that small-magnitude reinforcers, low-quality reinforcers, and long delays between the target behavior and reinforcement all produce poor conditioning. This theory suggests that all these circumstances lead to poor conditioning because they lead to poor classical conditioning of goal responses. Thus, under all these conditions, fractional anticipatory goal responses are less likely to occur. This means that under these conditions there will be fewer stimuli available to elicit or promote performance of the operant behavior. Small-magnitude reinforcers do not reduce associations between stimuli and emitted responses; they produce less in the way of classically conditioned response elicitation.

Despite the power and early appeal of Spence's position, this view of reinforcement is no longer favored by most researchers (see, for example, Adams & Dickinson, 1981; Bolles, 1975; Mackintosh, 1983). The reason for this loss of favor is clear. The main premise in the Spence theory is that classically conditioned goal responses help to motivate or promote operant behaviors. If we accept this basic assumption, Spence's theory accounts for a number of reinforcement effects. However, there is little or no experimental support for this most basic premise. Researchers simply have been unable to find evidence that conditioned goal responses affect the performance of operant behaviors.

For example, several researchers have tested this assumption by conducting two-stage experiments. In stage 1, animals receive pairings of a specific CS with a food US, to condition goal responses such as salivation to the CS. Upon completion of this conditioning, the animals enter stage 2 of the experiment, in which they are trained to perform some operant response for a food reward. During training, some of the animals receive the CS from stage 1 while they are performing the operant response. According to Spence, the presentation of the CS should produce goal responses, which should act to enhance the operant behavior. Yet most such studies have found either that the CS has no effect on responding or that the CS actually retards performance of the operant behavior (Azrin & Hake, 1969; Hake & Powell, 1970; Miczek & Grossman, 1971).

Another approach to testing this premise of Spence's theory has been to measure conditioned goal responding and operant responding concurrently in the same experiment. If the Spence notion is correct, we should find that conditioned goal responses develop before operant responses, since the goal responses presumably help to produce the operant behaviors. We would also expect to see a strong correlation between these two kinds of responses. That is, operant responding should increase as the occurrence of goal responding increases. These predicted relationships between operant and goal responses have seldom been found. In one study that typifies this approach, D. R. Williams (1965) trained dogs to press a lever to obtain a food reward on a fixed-ratio schedule. As you may recall, organisms placed on this type of schedule usually make no responses for a short period of time after each reward. However, once they have resumed responding, they typically do so at a reasonably constant rate until the next reward occurs. In this particular study, Williams measured both the rate of lever pressing and the amount of salivation that occurred throughout training. He was interested in how long it would take the dogs to resume pressing after each reward. He also wanted to know when salivation would occur relative to the pressing response.

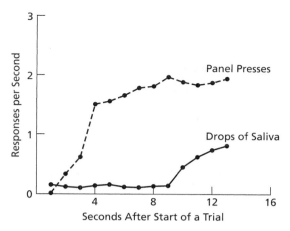

FIGURE 5.6 A Fixed Ratio Trial. Number of panel presses and drops of saliva as a function of time since the start of a fixed ratio trial. From *Classical Conditioning: A Symposium* © 1965 by Appleton-Century Crofts.

According to the Spence theory, we would expect the dogs to begin salivating before resuming the lever-press response on each trial. Yet Figure 5.6 shows that this is not what Williams found. This figure illustrates lever-press and salivary responding by one of the dogs in this experiment. We see that on average the dog resumed the lever-press response within 4 seconds after each reward. However, no significant salivation tended to occur until about 10 seconds after each reward. In other words, the goal response of salivation, which according to Spence should be helping to promote the operant response, did not begin to occur until well after the operant response was occurring maximally (see Deaux & Patten, 1964, for a similar result in a runway experiment).

It is notable that Spence's prediction also appears to fail in studies that have attempted simply to correlate operant and goal responding. Several studies that have measured responses of both kinds in the same situation have found that the degree of operant responding is often unrelated to the degree of goal responding (see, for example, Kintsch & Witte, 1962; Miller & Debold, 1965). Such findings have done little to bolster the Spence version of reinforcement effects.

Response-Outcome Theories

Both reinforcement theories discussed so far take the position that stimulus–response associations are formed during instrumental and operant conditioning. Reinforcement is viewed as an event that either strengthens these associations or helps to translate them into performance. Most contemporary theories of reinforcement take a different view of operant learning and of the role of reinforcement. Probably the most common notion is that instrumental and operant conditioning involves learning about the reinforcer itself and about the relationship between a response and the consequences of that response (see Mackintosh, 1974). In this view behaviors are controlled by their consequences, rather than stimuli that occur before the response. The theories we have discussed previously proposed that reinforcement played a secondary role in learning by influencing how organisms learned about other events (stimuli and responses). According to this approach, illustrated in Figure 5.7 (p. 154), reinforcement no longer plays a secondary role, but instead is part of what the organism learns about during conditioning.

The idea that operant learning involves learning about the reinforcer is entirely consistent with the evidence we have discussed. For example, the results of contrast–effect experiments strongly suggest that during instrumental and operant conditioning organisms learn about the characteristics of the reinforcer. In these experiments, we find that the rate of a learned behavior changes when the amount or quality of reinforcement is changed. If reinforcement only helped to forge stimulus–response associations, a change in the reinforcer should not affect those stimulus–response associations that have already been learned.

Likewise, the latent-learning experiments suggest that an organism's performance will change when reinforcement is introduced to the learning situation. Thus, the organism's behavior changes if there is the opportunity to learn that a particular behavior is followed by a particular

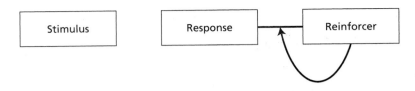

FIGURE 5.7 **Response-Outcome Theories.** The organism learns the relationship between a response and a particular reinforcer. Reinforcement contributes to learning this association.

consequence. Again, this phenomenon is consistent with the view that behavior changes during instrumental and operant conditioning because organisms learn about the relationship between the response and the reinforcing events.

Other evidence that operant conditioning involves learning about the response-consequence relationship comes from a series of experiments conducted by Adams and his colleagues (see Adams, 1980, 1982; Adams & Dickinson, 1981). Basically, Adams trained rats to bar-press for sucrose pellets and later paired sucrose consumption with a lithium chloride injection. As we have seen in our discussion of taste aversion learning in chapter 2, lithium chloride usually results in nausea, and organisms normally form aversions to tastes experienced prior to injections with this substance. The point of the treatment was to make the taste of sucrose aversive or less palatable. After the treatment, the rats were returned to the operant chamber and were given the opportunity to press the bar. This phase of the experiments actually involved extinction, since no sucrose pellets were ever delivered. Adams found that rats that experienced the pairing of sucrose with illness pressed much less than did the control animals. This finding shows that the lithium chloride injection paired with sucrose had changed the rate of behavior that was previously reinforced with sucrose. One would expect such a decrease only if, during the bar press training, the rats had learned about the relationship between their responses and the delivery of sucrose pellets.

These lines of evidence suggest that reinforcers play more than a supporting role in instrumental and operant conditioning. Such data are consistent with the notion that in instrumental conditioning organisms learn about the response-reinforcer relationship. In effect, instrumental and operant conditioning seems to involve learning that a particular response reliably leads to a particular outcome. This position is summarized together with the Thorndike-Hull and Spence-Hull theories in Table 5.2.

THEORIES OF EXTINCTION

Numerous theories of extinction have been proposed, but no single theory adequately explains all of the facts concerning extinction. Consequently, the next discussion will focus on only four of the theories that have been suggested. These theories represent different approaches to extinction, and each theory contains ideas that have contributed to our understanding of the extinction process.

Amsel's Frustration Theory: A Competing-Response Hypothesis

It is well known that during the extinction of a learned behavior, organisms often begin to perform new alternative responses. For example, when a bar-press response undergoes extinction, rats often exhibit an increase in such behaviors as grooming, exploration, and rearing. Based on this, several theorists have suggested that during extinction organisms develop responses that compete or interfere with the behavior being extinguished. According to these theories, the operant response diminishes because other incompatible responses develop and become more probable.

Without doubt, the most influential competing-response theory that has been

Table 5.2 Three Theories on the Role of Reinforcement in Instrumental Conditioning.

	ROLE OF REINFORCEMENT
Thorndike-Hull Hypothesis (Thorndike, 1913; Hull, 1943)	Reinforcement causes organisms to learn stimulus-response associations.
Spence-Hull Hypothesis (Spence, 1956; Hull, 1952)	Organisms learn stimulus-response associations whenever a particular stimulus and response occur together consistently. Reinforcement serves to motivate and increase the performance of learned behaviors.
Response-Outcome Theories (e.g., Mackintosh, 1974)	Organisms learn about the reinforcer itself and the relationship between the behavior and that reinforcer.

proposed is Amsel's frustration theory of extinction (Amsel, 1958, 1967, 1972). Amsel's ideas were initially influenced by the observation that during extinction, animals display a number of reactions that appear to be emotionally charged. To the casual observer, such animals appear to be frustrated or angry when reinforcement is eliminated. Thus, Amsel proposed that the elimination of an expected reward resulted in a state of frustration that produced a number of new responses. These responses were usually incompatible with the ongoing operant behavior. As extinction progressed, organisms became increasingly frustrated, and the incompatible responses began to block the performance of the operant response. Thus, extinction was viewed as resulting from competition between the previously learned response and incompatible behaviors produced by frustration.

In support of this view, several researchers have reported that the elimination of an expected reward does appear to produce an increase in the rate of other behaviors (see, for example, Amsel & Roussel, 1952; Amsel & Ward, 1965; Hug, 1970; Peckham & Amsel, 1967; Wagner, 1959). To elaborate, Amsel and Roussel (1952) trained rats to traverse a double alley runway. In essence, the apparatus consisted of two runways laid end to end. The rat was placed in the start box; then it ran down the first runway and into the first goal box. Goal box 1 served as the start box for the second runway and ended with the rat receiving reinforcement in the second goal box. Amsel

and Roussel rewarded their rats in both goal boxes three trials per day for 28 days.

Following acquisition training the rats ran an additional 36 trials. During these trials, rats received reward in goal box 1 on 50% of the trials determined randomly. They were rewarded in goal box 2 on all trials. Amsel and Roussel showed that on those trials in which the rat was not rewarded in goal box 1 it ran faster down runway 2 than on those trials in which it received reward. Amsel and Roussel interpreted this finding as showing that the rats had formed an expectancy for reward in goal box 1 and that when this expectancy was disconfirmed it resulted in frustration. Frustration was considered a motivating force and the reason the rats ran faster down runway 2 is because they were escaping the frustrating conditions of goal box 1. Wagner (1959) used two control groups, one that never received rewards in goal box 1 and one that always received rewards in goal box 1, to show that the effect was a result of the frustrating effects of nonreward and not demotivation.

By extrapolating certain ideas in this theory, Amsel has been able to account for a variety of extinction phenomena. For example, we saw earlier that extinction is usually fastest when the magnitude of reward during learning is large. According to Amsel, the larger the reward during learning, the greater the level of frustration when the reward is eliminated. This means that when large rewards cease, frustration-produced incompatible responses in extinction are stronger and more numerous. For this reason, the operant response is more quickly replaced or extinguished.

Although this theory does an adequate job of explaining a number of extinction phenomena, the impact of the theory is based largely on its ability to account for the partial reinforcement extinction effect (PREE). As you may recall from chapter 4, the PREE refers to the fact that behaviors learned and maintained through partial reinforcement extinguish more slowly than those given continuous reinforcement. Amsel explains this effect by suggesting that partial reinforcement of a behavior also results in organisms learning to respond in the presence of frustration during learning. In other words, on nonreinforced trials these organisms experience frustration and exhibit frustration-produced responses. However, they continue to perform the operant response because they have learned to continue responding despite this frustration and this continued responding eventually is reinforced. In such a situation, the stimulus aftereffects of frustration may come to serve as discriminative stimuli that signal that continued responding will result in reinforcement. Amsel proposed that in such cases, frustration might actually evoke continued responding.

When extinction begins, both partially and continually reinforced organisms experience frustration. In the case of the continually reinforced response, frustration-produced responses begin to interfere with the operant behavior and extinction occurs rapidly. However, in partially reinforced organisms, the frustration of extinction actually helps to maintain responding, since initially it was associated with the operant behavior. Thus, during extinction, partially reinforced organisms continue to perform the operant behavior for a substantial period of time.

As we have noted, Amsel's frustration theory successfully accounts for a variety of extinction effects. Still, this theory cannot stand as a complete explanation of the extinction phenomenon.

One major problem is that the theory fails to account for some of the finer aspects of the PREE. For example, Amsel emphasizes that frustration should begin to occur only after a long history of reinforcement has occurred. To support this idea, Hug (1970) has shown that the elimination of reward has no motivating effects unless an organism has had approximately 8 to 12 prior reinforcements. Still, a significant PREE has been obtained in studies using only five or six learning trials. This means that after only two or three reinforcement experiences intermingled with two or three nonreward experiences, animals exhibit slower extinction (see, for example, McCain, 1969; Ziff & Capaldi, 1971). This suggests that a PREE can occur in the absence of frustration.

In fact, accounting for various aspects of the PREE has proven to be a major issue for all theories of extinction. Although many theories easily explain the extinction of a continuously reinforced behavior, few theories adequately account for the PREE. Accordingly, the ability to account for the PREE became a major criterion for evaluating theories of extinction.

The Discrimination Hypothesis of Extinction

One theory of extinction that can account for the PREE is the discrimination hypothesis. Mowrer & Jones (1945) proposed that the reduction in behavior during extinction occurs only when the organism is able to discriminate a change in the reinforcement contingencies for the behavior. Simply stated, can the organism perceive a change in reinforcement contingencies once extinction has begun? If the change is quite noticeable, the reduction in behavior should be rapid, while changes to extinction that are less noticeable will result in a slower reduction in behavior.

This theory offers a rather simple account of the PREE. Under procedures where every response is reinforced, the change from continuous reinforcement to extinction is quite noticeable. On the other hand, under partial reinforcement, the change from the variable reinforcement contingency to extinction is far less noticeable; it takes more time for a reduction in behavior to occur. For example, when you insert and turn the key in your car's ignition the car always starts; this behavior is continuously reinforced. If some malfunction occurs so that your car will not start and your behavior is under extinction, the change would be obvious and you would not continue to try to start your car for very long. On the other hand, if your car only starts after a number of attempts, it would take much longer for you to discriminate the change to extinction and you would likely continue trying to start your car for quite some time.

The discrimination hypothesis provides a very appealing and straightforward account of the PREE, but findings from several experiments suggest that this hypothesis does not adequately account for the PREE (Capaldi, 1966). In the face of this evidence Capaldi proposed a somewhat different theory of extinction, known as the generalization decrement hypothesis.

Capaldi's Generalization Decrement Hypothesis

Capaldi argues that extinction is primarily the result of a stimulus-generalization decrement. We will discuss the topic of stimulus generalization in greater detail in chapter 7. However, for present purposes, stimulus generalization simply refers to the fact that when organisms learn a response in one stimulus situation, they tend to perform that response best in the same or a similar stimulus situation. When learning occurs in the presence of one stimulus set and testing occurs in the presence of a different stimulus set performance of the learned response tends to decrease. The decrease in learned responding that results from stimulus change is called a stimulus-generalization decrement.

Capaldi argued that during learning the reinforcer becomes a critical part of the stimulus situation. In this sense the reinforcer is analogous to contextual stimuli that are present during classical conditioning situations. In extinction, the elimination of the reinforcer changes the stimulus situation dramatically. Thus, organisms cease responding for the same reason they would fail to respond if they were placed in a novel apparatus or context: because the stimulus situation is different from the one in which they learned.

Despite the success of Capaldi's theory in accounting for extinction phenomena, some theorists have questioned whether this or any other stimulus-generalization decrement theory can stand as a complete explanation of extinction (see Mackintosh, 1974). Most important are several studies that have shown that extinction occurs readily even under circumstances in which generalization decrements should be minimal (Rescorla & Skucy, 1969; Uhl & Garcia, 1969). Stimulus-generalization decrements appear to contribute substantially to the extinction of instrumental behaviors, but such decrements may not provide a complete account of extinction phenomena. In 1967, Capaldi proposed an extension and modification of generalization-decrement theory. This revised position is known as sequential theory.

Capaldi's Sequential Theory

Capaldi's (1967, 1971) sequential theory builds on the contention that extinction results from the stimulus discrepancies between acquisition and extinction. The argument is made that animals have memories or representations of responses that are recalled in the presence of the cues of the apparatus. For example if a rat runs down a straight alley maze and receives reinforcement it will form a memory of that event. On the next trial the maze cues present in the start box will cause the retrieval of the previous event and the animal will run down the maze. Similarly, if the rat runs down the maze and does not receive reinforcement it will form a memory of that event and on the next trial the rat will recall the nonreinforced trial. The effect of these retrieval cues will be to decrease the maze-running response.

Sequential theory offers a novel account for the PREE. The animal is intermittently reinforced during acquisition; it will run down the alley and sometimes be reinforced and sometimes not. Assume that the animal has a sequence of rewarded (R) and nonrewarded (NR) trials that consists of NRNR. On the first trial of this sequence the animal is not rewarded. On the next trial, the maze cues retrieve the memory of no reinforcement and when the rat runs down the alley in the presence of these cues it receives a reward. According to Capaldi, animals take longer to extinguish when they are partially reinforced because they have been reinforced for running in the presence of the nonreinforcment cues. Animals reinforced continuously have not been reinforced for running in the presence of these cues.

Capaldi's Sequential Theory is compelling because it makes unique predictions that cannot be made by Frustration Theory or Discrimination Theory. Capaldi maintains that the degree to which the animal is reinforced for running in the presence of nonreinforcement cues is critical. This, of course, is determined by the sequence of rewarded and nonrewarded trials. For example, imagine that a rat is given four trials per day for 25 days. Each day the rat is reinforced according to the sequence NRNR. Now imagine a rat in a second group that also receives four trials per day for 25 days, but for this rat the sequence of trials is RNRN. Capaldi is able to make the prediction that the rat in the group receiving the NRNR sequences will extinguish more slowly than the rat that receives the sequences RNRN. This is because the NRNR rat actually gets rewarded twice for running in the presence of nonreinforcement cues, whereas the rat in group RNRN is rewarded only once. Capaldi calls these sequences N-R transitions and he maintains that they play a critical role in extinction.

Capaldi also maintains that a second variable is critical. This variable is termed *N length*. N length refers to the number of nonreinforced trials that occur prior to reinforcement. A rat that receives the sequence NRNRNR will extinguish more quickly than a rat that receives the sequence NNRNRR. This is because the animal remembers more than one past event. If it is rewarded for responding in the presence of a long string of nonreinforced trials, it will show greater

resistance to extinction than if it reinforced for responding in the presence of fewer nonreinforced trials.

In Capaldi's theory, extinction results when the animal has retrieval cues representing a long string of nonreinforced responses and it has not been rewarded for responding in the presence of these cues. To elaborate, imagine a rat that has received a sequence of trials in which there are 10 NR transitions and the N length is always one. During extinction it will quickly encounter an N length greater than one and it will stop responding. Now contrast this rat's experience with a rat that has had the same number of rewarded and nonrewarded trials, but has had N lengths of two and three. During extinction this rat should extinguish more slowly because it will remember being reinforced in the presence of memory cues indicating longer periods of no reinforcement.

As we alluded to above, Capaldi's theory makes unique predictions. For example, imagine a rat that receives the sequence RRN and a rat that receives the sequence RNR. Discrimination theory predicts no difference between these two groups, but Capaldi does. The rats receiving the RNR sequence should show greater resistance to extinction than the RRN rats. Indeed, the last trial has no effect on performance because it will not have been associated with reward. Capaldi and Kassover (1970) showed the importance of this point. One group of rats was trained with three times as many nonreinforced trials as rats in a second group. However, for the rats with more nonreinforced trials, the nonrewarded trials came at the end of the sequence. It was predicted that these nonrewarded trials would have no effect on extinction performance and they did not. This study clearly shows the importance of sequence during acquisition.

Conclusions Concerning Extinction Theories

Table 5.3 provides an overview of the four theories of extinction. Both Amsel's frustration theory and Capaldi's sequential theory have received

Table 5.3 Summary of Four Theories of Extinction.

THEORIES OF EXTINCTION	
Frustration hypothesis (Amsel, 1958)	Extinction occurs because the absence of reinforcement elicits emotional responses that interfere with the operant behavior. Resistance to extinction increases as the animal learns to run in the presence of frustrating conditions.
Discrimination hypothesis (Mowrer & Jones, 1965)	Extinction occurs because organisms discriminate the absence of reinforcement in the learning situation.
Generalization-decrement hypothesis (Capaldi, 1966)	Extinction occurs because the absence of reinforcement changes the learning context. Behaviors learned under the context of reinforcement do not generalize to the new context (absence of reinforcement).
Sequential theory Calpaldi (1967, 1971)	Extinction occurs as a result of the animal learning not to run in the presence of retrieval cues predicting no reward. Resistance to extinction increases as a function of the number of times it is reinforced for running in the presence of retrieval cues that predict nonreward. Of importance are the number of N–R transitions and N length.

considerable coverage in the literature (see Amsel, 1992; Capaldi, Alptekin, & Birmingham, 1996; Haggbloom, Lovelace, Brewer, Levins, & Owens, 1990). However, neither theory has been able to account for all of the data. For example Amsel has trouble accounting for some of the sequence effects shown by Capaldi, and Capaldi has trouble accounting for the speed increases in animals that have experienced frustrating nonreward. Most likely, extinction is a phenomenon that results from a variety of factors including generalization decrements, competing emotional responses, and reinforcement for running in the presence of memory cues that predict no reward. Future theories of extinction may need to include all these mechanisms to provide a complete account of why the elimination of reinforcement abolishes instrumental responding.

PUNISHMENT: THEORETICAL ISSUES

Issues surrounding the use of punishment are numerous and quite familiar. Folk wisdom such as "spare the rod, spoil the child" suggests that punishment is a useful and necessary (although unpleasant) means of changing behavior. On the other hand, many individuals believe that it is undesirable or even unacceptable to punish children's behavior. Although our criminal justice system attempts to reduce criminal behavior through punishments such as incarceration or fines, many of us question whether these consequences are truly effective in changing behavior.

Punishment certainly plays a number of roles in our lives. For example, how often have you received a traffic ticket for speeding, or been fined for returning library books late? In contrast, how often have you received some reinforcer for driving responsibly or returning library books promptly? For most of us, our answer would be that our inappropriate behaviors are frequently punished, while our appropriate behaviors are rarely reinforced. In this light, we see that the question of whether we should use punishment affects many aspects of our lives, such as child rearing, education, employee management, criminal justice, and even training our pets. A second important question surrounding punishment is how to use it effectively if we choose to use it.

We will first turn our attention to examining two theoretical issues that are directly related to these questions regarding the use of punishment. First, we will look at the effects of punishment by asking whether punishment simply causes a temporary suppression of a behavior or causes a more lasting reduction in the behavior. Second, we will ask whether punishment results in an overall reduction in all behaviors or if punishment reduces only the rate of the punished behavior. Both of these issues have clear implications for whether we should use punishment to control behavior, and how we should use punishment if we use it at all. Finally, we will return to our discussion of the response-disequilibrium hypothesis to examine the predictions this theory makes regarding the necessary and sufficient conditions for effective punishment.

One theoretical question concerning punishment asks whether punishment contingencies produce only a temporary suppression of the punished behavior, or if punishment actually functions to produce lasting reduction or elimination of the punished behavior. Our definitions of reinforcers and punishers in chapter 4 indicated that punishment is the opposite of reinforcement. Reinforcement increases behavior while punishment decreases behavior. Although this view is appealing, theorists have disagreed over the question of whether punishment is, in fact, the opposite of reinforcement. If punishment only temporarily suppresses behavior rather than reducing or eliminating behavior, it would seem clear that punishment is not a reliable means of producing lasting changes in behavior. Such a conclusion could have profound implications for both child rearing and our criminal justice system.

One of the earliest answers to this question was proposed by Skinner (1938). He exposed two groups of rats to three 120-minute sessions of a VI reinforcement schedule followed by two 120-minute sessions of extinction. For one group of rats, nothing unusual happened during the extinction sessions. The second group of rats, however, received a mild punishment each time they pressed the bar during the first 10 minutes of the first extinction session. For these rats, each press during the punishment condition resulted in the lever jolting upward and slapping their paws.

Figure 5.8 shows the cumulative records for each group of rats during the two extinction sessions. The upper record was produced by the control group, and the bottom record was produced by the group that received punishment during the first session. These cumulative records show that the punishment procedure did produce a decrease in responding for the punished group. What is most important about this data, however, is the fact that the rate of bar-pressing in the punishment group increased after the punishment procedure ended. As the cumulative records show, by the end of the second extinction session, both groups of rats had made approximately the same number of responses. Skinner concluded that punishment was not the opposite of reinforcement because the effects of punishment were not permanent, and it appeared that punishment only produced suppression of the behavior for a short period of time.

If we examine some problems with Skinner's experiment, though, we find reasons to question his conclusion. First of all, the rate of responding did decrease while the punishment was delivered. More importantly, it was only after the punishment was removed that the behavior increased. This is analogous to extinction of reinforced responding where the effects of reinforcement begin to fade after reinforcement is stopped. One might argue that the results of Skinner's experiment actually support the position that punishment is the opposite of reinforcement. The temporary effects of punishment observed by Skinner were probably a result of the fact that the punishment itself was temporary. Accordingly, we should view Skinner's conclusion with some caution.

A number of experiments have since addressed the question of whether punishment only temporarily suppresses behavior (see Azrin & Holz, 1966, for an excellent review of these studies). In these experiments (unlike Skinner's), the punishment was delivered throughout the experiment, much the same as reinforcement is normally delivered throughout experiments examining the effects of reinforcement. The results of experiments like these suggest several

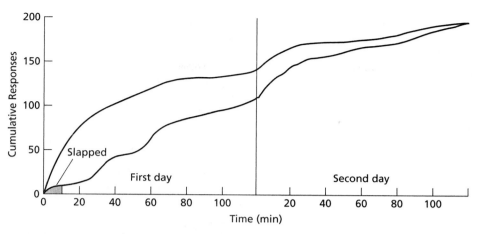

FIGURE 5.8 Effects of Punishment. Effects of mild punishment, paw-slapping, on cumulative bar presses in extinction. Punishment was administered to experimental group only during first 10 minutes of first extinction session (Skinner, 1938).

conclusions concerning punishment. In one such experiment, Azrin (1960) first trained pigeons to respond steadily in an operant key-peck procedure. He then introduced a punishment procedure wherein each response was followed by electric shock and these conditions remained in effect for the rest of the experiment. Azrin varied the level of shock intensity across groups of pigeons and he found that a relatively mild shock produced results similar to those from Skinner's experiment. That is, the rate of key-pecking decreased when the mild shocks were first introduced, but the pigeon's behavior ultimately returned to almost the same rate as before the punishment was introduced. Azrin concluded that these birds habituated to the mild punisher. It appears, then, that the effects of punishment were temporary in this condition.

In contrast, Azrin found that with high shock intensities, the punishment contingency produced a dramatic reduction in response rates, and in some cases eliminated key pecking altogether. In addition, the rate of responding did not recover during the rest of the experiment for those

birds that received more intense punishers. This experiment, together with many others that followed, clearly support the conclusion that punishment is the opposite of reinforcement and that sufficiently intense punishment will produce lasting reduction in behavior (Azrin & Holz, 1966). Also, as with reinforcement, the effects of punishment tend to weaken when the punishment contingency is no longer present.

Another theoretical issue concerning punishment asks whether the effects of punishment are specific to the behavior being punished, or if punishment instead results in a reduction in the rate of all behaviors. This theoretical question is also related to the question of whether punishment is the opposite of reinforcement. We saw in chapter 4 that reinforcement contingencies are quite specific in increasing only the rate of the behavior that produces the reinforcer. In the case of punishment, however, some theorists have proposed that punishment simply reduces the rate of all behaviors, while other theorists have argued that punishment functions by specifically reducing the behavior that results in punishment.

Estes (1944) proposed that punishment reduces the rate of all ongoing behaviors. We see one example of Estes's theory when we reconsider the CER (conditioned emotional response) procedures used to study classical conditioning. To briefly review this procedure, rats are first trained to press a bar for food reinforcement, then some CS is paired with shock, and finally the CS is presented while the animal is responding for food reinforcement. Successful conditioning is demonstrated when the CS that was paired with shock suppresses the ongoing operant response (bar-pressing).

Note that in this situation, the shock never follows bar-pressing. Thus, the aversive stimulus (shock) is never presented contingent upon a particular response. Nonetheless, we saw that presentation of the CS resulted in suppression of the bar-pressing response. These findings led Estes to propose that the effect of punishment is to suppress the rate of all ongoing behaviors, not just the behavior that is being punished.

In contrast to Estes's proposal, the bulk of experimental evidence suggests that the effects of punishment are specific to the response that is punished. Schuster and Rachlin (1968) best demonstrated this effect. Pigeons could respond on one of two keys that both produced the same VI schedule of reinforcement. Only one of the keys was activated at any time, and the active key was illuminated. Thus, during the reinforcement phase of this experiment, the keys were functionally equivalent because both produced the same schedule of reinforcement. After the reinforcement phase of this experiment, however, the two keys resulted in different schedules of shock presentation. When the left key was illuminated, some responses were followed by shock. When the right key was illuminated, shock was sometimes presented regardless of the birds' behavior.

Note that Estes's account would predict that responding to both keys should decrease because the presentation of the punisher (shock) should reduce all ongoing behaviors. The results of this experiment, however, clearly indicated that the punishment contingency on the left key reduced only responding to the left key, because the pigeons' rate of pecking the right key changed very little. This study and several subsequent experiments have shown that punishment contingencies result in the specific reduction of the punished response and not an overall reduction in the rate of ongoing behaviors.

Should We Use Punishment?

The theoretical analysis of punishment we have just discussed certainly provides some help in deciding whether or not to use punishment to control behavior. Unfortunately, this issue is too complex to address adequately here. However, we can offer some general statements about punishment.

The effectiveness of punishment depends upon including severity of punishment, schedule of punishment, initial rate of the target behavior, and many other factors. (Azrin & Holz, 1966). To use punishment effectively, one must be familiar with the various factors that affect punishment procedures. Still, we have seen that it is at least possible to use punishment to reduce the rate of undesirable behaviors.

On the other hand, several features of punishment that suggest that its use should be avoided whenever possible. One such undesirable effect of punishment is that it can elicit a range of emotional reactions, particularly fear and anger. Think about the last time your behavior was punished. You probably felt a strong reaction of fear, anger, or both. These emotional behaviors can interfere with learning and performance. For example, it is hard to return to your job and perform well after your supervisor has yelled at you.

In more extreme cases, punishment contingencies can lead to aggressive behavior. This aggression can be directed toward the source of punishment, or any other organism present in the situation. Experiments have shown that rats that consistently interacted peacefully under normal circumstances began fighting viciously when shocks were delivered (Ulrich & Azrin, 1962).

Punishment often causes organisms to avoid the situation where punishment is delivered. One example of this effect is that students who experience a great deal of punishment at school will begin to play hooky and skip school. In such a situation the result is that educators have reduced the opportunity to teach these students and encourage appropriate behavior.

Given these disadvantages of punishment, it seems that the use of punishment should be avoided whenever possible, and especially in situations where it is possible to use reinforcement procedures to increase desirable behavior. Azrin and Holz (1966) conclude that punishment should be used only as a last resort and this view is shared by many learning theorists (e.g., Axelrod, 1990). On the other hand, some individuals argue that punishment should never be used under any circumstances (for example, Freagon, 1990).

Response Disequilibrium and Punishment

The response-disequilibrium hypothesis is an excellent predictor of the necessary and sufficient conditions for reinforcement. In the case of punishment, the response-disequilibrium hypothesis also allows us to predict the necessary and sufficient conditions for punishment. To review briefly, this theory states that reinforcement will occur when our reinforcement contingencies satisfy the following inequality:

$$Rt/Rc > Bt/Bc \quad \text{Inequality 5.1—repeated}$$

The application of response disequilibrium to punishment is simply a matter of reversing this inequality:

$$Rt/Rc < Bt/Bc \quad \text{Inequality 5.10}$$

This inequality specifies that punishment of the target response Rt will occur when we create a situation in which the required ratio of the target response (Rt) to the consequence response (Rc) is less than the baseline ratio of the target behavior (Bt) to the consequence behavior (Bc). According to the response-disequilibrium

hypothesis, then, Inequalities 5.11a and 5.11b present the conditions necessary for reinforcement and punishment, respectively.

a) Reinforcement $Rt/Rc > Bt/Bc$
b) Punishment $Rt/Rc < Bt/Bc$ Inequality 5.11

Once again, we will attempt to clarify this situation by considering our earlier example of modifying the rates of reading and playing in a second-grade student. Recall that for this student Bt (the baseline rate of reading) was 10 minutes in a one hour period compared to Bc (the baseline rate of playing) which was 50 minutes in the same one hour period. By substituting these values into Inequality 5.10, the result is

$$Rt/Rc < 10/50 \quad \text{Inequality 5.12}$$

and we can simplify these values to

$$Rt/Rc < 1/5 \quad \text{Inequality 5.13}$$

In this case, then, the response-disequilibrium hypothesis predicts that punishment of reading RT will occur when we create a situation that requires a ratio of RT to RC (reading to playing) that is less than 1/5.

To put this theory to work, suppose that you implement a program where this student must play for 55 minutes to earn the opportunity to read for 5 minutes. When we substitute these values in our equation, we get

$$5/55 < 1/5 \quad \text{Inequality 5.13}$$

which simplifies to

$$1/11 < 1/5 \quad \text{Inequality 5.14}$$

In this case, 1/11 is less than 1/5 so the response-disequilibrium hypothesis predicts that reading would be punished for this student.

As this example illustrates, the response-disequilibrium hypothesis, allows us to predict the conditions that will lead to punishment of a target response. A number of studies have confirmed these predictions of the response-disequilibrium hypothesis in laboratory experiments (Heth & Warren, 1978; Mazur, 1975) and in clinical settings (Dougher, 1983). The response-disequilibrium hypothesis currently appears to be the best statement of the necessary and sufficient conditions for reinforcement as well as punishment in operant learning situations. Despite this success, the response-disequilibrium hypothesis still awaits further experimental evaluation.

SUMMARY STATEMENTS

We have examined four theoretical issues concerning instrumental and operant conditioning. We found that there is no adequate theory to characterize the nature of reinforcement. However, recent theories emphasizing the kinds of response opportunities that occur after the operant response appear promising. The response-disequilibrium hypothesis provides the best available specification of the necessary and sufficient conditions for reinforcement.

We noted the various attempts to explain how reinforcement functions in instrumental and operant conditioning. We saw that problems arise from the view that a reinforcer strengthens stimulus-response associations. We also found that the notion that a reinforcer provides incentive or motivation does not cover all situations. Here, the best explanations appeared to be those in which the reinforcer is viewed as an element in the operant association itself.

We looked at two different types of operant extinction theories. One was based on a competing response notion, while others emphasized discrimination between reinforcement and extinction situations, or sequential decrements that occur during extinction. We found that Capaldi's generalization decrement theory accounts for a wide range of extinction data. Still, we noted the possibilities that extinction may be caused by multiple factors and that a combination of theoretical ideas may be necessary to provide a satisfactory explanation.

Finally, we examined theoretical issues surrounding punishment. In this case, it appears that punishment is the opposite of reinforcement and that it functions to reduce the punished response. We saw that punishment is effective for reducing or eliminating undesirable behavior, but we also saw that punishment produces a number of troublesome side effects. It seems fair to conclude that punishment should be avoided whenever possible, but the question of whether it should be used at all remains an ongoing controversy. To end the chapter, we returned to the response-disequilibrium hypothesis and examined the predictions this theory makes regarding the necessary and sufficient conditions for punishment. We again found that the theory provides a useful and promising theoretical account of punishment.

6

The Interaction of Classical and Operant Conditioning

CHAPTER OVERVIEW

Classical and operant conditioning are not separate processes. Classical conditioning involves pairing a neutral stimulus (conditioned stimulus or CS) with an unconditioned stimulus (US). Presentation of the US causes some reliable and measurable response. In addition, the US is presented regardless of the behavior of the organism. That is, the US is response independent. With repeated pairings the CS acquires the ability to elicit its own response, which is known as the conditioned response (CR). Instrumental conditioning on the other hand involves pairing a response with an outcome. To receive the outcome, the organism must emit a response. In instrumental conditioning, organisms emit responses and outcomes are response dependent. In classical conditioning, responses are elicited by stimuli and outcomes are response independent. With these definitions it is not apparent that instrumental conditioning could affect responding to a conditioned stimulus or that classical conditioning could modify an instrumental response.

This chapter demonstrates that classical conditioning and instrumental conditioning are not separate and independent processes. As the title of the chapter implies, we will examine situations where classical conditioning and operant conditioning interact. The interactions could take any of three forms. First, we will examine those instances where classical conditioning and instrumental conditioning are occurring at the same time. Under this topic we will examine avoidance learning, in which an animal learns first to escape and then to avoid dangerous or harmful situations. To demonstrate the possible role of classical conditioning and instrumental conditioning in avoidance learning, we will first consider a typical avoidance experiment. Then we will examine an explanation for avoidance learning that relies on both classical conditioning and operant conditioning. Supportive and nonsupportive evidence for this position will be discussed. Having considered the classic theory of avoidance learning, we will then examine more closely the implications of this theory and we will examine theoretical positions that take into consideration the organism's evolutionary past.

Marion and Keller Breland first alerted us to the role an organism's evolutionary past plays in behavior. The Brelands had difficulty training some animals to do certain tasks because the animals instinctive behavior interfered with its conditioned behavior. We will see that part of the problem that the Brelands encountered was an interaction among the influences of classical conditioning, instrumental conditioning, and the organism's evolutionary history.

Classical conditioning and instrumental conditioning also combine to influence behavior in those situations where cues are provided that indicate whether an animal will be rewarded or not. This section will discuss the role of discriminative stimuli. Such stimuli can elicit respondent or reflexive behavior. In addition, because of their association with primary reinforcers they are also able to reinforce behavior. Discussion of conditioned reinforcement leads to consideration of the observing response. Studies on observing examined why animals respond to obtain a signal that informs them what schedule of reinforcement is currently in effect.

Next we will examine cases where classical conditioning affects instrumental conditioning. We will also look at instances where instrumental conditioning influences classical conditioning. In earlier chapters, we alluded to the phenomenon of autoshaping. The autoshaping literature shows that you do not have to use elaborate shaping techniques to get a pigeon to peck a key. All you have to do is light a response key for a short period of time and follow that with access to grain. Once the animal makes the association between the light and food, the light will elicit an approach response. This approach response often terminates with a complex instrumental or operant response that for a pigeon is pecking the key. The procedure shows that classical conditioning can produce a complex operant response.

The chapter concludes with consideration of a mathematical model of operant conditioning offered by Dragoi and Staddon (1999). This model will not be considered in its full mathematical detail. However, enough information will be provided to understand the approach and the basic parameters that underlie operant behavior.

CLASSICAL CONDITIONING AND INSTRUMENTAL CONDITIONING IN AVOIDANCE LEARNING

Imagine that it is the first day of spring break and you are on your way to Cancun. When the flight attendant announces that it's time to board the plane, you walk through the gate and down to the plane, thinking you are the luckiest person around.

Seated comfortably in a window seat you gaze out as the plane takes off. After an hour you hear the pilot announce over the intercom that you should fasten your seat belt as there appears to be a little turbulence ahead. Suddenly you feel your stomach in your throat and you hear people screaming. You look out the window and see that the aircraft is hurtling straight toward the ocean. In seconds you hear the engines whining loudly as the plane begins to pull out of its dive. You are thrown back in your seat and feel your body being pressed hard against the cushions. Finally, the plane levels off and the pilot announces that the plane will be landing shortly.

After seven glorious days in Cancun, it is time once again to board the plane. This time your experience is far different. Now as you walk through the gate you find yourself sweating. Your heart is racing and breathing is difficult. You realize that you are very afraid, and you refuse to get on the plane. You run back out the gate, leave the airport, and stop running only after the airport is no longer in sight. Now you finally start to feel better. In minutes your heart rate decreases, you find breathing easier, and you stop sweating.

Mowrer's Two-Factor Theory

So how are we to account for your behavior? Clearly you were afraid. You probably will be afraid of flying for some time. Mowrer (1947) proposed that avoidance learning involved two processes, classical conditioning and instrumental conditioning. Dangerous, painful, aversive stimuli cause an innate fear response. When an or-

ganism encountered such a situation, stimuli that were present were associated with fear through classical conditioning. Thus when these stimuli were encountered again, they evoked a fear response. In the above example, the airport, gate, and plane were initially neutral stimuli. These stimuli were paired with a series of aversive events that constituted unconditioned stimuli. In this example the USs are (1) plummeting toward the ocean, (2) the sights and sounds of people screaming, and (3) getting sick. Following this experience, the presentation of the airport, gate, and the plane all evoke a fear response.

Mowrer argued that the presence of fear and all of its visceral effects was aversive and that any response that removed these stimuli would be negatively reinforced. The avoidance response therefore was reinforced through instrumental conditioning. In the example above, when you ran away from the plane, the gate, and the airport you started to feel better. This reduction of fear was rewarding and reinforced your behavior of retreating from airports.

The Avoidance Paradigm. A study by Solomon and Wynne (1953) illustrates the basic procedure for avoidance conditioning. Soloman and Wynne placed dogs one at a time in a chamber that contained two rectangular rooms separated by a barrier several centimeters high. Each compartment had a metal floor through which a strong electric shock could be delivered. Each compartment was illuminated by an overhead light. In each session dogs received 10 trials in which the light overhead was turned off for 10 seconds followed by electric shock. The dog could escape shock by jumping over the barrier to the lighted side of the apparatus. It could avoid shock by jumping to the lighted side before the 10-second period elapsed. On the subsequent trial, the dog is in the other compartment. The overhead light for this chamber is turned off and the dog is required to jump back to the previous site. The apparatus is called a two-way shuttle and the animal is required to jump back and forth in the presence of the conditioned stimulus to

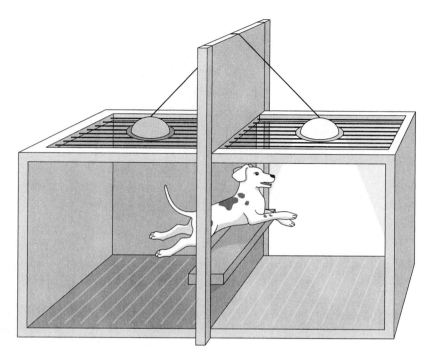

FIGURE 6.1 Experimental Apparatus. Soloman and Wynne's apparatus for studying avoidance learning in dogs.

either escape or avoid shock. Figure 6.1 shows a two-way shuttle apparatus and the acquisition of an avoidance response.

As you might expect, Soloman and Wynne's dogs readily learned. For the first few trials when the light went off the dogs stayed in the dark compartment until they received the shock. Then they quickly jumped over the barrier to safety. After a few trials, the dogs began to show generalized activity when the light was turned off and soon began jumping to the lighted side before the shock was delivered. From this point forward the dogs rarely, if ever, received shock.

A Problem for Psychologists: What Reinforces Avoidance Behavior?

Avoidance learning posed a problem that Mowrer found intriguing. It was easy to understand how the escape behavior persisted. The termination of the aversive stimulus would be rewarding. Escape behavior was maintained through negative rein-

forcement. But how was the avoidance response maintained? The paradox is that the animal continues to respond even though it no longer receives aversive stimulation. How could the absence of a stimulus reinforce or maintain a response?

Mowrer's two-factor theory offered a convincing explanation. In the Solomon and Wynne study, termination of the light served as a conditioned stimulus that was associated with electric shock. Given that electric shock was painful, the dark side became a feared stimulus. As such, light termination would be associated with visceral responses that might include an increase in heart rate, changes in breathing rate, increased sweating, etc. These visceral responses are unpleasant and any response that caused their reduction or elimination would be reinforced.

Mowrer argued that the termination or reduction of fear stimuli maintained the avoidance response. The argument, modified somewhat by

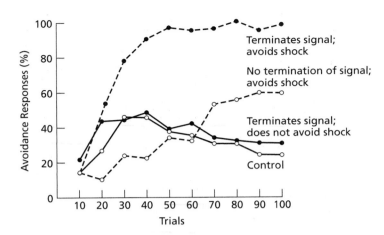

Schoenfeld (1950), stated that there really was no avoidance learning. There was only escape learning. In the initial trials the dog escaped electric shock that was painful and aversive. In later trials, once the CS had been associated with an aversive stimulus and elicited conditioned fear, the animal escaped these stimuli.

Support for Two-Factor Theory

Two-factor theory predicts that avoidance responding will be learned only to the extent that the warning signal terminates when a response is made. To test this prediction Kamin (1957a) trained four groups of rats in a two-chamber avoidance apparatus. One group was given typical avoidance learning trials in which moving from one compartment to the other during the signal led to both avoidance of shock and to termination of the warning signal. A second group was trained so that responding led to avoidance of the shock but not to the termination of the signal. Responses in the third group terminated the signal, but shock was delivered nevertheless. In the last group, both the signal and the shock occurred regardless of the response. Thus, this group received only classical conditioning trials with no instrumental contingencies in effect.

Figure 6.2 depicts the results of the experiment. The figure shows that a significant amount of avoidance responding occurred in the first group only. It is particularly notable that responding was poor in the group that was able to avoid shock but could not terminate the signal. This is precisely the result that would be predicted by two-factor theory.

As we have seen, the essence of two-factor theory is that the animal escapes a fear-producing stimulus. If the termination of a feared stimulus is reinforcing, it should be possible to reduce the level of reinforcement by introducing a delay between the response and termination of the feared stimulus. As we saw in chapter 4 delaying the onset of reinforcement reduces the effectiveness of reward. Kamin (1957b) conducted an avoidance study in which the termination of the CS was delayed by varying amounts. In one condition upon completion of the avoidance response the CS was immediately terminated. In other conditions termination of the CS was delayed by 2.5, 5, or 10 seconds.

As depicted in Figure 6.3 the effectiveness of termination of the CS to support avoidance conditioning was decreased by increasing delay. In the zero-delay condition animals successfully avoided shock over 80% of the trials. Animals in

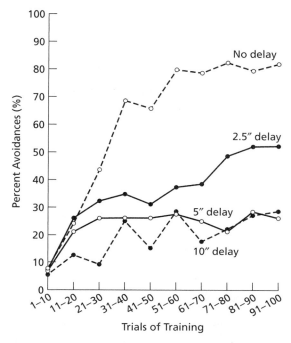

FIGURE 6.3 Kamin's (1957b) Results. Delay was introduced into an avoidance paradigm.

the 10-second delay condition avoided shock on fewer than 10% of the trials. The results of the Kamin study strongly supported the contention that the source of reinforcement in avoidance conditioning was the reduction of fear generated by termination of the CS.

A paper by Rescorla and LoLordo (1965) provides an example of two-factor theory in another class of experiments. Rescorla and Lolordo trained dogs to shuttle from one compartment to another to avoid shock. In their procedure shocks were delivered every 10 seconds unless the dog jumped to the other side in which case shock was delayed for 30 seconds. Next, away from the shuttle box, these dogs were given trials in which a tone was paired with shock. Then the dogs were returned to the shuttle box and avoidance trials resumed. During the avoidance session the tone was sounded but was not followed by shock. In the presence of the tone, the dogs made significantly more avoidance responses.

Rescorla and LoLordo also found the opposite effect. During the phase in which the tone was paired with shock, a second stimulus was presented and this stimulus was never followed by shock. Thus, the dogs learned that when this second stimulus was presented (a conditioned inhibitor) they would not be shocked; the stimulus was considered a safety signal. When Rescorla and LoLordo presented the conditioned inhibitor, the number of avoidance responses emitted by the dogs decreased relative to the number produced during the absence of the conditioned inhibitor. The two findings together show that it is possible to manipulate the level of avoidance conditioning by increasing or decreasing the level of fear by introducing stimuli associated with fear or safety. This finding is consistent with two-factor theory.

Contradictory Evidence for Two-Factor Theory

Not all of the evidence has supported two-factor theory. Sidman (1953) developed a procedure that posed a major problem for two-factor theory. Sidman placed rats in a Skinner box and programmed it to deliver shock every 5 seconds. If the rat pressed a lever before the 5-second period expired shock was delayed for 30 seconds. Rats were not able to accumulate shock-free periods. If the rat responded a large number of times consecutively, shock was delayed by only 30 seconds from the last response. Interestingly the rats were able to solve this problem and responded in such a way as to avoid many of the shocks.

The procedure used by Sidman generated theoretical interest because it appeared that Sidman had demonstrated avoidance learning in the absence of a conditioned stimulus. How could that be possible if maintenance of avoidance behavior required escape from a fear-eliciting stimulus? Anger (1963) pointed out that the passage of time could serve as a CS. Sidman's rats may have used the passage of time to predict the onset of shock and by pressing the bar and increasing the amount of time before the next shock was delivered may have reduced the fear elicited by time. This idea is not at all far-fetched as numerous studies have shown that animals are capable of timing events (Church, 1978).

A more significant challenge to two-factor theory came from a study by Herrnstein and Hineline (1966). These scientists placed rats in a Skinner box and programmed electric-shock delivery randomly according to a probability of .3 for each two-second period that elapsed. If the rat pressed a lever, the probability of shock was decreased from .3 to .1. Thus, by pressing a lever a rat could neither avoid nor escape shock, but it could reduce the number of shocks it received. Amazingly, Herrnstein and Hineline's rats learned the task and kept the lower rate of shock schedule in effect most of the time.

These results were significant because avoidance learning was demonstrated in a situation where there was no external stimulus to elicit fear, nor was there a possibility for an internal cue. Herrnstein and Hineline argued that avoidance conditioning could be accounted for by positing only one factor, reduction in shock rate. One did not have to invoke classical conditioning as a factor in avoidance learning.

The Herrnstein and Hineline position had an added advantage. It explained why rats learned more slowly in certain situations than others. When an animal can discriminate easily between conditions where shock is likely and where it is not, learning should proceed much faster. This analysis correctly predicts that avoidance conditioning in situations where shock probability is reduced from 1 to 0 would be much faster than in those cases where the probability of shock is reduced by a smaller margin. There is evidence both supporting and not supporting the shock-reduction hypothesis (see Hineline, 1977).

The Role of Discriminative Stimuli and Instinctive Drift

Imagine that you want to create your own animal-training business. You have been impressed by recent television and radio commercials that use animals to sell products and you think you can do better and more creative work.

As you sit watching myriad TV commercials, you realize that bank commercials are generally the most boring. How could animals be used to promote the banking industry? Suddenly, it hits you. Why not train a real pig to drop a coin into a piggy bank? That would certainly be cute and you have heard that pigs are smart and easy to train.

Arriving back at your apartment with your newly purchased pig, you develop a training strategy. The first step is to motivate the pig. You deprive the pig of food for 24 hours. The next day, having gotten the pig's attention, you train it to drop a coin on demand. You get a quarter, walk over to the pig, and when he looks up and opens his mouth you put the coin in his mouth. Not too surprisingly, the pig swallows your quarter.

You get a bigger coin, and you put it in the pig's mouth. As soon as he drops the coin, you reinforce it with a Pig Power Biscuit. The pig eats the biscuit and you put the coin back in its mouth and repeat the trials. After about 50 trials, the pig reliably drops the coin when you signal.

Next, you require the pig to drop the coin in a particular place before it gets the treat. The pig is then required to run from another location to the selected spot and drop the coin. Having trained the pig to drop the coin onto a certain spot from anywhere in the room, you begin having the pig drop the coin into a large piggy bank with a very wide hole on top. Training continues in this manner until the pig runs from any location across the living room floor and drops the coin into the bank.

You are completely excited as you call the marketing people at the local banks to see if any are interested in your promotion idea. Several are. You talk to the marketing specialist at United Bank & Trust, and you get an appointment for three weeks after to show off your pig. Now it's time to polish your act.

Following a few days off during which you thought of all the ways to spend the money you will make with your trained pig, you pull the piggy bank out of a sack and place it at the other end of your living room. As you do this, you notice your pig showing signs of excitement. Next you pull out the coin and place it in front of the pig. The pig shows an even greater level of activity and it starts salivating on the floor. You get a little nervous. The pig runs toward the coin and picks it up and runs toward the piggy bank. About half way across the floor, the pig flips the coin in the air. When the coin hits the floor the pig roots around for it and knocks over furniture as it chases the coin. At one point, you attempt to pick up the coin as it rolls by and the pig knocks you down. Then he accidentally knocks over the sack of pig treats. The pig roots its way to the treats and eats contentedly.

You are devastated. Your first major break in the animal-training business has gone awry. You decide you need to get the pig's attention, and the only way is through further hunger deprivation. You decide to try again in 48 hours. After all it will be two more weeks before the film crew comes with the bank representatives. There is nothing to worry about. After 48 hours, you try again. This time the problem is worse. The pig continues to misbehave. In fact it is acting very much like a pig. You decide to deprive the pig of food for 72 hours. With 10 days left to filming, there is nothing to worry about. Three days later you try again. This time, it appears that you have no control at all over the pig. He has completely lost his senses. Indeed, the pig is not only *not* doing what he was rewarded to do, he is doing things for which he has never received reward. You call the bank and cancel the deal.

Think about the chain of events that led to this errant pig behavior. The first thing you realize is that the behavior elicited by the coin changed during training. At first the coin had no effect on the pig; remember, he nonchalantly ate the first one. The bigger coin solved that problem, but it elicited no behavior initially. However, with training, it was clear that the coin, and the piggy bank for that matter, elicited species-

typical behavior. Both stimuli caused the pig to increase in generalized activity, but the coin also elicited salivation. For the first time you realize that this is the same thing that Pavlov's dogs did many years ago. It looked like the coin had been associated with food and now the pig was reacting to it as if it were food.

The coin served as a **discriminative stimulus** informing the pig when a particular response-reinforcement contingency would be in effect. And it was a conditioned stimulus that elicited respondent behavior.

Upon greater reflection you reasoned that there was even more going on than just classical conditioning and operant conditioning. The pig's response to the coin appeared to be behavior that it would naturally emit to food. That is, the sight or smell of food would elicit a series of behaviors that pigs throughout time have emitted. Pigs naturally dig for roots and tubers with their snouts knocking things over and throwing things around. The coin, which had been paired with food, now seemed to elicit pig typical foraging behavior.

Discriminative Stimuli Elicit Respondent Behavior. The above scenario is virtually identical to the experiences of Marion and Keller Breland. These research scientists worked with B. F. Skinner and were interested in applied animal behavior. In a paper entitled "The Misbehavior of Organisms," published in 1961, they reported on attempts to train a pig to drop a coin into a piggy bank. During the course of training the pig began acting toward the coin as it would toward food. This was especially disconcerting to the Brelands because at no time had they reinforced this type of behavior. Indeed, during the course of training the Brelands thought that the problem might lie in the motivation of the pig. As they increased the level of deprivation, the pig reverted more and more to its old self. The Brelands were forced to abandon the attempt.

The Breland's difficulty did not end with pigs. Raccoons were trained to do the same trick. Again, it became more and more difficult to train the animal to do the task. This time the problem was not one of rooting and running around but was one of washing. Once the raccoons had associated the coin with food they would treat it like food. When the raccoon picked up the coin it would walk over to the bank and start to drop in the coin but then pull it back out. It would then rub the coin against the side of the bank before attempting to drop it in again. Eventually the animal was successfully trained, but when the Brelands required the animal to drop two coins in the bank the raccoon's behavior became unpredictable. The raccoon would sit for seconds and even minutes washing the coins and not dropping them into the bank. The Brelands were forced to abandon this project as well.

The discovery that an animal's evolutionary history can compete with learned behavior was termed **instinctive drift**. In fact, the evolutionary history of the animal will often take precedence over learned behavior. During instrumental conditioning if the conditions for reinforcement require a response that is not compatible with the animal's evolutionary history, the latter takes precedence. Had the Brelands been interested in training a pig to push a soccer ball around a field they would have had no difficulty. And we might not have discovered the important role that evolution plays in dictating an organism's behavior.

You may have already noticed the adaptive nature of the responses produced by discriminative stimuli. The rooting behavior of the pig and the washing behavior of the raccoon are adaptive behaviors that promote survival. This finding and the whole notion of instinctive drift emphasizes the fact that behavior is adaptive and that it takes place within a biological context.

The Discriminative Stimulus Reinforces Behavior. Another instance in which classical conditioning and operant conditioning combine to produce behavior relates to the role of the discriminative stimulus as a conditioned reinforcer.

THE OBSERVING RESPONSE: THE POWER OF CONDITIONED REINFORCEMENT

A stimulus that has been associated with an aversive event can be used to punish behavior. It makes sense then that a stimulus that has been paired with reward can be used to reinforce behavior. Given that discriminative stimuli are often paired with food, such stimuli should strengthen the probability of the response that produced it.

Wyckoff (1952, 1969) placed pigeons in a Skinner box where a white light was projected onto the response key. During certain 2-minute segments, the pigeon was rewarded on a FI 30 sec schedule. That is, the pigeon was reinforced for the first peck on the key after 30 seconds had elapsed since its last reinforcement. During other 2-minute segments the pigeon was not rewarded. During the 30-minute session the pigeon responded under an FI 30 sec schedule one half the time and under extinction the other half. The segments of FI 30 sec and EXT were randomly distributed. There were no cues that the animal could use to determine which schedule was in effect. This schedule is known as a mixed schedule of reinforcement.

Wyckoff then introduced a second response. He placed a treadle in front of the food hopper and response key. This treadle could be depressed while the pigeon pecked the key and ate. For pigeons in the control group, depressing the treadle changed the response key color from white to either red or green. In the presence of either color the pigeon received either food or extinction segments. In the experimental group, pigeons pressed the treadle and the key color also changed to red or green. However, for this group if the food schedule was in effect the key turned red and if the extinction schedule was in effect the key turned green. Depressing the treadle provided information about which schedule was in effect.

Pigeons in the experimental group spent about 90% of their time in the Skinner box standing on the treadle. Control pigeons spent

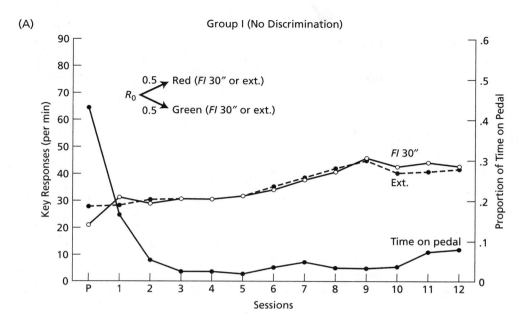

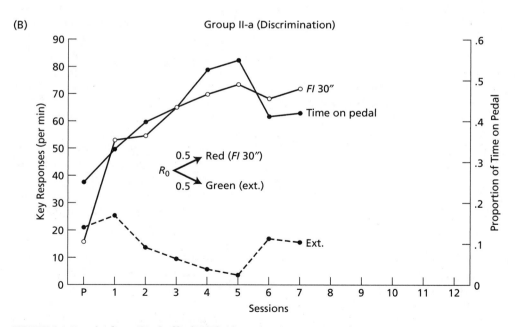

FIGURE 6.4 Results from Wyckoff's (1969) Observing Response Study.

significantly less time on the treadle. Wyckoff termed this behavior an **observing response**. In addition, pigeons in the experimental group pecked the key color associated with food significantly more than they pecked the key color associated with extinction. Control pigeons did not discriminate. The question of interest is why did Wyckoff's pigeons stand on the treadle at all? Figure 6.4 depicts the results of Wyckoff's (1969) study on observing.

Theoretical Explanations of the Observing Response

You probably have already thought of several reasons why pigeons observed. Perhaps they simply liked the change in key colors. This explanation is not supported, however. Pigeons in the control group also produced changes in key color, but these changes were not correlated with outcome. Because control pigeons did not observe, it appears that a critical element in the Wyckoff procedure is that the change in stimuli must reliably predict response outcomes.

An animal indeed may observe to be a more efficient forager. This argument relates to theoretical positions concerning **optimal foraging**, where it is assumed that natural selection would select animals that maximize energy intake and minimize energy output (Kamil & Sargent, 1981; Kamil, Krebs, & Pullium, 1987; Shettleworth, 1988). This argument has been supported in studies involving humans (Case, Fantino, & Wixted, 1985; Case, Ploog, & Fantino, 1990; Fantino & Case, 1983; Perone & Baron, 1980) and in studies involving rhesus monkeys (Lieberman, 1972; Steiner, 1967).

However, the optimal foraging argument has received no support in the pigeon literature. Dinsmoor has shown that pigeons will observe in situations where reward is response independent (Dinsmoor, Bowe, Green, & Hanson, 1988). In addition, Dinsmoor and his colleagues have shown that observing pigeons actually responded more during food segments than pigeons in the control group. In fact, the number of pecks generated by both experimental and control pigeons were about the same (Dinsmoor, Browne, & Lawrence, 1972; Mulvaney, Dinsmoor, Jwaideh, & Hughes, 1974). Thus, an argument based on optimal foraging theory accounts for some of the data, but it can not handle a number of studies from the pigeon literature.

Information theory provides the third account. Berlyne (1957) and Hendry (1969) argued that observing is reinforced through the **reduction of uncertainty.** Uncertainty is viewed as an aversive condition and observing persists because it reduces uncertainty about forthcoming events. Information theory makes the novel prediction that the stimulus associated with food (S+) and the stimulus associated with extinction (S−) are rewarding, because both stimuli reduce uncertainty equally.

No studies unambiguously support this position. In situations where S− has been terminated or not presented, the level of observing increased (e.g., Blanchard, 1975; Browne & Dinsmoor, 1974; Dinsmoor, Browne, & Lawrence, 1972; Mulvaney, Dinsmoor, Jwaideh, & Hughes, 1974). In these studies, S+ increased the probability of observing whereas S− decreased the probability. There are also studies where S− has been shown to be aversive (see for example, Purdy, Bales, Burns, & Wiegand, 1994).

Wyckoff (1952) argued that the observing response was maintained through **conditioned reinforcement.** The basic argument was that a stimulus that was associated with food became a conditioned reinforcer. When the animal produced S+ (the green or red light depending on which one was associated with food) its response was reinforced. In contrast, the stimulus that was associated with extinction was not reinforcing and possibly even punishing. Wyckoff maintained that on balance the rewarding properties of S+ outweighed the punishing properties of S− and observing persisted.

In a refinement of this argument, Fantino (1977) theorized that the strength of a conditioned reinforcer is determined by the degree of reduction in delay to reinforcement. Thus, a stimulus associated with a short delay to reinforcement will be a better secondary reinforcer than a stimulus associated with a longer delay to reinforcement. A stimulus associated with extinction would not serve as a secondary reinforcement.

Fantino also argued for the importance of a second factor. This factor concerns the relative reduction in time to reward as measured from the previous reward. A stimulus that predicts reward after a short delay in a schedule where the overall density of reward is low will be a better reinforcer than a stimulus that predicts reward after a short delay in a schedule where the overall density of reward is high. Imagine a red light that is associated with a 10-second delay to food in a schedule where food is presented every 10 minutes. The red light would be a stronger conditioned reinforcer in this situation than in a schedule where food is presented once a minute. Fantino maintains that the increase in reinforcing effect of delay reduction is greater in magnitude than the decrease in reward value of a comparable increase in delay to reward.

A great number of studies have found that S+ is rewarding and S− is not (e.g., Blanchard, 1975; Browne & Dinsmoor, 1974; Dinsmoor, Browne, & Lawrence, 1972; Mulvaney, Dinsmoor, Jwaideh, & Hughes, 1974; Purdy & Peel, 1988; Purdy, Bales, Burns, & Wiegand, 1994). Secondary reinforcement theory has accounted for the majority of studies on observing and appears to be the explanation of choice.

Generality of the Observing Response

The finding that an animal will work for a cue that informs it which schedule is in effect has been replicated numerous times and with a variety of species including goldfish (Purdy & Peel, 1988; Purdy, Bales, Burns, & Wiegand, 1994) pigeons (e.g., Blanchard, 1975; Browne & Dinsmoor, 1974; Dinsmoor, Browne, & Lawrence, 1972; Mulvaney, Dinsmoor, Jwaideh, & Hughes, 1974; Roper & Zentall, 1999), rats (Daly, 1985; Prokasy, 1956), rhesus monkeys (Lieberman, 1972; Steiner, 1967), and humans

(Fantino & Case; Perone & Baron, 1980). The observing response is a robust phenomenon and its discovery has generated considerable interest.

AUTOSHAPING AND SIGN TRACKING

We will now take a look at some situations in which classical conditioning influences the instrumental response.

Autoshaping: The Role of the Discriminative Stimulus as a Conditioned Stimulus

Sitting in his living room one afternoon, a man hears a funny scratching/knocking noise at the door. Disturbed, he walks over to the door and looks outside. No one is there. A few seconds later the knocking noise has returned. Again the man goes to the door and opens it. This time he looks down to discover a pigeon. The bird walks over to the couch and begins cleaning the carpet.

By the end of the week the man's apartment is looking good. During the second week, he decides that he will have to find the pigeon a source of entertainment. He remembers that a few months ago he had purchased a Skinner box at a garage sale hosted by a famous learning psychologist.

He dusts off the Skinner box, hooks up the controls, and tosses in the pigeon. But training a pigeon to peck a key is not simply a matter of putting the bird in the box and shutting the door. Something more is required. As the man stares at the pigeon thinking about how best to get this bird to peck that key, he notices that the bird is looking awfully plump. It occurs to the man that the bird has gained four pounds; perhaps it is simply not motivated.

After a 24-hour fast the bird is much more active. Still there is no attempt to peck the key.

The man picks up a psychology text and do a little studying about operant and instrum conditioning. It becomes obvious why the pigeon failed to peck the key. Once the animal is motivated, it has to be taught that food is available. So the man begins with a process called magazine training. He programs the food hopper to open at random intervals. The hopper contains the pigeon's favorite food (carpet crumbs) and the pigeon is allowed to eat as much as it can in 4 seconds. This contingency is in effect for 2 hours.

Now the pigeon's behavior has changed dramatically. Before magazine training there was an increase in activity but nothing else. Now, at the sound of the clicking, the pigeon races to the food hopper and eats voraciously when the door opens.

Now the man can start shaping the bird's pecking behavior. First he restricts the space in which the bird can receive a reward. He requires the pigeon to stand on the side of the box where the response key is located. If the bird moves to the side nearest the response key it will receive food. For the next 30 minutes or so the man reinforces the pigeon only if it is on this side. Gradually the man restricts the pigeon further.

Finally he achieves success. The pigeon actually strikes the key! Unfortunately, it does not strike the key hard enough to register. Still, the man reinforced the animal immediately after it pecked. Two hours later, the pigeon has finally been trained to key peck.

Shaping the Key-Peck Response Automatically.

For a great number of years, the above scenario accurately depicted how experimental psychologists trained pigeons (or any animal for that matter). Though researchers spent a few hours training their animals the effort seemed worthwhile. Once the animal was trained, the Skinner box was an ideal apparatus. It virtually ran itself and freed the experimenter to work on more human tasks such as writing manuscripts, teaching classes, and drinking coffee. The apparatus provided superb control of the environment making one confident of the cause-and-effect relations that were discovered.

Autoshaping Studies.

Still, one had to first shape the animal to produce the operant and that was generally the least interesting part of any experiment. Imagine then, the reaction when a paper came out by Brown and Jenkins (1968) showing researchers how to shape their animals automatically. Brown and Jenkins placed a hungry pigeon in a one-key Skinner box and trained it to feed from a food hopper.

Brown and Jenkins presented their pigeons with two conditioning sessions. Each session consisted of 80 pairings of 8 seconds of light followed by 4 seconds of access to grain. The light was projected onto the response key that was centered above the food hopper. The pigeon received these pairings of light and food on average every 60 seconds. Brown and Jenkins programmed one other contingency. A peck on the lighted key turned it off and resulted in access to food.

Twelve pigeons in a control group received backward conditioning trials. For these pigeons the food hopper suddenly opens and the pigeon is allowed access to grain. After the hopper closes, the response key is lighted for 8 seconds. All subjects receiving forward conditioning trials pecked the lighted key during CS presentations. Pecking was preceded by an increase in general activity levels and the first response was seen on average after 45 trials. The range was 6–119. All pigeons in the experimental group pecked the key even though there was no shaping and they did not have to respond to receive the food. The pigeons in the backward conditioning group did not acquire the key-peck response. The procedure became known as **autoshaping.**

The Brown and Jenkins paper revolutionized the means by which experimenters trained animals to produce operant responses. No longer did the experimenter have to spend long hours in the lab carefully shaping the pigeon to peck. Experimenters could simply place a hungry pigeon in a Skinner box and program paired presentations of the key light and food.

Much more important than reducing the workload of operant researchers were the theoretical implications. Brown and Jenkins appeared to have identified a new type of conditioned response. When a hungry pigeon is presented with the sight of food, it pecks. This is the unconditioned response. When a key light is paired with food the pigeon comes to peck the key as a conditioned response. Brown and Jenkins showed that complex motor behavior could be acquired through classical conditioning. Before 1968 this was considered the role of instrumental conditioning. The findings also suggested that classical conditioning might play a role in instrumental responding in ways not previously considered.

Generality of Autoshaping. We have seen that pigeons can be autoshaped to peck a key. A number of experiments with rats have demonstrated that they too will autoshape. The usual procedure involves the insertion of a lever into the chamber just before food is delivered. Once the rats make the association between the lever and food, they approach and contact the lever with their mouths and then with their paws. Eventually the rat pushes the bar with enough force to activate the feeding mechanism (for examples, see Cleland & Davey, 1983; Locurto, Terrace, & Gibbon, 1976).

Woodard & Bitterman (1974) autoshaped goldfish to strike a target for a food reward, Squier (1969) autoshaped tilapia (another species of fish), and Loop (1976) autoshaped monitor lizards. Interestingly, in each case the form of the conditioned response resembled the animal's species-typical feeding behavior. This finding led some researchers to question whether the US played a role in establishing the nature of the instrumental response.

Role of the US in Autoshaping. If classical conditioning influences the nature of the instrumental response then characteristics of the US should affect that response. Jenkins and Moore (1973) tested this hypothesis under two conditions. In one condition the US was food and in the second the US was water. The authors used high-speed photography to analyze the conditioned response. Under both conditions the key light elicited approach behavior. However, the key-peck response differed depending on the reward. Pigeons pecked the key that had been associated with food with open beaks and they pecked the key that had been associated with water with closed beaks. In nature, pigeons peck for food with an open beak and they peck for water with a closed beak. It appeared that the pigeon was responding to the CS as if it were food or water. Figure 6.5 (p. 180) shows the form of the key-peck response as determined by the US.

The Jenkins and Moore paper showed that characteristics of the US influence the nature of the instrumental response and confirmed that classical conditioning could play a role in the development of an instrumental response. The study also provided support for Pavlov's stimulus substitution model, which theorized that when the neural events produced in the brain by the presentation of the CS overlap with the neural events produced by the US there results an association. This stimulus–stimulus or stimulus-reinforcement bond implied that the CS became a substitute for the US. The results of the Jenkins and Moore study can be understood in this manner. The animals responded to the food signal as if it were food and to the water signal as if it were water.

According to Brown and Jenkins the autoshaped response was not supported solely by classical conditioning. The first peck on the key was due to the association between the light and the food. Subsequent pecks were maintained by both classical and instrumental conditioning because reward always followed key pecking. Williams and Williams (1969) tested whether the response-reinforcement bond was necessary to support the key peck behavior. In one experiment, they showed that autoshaped key pecking was maintained even under a negative-response contingency.

In the Williams and Williams study one group of pigeons received traditional autoshaping trials. The birds received paired presentations of the key light and food. A peck on the key terminated the CS and was followed by reinforcement.

FIGURE 6.5 Pigeons in Jenkins & Moore's (1973) Autoshaping Study. They pecked for food with an open beak and pecked for water with a closed beak. *From the Journal of the Experimental Analysis of Behavior*, 1973, 20, 163–181. ©1973 by the Society for the Experimental Analysis of Behavior.

A second group also received paired presentations of light and food. However, for this group if the animal pecked the key, the CS was turned off and no food was presented. Interestingly, both groups acquired and maintained the key-peck response. In fact, the performance of the negative autoshaping group fell to a level where the birds were collecting only 5 to 30% of the total possible rewards.

Williams and Williams' results demonstrated just how powerful conditioned stimuli could be in controlling behavior. Brown and Jenkins, Jenkins and Moore, and Williams and Williams showed that autoshaped key pecking was maintained by stimulus-reinforcement associations established through classical conditioning. These studies also provided evidence for Pavolv's stimulus substitution model and showed that it might be difficult to separate the effects of classical and instrumental conditioning. In situations once thought to be purely operant in nature, classical conditioning was at work to influence behavior.

Role of the CS in Autoshaping. Holland (1977) showed that characteristics of the CS played a role in the nature of the conditioned response. In situations where food served as the US, if the CS was light rats responded to the light by rearing up and if the CS was a tone, rats responded to the tone by jerking their head toward the sound. Characteristics of the key light might also influence the autoshaped response. In the Brown and Jenkins study, the pigeon was placed in a lighted Skinner box. The light provided general background illumination and in its presence the key light was turned on. In this situation, the key light was highly localizable, and the pigeon readily approached and made contact with the stimulus.

What would happen if the light were less easy to locate? Wasserman (1973) eliminated the background light and found that the autoshaped response did not develop as quickly nor to the same level. Wasserman attributed the attenuation in response strength to the fact that the key light was less localizable when it provided the only illumination in the apparatus.

Sperling and Perkins (1979) showed that the size of the CS also influences the autoshaped response. In one condition, the CS display consisted of four lighted elements all located within 40 cm of the center of the key. In a second condition, the four elements were spaced within 70 cm of the center. The number of pairings required to the first response was less if the four elements were spaced within 40 cm of the center.

It has been difficult to autoshape responses using auditory stimuli. Jenkins (1973) successfully autoshaped a pigeon's responding to an auditory stimulus but the amount of key pecking to a key located directly in front of the speaker was reduced relative to a key light. Cleland and Davey (1983) and Harrison (1979) were not successful in autoshaping bar-pressing behavior in rats. Auditory cues are much more difficult to localize relative to a single light confirming that spatial localization is important to the autoshaped response.

Sign Tracking Studies

Another variable that affects autoshaping is proximity of the key light to the food. In previous studies the CS and food were located near each other. Hearst and Jenkins (1974) examined the question of what would happen if the CS and US were separated spatially. They presented pigeons a green key light at one end of a six-foot-long box. The light was followed by four-second access to food, but the food hopper was located three feet away at the center of the apparatus. At the other end of the long-box a red key light was presented, but it was not correlated with food. On one half of the trials the correlated light was presented at one end of the box and on the other trials, it was presented at the other end.

Once the pigeons associated the correlated light with food they approached the key light and pecked it until the light went off. Then the pigeons would run as fast as they could to the center of the box. Often they failed to reach the food. The uncorrelated stimulus produced no approach behavior. Hearst and Jenkins termed this

Key light signaling food

Food dish

Key light uncorrelated with food

FIGURE 6.6 The Long-Box Experiment of Hearst and Jenkins (1974).

behavior **sign tracking.** Their apparatus is depicted in Figure 6.6.

Why would a pigeon approach a light and peck it and then try to run back to the food hopper before it closes? In fact, by running to the light the pigeon actually reduced the number of opportunities for food. The more efficient strategy would be for the pigeon simply to stand in the middle of the box and wait for the food hopper to open. Why wouldn't a hungry pigeon adopt such a strategy?

Hearst and Jenkins showed that pigeons would track the CS and not the US even when the CS and US were separated by 91 cm. However, not all animals sign track (Kemenes & Benjamin, 1989) and not all animals sign track all the time (Boakes, 1977; Brown, Hemmes, de Vaca, & Pagano, 1993; Holland, 1980; Silva, Silva, & Pear, 1992). Under certain conditions, animals approach the US instead of the CS, a phenomenon known as **goal tracking.**

In rats, separating the CS from the US by more than 30 cm disrupted sign tracking and led to greater goal tracking (Holland, 1980). In pigeons, separating the CS from the US by 60 cm reduced sign tracking and enhanced goal tracking (Silva et. al., 1992). However, note that Hearst and Jenkins separated the CS from US by 91 cm and still observed sign tracking.

A second variable that may affect whether an animal sign tracks or goal tracks is the nature of the US. Burns and Domjan (1996) showed that the dominant response of Japanese quail in a sexual conditioning paradigm was sign tracking. In the first experiment, Burns and Domjan separated the CS and US by 91 cm and observed sign tracking. In the second experiment quail received regular training with the CS and US separated by a constant distance. In test conditions the CS was moved variable distances from the US. Regardless of the distance, quail sign tracked. Burns and Domjan argued that sign tracking might be more likely in sexual conditioning because of characteristics of the US. In sexual conditioning, the US is not stationary and the animal must track a moving stimulus to contact the US. This characteristic may result in a predisposition to sign track.

For stationary USs, the predominate conditioned behavior might be goal tracking. If a given CS always predicts a stationary US to occur in a certain location, the animal could be predisposed to goal track. It is interesting to note that most of the studies of sign tracking have used a stationary US and most of these studies have produced goal tracking. Jenkins and Moore (1973) had shown that the nature of the autoshaped response depended in part on characteristics of the US. In that study, pigeons pecked for food with an open beak and pecked for water with a closed beak. Jenkins and Moore argued that their pigeons were responding to the CS as if it were the US. Burns and Domjan are making a similar argument.

Generality of Sign Tracking Sign tracking has been investigated in a variety of vertebrate species including crows (Powell & Kelly, 1976), Japanese quail (Burns & Domjan, 1996), monitor lizards (Loop, 1976), pigeons (Silva, Silva, & Pear, 1992), and rats (Locurto, et al., 1976). Sign tracking is also evident in fish and large-brained invertebrates.

A recent experiment tested whether fish sign track or goal track. Purdy, Ferguson, and Sieve (1998) randomly assigned 32 goldfish to one of four groups. Sign track experimental (STE) fish received four presentations of a red light (S+) at either end of a 140-cm tank. The red light was on for four minutes and food was delivered on average every 30 seconds through a tube located directly underneath the light. On other trials a green light (S−) was presented but was not followed by food. Stimulus lights appeared at the same end of the tank on any given day but were presented at either end equally. Fish in a goal track experiment (GTE) received the identical procedure except food was delivered to a point 46 cm from the CS. In the two control groups, conditions were identical to those of STE and GTE except target color was not correlated with outcome. Figure 6.7 depicts the apparatus and shows goldfish either sign tracking or goal tracking.

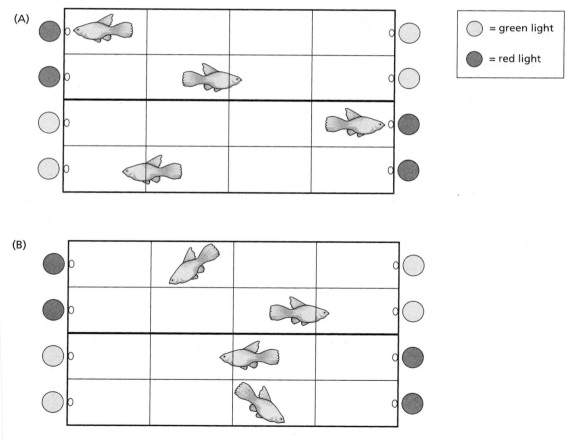

FIGURE 6.7 Depiction of Goldfish Goal Tracking. Study by Purdy, Ferguson, and Sieve (1998).

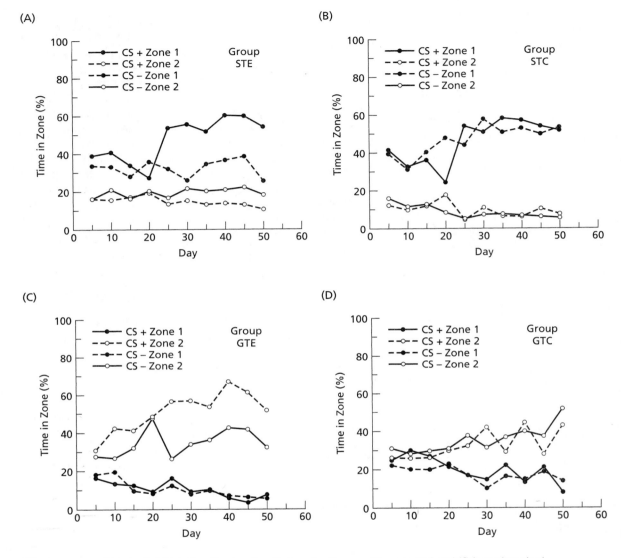

FIGURE 6.8 Tracking in Goldfish. Results showing that under the conditions tested, goldfish goal tracked.

Figure 6.8 shows the results. Goldfish were able to solve the discrimination task and they goal tracked. STE fish spent 60% of their time in zone 1 (where the CS and US were presented) in the presence of CS+ and 35% of their time during CS−. GTE fish spent 68% of their time in zone 2 during CS+ and only 40% of the time in zone 2, when CS− was presented. Food

was delivered to zone 1 for STE fish and zone 2 for GTE fish. Control subjects, both STC and GTC spent their time in the zone where food was delivered, but did not differentiate between CS+ and CS−.

In a further test of the generality of sign tracking and goal tracking, Purdy, Roberts, and Garcia (1999) tested cuttlefish (*Sepia officinalis*), a coleoid cephalopod. Cuttlefish are related to squid and octopus and are known to have the largest brain-to-body weight ratio among the cephalopods (Maddock & Young, 1987; Packer, 1972). Still, cuttlefish have been competing with fish for food for millions of years. Therefore it was an interesting comparative question to determine whether this large invertebrate was fishlike in its cognitive capabilities. (See Figure 6.9 for a picture of a cuttlefish.)

For cuttlefish in the experimental group, 30 seconds of bright flashing light was presented at one end of a long tank followed by food dropped into the center of the tank. For control cuttlefish, the bright flashing light and food were not paired. Cuttlefish in the experimental group showed greater orientation to the light, greater movement toward the light, and more attacks on the light. There was no tendency to move toward the food location until the prey item was dropped in the tank. Therefore cuttlefish sign tracked. Figure 6.10 (pp. 186–187) shows a sequence of pictures taken from a video clip where a cuttlefish swims toward a flashing light and strikes it with its tentacles. From the behavioral sequence it can clearly be seen that the cuttlefish is responding toward the CS as it would the US.

What Is Learned in Sign Tracking and Goal Tracking?

In experiments using autoshaping it appeared that stimulus-reinforcement associations initiated and maintained the key-peck response. These bonds might support sign tracking as well. Using an omission procedure Peden, Browne, and Hearst, 1977, found that terminating reward when the animal approached the CS reduced, but did not eliminate, sign tracking. Crawford and Domjan (1993) did not observe a reduction in approaching and observing a female quail when the approach response was not rewarded with the visual presentation of a female quail. Both studies support the notion of behavior being controlled by stimulus-reinforcement bonds.

FIGURE 6.9 The Cuttlefish (Sepia officinalis). A large-brained invertebrate.

The work with cuttlefish was particularly interesting in this regard. As shown in Figure 6.10, cuttlefish in the paired group oriented to the light and then approached it. On occasion, the cuttlefish attacked the light either by pouncing or striking it with their tentacles. The cuttlefish were reacting toward the light in the same manner that they would approach their natural prey. These observations support the contention that the animal had formed a stimulus-reinforcement bond. Note that these results also support Pavlov's stimulus-substitution hypothesis.

Goal tracking may involve response-reinforcement bonds. Farwell and Ayres (1979) showed that goal-tracking behavior in rats (head poking) was controlled by **response-reinforcer associations** and goal tracking in pond snails was reportedly maintained by **stimulus-reinforcer associations** in conjunction with response-reinforcement bonds (Kemenes & Benjamin, 1989).

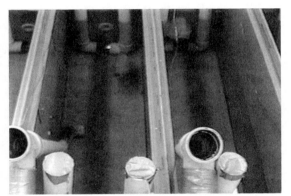

FIGURE 6.10 Cuttlefish Sign Tracking and Attacking the Conditioned Stimulus. Taken from Purdy, Roberts, & Garcia (1999).

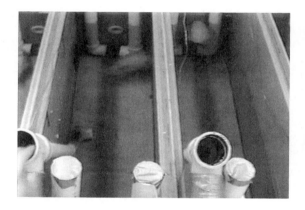

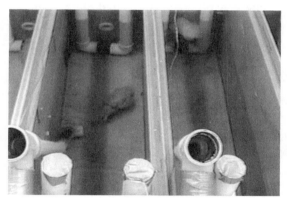

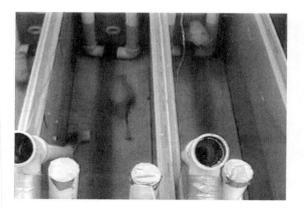

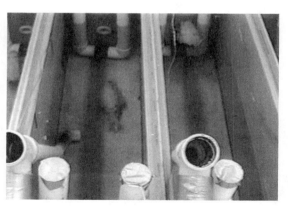

However, this is not the entire story. Several studies have shown autoshaping in fish (Brandon & Bitterman, 1979; Northmore, Skeen, & Pindzola, 1981; Squier, 1969; Woodard & Bitterman, 1974). Two of these studies provided evidence that the target-striking response was dependent on response-reinforcement associations as opposed to stimulus-reinforcement associations. Using an omission procedure, Brandon & Bitterman (1979) showed that target striking declined. Both Brandon and Bitterman (1979) and Northmore, et al. (1981) showed that separation of the CS and US disrupted performance. It appears that either stimulus-reinforcement or response-reinforcement bonds can support sign tracking. More work is required to determine if other types of associations can also support sign and goal tracking.

Why Would Animals Sign Track? Sign tracking might make sense when viewed from an ecological perspective. Many animals take part in predator/prey interactions and prey animals often avoid being eaten by hiding or escaping. As a result prey are not always in sight of the predator. One way for an animal to find food would be to look for stimuli that have been associated with prey. Such stimuli might include different types of plants, rocks, etc. When the animal approaches such stimuli, it is sign tracking.

Support for this idea comes from Sanders and Young (1940) who studied foraging cuttlefish in a large rectangular tank. The tank contained an enamel pail at its center and an enamel wall at one end. A shrimp was tied to a string and placed in front of the cuttlefish. The shrimp was then dragged around behind the pail and then behind the wall. The cuttlefish tracked the shrimp even though it moved out of the visual field. Sanders and Young commented "After a prawn has disappeared round a corner that corner exerts an attraction which it did not possess before" (p. 522). The ability to approach a stimulus that has been associated with food might be important for an animal that hunts live, hard-to-see prey.

SITUATIONS IN WHICH INSTRUMENTAL CONDITIONING INFLUENCES THE CLASSICALLY CONDITIONED RESPONSE

We have seen that a number of studies support the contention that classical conditioning influences the instrumental response. But you may be wondering if the opposite is true. Are there situations in which instrumental conditioning influences classical conditioning? We turn now to a brief discussion of this issue.

The Conditioned Response May Make the US More Reinforcing

One of the possible advantages of the conditioned response is that it may be reinforcing. That is, perhaps an organism produces a conditioned response and receives reinforcement. Perkins (1955) argued that one reason that animals might produce the observing response is because it provides an opportunity to prepare for periods of reward or nonreward. For example, if a pigeon produces an observing response, and the stimulus produced predicts impending reward, the pigeon might salivate. When the pigeon then receives the reward (4-second access to grain) the pigeon is better prepared for the reward and that improves the quality of the reward. Similarly, if the pigeon produces the observing response and no reward is predicted, then lack of salivation in its mouth would be less aversive. Thus, by making the observing response, the animal can prepare appropriately for reward and nonreward. Then, by preparing appropriately, the pigeon can increase the reinforcing aspects of the reward and decrease the aversive aspects of nonreward.

Classical conditioning might have the effect of increasing the rewarding properties of a reinforcer or decreasing the aversive properties of a punisher. If true, this suggests that the effect of the CR might be reinforcing. To test this notion, Coleman (1975) classically conditioned the eyeblink response in rabbits. For each of four groups, a tone was used as the CS and the US was a 5.0 mA electric shock delivered to the skin below one eye. For one group, if the rabbit produced a CR there was no reduction in the intensity of the shock. For two groups the intensity of shock was reduced and in a fourth the shock was not delivered if the rabbit produced an eye blink in the presence of the tone.

If the CR is rewarding in an instrumental-conditioning sense, then it would stand to reason that by reducing the shock when the rabbit produced a CR, one should increase the number of conditioned responses. On the other hand, if the CR is not rewarding there should be no effect on the CR. Interestingly, there was no effect of reducing the level of shock as a result of producing a CR. It should be noted that the group that did not receive electric shock in the presence of a CR did not perform at as high a level as the other three groups. However, this result was attributed to the fact that this group received the US on less than 100% of the trials.

The CR May Be Reinforced by the US

It is possible that the CR produced by the organisms is reinforced by the presentation of the US. For example in a typical autoshaping study with pigeons, a key light is lighted; this is followed by a reward. If the pigeon approaches the key and pecks, it is also reinforced. There is the possibility then that the approach and peck response was reinforced through an instrumental conditioning procedure. If this is the case then omitting the reward for approaching the stimulus and pecking it should decrease the autoshaped response. Peden, Browne, and Hearst (1977) conducted just such an experiment. They trained pigeons under an **omission procedure** in which a light was paired with access to grain. If the pigeon approached the key and pecked it, the reward was not given and the next trial began. Peden, Browne, & Hearst found that their pigeons still acquired the key-peck response supporting our contention above that classical

conditioning was influencing the pigeon's behavior. However, when Peden et al. removed the omission contingency, responding to the key light increased significantly. This result showed that the autoshaped key-peck response in pigeons could be reduced by omitting the reward if the pigeon pecked the key and that instrumental conditioning might be influencing the classically conditioned response.

CLASSICAL AND OPERANT CONDITIONING: ONE PROCESS OR TWO?

It is important to understand that classical conditioning and operant conditioning were considered two separate and independent processes. This chapter provides evidence that these two modes of conditioning can not be so clearly delineated. We have seen that classical conditioning and instrumental conditioning combine to influence behavior. And we have also shown evidence that classical conditioning affects the instrumental response and that instrumental conditioning can influence the classically conditioned behavior.

We could argue that classical conditioning requires that the animal associate a stimulus with an outcome (bell = meat powder, for example) and that operant conditioning requires the animal to associate a response with reinforcement (bar press = food, for example). However, as we learned in this and previous chapters, this distinction also fails. Animals do make stimulus–reinforcement associations, response–reinforcement associations, and stimulus–response associations. Any or all of these associations can be formed during classical conditioning or instrumental conditioning.

Our best bet may be to acknowledge that animals can form most if not all of these various associations and ask to what extent these associations guide classical or operant behavior. Indeed, we could argue that the two procedures are separable, but are not independent. Dragoi and Staddon (1999) took this approach. They developed a mathematical model of operant conditioning that relies on two types of association—response reinforcement and stimulus reinforcement. We examine this model in the next section.

A Mathematical Model of Operant Conditioning

The Dragoi and Staddon (1999) model combines elements of classical conditioning and operant conditioning. The model attempts to define the fundamental variables controlling operant conditioning. According to Dragoi and Staddon, the dynamics of operant behavior are contingent upon several factors. First, operant behavior depends upon the associative strengths of the stimulus reinforcer and response reinforcer bond. The strengths of these associations increase when discriminative stimuli and responses are followed consistently and closely by reinforcement.

Second, when an animal perceives a stimulus or makes a response, a brief decaying **short-term memory trace** of the event is formed. In addition, each association between a stimulus and reinforcement or a response and reinforcement leaves a decaying memory trace. It is assumed that the memory traces left by simple stimuli and responses leave brief memory traces whereas the memory traces for stimulus-reinforcer and response-reinforcer associations are longer. It is further assumed that associations leave both short-term and long-term memory traces.

Third, Dragoi and Staddon argue that stimulus and response traces, multiplied by their associative strengths determine **short-term learning expectancy** and **long-term learning expectancy.** Short-term learning expectancy provides a measure of experienced reinforcement and long-term learning expectancy provides a measure of expected reinforcement.

According to the model, operant behavior is controlled by the integration of short-term and long-term learning expectancy. Whenever the short-term learning expectancy is greater than the long-term learning expectancy behavioral

excitation occurs. In other words, when reinforcement conditions improve (for example through larger size, shorter delay, increased duration, or higher probability) the animal compares currently experienced conditions with expected conditions and if current experience is greater, behavioral excitation occurs. Whenever the short-term learning expectancy is less than the long-term learning expectancy, behavioral inhibition occurs.

Finally, Dragoi and Staddon assume that both short-term and long-term expectancies are transient and eventually decline to zero. More persistent changes are represented by consolidated long-term memory. These long-term changes occur with slow changes in the association between behavioral excitation and the response and are used to account for phenomena that rely on extended training.

The Dragoi and Staddon mathematical model can be used to account for a wide range of operant behaviors. It is particularly suited to account for recurrent-choice behavior with food as reinforcement. The model accurately depicts operant performance under continuous and intermittent reinforcement schedules during both acquisition and extinction. It also accounts for performance during discrimination learning, stimulus generalization, and how reinforcement selectively strengthens certain responses.

The model correctly simulates matching behavior and successive and simultaneous behavioral-contrast effects. By using the consolidated long-term memory principle the model can account for long-term spontaneous recovery from extinction and serial reversal learning.

If rats are trained to traverse a straight alley maze for a large reward and they are suddenly shifted to a small reward, they will decrease their response to a level below that of the rat that had received the small reward all along. The phenomenon was termed successive-negative contrast. Dragoi and Staddon would argue that the rats in both groups acquired both a short-term and a long-term expectancy for reward. When the rats receiving the large reward were shifted to the small reward their currently expected reinforcement conditions decreased relative to their long-term learning expectancy. The effect of this discrepancy is behavioral inhibition and the rat reduces its rate of response considerably.

The model accounts for a wide range of operant behavior using associations developed through classical and operant conditioning. These associations and the memory traces of the stimuli and responses combine to form short-term and long-term expectancies that in turn produce behavioral change. The model reminds us that it is really not possible to separate the effects of classical and operant conditioning in an operant setting. Both types of conditioning are occurring and are influencing performance.

SUMMARY STATEMENTS

Chapter 6 discusses the interaction between classical conditioning and operant conditioning. Avoidance conditioning involves presenting a signal that predicts some noxious or aversive event. The signal is turned on and a short while later the aversive event is presented. In a typical situation the animal can make a response that terminates the aversive event. This response is called an escape response. With continued training the signal elicits fear through classical conditioning. Now, when the signal is presented the animal shows a fear response and it attempts to escape the fear-eliciting stimulus. At this point the animal responds before the aversive event occurs and successfully avoids it.

Avoidance conditioning is unique in that it is very difficult to extinguish. That is, as long as the stimulus is presented, the animal will emit the avoidance response. One of the difficult problems that faced psychologists was explaining how the absence of a stimulus can reinforce behavior. Mowrer solved this problem by developing two-factor theory. In this theory, a stimulus elicited fear through classical conditioning. The fear elicited by this stimulus was aversive and the animal responded to terminate the stimulus. Thus,

the animal's behavior was not controlled by the absence of a stimulus but was maintained by negative reinforcement. In both escape training and avoidance training, the animal terminated an aversive event.

Two-factor theory represented a major breakthrough. It accounted for a wide range of findings and made predictions that were later supported. Studies by Kamin (1957a, 1957b) and Rescorla and LoLordo (1965) showed the validity of the position. Still, two-factor theory could not account for all results. Herrnstein and Hineline (1966) showed that animals could learn to avoid aversive events even in the absence of external or internal stimuli that could be used to condition fear. In their study the reduction of shock played the major role in avoidance conditioning.

The discriminative stimulus through its association with reward can disrupt instrumental behavior. Such behavior was termed instinctive drift and led Breland and Breland to abandon attempts to train pigs and raccoons to drop coins into piggy banks. The discriminative stimulus, through its association with reward, can become a secondary reinforcer. Wyckoff (1952) showed that this stimulus reinforced behavior whose only outcome was information regarding which schedule of reinforcement was currently in effect. Such a response was termed the *observing response*.

Several explanations were offered to account for observing behavior. Berlyne (1957) argued that the observing response was maintained because the response reduced uncertainty as to which of two events would be forthcoming. Uncertainty was regarded as aversive and its reduction would be rewarding. Others (Wyckoff and Fantino) argued that the observing response was maintained by secondary reinforcement. Numerous studies were conducted by Dinsmoor, Fantino, and others showing that indeed S+ was rewarding and S− was not. A third explanation was that animals observed because it allowed them to be more efficient foragers. This position accounted for some of the literature with humans and monkeys but could not account for the

pigeon literature. The observing-response literature showed that stimuli that had been paired
with primary reinforcers could be used to reinforce other behaviors and that stimuli that had
been paired with extinction did not acquire reinforcing strength.

The chapter continued with a discussion of
autoshaping and sign-tracking behavior. In both
procedures one pairs a localized stimulus with
food and the stimulus elicits an approach response
(Brown & Jenkins, 1968). Jenkins and Moore
(1973) showed that the autoshaped stimulus elicits a response that is typically followed by behavior appropriate to the reward. Thus when one
pairs a lighted key with a food reward a pigeon
comes to peck the key with an open beak. When
pigeons receive pairings of a light with water they
peck with a closed beak.

Characteristics of the CS also affect autoshaping and sign tracking. Here the degree of localiz-
ability was an important variable as was the
distance separating the CS and US. By separating
the two spatially, one can determine whether the
animal is sign tracking (approaching the CS) or
goal tracking (approaching the US). Two vari-

ables that appeared to influence which behavior
would result were the degree of separation between the CS and the US and the nature of the
US. The section ended with a discussion of the
generality of the phenomena, the nature of the
learned associations supporting sign or goal
tracking, and a rationale for why an animal might
sign track.

The final section of the chapter examined a
mathematical model of operant conditioning
developed by Dragoi and Staddon (1999). The
model assumes that stimuli and responses leave
memory traces and that associations between
stimuli and reinforcement and responses and reinforcement leave both short-term and long-
term memory traces. These memory traces are
used to determine currently experienced rates
of reinforcement and expected rates of reinforcement. Differences between experienced
and expected reinforcement determine operant
behavior. The model is important in that it ac-
knowledges both stimulus-reinforcement and
response-reinforcement associations as important variables in operant conditioning.

7

Generalization, Discrimination, and Concept Learning

CHAPTER OVERVIEW

Don Meyer, a researcher, is in Africa studying vervet monkeys. One day as he watches, an eagle flies overhead and one monkey emits a cry and dives into the brush. Immediately afterward all of the monkeys look to the sky and then dive into the brush. Once the eagle has passed by, the monkeys return to their usual monkey business. That night Don plays back the monkeys' vocalization into a computer loaded with sound-analysis software. He begins mathematically characterizing the sound.

A week later another amazing event occurs. A leopard passes within 50 meters of the monkeys and one of the monkeys emits a cry. This time all the monkeys in the troop head for the trees. That night as Don analyzes the call he observes that it is different from the one that was emitted in response to the eagle.

A month later, a python slithers through the vervet's territory and is spotted by the matriarch of the vervet colony. She emits a call and in response all monkeys in the immediate vicinity stand up on their hind legs and look around in the grass (see Figure 7.1). Several of the monkeys grab sticks and they all appear to be agitated. Once the threat has passed, the monkeys return to their normal habits. Again, as Don analyzes the data that night, it is clear that the signal produced by the matriarch monkey is significantly different from the other two calls.

So what is going on here? Three different predators have invaded the vervets' territory and they have emitted three different calls that produced three different, yet appropriate antipredatory behaviors. Were the monkeys really identifying the type of predator and alerting their fellows to the danger? Don concludes that these monkeys have a vocabulary that consists of signals that identify certain predator types (bird, cat, and snake). The calls elicit the same behaviors each time and the behaviors are predator specific and appropriate.

It appears that these monkeys are forming concepts and are classifying different predators on the basis of type. Vervet monkeys emit one type of sound to aerial predators, a second sound to land or mammal predators, and a third sound to snake predators. Some other aerial predators elicit the same monkey call as the eagle, but other nonpredatory birds do not. This means that the monkeys are able to determine similarities and differences among the bird, reptile, and mammal predators and nonpredators they encounter. So, how do these monkeys acquire these concepts of aerial predator, mammal predator, and reptile predator? The process probably involves stimulus generalization and discrimination learning.

FIGURE 7.1 Vervet Monkeys Reacting to the Presence of a Python. Monkeys are pictured standing bipedally and giving alarm calls to the python's presence. From *How Monkeys See the World.* Reprinted by permission of The University of Chicago Press.

The above scenario was drawn from actual research. Struhsaker (1967) made the initial observations of the behavior. Dorothy Cheney and Robert Seyfarth extended the observations and the implications of the behavior dramatically (Cheney & Seyfarth, 1980, 1986; Seyfarth & Cheney, 1986). If you are interested in further exploring this line of investigation see Cheney and Seyfarth (1990) and Seyfarth and Cheney (1997). Figure 7.2, taken from the work of Cheney and Seyfarth (1990), shows that male and female vervet monkeys are able to classify different predators and communicate to other vervets about their presence.

The example of the vervet monkey points to the conditions required for human and nonhuman animals to form **concepts.** When an organism learns some new response to a particular stimulus it tends to make the same response in the presence of other similar stimuli. This natural tendency to do so is called **stimulus generalization.** When an organism learns to make one response in the presence of one stimulus and a different response in the presence of a second stimulus, it has learned to discriminate between the two stimuli.

The tendency to generalize from one stimulus to another means that organisms do not have to experience all possible stimulus situations in order to make

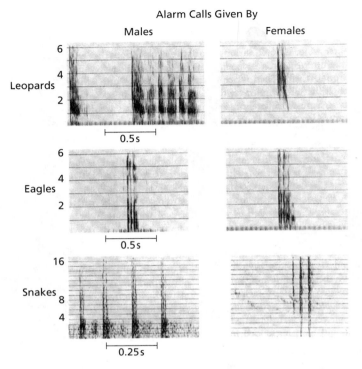

FIGURE 7.2 Alarm Calls. Vervet monkeys classify different predators and communicate to other vervet monkeys about their presence. Depicted are the different spectrograms of the calls given to
leopards, eagles, and snakes. For each spectrogram the X-axis
indicates time and the Y-axis indicates frequency. From *How Monkeys See the World.* Reprinted by permission of The University of
Chicago Press.

appropriate responses in those situations. For example, if a snake bites your leg,
you soon develop a healthy respect for that particular animal. Because of stimulus generalization, you will show similar respect for other snakes without having to be bitten by each of them.

On the other hand, the natural tendency to generalize can sometimes result in
inappropriate or maladaptive responses. For example, some people have experienced near-death drowning situations and have been afraid ever since to take
a bath. On occasion, overgeneralization can lead to inappropriate responses.

The second important learning process that is involved in concept formation
is **discrimination learning.** In this process we learn to make a response
in the presence of one stimulus and to make a different response to other

similar stimuli. Thus, in one sense, discrimination learning can be viewed as a process that counteracts a seemingly natural tendency to generalize.

For human and nonhuman organisms stimulus generalization and discrimination learning play an important role in concept formation. A concept is a group of objects or ideas that fall into a given category because they share certain characteristics or features. For example, for vervet monkeys, the concept of *aerial predator* includes a number of objects that all have wings, sharp claws, and a curved beak. To form a concept an individual must be able to attach labels or feelings to one set of stimuli and not to others. As we will see, this can be a rather complex endeavor. In addition, the ability to discriminate is essential for the process of concept formation. The ability to discriminate allows the vervet monkey to distinguish a dangerous bird from a nonthreatening bird.

In addition to an in-depth look at stimulus generation and discrimination learning, this chapter will cover continuity theories as espoused by Pavlov and Spence. These theories are contrasted then with noncontinuity theories as proposed by Krechevsky, Lashley, Sutherland, and Mackintosh. The chapter will also address theories of concept representation including attribute theory, the Collins and Loftus network model, exemplar theory, and prototype theory. The chapter ends with a discussion of whether nonhuman animals are capable of concept learning.

STIMULUS GENERALIZATION

Methods for Studying Generalization in the Laboratory

Pavlov (1927) carried out some of the earliest stimulus generalization experiments. In one experiment, Pavlov conditioned dogs to salivate to a touch on the dog's leg. In later tests, Pavlov measured the responses to touches placed at varying distances from the original point. As he moved increasingly far from the original training point, the amount of salivation to the touch decreased. Pavlov had shown that dogs could generalize along a distance dimension where tactile stimulation was the stimulus of choice.

Numerous generalization studies have also been done using instrumental and operant conditioning paradigms. In these experiments organisms are usually trained to respond in the presence of one stimulus and then tested to see whether they will respond in the presence of similar stimuli. The later trials constitute **stimulus generalization tests.**

During these test trials the animal is not rewarded. This eliminates the argument that the animal's behavior is being reinforced for responding, but it does cause a problem in that the animal's responses will begin to extinguish. For this reason, generalization tests are usually short in duration. A second commonly used method to test for generalization involves the use of probe trials. These trials are randomly presented during the training conditions. Thus during training every now and then a different stimulus is presented for a short time and the number of responses to the probe is recorded. In both cases, the typical finding is that the original stimulus produces the greatest amount of responding with decreased responding to stimuli as you get further and further from the original stimulus.

Guttman and Kalish (1956) conducted a classic study showing stimulus generalization. Four groups of pigeons learned to peck a key on a variable-interval one-minute schedule of reinforcement. Each group of pigeons pecked a key that was illuminated with a different color, 530 nm, 550 nm, 580 nm, or 600 nm. Once response rates had stabilized, the researchers tested for stimulus generalization. Pigeons were presented with 10 variations of color and the original color. The 11 colors were presented in a random order, each color for 60 seconds. Although key pecks were not reinforced during test trials, it was assumed that extinction rates would be comparable across colors.

Figure 7.3, taken from one group of pigeons, shows the amount of responding to both the original training stimulus (a 600 nm light) and other similar but nontrained stimuli. The graph depicts a **stimulus generalization gradient.** Most such gradients have a similar form. That is, the greatest level of responding typically occurs to the previously trained stimulus or to stimuli that are very similar to the trained stimulus. Progressively lower levels of responding result as the test stimuli become less similar to the original training stimulus.

The slope of the generalization gradient measures the amount of generalization an organism exhibits on a particular test. Figure 7.4 illustrates two gradients having very different slopes. Gradient A is termed a **steep gradient** because responding decreases substantially even when minor changes in the training stimulus occur. Obviously, a steep gradient indicates very little stimulus generalization. Gradient B, on the other hand, is called a **shallow gradient,** indicating that substantial responding occurs even to stimuli that are highly dissimilar to the training stimulus. The occurrence of a shallow gradient shows that significant stimulus generalization has taken place. Thus, the shape of the generalization gradient reflects the degree of stimulus generalization that an organism exhibits.

Three further points concerning generalization gradients should be noted. First, the abscissa or X-axis of a gradient always represents a scale along which stimuli can be ordered according to some characteristic. For example, color, size, height, distance, and loudness are **stimulus**

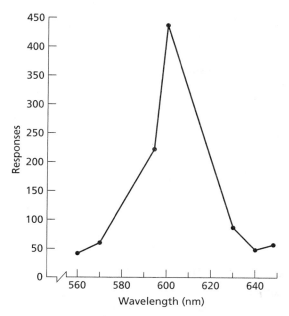

FIGURE 7.3 A Stimulus-Generalization Gradient. (From Guttman & Kalish, 1956).

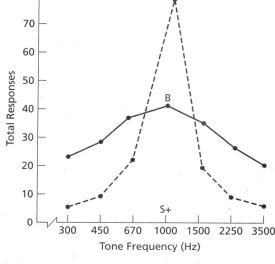

FIGURE 7.4 Generalization Gradients. Examples of steep (A) and shallow (B) generalization gradients after training on a 1000-Hz tone.

dimensions that could be generalized. Each of these stimuli represents a physical scale.

A second point concerns the ordinate or Y-axis. We have considered only gradients based on an absolute measure of the number of responses made to each stimulus. A gradient that is based on the total number of responses is called an **absolute generalization gradient.**

We might wish to know how some variable, such as the amount of reward during training, affects subsequent generalization. To answer this question we might give two groups of organisms different amounts of reward during training and then test both groups on the training stimulus and on a set of nontrained stimuli. What we are likely to find if we measure the absolute number of responses is that the small-reward group makes fewer responses to all stimuli, including the training stimulus. In other words, the height of the generalization gradient will be depressed in the small-reward group. This means that the gradient will tend to flatten out or become shallow, not

necessarily because of any change in generalization, but because overall responding has been depressed.

To rectify this measurement problem, several researchers have used what are termed relative measures of generalization. In other words, on a generalization test the experimenter notes the total number of responses made and then calculates the percent of this total that was made in the presence of each stimulus. This procedure results in a **relative generalization gradient.** Such gradients are less affected by changes in absolute responding to all stimuli.

One final point concerning generalization gradients is the measurement of either excitatory or inhibitory gradients. **Excitatory gradients** are formed when organisms are first trained to emit some response in the presence of a given stimulus. Then this tendency is tested to determine whether a response generalizes to other stimuli. All the types of gradients discussed thus far fall into the category of excitatory gradients.

On the other hand, an organism may also be trained to inhibit or withhold a response in the presence of a given stimulus. This is the kind of training that occurs in classical inhibitory conditioning. If an organism is trained to inhibit responding in the presence of one stimulus, this tendency to inhibit responding will generalize to other similar stimuli. The curve in Figure 7.5, a graphical representation of an organism's tendency to generalize the inhibition of responding, is termed an **inhibitory generalization gradient.**

Variables That Affect Stimulus Generalization

As noted earlier, when people learn some new response, they tend naturally to generalize that response to novel stimulus situations. The tendency to generalize can have important consequences for everyday behaviors. For this reason it is helpful to understand which circumstances tend to promote generalizations and which factors tend to inhibit them. To make such a determination, researchers have examined how a variety of variables affect the shape of generalization gradients. Many of these studies have been concerned with a single question: Does the way we learn influence our tendency to generalize? We will attempt to answer this question by looking at some of the learning variables that have been studied in generalization experiments.

Degree of Original Learning. It seems reasonable to assume that our tendency to generalize depends on how well we have learned a particular response. At least some experiments support this assumption. For example, Hearst and Koresko (1968) trained pigeons to peck a key that had a vertical black line on its surface. Pecking in the presence of this stimulus was reinforced on a variable-interval schedule. Various groups of pigeons received either two, four, seven, or fourteen sessions of training. Then all the pigeons were presented with a key having either a vertical line or lines that were tilted away from the

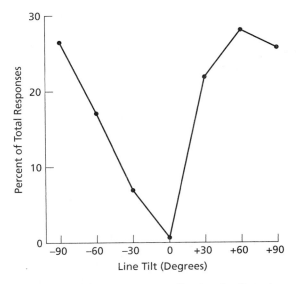

FIGURE 7.5 An Inhibitory Generalization Gradient. In this study, pigeons were trained to peck a blank key and were not reinforced for pecking a key with a vertical line (0° tilt). Then they were tested using different line tilts. (From Zentall, Collins, & Hearst, 1971.)

vertical position. No responses were reinforced during testing. Figure 7.6 shows that the more training pigeons received with the vertical-line stimulus, the greater was the level of responding to this stimulus on test trials. Increased training also appeared to reduce generalization, as evidenced by the increasingly steep generalization gradients.

This effect of degree of training on absolute generalization gradients is reasonably common (see, for example, Brown, 1970). There is, however, some disagreement as to whether increased training on the original stimulus (S+) reduces generalization in a relative sense. The data produced by Hearst and Koresko suggest that increased training does decrease the relative proportion of responses allotted to the nontrained stimuli. However, other studies have reported that in some cases increased training can actually increase relative generalization (Margolius, 1955).

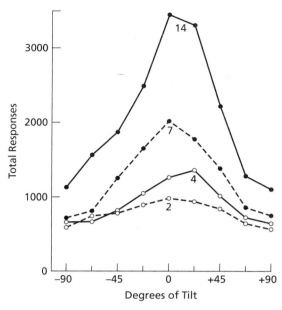

FIGURE 7.6 Generalization. Generalization among tilted lines after 2, 4, 7, and 14 training sessions with a vertical line as S+. (From Hearst & Koresko, 1968).

Motivational Level. Another variable that appears to influence the shape of generalization gradients is an organism's level of motivation at the time of original training. However, just as with the degree of learning variable, the effects of motivational level have not always been consistent. Kalish and Haber (1965) trained pigeons to peck a key of a certain color and then tested for generalization using a range of different colored keys. Before training, these experimenters reduced their pigeons to either 90, 80, or 70% of the normal body weight. Pigeons that were deprived of food to 70% of their freefeeding body weight were considered more motivated than pigeons deprived to 80 or 90%.

Kalish and Haber found that increased levels of motivation resulted in greater responding to the S+ during the generalization test. They also found that higher levels of motivation tended to produce steeper absolute-generalization gradients. Newman and Grice (1965) have reported

similar findings. There are exceptions to the finding that increased levels of motivation decrease generalization. Jenkins, Pascal, and Walker (1958), Thomas and King (1959), and Coate (1964) each reported that increased levels of motivation flattened the generalization gradient. In these studies relative generalization gradients were measured.

It is obvious from the above that the variables affecting generalization gradients are complex and are dependent to some degree on the manner in which the gradients are measured. There is no general agreement with respect to which measurement best reflects the underlying process of stimulus generalization. Thus, as Morgan (1969) reported, conclusions about the slopes and different effects of training are safest when the results of absolute and relative gradients coincide.

Schedules of Reinforcement. Hearst, Koresko, and Popper (1964) trained five groups of pigeons to peck a key marked with a vertical line. Although all pigeons were exposed to a variable interval schedule, the average length of the interreinforcement interval was 30 seconds or 1, 2, 3, or 4 minutes in the five groups, respectively. After training, all pigeons were tested using a variety of tilted lines on the response key.

Figure 7.7 shows the relative generalization gradients for these five groups. As you can see, the different training schedules produced markedly different gradients. When subjects had been trained using longer interreinforcement intervals, they displayed a greater tendency to generalize. Shorter interreinforcement intervals reduced generalization significantly. Schedules of reinforcement that are relatively rich or dense (that is, schedules that provide more frequent reinforcement) typically tend to reduce subsequent generalization to nontrained stimuli (Haber & Kalish, 1963).

Duration of the Training–Test Interval. Another variable that has a consistent effect on generalization is the length of time that separates training on S+ and the subsequent test. Several

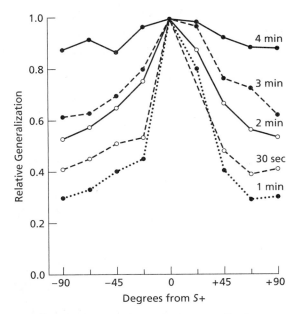

FIGURE 7.7 Relative Generalization. Generalization on a line tilt dimension after training on a vertical line using different VI schedules of reinforcement. (From Hearst, Koresko, & Popper, 1964. *Journal of the Experimental Analysis of Behavior*, 7, 369–380. © 1964 by the SEAB.).

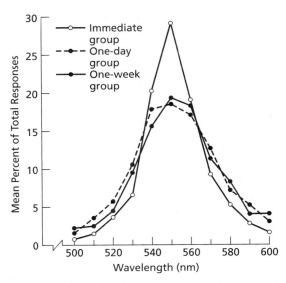

FIGURE 7.8 Training-Test Interval. Generalization as a function of the training-test interval. (From Thomas & Lopez, 1962.)

studies have shown that the tendency to generalize increases as the training-test interval is lengthened. For example, Thomas and Lopez (1962) trained pigeons to peck a colored key and later tested them using keys of different colors. Pigeons were tested 1 minute, 1 day, or 1 week after training. Figure 7.8 shows the effect in terms of relative generalization gradients. Pigeons tested after 1 minute exhibited very steep generalization gradients. Those tested 1 day or 1 week after training showed somewhat flatter gradients. This effect is often interpreted as an example of forgetting. That is, over time subjects forget the specific characteristics of the S+ and tend to respond more often to relatively similar stimuli. (For other findings of this nature, see Burr & Thomas, 1972; McAllister & McAllister, 1963; Perkins & Weyant, 1958; Thomas et al., 1985). For a recent excellent review of this research area see Bouton, Nelson, and Rosas (1999).

Prior Discrimination Training. Discrimination training involves presenting two or more stimuli to an organism during the training phase. For example, an organism may be confronted with one stimulus on some trials and another stimulus on the remaining trials. The organism is reinforced for responding in the presence of one of these stimuli (S+) and is not reinforced for responding to the other stimulus (S−).

The effect of discrimination training on subsequent generalization is usually pronounced. For example, Jenkins and Harrison (1962) reinforced pigeons' pecking in the presence of a 1000-Hz tone. These pigeons were also trained *not* to peck to a 950-Hz tone. Subsequently, the experimenters tested the pigeons for response to a range of tone frequencies. Discrimination training led to very steep generalization gradients relative to those produced by pigeons that had been trained to respond to the 1000-Hz tone only. In effect, prior discrimination between two tones reduced later generalization along the tone frequency dimension. The same effect has been reported in numerous experiments involving a wide variety of

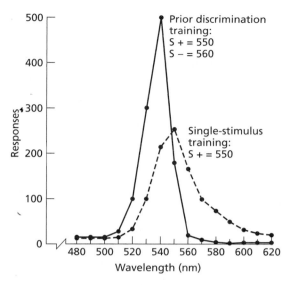

FIGURE 7.9 Comparing Training Strategies. Different generalization gradients resulting from single-stimulus and discrimination training. (From Hanson, 1959.)

stimulus dimensions (see, for example, Friedman & Guttman, 1965; Hanson, 1959, and Thomas, 1962).

Aside from reducing generalization, prior discrimination training can result in two other effects, as illustrated in a study with pigeons conducted by Hanson (1959). We will consider only two of Hanson's groups. One group of pigeons (the no-discrimination group) was reinforced for responding to a colored light having a wavelength of 550 nm. A second group (the discrimination group) was reinforced for pecking a 550 nm key (the S+) and was not reinforced for pecking 560 nm key (the S−). Both groups were then given a generalization test in which no responses were reinforced.

Figure 7.9 shows the results of this generalization test. Prior discrimination training resulted in a significantly steeper generalization gradient. In addition, two characteristics of Figure 7.9 are notable. First, in the no-discrimination group maximal responding occurs to the previously trained wavelength (550 nm). In the discrimina-

tion group, however, maximal responding occurs not to the original S+ (550 nm) but instead to a key having a wavelength of 540 nm. In other words, the peak of the generalization gradient is not at the original S+ but is shifted away from the original S− (560 nm).

This effect, which is called the **peak-shift phenomenon,** is inherent to a number of studies and is the direct result of prior discrimination training (see, for example, Purtle, 1973; Wills & Mackintosh, 1998). It is important to emphasize that the peak shift always occurs in a direction away from the S− used in discrimination training.

Discrimination learning appears to enhance peak responding substantially. Hanson's discrimination group had a mean of more than 500 responses to the 540-nm key, whereas the no-discrimination group had between 200 and 300 responses to the 550-nm key. This behavioral contrast results from giving organisms a comparison between the reinforcing values of two stimuli. If two organisms receive the same percentage of reinforcement for responding to a stimulus (S1) and one organism is also given a lower percentage of reinforcement for responding to another (S2), the organism that experiences both stimuli often responds more to S1. This is the case even when responding to S2 does result in some degree of reinforcement (see, for example, Reynolds, 1961; Williams, 1974; Williams, 1976).

To this point we have considered only situations in which discrimination training occurs among stimuli that later will be present during the generalization test. Somewhat surprisingly, discrimination training can apparently affect generalization gradients even when the stimuli an organism must discriminate are not the same as the stimuli on the generalization test. One example of this effect comes from a series of experiments conducted by Thomas, Freeman, Svinicki, Burr, and Lyons (1970). In one of their experiments, one group of pigeons (true discrimination group) learned to discriminate between two different colored keys. They were rewarded for responding in the presence of one color and not rewarded for responding to the other. Superimposed on both the S+ and S− keys was a vertical white line. A second group of pigeons (psuedodiscrimination group) also was presented the different colored keys bearing a vertical line. However, for this group, responding to either key resulted in reinforcement on the same variable interval schedule. The group was not required to learn any discrimination between the two colors.

After training both groups were given generalization tests using keys marked with lines that were either vertical or tilted from the vertical position. Recall that even though all pigeons had seen a vertical line during training, the discrimination task involved learning a color discrimination. These researchers found that the true discrimination group exhibited a steep generalization gradient, with peak responding occurring for the vertical line.

The pseudodiscrimination group produced an extremely flat generalization gradient, with no clear response advantage for the vertical line. This study shows that discrimination training on one stimulus dimension can reduce later generalization along a totally different stimulus dimension. This finding has been replicated in a number of experiments (see, for example, Honig, 1970; Mackintosh & Honig, 1970). It suggests that practice in discriminating among stimuli may result in some general set or predisposition that makes organisms more discriminating even in different stimulus situations.

The Basis for Generalization Gradients

The phenomenon of generalization is a basic characteristic of living organisms. However, so far this text has not considered the important question of *how* organisms generalize.

Traditional Explanations for Generalization

For several years two predominant theories attempted to explain generalization. One theory, proposed by Hull (1943), suggested that generalization results because during learning, organisms associate several different stimuli with the correct response. According to this view, although an experimenter may attempt to condition a response to a single stimulus, such an endeavor can never succeed completely. On many occasions the subject's sensory system senses the level of the stimulus the experimenter actually intends. On other occasions, however, the subject senses the stimulus as being slightly different from the one presented. This means that conditioning actually occurs to a zone, or range, of stimuli. Maximal conditioning occurs to the target stimulus, but some conditioning also occurs to variations of the target stimulus (that is, to stimuli that are similar to the target stimulus). This, according to Hull, is the basis for the stimulus generalization gradient.

Lashley and Wade (1946) directly opposed Hull's position. They suggested that organisms generalize because of confusion at the time of a generalization test and that at the time of testing subjects often are unable to distinguish the training stimulus from similar testing stimuli. As a result, responses are made to test stimuli as well as to the original training stimulus.

This view states that such test confusions can be eliminated by giving a subject prior discrimination training with the stimulus dimension involved. If a subject has learned to discriminate between the training and testing stimuli, the tendency to confuse these stimuli during testing will be diminished. Thus, Lashley and Wade hypothesized that generalization will always depend on an individual's prior experiences with the stimulus dimension in question. The more discrimination experience a subject has, the less generalization the subject should show.

Clearly, both of the foregoing theories provide reasonable potential explanations for the occurrence of generalization effects. Unfortunately, researchers have found it difficult to distinguish between these views experimentally. In many cases the two theories simply make the same predictions concerning the effects of experimental manipulations. One of the few differences between these theories concerns the role of prior discriminative experience. According to Hull's position, such experience should play an insignificant role in determining the shape of a generalization gradient. Lashley and Wade, however, viewed prior discriminative experience as a critical variable.

In an attempt to determine whether prior experience affects generalization gradients, several experimenters have varied the rearing conditions of organisms before training with a given stimulus. For example, in some studies animals have been reared in environments that are virtually devoid of color in an attempt to prevent them from learning to discriminate colors. The question of interest is whether such manipulation does in fact affect later generalization along the color dimension.

The results of such studies have been mixed. Some experimenters have found that prior experience manipulations clearly influence the shape of generalization gradients (see, for example, Ganz & Riesen, 1962; Peterson, 1963). However, others have reported that these manipulations have little effect on generalization performance (see Riley & Leuin, 1971; Rudolph & Honig, 1972; Tracy, 1970). These conflicting results provide little basis for effectively choosing between Hull's explanation and the interpretations proposed by Lashley and Wade.

It is also clear that neither view can provide a complete explanation of generalization training on a totally different dimension (see Thomas, Freeman, Svinicki, Burr, & Lyons, 1970). It is possible that both multiple associations formed during training and stimulus confusions at the time of testing contribute to generalization performance. However, the problems just outlined have led other theorists to search for additional generalization mechanisms. One promising contemporary approach focuses on the role of incidental or contextual stimuli in producing generalization.

The Role of "Incidental Stimuli" in Generalization

The Rescorla–Wagner model (Rescorla & Wagner, 1972) views contextual or background stimuli as functioning like the nominal CS in a conditioning experiment. Thus, in any conditioning situation not only will the CS acquire the capacity to produce a response, but contextual stimuli will also acquire this capacity to a lesser degree.

Based on this view, Mackintosh (1974) has suggested that these incidental or contextual stimuli may be critical for understanding generalization phenomena. According to this view, responding during a generalization test is determined by the associative strength of all the stimuli present on that test.

This contextual view further states that prior discrimination learning (even on a dimension different from the test dimension) should steepen the gradient by reducing associations to the background stimuli. In other words, during discrimination training, responses in the presence of the background stimuli are sometimes reinforced and sometimes not reinforced. This means that such stimuli will become poor predictors for reinforcement and will not acquire much associative value relative to the S+ that is always followed by reinforcement. On a subsequent test, S+ will produce substantial responding. However, any change in S+ will decrease responding drastically, since the background stimuli present will have little capacity to produce a response.

Mackintosh (1974) demonstrates that this approach is consistent with a large proportion of generalization findings. Clearly, such an explanation is promising, and it deserves increased attention by experimenters.

Two Recent Theoretical Interpretations of Stimulus Generalization

Elemental Model of Stimulus Generalization. Recent papers on stimulus generalization extend the positions of Lashley and Wade and Hull. These papers highlight two different mechanisms for stimulus generalization. Wills and Mackintosh (1998) conducted a series of experiments designed to test Blough's (1975) theory of stimulus generalization. Blough (1975), building on the theoretical positions of Hull (1943) and

Spence (1937), proposed that physical dimensions such as color and size are overlapping sets of elements. Each stimulus within a dimension is assumed to activate elements most strongly at a particular point along a continuum. At points removed from this particular point elements are activated less strongly. When an animal is reinforced in the presence of a stimulus all elements of that stimulus acquire associative strength. Since a stimulus removed a short distance from the target would share many of the same elements with the target stimulus the second stimulus would also elicit responding. Stimuli farther removed from S+ would share fewer elements and hence would elicit a reduced level of response.

Blough explained peak shift as follows. During discrimination training, associations form between the elements of the discriminative stimuli and the availability of reward. Elements present in S+ but absent in S− acquire strong positive associative value. Elements present in S− but absent in S+ acquire strong negative associative value. Elements that are shared by both S+ and S− acquire both positive and negative value. Responding is dictated by the net strength of the associative value.

Consider a stimulus that is located a short distance from S+ away from S−. Following discrimination training, this stimulus will have a higher proportion of positive value and a lower proportion of negative value than the original S+. The organism would show greater responding to this stimulus than to S+. Similarly, a stimulus located a short distance from S− away from S+ will have a greater proportion of negative value and a smaller proportion of positive value than S−. The organism would show greater inhibitory responding to this stimulus than to S−. These two phenomena are termed positive peak shift and negative peak shift, respectively. Both positive peak shifts (Hanson, 1959) and negative peak shifts (Guttman, 1965) have been reported in the literature.

Wills and Mackintosh (1998) attempted to test Blough's extension of the Hull and Spence position. These researchers used computer-generated stimuli to develop an artificial stimulus dimension. In essence each stimulus was a composite of elements shared by stimuli along the continuum. S+ and S− could be made to share a given number of elements. Stimuli located further away from S+ and S− shared fewer elements. In Experiment 1 pigeons were trained to discriminate two neighboring stimuli and their responses to test stimuli were assessed. Pigeons solved the complex discriminations and then showed the typical generalization gradients to stimuli removed from S+ and S−. Indeed, the data revealed both the presence of positive and negative peak shift. Experiment 2 employed human subjects in a similar task. The results were analogous. Figure 7.10 shows a typical stimulus used in Experiment 1 and the entire set available to the experimenters. Stimuli used in the human studies were similar.

Forgetting and Context Change Model of Stimulus Generalization. A second line of reasoning regarding the mechanism underlying stimulus generalizations builds on the work of Lashely and Wade. Those theorists you will recall felt that generalization resulted from confusion. During stimulus-generalization test trials, subjects often are unable to distinguish the training stimulus from similar testing stimuli. As a result, responses are made to test stimuli as well as to the original training stimulus.

Consistent with this view is the notion that confusion results from forgetting. Organisms may learn about the features of S+ and/or S− and then over time or through interference may forget some of what they have learned and respond to similar stimuli. Obviously, the more the animal has learned about the stimulus the less likely it will be to forget and the steeper will be the resulting generalization gradient.

One reason for memory failure may be retrieval failure (Bouton, Nelson, & Rosas, 1999; Deweer, 1986; Gordon, 1981; Tulving & Pearlstone, 1966). Bouton and others (Bouton, 1993; McGeoch, 1942; Mensixk & Raajmakers, 1988; Spear, 1978) have proposed a second reason.

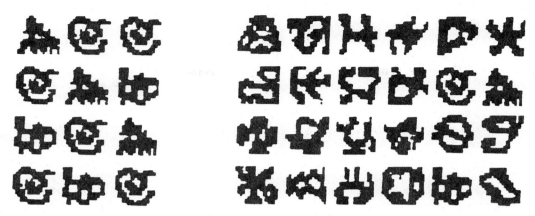

FIGURE 7.10 Testing Blough's Extension of Hull and Spence. The left panel depicts a typical stimulus used in Experiment 1 of the paper by Wills and Mackintosh (1998). As indicated the stimulus contains three instances of one element type, six instances of a second type, and three instances of a third type. The right panel depicts all 24 icons available to the experimenters. This figure is taken from Wills and Mackintosh (1998), "Peak shift on an artificial dimension," in *The Quarterly Journal of Experimental Psychology,* 1998, *51B*, 1–31. © 1998 by The Experimental Psychology Society.

These theorists suggest that the passage of time may change the background stimuli making retrieval more difficult. The basic argument here is that background or contextual stimuli provide the cues necessary for remembering. If these contextual cues change memory deficits can occur.

An interesting source of evidence for this position comes from Bouton (1993), who argues that extinction may not produce a weakening of a response or unlearning but may involve learning that a given relation no longer holds. For example, if an animal learns that food is presented following some stimulus event, then in the presence of that stimulus event the animal will emit a conditioned response. If the response is then extinguished, the animal stops responding to the stimulus. Bouton showed that the effect was primarily dependent on contextual stimuli. It is clear that contextual stimuli can affect stimulus generalization (Mackintosh, 1974). It may be that changes in contextual stimuli over time effect retrieval ability, which leads to greater generalization (Bouton, Nelson, & Rosas, 1999).

Generalizations Mediated by Internal Responses

Earlier in this chapter we mentioned that humans generalize not only between physically similar stimuli but also between words that have similar meanings. Lacey and Smith (1954) conducted a classic experiment demonstrating this effect. These experimenters first had participants do free association with each word in a list. Through this technique they were able to determine clusters of words with similar meanings. They then chose one word such as *cow* and followed the presentation of the word with a shock. They found that the word *cow* began to elicit a conditioned elevation in heart rate. They also found that words in the same conceptual category (for example, *plow, corn,* and *tractor*) produced a conditioned response even though these words had never been paired with shock. No responding occurred to unrelated words such as *paper*. This is an example of semantic generalization (Maltzman, 1977).

These findings are reminiscent of the generalization that occurs among physically similar stimuli. However, it is difficult to account for such findings with any of the explanations of generalization we have considered. The problem is that all these theories are based on the physical differences between training and test stimuli. As a result, theoretical explanations of semantic generalization have differed somewhat from theories of the kinds we have described.

Most attempts to explain semantic generalization have centered on the idea that a meaningful word always produces certain internal responses within an individual (see Jenkins, 1963). These internal responses may be conceptualized as either thoughts or emotional reactions triggered by the meaning of a word. So, for example, the presentation of the word *cow* may trigger thoughts about farms or rural settings. This implies that if a given word is paired with a US, not only will the word itself become capable of eliciting a CR, but also any thoughts provoked by that word will become conditioned. Following our example, if the word *cow* is presented and is followed by shock, both the word *cow* and any thoughts about farms will become associated with shock. Participants will generalize responding between any words that provoke the same thoughts or emotional reactions. These internal responses mediate or provide a link between physically dissimilar words. In general, this kind of theorizing accounts rather well for semantic generalization effects.

DISCRIMINATION LEARNING

In our discussion of stimulus generalization, we described some of the necessary conditions for discrimination learning. We know, for example, that such learning involves presenting different stimuli to an organism and then differentially reinforcing responses to those different stimuli. Typically, responses in the presence of one stimulus are reinforced, whereas responses in the presence of another stimulus are not. As a result of such differential reinforcement, we begin to establish **stimulus control** over behavior.

On the surface at least, the process of discrimination learning appears rather simple. However, discrimination learning in the real world is seldom simple. The complicating factor is that stimuli are rarely encountered in isolation. Thus, we are never differentially reinforced for responding to isolated stimuli.

To illustrate how this fact complicates the discrimination process, return for a moment to the field research project in which vervet monkeys produced different sounds to different predators and discriminated actual predators from nonthreatening animals. Cheney and Seyfarth (1990) argued that much of this behavior is learned. But how is the behavior *acquired?* Imagine how difficult it would be to teach a young vervet monkey to discriminate aerial predators from nonpredators and to emit a specific call in the presence of such a predator. One might begin by presenting a model or picture or the actual predator itself to the monkey and recording the response. Assume that the monkey responds to the presentation of the aerial predator with a startle response and with a call that resembles the actual call produced by adults. Upon completion of the response the trainer rewards the response with a monkey treat.

After several trials in which the trainer rewards the response, she begins to withhold the reward except on those occasions when the monkey emits a vocal response more like the adults. With this type of shaping over the course of several weeks, the animal might be responding to the predator with the appropriate adult response. But is training complete? The answer is no. Now the monkey must learn to respond to the aerial predator but not to nonthreatening species.

So in the next phase the trainer presents the aerial predator and a nonthreatening species. On those trials in which the monkey responds to the predator the trainer reinforces the call. But when the monkey responds in a similar fashion to the nonthreatening bird the trainer withholds reinforcement. After numerous trials the monkey responds to the predator but not to the other bird. The monkey has learned to respond in the presence of one stimulus but not in the presence of another. It has clearly learned the discrimination. But is training complete?

No, the question remains: What has the monkey learned? Is it responding to the silhouette of the predator, its color, its size, its beak, its claws, some combination of stimuli? Many experiments are needed to determine just what the animal is using as stimuli to make the discrimination. Finally, the trainer needs to know if the monkey will respond to all predator birds or just the one on which it was trained. That is, will it generalize its responses both within a species of predator and between species? After all, to be useful, the antipredator behavior must be exhibited in the presence of all aerial predators.

The same kinds of complication arise even in relatively simple laboratory experiments. We may, for example, attempt to train a rat to choose the white arm of a T-maze as opposed to the black arm. We might do this by rewarding the animal each time it enters the white arm and not rewarding entries into the black arm. Even this discrimination problem is complicated by the fact that on any given trial the white arm must be either on the left or the right of the central maze runway. Thus, if the rat turns, enters the white arm, and is reinforced, it may well be learning to turn right instead of learning to enter the arm that happens to be white instead of black.

Apparatus, Methods of Training, and Types of Discriminations

Discrimination learning can be quite complex and difficult to control. Still, psychologists have devoted much attention to discrimination learning, and they have learned a great deal about the process.

Common Apparatuses. Over the years, various discrimination-learning experiments have involved many different kinds of apparatus. Figure 7.11 shows the most popular apparatuses. Figure 7.11a shows the apparatus used by Karl Lashley. The **Lashley jumping stand** requires that the animal jump from the stand to one of two windows placed about three feet off the ground. If the animal makes a correct choice the window falls backward and the animal, usually a rat, lands on the platform behind the window. There is food located in a dish on this platform and the rat eats. If the rat makes an incorrect choice, the window does not fall back and the rat falls three feet to a net below.

Rats learned to discriminate in this apparatus, but the task was aversive. Rats, who do not see too well, are reluctant to jump off into space only to hit against a solid wall and then fall to a net below. To the myopic rat this fall may appear to be a very long distance. As a consequence Lashley often had to prod the animal to respond by blowing on it (rats do not like to have air blown on their faces) or by hitting its tail with a stick. The aversiveness of the situation posed a problem for experimenters who were interested only in discrimination learning and the apparatus was modified.

Figure 7.11b shows a **modified Lashley jumping stand.** In this apparatus the rat jumps from the stand to a ledge where it can then push the door down to receive a reward. If the rat makes a correct choice, it receives a food reward. If the rat is incorrect it simply stays on the ledge until the experimenter picks it up and places it back in the home cage.

Figure 7.11c shows an early version of the **Grice box,** in which there were two back walls with cards inserted into slots. The cards were interchangeable. Food dishes were attached to the stimulus cards and the animal responded by choosing the right or left door. In later versions of the Grice box, there were three back walls that could be painted any color. For example, the middle wall might be black and the two ends white. By moving the start box from one side to the other one could counterbalance which side S+ and S− are located. Figure 7.11 also shows other popular apparatuses for teaching discrimination problems. These include the T-maze, Y-maze, runways, and Skinner boxes. In the last panel of the figure is depicted a **Wisconsin General Test Apparatus.** This apparatus was

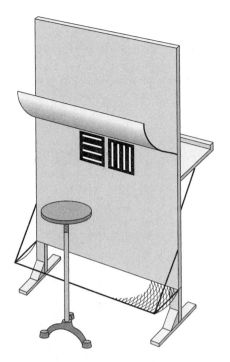

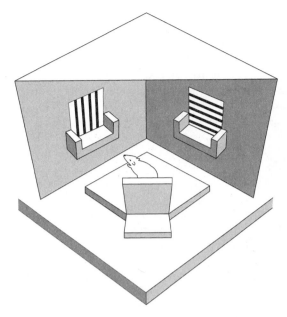

(B) Modified Lashley Jumping Stand

(A) Original Lashley Jumping Stand

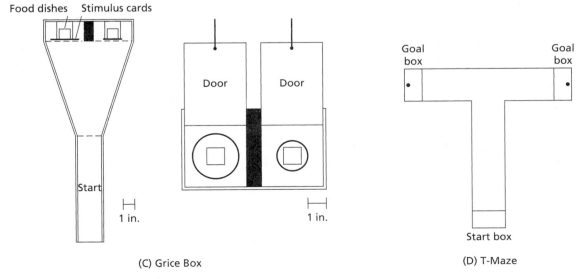

(C) Grice Box

(D) T-Maze

FIGURE 7.11 Popular Apparatuses for Teaching Discrimination Learning Problems.

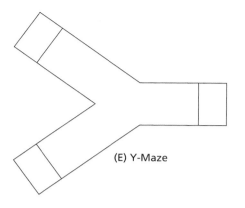

(E) Y-Maze

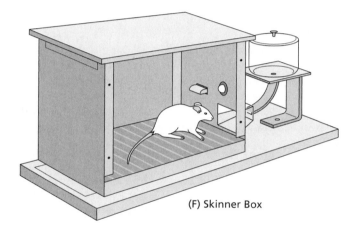

(F) Skinner Box

(G) Wisconsin General Test Apparatus

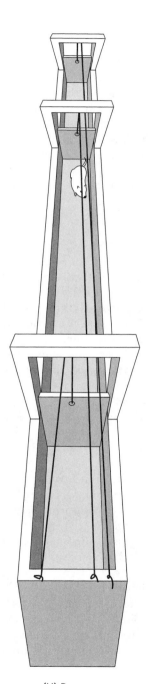

(H) Runway

used a great deal to teach two-choice discrimination problems to primates, birds, and humans.

Methods of Training. There are two basic methods for teaching discrimination learning. These are the **successive method** and the **simultaneous method.** In the successive method the stimuli are presented one at a time successively. Subjects are given randomly alternating trials of S+ and S−. In this method the subject is not able to compare the two stimuli and must remember from one trial to the next which stimulus is rewarded and which is not. With training, subjects come to respond in the presence of S+ and not respond in the presence of S−. In the simultaneous method the subject is presented S+ and S− at the same time and the animal is allowed to choose between the two stimuli.

Common Types of Discrimination Problems. There are numerous types of discrimination problems. We will discuss only the most popular. One of the least difficult discrimination problems is the position discrimination. In nondiscriminable goal boxes the animal learns always to respond to the left or right goal box. If the animal, usually a rat, prefers going to the right as opposed to left, then the goal would be to train this animal to go left.

Other, more complicated discriminations include **brightness** (black vs. white, different shades of gray, or bright vs. dim light) and **color discriminations.** Researchers have also taught form (circle vs. square), size (large square vs. small square), and line orientation (horizontal vs. vertical, or left diagonal vs. right diagonal) discriminations. Two other common discrimination problems should be mentioned. The first is the successive conditional discrimination. In this problem both stimuli are the same. The animal is taught that in the presence of one stimulus it responds one way, and in the presence of another stimulus it responds in a different fashion. For example, in a modified Lashley jumping stand we could teach a rat to jump left if both cards are white, and to jump right if both cards are black.

Finally, there are **discrimination reversal problems.** In these, the animal is originally trained to solve a problem to some criterion level. Once the problem is solved, the reward conditions are reversed. For example, imagine a rat in a T-maze. There are two goal boxes and one is painted white and the other is painted black. The rat is rewarded for choosing black and not rewarded for choosing white. The black and white goal boxes are alternated randomly so that they occur an equal number of times on the left and the right side of the T-maze. The animal receives 10 trials per day and we set our performance criterion at 9 out of 10 correct choices on any given day. Once the rat has solved this problem to criterion the situation is reversed. Now the rat is rewarded for choosing white and not black. Trials are conducted until the rat learns the reversal problem to the same criterion as the original problem. An interesting fact about reversal problems is that they are always harder than the original problem.

Theories of Discrimination Learning

The examples raise an important question. How is it ever possible to attach a response to one specific stimulus and not to others when the specific stimulus never occurs alone? For years this question has perplexed researchers interested in discrimination learning.

Continuity Theories of Discrimination Learning Using a classical conditioning paradigm, Pavlov taught dogs to differentiate between S+ and S−. Pavlov noted that in any discrimination task there were three states of differentiation. First, the level of response to S− was low. This was due to competing responses, presumably the **investigatory reflex.** Second, the level of responses to S− increased due to generalization from S+. Finally, the animal responded to S+, but not to S−.

Pavlov believed that there were two competing critical processes in learning. These processes were called **excitation** (which increased gradually with continued presentations of S+) and **internal**

inhibition (which increased gradually with continued presentations of S−). Behavior was considered the joint outcome of these two processes. Pavlov believed that excitation and internal inhibition increased slowly and continuously over trials. They were not all-or-none events.

In 1936, Spence built on the theoretical groundwork laid by Pavlov and Hull. He proposed that discrimination learning could be explained solely on the basis of the way that reinforcement and nonreinforcement tend to affect stimulus-response associations. Central to this theory were two simple principles. First, whenever an organism is reinforced for responding in the presence of a stimulus, the association between that response and all the stimuli making up that object will be strengthened. Second, whenever an organism makes a response in the presence of an object and is not reinforced, the association between that response and all stimuli comprising that object will be weakened. In effect, all stimuli present when a response is reinforced become excitatory and all stimuli present when a response is not reinforced become inhibitory.

By using these simple reinforcement principles, Spence was able to account for the occurrence of specific discriminations even in relatively complex situations. To illustrate the power of this approach, imagine a pigeon who is learning to discriminate colors. On trial 1 the pigeon is presented with two plastic keys that are identical except that one is red and other is green. The pigeon selects the red key and is reinforced. This means that the small size, the round shape, the position of the key on the panel, and the red color all become associated with reward.

On trial 2 the pigeon pecks the green key and is not reinforced. This means that the association between the color green and pecking will be weakened. It also means that the associations between pecking and the small size and the round shape and the position of the key are also weakened. Thus, after two trials the pigeon has an excitatory association between the color red and pecking. There is also an inhibitory association between the color green and pecking. The other

stimuli in the situation, the small size and the round shape and the position of the key, have both excitatory and inhibitory associations that tend to cancel each other out.

As more and more reinforced and nonreinforced responses occur, a clear pattern will emerge. The only strong excitatory association will be between the color red and the pecking response, since the pigeon is consistently reinforced for pecking red. The only strong inhibitory association will be between the color green and pecking, since the pigeon is consistently not reinforced for pecking the green object. All other stimuli that comprise these objects will be reinforced sometimes and not reinforced sometimes, depending on whether they occur in compound with the color red or the color green. Thus, these stimuli will have a net association of zero with the pecking response.

Two aspects of Spence's theory are important. First, organisms attend to all stimuli equally and all stimuli present at the time of reinforcement are associated with the response. Thus, in Spence's view, animals are **not selectively attending** to stimuli in their environment. Second, animals respond to the **absolute properties of stimuli.** For example in a black-and-white discrimination where the black stimulus is positive, the animal learns that black is rewarded and white is not. An animal does not learn about relationships between stimuli. That is, the animal is not learning that the darker of two stimuli is rewarded and the lighter of two stimuli is not.

In 1937 Spence further elaborated his position with the development of his **algebraic summation theory.** There were five postulates to Spence's theory, as follows:

- Every reinforced trial leads to an increase in the excitatory strength for a given stimulus and its reinforced response.

- Every nonreinforced trial leads to an increase in the inhibitory strength for a given stimulus and its nonreinforced response.

- Both excitatory and inhibitory tendencies generalize along a stimulus dimension.

- There is an algebraic summation of the excitatory and inhibitory gradients.
- The generalization gradient obtained following intradimensional training is the result of the algebraic summation.

Spence's position can be depicted graphically. Figure 7.12 shows the net associative strength of stimuli along a brightness gradient. The values along the abscissa represent degrees of brightness. In the figure, an animal is trained on a brightness discrimination where the brighter of the two stimuli is positive. The figure shows the excitatory gradient drawn around S+ and the inhibitory gradient around S−. A third curve depicts the net associative strength. This curve is obtained by subtracting the inhibitory strength from the excitatory strength. Note in the figure that the net excitatory strength around S+ is higher than the net excitatory strength around S−. Thus given a choice between S+ and S−, the animal would choose S+.

The algebraic summation theory can be used to account for peak shift. The peak shift phenomenon is the finding that in a discrimination setting, the maximum amount of responding to stimuli is not at S+, but is at a point removed from S+ and S− (Hanson, 1959). In Figure 7.12, you will observe that the net excitatory strength is highest at a point removed to the right of S+. Spence predicts, and correctly, that an animal will respond more to this stimulus than to the original S+. However, Spence's summation can not account for the contrast effects found by Hanson.

Noncontinuity Theories of Discrimination Learning. Spence's view of discrimination learning is termed a continuity theory because it assumes that discrimination learning is a continuous process. The formation of any discrimination begins on trial 1 and emerges gradually over several reinforced and nonreinforced trials. The appeal of such a view is that it can account for discrimination learning solely on the basis of reinforcement principles. Such a theory contrasts

sharply with a second type of theory, which claims that discrimination phenomena cannot be accounted for simply by understanding how stimulus-response associations become stronger or weaker. Theories of the latter type, termed **noncontinuity theories,** focus on the role of **attentional** mechanisms in the discrimination learning process.

Spence assumed that when an organism is confronted with a stimulus object, it noticed or perceived a large number of the individual stimuli that made up the object. This assumption is the basis for the idea that a simple reinforcement can affect numerous stimulus-response associations. Other theorists, however, have questioned this assumption. They believed it was impossible for an organism to learn about all the stimuli that impinged on its sense receptors at any given time. Organisms have a limited capacity for processing stimulus information; they have developed filtering mechanisms. Such mechanisms, which allow an organism to select or notice only a small subset of the stimuli actually present in a given instance, ensure that the organism's processing capacities will not be overwhelmed. It is this process of selecting out only a portion of the total stimulus array that we call attention.

Several theorists (Krechevsky, 1932; Lashley, 1942; Sutherland & Mackintosh, 1971) have proposed that discrimination learning involves two distinct but interacting stages. One stage involves learning to attend to the correct stimulus dimension (for example, color, shape, size, or some other aspect of that object). To do this, the organism initially focuses its attention on one dimension (for example, shape) and through its experience with reinforcement determines whether this dimension is critical for solving the problem. If not, the organism shifts its attention to a second dimension.

Once the organism determines that it is attending to the correct dimension, it begins the second stage of the discrimination process. In earlier versions of the noncontinuity position (Krechevsky, 1938; Lashley, 1942) this second stage of learning occurred rapidly. The animal quickly formed an association between the stimulus and the response. Thus, according to noncontinuity theory, animals try out different hypotheses and when they finally hit upon the correct one, they quickly solve the problem.

Later versions of this theory (Sutherland & Mackintosh, 1971) found that once the animal has selected the correct hypothesis, learning proceeds in basically the same manner suggested by Spence. That is, at this point the organism begins to associate the response with one stimulus on the correct dimension (for example, red) and to weaken the association between responding and another stimulus on that same dimension (for example, green). As in Spence's theory, these associations are strengthened or weakened depending on the occurrence of reinforcement.

This kind of theory has usually been called either a **noncontinuity** or a **hypothesis-testing theory.** The term **noncontinuity** often is applied because such theories view discrimination learning as a two-stage process. The term *hypothesis-testing theory* denotes that in learning to attend to the correct dimension, organisms begin by forming a hypothesis about what the correct dimension might be. They then test the hypothesis by determining whether their attention to that dimension increases their probability of reinforcement.

In noncontinuity theories, the animal is viewed as an active learner. That is, the animal selectively attends to stimuli in its environment, it actively tries out hypotheses, and once it hits upon the correct hypothesis, learning occurs rapidly. This view is in sharp contrast to continuity theory, which views animals as passive learners.

One difficulty with the early noncontinuity theories is that they were not explicit about what was involved in learning to attend to the correct dimension. They also were not entirely clear about how the two stages of discrimination learning were supposed to interact. Later versions of the noncontinuity position have been far more precise in their formulation. (See, for example, Lovejoy, 1968; Sutherland & Mackintosh, 1971;

Zeaman & House, 1963; for details on these noncontinuity approaches.)

A critical difference between the continuity and noncontinuity views stems from the degree to which individuals learn to focus on a stimulus dimension during discrimination learning. Experiments of several types have examined this question (see Sutherland & Mackintosh, 1971). For the most part, the studies have led to the same conclusion. Just as the noncontinuity view suggests, subjects learning a discrimination problem do appear to learn about stimulus dimensions as well as about stimulus–response relationships. In the next section we consider several different types of studies that shed light on the validity of the continuity and noncontinuity approaches.

Do organisms learn about relations or the absolute properties of stimuli? Spence believed that animals learned about the absolute properties of stimuli. In contrast, Kohler (1939) believed that animals learned about the **relationship between two stimuli.** To support his position, Kohler trained chickens on a brightness discrimination by presenting a light gray card and a dark gray card simultaneously. The chicken was rewarded for choosing the light gray card. After original training, Kohler presented his chickens two stimuli. One of the stimuli was the original light gray card that had previously been reinforced. The second card was an even lighter gray card. Kohler reasoned that if the chicken had learned about the absolute properties of stimuli that it should choose the light gray card that it had previously experienced.

On the other hand, if the chicken were making decisions on the basis of relationships, i.e., it had learned to choose lighter over darker, then it should choose the lighter gray card it had not encountered previously. Interestingly, Kohler's chickens chose the lighter gray card over the original S+. Kohler's findings supported his contention that animals learn about *relationships* and not about the absolute properties of stimuli. Kohler termed this phenomenon

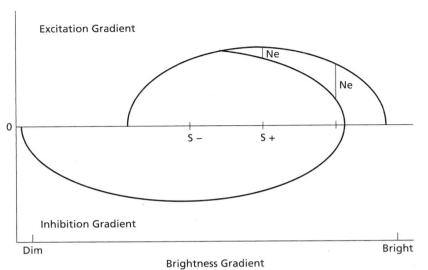

FIGURE 7.12 Transposition Effect. Depiction of summation of excitatory and inhibitory gradients resulting in net excitatory and inhibitory strength according to Spence's algebraic summation theory.

the **transposition effect** and he was able to demonstrate the effect in chickens and in chimpanzees.

The transposition effect posed a difficulty for continuity theories. That an animal would choose a stimulus it had not encountered over a stimulus that it had associated with reward did not make sense. On the other hand, the data fit the relational position quite well.

Figure 7.12 shows that Spence was able to predict the transposition effect. Indeed the same explanation that allows him to account for peak shift provides an explanation for transposition. Examining the net associative strengths of stimuli to the right of S+ we see they are higher than the net associative strength of S+.

So how are we to decide whether Kohler or Spence is correct? Both theorists make the same prediction. However, note that as the animal moves further to the right of S+ the net associative strength of these stimuli decreases. This is because the generalization gradient around S+ decreases as the animal moves further away from S+. Spence predicts that as it moves further and further away from S+ and S− there should be a weakening of the transposition effect and even-

tually a reversal of transposition. In other words, at some point along the continuum the animal will stop choosing the brighter stimulus and choose the dimmer stimulus.

Kohler cannot make this prediction. If the animal is learning about relationships between stimuli then it should always choose the brighter stimulus. Kohler cannot predict either a weakening of the transposition effect or a reversal of the effect. Kendler (1950) and Ehrenfreund (1952) reported evidence for a **weakening of the transposition effect** and a **reversal of the transposition effect.** On the basis of these data it seems clear that animals are learning about the absolute properties of stimuli.

But can animals also learn about relationships between stimuli? Lawrence and DeRivera (1954) conducted an ingenious study that shed light on this question. Using stimulus cards that had two shades of gray painted on them, these researchers trained rats on a successive conditional discrimination. The shades of gray ranged from light (stimulus 1) to dark (stimulus 7). For each stimulus card the number 4 gray was always on the bottom half of the card. The top half could be anywhere in the range from 1 to 3 or from 5 to 7.

In a Lashley jumping stand rats were presented with two identical stimulus cards. On some trials lighter shades of gray were over darker shades of gray. On other trials darker shades of gray were over lighter shades of gray. When the rat encountered the condition lighter over darker it was reinforced for jumping to the right and when it was presented darker over lighter it was reinforced for jumping left.

Once the rats had solved this discrimination problem Lawrence and DeRivera presented test trials in which the cards were turned over. The possible combinations were 4/1, 4/2, 4/3, 4/5, 4/6, or 4/7. Rats were presented with these combinations and their choices were recorded. Lawrence and DeRivera reasoned that if animals are learning about the absolute properties of stimuli, then turning the card over should make no difference in their responses. For example if a rat was reinforced for jumping left in the presence of 7/4, then when presented with 4/7 it should also jump left. At no time was the animal reinforced for jumping right in the presence of this stimulus.

On the other hand, if rats are learning about relations, then one would predict a different outcome. For example, if rats are learning darker over lighter jump left and lighter over darker jump right, then turning the card over makes a big difference. In the presence of 7/4, the animal should jump left (darker over lighter), but in the presence of 4/7 the rat should jump right (lighter over darker). Lawrence and DeRivera's rats all did the same thing. They jumped left to 7/4 and they jumped right to 4/7. Clearly, these rats had learned about the relation between the different shades of gray.

So which explanation is correct? Do animals learn about the absolute properties of stimuli or do they learn about relations between stimuli? It appears that the answer is not one or the other, but rather animals are capable of learning both about the absolute properties of stimuli and about the relationships between stimuli. The circumstances of the testing situation may play a role in whether animals show one type of learning over another. One thing does seem consistent: When the discriminations are taught successively, animals tend to learn about the absolute properties of stimuli. When they are taught a discrimination problem using the simultaneous method, they tend to learn about the relationship between the two stimuli.

Attacks on the Continuity Position

Spence believed that all stimuli that impinged upon the senses were learned about. On the other hand, noncontinuity theorists argue that animals only learn about the stimuli to which they are attending at any given point in time. If an animal is attending to position cues to solve a discrimination problem, it will not be learning about brightness cues at the same time.

Lashley (1942) trained rats to a high criterion on a size discrimination. Rats learned that a 10-cm circle was associated with a reward while a 6-cm circle was not. In phase 2, Lashley changed the stimuli by substituting a 10-cm triangle for the large 10-cm circle. In this phase, the large triangle was correct and the small circle, as before, was not. Subjects were trained under these conditions until the rat responded correctly for 10 successive trials. In phase 3 all rats received 200 further trials wherein the large triangle was correct and the small circle was not. Phase 4 was a test phase in which rats were presented with an 8-cm circle or an 8-cm triangle.

Lashley reasoned that in phase 1 the rats solved the problem on the basis of size. In phases 2 and 3 this hypothesis was not disconfirmed and would not be discarded. Therefore in phase 4, given a choice between an 8-cm circle and an 8-cm triangle, the rats should show no preference. Spence, on the other hand, would argue that in phase 1 excitatory strength to the 10-cm circle would increase and inhibitory strength would increase to the 6-cm circle. In phase 2, there would be a continued increase of inhibitory strength to the small circle, but now excitatory strength would develop to the large triangle. In phase 3, there would be a continued increase of excitatory strength to the large triangle and inhibitory strength to the small circle. During the test phase, Spence would predict that through stimulus generalization there would be an excitatory gradient around the 8-cm triangle and an inhibitory gradient around the 8-cm circle. Thus, given a choice between these two stimuli, the rat should choose the triangle.

As Lashley predicted, rats showed no preference for the 8-cm circle or the 8-cm triangle. In phase 5 Lashley once again returned to the large triangle/positive and the small circle/negative problem. Rats received these conditions until they had responded for 20 successive correct trials. Then in phase 6 they were tested on a new problem. This time a 6-cm triangle was presented along with a large 10-cm circle. Lashley argued that because the size hypothesis had never been disconfirmed, rats should choose the large circle. Spence would have trouble making this prediction. As predicted by Lashley, all rats chose the large circle.

Lashley's study offered strong support for noncontinuity theory. But Spence did not give up. In 1945, he published a study supporting the continuity position. Using an apparatus that had two runways and a common start box, Spence rewarded two groups of rats (experimental and control) on the basis of position for 30 trials. One half of the rats in each group were reinforced for choosing the left runway and the other half were reinforced for choosing the right runway. Both alleys were painted a neutral gray.

In phase 2 Spence introduced black and white alleys for 20 trials. In the experimental group one half of the rats learned that white was positive and the other half learned that black was positive. Rats in the control group were rewarded for 50% of the trials for black and white. In phase 3, Spence reintroduced the gray alleys. Working against the original position preference Spence trained all rats to a criterion of three successive correct trials. Finally, in phase 4, Spence reintroduced the black and white alleys and reversed training of the experimental subjects. He predicted that the black/white training the rats had

in phase 2 would interfere in their learning the reversal problem.

Noncontinuity theory would make a different prediction. Because the rats originally used a position hypothesis to solve the problem in phase 1, they would keep this hypothesis in phase 2. Given that there were only 20 trials of phase 2 and that Spence's rats continued to respond on the basis of position, noncontinuity theory would predict that the animals would not learn anything about black and white. The position hypothesis would still hold in phase 3, and noncontinuity theory would predict that the animals would not show negative transfer and that both the control and experimental subjects would solve the black/white problem in phase 4 at the same rate. They did not. The experimental group took significantly longer to solve the black/white problem in phase 4 than the control group. Spence interpreted his finding as supporting continuity theory.

Additional Attacks on Continuity Theory

The Acquired Distinctiveness of Cues. One finding that is clearly in accord with the noncontinuity approach comes from a series of experiments conducted by Lawrence (1949, 1950, and 1952) to evaluate what he called the **acquired distinctiveness of cues.** In the first experiment of this type, Lawrence (1949) trained three groups of rats on a discrimination problem in a T-maze. For one group, the arms differed in terms of brightness and the S+ was either a black arm or a white arm. For the second group the critical cue was floor texture; the S+ was either a rough floor or a smooth floor. The third group learned to discriminate between arms that were of different widths.

After this training, all three groups were placed in a T-maze that had two white arms on some trials and two black arms on other trials. Their task was to learn to turn in one direction (for example, right) when the arms were black and to turn in the other direction when the arms were white. Lawrence reasoned that none of the groups had learned a specific stimulus–response association in problem 1 that should help them learn the discrimination in problem 2. However, the group that had learned the black–white discrimination in problem 1 would have an advantage in learning problem 2 if, in learning problem 2, they learned to attend to the brightness dimension.

Lawrence's prediction was well supported by his data. The second problem was most quickly learned by the group that had previously learned the black–white discrimination. Similar findings have supported Lawrence's conclusions (see, for example, Mackintosh & Holgate, 1967; Mumma & Warren, 1968). These data clearly indicate that when an organism learns to discriminate between a black stimulus and a white stimulus, it does more than simply attach specific responses to these stimuli. The data suggest that organisms also learn to attend to the stimulus dimension on which the stimuli are located.

Intradimensional versus Extradimensional Shift Problems. A second set of data clearly favoring the noncontinuity position comes from studies that compare **intradimensional** and **extradimensional shifts.** Basically, any discrimination-shift paradigm involves two stages. A subject is trained first to discriminate between stimuli and then to discriminate between two other stimuli not encountered in the first stage. In an intradimensional shift, all the stimuli used in both stages are from the same stimulus dimension. An example would be to train an organism to discriminate between the colors red and green and then to shift to a discrimination problem involving the colors yellow and blue. In an extradimensional shift, the stimuli used in stage 1 and stage 2 are from different dimensions. For instance, an organism might learn to discriminate first between red and green and then between squares and circles.

The question of interest in most shift-paradigms studies has been whether subjects will learn the second stage of an intradimensional shift faster than the second stage of an extradimensional shift.

Spence's continuity view predicts no difference in the rate at which the second stage of intradimensional and extradimensional shifts will be learned. In both paradigms the stage 2 stimuli are entirely different from the stage 1 stimuli. No associations formed in stage 1 of either paradigm should carry over to aid learning in stage 2. On the other hand, noncontinuity theories predict clear advantages for subjects learning an intradimensional shift. According to this view, in stage 1 a subject learns to attend to a particular stimulus dimension. If the stage 2 problem involves stimuli from the same dimension, participants will learn very quickly because they have already learned to attend to the stimulus dimension that is critical for solving the stage 2 problem.

Many experiments have been conducted to test these differing predictions. In most cases, the evidence favors the conclusion that organisms learn intradimensional shifts more quickly than extradimensional shifts.

The Overlearning Reversal Effect. A study by Reid (1953) provides an example. Reid trained rats on a black/white discrimination to a criterion of 9 out of 10 correct with the last five trials all correct. At the end of criterion training Reid subjected his rats to one of three conditions. In one condition rats were reversed immediately upon reaching criterion. Rats in a second condition received 50 additional trials of the original discrimination problem and then were reversed. Rats in the third group received 150 additional trials of the original problem and then were reversed.

Continuity makes a clear prediction. The greater the number of overtraining trials the rat receives, the greater the associative strength for responding to S+ should become. As a consequence it should be more difficult for the rats to reverse the discrimination problem as the number of overtraining trials increases. Thus, rats in the immediate reversal group should reverse faster than the group receiving 50 trials of overtraining. Rats given 150 trials of overtraining should solve the discrimination reversal problem at the slowest rate.

Reid found that on average the immediate reversal group required 138 trials to learn the reversal problem to criterion. The group that received 50 trials of overtraining required 129 trials on average to solve the reversal problem. Interestingly, rats that received 150 additional trials past criterion solved the reversal problem in just 70 trials. The effect, which became known as the **overlearning reversal effect** (ORE), was considered highly unusual and posed a grave difficulty for continuity theory. How could training that increased the associative strength of responding to one stimulus give the animal an advantage when it has to extinguish responding to the old positive stimulus and learn to respond to the new positive stimulus? The ORE proved to be robust. More than 60 papers have been published examining the effect (Sutherland & Mackintosh, 1971).

Continuity theory did not have a ready answer for why increased training on the original discrimination facilitated learning the reversal problem. Noncontinuity theory on the other hand could account for the results. Sutherland and Mackintosh proposed that in any discrimination-learning situation, animals build strengths in two areas. One of these refers to the type of problem the animal encounters and is called **analyzer strength.** Examples of different analyzers include position, brightness, orientation, and size. In essence analyzers are the hypotheses that animals try out when solving a discrimination problem. Sutherland and Mackintosh proposed that analyzer strengths sum to a constant amount so that as the strength of one analyzer increases, the others decrease by a comparable amount.

Another important factor in all this is that animals enter a learning situation with analyzer strengths at different levels. For example, rats live in burrows and spend a significant portion of the their lives making left and right turns. Sutherland and Mackintosh claim that the rat comes into the laboratory with high position-analyzer strength. Thus, a rat may try to solve any discrimination problem on the basis of position first. When this analyzer fails to yield consistent results, the rat

must switch to a different analyzer. One prediction made by this theory is that rats should find position problems easier to solve than brightness or orientation problems (Sutherland & Mackintosh, 1971).

Along with analyzer strength, animals also build **response strength.** Increases in response strength cause an animal to respond to one stimulus or another within a specific analyzer. For example, if an animal is learning that black is positive and white is negative and it has the brightness analyzer switched in, then each reinforced trial will increase response strength to black and each nonreinforced trial will decrease response strength to white.

So how do Sutherland and Mackintosh account for the overlearning reversal effect? Imagine that experimenters are training a rat on an orientation problem where the horizontal stripes are positive and the vertical stripes are negative. Initially, the rat has the position analyzer switched in and it attempts to solve the problem on this basis. This does not result in consistent predictions regarding reward outcome, so eventually the rat switches out the position analyzer and switches in the orientation analyzer. Now the rat is getting consistent results and response strength starts to build to horizontal and decrease to vertical. Finally, the animal's response strength for horizontal builds to a high level and the animal reaches criterion.

Sutherland and Mackintosh assume that analyzer strength reaches an asymptotic level at a slower rate than does response strength. At the end of criterion training, response strength is high but analyzer strength is not. During overtraining, analyzer strength continues to build and reaches asymptote. Response strength remains high. At reversal, correct predictions are no longer being made, so both response strength and analyzer strength decrease. For the criterion-trained animals, because analyzer strength is not very high, it decreases to a point where other analyzers are switched in.

Overtrained animals have much stronger analyzer strength. At reversal, analyzer strength does not decrease to the point where the animal switches the relevant analyzer out. Therefore, when response strength for horizontal reaches the point where the animal can switch to responding to vertical, it is still solving the problem on the basis of orientation. The overtrained animal does not switch to the nonrelevant analyzer and, consequently, it is able to solve the problem more quickly than the criterion-trained animal.

Sutherland and Mackintosh's position was able to account for a wide range of phenomena related to the overlearning reversal effect. For example, it correctly predicted that overtrained animals would respond to the old S+ for a longer period of time than criterion-trained animals and that criterion-trained animals would respond on the basis of position for a longer period of time following the reversal than the overtrained animals.

Sutherland and Mackintosh also explained why it was more difficult to obtain the ORE with simple problems than with difficult problems. For example, it has been difficult obtaining the ORE in rats using a position discrimination. Most of the studies that did obtain the ORE in rats used brightness or line orientation problems (Sutherland & Mackintosh, 1971). Sutherland and Mackintosh pointed out that, given their nature, rats would come into a laboratory setting with high position analyzer strength. This would mean that rats would solve position problems easily and that at the end of criterion training, analyzer strength for position might already be at asymptote. As a result one would not expect to observe the ORE using a position discrimination problem when rats were the subjects of choice.

Sutherland and Mackintosh's position was well supported, but it could not account for all findings. For example, Hall (1974) trained rats to criterion on a horizontal/vertical discrimination problem. One of the groups was then taught a black/white problem immediately afterward, and the other group was overtrained 150 trials on the horizontal/vertical problem. Then the overtrained group learned a black/white problem. Once the rats reached criterion on the black/

white problem they were reversed on the black/white problem.

Sutherland and Mackintosh made two predictions. First they predicted that the overtrained group should solve the original black/white problem at a slower rate than the criterion trained rats. Second, they predicted that both groups would solve the black/white reversal problem at the same rate. They made these predictions because of the differences in analyzer strength of the orientation analyzer. The rats that were overtrained on the horizontal/vertical problem had the orientation analyzer at a high level and this would have to decrease to a point where the rat could switch in the brightness analyzer to solve the black/white problem. Because the horizontal/vertical criterion-trained rats have lower orientation analyzer strength, they should break out of the incorrect analyzer more quickly and switch in the relevant analyzer.

The results were not consistent with these predictions. Both groups of rats solved the original black/white problem at the same rate. Even more damaging was the finding that the group that had been overtrained on the horizontal/vertical problem solved the reversal of the black/white problem more quickly than the rats that had been criterion trained on the horizontal/vertical. Sutherland and Mackintosh could not account for the finding that overtraining a rat in one dimension could facilitate the learning of a reversal in a second dimension.

Another study that proved difficult for Sutherland and Mackintosh was conducted by Purdy and Cross (1979). These researchers presented the results of four studies, but we will consider only the third experiment. Four groups of rats were trained in a modified Lashley jumping stand to solve a horizontal/vertical problem to criterion. Following this training one group was overtrained 150 trials and then reversed. A second group was immediately reversed. A third group was transferred to a different Lashley jumping stand. This stand was identical to the first except it had only one window in the center. Rats received 150 trials where they were rewarded in 100% of the trials for jumping to the single gray card. Rats in a fourth group also received 150 trials in the single window jumping stand, but they were rewarded only 50% of the time.

Sutherland and Mackintosh would predict that only the rats overtrained on the horizontal/vertical discrimination would show the overlearning reversal effect. Rats receiving the additional trials in the single-window jumping stand would show no facilitation of reversal performance. These rats could not build orientation analyzer strength while responding to the single gray card. The results contradicted these predictions. As expected, rats that were overtrained on the horizontal/vertical discrimination solved the reversal faster than rats in the criterion-trained group. Surprisingly, rats that received 150 additional trials in the single window jumping stand and that were rewarded for 100% of those trials reversed as quickly as the overtrained rats did. Rats that received 150 additional trials in the single-window jumping stand but were rewarded only 50% of the time reversed at the same rate as the criterion trained rats.

Purdy and Cross argued that in any discrimination problem animals were learning two things. First they learned which stimulus was correct and which was not. Second, they learned that their responses were followed by reinforcement. It is the latter type of learning, they argued, that might effect the ORE. In essence, the authors argued that at the end of criterion training animals know which stimulus is correct. What is different is the strength of their response learning. For the criterion-trained animals their expectancy for reward is considerably less than 100%. That is criterion-trained animals might expect reward just a little over 50% of the time. Overtrained animals on the other hand have a higher expectancy for reward. They expect to receive reward on nearly every trial. This difference, they argued, effects the learning rate of the animal. The fact that the animals that received reward 100% of the trials when approaching the gray card outperformed the animals that received 50% reward

during these overtraining trials supports their position. The finding that these animals solved the reversal at the same rate as the traditionally overtrained group is also supportive.

Conclusions

One of the obvious advantages of Spence's original discrimination theory was its simplicity. Most experiments suggest that discrimination learning involves more than simply associating a specific stimulus and response. It also seems to involve learning to attend to stimulus dimensions that are important in solving the discrimination problem.

CONCEPTS LEARNING

Unless you live in southern Florida or have access to a particularly good zoo, it is unlikely that you have ever seen a roseate spoonbill. Still, if someone were to point out a spoonbill to you, you would immediately recognize it as a bird. You would not need to observe the spoonbill's mating rituals or its food-gathering behavior. You would not need to read about the physiology of the spoonbill, nor would you need to research its diet. You would make your judgment based on your **concept** of what a bird is.

The spoonbill example illustrates an important point. Much of people's knowledge about the world and many of their reactions to novel objects depend on concepts that they have formed from their experiences. We can define a *concept* as a distinct category of objects or events that are all generally related on the basis of certain features or characteristics. In other words, every concept is defined in part by a set of stimulus features. Objects that contain these features usually are viewed as part of the concept, while objects that do not have these features usually are excluded. The concept of an automobile, for example, contains for most people a wide variety of objects. Sports cars, station wagons, and limousines all fit into this concept, even though the objects named differ along a number of dimensions. All are usually included because they share certain features, such as four wheels, seats, and an engine.

Just from this brief description, it may be obvious why some researchers think that concept formation is related to the processes of generalization and discrimination. On the one hand, to form a useful concept we must be able to distinguish between objects that have different features and then respond to these objects accordingly. Certainly, such a process is similar to what we do when we learn a discrimination. At the same time, learning a concept involves learning to respond similarly to related objects even if they differ in some ways. This, of course, is similar to the process of generalization.

Representation of Concepts

Representation is a particularly difficult topic to study. In learning studies, it is relatively easy to control or observe what a person studies. It is also easy to measure what a person remembers at the time of the test. However, it is difficult to infer the nature of the memory representation that exists internally following learning but before the memory is retrieved. The inactive but present contents of memory are called representations. The organization of representations is of particular interest to cognitive psychology.

Family Resemblance. Why do we group various birds together under the common concept called *bird*? Birds are similar in some ways but quite different in others. Hummingbirds are closer in size and shape to bumblebees than they are to ostriches, but we identify the hummingbird and the ostrich as members of the same category, bird, and we exclude the bumblebee from the concept. We would also be more likely to list a sparrow as a typical member of the concept than either the hummingbird or the ostrich.

It is often difficult to identify the common feature that all instances of a particular concept share. With birds, for example, common features might include feathers, ability to fly, beak, etc.

However, there are types of birds that do not fly or that lack one or more of the other features we associate with the concept of *bird*. Therefore, we cannot say that a single feature marks all instances of a particular concept. Rosch and Mervis (1975) have proposed the idea that members of a concept share in common **family resemblances** (see Wittgenstein, 1953). Family resemblance refers to the idea that each member of a concept shares something in common with other members of a concept, although they may not all share the same thing. Thus, a penguin and an ostrich may not fly, but they both have feathers.

Theories of Concept Representation

Attribute Theory. Attribute theory (also known as **feature comparison theory**) argues that concepts are represented mentally in terms of a list of features. These features are the shared characteristics of all members of that concept. The features usually are divided into two types. Defining features are those characteristics that are necessary for inclusion in a particular concept. For example, the defining feature of a chair is that it is an object that a person can sit in or on. Characteristic features are those aspects of a concept that most instances share in common. Four legs, for example, are common characteristic features of chairs.

In its simplest form, attribute theory postulates that each concept is represented by a concept and a list of features. For example, "chair" might be represented as:

object for sitting

made of wood, metal, or plastic

cushioned for comfort

adaptable for indoor and outdoor use

We decide whether a particular object is a chair by comparing the features of a particular object to the features of the concept stored in memory. Typically, models based on this theory are much more complex (e.g., Anderson, 1990;

Collins & Loftus, 1975). Concept representation is a complex network of interacting nodes representing concepts and features.

Collins and Loftus Network Model. Models attempt to simulate some aspect of human behavior or cognition. Models are necessarily simplifications because they cannot capture the complexity of the human brain. Their simulation of human behavior allows for careful predictions about how people will behave under different circumstances. The Collins and Loftus (1975) model is no exception.

The model simulates the representation of cognitive structures that support concept formation. The model is based on the idea of networks of associativity. The networks connect various **nodes,** which represent individual concepts or memories. Figure 7.13 illustrates the idea that

each node represents a concept, and it is connected to other existing nodes through a series of connections.

The key to understanding the Collins–Loftus model is the concept of spreading activation. Spreading activation refers to how one node stimulates other nodes. In the model, when a concept is spoken or thought of, it stimulates the activation of all nodes connected to it. Thus, when the node *bird* is activated, it stimulates any node connected to it, such as *feathers, wings, Thanksgiving,* and *Larry.* The activity then spreads from these nodes to nodes connected to them. However, the degree of activation dissipates as it spreads out across the network. Thus, although *bird* stimulates *Larry,* and *Larry* stimulates *Moe,* there is much less activation of the concept *Moe* (of the Three Stooges) than there was for *Larry* (Larry Bird, the basketball player, and Larry, also

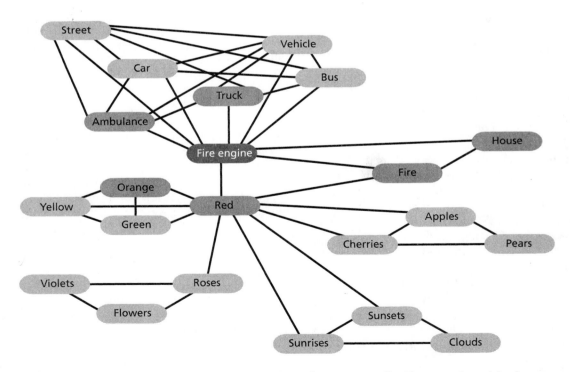

FIGURE 7.13 Networks of Associativity. A semantic network as conceptualized in network models of concept formation. Figure 7.13 is taken from Weiten (1999) as adapted from Collins & Loftus (1975).

one of the Three Stooges). Thus, if the person is asked whether a spoonbill is a bird, the activity generated by the item *spoonbill* will pass through all of its connections, including to the connection *bird*. Thus, the model (and the person) generates a positive answer.

Spreading activation also occurs faster when two nodes are strongly connected. And frequency of use strengthens connections. Thus, concepts such as *Bird* and *basketball* may be more strongly connected for older Boston Celtic basketball fans than for other individuals. As a consequence, Boston Celtic fans might answer more quickly if the question is "Was Bird a basketball player?" than would soccer fans from Southern California.

The Collins-Loftus model is considered a feature comparison model because it is based upon interconnections between the various features (nodes) that make up a given concept. The associations or connections between the nodes hold the concepts into coherent wholes.

One experiment that supports the Collins-Loftus model was done by Meyer and Schvaneveldt (1976). In the experiment, participants were asked to make speeded lexical decision judgments, that is, to determine as quickly as possible whether a presented string of letters was a word ("camel") or a nonword ("fwelp"). In the experiments, some words were preceded by primes. Primes were either words that were related to the target or word or unrelated. For example, using the word "cherries" as a prime for "apples" is a related prime, whereas "street" would be an unrelated prime for the word "apples." The results were that lexical decision times were faster following related than unrelated primes. The priming effect of related items supports the Collins-Loftus model.

Exemplar Theory. Exemplar theory postulates that concepts are represented by specific instances of that concept. Concepts are not broken down into component parts, as they are in attribute theory, nor are they abstracted as they are in prototype theory. Each concept is represented by any number of specific members of the concept. For example, the concept *dog* is represented by specific memories of individual dogs a person has known. The tricky aspect of exemplar theory is how we decide whether a new member is an instance of a particular concept. To make this decision, a new example must be compared to each exemplar of the concept. If there is a close match between the prospective member of the concept and the existing one, the new member is considered part of the concept.

Typicality refers to how representative a particular example is of a particular concept. Rosch (1973) has shown that more typical members of a category (e.g., *robin* in the category *bird* or *retriever* in the category *dog*) are verified as being a member of the category more quickly than less typical examples (e.g., *spoonbill* or *Mexican hairless*). Exemplar theory can explain these data because more typical examples are more likely to be stored as the exemplars.

Part of the success of exemplar theory is explaining people's abilities to learn poorly defined categories. For example, the concept of *games* includes card games, party games, ball games, etc., which may not have any apparent connections. On the other hand, exemplar theory has difficulty explaining how concepts form in the first place.

Prototype Theory. Prototype theory accounts for concepts by arguing that people abstract the common elements of a particular concept and then store an abstracted prototypical representation in memory (see Rosch, 1973). **Prototypes** are formed by averaging over large number of examples of the concept. By this process, prototypes become idealized representations of the particular concept. New examples are then compared to the prototype to determine whether the new member is an example of the concept. The prototype, unlike the exemplars of the previous theory, is not a real example. Rather it is an abstraction based on assimilation of many different examples of the concept.

It is presumed that objects in the same category share what is called family resemblance

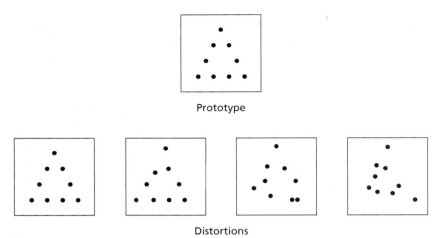

Prototype

Distortions

FIGURE 7.14 Prototype Formation. An example of one prototype and distortions of that prototype used by Posner and Keele to study prototype formation. (From Posner, Goldsmith, and Welton, 1967.) From the *Journal of Experimental Psychology,* 1967, *73,* 28–38, © 1967 by the American Psychological Assn. Reprinted with permission.

(Rosch & Mervis, 1975; Wittgenstein, 1953). This means that each object in a concept shares at least some features with other objects in that concept. If an object has close family resemblance to the prototype, it will be considered a good example of that concept. An object that has only a slight family resemblance usually is considered to be a marginal member of that concept.

Experimental support for this general prototype view has come from a variety of sources. First of all, there is evidence that participants do form abstract prototypes on the basis of their experience with a number of related objects. In one set of experiments, Posner and Keele (1968, 1970) constructed four geometric shapes with black dots. These shapes were considered as prototypes. They then created a series of distorted shapes by rearranging some of the dots used to form each of the original prototypes. Figure 7.14 shows one of the prototypes used, as well as the distortions created for that prototype.

The participants in these studies were first given all the distorted figures in a random order and were asked to sort them into four categories. It is important to note that at this point the participants had not seen the prototypes. Still, to be correct they had to sort all the distortions of a given figure (for example, the triangle) into one group, all the distortions of the second figure into another group, and so forth. Once the distorted figures had been sorted correctly, the participants were given a second set of figures to sort. Some of these figures were the old distortions they had already sorted, while some were new distortions of the same prototypes. Also included in set 2 were the four prototype figures that the participants had never seen.

Posner and Keele found that the participants sorted the prototypes into the correct categories along with their distortions. They were able to sort the prototypes much more easily than the new distortions, even though they had never seen either type of item before. This finding suggested that in the original sorting task, the participants had formed a mental representation for each category that approximated the prototype for that category.

Metcalfe, Funnell, and Gazzaniga (1995) conducted an ingenious extension of this study, using a **commissorotomy** patient. A commissorotomy is an operation that cuts the corpus collusum, severing the neural connections between the left hemisphere of the cerebral cortex and the right hemisphere of the cerebral cortex. Patients undergo commissorotomies for medical reasons related to intractable epilepsy. The operation leaves the left hemisphere of the brain unable to communicate with the right hemisphere when information is presented to only one hemisphere (see Gazzaniga, 1995).

Metcalfe and colleagues presented distortions of the prototypes developed by Posner and Keele to both the left hemisphere and right hemisphere of a commissorotomy patient. They asked the patient to sort the exemplars into one of two categories. Then, like Posner and Keele, Metcalfe's team gave a test phase in which original distortions, new distortions, and the previously unseen prototypes were presented. The test phase consisted of both a category judgment task and an old-new recognition test (participants had to decide whether or not they had seen the figures previously).

The results were intriguing. The left hemisphere of the commissorotomy patient performed much like the participants in the original Posner and Keele experiment. The left hemisphere quickly learned to categorize the figures. It also assigned the new distortions to the correct category, and did better on the prototypes themselves. The right hemisphere, however, did poorly at categorizing both the old distortions and the new distortions. However, the right hemisphere outperformed the left on the recognition test. Unlike the left hemisphere, the right easily distinguished between old and new distortions. Thus, it appeared that prototypes were formed and represented in the left hemisphere at least for commissorotomy patients.

In recent years, there has been a general consensus among cognitive scientists that prototype theory best explains the representation of concepts. This consensus derives from several different lines of evidence. We have already discussed some of the evidence that supports this view, namely the prototype abstraction experiments of Posner and Keele and Metcalfe et al. However, there are many more psychological data to support the prototype view.

Rosch (1975) asked participants to make explicit judgments about category membership. She asked people whether certain examples were typ-ical of a particular category. Rosch found that participants were consistent with one another as to which member of a well-known category was typical or not.

Rosch, Miller, and Simpson (1976) used participants' typicality ratings in a different kind of experiment. Participants were asked to verify as quickly as possible whether a particular example was a member of a concept or not. This task is called the sentence-verification task. Thus, a participant would decide as quickly as he or she could whether the following sentences were true:

A canary is a bird.

A Labrador retriever is a bird.

An ostrich is a bird.

Rosch and her colleagues found that items that were closer to the prototype (such as canary) were verified more quickly than were items that deviated from the prototype (such as ostrich). If people implicitly compare examples to a representation of a prototype, this is exactly the expected pattern of results. In a related study, Barsalou (1983) found that when people were asked to generate examples of a concept, they generated typical members first and atypical members later, also consistent with the prototype view.

Although there is some agreement that prototype theory offers an important understanding of how adults represent concepts, much remains to be determined.

Concepts in Nonhuman Species

Prototype theories were developed around the notion that many of our natural or real-world concepts cannot be defined on the basis of one or two critical stimulus features. Unlike the concepts often learned in laboratory experiments, **natural concepts** are often fuzzy and ill defined (see, for example, Rosch, 1977). This distinction raises an interesting question. We have already seen in our discussions of discrimination learning that rats and pigeons can form concepts based on a few stimulus features. For example, a pigeon can learn to respond to red objects and not to green ones. But are nonhuman organisms capable of acquiring natural concepts, which are less easily discriminated?

There is a growing body of literature that suggests that nonhuman animals can acquire natural concepts (see, for example, Herrnstein, 1979; Herrnstein & deVilliers, 1980; Herrnstein, Loveland, & Cable, 1976; Seyfarth, Cheney, & Marler, 1980; Wasserman & Astley, 1996). Herrnstein and deVilliers (1980) presented a set of 80 slides to a group of four pigeons. Half the slides showed underwater pictures of fish. These slides differed dramatically in terms of the type of fish, the position and size of the fish, and the physical context. The remaining 40 slides also showed underwater scenes, but no fish were present. The pigeons' behavior was reinforced on a variable interval schedule for pecking at the fish slides and were given no reinforcement for pecking at the others. Herrnstein and deVilliers found that all four pigeons rapidly acquired this discrimination even though the slides with fish shared few common features and the features in the fish and nonfish slides overlapped considerably.

Even more impressive was the behavior of the pigeons when they were presented with an entirely novel set of fish and nonfish slides. Based on the discrimination training, the pigeons showed a clear facility for responding to the new fish slides and not to the new nonfish slides. This result suggested that the pigeons had somehow acquired the concept of *fish* and were able to categorize novel objects into the natural concepts they had formed.

More recently Bhatt, Wasserman, Reynolds, and Knauss (1988) tested pigeons' ability to classify objects. Pigeons were trained to peck one of four different response keys depending on whether objects belonged to the general concept of cats, flowers, cars, or chairs. Pigeons reached a criterion of 80% correct after 30 days. Following this acquisition stage, pigeons were given a generalization test consisting of completely novel slides. Pigeons correctly categorized 64% of the novel slides suggesting a capacity to generalize their categorization ability. One observation of interest to the authors was that the pigeons' ability to categorize was not influenced by the nature of the class used. That is pigeons were able to classify natural stimuli (cats and flowers) as readily as nonnatural or artificial stimuli (cars and chairs). This result contradicted those of Herrnstein (1985) whose pigeons had difficulty discriminating between presence and absence of artificial stimuli including chairs, vehicles, and bottles.

A second point of interest in the Bhatt study was that pigeons could acquire these categories by one of two methods. In the first two experiments, pigeons received repeated presentations of 10 different exemplars of cats, flowers, chairs, and cars. In a third experiment, pigeons received presentations of 2,000 different slides. Pigeons viewed each slide only once and each category was represented by 500 slides. Pigeons learned to respond correctly at a level above chance and they generalized their skill to novel stimuli. It appeared that pigeons could learn to categorize by viewing a limited number of class representatives a large number of times, or by observing a large number of class representatives only once.

One further important point should be considered. Herrnstein (1990) argued that a true concept comprised stimuli that were not linked solely by perceptual similarity. Thus stimulus generalization is not the whole story in concept formation. Rosch, Mervis, Gray, Johnson, & Boyes-Braem (1976) asserted that linguistic labeling techniques have a decidedly hierarchical nature. Certain categories such as tree, bicycle, or flower are at a **basic level.** Categories nested within the basic level are called **subordinate categories.** Oak trees and apple trees are subordinate categories as are street bikes and mountain bikes. A third level of categorization is the **superordinate** level. Trees and a variety of other concepts can belong to the superordinate plants, and bikes of all kinds as well as other vehicles can be considered modes of transportation.

Rosch et al. (1976) determined that the basis for superordinate categories is not perceptual similarity. Superordinate categories are simply too perceptually diverse. An interesting question then is whether animals can form superordinate categories.

Wasserman, DeVolder, and Coppage (1992) and Astley and Wasserman (1998) provide evidence that they can. Wasserman, DeVolder, and Coppage (1992) trained pigeons to make one response (R1) in the presence of slides of people and flowers and a second response (R2) in the presence of slides of cars and chairs. In a second phase, pigeons were trained to make a third response (R3) in the presence of people slides and a fourth response (R4) in the presence of car slides. Following this reassignment phase, pigeons were tested on people, flowers, cars, and chairs. Wasserman and colleagues predicted that if pigeons had formed a superordinate category between people and flowers then during the test phase pigeons should make the R3 response to slides of flowers even though they had never been reinforced for doing so. Similarly if pigeons had formed a superordinate category between cars and chairs then they should make the R4 response when shown slides of chairs. It was not possible for the pigeons to make responses R1 and R2 during this test phase.

When pigeons encountered slides of people or cars they responded with the reassigned response R3 or R4 in 87% of the trials. When they encountered slides of flowers or chairs they responded with R3 or R4 in 72% of the trials. Thus, it appeared that pigeons had formed superordinate categories. Astley and Wasserman (1998) extended this finding to include novel stimulus. Thus, pigeons acquired a superordinate category through a common response procedure. Then reassignment training was given to one of the categories and the pigeons were tested on the other category as well as novel stimuli. Though performance on the novel-trained stimuli was not as high, pigeons still responded above chance to novel reassigned and novel nonreassigned stimuli. Astley and Wasserman concluded that superordi-

nate categorization ability in pigeons is a "robust" effect.

SUMMARY STATEMENTS

In this chapter's initial vignette vervet monkeys responded to aerial predators by running into the bushes. If vervets view a leopard, they run into the trees and in response to a snake, they stand on their hind legs and locate the snake. From this behavior, Cheney and Seyfarth (1990) concluded that vervets were able to categorize different predators and communicate to others when members of the troop were in danger. The ability to categorize or form concepts was the focus of this chapter.

The ability to form a concept requires an organism to determine how stimuli are similar and how stimuli differ. These two abilities are known as stimulus generalization and discrimination learning, respectively. Psychologists typically study stimulus generalization in the laboratory. Organisms are taught to respond to one stimulus and then are tested on other stimuli that vary along a single dimension. The standard finding is that the original stimulus produces the greatest amount of responding with decreased responding to stimuli as one moves further from the original stimulus. The generalization gradient is effected by several variables including degree of original learning, motivational level, the schedule of reinforcement used in training, the duration of the training-test interval, and prior discrimination learning.

Hull (1943) formulated one of early theories of stimulus generalization. He claimed that during training the organism's sensory system or the environment itself may cause changes in the stimulus from trial to trial. Thus organisms may associate several different stimuli with reward and this can lead to generalized responding. Lashley and Wade rejected this idea. They felt that organisms generalize because of confusion at the time of the generalization test. Blough (1975) extended the arguments of Hull and proposed an elemental model of generalization. Others (for example, Bouton, Nelson, & Rosas, 1999) have built upon the position of Lashley and Wade and have argued that forgetting and context are important components of stimulus generalization.

When an animal learns to respond one way to one stimulus and another way to a second stimulus it is said to have learned to discriminate. Discrimination learning leads to a steep stimulus-generalization gradient and demonstrates a greater degree of stimulus control. Two major theoretical approaches to discrimination learning have been proposed. One position proposes that learning is a continuous process that develops gradually over time. Proponents of this position argue that organisms gradually build habit strength to one stimulus and not another. Proponents of this position included Pavlov, Thorndike, Hull, and Spence. Spence offered the clearest theory with his algebraic summation theory. The second major view of discrimination learning contends that learning is discontinuous. Here the organism is pictured as an active learner that tries out different hypotheses and, upon hitting the correct hypothesis, solves the problem quite rapidly. A complementary view to discontinuity theory holds that animals learn about relations and not about the absolute properties of stimuli. Proponents of this view included Lashley, Krechevsky, Sutherland, and Mackintosh.

There is much evidence for the continuity and noncontinuity positions and it appears that organisms are capable of both forms of learning. Still, a significant number of studies have called into question the predictions made by continuity theorists suggesting that the predominate mode of discrimination problem solving may be more in line with the discontinuity approach. One of the more remarkable findings supporting this approach comes from the finding that animals overtrained on a discrimination task are actually better at solving the reversal of that problem than animals that are simply trained to criterion and reversed.

A concept is defined as a distinct category of objects or events that are all generally related on the basis of certain features or characteristics. One of the difficulties in the study of concept learning is determining how concepts are represented in the brain. Several theories of representation are considered including attribute theory, the Collins and Loftus network model, exemplar theory, and prototype theory. The chapter concludes with recent evidence that nonhuman animals are capable of forming concepts in a manner similar to humans.

8

Sensory and Short-Term or Working Memory

CHAPTER OVERVIEW

Most people become aware of their memories when they have to work to recall something. For example, if asked how many doors you have in your house or apartment, you probably could not answer immediately, because you have probably never counted them. Still, most people would be able to answer this question after a few moments. They would probably do this by imagining each room in the house and then counting the number of doors in each room.

Through their experiences, people form an internal representation of what their homes look like. Second, this is an enduring representation that can last for long periods of time. Third, they select or activate this representation from among thousands of memories they carry in their brains. Finally, they are able to use this representation to answer questions that guide their behaviors.

As human beings we tend to become aware of our memories only when we are asked a specific question; therefore it is easy to underestimate the role that memories play in our everyday behaviors. When we walk across a room, for example, we seldom consider that this is a learned behavior and that each step requires a memory of which motor movement occurred last and which one should follow. Likewise, carrying on a simple conversation involves remembering how to form sounds with our mouths, which sounds represent appropriate words, and which words we have already spoken. It also involves remembering which social cues signal that it is our turn to talk. In effect, we use our memories not only to answer specific questions, but also to perform behaviors so simple that we consider them to be automatic.

In the past 30 years, thousands of studies have examined various aspects of the human memory system. In this text's remaining chapters we will discuss some of the most important theories and experiments that have come out of this work. This chapter will focus on how memories are acquired, held, and retrieved over the short term. Chapter 9 will address the question of how long-term memories are organized or structured. Chapter 10 will examine various ideas concerning how people retain and forget information from long-term memory. Chapter 11 will examine implicit or nonconscious memories and consider the conscious strategies in memory and higher-order processing in memory.

This chapter's discussion begins by focusing on the processes involved in sensory and short-term memory, the formation and retention of memories over very short periods of time. By way of introducing this topic, it is helpful to take note of one of the more important developments in the study of memory, the use of the computer analogy as a way of conceptualizing the memory system.

INFORMATION PROCESSING

Memory in humans is complex and often mysterious. Scientists try to isolate the commonalities among the complexities. To understand these complexities, researchers look at simpler memory systems to get some idea of how human systems might operate. Since the mid-1960s, many researchers have examined the analogy between the information storage capabilities of computers as a way of conceptualizing memory in living organisms. This approach was not founded on the idea that computers (silicon and plastic) and living organisms (biological tissue) function in the same way. However, computers store and retrieve information in ways that might provide some clues to how organisms form and use memories.

This conceptual framework which is usually called the *information-processing approach,* takes the position that both computers and living organisms are information-processing systems. Both computers and living organisms begin by acquiring information from the environment in the form of stimulus inputs. In other words, both systems are capable of learning. Next, they convert these inputs into a usable format or code. The next step is to store this coded information in the memory system. Later, when the information is needed, the memory is retrieved and the information is used.

Through the use of this computer analogy, researchers have realized that an understanding of memory requires a knowledge of at least two aspects of memory: memory processes and memory systems (or structures). *Memory processes* include the operations people perform on stimulus inputs to convert them into usable memories, as well as the operations people go through to search memories out and retrieve them when needed. Most researchers agree that three processes are of critical importance: encoding, storage, and retrieval. Chapter 1 defined these terms, but we will review them again here as they are used in the fundamental information processing analogy (see Figure 8.1)

Encoding

The *encoding process* is characterized as the set of operations that people perform on incoming stimuli to convert them into a usable format or code. Organisms must modify incoming stimuli into codes that the brain can understand and use. In addition, encoding involves organizing or tagging stimuli by relating them to other bits of information in memory. Just as computers create files for inputs that belong together, we human beings organize our own inputs into groups of related bits of information. All these operations that result in an organized format are called encoding processes.

Storage

The second major memory process is *storage*. Simply, storage refers to the operation of placing information into the memory system and maintaining it there for later use. Anyone who has ever used a computer for word processing will quickly recognize the difference between encoding and storage. When you type a document into the computer, you can give that document a particular file name so that it will be kept separate from documents you have previously entered. This procedure is, of course, analogous to encoding, because the document is being organized or tagged in a certain way. However, until you direct your computer to save or store the new document, it does not become a permanent part of the computer's memory. Until a document is actually stored, it can be written over or lost from the system regardless of how well it has been encoded. Storage, then, involves the registration of information in the memory system. Many cognitive psychologists use the term *representation* to mean storage. However, in this chapter, we will use the term *storage*.

Retrieval

After a memory has been encoded and stored, it becomes subject to the process of *retrieval,*

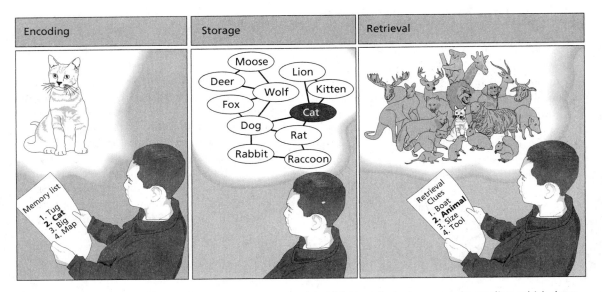

FIGURE 8.1 Basic Memory Processes. Human memory consists of three principal processes: *encoding,* which determines and controls how memories are initially acquired; *storage,* which determines how memories are represented and maintained over time; and *retrieval,* which controls how memories are recovered and translated into performance. In panel 1, how the subject thinks about the word *cat* will affect how that word is encoded into memory. Panel 2 shows how *cat* might be stored in long-term memory through the activation of existing knowledge structures. In panel 3, the subject uses the cue *animal* to help retrieve the memory of *cat.*

which involves the operations necessary for locating and calling up specific information from a memory store. Again, computers, like living organisms, are capable of storing thousands and thousands of individual memories. Yet, by giving a computer an individual file or code name, we make it possible for the computer to find the information attached to that name and display it on a screen. The same is true of our own memory systems. When we attempt to learn a person's name, we often relate the name to the person's facial features or to environmental stimuli that are present when the person is introduced. Later, when we see these facial features or stimuli, we are able to use the cues to help us retrieve the name from among all the other memories that we have represented in storage. The operations we go through to locate a particular memory in storage are called retrieval processes.

Storage, encoding, and retrieval processes are highly interrelated. Although these processes are classified separately, they are actually constantly interacting. Retrieval is impossible without storage because unless storage has occurred there will be no memory in the system to be retrieved. However, retrieval is equally dependent on the encoding process. For example, a memory in storage that is not properly encoded may be impossible to access. Retrieval of a document depends on whether the document was filed correctly; otherwise, when we search the filing cabinet in the logical, or proper place, we will not find the document.

Memory Systems

The computer analogy has drawn our attention to *memory systems,* a second aspect of memory that must be considered. We know, for example, that a computer has certain prewired circuits designed to hold information at various stages. For example, buffer circuits hold temporarily new information that is being entered into the computer. While information is held in buffer circuits a user can make changes in a document, combine one document with another, or change the file or code name attached to a document. In effect, these buffers hold our rough drafts of a document long enough for us to make whatever changes we desire. When we are satisfied with the form of a document that is located in a buffer, we can save the document or store it permanently in the computer's memory. Permanent storage requires shifting the document from the buffer circuits to another set of circuits designed to hold information indefinitely. As humans, we transfer information from short-term memory to long-term memory.

It is important to stress that the computer analogy is a model for information processing in biological organisms. Humans and other animals are not computers. Humans are the product of millions of years of adaptations in a biological context. Learning and memory have evolved in that context. Computers are artificial devices constructed by humans. The analogy exists because of certain formal similarities in the processing of information. And, as we will see, models based on information processing, have generated a rich data base in experimental psychology. However, many researchers are beginning to see these models as outdated now (Bjork, 1989).

This chapter is concerned with sensory and short-term memory. To focus this discussion, we will begin by looking at a *stage model* of memory formation—that is, the notion that a memory must pass through a sequence of structures and processes between the time of stimulus input and the time of permanent memory registration.

THE ATKINSON-SHIFFRIN MODEL

Several theorists have proposed memory models that have been based at least loosely on the computer analogy (see, for example, Broadbent,

1958; Waugh & Norman, 1965). However, the information-processing model proposed by Atkinson and Shiffrin (1968, 1971) is probably the best-known model of this type. According to Atkinson and Shiffrin, the human memory system is best conceptualized as a *series* of memory systems through which information must pass. In other words, information from the environment moves through a set sequence of memory systems before the memory of that information can be permanently stored. A basic assumption of this model is that information is processed differently in these various memory systems.

To illustrate how this model works, Atkinson and Shiffrin devised a flowchart that characterizes how information might move through memory. This flowchart, shown in Figure 8.2, shows three memory structures, lists the processes that can occur in certain structures, and includes directional arrows showing how information flows from one structure to another. We will use this chart as the basis for our description of the Atkinson-Shiffrin model.

The model begins with a simple assumption. When an individual first notices a stimulus in the environment, only the raw physical features of that stimulus become represented in memory. These physical features are stored in a memory structure called the *sensory register* or the *sensory memory store*. Atkinson and Shiffrin suggest that stimulus features remain represented in sensory memory only briefly (0.5–1.0 second, for visual stimuli). They further propose that there are different sensory registers for stimulus features of different types. Thus, the visual features of a stimulus are presumably represented in a visual register, the auditory characteristics are thought to reside in an auditory register, and so on, down to the characteristics experienced through the sense of touch, which would belong in the haptic register.

The sensory registers provide a brief stimulus aftereffect for each stimulus an organism encounters. For example, it is presumed that once an auditory stimulus has disappeared, its sound will remain briefly in the auditory register much like

The Atkinson-Shiffrin Model

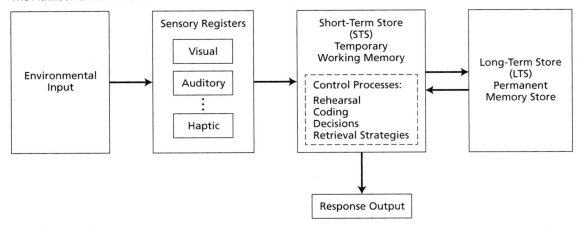

FIGURE 8.2 The Atkinson-Shiffrin Information Processing Model. (From Atkinson and Shiffrin, 1971.) © 1971 Scientific American.

a short-lived echo. Likewise, visual stimuli are presumed to leave behind a brief image in the visual register. Although these registers are thought to hold sensory information only briefly, Atkinson and Shiffrin propose that the sensory memory store has an extremely large capacity, permitting the holding of many bits of sensory information at any given time.

Organisms cannot possibly process all the incoming stimuli. Instead they attend to only a small proportion of the stimuli their sensory systems detect. According to Atkinson and Shiffrin, this selection process occurs while stimuli are represented in sensory memory. They propose that our attentional mechanisms scan through the stimuli represented in the sensory registers and select certain stimuli for further processing in the memory system. Stimuli that are not selected by the attentional mechanism never become represented permanently in memory. Sensory information that is not attended to cannot be maintained in the sensory registers and simply decays or deteriorates in fractions of a second. Sensory information that is selected by attentional mechanisms is transferred to the short-term memory store for further processing.

According to this model, the first time a person becomes consciously aware of a stimulus input is when that input enters the short-term memory store. This store holds all the information the person is currently thinking about or conscious of. For this reason, Atkinson and Shiffrin suggest that the short-term store must have a limited capacity. They assume that because a person can be conscious of only a limited number of items at one time, the short-term store must be able to hold only a few bits of information at once.

Aside from being a structure of limited capacity, the short-term store is viewed as being a temporary facility. That is, unless information is actively processed upon entering this store, it can remain there for only a matter of seconds.

Unlike information in the sensory store, however, information in the short-term store can be maintained there indefinitely if it is processed or rehearsed.

The true importance of the short-term store is that this is where human beings consciously or purposely rehearse and encode information for permanent storage. This model suggests that the short-term store contains a separate system called a *buffer.* As suggested earlier, information in the short-term store can be selectively placed into this buffer, where it can be rehearsed and encoded. The buffer is presumed to have a very limited capacity, such that only a few items can be actively rehearsed at once. New information placed into the buffer automatically displaces information that is already there. This displaced information then goes back into the short-term store, where it decays over time. Information that remains in the buffer and is actively processed becomes transferred into the *long-term memory store,* where it is permanently represented. Thus, much of the active memory processing that we do is presumed to occur in short-term memory. For this reason, several researchers have called short-term memory the *working memory store* (Baddeley, 1986).

Although Atkinson and Shiffrin assume that information processed in the short-term buffer is transferred to long-term memory, they also suggest that under some circumstances it may be possible for information to reach long-term storage without such processing. They assume, for example, that some information may be transferred to long-term storage simply by remaining in the short-term buffer for some period of time (Atkinson & Shiffrin, 1968). This point suggests that we may store some information that we have not consciously processed. Thus, we may sometimes be surprised by the contents of our permanent memories. Chapter 11 will elaborate on nonconscious memories.

The long-term memory store is characterized in this model as having an unlimited capacity. In other words, long-term memory is capable of holding as many memories as we can acquire in a lifetime. This model also assumes that once represented in long-term storage, memories can be maintained there almost indefinitely without any need for active processing. This model assumes that memories are lost from the long-term store through processes such as decay or interference resulting from the storage of new memories. Still, this store is thought to be a relatively permanent storage place, which serves as a vast repository for formed memories.

Two additional points about the Atkinson-Shiffrin model should be mentioned. Figure 8.2 shows that information can move not only from the short- to the long-term store but also from long- to short-term memory. This bidirectional flow of information is meant to represent the retrieval of memories from the long-term store. In other words, when a long-term memory is retrieved, a copy of that memory reenters short-term storage, where it becomes a conscious thought. This process has one important implication for the formation of a memory. Once information has been retrieved into the short-term store, it can be rehearsed along with new information that has entered short-term storage via the sensory registers. Thus, this model presumes that some memories may be the product of the combination of new information with old information from long-term storage.

In the Atkinson-Shiffrin model, decision making occurs in short-term memory. That is, as human beings, we decide how to respond based on information that is in that store at a given time. As we have seen, some of our decisions may be based on new information coming from the sensory registers, whereas others may be determined by information retrieved from long-term memory. These points emphasize the important role of short-term memory processes in the formation and use of memory.

Although some researchers have argued that sensory memory is an unnecessary concept (Haber, 1983), there is a substantial body of research supporting the existence of sensory memory and describing the characteristics of sensory memory for each modality. Second, we will consider the characteristics of short-term memory. A large body of data has accumulated on short-term memory, most, but not all, supporting the Atkinson-Shiffrin conception.

SENSORY MEMORY

According to the Atkinson-Shiffin model, sensory memory maintains information for a brief period of time after a stimulus is no longer available. Information in sensory memory is thought to be kept in an unprocessed form. By referring to this information as unprocessed, we are indicating that little coding or storage of that information has occurred. Furthermore, information capacity in sensory memory is not limited, but that information can be maintained for only a short period of time. In addition, a separate sensory memory system exists for each sensory modality. For visual information, we call it *iconic memory*, whereas for auditory information, we call it *echoic memory*. Finally, sensory memory is a largely non-conscious system. In other words, we cannot introspect or become aware of our sensory memories.

Because we are not aware of the contents of our sensory memory, it is the most difficult stage of the Atkinson-Shiffrin model to understand. It is different from short-term memory. Short-term memory is accessible to consciousness, but sensory memory is not. Sensory memory is different from visual persistence. Visual persistence refers to the phenomenon that stimuli may continue to excite the retina of the eye at some point after the stimuli is no longer visible. However, visual persistence is a peripheral phenomenon, which means it takes place in the eye. Sensory memory is a central phenomenon, which means it takes place in the brain. We will now consider the evidence that supports the existence of sensory memory.

Atkinson and Shiffrin (1968, 1971) based their notions of sensory memory on the pioneering work of Sperling (1960), who performed experiments to study memory in terms of visual stimuli. Because brief visual memories often are referred to as *icons,* Sperling's work is usually described as dealing with *iconic storage.* Basically, Sperling was interested in two questions. First, when an individual sees a visual display, how much of that display is stored in the sensory registers? Second, how long does this visual information last in storage?

To address these questions, Sperling conducted a series of experiments in which partici-pants were briefly presented with an array of 12 letters such as the following:

A   R   Q   N
Z   L   P   F
M   B   E   V

In his first experiment, Sperling presented the array for 0.05 second. The participants had been instructed to write down as many of the letters as they could once the array disappeared. Sperling found that participants consistently recalled an average of four to five letters. This method is the *whole-report technique* because participants must report all letters in the array.

Sperling realized that this finding could be interpreted in one of two ways. First, the results could indicate that when a visual display is presented, participants store only four to five of the items in memory. Another possibility, however, is that participants store a much larger number of items, but the memory for these items decays rapidly. By the time a participant has written down four or five of the items, the remaining items may have decayed from memory. To distinguish between these two interpretations, Sperling devised what is called the *partial report procedure* (see Figure 8.3). Once again, a 12-letter array was presented. When the array had disappeared, however, participants were presented with one of three tones. Each tone stood for one row of four letters in the array. If tone 1 was presented, participants were to report the top row in the array. Tone 2 indicated that the second row should be reported, and tone 3 signaled that a report of the bottom row was required. Thus, participants did not know which row would be tested until after the array disappeared.

Sperling reasoned that if participants were storing only four or five items from the entire array; then on the average they should be able to report only one or two items from a given row. If, instead, participants were storing all the items in the array but simply were having difficulty reporting more than four or five before memory decay set in, a different result would be expected. Under these circumstances, one would predict

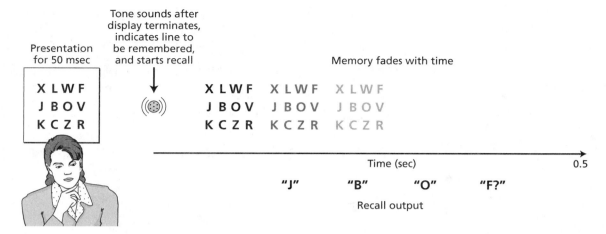

FIGURE 8.3 The Partial Report Technique. In the partial report technique, a tone sounds after presentation of the display, indicating which row of letters is to be recalled. As the subject attempts her recall, the visual iconic memory fades and becomes increasingly less accurate. But when recall of only part of the display is required, most of the relevant information can be reported before the image has been completely lost.

that a participant should be able to report almost all the items in a given row, since each row contained only four letters.

In his second experiment, Sperling used this partial-report procedure. He also varied the time between the disappearance of the array and the onset of the tone. On various trials the tone occurred either 0, 0.15, 0.30, or 1.0 second after the offset of the letters. The purpose of this manipulation was to determine how quickly visual memories are lost from the sensory register.

This experiment resulted in two important findings. First, when participants were given the tone immediately after the offset of the letters, they were able to recall three to four of the letters from whatever row had been signaled. Since this level of recall occurred regardless of which row had been signaled, the result suggests that for a brief period of time virtually all the letters in the array had been represented in the sensory store. The second significant finding was that recall of the letters decreased as the onset of the tone was delayed. For example, when a full second elapsed between the array offset and the tone onset, participants were able to recall only one or two letters from the signaled row instead of three

to four (see Figure 8.4). This result indicates that while several letters are originally stored in sensory memory, the memory for these stimuli decays very rapidly. Participants who have to wait even 1 second before reporting the letters show very poor levels of recall. Sperling concluded from this study that iconic memory has a reasonably large capacity for the storage of items, but items can remain in iconic storage for only a brief time.

Another experiment by Sperling was directed at still another characteristic of sensory memory—specifically, the type of information that is stored in the sensory registers. On the one hand, it is possible that the sensory store contains only the physical features of the stimuli we sense (for example, the size, color, or shape of an object). Sensory memory might include information about the meanings of sensory events as well. It is possible, for example, that when we see a set of items, these items automatically may be classified in sensory memory according to what the visual symbols mean. We might, for instance, organize our sensory information into groupings such as vowels and consonants, letters and digits, or uppercase and lowercase letters. In effect, we find

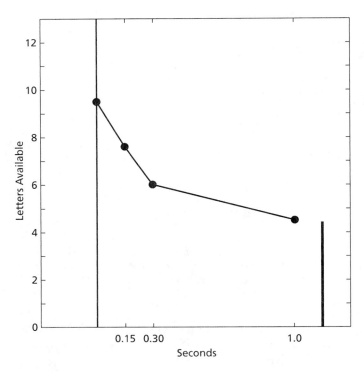

FIGURE 8.4 Recall as a Function of Delay of a Signaling Tone. From "The Information Available in Brief Visual Presentations," by G. Sperling, 1960, *Psychological Monographs, 74* (No. 498). Copyright 1960 by the American Psychological Association.

that the question of interest is whether we analyze or process the information in sensory memory or whether these memories are little more than pictures or traces of environmental stimuli.

To answer this question, Sperling presented his participants with an array such as the following:

R 4 6 C
3 B 9 S

As you can see, half the symbols in each row were letters and the other half were digits. On some trials the participants were asked to report all the symbols in the array. On other trials they were asked to report only the symbols in a given row. This, of course, is analogous to the partial-report procedure. Finally, on some trials the participants were asked to report either all the digits or all the letters in the array. This is like a partial-report procedure, except that participants must analyze the difference between letters and digits

instead of simply responding on the basis of location within the array.

Sperling found that when participants were asked to report the symbols in a given row, they consistently recalled three to four symbols correctly. When asked to report all the digits or letters, however, most participants gave only one or two correct responses. This result indicates that participants are able to use sensory memory to identify items that have specific physical features, such as items appearing in a particular spatial location. However, they are unable to use sensory memory to identify items according to a meaningful category such as letters or digits. This finding is consistent with the idea that sensory memory is like a brief picture of stimulus input. It is not a place in which items are organized in terms of meaning or conceptual class.

Since Sperling's original experiments, several researchers have replicated and extended his basic findings. For example, Averbach and Coriell

(1961) presented letter arrays to participants and asked for the recall of a single letter after the array had disappeared. One procedure presented the array on a visual field for 50 milliseconds. When the array had disappeared, they presented a black bar adjacent to the position that one of the letters had occupied in the array. The participant was required to identify the letter marked by the position of the bar. The investigators found that participants were able to recall the letter with a high degree of accuracy as long as the bar was presented immediately after the offset of the letter array. However, if more than 0.25 second elapsed between the offset of the array and the presentation of the bar, recall performance dropped to a very low level. This finding replicates Sperling's data and attests to the brief duration of iconic storage.

In a related study, Averbach and Coriell (1961) pointed out another important characteristic of sensory memory. This procedure was identical to the one discussed above except for the kind of marker used to denote the target letter. Instead of placing a bar next to a letter's position, the experimenters placed a circle around the position a letter had occupied in the array. They found that if the circle was presented immediately after the array, participants were able to recall the letter very easily. However, as soon as any delay occurred between the array offset and the onset of the circle, performance dropped to extremely low levels. In other words, the circle marker resulted in much poorer letter recall than did the bar.

Averbach and Coriell suggested that because the circle surrounded the entire position in which the letter had been, the circle was perceived as a new stimulus occupying the same position. They proposed that if one stimulus is stored in sensory memory and another stimulus occurs in the same physical location shortly thereafter, the second stimulus will erase the first from the sensory register. In other words, the second stimulus was thought to *mask* the first by being stored on top of it. This phenomenon has now been reported in numerous experiments and

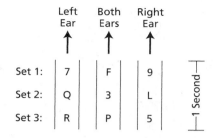

FIGURE 8.5 Procedure used by Darwin, Turvey, and Crowder (1972) to Study Auditory Sensory Memory. In each set, which consisted of three symbols presented simultaneously, one symbol went to a subject's left ear, another to both ears, and the last to the right ear. Then the next set was presented. Total time for all set presentations was 1 second.

is called *backward masking* (see, for example, Breitmeyer & Ganz, 1976). The importance of backward masking is that it indicates that sensory memories may be lost not only by decay, but also by being displaced when new stimuli are sensed.

Although much of the evidence pertaining to the sensory store has dealt with visual stimuli, there is evidence for the existence of an auditory sensory register. This auditory register has been termed an *echoic store,* as it appears to hold an echo of any sound we sense from the environment (Neisser, 1967). Although the results of several studies provide evidence of such a store, there has been little agreement with respect to how long auditory information is held there.

For example, Darwin, Turvey, and Crowder (1972) performed an experiment with auditory stimuli that was much like Sperling's studies using visual stimuli. These researchers presented strings of spoken symbols (letters or digits) to participants through earphones, using the protocol illustrated in Figure 8.5. One string of three symbols was presented through the left earphone, while a second string of three symbols was spoken through the right. A third string of three symbols was presented simultaneously through both earphones so that the participants perceived this string as being spoken in front of them. The three different strings were presented simultaneously, such that all the first symbols in each string occurred together, then the second symbols in each string, and finally the third. All symbols were presented in a span of 1 second.

On some occasions participants were asked to recall as many of the nine symbols as possible immediately after the presentation was over. As in Sperling's experiments, participants averaged about 4.2 correct symbols on this kind of test. On other occasions, however, a partial-report procedure was used. Participants were given a visual signal indicating that they should report only the symbols presented to the left ear or to the right ear, or in front of them. The visual signal occurred either 0, 1, 2, or 4 seconds after the symbols had been heard. When a 0-second interval was used, participants were able to report approximately two of the three symbols from a given string. This suggests that the participants had more than 4.2 symbols in the auditory register immediately after the symbol presentation. Recall dropped steadily, however, as the symbol-signal interval was increased. The experimenters estimated that symbols remain in the auditory register for up to 2 seconds. When 4 seconds elapsed between the symbols and the signal, participants performed no better than they did when they were asked to recall all the symbols.

The duration of auditory memory has been studied most extensively by Crowder and his associates using still another procedure (Crowder, 1971, 1976; Crowder & Morton, 1969; Morton, Crowder, & Prussin, 1971). This technique is based on certain characteristics of the serial position effect, which are best illustrated by the results of a study by Conrad and Hull (1968). These experimenters presented participants with a list of seven digits visually. Some participants were asked to look at the digits, while others were required to repeat each digit aloud as it was presented. Shortly after the last digit disappeared (400 milliseconds), the participants were asked to recall the digits *in order*.

As the results shown in Figure 8.6 suggest, a typical serial position effect occurred only when

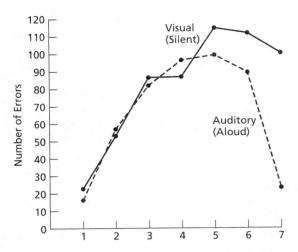

FIGURE 8.6 Serial Position Effect. Retention of a seven-digit serial list when the digits are seen, as opposed to being spoken aloud. (From Conrad and Hull, 1968.)

participants repeated the digits aloud. Participants who received only the visual presentation did not show the usual excellent recall of the most recently occurring item (digit number 7). Conrad and Hull attributed their finding to differences in the duration of auditory and visual memories in the sensory memory store. They suggested that visual information concerning the last few digits decays rapidly, preventing participants from remembering these digits any better than digits in the middle of the list. However, the digits stored in the auditory register (as when digits are spoken aloud) remain there much longer, making it relatively easy for participants to remember the last item in the list. Good retention of the early items is generally attributed to the ease with which these items are transferred into long-term memory.

Given this finding, Crowder began to use the serial-position paradigm as a way of studying the duration of memories in the auditory register. In these experiments, Crowder presented a list of eight digits to participants auditorially. At the end of the list the word "zero" or "naught" (the British term for zero) was presented as a signal that the participants should recall the digits in order. Participants had previously been told that zero or naught was simply a signal and should not be recalled as one of the digits. Crowder found that the use of the word *zero* as a signal disrupted a participant's ability to recall the last digit in the serial list. In other words, participants performed as if the list had been presented visually instead of having been spoken. They did not show the usual excellent recall for the last digit (Crowder & Morton, 1969).

Crowder labeled this phenomenon the *suffix effect*. That is, if an auditory suffix is attached to the end of a list that is spoken, the suffix blocks out the auditory memory of the final listed item. The suffix replaces the last digit or pushes it out of the auditory register.

Using this procedure, Crowder and his associates have attempted to assess how long memories remain in the auditory sensory store. For example, in one experiment (Crowder, 1971) participants were given a digit list followed either by no word or by the suffix word *zero*. Some participants received the suffix 0.5 second after the end of the list, while others received the word 2 seconds after the list was complete. Figure 8.7 shows the results of this manipulation. Basically, participants receiving no suffix word (control group) exhibited excellent recall of the last digit. Slightly poorer recall of the last digit was found when the suffix word occurred 2 seconds after the list. When only 0.5 second elapsed between the list and the suffix, participants showed very poor recall of the final digit.

This finding suggests that when participants hear a digit list, the final digit remains in auditory memory for only a few seconds. For this reason, if a suffix occurs almost immediately after the final digit, the memory of this digit will be displaced and forgotten. Apparently if at least 2 seconds elapse between the final digit and the suffix, the final digit has time to transfer into short-term storage and the suffix has little or no effect on its subsequent recall. Various experimenters using this procedure have estimated that memories remain in the auditory register for 2 to

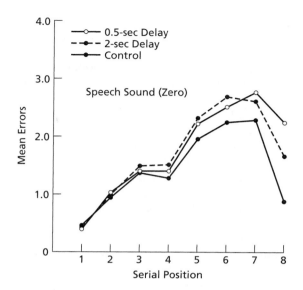

FIGURE 8.7 Crowder's Results. Retention of a serial digit list when the word *zero* is heard at various delays after the list presentation. (From Crowder, 1971.) Reprinted by permission of Psychology Press.

6 seconds (but, for another view, see Massaro & Loftus, 1996).

The Adaptive Value of Sensory Memory

The concept of sensory memory has been challenged on the grounds that it serves no function in everyday life and has no adaptive value. Haber (1983) sarcastically wrote that the only adaptive value that visual sensory memory has is that it allows us to read during a lightning storm. However, Loftus, Johnson, & Shimamura (1985) conducted a series of studies that provide an adaptive basis for sensory memory systems. They presented slides of naturalistic scenes for durations ranging from very fast (62 milliseconds) to quite long (1,300 milliseconds). On some of these presentations, the picture was followed by an immediate mask, similar to the ones used by Averbach and Coriel (1961). The purpose of the mask was to eliminate the iconic storage of the naturalistic scene. For other scenes, Loftus et al. did not present a mask after showing the scene.

Following a presentation of 72 scenes, Loftus et al. tested for recognition of the scenes.

Participants' accuracy was determined by looking at the percent correctly recognized as a function of the total number of scenes in the particular condition. Loftus et al. found that accuracy was higher in the condition in which no mask had been presented. The mask, which eliminated the iconic memory of the scene, interfered with correct recognition. In fact, to achieve similar accuracy in the mask condition, one had to look at longer stimulus durations, roughly 100 milliseconds. Loftus and his collegues concluded that the icon provides additional time in which to process a stimulus. They argued that the icon is worth 100 milliseconds of actual stimulus presentation.

Sensory memory provides with a very brief buffer of time in which we represent a large number of stimuli. This brief buffer gives us just a little more time to process the information.

There is substantial evidence for the existence of both a visual and an auditory sensory store. The visual store, which appears to have a reasonably large capacity, is believed to maintain items for very brief time periods. While the auditory store also appears to hold items only briefly, estimates of the duration and capacity of this store vary widely. Both the visual and auditory stores seem to be structures that hold only the physical characteristics of stimuli.

SHORT-TERM MEMORY

Consider the following scenario. You have spent a long day at work or school, and you arrive home too tired to cook dinner. You decide to call for a pizza. You know the name of your favorite pizza shop, but you do not have their phone number written down. You dial information to get the number. When the operator tells you the phone number, chances are that you will repeat it, either aloud or silently, to yourself for as long as it takes you to hang up the phone and dial it again. Although you are more concerned about

your pizza than your memory skills, you are using your short-term memory to store the phone number. Seven-digit phone numbers are relatively easy for most people to keep in short-term memory. However, consider that you need to dial a different city to order from a particular catalog. You may now have a 10-digit phone number to remember. In this case, chances are that you will look for a pencil and paper because 10 digits exceeds most people's short-term memory span.

Now consider how many phone numbers you know by heart. You probably have quite a few phone numbers memorized. You may also have your nine-digit social security number committed to memory. However, it is only after repeated exposure, or in the case of phone numbers, dialings, that you come to memorize the numbers. How is it that we have so many sequences in memory but find it so difficult to keep the pizzeria's phone number accessible when information provides it?

One hallmark of the Atkinson-Shiffrin model is the idea that a distinction can be drawn between short- and long-term memory. Regardless of how information is selected from sensory memory, this model proposes that the information must be stored and processed in short-term memory before a permanent record of that information can be registered. According to this model, the short-term memory store differs from the long-term store in a number of important respects. First, short-term memory is believed to have a limited storage capacity whereas the capacity of long-term memory is large. Second, the short-term store can hold memories only for a limited period unless rehearsal is used to maintain information in that store. Obviously, the long-term memory store is capable of holding memories for years. Finally, Atkinson and Shiffrin hypothesized that short-term memory is the locus of the important controlled processing of information.

Other researchers have suggested that short- and long-term memories may differ in additional ways. For example, some researchers have suggested that short- and long-term memories may be represented in terms of different memory codes. Others have hypothesized that these two memory stores may be susceptible to different sources of forgetting.

The Characteristics of Short-Term Memory

The Capacity of Short-Term Memory. How many items of information can we hold in conscious awareness at any given point in time? Since Atkinson and Shiffrin equated short-term memory with conscious awareness, this is the question we must answer in assessing the capacity of short-term memory. The most common answer comes from a paper by G. A. Miller (1956) entitled "The Magical Number Seven, Plus or Minus Two: Some Limits on our Capacity for Processing Information." As the title suggests, Miller proposed that on average it is possible to hold seven separate items of information in short-term storage at one time. Miller based his estimate on experiments in which participants heard long lists of words, digits, or numbers and then tried to recall as many items as possible (see, for example, Hayes, 1952; Pollack, 1953). These studies showed that participants invariably were able to report five to nine items accurately. Such results suggested that this was the maximum number of items a participant could hold in short-term memory at once. Several later studies have tended to confirm this earlier estimate (Cavanagh, 1972).

One source of ambiguity in this literature, however, concerns the definition of "items of information." Miller proposed that it is possible for an individual to maintain approximately seven chunks of information in short-term storage. Chunks are the fundamental unit of short-term memory. Thus, a chunk may be a single letter when we are focusing on recall of individual letters, or it may be a grouping of letters that form a single word or idea, depending on the focus of the task at hand. A word, for example, is actually a grouping of letters that represents one chunk of information. In long-term memory, we may be able to decode a chunk into more information,

but in short-term memory, it is an indivisable whole. Therefore, it is possible to maintain about seven words in short-term memory even though these words may contain 30 or more individual letters.

This notion of chunks of information is important because it points to a strategy we often use to retain more information in short-term storage. When called on to remember a long string of letters or digits, we often chunk related items together and then remember the chunks rather than attempting to recall each item individually. To show how this strategy works, consider the following string of 12 letters: A P E X S H U T F R O G. If these letters were presented one at a time or in a different order, it would be difficult to remember accurately more than seven of them. However, when the letters are presented in the order shown above, it is easy to chunk the letters into three words: APEX, SHUT, and FROG. These words are three chunks of information, and they easily fit the capacity of short-term memory. By using this chunking strategy, we can remember all 12 letters without difficulty.

Recently, however, some researchers have challenged the notion that short-term memory capacity is limited by the number of items or chunks. These researchers have challenged the idea that short-term memory is solely based on the amount of information that can be stored in a chunk. They argue that other processes are also important in determining the capacity of short-term memory. Foremost of these is phonological processing, as we shall see shortly. Indeed, these researchers have stressed that it is pronunciation time of items (i.e., the amount of time it would take to say them aloud) being rehearsed that more strongly affects the capacity of short-term memory. The argument here is that short-term memory is not limited by a fixed number of items, but rather by how much a person can pronounce in approximately 1.5 seconds (Schweickert & Boruff, 1986). In English, a person can pronounce about six words in 1.5 seconds (Matlin, 1998).

To test this hypothesis, Naveh-Benjamin and Ayres (1986) conducted an ingenious experiment based on the fact that the digits 1 through 10 require different pronunciation times depending on the language. In English, there is only one multisyllabic word in the 10 digits, whereas in other languages such as Hebrew, Spanish, and Arabic, more digits are multisyllabic and therefore take longer to pronounce. Naveh–Benjamin and Ayres predicted that English-speaking people would have longer digit spans than speakers of Hebrew, Spanish, or Arabic. Indeed, that is exactly what they found (see Figure 8.8). Digit spans were better than 7 for the English speakers, around 6.5 for Spanish and Hebrew speakers, and less than six for the Arabic speakers. This decline in digit span parallels the increase in time it takes to pronounce the digits in each language. Therefore, both pronunciation time and the number of actual items of information are both relevant in describing the capacity of short-term memory.

Regardless of the precise estimate of short-term memory capacity and regardless of how we define an "item of information," one point is clear. The capacity of conscious awareness is strictly limited. This restriction is one of the major reasons for distinguishing between short-term memory and the long-term store, which can hold an unlimited number of representations at any given time.

Control Processes in Short-Term Memory

According to Atkinson and Shiffrin, the fate of information in short-term storage depends on how that information is processed. In effect, they viewed the short-term store as the location for conscious manipulation of memories. They assumed that the way an individual chooses to process short-term memories determines how these memories are encoded and whether they are stored permanently. They called these conscious manipulations control *processes.*

Individuals can choose whether to rehearse the information of which they are consciously aware. Failure to rehearse can lead to rapid for-

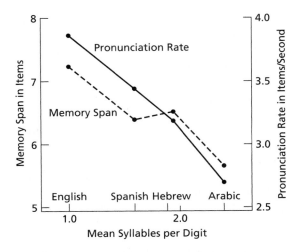

FIGURE 8.8 Memory Span and Pronunciation Rate for Numbers in Four Different Languages (Naveh-Benjamin & Ayres, 1986). Reprinted by permission of Psychology Press.

getting, while rehearsal can prolong a memory's availability. There is additional evidence, however, that the fate of a memory depends on more than whether the memory is or is not rehearsed. It also appears to depend on the type of rehearsal that occurs.

Some of the best evidence that different types of rehearsal exist comes from experiments called *directed forgetting studies* (see, for example, Bjork, 1972, 1975, 1989; Geiselman, 1975). In these studies participants are presented with a number of items and are told to retain particular items in memory and to forget others. Then, after viewing many items, participants are given a surprise retention test that includes both types. Typically, participants are unable to recall to-be-forgotten items, even though often participants were exposed to them for just as long as they saw the to-be-remembered items. Directed forgetting studies suggest that one can rehearse items solely to keep them in one's awareness but this rehearsal does not automatically lead to storing the items in long-term memory.

One study by Bjork and Jongeward (Bjork, 1975) illustrates this procedure. The participants were given a sequence of six-word sets. Each set was rehearsed for 20 seconds, after which a retention test was given. Some participants were instructed to forget each set immediately after the retention test. Others were instructed to keep all sets in memory even after testing. When all sets had been presented and tested, a surprise retention test was given for all the word sets.

Bjork and Jongeward found that the two groups of participants performed equally well on the immediate retention tests. That is, the two groups were equally capable of remembering each set of 6 words after 20 seconds of rehearsal. However, on the surprise retention test the two groups differed dramatically. The group told to retain all the words performed very well on this test, while the group told to forget did just that. The latter participants showed very poor recall even though they had rehearsed the words for the same period of time as the participants in the other group.

Because in this experiment total rehearsal times were equal, the results suggest that the two groups must have rehearsed the words in different ways. One group apparently rehearsed the items solely to keep them in conscious awareness for a brief period of time. The other group seemingly managed their rehearsals to ensure that the words were encoded and stored in long-term memory. The first type of rehearsal has been called *maintenance rehearsal,* whereas the second type has been termed *elaborative rehearsal* (Craik & Watkins, 1973).

Other researchers have suggested additional rehearsal distinctions (Craik & Lockhart, 1972). Such distinctions have been based on the apparent capacity of participants sometimes to process only the physical features of items, while at other times to process items in terms of meaning. These findings, combined with the data from directed forgetting studies, provide strong evidence for the existence of control processes. It is apparent that once we have become aware of an item of information, we can choose to rehearse that information in different ways. Furthermore, the way we choose to rehearse determines how well information can be recalled and what aspects of that information remain in memory.

Codes Used in Short-Term Memory

Another distinction sometimes drawn between short- and long-term memory stores concerns how the memories in these two stores are coded or represented. There is substantial evidence to suggest that long-term memories may be stored in terms of *meaning-based codes.* Over long periods of time we may tend to remember the meaning of a stimulus input much more readily than the physical features of that input. On the other hand, some have suggested that the information in short-term storage is usually represented in terms of *acoustic codes.* This proposal states that even visual information is transformed into sounds or acoustic codes once the information has entered short-term storage.

Whether we rehearse aloud or subvocally, most of our rehearsal involves the formation of sounds that we speak to ourselves in a repetitive fashion. If, for example, we hear a sentence that we wish to remember, we say those words to ourselves over and over. We go through the same process even if the sentence is presented visually. Instead of trying to visualize the presented sentence, we often read it to ourselves and then speak the material again and again.

Given the acoustic nature of the rehearsal process, many early theorists assumed that all memories are translated into acoustic codes for short-term processing. This was presumed to be the case regardless of how a memory was originally coded in the sensory store. There is at least some evidence to support this view. Recall that Sperling (1960) used a partial-report procedure to study the capacity of sensory memory. In these studies he presented a large array of visual stimuli (letters) and asked participants to report the stimuli from one location in the array. He found that participants were able to report small segments of an array quite accurately, indicating that the capacity of sensory memory is reasonably large.

Most pertinent to our present discussion, however, are the errors Sperling's participants made in attempting to report the letters. When participants reported a letter incorrectly, it was almost always one that *sounded* like the letter that should have been reported—an *E* for a *V,* for example, but rarely an *E* for an *F,* which looks like *E* but sounds quite different. Sperling suggested that errors are made in this paradigm when the original letter is no longer in visual sensory memory to be read. He suggested that as the visual aspects of a stimulus begin to decay from sensory memory, participants translate these stimuli into an acoustic code for short-term processing. This, he proposed, was the basis for the acoustic confusion errors his participants often made. These sound-based errors were, therefore, a product of short-term coding and not sensory memory.

Similar findings have been reported by Conrad (1964), who specifically measured short-term recall of visually presented letters. Participants were asked to maintain an entire set of letters in memory for a short period of time. Like Sperling, Conrad found that most recall errors involved the incorrect production of letters that sounded like those actually seen. Conrad interpreted this finding as showing that even visual stimuli are transformed to acoustic codes for short-term rehearsal (Conrad & Hull, 1964; Sperling & Speelman, 1970; Wickelgren, 1966). This conclusion is further reinforced by studies that have looked at short-term recall of geometric figures (see, for example, Glanzer & Clark, 1962). These studies have shown that recall of shapes depends more on the names given to the figures than on the shapes of the figures themselves. Again, such findings suggest that humans translate visual stimuli into acoustic codes for short-term processing.

These and other studies support the idea that short-term memories are coded in terms of acoustic features. But does this mean that we use *only* acoustic codes during short-term processing? The answer to this question is quite clearly no. The very fact that congenitally deaf people show evidence of short-term memory processing tells us that humans are able to use short-term codes of other kinds. If one has been deaf since birth, it is impossible to use acoustic codes for processing. Yet, congenitally deaf people are clearly able to recall information after either short or long retention intervals. It is interesting to note that Conrad (1972) examined short-term letter retention using deaf participants. He found that these participants made errors based on visual confusions, not on the basis of how letters sound. This suggests that deaf individuals use visual codes during short-term memory processing.

There is also substantial evidence that hearing-intact participants sometimes use visual codes for short-term memory. Some of this evidence comes from a set of experiments conducted by Posner and his colleagues (Posner, 1969; Posner, Boies, Eichelman, & Taylor, 1969; Posner & Mitchell, 1967). In these studies participants were shown a letter and then, after a brief interval, another letter. Their task was to state as quickly as possible whether the two letters had the same name. For example, they were to respond "same" to the pair *A-A* or the pair *A-a* and "different" to the pair *A-B.* The data of interest were the participants' reaction times in making these "same" or "different" decisions.

Posner found that participants responded most quickly when the two letters were physically identical (for example, A-A or b-b). Reaction times were somewhat slower on trials requiring a "different" response and on trials in which the letters had the same name but were different cases (for example, A-a or b-B). Posner attributed these differences in reaction times to differences in letter coding on the different trial types. He suggested that when letters are physically identical, a participant can use a visual code of the stimuli to determine whether the letters have the same name. However, when letters are not physically identical, participants must translate the visual code into a name or acoustic code to decide whether they are or are not the same. This translation, according to Posner, requires more time. Thus, a participant responds to A-A faster than to A-a because the first pair can be matched on the basis of visual codes, whereas the second requires some transformation from visual to acoustic codes.

If we accept Posner's interpretation of these findings, one of his results has important implications for our attempt to determine whether visual codes exist in short-term memory. Posner found that the reaction time advantage for the identical letter pairs remained even when the letters in a pair were separated by as much as 2 seconds; participants still reacted faster to A-A pairs than to A-a pairs. This suggests that participants were still able to use the visual code for the first letter 2 seconds after that letter had disappeared. Recall that visual stimuli apparently remain in sensory memory for only about 0.5 second. Thus in Posner's experiments participants apparently were using a visual code beyond the time of sensory storage. Even after a letter became represented in short-term storage, in other words, participants seemed to be using a visual code. Although such evidence is somewhat indirect, it does suggest that participants sometimes rely on visual codes for representing short-term memories.

Forgetting from Short-Term Memory

Now return to the experience of looking up a telephone number in a directory and trying to remember it just long enough to dial the phone. This is a relatively easy memory task as long as we are able to rehearse the number continuously between seeing it and dialing it. By constantly rehearsing the number, we can usually maintain it in memory for several seconds at a minimum.

One theory says that we forget phone numbers simply because we have ceased rehearsing them. This view, called the *decay theory*, states that a short-term memory has a limited life span and can be maintained only by constant rehearsal.

Another view worth discussing is the *interference theory*. According to this position, we forget when rehearsal is disrupted, not because continuous rehearsal is necessary for maintaining the memory. We forget because the questions or inputs that disrupt our rehearsal interfere with our ability to remember the number.

Both of these theories are consistent with the Atkinson-Shiffrin model, which proposed that short- and long-term memory differ not only in terms of capacity but also in terms of storage duration. Atkinson and Shiffrin suggested that while memories may remain in long-term storage for several years, memories that are not rehearsed can remain in short-term storage for only a matter of seconds. They presumed that memories are lost from short-term storage via two mechanisms. First, they hypothesized that in the absence of rehearsal, memories fade or decay from the short-term store. Second, because the short-term store has a limited capacity, they assumed that memories can be displaced or pushed out by incoming information. Because of the combined effects of these two mechanisms, short-term memories were presumed to be short-lived.

Support for the notion that forgetting from short-term memory arises from decay comes from two classic studies, one by Peterson and Peterson (1959), the other by J. A. Brown (1958). The methodology has come to be known as the Brown-Peterson paradigm. The Peterson and Peterson study gave participants a single trigram such as *RZL,* presented acoustically, and asked them, after a retention interval, to recall it (see Figure 8.9). The retention intervals used in this experiment varied between 0 and 18 seconds. The Petersons had wanted to determine how long a participant could retain the trigram in short-term memory if the trigram was not rehearsed. Thus, to prevent rehearsal, participants were given a three-digit number immediately after the trigram and were told to repeat this number and begin counting backward by threes. The counting was done aloud and participants were required to say a three-digit number about every half-second. Counting backward by threes

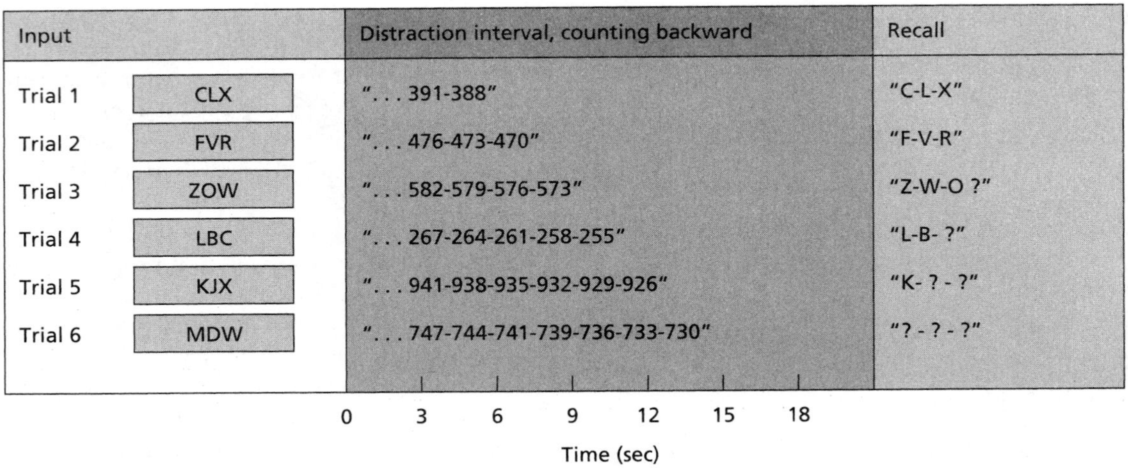

Input		Distraction interval, counting backward	Recall
Trial 1	CLX	"... 391-388"	"C-L-X"
Trial 2	FVR	"... 476-473-470"	"F-V-R"
Trial 3	ZOW	"... 582-579-576-573"	"Z-W-O ?"
Trial 4	LBC	"... 267-264-261-258-255"	"L-B- ?"
Trial 5	KJX	"... 941-938-935-932-929-926"	"K- ? - ?"
Trial 6	MDW	"... 747-744-741-739-736-733-730"	"? - ? - ?"

```
         0    3    6    9    12   15   18
                   Time (sec)
```

FIGURE 8.9 The Petersons' Distractor Task. On each trial, subjects were asked to recall three letters, in correct order, after counting backward aloud for a period lasting from 3 to 18 seconds. The longer the subjects counted, the less likely they were to recall the letters correctly.

requires a great deal of concentration. It is virtually impossible to rehearse an item such as a trigram and at the same time count backward. This was termed a *distractor task* because it was sufficiently difficult to prevent a participant from rehearsing the trigram presented originally. Thus, by means of such a procedure it becomes possible to determine the fate of the unrehearsed trigram.

The results of this study (Figure 8.10) indicate that retention of the trigram decreases rapidly as the retention interval is lengthened. Retention is excellent using a 0-second interval. After 18 seconds, however, recall of the trigram occurs on only about 10 percent of the trials. Peterson and Peterson interpreted these results as an indication that short-term memories decay rapidly unless they are rehearsed. They estimated that within 15 to 18 seconds, nonrehearsed memories become lost from short-term storage.

These findings show unambiguously that short-term memories can be lost in a matter of seconds. However, this experiment does not necessarily show that short-term memories decay without rehearsal. An alternative interpretation of these results is that short-term memories may be lost simply by being displaced from short-term storage by incoming information. In other words, participants may have had difficulty remembering the trigram because counting backward placed into short-term memory a series of digits that displaced the trigram. According to this interpretation, forgetting of the trigram is greater after longer retention intervals because longer intervals permit more incoming stimuli and a greater probability for displacement of the trigram.

Interference Theory. There are several different versions of interference theory. However, they do make the common assumption that memory representations do not change in strength simply as a function of time. Once formed, a short-term representation can, at least in theory, remain intact indefinitely. Interference theories also assume that the forgetting of one representation is always due to the presence of other representations we form. In other words, it is the formation of nontarget representations that

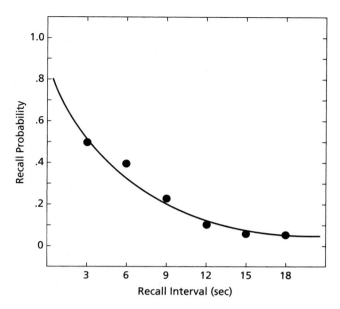

FIGURE 8.10 Correct Recall as a Function of Recall Interval. From "Short-Term Retention of Individual Verbal Items," by L. R. Peterson and M. J. Peterson, 1959, *Journal of Experimental Psychology*, 58, 193–198. Copyright 1959 by the American Psychological Association.

interferes with our ability to remember a given target representation.

The specific mechanism by which interference causes forgetting varies from one version of this theory to another. Some versions make the assumption that the short-term memory store has a limited capacity (see Atkinson & Shiffrin, 1968). Thus, if a person has registered one representation in short-term storage and then another representation is formed, the second representation tends to bump or displace the first from storage. Other variations simply say that whenever multiple representations reside in short-term storage at the same time, these representations tend to alter or distort each other. Forgetting would occur because a target representation becomes altered or unrecognizable due to the presence of other representations also in storage. Regardless of the specific mechanism involved, however, all interference theories suggest that forgetting of a target memory always is due to the formation of other nontarget memories.

Finally, the interference theories presume that rehearsal is not necessary for maintaining the strength of a representation. Instead, rehearsal

functions to keep us from forming new, interfering representations. The idea is that if a person is rehearsing one memory, it is difficult at the same time to attend to new inputs from the environment. Thus, rehearsal prevents forgetting by blocking the registration of new memories in short-term storage.

Evidence Pertinent to the Decay and Interference Theories

Since both decay and interference theories are capable of accounting for simple, short-term forgetting, several researchers have attempted to develop paradigms to distinguish between these points of view. Most of these studies have focused on the question of whether forgetting is caused by the passage of time or whether it is due to events that occur during the passage of time. One paradigm developed to answer this question is called the *probe-digit procedure*.

The Probe–Digit Paradigm. The probe-digit procedure was initially used in a study by Waugh and Norman (1965), who presented participants with a long list of digits over an interval of several seconds. The final digit in the list was accompanied by a tone. The final signaled digit was called a probe digit because in every case it had occurred earlier in the digit list. For example, participants might receive the list 1, 7, 3, 9, 4, 6, 9, 7, 2, 1, 8, 5, 0, 4, with the last digit being signaled by a tone, which served to flag the last digit in the list and to indicate that this number had appeared earlier in the same list. The participant's task was to attempt to remember the digit that had come after the probe in its earlier appearance on the list. Thus, in the list of digits presented above, the correct answer would be 6, because *4* was the probe digit and 6 followed that probe when it first occurred in the list.

Using the probe-digit procedure, it is possible to vary the number of digits between the probe and its earlier appearance on the list. In the example above, there were 8 digits between the original appearance of 4 and its final appearance as the probe. If, however, we were to vary the original position of 4 in the list, we could evaluate the effect of the number of intervening digits on a participant's ability to remember. This manipulation provides some assessment of how forgetting is influenced by changes in the number of interfering items.

It is also possible using the probe-digit paradigm to vary independently the passage of time between a probe and its prior appearance. To do this, Waugh and Norman sometimes presented the list very quickly (4 digits per second) and sometimes at a slower rate (1 digit per second).

By manipulating both the position of a probe digit and the rate of presentation, Waugh and Norman made an interesting discovery. Correct recall depended on the number of items that intervened between the probe and its earlier appearance (see Figure 8.11). Recall was unaffected by the time that separated these events. Specifically, the greater the number of digits that intervened between the probe and its earlier appearance, the poorer the participants' recall performance. If on two trials, however, the number of intervening digits was the same, but the

rate of digit presentation differed, recall was unaffected by the second variable-that is, the difference in presentation rate. These data suggest that short-term forgetting is controlled by the number of interfering items a participant must keep in short-term storage. The data also indicate that the simple passage of time has little influence on forgetting. Thus, the Waugh and Norman results clearly favor an interference explanation of forgetting over a decay approach.

A Modified Distractor Paradigm. In the Peterson and Peterson experiment, participants were distracted from rehearsing the items to be retained by having to repeat digits aloud. Problems with the interpretation of the Petersons' findings arose because of the nature of the distractor task. It was clear that speaking digits aloud led to forgetting of the test material, which consisted of consonant trigrams. However, it was not clear why the distractor produced forgetting. On the one hand, some researchers claimed that the distractor task simply blocked rehearsal and allowed the trigram memory to decay. Others, however, saw the distractor as providing new memories that could have interfered with the trigram memory.

In an effort to circumvent the interpretive problems inherent in the Peterson-Peterson experiment, Judith Reitman attempted to develop a modified distractor paradigm (see Reitman, 1971, 1974). Basically, Reitman's idea was to find a distractor task that would effectively block rehearsal but would not produce interference with the target memory. She reasoned that if such a task could be developed, it would be possible to determine whether memories do in fact decay in the absence of rehearsal or whether forgetting occurs only with the formation of interfering memories.

Reitman's earliest experiments were very similar to the one conducted by Peterson and Peterson. She presented her participants with a set of three words and asked for recall after 15 seconds. However, she filled the retention intervals with a distractor activity featuring white noise (a mix-

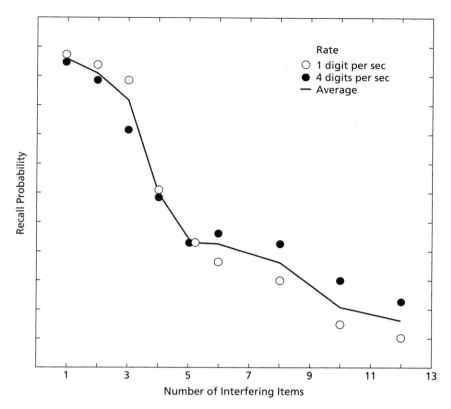

FIGURE 8.11 Effect of Rate of Presentation and Number of Interfering Items on Recall Probability. From "Primary Memory," by N. C. Waugh and D. A. Norman, 1965, *Psychological Review, 72,* 89–104. Copyright 1965 by the American Psychological Association. Reprinted by permission.

ture of tone frequencies that sounds like static or rushing air). Occasionally embedded in this noise was a pure tone signal. Participants were instructed to monitor the noise during each interval and to press a button whenever the signal occurred. Detection of the tone was so difficult that participants were able to perceive it only about half the time.

Reitman reasoned that the difficulty of her distractor task would make it almost impossible to rehearse the words and still detect the tones successfully. She also reasoned that this signal detection task should provide little in the way of interference for the word memory. The use of such a distractor should help to reveal

whether short-term forgetting occurs because of decay or whether there must be interfering items. Her results were very clear. Under this paradigm, participants showed almost no evidence of forgetting even when a retention interval of 15 seconds was used. Using a similar paradigm, Shiffrin (1973) found little forgetting over intervals as long as 40 seconds. These results indicate that the disruption of rehearsal does not inevitably lead to forgetting. Distractors appear to cause forgetting only if they produce interfering memories. Such results strongly support the interference theory of short-term forgetting and seem to provide overwhelming evidence against the notion that short-term memories decay. In subsequent research, however, the results are not as clear as Reitman had initially hoped.

Reitman herself became concerned about the validity of her findings. She wondered whether her distractor task had, in fact, blocked rehearsal completely. Analyzing each participant's data, she found that some participants had performed rather poorly on the signal detection task, which suggested that they might have been rehearsing the words during the retention interval. Reitman also became concerned that her memory task might have been too easy, so that if participants had rehearsed even briefly, they would have been able to recall the words.

To compensate for these potential problem areas of the first experiment, Reitman (1974) conducted a study in which the difficulty of the task was increased by using sets of five words rather than three. She also established stringent criteria for determining when participants might be rehearsing during the distractor task and when they might not. Using these more stringent criteria, she found that only about 20 percent of her participants actually seemed not to rehearse during the distractor task. Thus, she used only the data from the nonrehearsing participants. The results of this study were not nearly as clear as those from the initial experiment. Reitman found that participants showed evidence of forgetting even when the distractor task was noninterfering. On the other hand, Reitman found much less forgetting than Peterson and Peterson had reported earlier. In the 1959 experiment, participants averaged only 15 to 20 percent recall after a 15-second retention interval. Reitman found that participants averaged about 75 percent recall over the same interval.

Reitman reached an important conclusion. Some short-term forgetting does appear to result solely from decay when rehearsal is blocked. However, much of the forgetting found by Peterson and Peterson appears to have been due not to decay of the original memory but rather to the interfering effects of their distractor. Thus, interference appears to be the primary determinant of short-term forgetting, although memory decay also may contribute to this process.

The Role of Proactive Interference in Short-Term Forgetting. To this point, we have discussed the possibility that new memories formed during a retention interval may interfere with the retention of another memory formed earlier. This type of interference is called *retroactive interference* (RI), to reflect the capacity of newly formed memories to block the retention of memories previously formed. However, another type of interference appears to play a role in short-term forgetting. This second type of interference is called *proactive interference* (PI) (see Figure 8.12).

In proactive interference, retention of a currently forming memory is disrupted by memories that were formed earlier. For example, assume that you have been given a trigram to remember. If you are asked to say digits or letters during the retention interval, these new memories can interfere with your ability to recall the trigram. This is an example of retroactive interference. Assume now that you are presented with several trigrams and afterward you are asked to remember a target trigram from the end of the list. Your ability to remember the target trigram would likely be blocked by the trigrams you heard first. This is an example of proactive interference. Figure 8.12 illustrates the difference between these two types of interference.

Much of the forgetting in the Peterson-Peterson study was most likely due to retroactive interference produced by the distractor task these experimenters selected. Others, however, have offered a rationale for suggesting that at least some of the forgetting may have been caused by proactive interference. Peterson and Peterson required their participants to take part in numerous test trials; consequently, all participants actually received several trigrams, each followed by a retention interval and a test. Thus, it is possible that some of the forgetting that occurred on later trials resulted from the memory of trigrams presented on earlier trials.

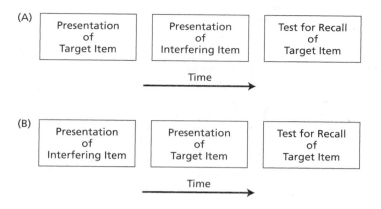

(A)

| Presentation of Target Item | Presentation of Interfering Item | Test for Recall of Target Item |

Time →

(B)

| Presentation of Interfering Item | Presentation of Target Item | Test for Recall of Target Item |

Time →

FIGURE 8.12 Proactive Interference. The arrangement of item presentations that can lead to (a) retroactive interference and (b) proactive interference in a short-term retention paradigm.

Keppel and Underwood (1962) replicated the Peterson–Peterson experiment and noted the forgetting each participant showed from one trial to the next. Figure 8.13 shows the participants' forgetting curves on the first three trials. On trial 1, participants showed very little forgetting even when the retention interval was as long as 18 seconds. On trial 2, however, recall performance was somewhat poorer. Performance decreased even more on the third test trial. This finding supports the idea that the more prior trigrams a participant has heard, the less able that participant will be to recall a current trigram. This indicates that proactive interference can produce short-term forgetting. It further suggests that such effects were probably at work in the Peterson–Peterson experiment (see also, Loess, 1964).

Another factor that influences the degree of proactive interference is the similarity of the interfering and the target items. This was demonstrated convincingly by Wickens (1972), who conducted "release from PI" experiments. These studies consisted of trials in which participants were presented with a common word, directed to count backward for 20 seconds, then asked to recall the word. One group of participants (control group) received four such trials, all involving words belonging to the same conceptual category (for example, names of animals). A second group of participants (shift group) received the same words as the control group of trials 1 through 3. However, on trial 4, these participants received a word from a totally different conceptual category (for example, a type of fruit). Figure 8.14 shows the kinds of results these manipulations produced.

First, note the performance of the control participants in Figure 8.14. These participants show excellent recall on trial 1, but their performance declines steadily on the subsequent trials. This result is similar to that reported by Keppel and Underwood: performance deteriorates as more and more prior words are accumulated. In effect, proactive interference builds up as more trials occur and this buildup produces progressively more forgetting. We can note the same phenomenon in the first three trials of the shift participants. However, on trial 4, the shift participants show a clear *increase* in recall performance. It is as if the effects of proactive interference are lifted or released. Clearly, the detrimental effects of proactive interference are reduced substantially when a participant is shifted to a target word that is dissimilar to the previously presented words. Such results indicate that proactive interference depends on the similarity of the interfering and the target items. When these items are dissimilar, the effects of proactive interference are lessened. It is interesting to note that retroactive interference also appears to depend on the similarity of the target and interfering items (see, for example, Reitman, 1971).

All the studies we have reviewed point to the importance of interference in the production of

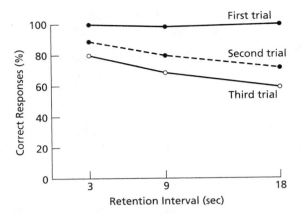

FIGURE 8.13 **Forgetting Curves.** Short-term retention of a trigram as a joint function of retention interval and number of preceding trials. (From Keppel and Underwood, 1962. From the Journal of Verbal Learning & Verbal Behavior, 1962, 1, 153–161. © 1962 by Academic Press. Used by permission.)

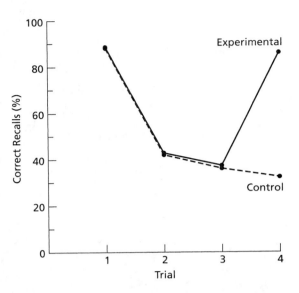

FIGURE 8.14 **An Example of Release from PI.** Both control and experimental subjects receive stimuli belonging to the same conceptual category on trials 1 through 3. On trial 4, the experimental subjects are switched to a different category, while the control subjects are not. (From Wickens, 1972.)

short-term forgetting. It is clear from these experiments that if a participant is given a target item to remember, the participant's retention can be diminished by either previously presented items (PI) or by items presented during the retention interval (RI). What is less clear is the degree to which memory decay might also contribute to the forgetting process. The studies conducted by Reitman are probably the most informative with respect to the role of decay. These studies suggest that at least some of our short-term forgetting may result from the deterioration of a memory representation over time. Still, even these experiments lead us to conclude that decay contributes only minimally to short-term forgetting. The predominant factor in such forgetting appears to be the presence of interfering memory representations, although some forgetting does take place strictly as a function of decay. Can we estimate the duration of short-term memories? Most likely we cannot because it will depend on the amount of interfering material. Nonetheless, it is safe to say that short-term memory cannot maintain unrehearsed information for more than one minute. Some estimates of the duration of short-term memory are much

lower, on the order of 20 seconds (e.g., Peterson & Peterson, 1959). Thus, 20 seconds and 60 seconds may represent the minimum and maximum estimates for the duration of short-term memory.

WORKING MEMORY

In the Atkinson-Shiffrin model, all information is processed while in the same short-term store. Therefore, all the processing in short-term memory occurs by the same governing rules. However, some theorists have challenged the idea that short-term memory is a single system. This section presents an alternative to the Atkinson-Shiffrin model, Alan Baddeley's working memory model (Baddeley, 1986, 1990, 1994, 1996), which is generally preferred by contemporary researchers (Schacter, 1996). Baddeley's model views short-term memory as a set of interacting systems that work together but are functionally separate. Indeed, he thinks of two

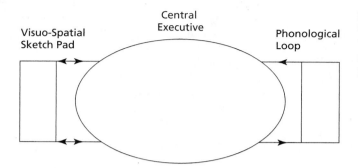

Central
Executive

Visuo-Spatial
Sketch Pad

Phonological
Loop

FIGURE 8.15 Baddeley's (1990) Model of Working Memory. From *Human Memory: Theory and Practice,* by A. Baddeley. Copyright © 1990 by Allyn and Bacon. Reprinted by permission.

separate modality-specific systems, one visually based, the other phonologically based. Connecting the two is an attentional, or *executive,* system (see Figure 8.15).

Baddeley's model should be considered as an expansion of the Atkinson-Shiffrin model; it does not contradict or replace it. Atkinson and Shiffrin thought of short-term memory as a working memory, a system for the temporary holding and manipulating of information. However, short-term memory frequently is thought of as a passive store of information on the way to or from long-term memory. Like Atkinson and Shiffrin, Baddeley views short-term memory as a means of holding and processing information in the service of complex learning and thinking. Therefore, Baddeley replaces the term *short-term* with *working* to describe this immediate form of memory. However, unlike Atkinson and Shiffrin, Baddeley does not consider working memory a unitary system.

Baddeley views working memory as multi-component system. In the model, there are three components of working memory, the **phonological loop,** the **visuo-spatial sketch pad,** and the **central executive.** Each of these subsystems is specially designed to handle some, but not all, of the tasks of holding and manipulating information. The phonological loop is an auditory subsystem that holds information in an acoustic format. Its existence is supported by research that suggests that information in short-term memory is coded in an auditory format.

The visuo-spatial sketch pad is a visual short-term memory system. Some research suggests that information can be held in visual code in short-term memory. According to Baddeley, the visuo-spatial sketch pad accomplishes that. Finally, the central executive is the system that accomplishes control functions. It allocates attention and directs rehearsal.

Why does Baddeley view these three functional systems as separate? The main evidence for separate subsystems is the idea that these systems are dissociable. A dissociation occurs when a single independent variable affects two dependent variables differently. In the context of working memory, Baddeley has shown that certain manipulations affect one subsystem without affecting another subsystem.

Evidence for Subsystems

Baddeley and Hitch (1974) originally were interested in testing the assumption that working memory serves a temporary store that helps people perform other cognitive tasks. The experimenters decided to test this hypothesis by using a dual-task procedure, in which participants were asked to perform one demanding task that was designed to take up most of the capacity of short-term memory. A second task involved trying to do a relatively complex cognitive task such as verifying the truth value of simple sentences. Baddeley and Hitch expected that the demanding task they designed to occupy short-term memory would make it difficult—if not impossible—to do the complex cognitive task.

The demanding short-term memory task chosen by Baddeley and Hitch involved requiring participants to repeat a sequence of digits. The numbers of digits in the sequence varied from zero to eight. Baddeley and Hitch expected that repeating the digits would occupy working memory. Therefore, the more digits the participant was storing and repeating, the more difficult it should be to carry out the other task. The second task involved a simple reasoning test. Participants were asked to verify a set of sentences concerning the order of presented letters. As the task was easy and 100% accuracy was expected, Baddeley and Hitch instead measured the response time to conclude whether a sentence was correct or incorrect.

The results from this experiment were completely unexpected. Based on the traditional model of a single short-term system, increasing digit rehearsal should have catastrophic effects on response time to the sentences. However, Baddeley and Hitch found that response times on the sentences did not vary greatly as a function of the number of digits being rehearsed. Seemingly, participants could occupy working memory with the digits and still have cognitive resources left for the sentence verifications. One conclusion could have been that thinking of short-term memory as a work space for cognition was a misconception. However, Baddeley thought that perhaps these data indicated that several independent short-term stores are at work. Because the sentence information could be handled by one working memory system (i.e., the visuo-spatial sketch pad), another system (i.e., the phonological loop) could handle the digit span.

In another experiment designed to test Baddeley's idea of working memory, Logie (1986) had participants learn digit-word pairs (e.g., 45–bracket) using a visual imagery mnemonic. Other participants learned through a rote rehearsal strategy. The visual imagery strategy was designed to occupy the visuo-spatial sketchpad, whereas the rote rehearsal strategy was designed

to occupy the phonological loop. Logie then distracted his participants by presenting pictures or by having an experimenter read names. The pictures should also occupy the visuo-spatial sketchpad and should therefore interfere more with learning when a visual-imagery strategy was being used. In contrast, reading names should occupy the phonological loop and, therefore, interfere more with rote rehearsal.

Logie's findings were consistent with Baddeley's model. First, pictures interfered with learning more when people were using the visual-imagery strategy than when they were using the rote-rehearsal strategy. Second, the names interfered more with learning when the participants were using rote-rehearsal strategy than when they were using the visual imagery strategy. In other words, the visual task interfered with short-term memory rehearsal that was visually based, and the auditory task interfered with short-term memory rehearsal that was auditorally based. This pattern of results supports the idea that the visuo-spatial sketchpad and the phonological loop may be distinct memory systems, just as Baddeley suggested.

Phonological Loop

The phonological loop is a short-term memory subsystem that maintains speech-based information for short periods of time (Baddeley, 1990). If information is not rehearsed, the memory trace decays. However, the phonological loop can retain information for longer periods of time by use of an articulatory control process that rehearses the information.

This model can also account for a variety of phenomena, including the word-length effect (Baddeley, Thomson, & Buchanan, 1975). In the word-length effect, longer words are harder to maintain in working memory than shorter words. (This goes against the idea of Miller (1956) that short-term memory's capacity can be measured in chunks.) For example, Matlin (1998) asked her readers to try to keep the following names of nations in short-term store: Chad, Burma, Greece,

Cuba, and Malta. Then, she asked her readers to try Czechoslovakia, Somaliland, Nicaragua, Afghanistan, and Venezuela. This quick demonstration suffices to show the word-length effect. People can maintain more short words than long words in the immediate span. Baddeley accounts for this effect by invoking the phonological loop. Because information is stored and rehearsed in acoustic format in the loop, those items that take longer to pronounce or say use up more of the phonological loop. The differences in digit-spans across different languages is also consistent with the word-length effect and the concept of a phonological loop.

Some of the most convincing evidence for the existence of a phonological loop comes from the neuropsychological domain. Vallar and Baddeley (1984) studied a patient who seemed to have selective damage to the phonological loop. The patient, appeared to be intellectually normal in most areas. Her short-term memory, however, was severely impaired. Nonetheless, she scored well on verbal and performance IQ tests and showed no impairment of language or other intellectual abilities. However, she did not show a word-length effect and her short-term memory was not affected by phonological similarity. Because these are variables that affect the phonological loop, Vallar and Baddeley concluded that her phonological loop was damaged.

Visuo-Spatial Sketch Pad

The visuo-spatial sketch pad handles visual and spatial information. It is also assumed to consist of a brief store, analagous to the iconic memory and a control process, analagous to short-term memory, that keeps information refreshed. In contrast to the phonological loop, auditory information does not interfere with processing on the sketch pad. However, visually presented information *can* interfere. Nonvisual spatial tracking can also interfere (Baddeley, 1994).

Evidence for the visuo-spatial sketch pad mirrors that used to demonstrate the phonological loop. For example, Logie (1986) presented participants with color patches while they were using visual imagery to learn cue-target word pairs. Participants were instructed to ignore the color patches. However, the color patches interfered with learning processes that used visual imagery. A second set of participants was given rote encoding instructions (e.g., "keep repeating the to-be-remembered words"). The color patches did not interfere with this kind of learning.

Central Executive

The central executive is the third component of Baddeley's model. It integrates information from the phonological loop and the visuo-spatial sketch pad. The central executive is also involved in attention, planning, and controlling cognition. Baddeley argued that it is also important in the ability to do more than one task at once. However, the central executive may be the aspect of working memory to which the least experimental work has been devoted (but, for another view, see Baddeley, 1996).

Most theorists consider the central executive the weakest dimension of Baddeley's theory. Whereas there are firm reasons to suspect that the visuo-spatial sketch pad and the phonological loop are separate memory processes, it is unclear how to consider the central executive. It is properly more in the domain of attention, which is of course important for memory processes.

THE NEUROPSYCHOLOGY OF SHORT-TERM MEMORY

Short-term memory is functionally separate from long-term memory. It differs from long-term memory with respect to capacity, duration, coding, and forgetting. However, when studying whether memory exists within a biological context, it is important to see if the differences between short- and long-term memory have a basis in the brain. There is evidence to support a biological distinction between short- and long-term memory. Therefore, it is important to show that differences between cognitive systems have their roots in differences in brain organization.

Research supports the possibility that different neural mechanisms underlie short- and long-term memory stores. This distinction is based on clinical evidence from individuals who had experienced various types of brain injury. For instance, there have been many reports that individuals having long-term memory deficits have no difficulties with short-term memory, and there have been several reports of patients with short-term memory deficits, but seemingly no difficulties in learning or retrieving from long-term memory (see, for example, Baddeley, 1990; Milner, 1966; Shallice & Warrington, 1970).

We will contrast two classic studies the case histories of HM (Milner, 1966) and KF (Warrington & Shallice, 1969). KF was a young man who injured his head in a motorcycle accident. HM underwent brain surgery to relieve severe epilepsy. Both men wound up with severe damage as a consequence. However, the pattern of deficits was different. KF's long-term memory was unaffected. On tests of paired-associate learning, he did not differ from normal people. On tests of short-term memory, however, he was severely impaired. Warrington and Shallice estimated his immediate memory span at two items, when tested auditorily, four when tested visually. Compare this with the "normal" seven plus or minus two.

HM was of normal intelligence. In contrast to KF, he had normal short-term memory. His memory span was in the normal range. However, he had severe difficulties in learning new information (over longer durations) and remembered little from his life since his surgery. Despite a normal short-term memory, his long-term amnesia was nearly complete. He cannot consciously maintain information for more than a few minutes.

The region of the brain that was damaged in each patient was different. KF suffered damage to the left hemisphere of the brain. Localization of the lesion revealed that it was close to the Sylvan fissure. This area of the brain usually involves lan-

guage formation and processing. Thus, it is possible to see KF's deficit as consistent with the theory that coding is acoustic in short-term memory. HM, like many amnesic patients, suffered damage to the hippocampus and adjacent temporal-lobe structures. Thus, the neuropsychological evidence argues for a distinction between long-term and short-term memory.

The comparison of HM and KF supports a general difference between short-term and long-term memory. However, recent neuroimaging data support differences between the phonological loop and the visuo-spatial sketchpad. Using PET technology, Jonides (1995) scanned different regions of the brain while participants were engaging in tasks designed to tap either the phonological loop or the visuo-spatial sketchpad. In the task designed to occupy the phonological loop, participants saw a sequence of letters at a rate of one letter every three seconds. If a given letter was the same as a letter shown two spaces places back, the participant was required to say "yes." If the letter had not been shown two spaces earlier, the response was "no." Jonides hypothesized that this relatively complex task would tap the phonological loop.

To engage the visuo-spatial sketchpad, Jonides presented three dots in different spatial locations for a 200-millisecond span. The screen then went blank for three seconds. A circle then appeared on the screen, and the participant was required to determine whether the location was one of the positions where a dot had been previously.

The PET imaging results showed that the two tasks led to very different activation patterns in the brain. The phonological task engaged Broca's area (known to be involved in language processing) in the left frontal cortex and also parts of the left parietal lobe. The visuo-spatial task led to activation in the occipital lobes, and activity in the right frontal lobe and right parietal cortex. Not only do these data support a theoretical difference between the phonological loop and the visuo-spatial sketchpad, but they suggest that the two hemispheres of the brain may engage in different kinds of short-term memory processing.

SUMMARY STATEMENTS

We began by describing the Atkinson-Shiffrin model of memory formation, which emphasizes that a memory must pass through multiple structures or memory stores before permanent registration of the memory can occur. We reviewed evidence in support of this model and also pointed out the difficulties inherent in such a view. We then described what sensory memory is and how iconic and echoic memory have been studied.

We then addressed the issue of short-term memory. We described short-term memory in terms of its capacity, control processes that guide it, coding in short-term memory, and forgetting from short-term memory. We emphasized for each of these characteristics how short-term is similar to or different from long-term memory. We also described neuropsychological evidence that supports a difference between short- and long-term memory. Finally, we adressed the newer conception of working memory.

9

Encoding in Long-Term Memory

CHAPTER OVERVIEW

For a student, studying for an exam is a common experience. The student has three goals when studying new material. The first is to understand the material that he or she is reading. The second is to remember it on an upcoming exam. The third is to retain the information past the exam and to be able to retrieve and use it. All of these goals are important. If the student understands the material but does not remember it the next day on the test, it is doubtful that she will get a good grade. If she doesn't remember it when necessary later in life, she didn't get much benefit out of studying in the first place.

This chapter will consider the topic of encoding in memory. As defined in chapter 8, the encoding process is characterized as the set of operations we perform on incoming stimuli to convert them into a usable format or code. Encoding new information into memory is clearly an important process in human beings.

Bear in mind the distinction we made earlier between the nature of long-term and short-term memory. The theoretical distinction is important because it differs from the popular usage of these terms. Short-term memory refers to a working memory system that holds information briefly so that it can be used or processed. If information is not continually rehearsed, and successful retrieval occurs over time, the memory was most likely stored in long-term memory. For example, if a person can remember what he did five minutes ago, psychologists would consider this to be retrieval from long-term memory. However, long-term memory extends far beyond that. We can remember events that took place years and years ago. Older people often can accurately recall events that took place 80 years ago!

Long-term retention can be quite remarkable. For example, while it may seem that considerable amounts of what they learn in high school and college is lost, most people would be surprised by how much they do retain from those classes. Clearly one of the important factors in long-term retention is how you learned or encoded the material in the first place.

Several studies have looked at retention or maintenance of knowledge across long periods of time (Bahrick, 1984; Bahrick & Hall, 1991; Conway, Cohen, & Stanhope, 1991). The findings of these studies are quite intriguing. For example, Bahrick and Hall looked at retention of high school algebra in former students, some of whom had graduated high school more than 50 years earlier. In the study, they tested only those individuals who did not use mathematics at that level in their lives or careers. However, they still found measurable levels of retention 50 years later. In fact, most of the forgetting appears to take place in the first few years after the material was learned. Bahrick and Hall also found that one important predictor of retention was whether the individuals had also taken math in college. Those who did remembered more of their high school work. Bahrick and Hall reason that the college math provides those individuals with a better cognitive organization of the information they learned. Indeed, organization appears to be an important variable in encoding.

Conway et al. (1991) did a similar study, although across a more modest time span, on the retention of concepts learned in cognitive psychology classes. They also looked at the retention of proper names associated with the field. Do you think you will remember the name of George Sperling five years from now? Conway et al. made some interesting discoveries. First, like Bahrick and Hall, they found that most of the forgetting took place in the first three years. After that, knowledge decays slowly (see Figure 9.1). Second, they found that concepts showed a slower decay than names. This suggests that organization is

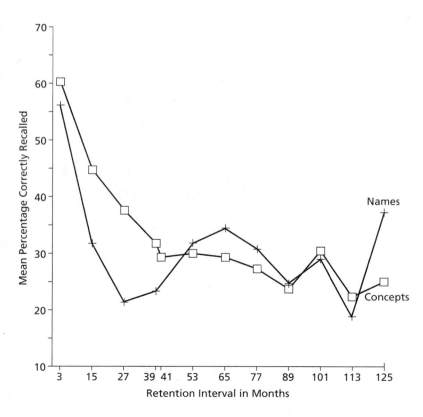

FIGURE 9.1 Mean Percentage of Correctly Recalled Names and Concepts for Different Retention Intervals. From "On the very long-term knowledge acquired through formal education: Twelve years of cognitive psychology," by M. A. Conway, G. Cohen, and N. Stanhope, 1991, *Journal of Experimental Psychology: General, 120,* 395–409. Copyright 1991 by the American Psychological Association. Reprinted by permission.

important; it is easier to organize ideas into a coherent whole than it is to find a pattern in a series of names. Third, they found that those who had received higher grades originally were also likely to retain more over the years. These studies emphasize the interdependence of learning and remembering. The good learners in the Conway et al. study were also the good rememberers years later.

These encouraging findings emphasize the importance of encoding processes in long-term memory. Retention in long-term memory, even for intervals up to 55 years, are a function of initial encoding. Conway et al. (1991) found that better grades led to more long-term retention. Bahrick and Hall (1991) found that high school algebra was remembered better if it was reinforced by college math. This chapter will outline a number of important dimensions of encoding.

THE LEVELS-OF-PROCESSING APPROACH

The levels-of-processing approach usually is attributed to two University of Toronto psychologists, Fergus Craik and Robert Lockhart (Craik & Lockhart, 1972; see also Melton, 1963). What Craik and Lockhart proposed is more a set of ideas than a formal model or theory. They disagreed with the standard Atkinson-Shiffrin model. They wanted to account for both short-term memory effects and long-term memory effects in a single memory system, questioning the proposition that memories must move through a sequence of structures or stores on the way to permanent registration. Instead, they proposed that there is a single memory store that holds all memories regardless of when those memories entered the system. In many respects this single store was presumed to be similar to the long-term store suggested by Atkinson and Shiffrin. That is, it was presumed to have an unlimited capacity and to be capable of holding memories for extremely long periods. Most researchers today accept the difference between short-term and long-term memory, but they also recognize the importance of the levels-of-processing approach for understanding encoding processes.

Intentional vs. Incidental Learning

Craik and Lockhart were interested in the manner in which people encode information. They were concerned that most research on memory was about intentional learning. **Intentional learning** means that the people actively engage in learning information because they know that their memories may be tested. Typical memory experiments (for instance, free recall) involve intentional learning. In contrast, Craik and Lockhart observed that most learning in the real world was not intentional. Rather, they argued most encoding occurred through incidental learning. **Incidental learning** means that people encode information into long-term memory not by actively trying to remember the information, but rather as a by-product of perceiving and understanding the world (see Table 9.1).

Craik and Lockhart point out that in real life a person seldom says to himself, "I have to remember that." Perhaps this happens when a person is reading the instructions for installing new stereo speakers. However, typically, people engage in their daily work and leisure activities and do not actively try to remember new information. When watching a favorite TV show, a person is not trying to remember the storyline. When reading a novel for leisure, she is not trying to remember the plot or the characters' names. Yet in each case, the person does encode something. Craik and Lockhart consider this incidental learning to be the most common and most important part of encoding.

Craik and Lockhart assumed that we are capable of applying control processes to only a small subset of memories at any given time. In other words, our capacity for actively processing information is limited. In most cases we choose to process information that has just entered storage, because we must always adjust our behaviors to

Table 9.1 Intentional and Incidental Learning.

Type of Learning	Real-World Example	Applicability
Intentional	Learning all the presidents of the United States	Educational testing and some work settings
	Learning a locker combination	
Incidental	Learning the plots of TV reruns	Daily life
	Learning where to find the peanut butter section in the supermarket	

new incoming stimuli. We can, however, choose to focus our processing on memories that have been in storage for a longer time.

Rehearsal. The most important idea in this approach concerns the nature of the processes we employ once certain ongoing events or memories have been selected for processing. Craik and Lockhart proposed that we are capable of processing selected memories in a variety of ways. First, they distinguished two types of rehearsal. **Maintenance rehearsal** is a process by which we keep a memory in conscious awareness for a period of time, whereas **elaborative rehearsal** involves the encoding of a memory so that it can be recalled even after long retention intervals. Maintenance rehearsal usually involves the repetition of the to-be-remembered item over and over in short-term memory. Elaborative rehearsal involves relating the item in memory to other items in memory. Craik and Lockhart suggested that we can choose to rehearse a memory in either of these ways, and that our choice will often determine how well a memory can be retained over time.

Levels of Processing. Importantly, Craik and Lockhart also assume *different levels of processing.* The level of processing refers to the idea that the manner in which information is first encountered and rehearsed leads to a different depth of processing. Elaborative processing leads to deeper processing, whereas maintenance rehearsal leads to shallow processing. For example, watching a movie and attending only to the attractiveness of the actors and the style of clothes they wear generally results in poor memory of the film's content. This is considered "shallow" processing. In contrast, attending to the possible message of the director and looking for allusions to earlier films is considered deep processing. This should lead to better memory of content.

In the verbal-learning experiments that Craik and Lockhart wished to explain, levels of processing assumed a more specific meaning. If we hear a spoken word, we may choose to process it at a

shallow or surface level, focusing on only how it sounds. We might also decide to process the word at a somewhat deeper level, perhaps taking note of whether the word begins with a consonant or a vowel. This would constitute a deeper level of analysis because it would require a recognition of the word's first letter and a categorization of that letter as either a vowel or a consonant. Finally, we might choose to process the word in terms of its meaning or its symbolic characteristics. This would call for a comparison of the word to similar words stored in memory, followed by a decision of what the word is comparable to in terms of meaning. Attending to meaning involves the deepest level of analysis. Therefore, processing for meaning is the best encoding strategy and results in the best retention.

According to Craik and Lockhart, these different levels of processing are not necessarily sequential. Given enough processing time we do not necessarily move from the surface to a deeper level of processing. Two individuals may, for example, rehearse the same item for the same period of time. However, one may spend the entire time processing at a surface level, whereas the other may spend the whole time processing meaning. In effect, a person can choose how a given memory is to be processed. This choice will depend on a variety of factors, such as individual characteristics, how the person plans to use the memory later, and the features of a given input that seem most pertinent at the moment.

The importance of these different processing levels is that Craik and Lockhart assume that the processing level a person chooses determines how a stimulus input will be coded or represented in memory. That is, the level at which the person processes a given stimulus determines which features of that stimulus become stored in the memory system. For example, a word that is processed at a surface level may end up being represented in memory only in terms of its sound. On the other hand, if a deeper level of processing is used, the same word might become represented in terms of its meaning.

Assuming that this view is correct, we might ask whether it really matters how a stimulus is coded as long as the stimulus does get represented in memory. Craik and Lockhart suggest that the type of representation we form is critical for at least two reasons. First, the type of input representation formed determines which features of an input we will be able to remember later. If a stimulus is represented in terms of its sound alone, then later we will be able to remember its sound but not its visual features or its meaning. Second, Craik and Lockhart propose that certain types of representations are longer lasting than others. Specifically, they hypothesize that meaning codes last longer than physical-feature codes. This implies that an input represented in terms of meaning should be remembered longer than an input represented in terms of its sound.

Evidence Supporting the Levels-of-Processing Approach

Probably the most salient point in the levels of processing approach is that the fate of a memory depends on how a memory is processed, not on how long it is processed. This point has been supported in a number of different experiments. First, long-term retention appears to depend on whether individuals engage in maintenance or elaborative rehearsal (see, for example, Bjork, 1975). Such a result is clearly consistent with this general view. There is equally strong evidence that when subjects process the same input at dif-

ferent levels, they form memories that are forgotten at different rates.

Craik and Tulving (1975) tested the levels-of-processing approach in a series of experiments using a new technique to simulate incidental learning. When subjects were exposed to words that they would later be asked to recognize, they were not told that there would be a later memory test. Rather, the subjects thought they were being tested at the speed at which they could perform an **orienting task,** which is the simple activity that subjects were asked to perform on each item. Thus, if subjects were exposed to the word *crate*, they might be asked to make a quick judgment as to whether the word was printed completely in capital letters. This orients the subject toward the word, but does not tip off that the word will appear on a recognition test (see Table 9.2).

In one of these studies, subjects were first asked a question (the orienting task), without being told what word the experimenters had in mind. Then they were given a brief visual presentation of a specific word and were asked to answer the preceding question with a yes or a no as quickly as possible. Some of the questions used concerned only the physical features of the words that followed (for example, "Is the word in capital letters?"). A second set of questions dealt with the sounds of the target words (for example, "Does the word rhyme with "weight?"). A final group of questions concerned whether the target word would fit a blank in a given sentence (for

Table 9.2 Levels-of-Processing Theory. According to Craik and Lockhart (1972), structural, phonemic, and semantic encoding—which can be elicited by questions such as those shown on the right—involve progressively deeper levels of processing, which should result in more durable memories.

	LEVEL OF PROCESSING	TYPE OF ENCODING	EXAMPLE OF QUESTIONS USED TO ELICIT APPROPRIATE ENCODING
	Shallow processing	Structural encoding: emphasizes the physical structure of the stimulus	Is the word written in capital letters?
Depth of Processing	Intermediate processing	Phonemic encoding: emphasizes what a word sounds like	Does the word rhyme with weight?
	Deep processing	Semantic encoding: emphasizes the meaning of verbal input	Would the word fit in the sentence: "He met a _____ on the street"?

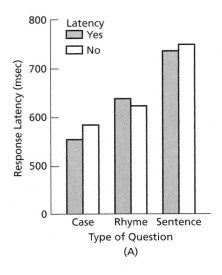

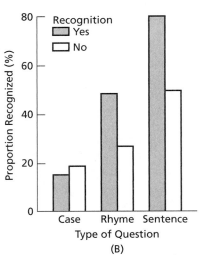

FIGURE 9.2 Results of Surprise Recognition Tests.
(A) Mean latency to answer questions about the case of a word, whether a word rhymed with another, or whether a word fit a particular sentence. (B) Proportion of these words that were recognized on a subsequent test. (From Craik and Tulving, 1975.)

example, "Does the word fit the following sentence? He met a _____ in the street.").

The purpose of the orienting task was to bias subjects toward processing the words at different levels. It was assumed that questions concerning features such as capital letters would lead to a shallow level of processing for the word that followed. Questions having to do with word sounds were intended to result in an intermediate processing level, because to answer these questions one at least would need to sound out the entire word. Questions about whether a word would fit a sentence were intended to prompt a deep level of processing, by requiring subjects to attend to the meanings of words.

After all the questions had been answered, Craik and Tulving gave the subjects a surprise recognition test to determine how many words they remembered. Figure 9.2 shows the results of this test for each of the word categories, as well as the subjects' reaction times. At least two important results are contained in this figure. First, it is clear that subjects take longer to answer the sentence questions than questions concerning letter cases or rhymes. Second, the recognition results are precisely what one would predict from the levels–of–processing approach. Retention is best for words that had to be processed for mean-

ing (sentence condition). Retention is somewhat poorer in the rhyming condition and is very poor in the condition requiring a decision on letter case.

There are two possible interpretations for these results. One is that different levels of processing led to different levels of retention. The second possibility is that different *amounts* of processing led to different levels of retention. The latter interpretation is feasible because subjects took more time to answer the rhyme questions than they did to answer the letter case questions, suggesting subjects took longer to process words for the rhyme condition than for the letter case distinction. The longest processing time apparently occurred in the sentence-completion condition, as these were the questions eliciting the longest reaction times.

To distinguish between these interpretations, Craik and Tulving next attempted to disentangle depth of processing and total time of processing. The procedure used an orienting task that was similar to the one employed in the first study. That is, subjects received a question followed by a word, whereupon they were to answer the question as quickly as possible. In this study only two types of questions were used. The first type was intended to induce surface processing;

however, these questions were also designed to require extensive processing time. These questions concerned the sequence of vowels and consonants in a word ("Does the word match this pattern: vowel-consonant-vowel-consonant?"). The second type of question was similar to the sentence-completion questions in the experiment summarized in 9.4. These questions were relatively easy to answer, so that processing time would be minimal, but they required a deep level of semantic processing.

The results of this experiment strongly supported the idea that it is the level rather than the amount of processing time that is critical. Reaction times to the vowel-consonant questions were actually longer than those to the sentence-completion questions. Still, words that followed the sentence-completion questions were recognized much better on the retention test than the words that followed the vowel-consonant questions. This finding indicates that retention may depend very little on how long a word is processed, but it may depend a great deal on the type of processing that occurs. Similar conclusions have come from a variety of experiments (see, for example, Bellezza, Cheesman, & Reddy, 1977; Moeser, 1983; Packman & Battig, 1978).

The Status of the Levels-of-Processing Approach

There is much to recommend the levels-of-processing approach to the study of memory formation. First of all, it is able to account for different degrees of retention, as well as capacity limitations in memory and even differences in memory codes. In addition, there is substantial support for the idea that different types of processing result in differential retention of memories. Still, this approach has not gone without criticism, much of which has centered on the definition of the term *level* or *depth* of processing.

Defining Processing Levels. In the studies we have reviewed thus far, the rules for defining different processing levels have seemed self-evident.

For example, it makes intuitive sense to say that an analysis of meaning represents a deeper level of processing than does an analysis of visual features. Still, Craik and Lockhart were somewhat vague in discussing what really constitutes a given level of processing. They did not say, for example, whether there are different levels of processing for meaning. Likewise, they did not explain fully why dealing with the sound of a word should involve a deeper level of processing than dealing with a word's visual characteristics. This lack of explicitness has been viewed by some theorists as a serious flaw in the levels-of-processing approach (see Baddeley, 1978; T. O. Nelson, 1977; also see Lockhart & Craik, 1978). The absence of general agreement about what constitutes a level of processing has made it difficult to interpret a number of experimental findings. Packman and Battig (1978), for instance, had subjects rate each word on a list on one of several dimensions. Words were rated in terms of concreteness, meaningfulness, imagery value, familiarity, or pleasantness. Certainly, Craik and Lockhart would have to agree with the notion that each of these rating tasks should promote deep semantic processing. Yet, Packman and Battig found that words rated in terms of pleasantness were recalled much better than words rated along the other dimensions. Does this mean that a pleasantness rating involves a deeper level of processing than a rating in terms of meaningfulness? Without a more explicit definition for processing levels, we have no way of answering this question.

A similar question about the precision with which *level of processing* can be defined arises in connection with the results of Craik and Tulving (1975), discussed earlier. Recall that in these experiments subjects were given questions designed to induce different processing levels for different words, and the only answers possible were yes and no. The results clearly showed that words could be retained differentially depending on the level of processing induced. There was, however, an additional result of these experiments, one passed over in our original discussion. As Figure 9.2

indicates, in both the sentence-completion and the rhyming conditions, subjects remembered words that required a yes response much better than they remembered the words that required a no response.

Does this finding imply that different levels of processing are involved in making yes and no decisions about the fit of a word in a sentence? Again, the levels-of-processing approach would suggest so because the decisions resulting in these two responses produce different levels of retention. However, there is little basis for suggesting that a yes decision should require deeper processing than a no decision. In effect, Craik and Lockhart have failed to provide a set of rules or conditions for determining when processing levels are deep and when they are shallow. Without such a set of rules, it becomes difficult to use this hypothesis to make predictions concerning retention performance.

The Connection Between Deep Processing and Retention. Another problem associated with the levels-of-processing approach is that some findings seem to contradict the idea that deep processing is always necessary for good long-term retention. In contrast to the conclusions drawn by Craik and Tulving (1975), some studies have shown that retention sometimes is improved by increases in processing time, regardless of the level at which processing occurs (Dark & Loftus, 1976; T. O. Nelson, 1977; Rundus, 1977). Other studies have shown that such physical features of stimuli as the location of a sound or the voice in which a word is spoken can be recognized long after the presentation of the stimuli (see Craik & Kirsner, 1974; Fisher & Craik, 1977; Kolers, 1979; D. L. Nelson, 1979; Rothkopf, 1971). These studies seem to refute the notion that only meaning codes remain in memory for long intervals.

There have been several recent attempts to modify or make more explicit the levels-of-processing hypothesis. Instead of simply showing that different types of processing lead to different degrees of retention, these hypotheses have ad-dressed the question of why processing levels influence retention.

Distinctiveness

Consider the two following sentences. Sentence 1: *One possible alternative to the levels-of-processing approach is to consider the role of distinctiveness in the formation of new memories.* Sentence 2: *The largest mountain in New York State is known by the name of Mount Marcy.* Note that both of these sentences are grammatical and written in English. Both contain one idea. However, the second sentence is highly distinctive. It really does not fit in with the ongoing discussion of memory encoding. Thus, this oddball sentence stands out. According to the idea of distinctiveness, such oddball items are frequently highly memorable.

Research supports the idea of distinctiveness as being important in memory encoding. That is, the more distinctively a memory is coded, the easier it will be to recall that memory later. According to this view, semantic or meaningful processing usually leads to better retention because it increases the distinctiveness of the memory code that is formed. To illustrate this point, consider what we normally do when we read a printed page. While we read, we normally think about the meanings of the words we are reading. That is, we process the printed words at a semantic level. By doing this we create a set of distinctive memory codes. The meaning found on one page is seldom the same as the meaning found on another page. Thus, each meaning code is reasonably distinct from the others we form.

Now consider what would happen if we simply noticed the letters in each word that we read. We would be processing the words at a shallow level and creating memory codes based on the physical features of the letters. As the same letters occur over and over again, each of these codes would overlap significantly with numerous other codes from the same page. In other words, codes based on physical features are less distinct from one another than are codes based on meaning. As a result, at the time of recall it is much easier to remember the semantically processed words, because they can be differentiated easily from other coded words.

Distinctiveness appears to account for a number of encoding effects. One such effect is the von Restorff effect (Hunt, 1995; von Restorff, 1933). In the von Restorff effect, participants are given a list of words to commit to memory. The words on the list are all homogenous along a certain dimension except for one item. For example, participants might study the names of 11 birds (e.g., sparrow, pigeon, owl, pelican, etc.), but also see the name of one boat (e.g., kayak). Or they might study 11 numbers (8, 43, 68, etc.) along with one nonsense syllable (XUP) (see Table 9.3). After studying the list, participants are either given a free-recall test or a recognition test. The question of interest is how well recalled or recognized are the distinctive items (in this case, kayak or XUP). The general finding is the distinctive item is recalled or recognized at higher levels than category-consistent words occupying the same serial position. According to distinctiveness, it is the unique encoding of the distinctive item that produces the better memory retention.

In effect, the distinctiveness view disputes the rather circular idea of the levels-of-processing framework that meaning codes are remembered better because they last longer in memory. Meaning codes are remembered better because usually they are more distinctive. This view implies that words processed at a surface level should also be recalled better if the physical features of the words are made particularly distinctive. This has been supported in a number of experimental situations (Kolers & Ostry, 1974; Stein, 1978). Indeed, von Restorff's experiments show that nonsense syllables become more memorable than meaningful words when the nonsense syllable is the isolated item on the list (Hunt, 1995).

Effort of Processing

Consider this sentence: *Understand to hard is sentence this think you perhaps.* What? Did the authors lose their minds? Now try reading that sentence

Table 9.3 The Von Restorff Effect.

List 1	List 2
SALT	LAKE
MUSTARD	VALLEY
PAPRIKA	RIVER
CURRY	TUNDRA
GINGER	CANYON
DILL	CAVE
PARSLEY	PUMPKIN
BISHOP	GLACIER
SESAME	DESERT
OREGANO	RAVINE
CUMIN	CRATER
PEPPER	RIDGE
BASIL	STREAM
GARLIC	MOUNTAIN

backwards. Suddenly it makes sense. Reading sentences backwards takes more effort than normal reading. Some researchers have argued that effort and memory are closely linked. In fact, elaborative rehearsal may lead to stronger memory encoding because it involves more effort than does maintenance rehearsal. Therefore, some researchers have proposed that the effects of processing levels may really depend on the amount of effort or processing capacity involved in coding a given memory (Craik & Simon, 1980; Ellis & Hunt, 1993; Ellis, Thomas, & Rodriguez, 1984).

This idea is based on the notion that we have a limited capacity for processing new inputs (Kahneman, 1973). It is hypothesized that retention will depend on how much of our processing capacity we allocate to the coding of a given memory. The more capacity we use or the more effort we devote to processing a particular input, the better we will retain that input over time. According to this view, semantic processing usually produces better retention, because it involves a greater amount of effort than does processing in terms of physical features.

At least two lines of evidence lend support to this hypothesis. First, some studies have shown that a subject's ability to detect and process one stimulus depends on the level at which he or she is processing a second input. If, for example, a subject is processing words at a semantic level, it is difficult for that subject to detect other stimulus inputs. However, if a subject is processing words in terms of physical features, detection of a second incoming stimulus is much easier (see, for example, Eysenck & Eysenck, 1979). This suggests that semantic processing may require a greater allocation of processing resources than other types of processing do. Second, there is growing evidence that retention does depend on the amount of processing effort involved in coding a memory. One example of this line of research comes from studies dealing with a phenomenon called the *generation effect* (see, for example, Begg, Vinski, Frankovich, & Holgate, 1991; Graf, 1982; Jacoby, 1978; McFarland, Frey, & Rhodes, 1980; Slamecka & Graf, 1978).

A popular topic of research in recent years (Greene, 1992), the generation effect shows that you remember things better if you thought of them yourself than if someone else tells them to you. It is similar to the idea that you perform a task better if you try it yourself rather than watch someone else do it. Indeed, the generation effect shows that this is true for memory encoding. In the generation effect, memory for items that the subject generates is compared to memory for items provided to the subject by the experimenter. Through clever manipulations, the items themselves can be controlled. Not surprisingly, the self-generated items are better remembered than the experimenter-provided items.

Consider a typical generation-effect experiment. Replicating the generation-effect experiments of Slamecka and Graf (1978), Schwartz and Metcalfe (1992) compared two conditions, a generate condition, in which subjects self-generated the targets in cue-target pairs, and a nongenerate condition, in which subjects read

Table 9.4 The Generation Effect.

At Time of Encoding		At Time of Test
light—F	(generate item)	save —
long—SONG	(read item)	lamp —
seat—M	(generate item)	hold —
ring—K	(generate item)	long —
house—MOUSE	(read item)	seat —
save—CAVE	(read item)	light —
Lamp—D	(generate item)	house —
hold—COLD	(read item)	ring —

both the cues and targets provided by the researcher. In the generate condition, subjects were presented with the cue word and the first letter of the to-be-generated target word, as in *seat—m* _____. They were instructed to generate a word that rhymed with the cue and started with the letter provided. Nearly every subject (98%) would generate the word *meat*. This could be compared to the read condition, in which subjects simply saw *house-mouse* (see Table 9.4). Under these conditions, later recall performance was better for the self-generated words than for the read words (see Figure 9.3). Slamecka and Graf (1978) found this effect under a number of generating rules, such as synonyms (e.g., *fast—quick*), antonyms (e.g., "tall—short") and associates (e.g., *cloak—dagger*).

Thus, one way to interpret the levels of processing data is to say that deeper levels of processing require more effort than do shallow processing levels. This interpretation, however, is not necessarily incompatible with the coding-distinctiveness idea discussed earlier. It is certainly possible that greater processing effort leads to a more distinctive memory code (see, for example, Jacoby, 1978). Thus, these two views concerning processing levels may actually focus on the same underlying mechanisms. Indeed, the theoretical explanation of the generation effect has been elusive (Green, 1992), but it is certainly a variable that improves memory encoding.

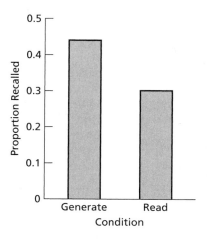

FIGURE 9.3 Results of Testing the Effect of Generation on Retention.

Elaborative Processing

Elaborative processing means that new information being encoded into memory is related to other already-learned information. Elaboration is the process by which we encode new targets by relating them to already known facts (Anderson & Reder, 1979). Relating information to existing information can lead to better memory performance.

Elaborative or relational processing has been used to explain phenomena that usually are explained by levels of processing. It has also been used to explain generation effects. McDaniel, Wadill, and Einstein (1988) argue that the advantage of generated items over read items is explicable because generated items are related to self-knowledge and existing memory structures. The act of generating forces one into invoking elaborative processing in a way that simply reading the association cannot. Indeed, many books on memory improvement list relational processing as an important mnemonic aid.

Retrieval Conditions Matter

The effects of encoding can be assessed only by testing. Therefore, any study of encoding necessarily depends upon the retrieval conditions given.

Semantic processing may produce a memory code that is more useful, given the kinds of retention tests normally employed in experiments. It may well be that with retention tests of certain kinds, surface processing may produce the best performance. It is interesting to note that several studies have found that retention performance depends *jointly* on the level of processing and the type of information requested on a retention test (see, for example, Bransford, Franks, Morris, & Stein, 1979; Stein, 1978).

Fisher and Craik (1977) provided a particularly striking example of this view. They were interested in whether the levels of processing were dependent upon the kind of test given to subjects at the time of retrieval. To study this, they used a design similar to that of Craik and Tulving (1975). It was similar in that both experiments used orienting tasks to promote differing levels of processing through incidental learning. However, Fisher and Craik varied the conditions at retrieval as well.

Like Craik and Tulving, Fisher and Craik used one of three kinds of questions for their orienting task. The first asked whether a word rhymed with the target word, the second asked whether the target was a member of a given category, and the third asked whether the target would fit into a particular sentence. The levels-of-processing approach would predict that rhyme encoding would lead to worse recall than the category question or the sentence-context question. However, Fisher and Craik also introduced a variable during the testing phase, a cued recall test. Fisher and Craik varied the kind of cue that subjects saw. Some cues were rhymes, others were categories, and still others were sentence contexts. Thus, one-third of the cues were identical to the orienting task during study. Fisher and Craik found that recall was highest when the original orienting item was given as the cue for recall, even when the subject had originally used a rhyme as the orienting task (see Table 9.5, p. 276).

Table 9.5 Proportions of Words Recalled as a Function of Encoding Questions and Retrieval Cues (Experiment 1)

	ENCODING QUESTION							
	POSITIVE RESPONSES				NEGATIVE RESPONSES			
Retrieval Cue	Rhyme	Category	Sentence	M	Rhyme	Category	Sentence	M
Rhyme	.40	.43	.29	.37	.26	.28	.28	.27
Category	.15	.81	.46	.47	.10	.28	.11	.16
Sentence	.10	.50	.51		.15	.25	.16	
M	.22	.58	.51		.15	.25	.16	

Note that this result is not completely consistent with the predictions of levels of processing, which predict that deeper encoding creates stronger memory traces, which are then better recalled. Deep encoding did have a main effect: Overall semantic encoding led to better performance. However, in Fisher and Craik deeper encoding did not *always* lead to better memory performance. Indeed, when the retrieval cues were rhymes, memory performance was highest for those items that had been encoded during the rhyming-orienting task. Thus, at least under some circumstances, shallow processing leads to better memory performance.

There is no clear resolution to this issue. It is obvious that retention is strongly affected by the type of processing in which a person engages. However, it remains unclear why different types of processing have these effects. In any event, the levels-of-processing approach has had an important impact on the study of memory formation. Although most researchers reject some of the original ideas of levels of processing—such as one memory system underlying both long-term and short-term memory—it has given rise to countless studies concerning the nature of memory processes. Moreover, under most circumstances, deeper levels of processing do lead to stronger memory traces. Such studies have clearly increased our understanding of how memory formation occurs.

DIMENSIONS OF ENCODING

One of the questions professors of learning and memory are most frequently asked is "How can I improve my memory?" Many people find that they forget important information when they most need it and do not remember the names of people they should know. Others feel that their lives would be enhanced if they could acquire new information more speedily. People realize that they would be better able to do their jobs, study for exams, and indeed, have more time for recreational activity if their memories were better.

Some dimensions of encoding are not within a person's control. More familiar, more meaningful, and more associatively strong information is better encoded. However, there are some ways in which people can improve their memory-encoding skills. Some people want a quick fix, an easy and guaranteed method that helps them remember. Such magic does not exist. But for people who are willing to work a little at improving their memory, there are a number of ways to study and encode information that will improve subsequent performance. As our previous discussion of effortful processing implies, improving memory takes hard work and diligence, but it can be done. In the following sections, we will explore a number of variables that affect encoding, and we will discuss why they affect encoding.

Historical Antecedents

In 1885, Herman Ebbinghaus, a German psychologist, carried out the landmark study on memory (Ebbinghaus, 1885; 1964). In Ebbinghaus's time, most psychologists thought that higher-level cognitive processes such as memory could not be studied scientifically. To those psychologists, research should look only at basic level sensory and perceptual issues. Introducing a methodology that is still current in memory research today, Ebbinghaus conducted a study that demonstrated that memory could be studied in scientifically meaningful ways.

When Ebbinghaus began to study verbal associations, his primary interest was in the effect of procedural variables in the rate of learning. For example, he was concerned with how factors such as the spacing and number of learning trials influenced acquisition of a serial list. He was interested in the issues of forgetting, relearning, and saving. He also invented a method for calibrating materials that revolutionized the way research addressed memory.

Early in his studies Ebbinghaus recognized the difficulties of studying the effects of these procedural variables using real words as the items to be learned. He realized that his own familiarity with the words he used had a powerful effect on the rate of learning and that this effect often overshadowed the influence of the procedural variables he wanted to study. For this reason, Ebbinghaus decided to use lists of syllables instead of real words in his learning experiments. He developed a set of three-letter syllables called *trigrams,* which consisted of either a consonant-vowel-consonant sequence (a CVC trigram) or three consonants in a row (a CCC trigram). He believed that all these syllables, called nonsense syllables, would be relatively meaningless to a human subject—thus, learning would not be as contaminated by a subject's prior verbal experiences.

The use of nonsense syllables in verbal learning experiments has been extensive, especially when such research has focused on procedural variables. It should be noted, however, that even trigrams have differential meanings among subjects. Glaze (1928), for example, presented 2,000 nonsense syllables and asked subjects to indicate whether the syllables were meaningful to them. He found wide variations in meaningfulness of different trigrams. As you might imagine, even though neither *BAL* nor *ZEQ* constitutes a real word, the syllable *BAL* is meaningful to most subjects, whereas *ZEQ* has little meaning. Thus, most of the syllables commonly used in verbal learning studies have been carefully scaled with respect to their meaningfulness (see, for example, Archer, 1960). By scaling these syllables, it is possible to make certain that one list of syllables is no more meaningful than another, so that procedural variables may be studied without the distorting effect of word meanings. Having established a method whereby he could look at procedural variables without contamination, Ebbinghaus explored the development of new memories, how associations are formed between items in memory, and how these memories fade with time and disuse.

In addition to the methodological contribution that Ebbinghaus made, he also made a number of important empirical discoveries. For example, he first observed the spacing effect. The spacing effect refers to the observation that a second study trial is a greater advantage for learning if it does not occur immediately after the initial study trial. Although Ebbinghaus used nonsense syllables, the effects he observed have been replicated with many more realistic kinds of information in recent years (see, for example, Dempster, 1996).

Learning and Practice

The fact that practice helps a person remember information is obvious. It almost seems superfluous to include it in a textbook on learning and memory. Most professors tell students to study each day to best learn the material. However, many of us wind up "cramming," or doing all of our studying the night before our examination.

But is the conventional wisdom correct? Should we *distribute* our study over an extended period of time, or should we *mass* it immediately before test. The answer is twofold. The ideal learner studies over an extended period of time and then concentrates his or her study just before the time of test. We consider this issue in the next section.

The Spacing Effect

Consider a student trying to learn vocabulary in a new language. Most people cannot acquire words in a new language without considerable study and reinforcement. Usually, they must study the items a few times before mastering them. If we need to repeat study of a particular item to remember it, is there an ideal way to space those repetitions? For example, if a person is trying to learn English-French pair, *sometimes—quelquefois,* should the second study trial of the pair occur right after the first, should the person intersperse it with other items, or should there be a time delay? From Ebbinghaus onward, research suggests that learning is more efficient when two study trials of the same item are spaced.

The spacing effect occurs when subjects are allowed more than one study trial. In general, memory performance is maximized when study trials for a particular item are separated in time or by the interim study of other items. This was formalized in Jost's law: "If two associations are of equal strength but of different age, a new repetition has a greater value for the older one" (McGeoch, 1943). Although most researchers nowadays would not consider the spacing effect a law, countless studies have documented that memory improves more when there is a lag between one study trial for a particular item and the next study trial for that item (Dempster, 1996).

For example, Glover and Corkhill (1987) tested subjects' memory for studied paragraphs. The subjects studied the paragraphs twice. Some were given their second study session immediately after the first session, whereas the other half were given a 30-minute break between studying. Consistent with the spacing effect, those subjects who were given a 30-minute interval between successive study sessions did better than those who had a 0-minute interval. Similarly, Dempster (1987) found that a 48-hour interval was superior to a 30-minute interval. Moreover, the spacing effect can be observed for verbal and nonverbal material, and classroom information as well as laboratory stimuli (Dempster, 1996).

Encoding Variability. One explanation of the spacing effect centers on the concept of encoding variability (Martin, 1978; Melton, 1972; Greene, 1990). Encoding variability means that greater differences in environmental and mental conditions occur when there is greater spacing between two study trials. These differences in conditions allow subjects to remember to use different associations and cues to encode the target item. These different associations and cues then make the item more memorable later. Greene (1992) compares encoding variability to leaving a different copy of an important paper in every room in your house. You will be less likely to forget the paper before you leave your house if you have a copy everywhere than if it were only in one room. Similarly, the multiple associations caused by studying the item under different conditions create a memory less likely to be forgotten. Because the mental and environmental conditions differ more when there is a greater lag between one presentation and the next, increased spacing will lead to better retention. Thus, encoding variability offers a potential explanation for the spacing effect.

Massed and Distributed Practice

Consider two students preparing for an exam. The first student waits until the day before the exam to begin studying. Then the student spends the entire day preparing for the test. The second student studies for a little while each day for several weeks before the exam, so that by the time the day before the exam arrives, he or she feels little necessity to study. Many of us guess that the second student will do better on the exam—

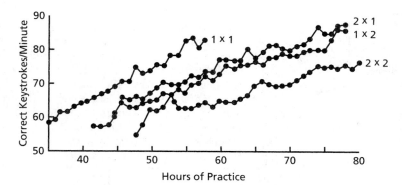

FIGURE 9.4 The Role of Distributed Practice. Rate of acquisition of typing skill for a range of training schedules: 1 × 1 = 1 session of 1 hour per day; 2 × 1 = 2 sessions of 1 hour per day; 1 × 2 = 1 session of 2 hours per day; and 2 × 2 = 2 sessions of 2 hours per day. From Baddeley and Longman (1978).

although there are more students similar to the first. The first student is said to be engaging in massed practice, study of particular items all at once. In contrast, the second student is engaging in distributed practice, study spaced out over a number of hours, days, or weeks.

Most research suggests that distributed practice leads to better long-term retention. For example, about 20 years ago, the British Post Office needed to teach a large number of its employees how to type. They asked two cognitive psychologists to devise an optimal practice regimen for the postal workers learning to type. Baddeley and Longman (1978) devised an experiment to study the effects of massed versus distributed practice with touch typing.

Four different groups were tested. In the first group, the employees practiced typing one hour per day. The second group practiced two hours per day. The third group had two sessions per day, each of one hour. The fourth group had two sessions per day, each for two hours. Performance was measured by the mean number of keystrokes per minute by the end of any training session. Note, here, that the amount of study per day varies from condition to condition. To compare groups one must first equate for numbers of hours actually practiced. The comparison was made on efficiency, or which group was typing better after *20 hours* of practice. As you can see from Figure 9.4, the group that studies one hour per day outperforms the other groups when the

amount of total practice time is equated. The group that has two separate one-hour study sessions per day outperforms the group that studies once for two hours each day. Therefore, these data strongly suggest that, in terms of learning efficiency, distributed practice is better than massed practice.

In general, distributed practice is superior to massed practice. However, Landauer and Bjork (1978) thought that, under some circumstances, massed practice might still lead to better performance, especially if it was combined with later distributed practice. Landauer and Bjork (1978) wanted to determine an optimal learning algorithm. They suspected that there may be some advantages to massed study if it was combined with distributed practice. They thought that massed study might allow easy acquiring (if easy forgetting), thereby establishing a memory trace that could then be strengthened by distributed practice. Therefore, Landauer and Bjork reasoned that an optimal learning strategy could be achieved by combining aspects of distributed practice with aspects of massed practice.

The technique they developed is known as *expanding rehearsal.* Expanding rehearsal means a gradual transition from massed to distributed practice. The massed practice establishes the memory trace, and the distributed practice keeps it from fading. Before considering the details of the expanding-rehearsal experiment employed by Landauer and Bjork, it is important to understand

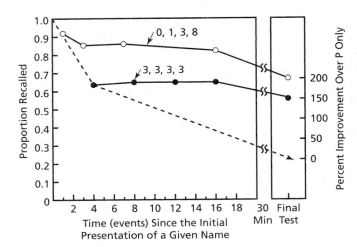

FIGURE 9.5 Results of a Study Using the Expanding Rehearsal Procedure. Three conditions are tested, a single presentation (P only), four presentations each separated by three other items (3, 3, 3, 3) and an expanding-rehearsal schedule in which number of items between successive presentations is increased (0, 1, 3, 8). From Landauer and Bjork (1978). From M.M. Gruneberg, et. al., *Practical Aspects of Memory,* pp. 625–632. Reprinted by permission of Academic ress, UK.

the other memory-enhancing technique they used in their study, the *retrieval-practice effect.*

Retrieval practice means that subjects are given an initial test as preparation for a later final test. It is similar to a technique many people spontaneously use while studying. Test yourself to see if you have learned the information. The testing can indicate which items require further study. However, Bjork and Bjork (1992) and others have shown that a retrieval-practice trial is a potent learning event in and of itself. Indeed, retrieval-practice trials are better at promoting long-term retention than is a learning trial (in which you study the entire item and do not rely on retrieval).

Landauer and Bjork combined these two ideas in a convincing experiment on how to maximize memory retention. Subjects were asked to learn English-French translation equivalents, such as *the cow—la vache.* In one condition, the subjects received only a single presentation. In the other two conditions, the subjects received five presentations of each word pair. However, the ordering of presentations within those two conditions was different. In one condition, the blocked condition, there was always an initial presentation followed by equally spaced retrieval practice. The spacing always involved three intervening items between each presentation of a

given pair. In this condition, there were five presentations each spaced by three intervening items (indicated as 3, 3, 3, 3). In the expanded rehearsal condition, the initial presentation was also followed by retrieval practice. However, in this condition the first two retrieval-practice trials were back to back (i.e., massed). Following those presentations, the number of intervening items between retrieval-practice trials increased. Thereafter, greater spacing occurred between the items (indicated 0, 1, 3, 8).

The results are quite convincing (see Figure 9.5). Despite the early massed practice, the expanding rehearsal strategy quickly outpaces the spaced condition. It is more effective at producing the correct target both during study (in retrieval-practice trials) and in a final test given 30 minutes later. The implications of this study are clear. First, one can improve one's memory strategy by adopting good learning techniques. Second, the expanding-rehearsal strategy is one of these good learning techniques. Landauer and Bjork's results show that a combination of initial massed practice followed by subsequent distributed practice leads to the best retention and performance.

There is a striking similarity in the results of Landauer and Bjork's study over relatively short retention spans and the results of Bahrick and

Hall's (1991) that we discussed earlier. Bahrick and Hall found that taking college math led to better long-term retention of high school algebra than could be attained without taking college math. In effect, the practice in algebra that occurs during a college math course serves as the expanding rehearsal. The algebra is initially encoded during high school in a massed format (relatively speaking), and the college math provides the later distributed practice, leading to good long-term retention. For college students in particular, the results of expanding rehearsal are worth keeping in mind.

Organization

Practice is not the only way of enhancing encoding. According to Craik and Lockhart (1972), anything that promotes a deeper level of processing will benefit encoding. In other words, semantic or meaning-based processing leads to long-term retention. One of the most important of these meaning-based techniques is organization. In this case, organization means grouping to-be-learned information into conceptual categories. For example, it may be easier to remember the names of 10 animals if we study the birds together and then the reptiles together. People may also use their own indiosyncratic organizational strategies. Organization is important to encoding for two reasons. First, there is an organization to the structure of items that you have stored in memory. New materials that fit this existing organization are more likely to be learned. Second, if there is organization already in the to-be-learned information, this may reduce the number of chunks that have to be encoded, and may allow more rapid assimilation into existing memory representations. For example, most people would find the following set of letters in a memory experiment to be quite difficult:

DIOFRAL NSSUNIHE

However, when confronted with the following set of letters, composed of exactly the same letters, most people would have an easier time of encoding:

FLORIDA SUNSHINE

Obviously, the meaning-based organization allows for much easier encoding. Like the levels-of-processing approach, organization stresses meaning-based processing. When you organize the above letter sequences, the meaning of the second example allows for easy encoding. Organization in memory has far-reaching consequences.

Subjective organization refers to the idiosyncratic meaning-based structures that each person maintains. Endel Tulving coined the term to describe a phenomenon he observed in experiments that involved the repeated presentation and retrieval of word lists (Tulving, 1962). This organization is based on each person's unique set of knowledge. Thus for one person the word pair *captain-carbon* may elicit no special association, whereas for another it may evoke memories of childhood cartoon heroes. Tulving assumed that these structures may be constructed as people learn information. Because subjects do use meaning-based encoding strategies to acquire new information, items will be linked in a person-specific manner.

Tulving tested these ideas in an experiment in which participants studied a list of words for free recall. This technique allowed participants to report all items, but in any order, with no experimenter-provided cues. The participants were then tested for those words. Following the initial study and test, participants again studied the words, but in a new random order. Again, they were tested for recall. This pattern was repeated several times. Tulving showed that as the number of recall tests increased, participants were more and more likely to report the words in particular sequences. For example, even when new random orders were presented, participants continued to output the items in the same manner they had done on earlier lists. Tulving argued that participants were developing organizational structures for the items that superseded the input structure.

Tulving's experiment was done in the context of the laboratory. But do people in real-life situations really use subjective organization to help them remember information? One set of studies comes from people who are required to remember a lot of information on the job, for example waiters and bartenders (Erickson, 1988). In many restaurants and bars, the wait staff does not write down customers' orders. Rather they use unique subjective organizations to help them remember people's orders. Beach (1988) studied both novice and experienced bartenders. The initial observation centered on the better memory of experienced bartenders in remembering the orders of customers. Beach was curious about whether the experienced bartenders had a more elaborate organizational framework for encoding the drink orders. Beach found that the expert bartenders placed a glass on the bar as the customer ordered. They would place a different kind of glass (mug, shot glass, wineglass, etc.) depending on the drink the customer ordered. The kind of glass then served as a retrieval cue for the order. Different kinds of glasses code for different kinds of drinks. In this way, bartenders can remember a great many drink orders without having to write them down.

Imagery

One of the most interesting and well-studied areas of memory encoding regards the effects of visual imagery on encoding in long-term memory. The use of imagery techniques to improve encoding and subsequent memory performance has a long and distinguished history. For the ancient Greeks, rote memory was a great and important skill. Because books were not widely available, most knowledge was only obtainable by listening to speeches. The ability to memorize large speeches became extremely important for both teachers (the orators) and students—who needed to memorize what they heard because it could not be also be acquired in books. It is widely believed that some ancient Greeks had far superior abilities to retain verbatim information than do most people today.

Perhaps the oldest recorded story involving the use of visual imagery is by the Greek poet Simonides in 477 B.C. According to the legend, Simonides was asked to give a speech at a large banquet in honor of the gods Castor and Pollux. The banquet was sponsored by a nobleman named Scopas. When Simonides arrived, Scopas offered to pay him only half the sum that had been agreed upon and challenged the gods themselves to pay the rest. Simonides agreed to give the speech anyway, despite the cut in pay. Angered by Scopas's disrespect, the gods decided to destroy the banquet. They sent a messenger to Simonides and called him out of the room. Just as he left the room, the banquet hall collapsed, killing Scopas and all the guests present except Simonides. Simonides had memorized exactly where every guest had been seated, and was therefore able to identify each body for the families (see Yates, 1966). Although this story may seem a bit violent and gruesome for a textbook on learning and memory, it is generally considered the first recorded use of imagery-based learning.

In modern times, memory-enhancement books have become big business (e.g., Fry, 1992; Higbee, 1977), and memory-enhancement specialists often end up on talk shows. The chief techniques taught by these books and shown off by their promulgators are based upon visual-imagery strategies. The question for memory researchers is whether or not these strategies really work. The answer is that they *can* work very well in some circumstances, but only in some circumstances. Indeed, in some circumstances, ordinary rote rehearsal may actually be preferable (Thomas and Wang, 1996). We will now review the major imagery techniques.

Method of Loci. In the method of loci, people learn to associate new to-be-learned items with a series of previously well-learned physical locations. The key to using the method involves visualizing a well-known place, such as your grandmother's house in the country or the buildings on your college campus. Then designate a

FIGURE 9.6 Illustration of the Loci Method. Items to be remembered: hot dogs, cat food, tomatoes, bananas, whiskey. Locations: driveway, garage, front door, closet, kitchen sink. (After Bower, 1970a). From "Analysis of a Mnemonic Device," by Gordon H. Bower, 1970. *American Scientist, 58,* 497–499. Copyright ©1970 Sigma Xi Science Research Society. Reprinted by permission.

series of landmarks as memory loci: the picket fence, the mailbox, the big maple tree, or the library, the biology building, and the cafeteria. Then associate each item of the to–be–learned information with the designated loci.

Assume you have the following serial list of items to learn: *dog, lamp, book, flower, sofa, horse, table,* and *chalk*. To learn the list you must not only learn each word, but you must also remember the order of presentation. One simple procedure for learning the list is to imagine each item at one of the spatial locations in your imaginary trip. For example, you might begin by forming an image of a dog (the first word in your list) sitting by the maple tree in front of your grandmother's house. You would then form an image linking the next word in your list to the second location in your trip. Once comparable images have been formed for each item, remembering the items in order is simple. All you have to do is imagine yourself walking from your grandmother's house. Each landmark you pass reminds you of the corresponding word in the list. In effect, you maintain the order of a new list by linking it to an imaginary list of spatial locations that already has a familiar order (see Figure 9.6).

This imagery strategy may sound complex. However, with minimal practice participants usually become proficient at it. Groninger (1971), for example, instructed college students to imagine a sequence of 25 spatial locations on their campus. He then gave the subjects a list of 25 words to learn using the method of loci. Students who used the technique showed significantly better recall of the 25 words than subjects who were given no imagery instructions.

Crovitz (1971) showed that memory loci improved performance when participants had more loci available. In his study, the participants were asked to learn a list of English words. They were also given a set of picture cards with which they could associate the words. Some groups of participants did not receive any cards, whereas other groups received up to 32 cards (the number of words in the list). The more cards that participants had to use as loci the better their memory performance was (see Figure 9.7, p. 284). Similar facilitation using the method of loci has been reported in other experiments.

Pegword Technique. A second imagery strategy that is highly related to the method of loci is the pegword technique. To use this technique, a

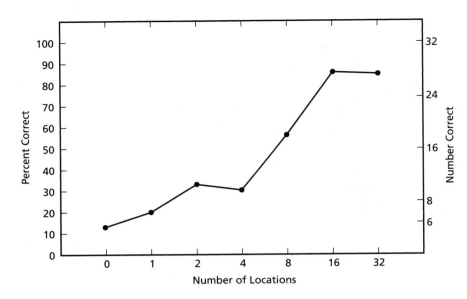

FIGURE 9.7 Recall of Items in Their Correct Order as a Function of the Number of Locations. From "The Capacity of Memory Loci in Artificial Memory," by J. F. Crovitz, 1971, *Psychonomic Science, 24,* 187–188. Copyright © 1971 by the Psychonomic Society, Inc. Reprinted by permission.

subject must begin by knowing a list of items in some order. For example, if you have a favorite major league baseball team, you probably know the names of the starting players and the order in which they usually bat. Alternatively, you may remember the grammar school teachers that you had in each of the first six grades. If you know such a list, you can use it to learn a novel list in much the same way as you would use the method of loci, simply by forming an image that links the first item in your familiar list with the first item in the novel list (see Figure 9.8). You would then form images for each subsequent pair of items from the two lists. To remember the novel list, you would merely recite the familiar list, and each item on it would serve as a cue for a novel list item. Several studies have documented the effectiveness of the pegword technique (Paivio, 1969).

Keyword Technique. The keyword technique was designed to allow the use of mental imagery in the learning of new vocabulary items. This method has been used with great success in the learning foreign-language vocabulary (see Bellezza, 1996; Desrochers & Begg,

1987). In the keyword technique, you identify a salient aspect of the to-be-learned word, make a visual image to that word, and then associate the visual image with the word's meaning. For example, suppose that you are learning French, and you need to remember the verb *endormir,* which means "to sleep." From the word *endormir,* you might imagine yourself sleeping in your college *dorm.* In this way, you form a chain of associations. When you encounter the word *endormir,* you think of the English word *dorm,* and you conjure up the image of yourself asleep in a college dorm-room. Kasper and Glass (1988) found that subjects learned more foreign-language vocabulary using the keyword technique than by simple rote repetition (see Table 9.6, p. 286).

On the other hand, a series of recent studies by Alvin Wang and Margaret Thomas (Thomas & Wang, 1996; Wang & Thomas, 1992, 1995) serve as a warning concerning the usefulness of the keyword technique for acquiring vocabulary in a new language. Wang and Thomas noticed that most studies testing the keyword mnemonic tested at relatively short retention interval. Earlier studies in their lab suggested that with time,

Number	Peg target	Interactive image

FIGURE 9.8 **The Peg-Word Technique.** In the peg-word technique, images of to-be-remembered material are linked visually to images of specific rhyme cues, or pegs. Here, an image of a bun from the rhyme "one is a bun" is linked to an image of an overdue library book, an image of a shoe is linked to an image of dog chow, and shirts are imagined to be hanging from a tree. The interactive visual image produces an elaborative memory tree, and the peg "cues" are easy to access.

forgetting occurred just as rapidly with the key-word technique as with other methods (see Mc-Daniel, Pressley, & Dunay, 1987). Wang and Thomas were concerned about the educational implications of this finding. Surely, the keyword technique could boost acquisition over the shorter periods of time, such as the delay between the study session the night before and the test the next morning, but they worried whether people would maintain this information over longer periods of time.

One concern of Wang and Thomas is that the keyword technique seems to run contrary to the principles of levels of processing. The linking keyword is often something that relates the appearance of a word to a *similar looking* word in English. This would be classified as shallow processing in the levels-of-processing model.

Table 9.6 A Sample of 20 Russian Words with Related Keywords. From "An Application of the Mnemonic Keyword Method to the Acquisition of a Russian Vocabulary," by R. C. Atkinson and M. R. Raugh, 1975, *Journal of Experimental Psychology: Human Learning and Memory, 104,* pp. 126–133. Copyright 1975 by the American Psychological Association. Reprinted by permission.

RUSSIAN	KEYWORD	TRANSLATION
VNIMÁNIE	[pneumonia]	ATTENTION
DÉLO	[jello]	AFFAIR
ZÁPAD	[zap it]	WEST
STRANÁ	[straw man]	COUNTRY
TOLPÁ	[tell pa]	CROWD
LINKÓR	[Lincoln]	BATTLESHIP
ROT	[rut]	MOUTH
GORÁ	[garage]	MOUNTAIN
DURÁK	[two rocks]	FOOL
ÓSEN	[ocean]	AUTUMN
SÉVER	[saviour]	NORTH
DYUM	[dim]	SMOKE
SELÓ	[seal law]	VILLAGE
GOLOVÁ	[Gulliver]	HEAD
USLÓVIE	[Yugoslavia]	CONDITION
DÉVUSHKA	[dear vooshka]	GIRL
TJÓTJA	[Churchill]	AUNT
PÓEZD	[poised]	TRAIN
KROVÁT	[cravat]	BED
CHELOVEK	[chilly back]	PERSON

However, levels of processing suggest that deeper meaning-based encoding is better. Therefore, levels of processing suggests that the keyword technique may be a temporary artifact of phonological similarities between the two languages. Instead, Wang and Thomas (1995) suggest that using strategies that emphasize the semantic context will result in better long-term retention, even if they suffer, relative to the keyword technique, under relatively short delays.

Wang and Thomas (1995) compared the keyword technique with semantic-context encoding in an interesting experiment. Participants were taught 24 vocabulary words in Tagalog, a language of the Philippines spoken by few American college students. Half of the participants learned via the keyword method. They were shown a Tagalog word followed by an English keyword followed by the English translation (e.g., *SALAMIN—salmon—eyeglasses*). Under these presentation conditions, most subjects would construct mental images of a funny-looking fish wearing glasses. In the semantic-context condition, they saw the Tagalog word in the appropriate context in two English sentences (e.g., *In order to read the menu, the man took out his SALAMIN and put them on*, and *Because of her diminished eyesight, the doctor prescribed SALAMIN*). Tests were given twice, once five minutes later, and a second time, two days later. In the tests participants were given the Tagalog word and asked to provide its English equivalent. The keyword was not given when the participants were tested.

Wang and Thomas found that at the five-minute delay, the keyword method resulted in higher recall than the semantic-context encoding. However, at the two-day delay, they found the pattern reversed. Recall was better after semantic-context encoding than with the keyword method. This is illustrated graphically in Figure 9.9.

Educational purposes are served by long-term retention, retention spans of time longer than five minutes. We want students to remember the information we teach them on the scale of years not minutes. Therefore, Wang and Thomas's results may suggest that the keyword technique in fact does people a disservice. Wang and Thomas argue that it may be premature to dismiss this encoding strategy. It has advantages at short delays and allows for rapid learning of paired associate stimuli. However, it does not promote retention over longer intervals. Therefore, Wang and Thomas suggest that people combine methods. They suggest that people initially learn new vocabulary using keyword methods, but then use deeper-level semantic strategies after the initial learning. The keyword method is not sufficient by itself, but may boost performance over longer

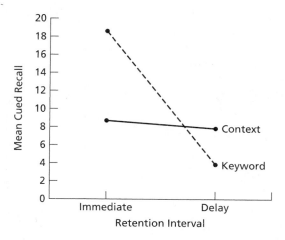

FIGURE 9.9 Retention Interval.

periods of time when it is combined with semantic encoding.

Notice that Wang and Thomas's conclusions are similar to those reached by Landauer and Bjork (1978). Rather than suggesting distributed practice is always better than massed practice, Landauer and Bjork suggest a mix of the two—massed study followed right away by distributed study. The latter suggest initial imagery-based learning be followed by subsequent meaning-based encoding. Perhaps the way to a good memory is to incorporate many of the learning strategies suggested here.

Imagery Mnemonics vs. Imagery-Based Memories

The method of loci, the pegword method, and the keyword technique are, in a sense, tricks. They allow us to learn information quickly, but often at the expense of deeper meaning, as the Wang and Thomas studies reveal. For example, one could acquire a large French or Tagalog vocabulary without being able to communicate in the language. Or perhaps one could learn the names of all the amino acids, useful in the study of biochemistry without understanding how these chemicals combine in proteins. The

mnemonic tricks are useful, but only to those who also enlist semantic processing in learning.

The use of imagery mnemonics is usually in the service of learning verbal information. It is obvious that under many conditions, manipulations that encourage the use of imagery facilitate encoding. Still, the effectiveness of the image-forming strategy depends on a variety of factors. First of all, some words provoke less vivid images than others. Although it is easy to form an image of an elephant, it is quite difficult to form an image that represents for example, justice. Paivio (1971) has suggested that our ability to form an image of a word depends on the word's concreteness. Concrete nouns represent visible objects in the environment. On the other hand, words such as *justice, integrity,* and *freedom* are abstract because instead of naming objects, they name states of being or nonphysical characteristics. According to Paivio, image-forming strategies are most effective when concrete terms are used simply because they provoke more vivid images.

A second factor that influences imagery effectiveness is the type of image a subject uses or is instructed to use. This point was illustrated by Wollen, Weber, and Lowry (1972) who sought to test the often-cited assumption that bizarre or unusual images are more effective than common images when it comes to learning verbal items. The experimenters gave subjects a list of paired-associates to learn. All the items were names for concrete objects. Instead of instructing the subjects to form images of each item pair together, they supplied pictures of each item pair and instructed the subjects to form an image of each picture. For example, if the words to be associated were *cigar* and *piano,* the subjects were shown a picture that contained a cigar and a piano in some arrangement.

In this experiment, however, the pictures of item pairs differed along two dimensions. First, some pictures contained bizarre or strange illustrations of the objects, while others contained ordinary drawings. Second, some pictures showed the two items together so that the items appeared to be interacting in some way. Other pictures

Noninteracting, Nonbizarre

Noninteracting, Bizarre

Interacting, Nonbizarre

Interacting, Bizarre

FIGURE 9.10 Examples of Noninteracting and Interacting Images. Examples of pictures used by Wollen, Weber, and Lowry (1972) to induce subjects to form images of different kinds. From *Cognitive Psychology,* Vol. 3, 518–523. © 1972 by Academic Press, reproduced by permission of the publisher. All rights reserved.

showed the items separately. Using such combinations produced four types of pictures, bizarre-interacting, bizarre-noninteracting, common-interacting, and common-noninteracting. Figure 9.10 contains examples of these four picture types of the words *cigar* and *piano.*

The results of this manipulation were surprising. Subjects who were encouraged to use interacting images learned the list of words better than those given the noninteracting pictures. However, the use of bizarre images did nothing to improve performance. Apparently, the effectiveness of image formation depends on how close together two objects are within the image. Once an interacting image had been formed, it seems to matter very little whether the image is commonplace or unusual. The same finding has been reported when young children, rather than young adults, are used as subjects.

In all of the mnemonic techniques and studies discussed in this chapter, imagery was used in the service of verbal learning. The general implication of this trend is that verbal learning is difficult but remembering visual images is easy. Indeed, much of our memory for episodic or autobiographical events is, in fact, visual. We remember the layouts of our houses, the way our grandmothers looked, our first home run in Little League, and so on. Visual memory, indeed, seems to come more naturally to us, and therefore impressing it into the service of verbal learning is adaptive.

Research supports the hypothesis that visual memory is exceptionally good. For example, Standing, Conezio, and Haber (1970) conducted a memory study using pictures of scenes and events. They presented more than 2,000 slides for 10 seconds each. Several days later, the subjects were tested with an old/new recognition test. They were able to identify as old approximately 90% of the slides they had seen earlier. Similarly, Goldstein and Chance (1971) also found good picture memory, not only for photographs of faces, but for magnified snowflakes and inkblots as well. Therefore, memory for visual images is rather good and we can capitalize on this when we engage in imagery techniques.

Paivio (1971) argued that we have two different ways of representing memories. One of these is in terms of a verbal code, in which the memory is stored in terms of its semantic content, or more simply, in words. The other code is an imaginal code, in which the memory is stored as an image or picture. Although this dual-code hypothesis is controversial, it is consistent with the work on imagery mnemonics developed here. Associating or elaborating between the codes may produce the advantages in memory seen when people use imagery techniques.

SUMMARY STATEMENTS

In this chapter, we considered the nature of encoding processes in human memory. We discussed the levels-of-processing framework and emphasized how it stressed both the importance of incidental learning and the importance of meaningful processes. We then considered several alternatives to the levels-of-processing framework. We discussed the theory that distinctive processing leads to good memory traces. We also discussed the theory that effortful processing is necessary for good memory. We also introduced the importance of the retrieval processes in the understanding of memory.

This chapter outlined a number of variables that promote good encoding. It discussed both those that focus on how to allocate study time and those that focus on using imagery to learn verbal information. A good learner uses these strategies expertly.

10

Retrieval from Long-Term Memory

CHAPTER OVERVIEW

Imagine for a moment that you have just purchased a new car. The engine is powerful and fuel efficient. The exterior sparkles, and the design is aerodynamically perfect. The steering and suspension systems enable the car to turn without a wobble. Your new car is ideal for your needs. There is, however, one small problem. The doors are welded shut, the windows will not budge from the closed position, and you do not have the key to the ignition. In other words, you cannot get in! This automobile is capable of doing everything you would want it to do, but its potential cannot be realized because you are unable to gain access to its controls.

In a very real sense, this automobile is what memory systems would be like without retrieval processes. The processes of storage and encoding enable people to represent experiences in memory. The mere fact that people are capable of forming such representations allows unlimited potential for profiting from past experiences. Retrieval is a key to memory stores. It allows access to use of representations at the appropriate time. Quite obviously, the retrieval process is critical if we are to use our memories in an adaptive way.

In its discussions of how memories are formed and represented, this text has alluded several times to the process of retrieval. For example, some researchers have used a participant's retrieval speed as a way of determining how memories are organized. This chapter will examine the retrieval process in more detail, discussing various ideas concerning the nature of retrieval and identifying the factors that appear to influence the procedure by which people access stored memories. The chapter will also discuss how retrieval is involved in the reencoding of a memory.

The process of retrieval from long-term memory is fascinating to almost everyone. The popularity of crossword puzzles and trivia games attests to the satisfaction people get from using subtle cues to retrieve information from long-term memory. By the same token, there are few things more frustrating than not being able to retrieve a fact when it is needed. For example, as Americans we count astronauts among our greatest heros. What was the name of the first person to set foot on the moon? Some people will recall that name instantly, but others, although they feel that they know it, will not be able to come up with the answer. If you cannot recall the name, you may already be experiencing exasperation. (You yourself may even feel as if the name is on the tip of your tongue. The feeling of frustration probably will increase as soon as you realize that this paragraph does not contain the answer.)

There are a number of different theories of long-term memory retrieval. These theories deal with how people use retrieval cues to locate and activate representations in long-term storage. Before going on, however, one piece of data should be supplied. The astronaut's name was Neil Armstrong. (If you have spent the past few moments trying to retrieve that name, you probably need to reread this paragraph. The work involved in retrieval can often interfere with the encoding of new material.)

One of the authors of this text regularly teaches a course on memory. In 1996, during a class discussion on the concept of retrieval, he asked the following question, "What did you do on April 4, 1996?" Even though this day was only a few months earlier, most people could not remember what they did that day when only the date was given as a retrieval cue. There was one student whose birthday was April 4. She remembered the date, but in general, dates of the year are usually not an effective **retrieval cue.** However, when the author told his class that April 4 was Easter Sunday, nearly everyone reported remembering where they had been, who they had been with, and what they had done. Names of holidays appear to be effective retrieval cues. As this chapter will clarify, the concept of a retrieval cue is extremely important to research and theory in memory retrieval.

TESTING MEMORY

Recall from chapter 9 the differences between intentional and incidental learning. Motivation under which retrieval testing occurs is important to consider as well. Two distinct types of retrieval situations must be considered. In one case, **explicit memory testing** (also known as direct testing), specifically asks a person to use his or her memory to retrieve information. For example, suppose the person has been asked to recall the name of the 1996 third-party candidate. He or she may be asked to retrieve the words from a study list or identify a face as having been the person at the crime scene. In each case, this person is aware of the existence of the answer somewhere in his or her memory and is trying to retrieve the information. This type of task is considered an explicit memory test (Richardson-Klavehn & Bjork, 1988).

An **implicit memory test** (also known as indirect testing) does not require a person to use memory to do the test (although the person may do so anyway). The implicit memory task does not require memory retrieval of an earlier episode, but it may make use of such an experience. Performance on the task may be influenced by information in memory without the person necessarily being aware of the influence (Roediger, Weldon, & Challis, 1989; Schacter, 1987). For example, in an experiment by Eich (1984), participants heard sentences such as "They had just enough money to pay the taxi fare," or "The lion's mane was of a soft and tawny fur." Later, participants were given a spelling test. Some of the words were homophones (i.e., two or more words pronounced the same, but spelled differently), such as *"mane/main," "fair/fare,"* or *"bare/bear"*. The participants were not asked to spell the words in the manner of the early sentence. Eich revealed that people did show an increased use for the biased form of the homophone. Thus, although the task did not require retrieval of an earlier event, it did influence task performance on the spelling test. Chapter 11 will consider indirect tests in greater detail.

Recognition Versus Recall

If you have a long list of words to memorize, your memory could be tested for that list in two ways. First, you might report the words on the list from memory. This is considered a recall test. If you are asked to write down all the words on the list without any cues other than the directions to recall the list, it is considered a **free recall** test. If, however, cues are provided to help you remember list items, such as the category certain words fall into, the test is called **cued recall.**

The second procedure we might use to test your memory involves a **recognition** test. That is, at the time of testing you are presented with a long list of words that includes items from the list learned previously, as well as new items not contained in the original list. The new items are usually called **distractor items.** Your task is to choose from the test list words that appeared on the list you were asked to learn. In other words, you see the items you have learned again, and you must simply recognize them among other words on a larger list (see Table 10.1).

Clearly, both recall and recognition tests are valid measures of how much a person remembers. In both cases, to perform well, one must have items represented in memory and be able to retrieve those representations at the time of testing. Yet, scores on recognition tests are usually much higher than scores based on recall.

In one experiment, for example, Shepard (1967) gave participants more than 500 words printed on cards. Then he tested their recognition of these words by means of word pairs. Each pair contained one word the participants had seen before and one distractor word. They were to choose the word in each pair that had been presented earlier. Participants recognized previously presented words about 90% of the time, even though they had seen each word only once. Shepard found that if he used pictures instead of words, recognition scores reached almost 100%, even though he increased the number of original items to 600 or more. Finally, Shepard found that recognition scores did decrease over long

Table 10.1 Recall vs. Recognition.

Name of Test	Retrieval Cue Given
Free recall	No cues given
Cued Recall	Retrieval cue given—person must still generate answer
Old/New Recognition	Target or distracter given—person must identify items presented earlier

retention intervals. However, most participants were still accurate more than 90% of the time when the test came a full week after viewing the original items.

Not all experiments using recognition tests have shown such outstanding results. In fact, there have been a number of situations in which recall performance is actually better than recognition (Watkins, 1974). Still, it is generally accepted that under most circumstances it is easier to recognize an item that has been stored in memory than to recall the same item. Thus any successful retrieval theory must explain why recall and recognition performance often differ.

Recognition is also more prone to errors than is recall. One problem in recognition is that it is often difficult to distinguish the correct answer from distractors that are not too different. Nickerson and Adams (1979) found that people were very poor at identifying the correct configuration of a penny from coins that looked very much like pennies (see Figure 10.1, p. 296). We see pennies all the time, but in the figure it is hard to tell the real penny from the distractors. Difficulty in recognizing the correct person among a lineup of similar distractors is a problem in the legal system as well.

Recall and recognition are ways of *testing* memory, not forms of memory in and of themselves. This is important to keep in mind as we discuss theories of retrieval. Jacoby (1991) argued that there is seldom a one-to-one relation between a given test or task and a given underlying psychological process. Furthermore, varying tests may have different relations to the underlying processes. Originally theories supported the assumption that recall and recognition both reflect the same underlying process, the only difference being that recognition is easier. Later theories assume a more complex relationship between the test and the process.

THEORIES OF RETRIEVAL

Most theories of retrieval agree that we use retrieval cues to locate and activate memory representations, whereupon we decide how to respond. There is some disagreement over how this process actually unfolds. Such disputes have often centered on the issue of whether recall and recognition involve retrieval processes of different kinds.

A Single-Process Model of Retrieval

One early point of view that developed among memory researchers was that recall and recognition involve the same underlying process. This is the process of activating a representation in memory. It is assumed that performance on a retention test depends on the degree to which an item in memory becomes activated. The greater the degree of memory activation, the greater the probability that an item will be remembered. According to this view, the degree of memory activation depends on two factors. First, activation depends on the strength of the memory representation. The stronger the memory representation, the easier it is to activate that representation to a high degree. Second, activation levels depend on the effectiveness of retrieval cues. Cues that are particularly effective may result in high levels of activation, whereas less effective cues may result in lower levels.

This single-process model makes the assumption that the retrieval cues on a recognition test are more effective than those on a recall test. After all, on a recall test, cues usually are merely related to the target item, whereas on a recognition test, the cue is the target item itself. Based on this assumption, this model makes several predictions. First, if an item is weakly represented in memory, there is little likelihood that it will be recalled, because a weak representation combined with less effective retrieval cues will lead to very low levels of activation. On the other hand, the same item may in many cases be recognized, because even though the representation is weak, the cues contained in the recognition test can lead to a high level of activation.

At least two implications of the single-process model appear to be incorrect. First, the model implies that recognition performance should always be better than, or equivalent to, recall performance. There are no circumstances, according to this model, under which recall should exceed recognition. However, as will be shown later in this chapter, there is now reason to question this implication. Some studies have shown that under certain conditions, participants are unable to recognize some items but do appear to be capable of

recalling them (see, for example, Tulving and Thomson, 1973; Watkins, 1974).

A second implication of the single-process model is that performance on recall and on recognition should be similarly affected by the same variables. This implication is based on the idea that both recall and recognition procedures result in the same process—the direct activation of a memory representation. The procedures differ only in the degree of activation they produce. Thus, any variable that leads to the increased strength of a representation should improve performance on both recall and recognition. Variables that reduce the strength of a representation should decrease both types of performance. This implication appears not to be correct. For example, we know that recall is better for words that are frequently used in our language than for less frequently used words (compare the high-frequency word *house* to the low-frequency word *kiosk*) (see Table 10.2). Word frequency has the opposite effect, however, on recognition performance (see Figure 10.2). When asked to recognize words from a previously presented list, participants tend to perform better with low-frequency words than they do with high frequency words (see Kintsch, 1970; Kinoshita, 1995). Such different effects would be unlikely if

Table 10.2 Examples of High- and Low-Frequency Words*

HIGH FREQUENCY	LOW FREQUENCY
act	harp
clay	ban
cold	matte
eye	fallow
river	taper
play	syntax
sun	equinox
farm	myrrh
college	orchard
husband	pawn

*adapted from Harley & Brown, 1998.
From the *British Journal of Psychology,* Vol. 89, Part I, pp. 151–174.
Reprinted by permission of the British Psychological Society.

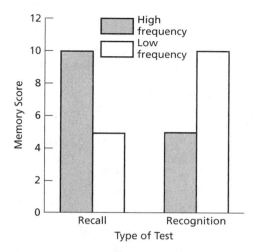

FIGURE 10.2 Effect of Word Frequency on Recognition Performance.

recall and recognition tests induced retrieval in the same way.

The Generation–Recognition Hypothesis.

Because of the problems associated with a single-process model, another type of retrieval theory has become popular. This view, proposed by Kintsch (1970), is often called the **generation-recognition hypothesis.** According to this view, the recognition of an item proceeds much as suggested by the single-process model. On a recognition test, that is, the presentation of an item can directly activate the representation of that item in memory. If such an activation occurs, an individual decides that the item has been presented before. If there is no activation (or only a weak one), the individual may decide that the item has not been presented in the past. Thus, recognition consists of a decision-making process based on how strongly a representation in memory is activated by some test item. This decision making is labeled the **recognition process** in Kintsch's theory.

Whereas Kintsch's hypothesis views recognition as involving only the single decision-making process, it suggests that recall most often requires an additional step before a decision can be made. The additional step is necessary because the retrieval cues presented on a recall test are incapable of directly activating the target memory. Instead, these cues activate their own representations in memory, whereupon the activation spreads to other related representations. Assuming that a given retrieval cue is strongly related to the target stimulus, this spread of activation eventually results in the activation of the target memory; consequently retrieval of that memory can occur. This spread of activation from the retrieval cue representation to the target memory is called the generation or search process.

When the generation process has been completed, Kintsch assumes that recognition or decision making begins, working the same way in recall as it would on a recognition test. That is, a participant decides whether an item has been presented before based on the degree to which the target memory is activated. Recall and recognition are presumed to be similar in that both kinds of tests involve a decision-making step. However, recall involves a prior search process that is not necessary when a recognition test is used.

Kintsch's model explains why some variables might affect recall and recognition differently. Basically, the generation-recognition hypothesis predicts that any variable that affects the strength of an item representation in memory should affect recall and recognition performance in the same manner. This is reasonable because increasing the strength of an item's representation should lead to greater activation of the target memory and easier decision making. Thus, manipulations such as increasing the degree of learning for an item should improve both recall and item recognition. This prediction is in accord with the existing data.

On the other hand, variables that affect the organization or the relation between representations in memory would be expected to influence recall, but not recognition. This prediction is based on the idea that the organization of items in memory determines the success of the search process but should have little to do with decision making once the search has been completed. This prediction is supported by data from a number of experiments.

The generation-recognition hypothesis can also explain why a variable such as word frequency might affect recall and recognition. It is reasonable to assume that frequently used words (e.g., *boat*) are more strongly associated with other words than are less frequently used words (e.g., *skiff*) (see Table 10.2). These strong associations should facilitate the process of searching through a network of related items. On the other hand, word frequency might be expected to have a detrimental influence on decision making after an item representation has been activated. To illustrate how word frequency might influence decision making, imagine that you are being tested on a list of commonly used words that you have just learned. The test is a recognition test containing both the learned items and, as distractors, words that are frequently used. If a test item leads to the activation of an item representation, it may be difficult to decide whether activation is occurring because the word was on the list or because the word is commonly used and therefore strongly represented in memory. There is a certain likelihood of incorrectly citing distractor words, because these words should be as strongly represented in memory as the listed words.

Based on this line of reasoning, it is possible to predict that high word frequency will facilitate a search process but might interfere with decision making. On a recall test, the net effect of these influences might be to enhance recall through the facilitation of the search. Recognition performance, however, might well be expected to be poorer because effectiveness in this task depends solely on decision making.

The generation-recognition hypothesis enjoys greater success than the single-process theory; however, it does not overcome all the problems inherent in the single-process view. Implicit in both approaches, for example, is the assumption that recognition performance should always be better than or equal to performance based on recall. We have noted before that this is not always the case.

Instances of Recall Exceeding Recognition

In 1973, Tulving and Thomson conducted an experiment designed to look at recognition and recall for a given set of common words. The experiment itself consisted of the following stages.

Stage 1: Pairs of words were presented. Participants were told to memorize capitalized words and to use lowercase words as cues.

Example: pretty—BLUE

Stage 2: Participants were told to free associate to given words, using words from Stage 1 if desired. Then participants were asked to list their associations and to circle any they had seen in Stage 1.

Example: Word	*Free associations*
lake	water
	ocean
	blue
	deep

Stage 3: Participants were given cue words from Stage 1 and were asked to recall the appropriate capitalized words.

Example: pretty—_____

Stage 1 was straightforward. Participants were asked to learn the capitalized word in each pair on a list, and were told that the lowercase word could be used as a cue. Thus, in the pair *"pretty-BLUE,"* participants were required to remember *"BLUE,"* and were encouraged to use *"pretty"* as a cue.

Stage 2 did not begin until the word pairs had been studied thoroughly. Then participants were given a series of target words that had not appeared in Stage 1 and were asked to write down any words that came to mind when each target word was presented. Some words presented in Stage 2 were weakly related to some of the capitalized Stage 1 words. The participants were told that their free associations could include any of the words they had learned in Stage 1. Thus, when *"lake"* was presented in Stage 2, many participants' free associations included *"blue,"* which had been learned in Stage 1. Upon completing the free associations, the participants were asked to recognize and circle any items that had appeared on the Stage 1 list.

After this de facto recognition test for the free-associated words, the participants were presented with lowercase cue words from Stage 1. The task in Stage 3 was to recall each of the capitalized words that had been learned in Stage 1. Tulving and Thomson found that during the free-association stage, several of the capitalized words were given as responses to the target words. However, participants were able to recognize only about 25% of the capitalized words they gave as responses. Surprisingly, when the participants were given the cued-recall test for these words, on the average they recalled more than 60% of the capitalized words. Using these procedures, participants showed that they were able to *recall* many words that they had not *recognized.* Apparently, retrieval of the capitalized words was easier with the lowercase words as cues than it was when a capitalized word itself was presented.

This finding that some recalled words are not recognizable is, of course, counterintuitive. We usually assume that if a word can be recalled, it can certainly be recognized. Because the results were so contrary to prevailing assumptions about retrieval, the Tulving and Thomson experiment was criticized on a variety of grounds. For instance, Martin (1975) argued that the experiment required participants to encode the capitalized words differently in stages 1 and 2. In Stage 1 the words are encoded in terms of the cue word given. In Stage 2 the words take on a different meaning because they are responses to a different stimulus. Martin suggests that the words are difficult to recognize because their meanings are essentially different in the original learning stage and in the free-association stage.

Although Martin's criticisms were valid, Tulving and Watkins (1977) demonstrated that the Tulving-Thomson result does not depend on a target word having different meanings at different stages of the experiment. In a refined study, they selected cue words that would give the capitalized words a particular meaning. The words used in the free-association phase were designed to evoke the same meaning for the capitalized words. Still, Tulving and Watkins found that recall performance was superior to recognition in this paradigm.

Others have argued that the Tulving and Thomson finding may have resulted simply from the complexity of the procedures used. There is no denying that the Tulving and Thomson procedure can be confusing. However, similar results have been obtained in a variety of experiments using relatively simple sets of procedures (see, for example, Watkins & Tulving, 1975; Wiseman & Tulving, 1976). Apparently, this is a robust phenomenon that can be observed under a variety of conditions.

Tulving's Synergistic Ecphory

Findings such as those reported by Tulving and Thomson (1973) led several theorists to reexamine the retrieval process involved in recognition

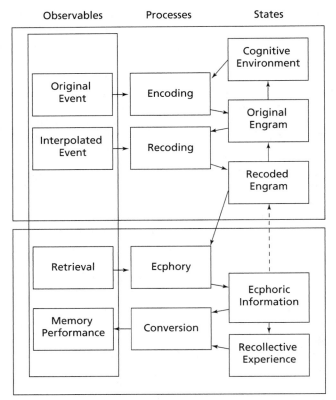

Observables Processes States

FIGURE 10.3 Elements of Episodic Memory and Their Relations. From *Elements of Episodic Memory* by Endel Tulving. © 1983 Endel Tulving. Reprinted by permission of Oxford University Press.

testing. As a result, many current theories of retrieval suggest that recognition may entail more than a simple decision-making process. According to these approaches, recognition may involve a preliminary search stage similar to the one proposed for recall. Tulving has introduced his theory of retrieval, which he calls **synergistic ecphory.** The term *ecphory* is based on a Greek word meaning "to be made known" (Schacter, Eich, & Tulving, 1978). The term *synergistic* implies that several processes are occurring at the same time and may be interacting. The term may seem like jargon, but Tulving argues that technical terms are important in psychological theory. According to Tulving, when we borrow terms from everyday usage, too often they carry connotative baggage. So Tulving tried to introduce terms that do not carry the everyday connotations that retrieval, recognition, and remembering do.

Tulving (1983) argued that the same processes are active in both recall and recognition. What differs between the two tests are the kinds of retrieval cues provided. In recognition, copy cues (the original stimuli) are provided. During the retrieval process, an **engram** (the memory trace or representation) is combined with a retrieval cue (see Figure 10.3). The engram is stored internally, whereas the retrieval cue is provided from outside. The engram and the cue are combined in ecphory. Ecphoric information is then converted into memory performance and also leads to a recollective experience.

Although it may sound complicated, Tulving's model is quite intuitive. Retrieval starts with an external retrieval demand, such as somebody asking you what you did on your last birthday. The retrieval cue "last birthday" is combined with your encoded memory of the event in the process known as ecphory. Ecphory, in turn, produces a certain kind of internal state that can be converted into the experience of remembering the various events surrounding your birthday. The memory report may consist of a description of that party (i.e., recall). Or it may be reported as specific answers to specific questions. Recognition works in much the same way. The major difference is that the cue is more informative, "Do you remember that delicious chocolate cake Margaret baked for you?" In recognition, a simple yes or no suffices. Notice that the important difference between recall and recognition is not the internal cognitive processes used but the external retrieval cues and required response.

This feature of Tulving's model can account for the Tulving and Thomson (1973) results described earlier. In Stage 1, the target *(blue)* is encoded in terms of the cue word *(pretty)*. The cue word forms part of the cognitive environment for the target word. Presumably, the engram that represents the memory has the word *blue* encoded in terms of something that is both pretty and blue, possibly a lake, but also possibly a pair of blue eyes or pair of turquoise earrings, but not with the sad music you listen to in a smoky bar.

In Stage 2, the recognition stage, the word *blue* has been generated while free associating to the word *lake*. The cognitive environment at this point may differ from that of the original encoding. The participant may be processing the word *blue* in terms of the color of a lake, not the sad jazzy music. The retrieval cue is a copy cue, but, when combined with the engram (which emphasizes the blueness of lakes), may not yield the recollection of the encoding of *"pretty-blue."*

In contrast, in Stage 3, the original encoding cue is given as the retrieval cue. This cue ("pretty") is episodically associated with the to-be-remembered target word. The retrieval cue now fits the cognitive environment that was present at the time of encoding. The cue word is now likely to combine with the engram that is representing the word *blue* as something pretty. Therefore, the original event is likely to be remembered.

Tulving makes an interesting point about what happens to a memory after it has been retrieved. The internal product of retrieval is a hypothetical entity called ecphoric information (see Figure 10.3). Ecphoric information is still hidden from the outside observer. It must be converted into a subjective experience for the rememberer and, potentially, a memory report for the outside observer. There are two ways in which the information is converted. One is behavioral—a process called *conversion* occurs resulting in observable behavior, such as a reporting that "it was a great big chocolate cake made with real butter and sour cream." The second is inherently cognitive and experiential. The process of ecphory leads to a memory experience. We see the experienced event again in our mind's eye, or in the current example, we taste the experience again in our mind's tongue. Indeed, the reexperiencing earlier events is really what we think of first when we hear the word *memory*.

Retrieval Strength and Storage Strength

Another theory of memory retrieval also focuses on the differences between what is stored and what can be retrieved. Bjork and Bjork (1992) postulate that any memory representation has two strengths associated with it; a storage strength, which represents the relative depth of encoding of a trace or how strongly it is represented in memory (storage), and a retrieval strength, which represents the relative ease of access of the trace (retrieval). Storage strength refers to how well stored the item is in long-term memory; the retrieval strength refers to how easily it is to actually pull that item out of memory. In this theory, the likelihood that an item will be recalled is completely determined by the retrieval strength, regardless of the storage strength. Recognition, however, is more dependent on storage strength. Moreover, storage and retrieval strength are potentially independent of each other.

Bjork and Bjork observed that some memories may be highly retrievable now but may be completely forgotten in a few seconds, hours, or days. For example, while on vacation, you do not forget your room number at your hotel, but soon after your return home, the number is completely forgotten. A hotel room number has high retrieval strength but low storage strength. In contrast, you may not be able to recall the phone number of a house you once lived in. The old phone number is an item with high storage strength because you used it for years, but it now has low retrieval strength because it has not been used in a long time.

A second aspect of the theory is that these strengths grow and change in different ways. Bjork and Bjork argue that storage strength increases as a function of study and retrieval opportunities. In other words, storage strength for an item can only increase. Retrieval strength, however, is limited. First, there is a limit on retrieval capacity; only a certain number of items can be retrieved at any one time, so retrieval strength for an item decreases when other items are studied or retrieved. Thus, the more time you spend learning the Latin names of tropical fish, the harder it will become to recall the names of the kings and queens of England. However, Bjork and Bjork argue that retrieval of items causes the biggest decreases in retrieval strength for those items related to the retrieved items. Therefore, retrieval practice on the kings of France will cause greater loss of access to the kings and queens of England than it will to the names of fish.

Bjork and Bjork make the following assumption about how items increase in storage and retrieval strength. Retrieving an item from memory or studying an item results in increments to both storage and retrieval strength. Storage strength changes are permanent—any study acts to strengthen the representation. However, retrieval strength goes up and down depending on usage. Recent usage causes retrieval strength to be high, and therefore, retrieval strength changes are temporary.

What relevance does this have to daily life? Bjork and Bjork maintain that usually the things we have retrieved recently are the things we may be likely to retrieve again in the near future. Consider the arena of interpersonal relationships. Imagine that you are dating a new person. You may be phoning that person frequently, and it is adaptive to remember your new friend's phone number—and not absent-mindedly dial your old boy/girlfriend's number. Perhaps a friend of yours has adopted her husband's last name. You want to remember the new last name, and not risk insulting your friend by using her former (maiden) name. In each of these examples, an item with high storage strength (the old name) is pitted against a newer item with lower storage strength. However, the desired response is the newer item (the new name). Relying on retrieval strength for recall allows suppression of the old name and recall of the new one. The distinction of storage/retrieval strength can be applied to medical scenarios as well. A doctor may have used a certain kind of treatment for an illness for many years. However, a better treatment may come along. Retrieval strength for the new and recently used procedure prevails over the older but more well-learned treatment. Bjork and Bjork's theory is consistent with the theme that learning and memory are adaptive processes. The items used most recently are, indeed, the items most likely to be needed (Anderson & Schooler, 1991).

An interesting corollary of Bjork and Bjork's theory is the possibility for spontaneous recovery of old memories (Postman, Stark, & Fraser, 1968). Compare an overlearned cue-target association that has not recently been practiced (high storage/low retrieval strength) to a newly learned cue-target association that has recently been practiced (low storage/high retrieval strength). If both cues are the same, a person will most likely respond with the newly learned target because it has been practiced recently and has high retrieval strength. However, if a week passes and the new association has not been practiced, its retrieval strength will wane. If later the cue is provided, then it is the older, previously "forgotten" target that may be recalled because of its high storage strength. Indeed, Wheeler (1995) has recently demonstrated that such spontaneous recoveries do exist.

THE ENCODING-SPECIFICITY HYPOTHESIS

Throughout our discussion of recognition and recall procedures, we have continued to talk about retrieval cues. Specifically, the term refers to any stimulus, or cue, occurring at the time of retention testing that an individual uses to aid in accessing a target representation. When you recall a person's name after seeing her face, the person's facial features seem to serve as retrieval cues for the memory of her name. Likewise, if you cannot remember a list of words, a hint such as "the first word began with the letter *A*" would constitute a retrieval cue. In some cases, retrieval cues are stimuli we notice in the external environment. For example, seeing a woman with a neatly pressed blouse may remind you that your clothing is ready at the dry cleaner's. At other times people seem to provide their own retrieval cues simply by thinking about an event they wish to remember. In any case, retrieval cues play an integral role in the retrieval process.

Now we will look more closely at what makes a retrieval cue effective. In other words, we will try to learn why some retrieval cues lead to immediate recollection, while others are relatively ineffective. Our discussion of retrieval-cue effectiveness centers on a deceptively simple hypothesis proposed by Tulving and his colleagues (Flexser & Tulving, 1978; Tulving, 1983; Tulving & Thomson, 1973; see also, Kintsch, 1974). This view is known as the **encoding specificity hypothesis.**

Simply put, the encoding-specificity hypothesis suggests that successful retrieval depends on the degree to which conditions of retrieval are similar to the conditions of encoding. More specifically, this hypothesis states that whenever a memory is stored, it is encoded in a unique fashion. The way a given memory is encoded de-

pends on the stimuli present at the time of learning as well as on other memories that are activated while learning occurs. Thus, if one is given a particular word to learn, that word does not occur in memory as an isolated representation. Rather, the representation of the word is connected to representations of environmental features (for example, time, place, odors, and sounds) that one notices when the word is learned. The representation of the word may also be connected to specific meanings or other words with similar sounds if those meanings or sounds are retrieved at the time of learning. In effect, a memory is always a complex of representations including not only the target event but also other events that are noticed as the memory is formed. The particular set of representations constituting a memory is what makes most memories distinct from one another to at least some degree (see Figure 10.4, p. 304).

According to Tulving, retrieval cues will be effective to the degree that they match the cues noticed by an individual when a memory was first encoded. Thus, if an individual notices the characteristics of a room while learning a list of words, the words will be at least partly encoded in terms of the room characteristics. Retrieval should then be facilitated by testing the individual in the room in which learning occurred. This environment would be expected to enhance retrieval because the retrieval cues would match a portion of the stimuli represented in the memory for those words.

This idea that retrieval should depend on test cues being similar to encoding cues does not seem revolutionary. However, this principle is often overlooked when retrieval problems occur.

Evidence Favoring the Encoding-Specificity Hypothesis

Although the earliest work on the encoding-specificity hypothesis was conducted by Tulving and his associates, a classic study on the topic was done by Godden and Baddeley (1975). They had participants learn a list of words for later recall.

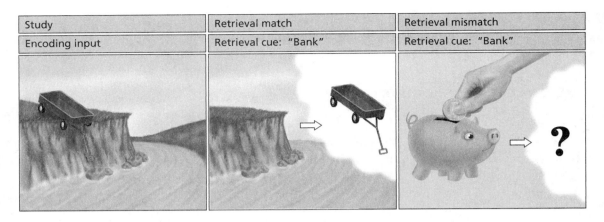

Study	Retrieval match	Retrieval mismatch
Encoding input	Retrieval cue: "Bank"	Retrieval cue: "Bank"

FIGURE 10.4 The Encoding-Retrieval Match. Memory often depends on how well retrieval cues *match* the way information was originally studied, or encoded. Suppose you're asked to remember the word pair *bank—wagon;* during study, you form a visual image of a wagon teetering on the edge of a riverbank. When presented later with the retrieval cue bank, you're more likely to remember wagon if you interpret the cue as something bordering a river than as a place to keep money.

These participants were trained scuba divers. The divers learned some words while submerged underwater. They learned other words on land. The divers returned later for a recall test of the words they had studied earlier. Testing was then conducted underwater and on land. Half of the words that had been learned underwater were tested underwater; the other half were tested on land. Half of the words learned on land were tested on land; the other half were tested underwater. The results of this study are rather dramatic (see Figure 10.5). Recall performance was relatively good in participants who were tested under the conditions they experienced during learning, regardless of whether on land or underwater. Performance was relatively poor, however, when participants learned and recalled under different conditions. Thus, making the conditions at retrieval (underwater) the same as those at encoding (also underwater) led to good retrieval.

One does not need such outlandish situations to demonstrate encoding specificity. Tulving and Pearlstone (1966) demonstrated the effect with word-list learning. They presented their partici-pants with a list of words that could be grouped into several conceptual categories such as types of vegetables or modes of transportation. The list they presented had all the words grouped by category, and each grouping was preceded by the appropriate category name. The purpose of this format was to bias the participants toward encoding the list in terms of specific categories. Following this procedure, the participants were asked to recall the words on the list. Half the participants were given the category names as retrieval cues, while the remaining participants were given no category names as cues. The participants who received the category names remembered significantly more words than the participants who received no cues. They suggested that the category names facilitated recall because these names had been presented at the time the list was encoded.

Similar results have been obtained by Tulving and Osler (1968) and by Thomson and Tulving (1970), in experiments involving the learning of free-recall lists. During learning some participants were given a meaningful word associate for each

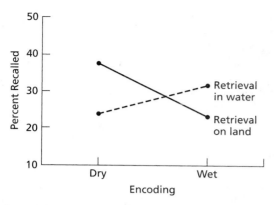

FIGURE 10.5 Results of Godden and Baddeley Experiments.

list item. For example, the word associate for the listed word *giant* might have been *tall*. Other participants learned the list without word associates. On a later test all participants were required to recall the listed words. Half the participants who learned using word associates were tested with the word associates as retrieval cues and half were tested without word associates. Likewise, half the participants who learned without word associates were given word associates as retrieval cues and half were not.

The results of Tulving's experiments were clear. The best recall performance occurred among participants who were given the word associates both at the time of learning and at the time of testing. The next best performance was by participants who received no word associates at the time of learning or testing (see Figure 10.4). The poorest performance was seen in participants who received the word associates *only* during testing. Such results are consistent with the idea that retrieval depends on the similarity of learning and testing conditions. Retrieval cues are effective to the degree that these cues are similar to those present at the time of encoding.

A study of recognition conducted by Morris (1978) is of particular interest because the results show that for the encoding-specificity rule to hold, retrieval cues need not be exact replicas of cues present at the time of learning. In this ex-

periment, Morris presented target words embedded in particular sentences. Some participants received the words in what were termed "congruous" sentences. These were sentences that described typical or normal situations. For example, for the target word *pickle,* Morris used the congruous sentence "The *pickle* was served with the slaw." Other participants received the target words embedded in incongruous sentences, or sentences that described a bizarre or atypical situation, such as "The *pickle* jammed the saxophone." On the test, participants received both old and new target words again embedded in either congruous or incongruous sentences. Their task was to recognize the words they had seen before. However, on the test all the sentences were new. For example, a pair of congruous and incongruous test sentences might be "The *pickle* was on top of the sandwich" and "The *pickle* was cut by the chain saw."

The results of Morris's experiment (Figure 10.6, p. 306) show the probability of correct recognition as a function of encoding and testing conditions. Participants who learned using congruous sentences clearly performed best when the words were embedded in congruous sentences on the test. However, when incongruous sentences were used during learning, performance was best when testing also involved incongruous sentences. These results occurred even though the actual sentences used in learning and testing were different. Apparently, all that is necessary for successful retrieval is relative similarity of encoding and retrieval conditions.

Encoding specificity appears to be an extremely robust generalization. It is clear that the encoding specificity principle holds up well in studies that use specific verbal cues at the times of learning and testing. Differing environmental contexts may also play a role (i.e., Godden & Baddeley, 1975). Several studies show that this principle extends to situations featuring the manipulation of more general contextual stimuli. Findings consistent with the encoding-specificity principle have also been reported when participants were asked to learn and remember

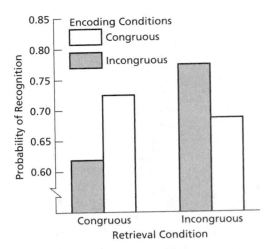

FIGURE 10.6 Recognition Performance As a Function of the Similarity Between Encoding and Retrieval Conditions. From *Memory and Cognition*, 6, 354–363. Reprinted by permission of the Psychonomic Society, Inc.

items in different postural positions. Greenspoon and Ranyard (1957) had participants learn a list of words either in a distinctive room sitting down or in a different room standing up. Then they tested their participants under the same or different conditions. Recall was highest when room and postural position were the same during learning and testing (Eich, 1995; Smith, Glenberg, & Bjork, 1978). Finally, encoding specificity can account for state-dependent learning.

State-Dependent Learning

Retrieval cues can be either objects, words, or events in the external world or they can be internal events; thoughts, images, and emotions. Often a particular thought may spur the memory of an important event in one's life. Being in a particularly good mood may remind one of a past experience with a similar good mood. Because the encoding-specificity hypothesis implies that people encode many features of an item or an event together, it also implies that internal events

may be encoded when the event is stored. Therefore, reinstating a similar internal state may help one retrieve that memory.

This hypothesis has been put to the test in a number of interesting ways. One involves altering the internal state by the use of drugs; another involves experimental manipulations aimed at affecting people's moods. The experimental design mirrors the experiments testing encoding specificity. That is, participants learn items while in one internal bodily state and are tested for retention in either the same or a different state.

To illustrate this kind of experiment, consider a study done by Eich, Weingartner, Stillman, and Gillin (1975). These experimenters had participants learn a list of categorized words after smoking a cigarette containing either marijuana or tobacco. Before testing, participants smoked another cigarette, which again contained either marijuana or tobacco. Half of the participants who smoked a marijuana cigarette smoked another marijuana cigarette before recalling the list (marijuana/marijuana). The other half smoked a tobacco cigarette before recalling the list (marijuana/tobacco). Of the participants who smoked tobacco when studying, half smoked marijuana (tobacco/marijuana) and half smoked tobacco (tobacco/tobacco) again during testing. The results were highly consistent with the notion of state-dependent learning and with the encoding-specificity principle. Recall was best when retrieval state matched encoding state. Thus, more words were recalled in the marijuana/marijuana and tobacco/tobacco conditions than the marijuana/tobacco or tobacco/marijuana conditions (see Figure 10.7).

Drug-dependent learning such as this is not an uncommon finding. In the Eich et al. (1975) study, two drugs (THC in marijuana, nicotine in tobacco) were used. Other studies have attempted to use placebo-control conditions. Goodwin, Powell, Bremer, Hoine, and Stern (1969) looked at the effects of alcohol on memory. Some people drank alcohol and were tested again either drunk or sober; others studied sober, but were either drunk or sober at test.

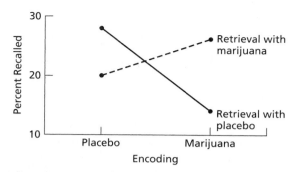

FIGURE 10.7 Results of State-Department Learning Experiment.

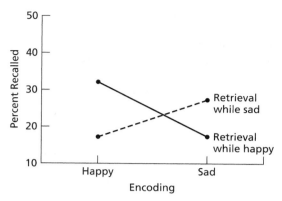

FIGURE 10.8 Effect of Mood-Dependent Learning Experiment.

Participants in the alcohol conditions consumed a large quantity of alcohol (10 ounces of 80-proof vodka). Sober participants recalled more when they had studied sober, but alcohol-drinking participants at test recalled more when they had also learned while drinking alcohol. In this study, there was a main effect of alcohol. Overall, alcohol decreased memory performance. But the decrease was not nearly as profound as the state-dependent effects (see Eich, 1989).

Other studies have shown that more naturally occurring internal states can also produce the state-dependent effect. Weingartner, Miller, and Murphy (1977), for example, did an experiment in which bipolar patients served as participants. A bipolar patient is one whose mood states swing rather violently between depression and mania or elation. These patients learned words in one mood state and attempted to recall the word in either the same or a different state. The experimenters found that recall was superior when the learning and testing mood states were the same.

There is now considerable evidence that similar results can be produced in normal people whose mood states are varied by experimental manipulations (Bower, 1981; Eich, Macauley, & Ryan, 1994). Consider a study by Eich and Metcalfe (1989) (see Figure 10.8), which tested normal Canadian college students by inducing them into either happy or sad moods through listening

to either happy or sad music. The experimenters instructed the students to think about pleasant or unpleasant incidents while listening to the music. Eich and Metcalfe waited until students reached a certain predetermined level of mood, and then asked them to learn a list of paired associates (e.g., "*silver—gold*"). The students returned to the laboratory two days later and were again induced into either a happy or a sad mood. Once they had reached the criterion level of happiness or sadness, they were given a cued-recall test for the words they had studied two days earlier. Consistent with earlier findings, students who were originally sad recalled more when sad, and those who were originally happy recalled more when happy again.

This text has discussed studies that are consistent with the encoding-specificity hypothesis for two reasons. First, it is important to realize the wide range of conditions to which this principle applies. Second, it is difficult to overemphasize the importance of this principle for understanding and predicting retrieval. Clearly, the effectiveness of a retrieval cue cannot be determined simply by looking at the nature of the cue itself. To predict the effectiveness of such a cue, we must know whether the cue is similar to cues present at the time of encoding. Both external (environmental) and internal (mental) may function as these cues.

Availability and Accessibility

Think again about the Eich and Metcalfe (1989) study. Participants were induced into either happy or sad moods at the time of test. The happy or sad students remembered more or less depending on their mood at the time of encoding. What if these students had been induced into the *other* mood at test? Presumably, they would have remembered more or less depending on the match to encoding conditions. The lower memory scores are not a result of inadequate learning, rather they are a consequence of less-than-ideal retrieval conditions. Thus, there is more information available (total amount of information in memory) than there is information accessible (information that can be retrieved under any one set of circumstances).

Availability refers to the hypothetical information present in the memory store whereas *accessibility* refers to that part of available information that can be retrieved at any particular point in time (Tulving, 1983). Availability can never be directly measured because the experimenter and the rememberer are constrained by the cues currently available. However, it is not difficult to demonstrate that material that is not retrievable under one set of cues becomes available under another (Tulving & Pearlstone, 1966).

The distinction between availability and accessibility is critical in understanding encoding specificity. There is a parallel between the availability/accessibility distinction and Bjork and Bjork's (1992) theory of retrieval discussed earlier. Retrieval strength, in the theory, is a measure of what is accessible at the current time. Storage strength is a measure of what is available in memory.

Availability and accessibility can be used to explain the part-set cuing effect (Nickerson, 1984; Roediger, 1974). In part-set cueing, participants study part of a set of well-learned items, such as the names of states, the names of parts of the body, or the names of fruits. In other versions of the part-set cuing procedure, participants study a list of newly learned items to a preestablished criterion. They then study half of these items again,

but not the other half. At some point later, they are asked to recall the entire set, both the studied items and the unstudied items. These participants are then compared to a control group. The control group does not engage in any studying. They are simply asked to recall the entire set. The intriguing finding is that the part-set study group recalls more of the studied items, which you should not find surprising, but fewer of the nonstudied items than the control group. In other words, studying some list members hurts retrieval of other lists members. For example, in one study, half of the participants studied the names of 25 U.S. states (the part-set study group). A control group studied the names of Asian and African countries. At some point later, both the control and part-set study groups were asked to free recall the 50 states of the United States. The part-set study group recalled more of the studied states, but fewer of the unstudied states than the control group.

Part-set cuing demonstrates two important points. First, it shows how some items are available (all 50 states), but that, at any particular time, some items may not be accessible (some of the unstudied states). A person cannot retrieve all the information he or she has stored in memory. Secondly, the part-set cuing results support Bjork and Bjork's theory of storage strength and retrieval strength. As one studies, some states increase in both storage and retrieval strength. However, the study of these states decreases the retrieval strength of nonstudied states. Indeed, Bjork and Bjork's model then predicts the outcome of the part-list cuing effect.

MEMORY CONSTRUCTION AT THE TIME OF RETRIEVAL

Virtually all theories of memory processing make the assumption that encoding takes place while memories are in short-term storage or while they are being actively processed (Atkinson & Shiffrin, 1968; Craik & Lockhart, 1972). In addition, most models assume that when a memory is retrieved from permanent storage, that memory or some copy of it reenters awareness or the short-term memory store. Combining these assumptions produces a peculiar implication: Once a memory has been retrieved, it may be susceptible to being reencoded in short-term storage. In other words, one might predict that a memory that has been retrieved is capable of being altered or modified in some way. This hypothesis raises an interesting possibility. It may be that retrieval is more than simply a process by which we activate and use stored memories. Retrieval may also be a process by which we are able to update or reencode memories that have long been in storage. This idea has some interesting implications. If we assume that retrieval is a process that can update or reencode memories from storage, it must all be able to change those encodings. Once a memory has been retrieved, its subsequent storage is altered (E. Loftus, 1992; Tulving, 1983).

Flashbulb Memories

Flashbulb memories are memories of an event that was surprising, emotionally arousing, or both (Brown & Kulik, 1977). Think of important life events—the birth of a sibling or the birth of your own child, the death of an important family member or friend, graduation from high school or college, and so on. These are events, both happy and sad, that people play over and over in their minds because of the importance or high emotional content associated with these events. Notice that according to the logic developed earlier, it is these memories that may be most susceptible to changes over the course of repeated retrievals because they are memories that people may be most likely to retrieve into short-term memory and then recode. However, Brown and Kulik argued that a special mechanism may print these events into memory. People are often very confident of the veracity of these memories.

A number of researchers have attempted to address this issue by studying public flashbulb memories. These public events, usually tragedies, include the explosion of the Space Shuttle Challenger, the assassination of John F. Kennedy, the assassination of Prime Minister Olaf Palme in Sweden, or the death of Princess Diana. Other researchers have looked at events such as the U.S. bombing of Baghdad. These public events offer a research advantage over private events in that many details can be objectively verified. Winograd and Neisser (1992) compiled an entire volume on the topic of flashbulb memories.

Weaver (1993) conducted a study comparing an ordinary memory and a flashbulb memory that occurred on the same day. He then traced the fate of each memory over a 12-month period. On January 16, 1991, Weaver asked the students in his Cognitive Psychology class to try to remember the details of an ordinary encounter with a college roommate or other friend. That same night (or the next morning in Baghdad), American warplanes began bombing Baghdad, Iraq, as the United States entered the Gulf War. On the next class meeting, January 18, Dr. Weaver asked his students to write down their memories of each event. For the ordinary event and the flashbulb event, students were asked to report who they were with and what they were doing, along with other information.

Then, three months later, Weaver asked the students to recount each memory. The students answered questions concerning the event and indicated their confidence in the accuracy of their memories. Eight months later (December 1991), the students were contacted again and queried about their memories. Weaver considered the first report (at two days) to be essentially correct, so he compared the later recollections to the report from Day 2. Weaver found that the amount remembered declined for both events in roughly the same manner. The students remembered approximately the same amount from the non-flashbulb event as they did from the flashbulb event. However, although their confidence in their memories declined for both events, it declined less for the flashbulb memories. Based on these data, Weaver concludes that there is nothing "special" about the mechanism whereby flashbulb memories are formed. Therefore, he argued against the "print" mechanism theorized by Brown and Kulik

(1977). Flashbulb memories seem to be susceptible to recoding and error just as ordinary memories. However, Weaver argued that the hallmark of flashbulb memories is high confidence—in some cases, unwarranted high confidence.

Not all researchers agree with Weaver, however. Conway and his colleagues (Conway et al., 1994) conducted an experiment on flashbulb memories for British and non-British participants for the resignation of Prime Minister Margaret Thatcher of Britain. Ms. Thatcher was Prime Minister for 11 years, and was a powerful and influential leader. Her resignation came as a complete shock to most British citizens. Conway et al. reasoned that many British people would experience flashbulb memories of her resignation, but that non-British people might not have the personal and detailed memories characteristic of flashbulb memories. Indeed, immediately following Thatcher's resignation, both British and a sample of Danish and American participants could remember the details of their lives surrounding Thatcher's resignation. However, approximately, 11 months later, at retest, the British participants showed very high consistency from one test to the next. However, the non-British participants showed much lower consistency. Moreover, the British participants were more likely to report a flashbulb memory than non-British participants when this concept was explained to them. Conway et al. reasoned that flashbulb memories are highly accurate, as originally suggested by Brown and Kulik. However, not all people experience flashbulb memories for a particular event. That is, the lower accuracy observed by Weaver may be a function of a mixture of flashbulb and non-flashbulb memories (see Conway, 1995).

Retrieval-Induced Forgetting

Retrieval appears to affect related memory representations as well as the retrieved representation. In fact, the retrieval of one memory may inhibit or impair the retrieval of another. This phenomena has been labeled **retrieval-induced forgetting** (Anderson, Bjork, & Bjork, 1994; Anderson & Neely, 1996; Anderson & Spellman, 1995). Anderson et al. comment that this phenomenon suggests that "the very act of remembering may cause forgetting." In retrieval-induced forgetting, remembering some information makes it more difficult to remember other related information. For example, if you are frequently asked to tell people your recipe for Louisiana Creole sauce, you may find it more difficult to remember the recipe for a good marinara sauce.

Anderson et al. (1994) studied retrieval-induced forgetting by asking participants to engage in extended retrieval practice (see Figure 10.9). Retrieval practice involves the repeated retrieval of certain items. The question Anderson et al. asked is what effect extended retrieval practice will have on other related items for which there was no retrieval practice. Anderson et al. presented their participants with long lists of category-example pairs from several categories (*Fish—marlin, trout, minnow, herring,* etc.). Participants then were given practice retrieving some pairs from the category (e.g., fish—marlin) but not other (e.g., *Fish—trout*). Retrieval practice consisted of a category cue and a stem from the example (*Fish—mar* _____). Other categories (*Trees—hemlock, oak, pine, palm*) did not receive any practice. Participants retrieved these examples up to three times before the final test was given. The final test was a free-recall test in which participants were asked to recall all of the originally studied examples from each category.

What did Anderson et al. expect on the final test? Consider first the practiced category *(Fish)*. There are two types of words in a practiced category. There are examples that have practiced (labeled RP+) and examples that have not been practiced (labeled *RP−*). Then consider the unpracticed category *(trees)*, labeled *Nrp*. Anderson et al. expected that RP+ items would be recalled more accurately than the NRP items (from the unpracticed category), and they found this pattern. More importantly, according to retrieval-induced forgetting, RP− items should be

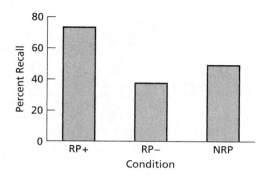

FIGURE 10.9 Results of Anderson et. al. Study on Retrieval-Induced Forgetting.

Condition 1: RP+ = Target items from practiced category that were practiced.

Condition 2: RP− = Target items from practiced category that were not practiced.

Condition 3: NRP = Target items from the nonpracticed condition.

forgotten. Therefore, Anderson et al. expected RP− items to be recalled at a lower rate than the NRP items. Indeed, this is the pattern they found (see Figure 10.9). In essence, the practice of some category members (e.g., *marlin*) caused retrieval-induced forgetting of other category members (e.g., *trout*).

Retrieval-induced forgetting is not limited to laboratory-based verbal learning. Shaw, Bjork, and Handal (1995) demonstrated retrieval-induced forgetting in an eyewitness paradigm. Participants viewed slides of a crime scene (a wallet had been stolen). The scene was a student's apartment. Scattered about the apartment were various college sweatshirts and textbooks. The sweatshirts and textbooks became the practiced or unpracticed category. Participants were asked repeatedly about the presence or absence of a Harvard sweatshirt (RP+), but not about a UCLA sweatshirt (RP−). Later Shaw et al. asked the witnesses to write down all of the sweatshirts (both RP+ and RP−) and textbooks (NRP) present at the scene. Compared to the items in the unpracticed category, witnesses remembered more of the practiced items from the practiced category but fewer of the unpracticed items from the practiced category. The danger for police investigators is clear—the more you ask about some detail of the crime, the less information may be accessible about other related aspects of the crime. However, there also is an advantage to repeated testing—the repeated items will be remembered better.

Misinformation Effect and Eyewitness Memory

Perhaps the most striking example supporting the idea that memories may be reencoded at the time of retrieval comes from the domain of eyewitness memory, in what has come to be known as the misinformation effect (Loftus & Hoffman, 1989). Elizabeth Loftus has pioneered this research area and still remains at the fore (Greene, Flynn, & Loftus, 1982; Loftus, 1979, 1992; Loftus & Hoffman, 1989; Loftus, Miller & Burns, 1978). Basically, Loftus began her studies by looking at a very practical question. Is eyewitness testimony of the type given in a courtroom really reliable? To test the reliability of such testimony, she first showed a film of an automobile accident. Then she asked her participants questions about the event they had witnessed. In one experiment (Loftus & Palmer, 1974), she asked some participants about the speed of the cars that had "smashed" into one another. To other participants, she asked how fast they were going when they "contacted" each other. This simple difference in instructions led to estimates that differed by 10 miles per hour (see Figure 10.10, p. 312). In Loftus and Palmer, participants were not given misinformation about the accident. In other studies, Loftus deliberately misinformed her participants. For example, during the series of questions, half the participants were asked "How fast was the white sports car going while traveling along the country road?" The other participants

Recall instructions	Schema	Response
"How fast were the cars going when they **smashed** into each other?"	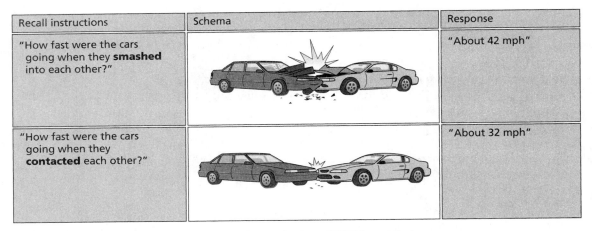	"About 42 mph"
"How fast were the cars going when they **contacted** each other?"		"About 32 mph"

FIGURE 10.10 Schema-Based Remembering. Loftus and Palmer (1974) found that students would "remember" cars traveling at a faster rate of speed when retrieval instructions used the word *smashed* instead of *contacted*. All subjects had seen the same film, but their different schemas for the words *smashed* and *contacted* presumably caused them to reconstruct their memories differently.

received a slightly different question. They were asked "How fast was the white sports car going when it passed the barn while traveling down the country road?" These questions differ only in that one mentions a barn and the other does not. The difference is important, however, because the videotape did not show a barn. Thus, half the participants were presented with subtle information about the presence of a barn that did not exist in the original stimulus and could not have been in their memory of the tape (Loftus, 1979).

After one week, Loftus asked her participants another series of questions about the same tape. One of these questions was "Did you see a barn?" Nearly 20% of the participants who had been given the barn question earlier answered yes. Fewer than 5% of the other participants responded that they had seen a barn. These data indicate that eyewitness accounts can be biased by the questions witnesses are asked. More important for present purposes is the implication that information can be added to a memory at the time that memory is retrieved. In the present case, participants were asked questions to get them to retrieve their memories of the tape. One

group was given additional information at the time of retrieval. Some of these participants may have incorporated the new information into the memory of the tape, even though this information was not present at the time the memory was originally formed. Such a finding suggests that people sometimes update or alter our memories at the time of retrieval based on any new relevant information that becomes available.

In a second, more complex study in this series, Loftus attempted to induce participants to alter information they had originally stored. To accomplish this she presented two groups of participants with a sequence of slides showing a red sports car progressively moving toward a collision with another car. Both groups received the same slides in the same sequence, except for one slide, which showed the sports car at an intersection. One group saw a slide that contained a stop sign, while the other group's slide showed a yield sign (Figure 10.11).

Immediately after seeing the slides, the two groups were asked questions about what they had seen. Half the participants who had seen a stop sign were asked a question in which the term

FIGURE 10.11 Eyewitness Reliability. A pair of photographs used in the experiment by Loftus, Miller, and Burns to test the reliability of an eyewitness account. (From Loftus, Miller, & Burns, 1978.)

"stop sign" was used (a consistent question). The other half received a question containing the term "yield sign" (an inconsistent question). Similarly, half the participants who saw a yield sign received a consistent ("yield sign") question, while the other half were asked an inconsistent ("stop sign") question. Several minutes later all participants were given a recognition test in which pairs of slides were presented. They were to choose the slide seen before. When slides showing the intersection were shown, 75% of participants given a consistent question recognized the correct slide. However, participants who received an inconsistent question were correct only 40% of the time. This result suggests that the inconsistent questions caused many participants to alter their retrieved memories so that they could no longer correctly recognize what they had originally seen (Loftus, 1979).

Both of these experiments can be labeled misinformation-effect experiments. In a misinformation-effect experiment, participants first witness an event. At some point later, the participants heard or read a description of the event or they are asked questions about the event. At this point in the procedure, the misinformation is introduced. The final phase is a recognition test for the witnessed event. The consistent finding is that witnesses tend to misattribute information they learned in the written description or questioning as having occurred in the original event. When this information is misleading, participants may occasionally report events or actions that never actually occurred.

Explanations for the Misinformation Effect. In general, we can advance two interpretations for the kind of findings Loftus reports. One explanation is that at the time of retrieval a memory reenters some active state (possibly short-term storage) and is at that time altered in accordance with new incoming information. This altered memory is then restored in its modified form. Thus the memory trace of the original event has been modified, impaired, or blended (Loftus, 1992; Metcalfe, 1990). Loftus's view is commonly known as the **trace-impairment hypothesis** because it argues that the original memory representation is altered. In contrast, McCloskey and Zaragoza (1985) argued that when the participant is initially asked questions about the event (some of which may contain misleading information), a second memory trace is formed. This second memory trace consists of retrieved information from the earlier memory and new information derived from the post-event questions. Therefore,

two memories exist, the modified copy and the original memory. In McCloskey and Zaragoza's view, it is retrieval of this second modified memory that causes participants to report the misinformation as part of the witnessed event in the final recognition test. This theory has been called the **coexistence hypothesis** because both the original and recoded memory are available (Lindsay, 1993).

To distinguish between these theories, one must look at the methodology more carefully. In Loftus's original experiments, the final recognition test would present participants with both a stop sign (correct) and a yield sign (incorrect). The two choices are based, however, on information from the experiment. One was actually in the slides, but the other was presented in the post-event narrative. This kind of memory test cannot distinguish between the two theories because both can explain poor memory accuracy. If there is only one memory trace, it may be of either sign. If both memory traces are present, the participant must select the one that he or she thinks is correct. In essence, the experiment cannot distinguish between the two theories (McCloskey & Zaragoza, 1985).

To test the two theories, McCloskey and Zaragoza introduced the modified-recognition test. In this test, the participant is asked to choose between the original event and an incorrect alternative, but the incorrect answer is *not* the item suggested in the misinformation (e.g., stop sign vs. no-parking sign). According to the trace-impairment hypothesis, the trace has been altered, and misinformation should show impairment even when the suggested item is not an alternative. In contrast, if two separate traces have been formed, then the participants should have no trouble picking the right one because the suggested memory is not an option. Using this modified recognition test, McCloskey and Zaragoza found no impairment of memory for the original item, thus supporting coexistence.

However, in subsequent work, researchers have found misinformation effects in the modified recognition test (Belli, Windschitl,

McCarthey, & Winfrey, 1992). For example, Belli et al. adopted the McCloskey and Zaragoza modified-recognition procedure and compared short retention intervals (15 minutes) to long retention intervals (5 to 7 days). Belli replicated McCloskey and Zaragoza; there was no misinformation effect for short retention intervals, but at the longer retention interval, control items (no misinformation given) were recognized better than misinformation items. This study, therefore, supports Loftus's idea of a single trace.

Other researchers have become interested in whether participants truly believe that the misinformation was seen or whether they simply report what they heard in the post-event narrative (Lindsay, 1990; Loftus, Donders, Hoffman, & Schooler, 1989; Weingardt, Loftus, & Lindsay, 1995). Because participants are seldom told that the misinformation is actually false, it is conceivable that they knowingly report information they heard in the narrative but know they did not actually witness. If so, it may be possible to ask participants to determine where or when they learned the information. Lindsay (1990), however, argued that people are not necessarily aware of the source of their memory. He showed that in some cases, participants may misattribute memories to the wrong sources. When they are explicitly asked to report where they learned something, they will sometimes report seeing what they actually heard. Lindsay's view is based on an assumption that, in some cases, there are two separate memories. What causes the misinformation effect, then, is an inability to monitor the source of that memory. Lindsay has labeled his explanation the **source–monitoring hypothesis** (see Johnson, Hashtroudi, & Lindsay, 1993, for a general review of source monitoring).

Implications of the Misinformation Effect. Although the theoretical understanding of the misinformation effect remains elusive, the practical implications are significant. If people's memory reports can be altered by post-event misinformation, then under those circumstances when accurate memory is crucial, precautions must be taken not to alter people's memories. For example, police must be careful not to inadvertently mislead a witness during an investigation. Even well-intentioned questions run the risk of changing memories if the police officer brings certain assumptions into the situation (Loftus & Palmer, 1974). For example, the police officer may assume that the bank robber was a man. Therefore, if the police officer asks the witness "What was he [the robber] wearing?" a witness who might not have been able to determine the gender because of concealing clothing may now remember the criminal as a man. Another real-world scenario where accurate memories may be crucial is in psychotherapy. Frequently, psychotherapists will ask their clients to retrieve childhood memories and, in some cases, recover lost memories. The therapist should be careful to avoid introducing leading or misleading information because the studies reviewed here suggest that memory for a past event can change with repeated remembering or from post-event information.

False Memory in List Recall. Because the retrieval process can alter what we remember about a particular event, researchers recently have become more interested in false memories, or memories of events that did not actually occur (see Roediger, 1996). False memories have enormous implications in the legal system, as we have seen, and for psychotherapy as we will see in the next section. For this reason, Roediger and McDermott (1995) introduced an experimental paradigm originally developed by Deese (1959) as a model for false memories (Read, 1996). Not all false memories, nor those induced by the Deese paradigm, may occur because of errors in retrieval (Roediger, 1996). However, retrieval errors have been implicated.

Roediger and McDermott presented participants with categorized lists (Table 10.3, p. 316). For example, participants might see the words *thread, pin, thimble, injection, syringe, haystack,* and *prick,* but not the critical word *needle.* Later, after study of these words, participants were asked to

Table 10.3 Creating False Memories. Stimuli used to induce false memories.

List 1	List 2	List 3
mad	water	butter
fear	stream	food
hate	lake	food
rage	Mississippi	sandwich
temper	boat	rye
fury	tide	jam
ire	swim	milk
wrath	flow	flour
happy	run	jelly
fight	barge	dough
hatred	creek	crust
mean	brook	slice
calm	fish	wine
emotion	bridge	loaf
enrage	winding	toast
anger	river	bread

From Roediger & McDermott (1995): Creating false memories: Remembering words not presented in lists. *Journal of Experimental Psychology: Learning, Memory, and Cognition, 21,* 803–814.

recall the words. At the time of test, participants recalled many of the list words, but also were very likely to intrude the word *needle*. In this case, recalling the word needle is a false memory. The word *needle* was not on the list; it was only an *associate* of all the words on the list. However, many participants were quite confident that it had been on the list and actually claimed to remember hearing the word being said in the experiment. Moreover, almost all people are susceptible to this effect.

The explanation of the Roediger-McDermott finding is still not clear. It may be that the critical intrusion word is somehow induced during encoding of the list. However, Roediger and McDermott argued that it is more likely to be a retrieval effect. When the list is being organized for recall, the critical intrusion may be the word with the most strength because it is an associate of all the other words, and therefore it comes to mind most easily. Perhaps most striking is the ease with

which false memories can be demonstrated in this procedure. These results have now been replicated many times (Roediger, 1996; Schacter, 1999).

The Deese-Roediger-McDermott procedure (DRM) has recently been used in neuroimaging studies. Most of these studies come from Schacter's lab (Schacter, 1999). For example, using fMRI technology, Schacter, Buckner, Koutstaal, Dale, and Rosen (1997) found that both true and correct recognition were accompanied by activity in the medial temporal lobes. However, the false recognitions were accompanied by slightly more activity in the frontal lobes. Schacter (1999) hypothesized that the increased activity in the frontal lobes may reflect an increased scrutiny on the false items. Nonetheless, the scrutiny is insufficient to weed these items out.

Recovery of Repressed Memories. A recent controversy on which the memory-retrieval literature can shed some light is the nature of repressed memories, and what, indeed is the recovery of these repressed memories (Lindsay & Read, 1994; Loftus, 1993). Recently, the question of whether repression is possible and whether repressed memories can be retrieved has generated considerable interest (Lindsay & Read, 1994; Hyman, Husband, & Billings, 1995). At the core of the controversy is whether repression is a viable mechanism of forgetting, and whether memories, if repressed, can later be retrieved. (Lindsay & Read, 1994; Read & Lindsay, 1994).

One issue is whether repression is an actual mechanism of forgetting or simply a label for a certain phenomena: namely, the forgetting of highly stressful or traumatic events. It is clear that extremely stressful memories can be forgotten. However, whether a specific mechanism of repression exists remains controversial. A repression mechanism is based on the idea that a person actively works to forget a traumatic event after it occurs (Cohler, 1994). If such mechanisms exist, how can they be documented? It is often quite difficult to verify claims of repressed memories at all. If repression is rare or if repressed memories cannot be recalled, what accounts for reports of repressed memories? Some researchers (Lindsay & Read, 1994; Loftus, 1993; Schacter, 1996) have advanced the notion that many reports of repressed memories may actually be *false* memories, accidentally induced through misleading information or some other technique.

It is important to note that traumatic information is sometimes forgotten. For example, Parker, Bahrick, Lundy, Fivush, and Levitt (1997) looked at children's memory for a traumatic event, a hurricane that devastated much of Miami in 1992. Parker et al. compared children who had been exposed to minor damage, medium damage, or severe damage as function of the storm. They found that the children exposed to severe damage recalled fewer details than did the children who had experienced only medium damage. Children exposed to minor damage also reported fewer details than the medium–damage condition. In other words, the severe damage led to more loss of memory detail than those simply exposed to medium amounts of damage. Other experiments are more directly relevant to the repression debate. Williams (1996), for instance, found that 38% of women with a documented history of childhood sexual abuse could not remember the abuse at an interview many years later. Moreover, many of these women were able to later recover memories of the abuse that were indeed accurate.

That repression may exist does not resolve the theoretical question as to whether repression is a special mechanism of forgetting or whether conventional theories of memory can account for it. On the one hand, many therapists argue that forgetting traumatic events is an active coping mechanism that enables people to block unpleasant memories. In contrast, many cognitive psychologists prefer to explain the forgetting of traumatic events through the same means as nontraumatic events are forgotten: combinations of difficulties encoding and difficulties in producing the correct cues. At this point, there has been little research directed at which of these two positions is correct.

Some cognitive psychologists suspect that some, perhaps many, recovered traumatic memories may in fact be false memories. Although no one knows how many recovered memories are true and how many are false, memory research has documented repeated instances in which people in laboratory settings remember false events. Researchers have tried to simulate situations in which false memories might arise in the course of trying to recover repressed memories.

Loftus and Coan (1995) demonstrated that people could create new memories of events that never occurred (also see Hymen et al., 1995). The researchers repeatedly questioned participants about childhood events. Loftus and Coan claimed that relatives of the participants had told them about the event, and they were testing on memory for details. One 14-year old participant was told that an older brother (a graduate student of Dr. Loftus's) had reported that the 14-year old had been lost at a mall as a young child. The participant denied it, but after repeated questioning, this changed. Indeed, not only did the participant later remember and describe the event, but even after being debriefed, still claimed the event actually occurred. This study has now been replicated several times. Therefore, it can be concluded that under realistic ecologically valid conditions, completely new memories can be implanted into some people. False memories may be created through the influence of a well-meaning but misguided therapist, or may result when imagination and memory are confused. There is no good estimate as to how many recovered repressed memories may actually be false memories generated in this fashion; nonetheless, this topic has generated a great deal of heated debate and vigorous research. Lindsay and Read (1994) provided an excellent overview of the empirical research and the cognitive criticisms of the repressed–memory movement. Cohler (1994) advances an equally well-articulated rebuttal.

The Cognitive Interview

As we have seen, memory fallability can have consequences in both the legal and psychotherapeutic domains. Can researchers structure retrieval conditions so as to maximize correct recall and minimize false recall? Fisher, Geiselman and their colleagues have developed a protocol for police investigators to facilitate the collection of unbiased reports from cooperative witnesses (Fisher & Geiselman, 1992; Fisher, Geiselman, & Raymond, 1987). Their *cognitive interview* is based on several of the principles of retrieval that we have covered in this chapter. The cognitive interview is designed to maximize the amount of information a witness can report without lowering the accuracy of that information. Let us consider two principles in the cognitive interview.

Fisher and Geiselman argued that police should ask open-ended questions, not direct questions. They claim that there are two possible mistakes in asking direct questions. First, the police officer runs the risk of asking leading (or misleading) questions, thus allowing for the possible inclusion of misinformation in the participants' report. Second, the witness may assume that information that the police officer does not ask for is not relevant, when in fact the police might not ask about a given detail because they do not know about it, even if it may be an important clue. Open-ended questions, by contrast, allow the witness to report anything that he or she may remember. Such questions are less susceptible to the effects of misinformation.

Fisher and Geiselman also encourage police officers, when possible, to ask witnesses to imagine themselves back at the scene of the crime. Fisher and Geiselman call this principle **context reinstatement.** Why is context reinstatement important? The claim is that it helps take advantage of the encoding-specificity principle. If witnesses at retrieval can reinstate their mental context at encoding, they may be able to retrieve more information. As we have seen earlier, the appropriate context can allow retrieval of previously unretrieved information.

The cognitive interview demonstrates two main points. First, it has important practical implications. If police officers can obtain more information from witnesses without compromising accuracy, more crimes may be solved. Second, the cognitive interview illustrates how principles obtained from the learning and memory research can be applied to real-world scenarios. The cognitive interview may be applicable beyond the police interview. Doctors could use the cognitive interview to get the information they need from patients. Auto mechanics could use it to get people who are otherwise car-illiterate to describe their car's problem. One could also use the cognitive interview to help someone find misplaced items.

SUMMARY STATEMENTS

This chapter dealt at some length with the nature of the retrieval process in long-term memory. It began by looking at retrieval from long-term storage. The chapter then reviewed a number of theories concerning the nature of this process, including single-process retrieval theory, the generation-recognition hypothesis, the synergistic ecphory theory, and theory of retrieval strength/storage strength. These theories differ primarily in terms of the distinction they draw between processes involved in recall and recognition. Most of the current evidence tends to favor the contemporary theories. Many try to account for the adaptability of human memory.

The chapter went on to discuss availability and accessibility, the encoding-specificity hypothesis, and state-dependent learning. These issues demonstrate the diversity of memory phenomena. The chapter closed with a discussion of the malleability of memory, focusing on three situations: flashbulb memories, retrieval-induced forgetting, and the misinformation effect, in which memory retrieval is susceptible to errors.

11

Conscious and Nonconscious Processes in Long-Term Memory

CHAPTER OVERVIEW

There is a famous story related by the Swiss psychiatrist Claparède. In 1911, Dr. Claparède described a meeting he had with a woman suffering from amnesia. Though densely amnesic, the woman was verbal and intelligent. When introduced to Dr. Claparède, she extended her hand to shake with him. Dr. Claparède had a pin hidden in his hand and when they shook, he gave her a painful jab. No serious damage was done, of course, and as the woman was amnesic, she forgot the incident within a few minutes. The following day, Dr. Claparède returned to call on the patient. She had no recollection of meeting him the day before, nor did he seem familiar to her. Yet, she steadfastly refused to shake his hand. When pressed, she could not come out with an explicit reason and demurred, saying, "That was an idea that went through my mind" (Tulving, 1983).

This story illustrates the striking differences between conscious and nonconscious forms of memory, the general topic of this chapter. Previous chapters have outlined various theories of encoding and retrieval and the differences between short- and long-term memory. In this chapter, we examine the differences between conscious and nonconscious processes in memory. We consider the possibility that retrieval of information is not always accompanied by awareness, or even a "feeling of pastness." Having then discussed the evidence that suggests nonconscious memory does exist, we compare conscious and nonconscious memory and discuss theories that have been advanced to explain the difference.

Nonconscious memory has become a major focus of contemporary memory research (Kelley and Lindsay, 1996; Schacter, 1996; Schacter & Tulving, 1994; Tulving & Schacter, 1990). Intriguing findings, originally with amnesic patients and then with normal people, suggest that human beings have complex abilities to process information and use it later without necessarily being aware of the knowledge. These findings have led researchers to hypothesize that humans have two or more independent memory systems. Some are used for conscious processing and others for nonconscious processing.

NONCONSCIOUS MEMORY

Nonconscious memory has some ominous overtones. It may evoke images of brainwashing or deeply repressed memories of traumatic events. In this chapter, nonconscious memory does not refer to such dramatic effects. Rather, nonconscious memory refers to the effects of earlier events that occur without the person consciously knowing that he or she is using memory. Nonconscious memory is often for complex perceptual and conceptual materials. Earlier in the text, we have considered nonconscious learning in nonhuman animals. Indeed, we acquire many skills without conscious awareness of them. The kinds of tests that are used to explore nonconscious memory are done consciously, such as spelling tests, word-fragment completion tests, and response-time tests. Because these tests are done consciously, the issue of conscious as opposed to nonconscious memory has become a controversial one.

Before we get to the core issues, however, it is important to define terms. The terminology often gets confusing here because different researchers used different terms to refer to similar concepts. First, in this chapter, *conscious memory* refers to the normal remembering process that produces in a person an awareness that he or she is using memory accompanied with a feeling of pastness. Thus, we are defining *conscious* here in terms of the experience of the remember. The term *recollection* is often used to refer to the conscious process of remembering. *Nonconscious memory,* in contrast, refers to a remembering process that may occur that does not produce an awareness of using memory nor does it elicit a feeling of pastness.

It is important to define a few other common terms used in memory research. Conscious memory may also be called *explicit memory* or *memory with awareness.* Nonconscious memory is sometimes called *implicit memory* or *memory without awareness.* This text prefers the terms *conscious* and *nonconscious* because the terms *explicit* and *implicit* have other uses in the memory literature

and *conscious* and *nonconscious memory* are more concise terms than *memory with and without awareness.*

As was discussed in the last chapter, *explicit memory tests* (also known as *direct tests*) are used to measure conscious memory. *Implicit memory tests* (also known as *indirect tests*) are used to measure nonconscious memory. In this chapter, the terms *conscious* and *nonconscious memory* refer to the kind of memory being tested. The terms *explicit* and *implicit memory tests* (or *tasks*) refer to the tools by which conscious and nonconscious memories are measured.

Implicit and Explicit Testing

Explicit testing means that the person participating in the memory experiment knows that his or her memory is being tested and that he or she should use memory to accomplish the task the researcher has assigned. Traditional explicit tests include recall tests and recognition tests. For example, in a standard free recall test, participants know that they are to retrieve items from a particular earlier list that they remember experiencing; they actively attempt to remember that experience. Similarly, in an old–new recognition test, participants attempt to verify whether an item that they are seeing has been presented to them earlier.

In implicit testing the person participating in the experiment does not know that his or her memory is being measured. Furthermore, the person is not asked to use memory to accomplish the task. However, in a typical implicit memory paradigm, participants are given earlier experiences that may influence their performance in the task. Implicit memory tests may include word-fragment completion tasks, word-stem completion tasks, spelling tests, lexical decision tasks, object-recognition tasks and many others, as shown in Table 11.1 (Schacter and Tulving, 1994).

Consider a spelling task. During a spelling task, the experimenter pronounces a word aloud, and the participant writes the word down on a piece of paper. The participant must know how

Table 11.1 Tests Used as Explicit and Implicit Memory Tests.

EXPLICIT TESTS	IMPLICIT TESTS
Free recall	Word-fragment completion
Cued recall	Word-stem completion
Old-new recognition	Lexical-decision tasks
	Perceptual identification
	Object-recognition tasks

to spell the word, but the task does not involve remembering any particular experience with the particular word. The participant simply retrieves the spelling from memory and writes it down. However, now consider what happens when the researcher says aloud the word *pear*. Without the appropriate context the participant does not know whether to write the word *pear* or *pair*, or *pare*. In English, there are a great many such homophones (e.g., bare/bear, too/two/to, steal/steel, etc.). Researchers know which spelling is more frequent in everyday usage and can use this as a measure by which to predict which of the two or more spellings is most likely.

Amnesics cannot remember what they read, but they can read aloud, interpret what they are reading, and write to dictation as well. Most amnesics can easily perform the spelling task. In an important experiment by Jacoby and Witherspoon (1982), amnesics were given a list of sentences to study, such as "The large <u>bear</u> ate fish caught from the river," and "The blacksmith forged a sword from <u>steel</u>." They were told to attend to and remember the words that were underlined. Being amnesic, they could not remember any of the critical underlined words on a later free-recall test. However, they were also given a spelling test. In the spelling test, they were more likely to spell the words in the manner in which they had studied them earlier. This occurred in the absence of any conscious recollection of studying the sentences.

This kind of effect is called *repetition priming*, or simply *priming* (Schacter, 1987). Priming is de-fined as the effect of an earlier episode on a later task. Thus, in the spelling task, the particular spelling of the homophone was primed by the earlier study of the sentences. Priming effects measure the extent to which the earlier experience affects later peformance. Thus, it is incorrect to equate priming with nonconscious memory although the terms are related. *Priming* is a term that refers to the difference in performance between performance with an earlier experience and performance without an earlier experience. Nonconscious memory refers to the memory process that produces the difference.

Repetition priming contrasts with semantic priming. In semantic priming, a word is presented (e.g., *doctor*) as a prime and then the person must make a decision about another word (e.g., *nurse*). If the two words are related, the first will often prime the second; that is, people will process the second word faster and make a response more quickly if the two words are related (Meyer & Schvaneveldt, 1976). The technique of semantic priming is usually used to examine associative networks and semantic memory, whereas the repetition priming is used to study nonconscious memory.

Similar priming effects occur with other kinds of tests. In the *word-fragment completion task* (Tulving, Schacter, & Stark, 1982), participants are first given a list of words to study, such as *assassin, sanctuary, perimeter,* and *sheriff.* After a designated retention interval, which varyies from just a few minutes to several months later, the participants are given a word-fragment completion task. In the task, they try to decipher a particular word from several of its letters. (see Figure 11.1). Word-stem completion is similar to word-fragment completion. In word-stem completion, the implicit memory task is to give the first part (and not random fragments) of the word. Priming effects—improved performance on previously presented items—have been observed in amnesics for both tasks (Schacter & Tulving, 1994).

Lexical-decision tasks also serve as implicit-memory tasks. As in the other implicit-memory tasks, the first stage is the priming task, in which

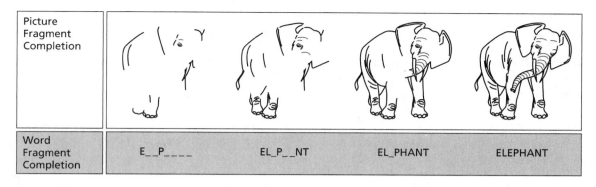

FIGURE 11.1 Implicit Memory Tests. A picture fragment completion task and a word-fragment completion task.

participants see lists of words. Sometimes they are given instructions to remember these words, but often the words are given in an orienting task. Later, these words, unstudied words, and non-words are included in a lexical-decision task. In the task, people verify whether a presented item is a word or not a word. The task is done at high speed, so both accuracy and response times are relevant measures. Participants might have to judge the words *sheriff* (old word), *cactus* (new word), and *climper* (nonword). The experimenter then measures response time and accuracy. The priming effect is defined as the difference in response time (or the difference in percent correct) between the old words and the new words. Priming effects are found in both amnesics and normals. Participants make faster "yes" responses to previously studied words than they do to unstudied words.

Because there are a great number of new terms in this section, it may be helpful to review the section before reading on.

Nonconscious Memory in Amnesics

We have already considered some of the research concerning priming in amnesics. The question is to what extent amnesics who may have severe deficits in episodic memory maintain memories in a nonconscious form that can be accessed implicitly. The modern origin of this research began with a series of studies of amnesics by two British psychologists, Elizabeth Warrington and Lawrence Weiskrantz (Warrington & Weiskrantz, 1968, 1970, 1974).

Warrington and Weiskrantz (1970) examined a sample of amnesic patients and normal controls on both explicit and implicit memory tests. Their explicit memory tests were free recall and recognition. Their implicit memory test was a word-stem completion task. On the explicit memory tests, the amnesics showed substantial deficits in performance relative to control subjects. However, on the word-stem completion task, the amnesics performed as well as the controls. This striking finding led to a completely new conception in how researchers think about memory (Schacter, 1996).

Since Warrington and Weiskrantz's original experiments, there have been numerous studies that have replicated and extended their results. Foremost in this effort has been Daniel Schacter of Harvard University (Schacter, 1996). Schacter and his colleagues conducted several important studies on nonconscious memory, priming, and amnesia.

In a representative study, Graf and Schacter (1985) were interested in whether amnesics would show priming for novel associations. This was important because the novel associations depend on new learning, not necessarily preexisting connections. In the study, the researchers gave amnesics unrelated word pairs to study, such as *"pasture—dragon."* The amnesics studied these words, which they did not later remember in explicit tests. However, Graf and Schacter tested them implicitly with a version of the word-stem completion task. During study the patients were shown either the original cue combined with the first three letters of the target word (*"pasture— dra_____ "*), or a new cue preceding the target word (*"window—dra_____"*). Priming was measured as the difference in completion of the target stem as a function of whether the cue was paired with the target in the earlier study phase. Although the results varied as a function of severity of the amnesia, the priming was larger when the semantic context was given. This finding suggests that nonconscious memory may not be limited to the perceptual domain. In this experiment, semantic context was important.

McAndrews, Gliksy, and Schacter (1987) conducted another important experiment demonstrating semantic effects in nonconscious memory in amnesia. They presented amnesics with sentences that were difficult to understand, such as "The haystack was important because the cloth ripped." This sentence is odd until a particular concept word is given; in this case, the word was *parachute*. Amnesics were provided with a word that disambiguated the sentence. A week later, the sentences were presented again to the amnesics. Densely amnesic patients were able to recognize only a limited number of the sentences, but they were able to "solve" the sentences by "thinking" of the solution word (e.g., *parachute*). They showed a classic priming effect; they were more likely to solve the sentences if they had been exposed to the solution a week earlier.

Nonconscious Memory in Normals

Amnesics seldom recall anything from a particular priming episode, and therefore must rely on nonconscious memory in implicit memory tasks. In contrast, normal people can remember consciously and often do recall items from the priming task. Thus, it is often difficult to determine whether a normal person is using conscious or nonconscious memory for an implicit-memory task. Therefore, nonconscious memory is not as easy to measure in normal subjects. Researchers must seek ways of rendering a normal person's conscious memory weak, so that they cannot explicitly recall the material, or find a way of conducting the implicit test such that the normal person does not try to recall items from the priming task. Both of these methodologies have been expanded and will be explored here.

One common implicit test that has been used successfully with normal people is called the *perceptual-identification task*. In this task, a participant sees a briefly presented target word. The word is presented so quickly that on some trials, the participant cannot read the word at all, usually about 15 milliseconds (.015 sec). The participant must try to read the word. Some of the words that the participant tries to read were presented earlier in a priming phase (at normal reading speeds). Thus researchers can compare accuracy rates for target words that have been primed (i.e., presented earlier) or unprimed (i.e., presented for the first time during the perceptual-identification procedure). The perceptual-identification procedure avoids the problem of conscious recall because the brief presentation time does not allow conscious strategies.

Jacoby and Dallas (1981) conducted a series of important experiments in which they compared performance on a perceptual-identification task with a standard explicit task, old-new recognition. In their first experiment, Jacoby and Dallas used the levels-of-processing technique during the priming phase. For some study words, the participants had to answer questions that oriented them toward perceptual aspects of the stimuli, such as "Does the word have the letter *e* in it?" For other study words, the participants answered questions that oriented them toward semantic aspects of the stimuli. This first phase served as a priming phase for the explicit and implicit memory tests. To test explicit memory, Jacoby and Dallas used an old-new recognition test, and to test implicit memory they used the perceptual-identification task.

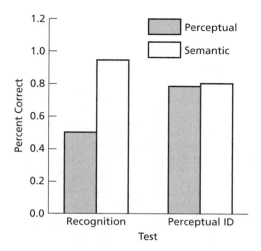

FIGURE 11.2 Effect of Levels of Processing on Recognition in Explicit and Implicit Tests. Jacoby and Dallas (1981) showed that levels of processing affected recognition, an explicit test, but did no affect perceptual identification, an implicit test.

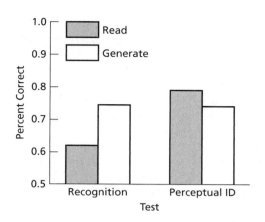

FIGURE 11.3 Generating vs. Reading a Target. Jacoby and Dallas (1981) showed that generating a target increased the likelihood of recognition but reading the target increased the likelihood of perceptual identification.

The results are shown in Figure 11.2. As can be seen in the figure, levels of processing affects the old–new recognition in the expected direction. Semantic processing leads to higher recognition performance than does perceptual processing. However, the interesting finding is the effect of the levels-of-processing manipulation on the implicit task. Notice that levels of processing has no effect on performance in the perceptual-identification task. There is an overall priming effect, but it is not enhanced by the semantic processing.

In a second experiment, Jacoby and Dallas used the generation effect to compare explicit and implicit performance. During the priming phase, participants either read a word (*moose*) or had to generate the word by unscrambling the letters (*osome*). Unscrambling the letters increases the difficulty of the priming task compared to reading the word in a normal presentation. Consistent with our discussion in Chapter 9 of the generation-effect, the read words were not recognized as well as the generated words in the old–

new recognition test. However, as you can see in Figure 11.3 above, during the perceptual-identification task, there was a greater priming effect for the read words than there was for the generated words.

There are two important points in this experiment. First, it is unlikely that the normal college students in this experiment used conscious memory in the perceptual-identification task. The task calls only for reading, not remembering, and people find it difficult enough to do the reading when the presentation is so brief. Second, variables such as semantic processing and generating the target, which lead to better performance in conscious memory, resulted in the same or worse performance during the priming on the implicit task. The finding that experimental variables affect implicit and explicit memory tests differently in normals is an important finding. Several theorists have used it as a basis for arguing that conscious and nonconscious memory are accomplished by different systems.

In Jacoby and Dallas's experiment, the priming phase was easy. Participants had ample time to read (or generate) the words. Thus, it is expected that normals would consciously remember some of the words from the priming phase. In the implicit test—perceptual identification—the words were presented too briefly for the participants to make use of these memories. Other researchers have tried the converse approach, that is, the priming phase is presented without the partipant's awareness. Thus, participants cannot consciously recollect the material studied in the priming phase because they were not consciously aware of it at the time. Eich (1984) used this strategy to study nonconscious memory in normal college students.

In Eich's experiment, students wore headphones. Eich played one message into the right ear and a different message into the left ear. Participants were instructed to attend to the message, an essay, given to the right ear. To ensure that the participants attended to the message, they were told that they would be tested later for their retention of the essay and were instructed to repeat the essay aloud as they heard it. In the left ear, the participants were presented with a series of words, some of which were homophones. As in the Jacoby and Witherspoon (1982) experiment discussed earlier, the homophones were preceded by a word that biased the homophone toward one of its multiple spellings. For example, the participants might hear *"sell/cell"* preceded by the word *"prison."* All of the biasing words were chosen to elicit the less-frequent spelling. Keep in mind, however, that the participants were not attending to these words. Indeed, they expected a test for the essay that was being played to the other ear.

Following the priming phase, participants were given a recognition test for the words presented in the unattended left ear. Like the amnesics, the participants were essentially at chance in the recognition test. In other words, they were unable to recognize the words presented to them. Following the recognition test, they were given the spelling test, which included the homophones. Although the subjects did not recognize the left-ear words, their spelling was affected by the priming phase. Participants were biased toward spelling the homophones toward the less-frequent alternative. The presentation of information to the unattended ear influenced how people would spell the words, even though the people did not consciously remember the words that were presented to them.

This striking finding has important implications. First, we have identified another variable, attention, which affects explicit and implicit memory tasks differently. Information presented to an unattended ear influenced performance only on the implicit-memory task. Second, nonconscious memory was observed here even though the participants exhibited no conscious memory at all. This finding rules out the possibility that participants were using conscious memory in the implicit-memory task. Third, in normals, priming can occur on a variety of different implicit-memory tasks, ranging from those that rely on perceptual processing, such as the perceptual-identification task to those that rely on semantic or meaning-based processing, such as the homophone spelling task.

In each of these experiments, normal humans use memory without being aware that they are doing so. However, the participants are aware that they are spelling words in a particular way or reading words at low presentation rates. How do people account for their own performance? Larry Jacoby has argued that people misattribute the effects of priming. He argues that because we do not know that they are memory effects, we attribute the improvement in performance to other factors. For example, Jacoby claims that his students often compliment him because they think he slowed down his pace of speech during the course of the semester, which the students think allows them to understand the material more readily. Jacoby, however, claims that his pace does not slow down. Rather the students are primed to his voice and to the topic of memory research. His voice sounds slower because they are familiar with it and with the topics discussed. Thus, the students attribute to Jacoby what is, in fact, a tribute to their own memories, which allows them to process his voice faster (see Jacoby, Kelley, & Dywan, 1989). We will illustrate Jacoby's point with another important study from his lab.

Jacoby and Whitehouse (1989) reported a priming study in which they exposed participants to novel names (such as Sebastian Weisdorf). The participants were informed that these names referred to ordinary people who were not famous. Later, however, the participants performed a fame-judgment task in which they were to decide whether a series of names were famous or not. In fact, some of the names were those of famous people, some were names that they had studied in the priming phase, and some were completely novel names. When the priming phase had occurred with the participants' full attention, the participants were able to reject correctly the primed names and label them "not famous." However, when the priming phase occurred under divided attention conditions similar to those employed by Eich (1984), the participants mistakenly labeled the primed names as famous (see Figure 11.4). Thus, the novel (but primed) names that the participants were told were not famous were later more likely to be judged as famous than the novel unprimed names. Jacoby, tongue-in-cheek, suggests that this is one way of making people famous overnight.

The Jacoby and Whitehouse results are explicable in terms of conscious and nonconscious memory. Under full attention, the primed names enter both conscious and nonconscious memory. When the participants are later asked to judge fame, they retrieve the names from conscious memory and correctly respond "nonfamous." However, under divided attention, the primed names enter only nonconscious memory. Because they do not attend to the names, they are not stored in the conscious portion of memory. Then, when the participants judge fame later, the nonconscious name gives a boost of familiarity to the primed names and people mistakenly judge them as famous (Jacoby et al., 1989).

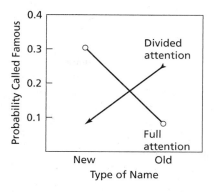

FIGURE 11.4 Effect of Prior Experience and Attentional Demand. The probability of judging a nonfamous name famous was affected by prior experience and attentional demand. From *Current Directions in Psychological Science*, 1, 174–178. © 1992 Blackwell Publishers.

In summary, nonconscious memory has been studied in both normal and amnesic people. In both cases, there is now convincing evidence that people can retain and later use information without being consciously aware of it. This nonconscious memory is revealed through the use of implicit-memory testing. Implicit-memory tasks do not require the use of memory, but prior experience with particular items may facilitate performance. Nonconscious memory often works by priming a particular response in an implicit-memory task.

SYSTEMS AND PROCESSES

The distinction between the systems and process approach should sound familiar. In Chapter 8, we considered the differences between long- and short-term memory. In that chapter, we noted that many researchers considered (and some still do) that there is only one memory system and that the differences between long- and short-term memory are a function of the fact that tasks call on different memory processes. In contrast, most researchers consider long- and short-term memory to be two separate systems that interact but operate by different rules and processes. With respect to long-term memory, some researchers argue that there must be independent memory systems that account for conscious and nonconcious memory. Some argue that there is only one system—long-term memory—and that the observed differences between conscious and nonconscious memory exist because different cognitive processes are used in implicit tasks than in explicit tasks.

A Systems View

At a basic level, the systems view is that there are two (or more) largely independent long-term memory systems. According to systems logic, these systems may operate by different rules, they may be affected differently by different variables, and they may be served by different underlying neurological systems. The process view suggests that there is only one long-term memory system. This single system, however, is capable of engaging in different processes to accomplish different aims. Different processes may rely on different underlying neurological pathways, but within a single system.

According to the systems approach, performance on implicit-memory tests and explicit-memory tests is based on two or more different underlying systems. According to this view, it ought to be possible to damage one without damaging the other. To support this view, systems theorists discuss the data from amnesic patients—impaired explicit performance and intact implicit performance. The process view, however, thinks of explicit tasks as simply being more difficult. When the system is damaged, the easier tasks based on fewer processes can still be carried out, but the patient is no longer capable of more difficult tasks.

Which view is correct? We do not know. Proponents of each admit that the issue is not entirely resolved. Nonetheless, there is a growing consensus that it is, in fact, no longer viable to think of long-term memory as being composed of a single system.

A representative example of the systems view is a recent account of long-term memory advanced by Daniel Schacter and Endel Tulving (1994), two researchers most associated with advancing the systems view. They state that their view is idiosyncratic and subject to revision. However, they believe it best accounts for the data observed to date.

Schacter and Tulving conceive of memory systems as follows:

1. Each system serves a different function for the organism and processes different kinds of information than other systems. Thus, one memory system may be designed to handle autobiographical information, another general information.

2. Each system operates according to different rules. This means that any particular variable may affect each system differently.

3. Each system is subserved by a different neural system. This means that the underlying brain system may be different for each system. Certainly, neurological evidence is needed to support the distinction between one system and another.

4. Each system may use a different representational format. This means that the way memories are stored may be different from one system to the next.

5. Each system has evolved independently. This is more speculative. It means that each system may have evolved at a different time during the course of human evolution. It also implies that developmental differences may be observed between systems.

Schacter and Tulving argue that there are five different memory systems that meet these criteria. One of the systems is short-term memory, but the other four are all long-term memory systems.

Short-Term Memory. Schacter and Tulving, like many other psychologists, view short-term and long-term memory as being different systems. This distinction was discussed in

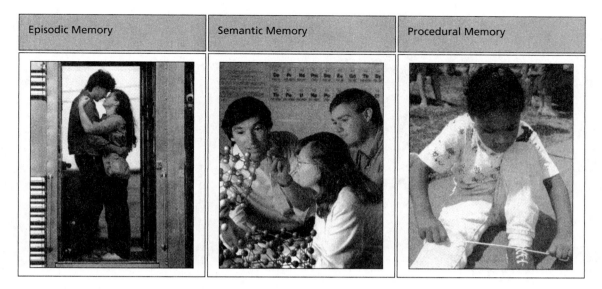

| Episodic Memory | Semantic Memory | Procedural Memory |

FIGURE 11.5 Episodic, Semantic, and Procedural Memories.

Chapter 8. Short-term memory is not relevant to the discussion of implicit and explicit testing.

Procedural Memory. Schacter and Tulving adopted Squire's (1987) term, *procedural memory,* to refer to skill memory. Skills may range from motor skills, such as remembering how to ride a bicycle, to mental skills, such as remembering how to play chess. Procedural memory is usually revealed in implicit tests. For example, people are seldom asked whether they remember how to ride a bicycle. But if they are asked, they can successfully demonstrate their knowledge and proficiency. Thus, procedural memory is demonstrated through action and conscious verbal output (see Figure 11.5). Neurologically, procedural memory is often associated with the part of the human brain called the cerebellum.

Semantic Memory. Semantic memory refers to any person's extensive knowledge of facts and ideas. For example, facts such as "Montreal is the second-largest French-speaking city in the world," "The American crocodile is only found at the very southern tip of Florida in North America," and "The New York Yankees have won more World Series than any other Major League Baseball team" are stored in semantic memory. One of the characteristics of semantic memory is that it is not necessarily tied to our lives, and our beliefs in these memories are not tied to our own experience.

Episodic Memory. Episodic memory is the encoding of knowledge about personal or autobiographical memories. It is also known as event memory. It concerns the ongoing events of one's life. For example, your memory of a recent vacation to the Everglades in South Florida, in which you saw crocodiles, constitutes an episodic memory. Or perhaps, you remember watching Michael Jordan's heroics in the final game of the 1998 NBA finals. Episodic memories are temporally organized. They are typically accompanied by a feeling of veracity.

Perceptual Representation System. This is not really one system but several, one for each

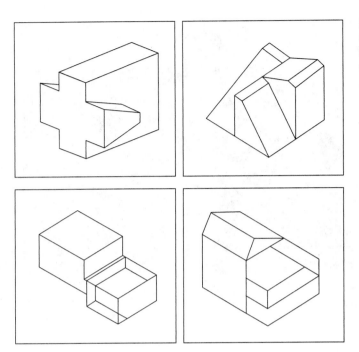

FIGURE 11.6 Possible and Impossible Stimuli. The upper stimuli are possible objects and the lower are impossible. From Schacter et al. (1990), p. 7.

perceptual modality. Thus, there may be a visual representation system, an auditory representation system, a haptic representation system, and so forth. The PRS (as Schacter and Tulving call it) holds information about the form and structure of a particular object or stimulus. Thus, it may represent the way a particular word looks or the way a particular voice sounds. However, the PRS is presemantic; it does not code nor represent meaning. Schacter and Tulving argue that it is the PRS that accounts for many of the priming effects observed. We are not consciously aware of the PRS; therefore its effects can occur without our knowledge.

Schacter and his colleagues have investigated the PRS in some detail (Schacter, 1992; Schacter, Cooper, & Delaney, 1990). For example, Schacter et al. (1990) showed line drawings to participants. Some of these drawings were of objects that were possible in 3-D, whereas others were impossible in 3-D (see Figure 11.6).

While viewing the line drawings, the participants made judgments about the orientation of the figures. This phase served as the priming phase for a later test. At some point later, the participants were given either an implicit or an explicit test. The explicit test was an old-new recognition. The implicit test involved making a speeded judgment about whether or not the objects were possible or not in the 3-D real world. Schacter et al. found that the primed objects were judged more quickly than objects that had not been seen earlier. However, this priming effect was seen only for the possible objects. Schacter and his colleagues have since replicated and extended this finding. Schacter interprets the findings as suggestive of a special memory system that stores structural descriptions about objects. These structural descriptions can later serve as a basis for identification of the object and also allow priming in implicit tests.

A Process View

Larry Jacoby has been one of the leading proponents of the process view of nonconscious memories. His view dovetails with Tulving and Schacter's in that it places considerable importance on nonconscious memory. However, the basis of the explanation lies in differences in processing, not in differences in systems. He thinks of two basic processes that operate in an explicit task, such as recognition. He calls these two processes recollection and familiarity (Jacoby, 1991). Recollection involves a conscious remembering of both the information required and contextual information surrounding it. It is the process by which we remember our last birthday or what we did over summer vacation. In this sense, it maps to Tulving's episodic memory system. Jacoby's second process, familiarity, occurs when a subjective feeling of pastness or remembering occurs without the accompanying contextual information. Although Jacoby's familiarity system bears some resemblance to Tulving and Schacter's perceptual representation system, familiarity still results in conscious experience (see Mandler, 1980, for a similar view).

Jacoby's research begins with the observation that any particular experimental task, whether it is recall, recognition, word-fragment completion, or homophone spelling is not "process-pure" (Jacoby, 1991). This means that there are no direct one-to-one relationships between a particular kind of test, explicit or implicit, and the underlying cognitive processes. In other words, both conscious memory and nonconscious memory, to varying extents, may be involved with performance on both implicit tests and explicit tests. Implicit tests may rely more heavily on nonconscious processes, and explicit memory may rely more heavily on conscious processes, but sometimes nonconscious processes may boost performance on explicit tasks and conscious processes will help performance on the implicit tasks. Therefore, one of Jacoby's goals was to develop a methodology that could separate the influence of conscious and nonconscious processes.

There are two central features to Jacoby's view. The first is that a task such as recognition can be accomplished by two processes. In the case of recognition, he labels the two processes *recollection and familiarity*. The second feature is that the tests psychologists develop cannot be process-pure, meaning that even the implicit tests developed to look at nonconscious memory may rely on some conscious processing. To test these core ideas, Jacoby developed an ingenious but controversial technique called the *process-dissociation procedure*. The function of the process-dissociation procedure is to derive estimates of the relative weights of the two cognitive processes that drive a task such as recognition. It tries to disentangle the two processes that drive recognition or any other task. However, its assumptions have been challenged (e.g., Gruppuso, Lindsay, & Kelley, 1997; Mulligan & Hirshman, 1997).

Recall the central problem that Jacoby and his colleagues face. They wish to investigate the underlying cognitive processes that allow us to recall, recognize, and complete implicit tests. However, they argue that any particular test is not process-pure. Therefore, studying recall as a measure of recollection is "contaminated" by the possibility that nonconscious processing may affect recall (e.g., Jacoby, Yonelinas, & Jennings, 1996). The goal of process dissociation becomes to separate the effects of the conscious and nonconscious process.

Jacoby and his colleagues achieved this by placing the two processes in opposition. Jacoby accomplished this by structuring a task so that when subjects used the conscious or recollective process, they would make one response, whereas when they used the nonconscious or familiarity process, they would make the opposite response. The opposition motif makes analogies easy. Consider two boxers. One may be taller and have longer arms, the other may be stronger and more experienced. Who is the better boxer? One doesn't know until they are put in opposition.

Putting boxers into opposition is comparatively easy, but how does one put two cognitive processes in opposition in an experiment? Here is the technique worked out by Jacoby and his colleagues. Consider a typical experiment from Jacoby's lab (Jacoby & Kelley, 1992). Subjects are asked to study a list of words (List A). Subsequently, they study a second list of words (List B). The two lists are separated in time to help the subjects distinguish them. So far, this seems straightforward enough. Now consider what occurs at the time of the recognition test.

Subjects are given careful instructions about what to do during the recognition test. They are told that they will see a series of words, some from List A, some from List B, and some new words that they have not seen before in the experiment. The instructions are to say "Old" only if the lists are from List B. Subjects are to say "New" to new words and words from List A. Why are these instructions important? They put the two cognitive processes, recollection and recognition, in opposition (see Table 11.2).

Consider the hypothetical process of recollection. If one recollects a List B item, one will assign it to the category "Old." However, if one recollects an item from List A, one will assign it to the category "New." Because recollection involves contextual information, recollecting the item will also allow the subject to assign it to the right list and make the right response. Therefore, the recollection process results in the response of "New" for List A items.

What about familiarity? Jacoby argues that the familiarity process results in an experience of pastness, but the subject cannot remember the context surrounding the experience. For a List B item, the familiarity process will result in an "Old" response, just as the recollection process. For List A items, however, the familiarity process results in an error. List A items are more familiar by virtue of the presentation of the list initially. Therefore, a familiarity response will occur whenever they are presented. But, because no contextual information is present, the subject does not know whether the item is from List A or from List B. Therefore, the familiarity process is likely to prompt the response of "Old" to List A items.

Table 11.2 Jacoby's (1991) Process-Dissociation Procedure.

	INCLUSION	EXCLUSION
Study	List A	List A
Study	List B	List B
Test for	List A and List B	List B, *not* List A
Analysis of old responses	*A items:* Recollection or familiarity	*A items:* Recollection or familiarity
	B items: Recollection or familiarity	*B items: Only* familiarity

The process-dissociation process puts the process of familiarity and recollection in opposition. Recollection, in this task, leads to one response for List A items, namely a "New" response. Familiarity, however, leads to the opposite response for List A items, namely an "Old" response. With the two processes now capable of producing opposing responses, Jacoby can manipulate experimental variables that foster one process or the other and determine which process they influence by looking at the number of "Old" responses to List A items. The tasks may not be process-pure, but by putting the two processes in opposition, Jacoby can isolate their functioning.

MONITORING AND CONTROL OF HUMAN MEMORY

As human beings we have the ability to monitor and also to exert conscious control over the workings of our memory systems. Monitoring allows us the ability to attend to how our learning is proceeding and whether our remembering is successful or not. Control allows us to adjust learning and alter our retrieval strategies (Nelson, 1996).

Consider a student studying a new language. In this ordinary scenario, it is the student who has control over the study parameters and not the professor or indeed, any experimenter. The student must decide which items to study, how long to study them, and by what methods to study them. These decisions are aspects of control that people can exert over their memory. How does a person go about making these decisions? The person must monitor his or her memory. He or she must be able to determine when the items are well learned, when the items are not learned sufficiently, and what method of study will maximize performance.

This perhaps uniquely human ability often is overlooked in memory experiments. However, in recent decades, there has been an increased interest in metamemory, how people monitor and control memory (Metcalfe, 1996; Nelson, 1996).

Metamemory is defined as the knowledge about how a person's memory works and the experiences that accompany ongoing memory processes (Flavell, 1979; Nelson, 1996; Schwartz, 1994). Each person has unique idiosyncratic knowledge about his or her own memory. This kind of knowledge may vary from broad claims, such as, "I don't have a good memory," and "I am good at remembering foreign-language vocabulary" to very specific kinds of claims such as "I can recall all of the U.S. presidents, if I say them in order."

Metamemory also includes experiences we have concerning our memory. For example, you may feel very unsure that you could remember the definitions of monitoring and control. This unsureness, or its converse, confidence, is also a kind of metamemory. You may not be sure why you are sure or unsure, but you may have a definite feeling associated with your likelihood of remembering. These kinds of feelings of confidence are called metamemory experiences (Flavell, 1979).

Thomas Nelson of the University of Maryland has made an important distinction between monitoring and control in metamemory (Nelson & Narens, 1990; Nelson, 1996). *Monitoring* refers to the cognitive processes involved in keeping track of the current status of the memory system. It involves assessing how strong memories are now and how they might change in the future. *Control* refers to those cognitive processes that allow us to direct or redirect our memory

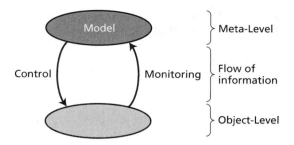

FIGURE 11.7 Nelson-Narens Model. From **Metacognition: Knowing About Knowing,** p. 11, by J. Metcalfe and A. Shimamura. © 1994 by Bradford Books. Reprinted by permission of the publisher.

processes. Control decisions are based on the output of the monitoring processes. For example, if a person feels she can remember a still unremembered name, the control processes can direct the memory processes to continue searching for the unrecalled word (see Figure 11.7).

The crucial dimension of monitoring is its accuracy. For control to be effective, monitoring must be able to measure accurately the underlying memory processes. In other words, it must be able to tell the weak memories from the strong and the easily remembered items from the more-difficult-to-remember items. Accurate monitoring provides useful information to the control processes. Therefore, one of the first issues that researchers addressed was whether monitoring was indeed accurate. This research began in the 1960s (Hart, 1965). Only later did researchers turn their attention to what the monitoring and control processes might actually be (Nelson, Gerler, & Narens, 1984).

Feeling-of-Knowing Judgments

To assess metamemory, subjects are asked to make explicit judgments concerning the state of their memory. These judgments are then used as the measure of metamemory. Judgments concerning the likelihood of recognizing an unrecalled item are called feeling-of-knowing judgments. Historically, feeling-of-knowing judgments have played a substantial role in the study of metamemory

Table 11.3 The Recall-Judgment-Recognition Paradigm. Developed by Hart (1965) and Nelson and Narens (1980) for studying feeling-of-knowing judgments.

Recall

What is the last name of the first person to set foot on the moon?

      Answer: _____

If "I don't know," then

Feeling-of-Knowing Judgments

      What is your feeling of knowing?

0 20 40 60 80 100

Recognition

What is the last name of the first person to set foot on the moon?

      1. Aldrin

      2. Glenn

      3. Armstrong

      4. Collins

      5. Jamison

From Nelson, T. O. (1996). *American Psychologist,* 51, 102–116.

monitoring (Nelson et al., 1984; Schwartz, 1994).

Feeling-of-knowing judgments are judgments that reflect the likelihood of being able to recognize or recall an item that is not yet recognized or recalled. They are made at the time of retrieval. Typically, a cued recall question is given. If the subject cannot recall the target answer, he or she makes a feeling-of-knowing judgment concerning the likelihood of later recognizing the answer. Finally, a recognition test is given. Starting with the seminal research of Hart (1965, 1967), this procedure has become known as the RJR procedure, referring to its three stages; recall, judgment, and recognition (see Table 11.3).

In Hart's experiments (1967), later refined by Nelson and Narens (1980, 1982), participants are given general-information questions, such as "What is the last name of the first man on the moon?" or "What is the name of the city destroyed by the volcano Mt. Vesuvius, in 79 A.D.?" In the RJR procedure, if the subject knows the correct answer, he gives it and moves on to the next question. However, if the subject does not know the answer, he instead makes a feeling-of-

knowing judgment. Feeling-of-knowing judgments are usually given numerically. For example, 1, 2, and 3 might indicate a low feeling of knowing, but 4, 5, and 6 might indicate high feeling of knowing. In Hart's paradigm, feeling-of-knowing judgments are only given on unrecalled items. After making a feeling-of-knowing judgment, participants then see the question again followed by a set of alternatives, such as "Glenn, Aldrin, Armstrong, Jamison," or "Pompeii, Rome, Carthage, Athens" and the participant then attempts to choose the correct answers.

Hart and many researchers subsequently found that feeling-of-knowing judgments were accurate at predicting recognition. High feeling-of-knowing judgments tend to correlate with correct recognition. However, the correlation is not perfect. People do make errors and give high judgments to items they do not know (Nelson, 1988; Schwartz, 1994). Therefore, feeling-of-knowing judgments can serve as markers of *possible* later retrieval.

An experience linked to feeling-of-knowing judgments is the *tip-of-the-tongue (TOT) phenomenon.* This is a feeling that retrieval of a target word is imminent. People who experience tip-of-the-tongue states feel as if they are just about to retrieve a person's name, a particular experience, or a word for a crossword puzzle. Brown (1991) reported that most people report experiencing a tip-of-the-tongue state at least once a week. The tip-of-the-tongue phenomenon and feeling-of-knowing judgments differ in two important respects. First, tip-of-the-tongue states are unsolicited feelings with strong emotional components. Feeling-of-knowing judgments are elicited by the experimenter and are not necessarily accompanied by strong feelings. Second, tip-of-the-tongue judgments are predictions about likelihood of recalling it on one's own, whereas feeling-of-knowing judgments typically are predictions concerning the likelihood of recognition. They are, of course, closely related. (see Brown, 1991; Schwartz, 1994).

Tip-of-the-tongue states are good examples of metacognitive experiences. When in a tip-of-the-tongue state, people report strong feelings that an item is known and will be recalled. Brown and McNeill wrote that tip-of-the-tongue states often feel like being on the "brink of a sneeze." Much earlier, William James (1890) wrote that tip-of-the-tongue states have the quality of "beckoning us in a given direction, making us at moments tingle with the sense of our closeness and then letting us sink back without the longed-for term" (p. 251).

Like feeling-of-knowing judgments, tip-of-the-tongue states are good predictors of performance. Tip-of-the-tongue states are predictive of recall of the missing target and later recognition of the target (A. Brown, 1991). Tip-of-the-tongue states are also predictive of knowledge concerning the unrecalled target. People experiencing tip-of-the-tongue states are more likely to recall partial information about the target such as its first letter or how many syllables it has. Furthermore, people are likely to recall words that sound alike or words that mean something similar to the target word when they are experiencing a tip-of-the-tongue state (A. Brown, 1991; R. Brown & McNeill, 1966).

Another important question about monitoring in metamemory is the issue of what kinds of processes people use when they make feeling-of-knowing judgments or tip-of-the-tongue states. Hart (1965) and R. Brown and McNeill (1966) showed that monitoring can be accurate, but did not explain the bases upon which people make these judgments. Any theory for the basis of metamemory monitoring must explain two aspects of their accuracy. First, the theory must address why the judgments are generally accurate, and second, it must address why the accuracy is not perfect.

Nelson et al. (1984) outlined two classes of explanations for feeling-of-knowing judgments. They label the first class of explanations *direct-access mechanisms*. Direct-access theory suggests that very often people can *feel* what they cannot *recall*. In other words, even though you cannot retrieve a word that is on the tip of your tongue, your monitoring system "knows" that it is there. The second class of mechanisms are called *inferential mechanisms*. Inferential theory states that the monitor cannot directly access an unretrieved item, and therefore must infer its presence. Inferential theory postulates that the monitor uses other kinds of information that it can retrieve or perceive. For example, Koriat (1993) thinks of the feeling-of-knowing as based on the retrieval of partial information. If a remember retrieves enough partial information about an unrecalled target, then he or she may infer that the target will be recognized (Nelson et al., 1984; Schwartz, 1994).

Until the 1990s most researchers favored the direct-access mechanisms. However, in the 1990s a wealth of data began to support the inferential view. Most researchers have considered tip-of-the-tongue states to be the product of direct-access mechanisms. However, Schwartz and Smith (1997) suspected that inferential mechanisms might affect tip-of-the-tongue states too.

Their hypothesis was based on theoretical work of Asher Koriat (1993, 1995). Koriat argued that feelings of knowing occur because people retrieve partial information or related

Maximum-Information Condition	Medium-Information Condition	Minimum-Information Condition

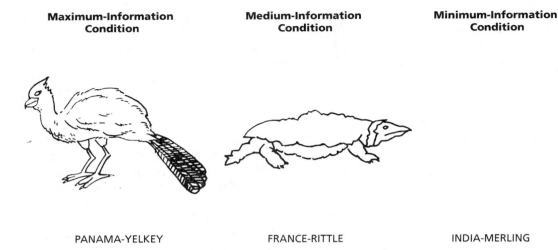

| PANAMA-YELKEY | FRANCE-RITTLE | INDIA-MERLING |

FIGURE 11.8 Examples of TOTimals. Used by Schwartz & Smith (1997).

information about a sought-for but unrecalled target. People then *infer* their feeling of knowing based on the amount or intensity of that retrieved knowledge. People base their judgments not on direct access to the target's strength—which they cannot retrieve—but rather on related knowledge that they can retrieve, such as semantically related information.

In the Schwartz and Smith study, participants studied nonsense words each paired with the name of a country. Eight of the twelve were also accompanied by line drawings of fictional animals (see Figure 11.8). Participants were told that each nonsense word was the name of an animal. The country name was the habitat of that animal. For example, participants might have seen *"Yelkey—Panama,"* which means that the "yelkey" is an animal that lives in Panama.

There were two main encoding conditions, called minimum-information (just the name-country pair), and maximum-information (name-country pair plus line drawing). Each condition was designed to allow a different amount of information to be retrieved at the time of test. At test, participants were given the country name as a cue for the retrieval of the animal name. Participants were asked to recall the name

of the animal. If they could not, they were asked for a TOT judgment and to guess at the first letter. Participants were also asked to retrieve as much related information as they could. Related information was defined as retrieving descriptions of the appearance of the animal.

The encoding manipulation did not affect recall of animal names (see Table 11.4). However, TOT states did vary as a function of condition. A greater number of TOT states were reported in the maximum information conditions than in the minimum-information condition. Moreover, this increase in TOT states was correlated with increased recall of related information, not recall of the sought-for name. The most succinct explanation is based on Koriat's theory. Participants retrieved pictorial information concerning the animal, and then inferred that, because they could recall the way the animal looked, they would be able to recall the animal's name. This inference drives the TOT state.

Judgments of Learning

Monitoring occurs when information is being learned as well as when information is being retrieved. Monitoring at the time of acquisition is

Table 11.4 Schwartz and Smith's Experiment 3.
Mean percent recall, percent likelihood of a TOT state per unrecalled target, mean related reported pictorial information, and percent recognized, as a function of presentation of related information.

	MINIMUM	MAXIMUM
TOT	.11	.19
Recall	.34	.33
Recognition	.66	.62
Related information	.19	.32

From Schwartz and Smith's (1997)

extremely important. People need to know whether their encoding processes have adequately done the job. Consider the consequences of improper monitoring of encoding. If a person does not know whether she has encoded new information adequately, she may study it insufficiently and subsequently forget it, or she may spend excessive time studying information that she will not forget.

Nelson and Narens have examined judgments of learning. Judgments of learning are defined as explicit assessments of the efficacy of study. Like feeling-of-knowing judgments, judgments of learning are predictions about the future. They ask the participant to assess the question "Will you remember this information at a later time?" In contrast to feeling-of-knowing judgments, judgments of learning are done during encoding, not retrieval. As with feeling-of-knowing judgments, judgments of learning typically are made on numerical scales.

Judgments of learning were first studied by Underwood in the 1960s (Underwood, 1965), but the most intensive studies of judgments of learning have come from Thomas Nelson and his colleagues. In a typical experiment, they gave participants word pairs to study, usually an English word and a foreign-language equivalent, such as *"the book—le livre."* The participants were then given adequate time to study the items. After studying each item for a set period of time, the participant made a judgment of learning concerning the likelihood of later recalling the French word if supplied given with the English word. At some point later, the participants were given the English word and asked to retrieve the French word (Dunlosky & Nelson, 1997; Nelson & Leonesio, 1988).

Judgments of learning are fairly accurate predictors of later recall. In other words, people's ability to monitor their encoding allows them to predict the future. By assessing the strength of a memory now, one can assess whether one will know the item later (Nelson & Leonesio, 1988).

The accuracy of judgments of learning varies as a function of how the judgments are made by the participants and with what information base they make the judgments of learning. Nelson and Dunlosky (1991) asked for judgments of learning at two different times. In one condition, the judgments of learning were made right after participants had studied a particular paired-associate. In the other condition, the judgments of learning were made at a delay of several minutes following initial study. Moreover, the judgments of learning were made only in the presence of the cue of the cue-target pair, rather than both items. Under these conditions, accuracy was much higher when the judgments were made at a delay. In fact, the judgments of learning were nearly perfect at predicting later recall performance. The result is paradoxical; a delay results in more accurate processing.

Nelson and Dunlosky (1991) argued that the paradox is a consequence of the way in which the judgments were made. When the judgments were made initially, the target word was still available in short-term memory, and the presence of the target in short-term memory impeded the prediction as to whether it had also been encoded into long-term memory. In contrast, when the judgments were made at a delay, the target word was no longer accessible from short-term memory. To make the judgment of learning, the participant had to rely on the target's representation in long-term memory. Because the final test was also one of long-term memory, the delayed judgment of learning better approximated the test situation and was consequently more accurate.

Are there any situations when people are not good at predicting later performance? Benjamin, Bjork, and Schwartz (1998) addressed this question and identified a situation in which people mispredict later performance.

In their experiment, Benjamin et al. asked participants to answer general-information questions, such as "What is the capital of France?" and "What is the capital of Croatia?" Participants were instructed to answer the question as quickly as possible. Once participants had retrieved the answer, they were asked how likely they were to be able to recall the answer later *without the question*. They were told that they would receive a free-recall test for the answers to the questions later. After answering 20 questions and making judgments of learning for these questions, they were given a final free-recall test for the answers.

Benjamin et al. were interested in the relationship between the judgments of learning and the likelihood of later retrieving the target answer in the free-recall test. They suspected that the judgments of learning might mispredict performance. Their reasoning was that some questions were easy to answer, such as "What is the capital of France?" Most people know this and the answer, "Paris," is retrieved easily and quickly. However, when posed with the question "What is the capital of Croatia?" most people have a much more difficult time retrieving the answer, "Zagreb." Based on an earlier finding by Gardiner, Craik, and Bleasdale (1973), Benjamin et al. suspected that initial ease of recall would be inversely related to later free recall.

The initial test, the general-information questions, relied on semantic memory. Names that were more strongly encoded into semantic memory were recalled more reliably and more quickly. However, they did not make a lasting episodic memory, whereas the more time-consuming difficult retrieval of an item such as "Zagreb" could very well make a lasting impression resulting in an episodic memory. The second test, the free-recall test, relied on episodic memory. Therefore, names that were initially difficult to retrieve from semantic memory should be easy to retrieve from episodic memory.

Benjamin et al. made a number of interesting discoveries. First, items that were initially difficult for participants to retrieve, as measured by response time, were in fact easier for them to remember later. However, this was not reflected in the participants' judgments of learning. Judgments of learning reflected the ease of initial retrieval. Names that were easy to retrieve from semantic memory were given high judgments of learning, whereas names that were initially difficult to retrieve from semantic memory were given low judgments of learning. The judgments of learning mispredicted performance.

Why is this finding important? First, it demonstrates that monitoring is not always accurate. In fact, in some situations it mispredicts performance. Because decisions concerning control are made based on monitoring, such mispredictions may cause less efficient performance. Therefore, people concerned about efficient learning methods should be interested in when monitoring mispredicts performance. Second, the Benjamin study's results suggest that judgments of learning, like tip-of-the-tongue states, are sometimes based on inferential sources. In the Benjamin study, initial ease of retrieval was used as a surrogate for episodic memory strength. The participants based their judgments on one variable, ease of retrieval, to predict another, memory strength. They considered this to be strong support for an inferential view.

Control Processes and Metamemory

We have shown that people can monitor their memories. Feeling-of-knowing judgments, tip-of-the-tongue states, and judgments of learning are generally accurate at predicting memory performance. However, monitoring offers little utility to the rememberer unless it can be used by the rememberer to effect change. Consider again the student studying English-French translation equivalents. During study, the student can make judgments of learning to assess which items are well learned and which are poorly learned. However, this information does not help the student until the knowledge about well-learned and poorly learned items is used to guide future study. Control processes in metamemory allow us to take what we learn from monitoring and adjust our behavior accordingly. Control processes are adaptive because they allow conscious decisions to influence our cognitive processes.

Let us consider control with respect to encoding first. Assessing the state of learning can influence control in several ways. First, if we assess that we have learned an item adequately, we may cease studying it. However, if the item is not learned adequately, we may continue studying it or give up if we think the item is too hard. In general, though, a good rule is that if an item is adequately studied, it need not be studied more; however an inadequately studied item requires more study. Therefore, there should be a negative correlation between judgments of learning and allocation of study time. This is exactly what has been found in several studies (Leonesio & Nelson, 1990; Mazzoni & Cornoldi, 1993).

Mazzoni and Cornoldi (1993) gave participants sentences to study. The participants, Italian college students, chose how much time to allocate to study each of the sentences. They were aware that they would be tested later and were instructed to allocate study time so as to maximize later performance. Mazzoni and Cornoldi found that allocation of study time was negatively correlated with judgments of learning. Sentences that received lower judgments of learning received more study time whereas sentences that received higher judgments of learning received less study time. Thus, participants devoted more time to the items they thought were more difficult. However, the researchers found that participants did not study the difficult ones enough. During the final recall test, the participants were still more likely to recall the ones that they had judged to be more easy (and indeed studied less) than the more difficult items that they had stud-

ied more. This basic finding has been replicated several times (Nelson, 1993).

This finding suggests that people use the output of their metamemory judgments to control encoding. Low judgments of learning resulted in more study than high judgments of learning. This is a good strategy. The higher judgments of learning imply that memory will be good for these items, as judgments of learning are highly accurate at predicting performance. Moreover, the difficulty of some items is also reflected in the judgments of learning. These items, however, receive more study to compensate for their overall difficulty.

Koriat and Goldsmith (1996) examined aspects of control at retrieval. They postulated that a retrieval process produces an answer, but then a conscious process must make a decision, and that is whether to speak or write the produced answer. This means making a control decision concerning the likely correctness of the answer. Thus, Koriat and Goldsmith examined the postretrieval decision of whether or not to output, or speak, a retrieved answer. In other words, their research addressed the age-old issue of whether one should say what one thinks.

In their experiments, they give Israeli college students general-information sentences such as "In what American state do you find Yale University?" Imagine if you were one of these students. You may come up with an answer such as "New Hampshire," and then realize it might be wrong because you know that Dartmouth is in New Hampshire. Therefore, even though you have retrieved an answer (albeit, a wrong one), you withhold from outputting it because you suspect that it may be incorrect. (By the way, Yale is in Connecticut.)

In Koriat and Goldsmith's experiments, some participants were placed into a forced-recall condition. In other words, they were required to output an answer, regardless of whether or not they thought it was incorrect. Other participants were allowed to answer only those questions to which they were relatively sure that their answer was correct. Koriat and Goldsmith compared two components of their memory performance, quantity and accuracy. They defined *quantity* as the total number of correct answers. The forced-recall participants showed a slight increase in quantity; they recalled somewhat more information than the free-recall participants. Koriat and Goldsmith also compared accuracy. Accuracy was defined as the number of correct answers as a function of total answers. Here, the free-recall participants were much more accurate than the forced-recall participants. In other words, participants can screen their answers for correctness. That is, all participants could retrieve information and then discard it as possibly incorrect. Thus, we can see another example of how people use metamemory control to improve their memory performance. Koriat and Goldsmith showed that people can monitor the output of their responses and use that to control the accuracy by eliminating wrong answers.

AMNESIA

Amnesia is often an early symptom of disorders such as Alzheimer's. The study of amnesia is both critical for understanding memory processes and helping those who suffer from memory disorders.

Amnesia refers to a deficit in the remembering of events. Thus, an aphasic (a person with a brain-based language disorder) may have difficulties remembering words, but is not classified as amnesic because event memory may be intact. Furthermore, amnesia usually occurs only for episodic memory. Most often, people remember semantic memories and also do not lose their own sense of identity. A person usually retains his or her intelligence, personality, and identity, but fails to learn new information or remember new people, and may sometimes fail to remember the past. And more often than not, it is permanent. In Hollywood portrayals, amnesics ultimately remember their identities and return to their former lives. Real amnesics usually spend the rest of their lives grappling with their impoverished memory.

Some amnesias are of psychiatric origin and are, therefore, reversible and temporary. However, amnesia caused by brain damage is often irreversible and permanent. Organic amnesias are caused by brain damage.

The most common forms of amnesia arise from four different causes. The first three are more typical in older people, and the fourth is most prevalent in younger people. The first form is the amnesia typical of Alzheimer's disease. Amnesia is the first symptom of the mental deterioration that occurs in the hundreds of thousands of people who suffer from Alzheimer's. Because the disease is progressive, patients are seldom used for psychological research. The second cause of amnesia common in older people results from strokes. Strokes result in a lack of blood supplied to particular areas of the brain. When a stroke affects blood supply to the areas of the brain involved in memory, amnesia can occur. The third major cause of amnesia is chronic alcoholism. Chronic alcoholism may induce a kind of amnesia called Korsakoff's disease, which we will consider at the end of the section. The fouth major cause of amnesia, most common among younger adults, is brain damage that results from accidents, particularly automobile accidents.

Forms of Amnesia

The major functional distinction in amnesia is the difference between anterograde and retrograde amnesia. *Anterograde amnesia* refers to difficulties in remembering new events or learning new information. Old memories may be intact, but the anterograde amnesic has difficulty forming new ones. General intelligence, short-term memory, and language skills remain intact in anterograde amnesics. *Retrograde amnesia* refers to difficulties in remembering old events or old information. Retrograde amnesics cannot remember information that they learned prior to their brain damage. Retrograde amnesia is usually accompanied by anterograde amnesia, but not always. Most anterograde amnesics, however, do not suffer retrograde amnesia (see Table 11.5).

Table 11.5 The Difference Between Anterograde and Retrograde Amnesia.

ANTEROGRADE	RETROGRADE
Inability to learn new facts and events	Often new learning is preserved
Old learning—both semantic and episodic—is intact	Deficits in remembering events prior to brain damage

Anterograde amnesia is common after strokes as well as head injuries. It is also a symptom of both Alzheimer's disease and Korsakoff's disease. Anterograde amnesia can vary in its severity. It may manifest as a minor difficulty in remembering new information that causes problems only in remembering such things as where the car keys are or learning a new name. However, anterograde amnesia can range to being nearly absolute, in which case no new learning is possible.

Anterograde amnesia often occurs after damage to the hippocampus and to surrounding regions of the medial temporal lobe. Damage to the hippocampus is not associated with retrograde amnesia, suggesting that the hippocampi are a part of the brain involved in encoding but not necessarily retrieval of information (see Parkin, 1996 for more information on the neuropsychological perspective).

The Amnesic Syndrome

Baddeley (1998) defines a certain class of symptoms that commonly occur together as the amnesic syndrome. The deficits characteristic of the amnesic syndrome seem to occur following damage to the hippocampus and the surrounding areas in the medial temporal lobe. Because these areas of the brain are particularly vulnerable to damage during a stroke, there are many patients with these characteristics. The amnesic syndrome is characterized by the following characteristics:

1. Normal short-term memory. Most amnesics can do digit-span tasks normally. Furthermore, they show a recency effect in immediate free-recall tests. Normal short-term memory allows amnesics to carry out simple tasks and hold conversations because they can maintain information indefinitely if they are rehearsing it.

2. Normal semantic memory. Semantic memory is unaffected by the amnesic syndrome as well. Amnesics may maintain a great deal of knowledge about the world. K.C., rendered amnesic in a motorcycle accident, was still able to remember who had won the Stanley Cup in hockey in each year prior to his accident (Tulving, Schacter, McLachlan, & Moscovitch, 1988).

3. General intelligence. General intelligence is unaffected by the amnesic syndrome.

4. Intact implicit memory. Patients with the amnesic syndrome show normal priming on implicit memory tasks (Schacter, 1992).

5. No or limited retrograde amnesia. There may be some retrograde amnesia for events just prior to the brain damage, but, in general, amnesia is restricted to after the brain damage.

6. Mild to severe anterograde amnesia. The patient has difficulty in learning and remembering new events.

These symptoms go together and tend to be associated with damage to the hippocampus and nearby medial temporal lobe, suggesting that these areas of the brain are crucial to the encoding of information.

Korsakoff's Disease

Korsakoff's disease results from a thiamine deficiency that usually is the consequence of long-term alcoholism, although occasionally, other abnormalities may be causative. The thiamine deficiency results in brain damage to areas of the brain other than the medial temporal lobes. Most prominent of these areas are subcortical structures in the diencephalon, such as the thalamus, and the mamillary bodies (Schacter, 1996). Damage to the frontal lobes of the cortex may also occur in Korsakoff's. Damage may also occur to the hippocampus and the medial temporal lobes.

Because of the number of regions affected, Korsakoff's syndrome tends to be much more debilitating than the amnesic syndrome. Korsakoff patients frequently have a variety of problems other than memory. Many Korsakoff patients suffer from motivational and cognitive problems. With respect to memory, they show anterograde amnesia similar to the Amnesic-syndrome patients. Moreover, they generally show some form of retrograde amnesia, sometimes going back years. For example, Jimmy, a patient studied by Oliver Sacks in 1975, suffered a retrograde amnesia back to 1945 (Sacks, 1985). Jimmy, a career Navy sailor, could not remember anything about his life dating back to his return from overseas after World War II. Sacks's eloquent description of a Korsakoff's amnesia is as poignant as it is accurate. The following interview took place in 1975 when Jimmy was 49 years old.

He [Jimmy] was a genial soul, very ready to talk and to answer any questions I asked him. He told me his name and birth date, and the name of the little Connecticut town where he was born. He described it in affectionate detail, even drew me a map. . . . He remembered the names of various submarines on which he had served [during WWII], their missions, where they had been stationed, the names of his shipmates. He remembered Morse code, and was still fluent in Morse tapping and touch-typing.

"What year is this, Mr. G.?" I asked, concealing my perplexity under a casual manner.

"Forty-five, man. What do you mean?"

He went on, "We've won the war, FDR's dead, Truman's at the helm. There's great times ahead."

"And you, Jimmie, how old would you be?"

Oddly, uncertainly, he hesitated a moment, as if engaged in calculation.

"Why, I guess I'm nineteen, Doc. I'll be twenty next birthday."

Korsakoff patients often have only a very dim awareness of their memory problems. When confronted with poor performance on a particular memory test, they will often blame the situation or perhaps claim that they were not paying attention. Amnesic patients are often more aware of their memory problems and are therefore more likely to use compensatory strategies. Korsakoff patients are not aware of their memory difficulties, and therefore, they do not try to compensate. For example, later in Sacks's interview with Jimmy, the following dialogue occurs.

"Okay," I said. "I'll tell you a story. A man went to his doctor complaining of memory lapses. The doctor asked him some routine questions, and then said, 'These lapses. What about them?' 'What lapses?' the patient replied."

"So that's my problem," Jimmie laughed. "I kinda thought it was. I do find myself forgetting things, once in a while—things that have just happened. The past is clear, though."

Sacks's patient had no idea of the severity of his amnesia.

Another feature characteristic of Korsakoff's patients is a tendency to confabulate. *Confabulation* means they construct memories that did not occur. It is sometimes called paradoxically "honest lying" (Moscovitch, 1989). Nonetheless, the patient earnestly believes them, at least as long as he or she is in the process of confabulating. When asked to retrieve the same memory later, the confabulation might be wildly different. Confabulation is extremely rare in people with the amnesic syndrome. When they cannot remember, they simply say so. Korsakoff's patients, however, are prone to confabulation.

Confabulation may arise because of disturbances to temporal sequencing of memory and it may also arise out of a failure of monitoring and control. The confabulatory patient may not be able to screen false memories and fantasies from real memories and thus may relate these confabulations. Consider the following interview between Morris Moscovitch, a leading expert on amnesia and patient HW (Moscovitch, 1989), who is suffering from Korsakoff's disease. The disease has affected his frontal lobes.

> HW: I'm 40, 42, pardon me, 62.
>
> MM: Are you married or single?
>
> HW: Married.
>
> MM: How long have you been married?
>
> HW: About four months.
>
> MM: What's your wife's name?
>
> HW: Martha.
>
> MM: How many children do you have?
>
> HW: Four. (He laughs.) Not bad for four months.
>
> MM: How old are your children?
>
> HW: The eldest is 32; his name is Bob; and the youngest is 22; his name is Joe.
>
> MM: (He laughs again.) How did you get these children in four months?
>
> HW: They're adopted.
>
> MM: Who adopted them?
>
> HW: Martha and I.
>
> MM: Immediately after you got married you wanted to adopt these older children?
>
> HW: Before we were married we adopted one of them, two of them. The eldest girl,

Brenda, and Bob, and Joe and Dina since we were married.

Another feature of Korsakoff's disease is poor metamemory. Shimamura and Squire (1986) conducted a study examining the accuracy of the feeling-of-knowing judgments in a group of amnesic-syndrome amnesics, Korsakoff's patients, and control subjects. The subjects were asked general-information questions such as "What is the capital of Chile?" If they did not know, they made a feeling-of-knowing judgment and then were given a multiple-choice recognition test. Shimamura and Squire found that the amnesic-syndrome patients showed normal accuracy that did not differ from the nonamnesic controls. The Korskakoff's patients, however, were severely impaired in this task. The correlation between their feeling-of-knowing judgments and their recognition did not differ from zero, meaning they did not know what they did or did not know. Like the confabulation results, the lack of metamemory accuracy suggests that Korsakoff's patients have very poor monitoring ability.

SUMMARY STATEMENTS

Amnesia is a neurological condition that results from brain damage to several areas of the brain including the hippocampus, the medial temporal lobes, the thalamus, the mamillary bodies, and frontal cortex. Amnesia is separable into two distinct varieties, anterograde amnesia, an impairment in new learning and remembering, and retrograde amnesia, an impairment in retrieving previously learned information. The amnesic syndrome, a consistent block of symptoms that follows hippocampal damage, is marked by impaired anterograde amnesia without any other cognitive impairments. Korsakoff's disease includes both anterograde amnesia and retrograde amnesia and is also accompanied by confabulation and difficulties with monitoring and control.

Glossary of Key Terms

absolute properties of stimuli—The contention that in a discrimination problem organisms learn about the specific properties of a stimulus (black vs. white) and not about relationships between them (darker vs. lighter)

absolute stimulus generalization gradient—A stimulus generalization gradient based on the absolute number of responses made to each stimulus in the generalization test

accessibility—The amount of information that can be retrieved from memory at any particular point in time

acquired distinctiveness of cues—Prior learning about stimuli in one setting will facilitate solving a different problem if the same stimuli are used

algebraic summation theory—Spence's theoretical account of discrimination learning that contends that excitatory gradients and inhibitory gradients summate to produce behavior

amnesic syndrome—A form of amnesia usually caused by damage to the temporal lobes and the hippocampus; characterized by anterograde amnesia

analyzer strength—A theoretical construct within Sutherland and Mackintosh's discrimination learning theory; analyzers identify the type of problem the

organism is solving and are considered the equivalent of hypotheses

anterograde amnesia—A deficit in memory that is characterized by an inability to acquire and retain new information

attribute theory—The theoretical position that concepts are represented mentally as a list of features

autoshaping—A procedure used in operant-conditioning studies to shape the operant response; the procedure involves the pairing of a localized CS with food and reinforcing the resulting approach and CS contact response

availability—The sum total of all information stored in memory

aversion therapies—A form of behavior therapy that utilizes classical-conditioning procedures to change behavior; for example, the taste of alcohol (CS) might be paired with a stimulus that causes illness (US); such a procedure reduces the occurrence of the target behavior

avoidance learning—A conditioning procedure in which an aversive event is signaled and the organism can avoid the aversive stimulus with a specified response

backward conditioning—A classical conditioning procedure in which the US precedes the presentation of the CS

backward masking—Occurs when immediately following the disappearance of a stimulus, a second stimulus occurs in the same spatial location, rendering the first stimulus more difficult to consciously process

basic level—Certain categories, like tree, are at a basic level; such categories are subsets of superordinate levels (plants) and contain subsets of subordinate levels (e.g., oak tree)

behavioral systems theory—An ecologically based classical conditioning theory used to predict the form of the CR depending on the temporal relation between the CS and the US and the organism's evolutionary and experiential history

blocking—A classical-conditioning procedure in which a previously conditioned CS is placed in compound with a second CS; the compound is then paired with the same US as before; blocking is demonstrated when there is little or no conditioning to the second CS

central executive—In the working memory model, an attentional mechanism

classical conditioning—A situation in which a contingency exists between a stimulus and an outcome; the outcome is presented independently of a response; also known as Pavlovian conditioning

classical excitatory conditioning—A type of conditioning that occurs when the CS acquires the capability of eliciting a response because of its association with the US

classical inhibitory conditioning—A type of conditioning that occurs when the CS is in a negatively contingent relation with the US; the CS predicts the absence of the US and it elicits a response that reflects this relation

coexistence hypothesis—A theory that explains the misinformation effect in which both the original and suggested memory are stored

cognitive interview—A technique developed for police to increase the amount of recalled information from cooperative witnesses

commissorotomy—A neurosurgical procedure in which the corpus callosum is severed, effectively breaking the connection between the left and right halves of the brain

concept—A distinct category of objects or events that are all related on the basis of certain features or characteristics

concurrent schedule—A schedule of reinforcement in which two or more independent schedules are operating simultaneously and independently in the presence of different external stimuli

conditioned emotional response—A conditioning procedure in which a CS is paired with an aversive US that is later used to disrupt ongoing operant behavior

conditioned reinforcer—A stimulus that has acquired reinforcing properties by being associated with a primary reinforcer

conditioned response (CR)—The response that is produced by the conditioned stimulus; the CR can differ from the unconditioned response both quantitatively and qualitatively

conditioned stimulus (CS)—An initially neutral stimulus that acquires the ability to elicit a response through its association with an unconditioned stimulus

confabulation—"honest" lying; occurs in amnesics, who often "remember" events that never occurred

consummatory response—The response used to acquire primary reinforcers such as eating or drinking

contextual stimuli—In classical conditioning all stimuli that impinge on the sensory systems of the organism other than the CS and US

contiguity theories—Theories of classical conditioning that contend that the temporal arrangements of the CS and US pairings dictate the necessary and sufficient conditions for conditioning

contingency theories—Theories of classical conditioning that contend that conditioning depends on the extent to which the CS is correlated with the presentation of the US

CS pre-exposure—A classical-conditioning procedure that involves presenting the CS alone for several trials prior to CS-US pairings; the typical effect is to retard conditioning (also called latent inhibition)

CS-US relevance—The contention that certain CS-US combinations are more easily conditioned than others; for example, rats quickly associate taste with illness, but do not readily associate audiovisual stimuli with illness

delayed conditioning—A classical-conditioning procedure in which the CS begins before the US and ends before the US ends; CS and US presentations overlap

delayed-judgment-of-learning effect—A condition in which judgments of learning are more accurate if they occur at a delay after the initial learning

differential reinforcement of high rates of response (DRH)—A schedule of reinforcement in which a response is rewarded only if a specified number of responses occurs within a specified period of time

differential reinforcement of low rates of response (DRL)—A schedule of reinforcement in which a response is rewarded only if a specified period of time has elapsed since the preceding response

direct access theory—A theory that postulates that metacognitive judgments reflect nonconscious access to an unretrieved target

directed forgetting—A condition that occurs when specific instructions to forget result in greater forgetting

discrimination hypothesis—A theoretical account of the partial reinforcement extinction effect (PREE), which contends that organisms take longer to extinguish under partial reinforcement because it is more difficult to distinguish between acquisition and extinction when reinforcement is intermittent than when reinforcement is continuous

discrimination learning—Occurs when an organism learns to make one response in the presence of one stimulus and a different response in the presence of a second stimulus

discriminative stimulus—A stimulus that predicts when a certain response-outcome relation will hold

distinctive processing—A condition in which information is processed according to unique aspects of the stimuli, which leads to good deep encoding

distributed practice—A condition in which learning is spread out over time; study is spaced out over a number of hours, days, or weeks

echoic memory—Auditory sensory memory

elaborative rehearsal—The process of encoding information by relating it to other information in memory

elicited responses—Responses that are elicited reflexively by certain stimuli of biological significance or by stimuli that have been associated with stimuli of biological significance

emitted responses—Responses that are produced by an organism often as a result of a learned association between the response and an outcome

encoding—Refers to the learning of events that can be represented internally, such as the memory for events, words, or faces

encoding specificity principle—A principle that maintains that retrieval is optimal when the retrieval conditions match the conditions at encoding

encoding variability—The idea that encoding leads to better storage and retrieval when the encoding takes place in a number of different physical and mental contexts

engram—A theoretical term that refers to the stored memory

episodic memory—A theoretical long-term memory system that represents memories of individual events from a person's life

excitation—One of two competing critical processes in Pavlov's theory of discrimination learning; excitation increases with each reinforced presentation of S+

excitatory stimulus generalization gradient—Gradients formed when organisms are trained to associate a reinforced response with a specific stimulus and then are tested to determine if this response is elicited by similar stimuli

exemplar theory—A theoretical account of cognition that postulates that concepts are represented in the brain as a specific instance of that concept

explicit memory tests—Memory tests in which memory is tested by conscious recollection

extinction—A procedure that involves the termination of reinforcement for a stimulus or a response that was previously reinforced; the normal outcome of extinction is a decrease and eventual cessation of responding

extradimensional shift problem—A discrimination problem in which the stimulus dimension is changed across successive problems; for example, the organism is trained on a size problem and then shifted to a color problem

false memories—Memories for events that never occurred, or memories that have become distorted

family resemblance—The idea that each member of a concept shares characteristics in common with other members of that concept; not all concepts share the same characteristics

feeling of knowing—A judgment concerning whether one will be able to recognize items that one cannot recall

fixed ratio (FR)—A schedule of reinforcement in which an organism is rewarded for a specified number of responses

flashbulb memories—Memories of an event that was surprising or emotionally arousing or both

flooding—A behavioral therapy for phobias in which an individual is exposed to the phobic stimulus for an extended period of time, which results in extinction of the phobic response

free recall—A memory task in which a person is asked to remember items or events without any cues

frustration—An aversive emotional response that results when an expected reward is withheld

frustration theory—A theoretical account of extinction in which competing responses are conditioned to stimuli that predict the absence of an expected reward

generalization decrement hypothesis—A theoretical account of the partial reinforcement extinction effect that contends that the absence of the reinforcer during extinction changes the stimulus conditions encountered during acquisition; this change results in a deficit in responding

generation effect—A condition in which items that are generated by a person are better remembered than those that are simply read by the person

generation-recognition hypothesis—A theory originally devised by Kintsch to explain retrieval processes; in the first stage, the person generates a set of possible memories, and the recognition phase identifies the correct memory

goal tracking—Behavior in which an organism approaches the US and not the CS as a result of a learned association between a CS and a US

habituation—A decrease in responding to a stimulus that is presented repeatedly and that is not associated with events of biological significance to the organism

higher order conditioning—A classical-conditioning procedure in which a stimulus (CS_2) is paired with a previously conditioned stimulus (CS_1); following these trials CS_2 is able to elicit a CR, also known as second order conditioning

hippocampus—A structure found deep within the limbic system of the brain that appears to play a role in learning and memory

iconic memory—Visual sensory memory

imagery—The forming of mental images of objects or sounds not physically present

implicit memory—Indirect memory tests in which the subject does not know that the memory can be or will be used to solve the problem

incidental learning—The process by which people encode information into long-term memory not by actively trying to remember the information

inferential theory in metacognition—The theory that states that metacognitive judgments are based on inferences that an item will be learned or can be remembered

information-processing approach—A major theory in cognitive psychology that postulates that cognition can be thought of as the flow of information through a series of systems and processes

inhibitory stimulus generalization gradient—Gradients formed when organisms are trained to associate a nonreinforced response with a specific stimulus and then are tested to determine if this response is elicited by similar stimuli

instinctive drift—Condition that occurs when instinctive behaviors prevent or interfere with the learning of a new response

instrumental conditioning—A situation in which a contingency exists between a response and an outcome; the outcome is dependent on a specific response

intentional learning—The process by which people actively engage in learning information because they know that their memories may be tested

intermittent reinforcement—A procedure in which responses are rewarded in less than 100% of the trials; also known as partial reinforcement

internal inhibition—One of two competing critical responses in Pavlov's theory of discrimination learning; inhibition builds with each nonreinforced stimulus presentation, and the animal actively withholds the response

interval schedules—Schedules of reinforcement in which the operant is rewarded following the passage of some specified interval of time

intradimensional shift problem—A discrimination problem in which the stimulus dimension remains constant through successive problems; for example, an organism may learn a red vs. green discrimination and then be shifted to a yellow vs. blue problem

investigatory reflex—An innate response in which attention behaviors are made to novel stimuli; in Pavlov's theory of discrimination learning, this response competes with approach responses resulting in low responses

judgments of learning—Judgments that predict whether an item has been adequately studied

keyword technique—A method that involves making a visual image of a salient aspect of the to-be-learned word and then associating the visual image with the word's meaning

Korsakoff's amnesia—A form of amnesia characterized by both retrograde and anterograde amnesia and frequently confabulation; caused by a thiamine deficiency usually induced by chronic alcoholism

learned helplessness—A condition in which organisms exposed to unavoidable and inescapable electric shock will have much more difficulty learning to avoid or escape shock in a later situation; the effect is often interpreted to mean that the organism has learned that its responses are ineffective

learning—A process by which a relatively permanent change in behavior occurs as a result of experience

levels of processing—A theory of memory to explain encoding effects; postulates that deeper or more meaningful encoding leads to stronger memory representations

lexical-decision task—An implicit memory task in which a person must decide as quickly as possible whether a letter string is a word or not

long-term learning expectancy—A hypothetical construct within the Dragoi and Staddon mathematical model of operant conditioning; the construct is a measure of expected reinforcement

long-term memory—A system or set of systems that stores an unlimited amount of information for up to the lifetime of the individual

maintenance rehearsal—A process by which a memory is kept in conscious awareness for a period of time but rehearsed in rote fashion

massed practice—A process in which all rehearsal is done at one time

matching law—A theoretical position that claims that when organisms are free to respond to two different schedules of reinforcement, they will allocate their responses in proportion to the rate of reinforcement on each schedule

median forebrain bundle—A large bundle of nerve fibers in the brain that is thought to be important in reinforcement and in species-typical behaviors

memory—An internal record or representation of some prior event or experience

memory processes—Theoretical functions of encoding, representation, and retrieval

memory systems—Theoretical neural/cognitive systems responsible for particular memory functions

metacognition—Awareness and knowledge of cognition

metacognitive control—The ability of a person to use metacognition to direct, alter, change, or affect the manner in which information is mentally processed

metacognitive monitoring—Cognitive processes involved in keeping track of the current status of the memory system; involves assessing how strong memories are now and how they might change in the future

metamemory—Awareness and knowledge of one's own memory

method of loci—The process of learning to associate new to-be-learned items with a series of previously well-learned physical locations

misinformation effect—A paradigm in which misinformation is presented to subjects and causes worse memory performance for recall or recognition of the original event

mixed schedule—A schedule of reinforcement in which two or more independent schedules of reinforcement are presented sequentially, each in the presence of the same external stimulus

multiple schedule—A schedule of reinforcement in which two or more independent schedules of reinforcement are presented sequentially, each in the presence of a different external stimulus

natural concepts—A distinct category of objects that are found in nature; such concepts are not well defined and are sometimes referred to as fuzzy concepts; they may include concepts such as tree, fish, or flower

necessary conditions—The minimum conditions in a cause-and-effect relationship

negative contingency—A condition in which the occurrence of the CS is correlated with the occurrence of the US such that the CS predicts the absence of the US

negative punishment—The termination of a positive reinforcer that results in the decrease of the probability of the response that produced it

negative reinforcement—The termination of an aversive stimulus that results in an increase in the probability of the response that produced it

network models—The position that concepts and ideas are represented mentally as nodes that are linked together by networks that vary in strength depending on the degree of association

neuroscience—A field of investigation dedicated to the discovery of the biological bases of behavior, including sensation and perception, motivation and emotion, and learning and memory

nodes—In network models of memory, representations of individual concepts or memories

noncontinuity theories—In contrast to the continuity position that habit strength or S-R associations build gradually with each reinforced trial, these theories contend that once the organism adopts the correct hypothesis, learning proceeds rapidly

NR transitions—Conditions that occur when a rewarded trial follows a nonrewarded trial in an instrumental task

observing response—A response that provides information about which of two possible outcomes is forthcoming

omission procedure—A procedure that involves the termination of reward if an organism makes a specified response

operant conditioning—A subset of instrumental conditioning in which the organism is free to emit specific behaviors at any time and the consequences of those behaviors change the rate of operant responding

optimal arousal hypothesis—The notion that organisms will behave in such a fashion as to maintain an optimal level of arousal

optimal foraging—A theoretical account of how organisms make decisions about where and when to forage and when to stop foraging in one place and move to another; it is assumed that natural selection has selected for organisms that maximize energy input and minimize energy output

overlearning reversal effect (ORE)—One of the paradoxical effects of reward in which organisms that are trained to criterion on a discrimination problem and then overtrained are able to solve the reversal of that problem more readily than organisms who are trained to criterion and reversed

overshadowing—The process by which certain CSs, by virtue of their greater salience, presented in compound with other CSs will have greater conditioned strength at the end of training

partial reinforcement extinction effect (PREE)—A paradoxical effect of reward in which organisms that are rewarded intermittently are more resistant to extinction than organisms who are reinforced continuously

pause after reinforcement (PAR)—A break in operant responding following reinforcement that is commonly observed in FR and FI schedules with high requirements for reward

peak-shift phenomenon—A condition in which an organism that has learned to discriminate between two stimuli that lie along the same dimension will, in a generalization test, respond more to a stimulus removed from both S+ and S− than the original S+

pegword technique—A mnemonic technique used to help remember lists, in which each to-be-remembered item is associated with a number-word association

perceptual-identification task—An implicit memory task in which a person is asked to identify a word that is presented at or around the person's conscious threshold (prior exposure will improve performance)

perceptual representation system—A hypothetical system of memory that stores information about the perceptual form of previously encountered items; used in implicit memory tasks

phonological loop—A hypothetical short-term memory system that rehearses auditory information for short periods of time

positive contingency—The occurrence of the CS is correlated with the occurrence of the US such that the CS predicts the presentation of the US

positive punishment—Involves the presentation of a stimulus that decreases the probability of the response that produced it

positive reinforcement—Involves the presentation of a stimulus that increases the probability of the response that produced it

Premack principle—The contention that a response that has a high probability of occurrence can be used to reinforce a response that has a lower probability of occurrence

priming—A phenomenon that occurs when an earlier presentation of a word or object facilitates performance on a later presentation of that word or object

proactive interference—When information presented before to-be-remembered information causes forgetting of the to-be-remembered information

procedural memory—A hypothetical system that stores information about both physical and mental skills

process dissociation—A technique devised by Jacoby to examine familiarity and recollective processes in recognition memory; separates the two processes by requiring a different response depending on whether the subject is using familiarity or recollection

prototype theory—A theoretical account of cognition that proposes that people abstract the common elements of a particular concept and then store prototypical representations in memory

punisher—A stimulus that decreases the probability of the response that produced it

punishment—A contingent relation in which a stimulus decreases the probability of the response that produced it

ratio schedules—Schedules of reinforcement in which rewards are determined by the number of responses emitted

recall—A memory task in which the person must produce or generate the target memory

recognition—A memory task in which the person must identify the target memory from a list of alternatives

reduction of uncertainty—A theoretical account of why organisms make observing responses; it is assumed that uncertainty is aversive and that the reduction of uncertainty is rewarding

reinforcement—A contingent relation in which a stimulus increases the probability of the response that produced it

reinforcer—Any stimulus or outcome that increases the probability of the response that produced it

relational learning—The notion that organisms learn about how stimuli relate (darker vs. lighter) and not about the specific or absolute properties of stimuli (black vs. white)

relative stimulus generalization gradient—A gradient based on the total number of responses made to all stimuli; the experimenter determines the percent of this total that was made in the presence of each test stimulus

representation—The inactive but present contents of memory

repressed memory—In some views of memory, active repression processes that cause the forgetting of psychologically painful information

Rescorla-Wagner theory—A mathematical modified contiguity theory of classical conditioning that asserts that a given US can support only a finite amount of conditioning and that stimulus salience and characteristics of the US affect the rate of conditioning

response deprivation—A state in which an organism is not allowed to make a response, with the result that there is an increase in the organism's preference for making that response

response disequilibrium hypothesis—If an organism is not allowed to maintain its baseline rate of a behavior, access to that behavior will reinforce other behaviors

response strength—A theoretical construct within Sutherland and Mackintosh's discrimination learning theory; response strength refers to the degree of habit strength for a specific stimulus

response-outcome theories—Theoretical positions that contend that instrumental and operant conditioning involves learning about response-reinforcer relations

response-reinforcer association—A theoretical position that posits that bonds can be formed between a response and a reinforcer with the result that the probability of the response is increased or decreased depending on the nature of the reinforcer

retardation test—A procedure that involves pairing an inhibitory CS with a US to determine if the CS is actually inhibitory

retrieval—The process by which memories are remembered, brought to awareness, or used in behavior

retrieval cue—A word or object that triggers the remembering of earlier events.

retrieval-induced forgetting—A phenomenon in which the retrieval of information inhibits or prevents the retrieval of related information

retrieval practice effect—A phenomenon in which practicing retrieval of a particular item induces storage of that item and strong likelihood of retrieval

retrieval strength—A hypothetical entity in Bjork and Bjork's model that indicates the likelihood that an item will be retrieved from memory

retroactive interference—When information presented after to-be-remembered information causes forgetting of the to-be-remembered information

retrograde amnesia—A deficit in memory characterized by an inability to remember past events

schedules of reinforcement—Rules that determine when a response will be rewarded and when it will not

selective attention—The contention that if an organism is paying attention to one event it cannot learn about other events

semantic memory—A hypothetical long-term memory system that holds general knowledge about the world

sensitization—A situation in which organisms show a greater response to mild stimuli as a result of an increase in arousal

sensory memory—Memory store that holds a large amount of sensory information for a very brief period of time

sensory preconditioning—A classical conditioning procedure in which two stimuli are paired; following these trials one of the CSs is paired with a US; demonstrated when the CS that was not paired with the US is able to elicit a conditioned response

sequential theory—A theoretical account of the partial reinforcement extinction effect that contends that resistance to extinction is a function of the number of NR transitions and reinforced N lengths that occur during acquisition

short-term learning expectancy—A hypothetical construct within the Dragoi and Staddon mathematical model of operant conditioning; the construct is a measure of the level of reinforcement the organism is currently experiencing

short-term memory—A hypothetical system in the brain that stores a limited amount of information for a relatively brief period of time

short-term memory trace—A hypothetical construct within the Dragoi and Staddon mathematical model of operant conditioning; it is assumed that when an organism perceives a stimulus or makes a response, there is a memory of the event that decays quickly

sign tracking—Occurs when an organism approaches the CS and not the US as a result of a learned association between a CS and a US

simultaneous conditioning—A classical-conditioning procedure in which the CS and US begin and end at the same time

simultaneous method—A procedure used in discrimination learning in which both stimuli are presented at the same time and the organism can directly compare the two discriminated stimuli

source-monitoring hypothesis—A theory of the misinformation effect that states that the poor memory performance observed in that effect is caused by an inability to discriminate between the original memory and the suggested memory

spacing effect—A phenomenon in which spreading learning out over time increases the likelihood of retrieving it later

Spence–Hull hypothesis—The notion that learning involves an association between a stimulus and a response, but that reinforcement is not required for the association; that is, the critical variable in the S-R bond is temporal contiguity

spontaneous recovery—The recovery of a response that has been extinguished; the response returns as a result of a period of time that has elapsed since habituation or extinction trials

state-dependent learning—Retrieval of information encoded during one particular state of the organism is better when the organism is in the same state at the time of retrieval; states usually refer to mood, physiological condition, or neurochemical effect

stimulus control—The degree to which a given stimulus elicits a response relative to other stimuli; discrimination learning results in steeper generalization gradients and hence greater stimulus control

stimulus dimensions—The modalities along which stimuli differ; examples include color, loudness, size, and so on

stimulus generalization—Organisms trained to respond to one stimulus tend to make the same response to similar stimuli

stimulus generalization gradient—A measure of the degree of stimulus generalization; steep gradients reflect very little generalization and shallow gradients reflect strong generalization

stimulus generalization tests—Procedures that determine the extent to which an organism has generalized across stimuli; the procedure usually involves nonreinforced presentations of stimuli that differ along the same dimension as the target stimulus

stimulus–reinforcer association—A theoretical position that posits that bonds are formed between a stimulus and a reinforcer with the result that presentation of the stimulus will retrieve a mental representation of the reinforcer; also known as a stimulus-stimulus association or S-S association

stimulus–response association—Through reinforcement an association is formed between a stimulus and a response such that the stimulus is able to elicit the response; this view was presented as the Thorndike-Hull hypothesis

storage—The processes that maintain memories when they are not being either encoded or retrieved

storage strength—A hypothetical entity in Bjork and Bjork's model that indicates the strength of the representation in long-term memory; does not ensure that it will be retrieved

subordinate level—Categories nested within the basic level (for example, oak trees are a subset of the basic level tree)

successive method—A procedure used in discrimination learning in which stimuli are presented one at a time successively; the organism is not able to directly compare the two discriminated stimuli

successive negative contrast—One of the paradoxical effects of reward in which an organism is trained at one level of reward and is then switched to a lower level; the switched organism responds at a lower rate than an organism trained originally on the lower level

successive positive contrast—One of the paradoxical effects of reward in which an organism is trained at one level of reward and is then switched to a higher level; the switched organism responds at a higher rate than an organism trained originally on the higher level

sufficient conditions—Conditions in a cause-and-effect relationship that should always produce a particular outcome

suffix effect—In serial position tasks, the effect of adding extra not-to-be-remembered information at the end of a list to prevent a recency effect

summation test—A procedure that involves pairing an inhibitory CS with a neutral stimulus to determine if the CS is actually inhibitory

superordinate level—Basic level categories nested within the superordinate level (for example, trees are under the superordinate level plant)

synergistic ecphory—A model of retrieval developed by Tulving, which centers on the importance of cues for retrieval

systematic desensitization—An effective treatment for phobias that involves gradual exposure to phobic stimuli combined with relaxation therapy

tip-of-the-tongue (TOT) state—A phenomenon in which a person feels that he will soon remember an item or word that he cannot retrieve at the moment

trace conditioning—A classical conditioning procedure in which CS begins and ends before the US begins and ends; the interval of time between the CS and US is termed the trace interval

trace impairment hypothesis—A theory of the misinformation effect that states that the poor memory performance observed in that effect is caused when misinformation causes memory for the original event to be impaired or weakened

transituational—Refers to the finding that a response or stimulus that reinforces behavior in one situation will also be reinforcing in other situations; for example, if a pellet of food will reinforce a rat for pressing a lever, that pellet will also reinforce the rat for running a maze

transposition effect—The effect in which organisms trained on a relational discrimination (dark gray vs. light gray) will, when presented with another relational problem (dark gray vs. darker gray), choose the darker stimulus over the original S+ in a test situation

two-factor theory—A theoretical account of avoidance learning that contends that the CS predicting an aversive event becomes a feared stimulus and the response that terminates the CS is maintained through negative reinforcement

typicality—Refers to how representative is a particular example of a particular concept

unconditioned response (UR)—The response elicited by the unconditioned stimulus

unconditioned stimulus (US)—A stimulus that naturally elicits a measurable and reliable response over an extended period of time

US pre-exposure—A classical-conditioning procedure that involves presenting the US alone before presenting CS-US pairings; the procedure typically retards conditioning

variable interval (VI)—A schedule of reinforcement in which an organism is rewarded for the first response after an average interval of time has elapsed; the time period being varied about a mean

variable ratio (VR)—A schedule of reinforcement in which an organism is rewarded on average for a specified number of responses; the specific number of required responses is varied about a mean

visual persistence—The phenomena by which stimuli may continue to excite the retina of the eye at some point after the stimuli is no longer visible

visuo-spatial sketch pad—A hypothetical system in Baddeley's working memory model that stores visual and spatial information for short periods of time

von Restorff effect—A phenomenon in which a unique or isolated item is recalled better than the more uniform items that surround it

Wagner's priming theory—A classical conditioning theory that contends that stimuli are associated through joint rehearsal in short-term memory; following such rehearsal the association is stored in long-term memory

word-fragment completion task—An implicit memory task in which subjects must fill in the missing letters of an unknown word; priming the word earlier facilitates performance

References

Adams, C. (1980). Postconditioning devaluation of an instrumental reinforcer has no effect on extinction performance. *Quarterly Journal of Experimental Psychology, 32,* 447–458.

Adams, C. (1982). Variations in the sensitivity of instrumental responding to reinforcer devaluation. *Quarterly Journal of Experimental Psychology, 34B,* 77–98.

Adams., C., & Dickinson, A. (1981). Actions and habits: Variations in associative representations during instrumental learning. In N. E. Spear and R. R. Miller (Eds.), *Information processing in animals: Memory mechanisms.* Hillsdale, NJ: Erlbaum.

Ader, R., & Cohen, N. (1993). Psychoneuroimmunology: Conditioning and stress. *Annual Review of Psychology, 44,* 53–85.

Akins, C. A.; Domjan, M.; & Gutierrez, G. (1994). The topography of sexually conditioned behavior in male Japanese quail (*Coturnix japonica*) depends on the CS-US interval. *Journal of Experimental Psychology: Animal Behavior Processes, 21,* 199–209.

Allen, M. (1968). Rehearsal strategies and response cueing as determinants of organization in free recall. *Journal of Verbal Learning and Verbal Behavior, 7,* 58–63.

Allison, J. (1976). Contrast, induction, facilitation, suppression, and conservation. *Journal of the Experimental Analysis of Behavior, 25,* 185–198.

Allison, J. (1983). *Behavioral economics.* New York: Praeger.

Allison, J. (1993). Response deprivation, reinforcement, and economics. *Journal of the Experimental Analysis of Behavior, 60,* 129–140.

Amsel, A. (1958). The role of frustrative nonreward in noncontinuous reward situations. *Psychological Bulletin, 55,* 102–119.

Amsel, A. (1967). Partial reinforcement effects on vigor and persistence. In K. W. Spence and J. T. Spence (Eds.), *The psychology of learning and motivation,* Vol. I (pp. 1–65). New York: Academic Press.

Amsel, A. (1972). Inhibition and mediation in classical Pavlovian and instrumental conditioning. In R. A. Boakes and M. S. Halliday (Eds.), *Inhibition and learning* (pp. 275–299). London: Academic Press.

Amsel, A. (1992). *Frustration theory.* Cambridge, England: Cambridge University Press.

Amsel, A., & Roussel, J. (1952). Motivational properties of frustration: Effect on a running response of the addition of frustration to the motivational complex. *Journal of Experimental Psychology, 43,* 363–368.

Amsel, A., & Ward, J. S. (1965). Frustration and persistence: Resistance to discrimination following prior experience with the discriminanda. *Psychological Monographs General & Applied, 79* (4, Whole No. 597).

Anderson, J. R. (1976). *Language, memory, and thought.* Hillsdale, NJ: Erlbaum.

Anderson, J. R. (1978). Arguments concerning representations for mental imagery. *Psychological Review, 85,* 249–277.

Anderson, J. R. (1983). A spreading activation theory of memory. *Journal of Verbal Learning and Verbal Behavior, 22,* 261–295.

Anderson, J. R. (1990). *The adaptive character of thought.* Hillsdale, NJ: Erlbaum.

Anderson, J. R., & Bower, G. H. (1973). *Human associative memory.* Washington, DC: Winston.

Anderson, J. R., & Bower, G. H. (1974). A propositional theory of recognition memory. *Memory and Cognition, 2,* 406–412.

Anderson, J. R., & Reder, L. M. (1979). An elaborative processing explanation of depth of processing. In L. S. Cermak & F. I. M. Craik (Eds.), *Levels of processing in human memory.* Hillsdale, NJ: Erlbaum.

Anderson, J. R., & Schooler, L. J. (1991). Reflections of the environment in memory. *Psychological Science, 2,* 396–408.

Anderson, M. C.; Bjork, R. A.; and Bjork, E. L. (1994). Remembering can cause forgetting: Retrieval dynamics in long-term memory. *Journal of Experimental Psychology: Learning, Memory, and Cognition, 20,* 1063–1087.

Anderson, M. C., & Spellman, B. A. (1995). On the status of inhibitory mechanisms in cognition: Memory retrieval as a model case. *Psychological Review, 102,* 68–100.

Anger, D. (1963). The role of temporal discrimination in the reinforcement of Sidman avoidance behavior. *Journal of the Experimental Analysis of Behavior, 6,* 477–506.

Archer, E. J. (1960). A re-evaluation of the meaningfulness of all possible CVC trigrams. *Psychological Monographs, 74* (10, Whole No. 497).

Ardrey, R. (1966). *The territorial imperative.* New York: Dell.

Armus, H. L. (1959). Effect of magnitude of reinforcement on acquisition and extinction of a running response. *Journal of Experimental Psychology, 58,* 61–63.

Asratyan, E. A. (1965). *Conditioned reflex and compensatory mechanisms.* Oxford, England: Pergamon Press.

Astley, S. L., & Wasserman, E. A. (1998). Novelty and functional equivalence in superordinate categorization by pigeons. *Animal Learning & Behavior, 26,* 125–138.

Atkinson, R. C., & Juola, J. F. (1973). Factors influencing speed and accuracy of word recognition. In S. Kornblurn (Ed.), *Attention and performance,* Vol. IV. New York: Academic Press.

Atkinson, R. C., & Shiffren, R. M. (1968). Human memory: A proposed system and its control processes. In K. W. Spence and J. T. Spence (Eds.), *The psychology of learning and motivation: Advances in research and theory,* Vol. 2. New York: Academic Press.

Atkinson, R. C., & Shiffren, R. M. (1971). The control of short-term memory. *Scientific American, 225,* 82–90.

Averbach, I., & Coriell, A. S. (1961). Short-term memory in vision. *Bell System Technical Journal, 40,* 309–328.

Axelrod, S. (1990). Myths that (mis)guide our profession. In A. C. Repp & N. N. Singh (Eds.), *Perspectives on the use of nonaversive and aversive interventions for persons with developmental disabilities.* Sycamore, IL: Sycamore Publishing.

Azrin, N. H. (1960). Effects of punishment intensity during variable-interval reinforcement. *Journal of the Experimental Analysis of Behavior, 3,* 123–142.

Azrin, N. H., & Hake, D. F. (1969). Positive conditioned suppression: Conditioned suppression using positive reinforcers as the unconditioned stimuli. *Journal of the Experimental Analysis of Behavior, 12,* 167–173.

Azrin, N. H., & Holz, W. C. (1966). Punishment. In W. K. Honig (Ed.), *Operant behavior: Areas of research and application.* Englewood Cliffs, NJ: Prentice-Hall.

Azrin, N. H.; Sisson, R. W.; Meyers, R.; & Godley, M. (1982). Alcoholism treatment by disulfiram and community reinforcement therapy. *Journal of Behavior Therapy and Experimental Psychiatry, 13,* 105–112.

Baddeley, A. D. (1976). *The psychology of memory.* New York: Basic Books.

Baddeley, A. D. (1978). The trouble with levels: A reexamination of Craik and Lockhart's framework for memory research. *Psychological Review, 85,* 139–152.

Baddeley, A. D. (1986). *Working memory.* Oxford, England: Clarendon Press.

Baddeley, A. D. (1990). *Human memory: Theory and practice.* Boston: Allyn and Bacon.

Baddeley, A. D. (1992). Working memory. *Science, 255,* 556–559.

Baddeley, A. D. (1994). Working memory: The interface between memory and cognition. In D. L. Schacter & E. Tulving (Eds.), *Memory systems* (pp. 351–367). Cambridge, MA: MIT Press.

Baddeley, A. D. (1996). Exploring the central executive. *Quarterly Journal of Experimental Psychology, 49A*, 5–28.

Baddeley, A. (1998). *Human memory: Theory and practice.* Allyn and Bacon: Boston. 2nd edition.

Baddeley, A. D.; Grant, S.; Wight, E.; & Thomson, N. (1975). Imagery and visual working memory. In P. M. Rabbit and S. Dornic (Eds.), *Attention and performance,* Vol. 5. New York: Academic Press.

Baddeley, A. D., & Hitch, G. (1974). Working memory. In G. A. Bower (Ed.), *The psychology of learning and motivation,* Vol. 8 (pp. 47–89). New York: Academic Press.

Baddeley, A. D., & Longman, D. J. A. (1978). The influence of length and frequency of training session on the rate of learning to type. *Ergonomics, 21*(8), 627–635.

Baddeley, A. D.; Thomson, N.; & Buchanan, M. (1975). Word length and the structure of short-term memory. *Journal of Verbal Learning and Verbal Behavior, 14,* 575–589.

Bahrick, H. P. (1984). Semantic memory content in permastore: 50 years of memory for Spanish learned in school. *Journal of Experimental Psychology: General, 113,* 1–29.

Bahrick, H. P., & Hall, L. K. (1991). Lifetime maintenance of high school mathematics content. *Journal of Experimental Psychology: General, 120,* 20–33.

Baker, A. G. (1977). Conditioned inhibition arising from a between-sessions negative correlation. *Journal of Experimental Psychology: Animal Behavior Processes, 3,* 144–155.

Baker, A. G., & Mackintosh, N. J. (1977). Excitatory and inhibitory conditioning following uncorrelated presentations of CS and US. *Animal Learning & Behavior, 5,* 315–319.

Baker, A. G., & Mercier, P. (1982). Manipulation of the apparatus and response context may reduce the U.S. pre-exposure interference effect. *Quarterly Journal of Experimental Psychology, 34B,* 221–234.

Baker, A. G.; Mercier, P.; Gabel, J.; & Baker, P. A. (1981). Contextual conditioning and the US pre-exposure effect in conditioned fear. *Journal of Experimental Psychology: Animal Behavior Processes, 7,* 109–128.

Balaz, M. A.; Capra, S.; Hari'l, P.; & Miller, R. R. (1981). Contextual potentiation of acquired behavior after devaluing direct context-US associations. *Learning and Motivation, 12,* 383–397.

Balaz, M. A.; Capra, S.; Kasprow, W. J.; & Miller, R. R. (1982). Latent inhibition of the conditioning context: Further evidence of contextual potentiation of retrieval in the absence of context-U.S. associations. *Animal Learning & Behavior, 10,* 242–248.

Balda, R. P., & Turek, R. J. (1984). The cache recovery system as an example of memory capabilities in Clark's nutcracker. In H. L. Roitblat, T. G. Bever, and H. S. Terrace (Eds.), *Animal cognition.* Hillsdale, NJ: Erlbaum.

Balsam, P. D., & Gibbon, J. (1988). Formation of tone-US associations does not interfere with the formation of context-US associations in pigeons. *Journal of Experimental Psychology: Animal Behavior Processes, 14,* 401–412.

Balsam, P. D., & Tomie, A. (1985). *Context and learning.* Hillsdale, NJ: Erlbaum.

Banyard, V. L., & Williams, L. M. (1996). Characteristics of child sexual abuse as correlates of women's adjustment: A prospective study. *Journal of Marriage & the Family, 58*(4), 853–865.

Barnes, J. M., & Underwood, B. J. (1959). "Fate" of first-list associations in transfer theory. *Journal of Experimental Psychology, 58,* 97–105.

Baron, M. R. (1965). The stimulus, stimulus control, and stimulus generalization. In D. I. Mostofsky (Ed.), *Stimulus generalization.* Stanford: Stanford University Press.

Barsolou, L. (1983). Ad hoc categories. *Memory & Cognition, 11,* 211–227.

Bauermeister, J. J., & Schaeffer, R. W. (1974). Reinforcement relation: Reversibility within daily experimental sessions. *Bulletin of the Psychonomic Society, 3,* 206–208.

Bartlett, F. C. (1932). *Remembering: A study in experimental and social psychology.* Cambridge: Cambridge University Press.

Baum, M. (1970). Extinction of avoidance responding through response prevention (flooding). *Psychological Bulletin, 74,* 276–284.

Baum, M., & Myran, D. D. (1971). Response prevention (flooding) in rats: The effects of restricting exploration during flooding and of massed vs. distributed flooding. *Canadian Journal of Psychology, 25,* 138–146.

Beecroft, R. S. (1966). *Classical conditioning.* Goleta, CA: Psychonomic Press.

Beecroft, R. S. (1956). Verbal learning and retention as a function of the number of competing associations. *Journal of Experimental Psychology, 51,* 216–221.

Beery, R. G. (1968). A negative contrast effect of reward delay in differential conditioning. *Journal of Experimental Psychology, 77,* 429–434.

Begg, I. (1971). Recognition memory for sentence meaning and wording. *Journal of Verbal Learning and Verbal Behavior, 10,* 176–181.

Begg, I.; Vinski, E.; Frankovich, L.; & Holgate, B. (1991). Generating makes words memorable, but so does effective reading. *Memory & Cognition, 19,* 487–497.

Bekerian, D. A., & Bowers, J. M. (1983). Eyewitness testimony: Were we misled? *Journal of Experimental Psychology: Learning, Memory and Cognition, 9,* 139–143.

Bellezza, F. S. (1996). Mnemonic methods to enhance storage and retrieval. In E. L. Bjork & R. A. Bjork (Eds.), *Memory* (pp. 345–380). San Diego, CA: Academic Press.

Bellezza, F. S.; Cheesman, F. L.; & Reddy, B. G. (1977). Organization and semantic elaboration in free recall. *Journal of Experimental Psychology: Human Learning and Memory, 3,* 539–550.

Belli, R. F.; Windschitl, P. D.; McCarthey, T. T.; & Winfrey, S. E. (1992). Detecting memory impairment with a modified test procedure: Manipulating retention interval with centrally presented event items. *Journal of Experimental Psychology: Learning, Memory, and Cognition, 18,* 356–367.

Benjamin, A. S.; Bjork, R. A.; & Schwartz, B. L. (1998). The mismeasure of memory: When retrieval fluency is misleading as a metamnemonic index. *Journal of Experimental Psychology: General, 127,* 55–68.

Berlyne, D. E. (1957). Uncertainty and conflict: A point of contact between information theory and behavior theory concepts. *Psychological Review, 64,* 329–339.

Berlyne, D. E. (1963). Motivational problems raised by exploratory and epistemic behavior. In S. Koch (Ed.), *Psychology—A study of science,* Vol. 5 (pp. 284–364). New York: McGraw-Hill.

Be'rsh, P. J., & Keltz, J. R. (1971). Pavlovian reconditioning and the recovery of avoidance behavior in rats after extinction with response prevention. *Journal of Comparative and Physiological Psychology, 76,* 262–266.

Bexton, W. H.; Heron, W.; & Scott, T. H. (1954). Effects of decreased variation in the sensory environment. *Canadian Journal of Psychology, 8,* 70–76.

Bhatt, R. S.; Wasserman, E. A.; Reynolds, Jr., W. F.; & Knauss, K. S. (1988). Conceptual behavior in pigeons: Categorization of both familiar and novel examples from four classes of natural and artificial stimuli. *Journal of Experimental Psychology: Animal Behavior Processes, 14,* 219–234.

Birch, D. (1965). Extended training extinction effect under massed and spaced extinction trials. *Journal of Experimental Psychology, 70,* 315–322.

Bitterman, M. E. (1964). Classical conditioning in goldfish as a function of the CS-US interval. *Journal of Comparative and Physiological Psychology, 58,* 359–366.

Bjork, R. A. (1972). Theoretical implications of directed forgetting. In A. W. Melton and E. Martin (Eds.), *Coding processes in human memory.* Washington, DC: Winston.

Bjork, R. A. (1975). Short-term storage: The ordered output of a central processor. In F. Restle, R. M. Shiffrin, N. J. Castellad, H. R. Lindman, and D. B. Pisoni (Eds.), *Cognitive theory,* Vol. 1. Hillsdale, NJ: Erlbaum.

Bjork, R. A. (1989). Retrieval inhibition as an adaptive mechanism in human memory. In H. L. Roediger & F. I. M. Craik (Eds.), *Varieties of memory and consciousness: Essays in honour of Endel Tulving* (pp. 309–330). Hillsdale NJ: Erlbaum.

Bjork, R. A., & Bjork, E. L. (1992). A new theory of disuse and an old theory of stimulus fluctuation. In A. F. Healy, S. M. Kosslyn, & R. M. Shiffrin (Eds). *From learning processes to cognitive processes: Essays in honor of William K. Estes,* Vol. 2. (pp. 35–67). Hillsdale, NJ: Erlbaum.

Black, A. H. (1959). Heart rate changes during avoidance learning in dogs. *Canadian Journal of Psychology, 13,* 229–242.

Black, R. W. (1968). Shifts in magnitude of reward and contrast effects in instrumental selective learning: A reinterpretation. *Psychological Review, 75,* 114–126.

Blanchard, R. (1975). The effect of S- on observing behavior. *Learning and Motivation, 6,* 1–10.

Blodgett, H. C. (1929). The effect of the introduction of reward upon the maze performance of rats. *University of California Publications in Psychology, 4,* 113–134.

Blough, D. S. (1975). Steady state data and a quantitative model of generalization and discrimination. *Journal of Experimental Psychology: Animal Behavior Processes, 1,* (Jan) 3–21.

Boakes, R. A. (1977). Performance on learning to associate a stimulus with positive reinforcement. In H. Davis & H. M. B. Hurwitz (Eds.). *Operant-Pavlovian Interactions* (pp. 67–97). Hillsdale, NJ: Erlbaum.

Boe, E. E., & Church, R. M. (1967). Permanent effects of punishment during extinction. *Journal of Comparative and Physiological Psychology, 63,* 486–492.

Bolles, R. C. (1969). Avoidance and escape learning: Simultaneous acquisition of different responses. *Journal of Comparative and Physiological Psychology, 68,* 355–358.

Bolles, R. C. (1970). Species-specific defense reactions and avoidance learning. *Psychological Review, 77,* 32–48.

Bolles, R. C. (1975). *Theory of motivation,* 2nd ed. New York: Harper & Row.

Bomba, P. C., & Siqueland, E. R. (1983). The nature and structure of infant form categories. *Journal of Experimental Child Psychology, 35,* 294–328.

Bourne, L. E. (1982). Typicality effects in logically defined concepts. *Memory and Cognition, 10,* 3–9.

Bourne, L. E., & Restle, F. (1959). A mathematical theory of concept identification. *Psychological Review, 66,* 278–296.

Bousfield, W. A. (1953). The occurrence of clustering in the recall of randomly arranged associates. *Journal of General Psychology, 49,* 229–240.

Bouton, M. E. (1991). Context and retrieval in extinction and in other examples of interference in simple associative learning. In L. Dachowski & C. F. Flaherty (Eds.), *Current topics in animal learning* (pp. 25–53). Hillsdale, NJ: Erlbaum.

Bouton, M. E. (1993). Context, time, and memory retrieval in the interference paradigms of Pavlovian learning. *Psychological Bulletin, 114,* 80–99.

Bouton, M. E. (1994). Conditioning, remembering, and forgetting. *Journal of Experimental Psychology: Animal Behavior Processes, 20,* 219–231.

Bouton, M. E., & King, D. A. (1983). Contextual control of the extinction of conditioned fear: Tests for the associative value of the context. *Journal of Experimental Psychology: Animal Behavior Processes, 9,* 248–265.

Bouton, M. E.; Nelson, J. B.; & Rosas, J. M. (1999). Stimulus generalization, context change, and forgetting. *Psychological Bulletin, 125,* 171–186.

Bouton, M. E., & Swartzentruber, D. (1986). Analysis of the associative and occasion-setting properties of contexts participating in a Pavlovian discrimination. *Journal of Experimental Psychology: Animal Behavior Processes, 12,* 333–350.

Bower, G. H. (1961). A contrast effect in differential conditioning. *Journal of Experimental Psychology, 62,* 196–199.

Bower, G. H. (1972a). A selective review of organizational factors in memory. In E. Tulving and W. Donaldson (Eds.), *Organization of memory.* New York: Academic Press.

Bower, G. H. (1972b). Mental imagery and associative learning. In L. Gregg (Ed.), *Cognition in learning and memory.* New York: Wiley.

Bower, G. H. (1981). Mood and memory. *American Psychologist, 36,* 129–148.

Bower, G. H.; Clark, M. C.; Lesgold, A. M.; & Winzenz, D. (1969). Hierarchical retrieval schemes in recall of categorized word lists. *Journal of Verbal Learning and Verbal Behavior, 8,* 323–343.

Bradshaw, C. M.; Szabadi, E.; & Bevan, P. (1976). Behavior of humans in variable interval schedules of reinforcement. *Journal of the Experimental Analysis of Behavior, 26*(2), 135–141.

Bradshaw, J. L. (1984). A guide to norms, ratings, and lists. *Memory and Cognition, 12*(2), 202–206.

Brandon, S. E., & Bitterman, M. E. (1979). Analysis of autoshaping in goldfish. *Animal Learning & Behavior, 7,* 57–62.

Bransford, J. D.; Barclay, J. R.; & Franks, J. J. (1972). Sentence memory: A constructive versus interpretive approach. *Cognitive Psychology, 3,* 193–209.

Bransford, J. D., & Franks, J. J. (1971). The abstraction of linguistic ideas. *Cognitive Psychology, 2,* 331–350.

Bransford, J. D.; Franks, J. J.; Morris, C. D.; & Stein, B. S. (1979). Some general constraints on learning and memory research. In L. S. Cermak and F. I. M. Craik (Eds.), *Levels of processing in human memory.* Hillsdale, NJ: Erlbaum.

Bransford, J. D., & Johnson, M. K. (1972). Contextual prerequisites for understanding: Some investigations of comprehension and recall. *Journal of Verbal Learning and Verbal Behavior, 11,* 717–726.

Breitmeyer, B. G., & Ganz, L. (1976). Implications of sustained and transient channels for theories of visual pattern masking, saccadic suppression, and information processing. *Psychological Review, 83,* 1–36.

Breland, K., & Breland, M. (1961). The misbehavior of organisms. *American Psychologist, 16,* 681–684

Brennan, M. J., & Gordon, W. C. (1977). Selective facilitation of memory attributes by strychnine. *Pharmacology, Biochemistry & Behavior, 7,* 451–457.

Briggs, G. E. (1954). Acquisition, extinction, and recovery functions in retroactive inhibition. *Journal of Experimental Psychology, 47,* 285–293.

Briggs, G. E. (1957). Retroactive inhibition as a function of the degree of original and interpolated learning. *Journal of Experimental Psychology, 53,* 60–67.

Broadbent, D. E. (1958). *Perception and communication.* Oxford, England: Pergamon Press.

Brogden, W. J. (1939). Unconditioned stimulus substitution in the conditioning process. *American Journal of Psychology, 52,* 46–55.

Brooks, D. C., & Bouton, M. E. (1993). A retrieval cue for extinction attenuates spontaneous recover. *Journal of Experimental Psychology: Animal Behavior Processes, 19,* 77–89.

Brooks, L. R. (1968). Spatial and verbal components of the act of recall. *Canadian Journal of Psychology, 22,* 349–368.

Brown, A. S. (1976). Catalog of scaled verbal material. *Memory and Cognition, 4*(IB), 45.

Brown, A. S. (1991). A review of the tip-of-the-tongue experience. *Psychological Bulletin, 109,* 204–223.

Brown, B. L. (1970). Stimulus generalization in salivary conditioning. *Journal of Comparative and Physiological Psychology, 71,* 467–477.

Brown, B. L.; Hemmes, N. S.; Cabeza de Vaca, S.; & Pagano, C. (1993). Sign and goal tracking during delay and trace autoshaping in pigeons. *Animal Learning & Behavior, 21,* 360–368.

Brown, J. A. (1958). Some tests of the decay theory of immediate memory. *Quarterly Journal of Experimental Psychology, 10,* 12–21.

Brown, J. S. (1942). The generalization of approach responses as a function of stimulus intensity and strength of motivation. *Journal of Comparative Psychology, 33,* 209–226.

Browne, M. P., & Dinsmoor, J. A. (1974). Wyckoff's observing response: Pigeons learn to observe stimuli for free food but not stimuli for extinction. *Learning and Motivation, 5,* 165–173.

Brown, P. L., & Jenkins, H. M. (1968). Auto-shaping the pigeon's key peck. *Journal of the Experimental Analysis of Behavior, 11,* 1–8.

Brown, R., & Kulik, J. (1977). Flashbulb memories. *Cognition, 5,* 73–99.

Brown, R. T., & Wagner, A. R. (1964). Resistance to punishment and extinction following training with shock or non-reinforcement. *Journal of Experimental Psychology, 68,* 503–507.

Brown, R. W., & McNeil, D. (1966). The "tip of the tongue" phenomenon. *Journal of Verbal Learning and Verbal Behavior, 5,* 325–337.

Bruner, A. (1965). UCS properties in classical conditioning of the albino rabbit's nictitating membrane response. *Journal of Experimental Psychology, 69,* 186–192.

Bruner, A. (1969). Reinforcement strength in classical conditioning of leg flexion, freezing, and heart rate in cats. *Conditional Reflex, 4,* 24–31.

Bruner, J. S.; Goodnow, J. J.; & Austin, G. A. (1956). *A study of thinking.* New York: Wiley.

Brush, F. R. (1957). The effects of shock intensity on the acquisition and extinction of an avoidance response in dogs. *Journal of Comparative and Physiological Psychology, 50,* 547–552.

Bugelski, B. R. (1938). Extinction with and without sub-goal reinforcement. *Journal of Comparative Psychology, 26,* 121–134.

Burkhardt, P. E., & Ayres, J. J. B. (1978). CS and US duration effects in one-trial simultaneous fear conditioning as assessed by conditioned suppression of licking in rats. *Animal Learning & Behavior, 6,* 225–230.

Burns, M. L., & Domjan, M. (1996). Sign tracking versus goal tracking in the sexual conditioning of male Japanese quail (*Coturnix japonica*). *Journal of Experimental Psychology: Animal Behavior Processes, 22,* 297–306.

Burr, D. E. S., & Thomas, D. R. (1972). Effect of proactive inhibition upon the postdiscrimination generalization gradient. *Journal of Comparative and Physiological Psychology, 81,* 441–448.

Bush, R. R., & Mosteller, F. (1951). A mathematical model for simple learning. *Psychological Review, 58,* 313–323.

Butler, R. A. (1954). Incentive conditions that influence visual exploration. *Journal of Experimental Psychology, 48,* 19–23.

Calhoun, W. H. (1971). Central nervous system stimulants. In E. Furchtgott (Ed.), *Pharmacological and biophysical agents and behavior.* New York: Academic Press.

Camp, D. S.; Raymond, G. A.; & Church, R. M. (1967). Temporal relationship between response and punishment. *Journal of Experimental Psychology, 74,* 114–123.

Campbell, B. A., & Kraeling, D. (1953). Response strength as a function of drive level and amount of drive reduction. *Journal of Experimental Psychology, 45,* 97–101.

Campbell, P. E.; Batsche, C. J.; & Batsche, G. M. (1972). Spaced-trials reward magnitude effects in the rat: Single versus multiple food pellets. *Journal of Comparative and Physiological Psychology, 81,* 360–364.

Canli, T.; Detmer, W. M.; & Donnegan, N. H. (1992). Potentiation or diminution of discrete motor unconditioned responses (rabbit eyeblink) to an aversive Pavlovian unconditioned stimulus by two associative processes: Conditioned fear and a conditioned diminution of unconditioned signal processing. *Behavioral Neuroscience, 106,* 498–508.

Capaldi, E. D. (1971). Simultaneous shifts in reward magnitude and the level of food deprivation. *Psychonomic Science, 23*, 357–359.

Capaldi, E. J. (1966). Partial reinforcement: A hypothesis of sequential effects. *Psychological Review, 73*, 459–477.

Capaldi, E. J. (1967). A sequential hypothesis of instrumental learning. In K. W. Spence & J. T. Spence (Eds.), *The psychology of learning and motivation* Vol. 1 (pp. 67–156). New York: Academic Press.

Capaldi, E. J. (1971). Memory and learning: A sequential viewpoint. In W. K. Honig & P. H. R. James (Eds.), *Animal memory.* New York: Academic Press.

Capaldi, E. J. (1978). Effects of schedule and delay of reinforcement on acquisition speed. *Animal Learning & Behavior, 6*, 330–334.

Capaldi, E. J.; Alptekin, S.; & Birmingham, K. M. (1996). Instrumental performance and time between reinforcements: Intimate relation to learning or memory retrieval? *Animal Learning & Behavior, 24*, 211–220.

Capaldi, E. J., & Bowen, J. N. (1964). Delay of reward and goal box confinement time in extinction. *Psychonomic Science, 1*, 141–142.

Capaldi, E. J., & Kassover, K. (1970). Sequence, number of nonrewards, anticipation, and intertrial interval in extinction. *Journal of Experimental Psychology, 84*, 470–476.

Capaldi, E. J., & Stanley, L. R. (1965). Percentage of reward vs. N-length in the runway. *Psychonomic Science, 3*, 263–264.

Case, D. A.; Fantino, E.; & Wixted, J. (1985). Human observing: Maintained by negative information stimuli only if correlated with improvement in response efficiency. *Journal of the Experimental Analysis of Behavior, 43*, 289–300.

Case, D. A.; Ploog, B. O.; & Fantino, E. (1990). Observing behavior in a computer game. *Journal of the Experimental Analysis of Behavior, 54*, 185–189.

Castelucci, V. F., & Kandel, E. R. (1974). A quantal analysis of the synaptic depression underlying habituation of the gill-withdrawal reflex in Aplysia. *Proceedings of the National Academy of Sciences, USA, 71*, 5004–5008.

Castellucci, V.; Pinsker, H.; Kupfermann, I., & Kandel, E. (1970). Neuronal mechanisms of habituation and dishabituation of the gill-withdrawal reflex in Aplysia. *Science, 167*, 1745–1748.

Cavanagh, J. P. (1972). Relation between the immediate memory and the memory search rate. *Psychological Review, 79*, 525–530.

Ceraso, J., & Henderson, A. (1965). Unavailability and associative loss in RI and PI. *Journal of Experimental Psychology, 70*, 300–303.

Cheney, D. L., & Seyfarth, R. M. (1980). Vocal recognition in free-ranging vervet monkeys. *Animal Behaviour, 28*, 362–367.

Cheney, D. L., & Seyfarth, R. M. (1986). The recognition of social alliances among vervet monkeys. *Animal Behaviour, 34*, 1722–1731.

Cheney, D. L., & Seyfarth, R. M. (1990). *How monkeys see the world.* Chicago: University of Chicago Press.

Cherry, E. C. (1953). Some experiments on the recognition of speech with one and with two ears. *Journal of the Acoustical Society of America, 25*, 975–979.

Chomsky, N. (1965). Aspects of the theory of syntax. Cambridge, MA: MIT Press.

Church, R. M. (1978). The internal clock. In S. H. Hulse, H. Fowler, & W. K. Honig (Eds.), *Cognitive processes in animal behavior* (pp. 277–310). Hillsdale, NJ: Erlbaum.

Church, R. M.; Raymond, G. A.; & Beauchamp, R. D. (1967). Response suppression as a function of intensity and duration of a punishment. *Journal of Comparative and Physiological Psychology, 63*, 39–44.

Cieutat, V. J.; Stockwell, F. E.; & Noble, C. E. (1958). The interaction of ability and amount of practice with stimulus and response meaningfulness in paired-associated learning. *Journal of Experimental Psychology, 56*, 193–202.

Clark, R. E., & Lavond, D. G. (1993). Reversible lesions of the red nucleus during acquisition and retention of a classically conditioned behavior in rabbits. *Behavioral Neuroscience, 107*, 264–270.

Cleland, G. G., & Davey, G. C. L. (1983). Autoshaping in the rat: The effects of localizable visual and auditory signals for food. *Journal of the Experimental Analysis of Behavior, 40*, 47–56.

Coate, W. B. (1964). Effect of deprivation on postdiscrimination stimulus generalization in the rat. *Journal of Comparative and Physiological Psychology, 57*, 134–138.

Cofer, C. N.; Bruce, D. R.; & Reicher, G. M. (1966). Clustering in free recall as a function of certain methodological variations. *Journal of Experimental Psychology, 71*, 858–866.

Cohen, N. J.; Eichenbaum, H.; Deacedo, B. S., & Corkin, S. (1985). Different memory systems underlying acquisition of procedural and declarative knowledge. *Annals of the New York Academy of Sciences, 444.*

Colavita, F. B. (1965). Dual function of the US in classical salivary conditioning. *Journal of Comparative and Physiological Psychology*, *60*, 218–222.

Coleman, S. R. (1975). Consequences of response contingent change in unconditioned stimulus intensity upon the rabbit (*Oryctolagus cuniculus*) nictitating membrane response. *Journal of Comparative and Physiological Psychology*, *88*, 591–595.

Coleman, S. R., & Webster, S. (1990). The decline of a research specialty: Human-eyelid conditioning in the late 1960s. *Behavior and Philosophy*, *18*, 19–42.

Collier, G. (1969). Body weight loss as a measure of motivation in hunger and thirst. *Annals of the New York Academy of Science*, *157*, 594–609.

Collier, G.; Knarr, F. A.; & Marx, M. H. (1961). Some relations between the intensive properties of the consummatory response and reinforcement. *Journal of Experimental Psychology*, *62*, 484–495.

Collins, A. M., & Loftus, E. F. (1975). A spreading activation theory of semantic processing. *Psychological Review*, *82*, 407–428.

Collins, A. M., & Quillian, M. R. (1969). Retrieval time from semantic memory. *Journal of Verbal Learning and Verbal Behavior*, *8*, 240–247.

Collins, A. M., & Quillian, M. R. (1972). How to make a language user. In E. Tulving and W. Donaldson (Eds.), *Organization and memory*. New York: Academic Press.

Commons, M. L.; Herrnstein, R. J.; & Rachlin, H. (Eds.) (1982). *Quantitative analysis of behavior, Vol. 2, Matching and maximizing accounts*. Cambridge, MA: Ballinger.

Conrad, C. (1972). Cognitive economy in semantic memory. *Journal of Experimental Psychology*, *92*, 149–154.

Conrad, R. (1964). Acoustic confusions in immediate memory. *British Journal of Psychology*, *55*, 75–84.

Conrad, R. (1972). Short-term memory in the deaf: A test for speech coding. *British Journal of Psychology*, *63*, 173–180.

Conrad, R., & Hull, A. J. (1964). Information, acoustic confusion and memory span. *British Journal of Psychology*, *55*, 429–432.

Conrad, R., & Hull, A. J. (1968). Input modality and the serial position curve in short-term memory. *Psychonomic Science*, *10*, 135–136.

Conway, M. A. (1995). *Flashbulb Memories*. Hillsdale, NJ: Erlbaum.

Conway, M. A.; Anderson, S. J.; Larsen, S. F.; Donnelly, C. M.; McDaniel, M. A.; McClelland, A. G. R.; Rawles, R. E.; & Logie, R. H. (1994). The formation of flashbulb memories. *Memory & Cognition*, *22*, 326–343.

Conway, M. A.; Cohen, G.; & Stanhope, N. (1991). On the very long-term retention of knowledge acquired through formal education: Twelve years of cognitive psychology. *Journal of Experimental Psychology: General*, *120*, 395–409.

Cooper, L. A., & Shepard, R. N. (1973). Chronometric studies of the rotation of mental images. In W. G. Case (Ed.), *Visual information processing*. New York: Academic Press.

Cooper, L. D. (1991). Temporal factors in classical conditioning. *Learning and Motivation*, *22*, 129–152.

Coppage, E. W., & Harcum, E. R. (1967). Temporal vs. structural determinants of primacy in strategies of serial learning. *Journal of Verbal Learning and Verbal Behavior*, *6*, 487–490.

Cotton, J. W. (1953). Running time as a function of amount of food deprivation. *Journal of Experimental Psychology*, *46*, 188–198.

Couvillon, P. A., & Bitterman, M. E. (1992). A conventional conditioning analysis of "transitive inference" in pigeons. *Journal of Experimental Psychology: Animal Behavior Processes*, *18*, 308–310.

Craik, F. I. M. (1970). The fate of primary memory items in free recall. *Journal of Verbal Learning and Verbal Behavior*, *9*, 143–148.

Craik, F. I. M., & Kirsner, K. (1974). The effect of a speaker's voice on word recognition. *Quarterly Journal of Experimental Psychology*, *26*, 274–284.

Craik, F. I. M., & Lockhart, R. S. (1972). Levels of processing: A framework for memory research. *Journal of Verbal Learning and Verbal Behavior*, *11*, 671–684.

Craik, F. I. M., & Simon, E. (1980). Age differences in memory: The roles of attention and depth of processing. In L. W. Poon, J. L. Fozard, L. S. Cermak, D. Arenberg, & L. W. Thompson (Eds.), *New directions in memory and aging: Proceedings of the George Talland memorial conference*. Hillsdale, NJ: Erlbaum.

Craik, F. I. M., & Tulving, E. (1975). Depth of processing and the retention of words in episodic memory. *Journal of Experimental Psychology: General*, *104*, 268–294.

Craik, F. I. M., & Watkins, S. M. J. (1973). The role of rehearsal in short-term memory. *Journal of Verbal Learning and Verbal Behavior*, *12*, 599–607.

Crawford, L. L., & Domjan, M. (1993). Sexual approach conditioning: Omission contingency tests. *Animal Learning & Behavior, 21*, 42–50.

Crespi, L. P. (1942). Quantitative variation in incentive and performance in the white rat. *American Journal of Psychology, 55*, 467–517.

Crowder, R. G. (1971). The sound of vowels and consonants in immediate memory. *Journal of Verbal Learning and Verbal Behavior, 10*, 587–596.

Crowder, R. G. (1976). *Principles of learning and memory.* Hillsdale, NJ: Erlbaum.

Crowder, R. G., & Morton, J. (1969). Precategorical acoustic storage (PAS). *Perception and Psychophysics, 5*, 365–373.

D'Agostino, P. R., & Deremer, P. (1973). Repetition effects as a function of rehearsal and encoding variability. *Journal of Verbal Learning and Verbal Behavior, 12*, 108–113.

Dallett, K. M. (1962). The transfer surface reexamined. *Journal of Verbal Learning and Verbal Behavior, 1*, 91–94.

Daly, H. B. (1985). Observing response acquisition: Preference for unpredictable appetitive rewards obtained under conditions predicted by DMOD. *Journal of Experimental Psychology: Animal Behavior Processes, 11*, 294–316.

D'Amato, M. R. (1973). Delayed matching and short-term memory in monkeys. In G. H. Bower (Ed.), *The psychology of learning and motivation: Advances in research and theory,* Vol. 7. New York: Academic Press.

D'Amato, M. R., & Fazzaro, J. (1966). Discriminated lever-press avoidance learning as a function of type and intensity of shock. *Journal of Comparative and Physiological Psychology, 61*, 313–315.

D'Amato, M. R.; Fazzaro, J.; & Etkin, M. (1968). Anticipatory responding and avoidance discrimination as factors in avoidance conditioning. *Journal of Experimental Psychology, 77*, 41–47.

D'Amato, M. R.; Schiff, D.; & Jagoda, H. (1962). Resistance to extinction after varying amounts of discriminative or nondiscriminative instrumental training. *Journal of Experimental Psychology, 64*, 526–532.

D'Amato, M. R., & Worsham, R. W. (1974). Retrieval cues and short-term memory in Capuchin monkeys. *Journal of Comparative and Physiological Psychology, 86*, 274–282.

Dark, V. J., & Loftus, G. R. (1976). The role of rehearsal in long-term memory performance. *Journal of Verbal Learning and Verbal Behavior, 15*, 479–490.

Darwin, C. J.; Turvey, M. T.; & Crowder, R. G. (1972). An auditory analogue of the Sperling partial report procedure. *Cognitive Psychology, 3*, 255–267.

Davison, M., & McCarthy, D. (1988). *The matching law.* Hillsdale, NJ: Erlbaum.

Deaux, E. B., & Patten, R. L. (1964). Measurement of the anticipatory goal response in instrumental runway conditioning. *Psychonomic Science, 1*, 357–358.

Deese, J. (1959). Influence of inter-item associative strength upon immediate free recall. *Psychological Reports, 5*, 305–312.

Deese, J. (1959). On the prediction of occurrence of particular verbal intrusions in immediate recall. *Journal of Experimental Psychology, 58*, 17–22.

Delgado, J. M. R. (1969). *Physical control of the mind.* New York: Harper & Row.

Delgado, J. M. R., & Hamlin, H. (1960). Spontaneous and evoked electrical seizures in animals and in humans. In E. R. Ramey & D. S. O'Doherty (Eds.), *Electrical studies on the unanesthetized brain* (pp. 133–158). New York: P. B. Hoeber.

Delin, P. S. (1969). The learning to criterion of a serial list with and without mnemonic instructions. *Psychonomic Science, 16*, 169–170.

Dempster, F. N. (1987). Effects of variable encoding and spaced presentations on vocabulary learning. *Journal of Educational Psychology, 70*, 162–170.

Dempster, F. N. (1996). Distributing and managing the conditions of encoding and practice. In E. L. Bjork & R. A. Bjork (Eds.), *Memory* (pp. 318–344). San Diego: Academic Press.

Denny, M. R. (1971). Relaxation theory and experiments. In F. R. Brush (Ed.), *Aversive conditioning and learning* (pp. 235–295). New York: Academic Press.

Deutsch, J. A., & Deutsch, D. (1963). Attention: Some theoretical considerations. *Psychological Review, 70*, 80–90.

Devilliers, P. A. (1974). The law of effect and avoidance: A quantitative relationship between response rate and shock frequency reduction. *Journal of the Experimental Analysis of Behavior, 21*, 233–235.

Dickerson, D. J. (1966). Performance of preschool children on three discrimination shifts. *Psychonomic Science, 4*, 417.

Dieter, S. E. (1976). Continuity and intensity of shock in one-way avoidance learning in the rat. *Animal Learning & Behavior, 4*, 303–307.

Dinsmoor, J. A.; Bowe, C. A.; Green, L.; & Hanson, J. (1988). Information on response requirements compared with information on food density as a reinforcer of observing in pigeons. *Journal of the Experimental Analysis of Behavior, 49*, 229–237.

Dinsmoor, J. A.; Browne, M. P.; & Lawrence, C. E. (1972). A test of the negative discriminative stimulus as a reinforcer of observing. *Journal of the Experimental Analysis of Behavior, 18*, 79–85.

Domjan, M. (1983). Biological constraints on instrumental and classical conditioning: Implications for general process theory. In G. H. Bower (Ed.), *The psychology of learning and motivation*, Vol. 17. New York: Academic Press.

Domjan, M.; Blesbois, E.; and Williams, J. (1998). The adaptive significance of sexual conditioning: Pavlovian control of sperm release. *Psychological Science, 9*, 411–415.

Donders, F. C. (1868). Over de snelheid van psychische processcn, *Ondersockingcn gedaan in het Psysiologisch Laboratium der Utrechtsche Hoogcschool, 2*, 92–120. Translated by W. G. Koster, Acta Psychologica, 1969, *30*, 412–431.

Donnellan, A. M.; LaVigna, G. W.; Negri-Shoultz, N.; & Fassbender, L. L. (1988). *Progress without punishment: Effective approaches for learners with behavior problems.* New York: Teachers College Press.

Dore, L. R., & Hilgard, E. R. (1937). Spaced practice and the maturation hypothesis. *Journal of Psychology, 4*, 245–259.

Dougher, M. J. (1983). Clinical effects of response deprivation and response satiation procedures. *Behavior Therapy, 14*, 286–298.

Dougher, M. J.; Crossen, J. R.; & Garland, R. J. (1986). An experimental test of Cautella's operant explanation of covert conditioning procedures. *Behavioral Psychotherapy, 14*, 226–248.

Dragoi, V., & Staddon, J. E. R. (1999). The dynamics of operant conditioning. *Psychological Review, 106*, 20–61.

Dunham, P. J. (1971). Punishment: Method and theory. *Psychological Review, 78*, 58–70.

Dunlosky, J., & Nelson, T.O. (1997). Similarity between the cue for judgments of learning (JOL) and the cue for test is not the primary determinant of JOL accuracy. *Journal of Memory & Language, 36*, 34–49.

Durlach, P. J. (1983). Effect of signaling intertrial unconditioned stimuli in autoshaping. *Journal of Experimental Psychology: Animal Behavior Processes, 9*, 374–389.

Durlach, P. J. (1989). Role of signals for unconditioned stimulus absence in the sensitivity of autoshaping to contingency. *Journal of Experimental Psychology: Animal Behavior Processes, 15*, 202–211.

Durlach, P. J., & Rescorla, R. A. (1980). Potentiation rather than overshadowing in flavor aversion learning: An analysis in terms of within compound associations. *Journal of Experimental Psychology: Animal Behavior Processes, 6*, 175–187.

Dweer, B. (1986). Pretest cueing after forgetting of a food-motivated maze task in rats: Synergistic action of context and reinforcement. *Animal Learning & Behavior, 14*(3), 249–256.

Dyal, J. A., & Holland, T. A. (1963). Resistance to extinction as a function of number of reinforcements. *American Journal of Psychology, 76*, 332–333.

Ebbinghaus, H. (1885). *Ober das Geddchtnis.* Leipzig: Dunker & Humbolt.

Edelmann, R. J. (1992). *Anxiety: Theory, research, and intervention in clinical and health psychology.* Chichester, England: John Wiley & Sons.

Efron, R. (1970a). The relationship between the duration of a stimulus and the duration of a perception. *Neuropsychologia, 8*, 37–55.

Efron, R. (1970b). Effect of stimulus duration on perceptual onset and offset latencies. *Perception and Psychophysics, 8*, 231–234.

Ehrenfreund, E. (1948). An experimental test of the continuity theory of discrimination learning with pattern vision. *Journal of Comparative and Physiological Psychology, 41*, 408–422.

Ehrenfreund, E. (1952). A study of the transposition gradient. *Journal of Experimental Psychology, 43*, 81–87.

Eich, E. (1984). Memory for unattended events: Remembering with and without awareness. *Memory & Cognition, 12*, 105–111.

Eich, E. (1989). Theoretical issues in state-dependent memory. In H. L. Roediger III & F. I. M. Craik (Eds.), *Varieties of Memory and Consciousness: Essays in honour of Endel Tulving* (pp. 331–354). New Jersey: LEA.

Eich, E. (1995). Mood as a mediator of place dependent memory. *Journal of Experimental Psychology: General, 124*, 293–308.

Eich, E.; Macauley, D.; & Ryan, L. (1994). Mood-dependent memory for events in the personal past. *Journal of Experimental Psychology: General, 123*, 201–215.

Eich, E., & Metcalfe, J. (1989). Mood-dependent memory for internal versus external events. *Journal of Experimental Psychology: Learning, Memory, and Cognition, 15*, 443–455.

Eich, J.; Weingartner, H.; Stillman, R.; & Gillian, J. (1975). State-dependent accessibility of retrieval cues and retention of a categorized list. *Journal of Verbal Learning and Verbal Behavior, 14*, 408–417.

Eisenberger, R. (1972). Explanation of rewards that do not reduce tissue needs. *Psychological Bulletin, 77(5)*, 319–339.

Eisenberger, R.; Karpman, M.; & Trattner, T. (1967). What is the necessary and sufficient condition for reinforcement in the contingency condition? *Journal of Experimental Psychology, 74*, 342–350.

Ekstrand, B. R., & Underwood, B. J. (1963). Paced versus unpaced recall in free learning. *Journal of Verbal Learning and Verbal Behavior, 2*, 288–290.

Ekstrand, B. R., & Underwood, B. J. (1965). Free learning and recall as a function of unit-sequence and letter-sequence interference. *Journal of Verbal Learning and Verbal Behavior, 4*, 390–396.

Elliot, M. H. (1928). The effect of change of reward on the maze performance of rats. *University of California Publications in Psychology, 4*, 19–30.

Ellis, H. C. (1969). Transfer and retention. In M. H. Marx (Ed.), *Learning: Processes*. New York: Macmillan.

Ellis, H. C., & Hunt, R. R. (1983). *Fundamentals of human memory and cognition*. Dubuque, IA: William C. Brown.

Ellis, H. C., & Hunt, R. R. (1993). *Fundamentals of cognitive psychology*, 5th ed. Madison, WI: Brown & Benchmark/William C. Brown.

Ellis, H. C.; Thomas, R. L.; & Rodriguez, I. A. (1984). Emotional mood states and memory: Elaborative encoding, semantic processing, and cognitive effort. *Journal of Experimental Psychology: Learning, Memory, and Cognition, 10*, 470–482.

Ellison, G. D. (1964). Differential salivary conditioning to traces. *Journal of Comparative and Physiological Psychology, 57*, 373–380.

Elmes, D. G., & Bjork, R. A. (1975). The interaction of encoding and rehearsal processes in the recall of repeated and nonrepeated items. *Journal of Verbal Learning and Verbal Behavior, 14*, 30–42.

Elmes, D. G.; Dye, G. S.; & Herdian, N. J. (1983). What is the role of affect in the spacing effect? *Memory and Cognition, 11*, 144–151.

Engle, R. W., & Bukstel, L. (1978). Memory processes among bridge players of differing expertise. *American Journal of Psychology, 91*, 673–689.

Ericsson, K. A. (1985). Memory skill. *Canadian Journal of Psychology, 39*, 188–231.

Estes, W. K. (1944). An experimental study of punishment. *Psychological Monographs, 57*, (3, Whole No. 263).

Estes, W. K. (1959). The statistical approach to learning theory. In S. Koch (Ed.), *Psychology: A study of a science,* Vol. 2. New York: McGraw-Hill.

Estes, W. K. (1960). Learning theory and the new "mental chemistry." *Psychological Review, 67*, 207–223.

Estes, W. K. (1969). New perspectives on some old issues in association theory. In N. J. Mackintosh & W. K. Honig (Eds.), *Fundamental issues in associative learning* (pp. 162–189). Halifax, Nova Scotia: Dalhousie University Press.

Estes, W. K. (1973). Memory and conditioning. In F. J. McGuigan and D. B. Lumsden (Eds.), *Contemporary approaches to conditioning and learning*. Washington, DC: Winston.

Estes, W. K., & Skinner, B. F. (1941). Some quantitative properties of anxiety. *Journal of Experimental Psychology, 29*, 390–400.

Etkin, M. W. (1972). Light-produced interference in a delayed matching task with Capuchin monkeys. *Learning and Motivation, 3*, 313–324.

Eysenck, M. W., & Eyesenck, M. C. (1979). Processing depth, elaboration of encoding, memory stores, and expended processing capacity. *Journal of Experimental Psychology: Human Learning and Memory, 5*, 472–484.

Fantino, E. (1977). Conditioned reinforcement: Choice and information. In W. K. Honig & J. E. R. Staddon (Eds.), *Handbook of operant behavior* (pp. 313–339). Englewood Cliffs, NJ: Prentice Hall.

Fantino, E., & Case, D. A. (1983). Human observing: Maintained by stimuli correlated with reinforcement but not extinction. *Journal of Comparative and Physiological Psychology, 40*, 193–210.

Farwell, B. J., & Ayres, J. J. B. (1979). Stimulus-reinforcer and response-reinforcer relations in the control of conditioned appetitive headpoking ("goal tracking") in rats. *Learning & Motivation, 10*, 295–312.

Fehrer, E. (1956). Effects of amount of reinforcement and pre- and postreinforcement delays on learning and extinction. *Journal of Experimental Psychology, 52*, 167–176.

Feigenbaum, E. A., & Simon, H. A. (1962). A theory of the serial position effect. *British Journal of Psychology, 53*, 307–320.

Feldman, D. T., & Gordon, W. C. (1979). The alleviation of short-term retention decrements with reactivation. *Learning and Motivation, 10*, 198–210.

Ferster, C. B., & Skinner, B. F. (1957). *Schedules of reinforcement.* New York: Appleton-Century-Crofts.

Finch, G. (1938). Salivary conditioning in atropinized dogs. *American Journal of Physiology, 124,* 136–141.

Fisher, R. P., & Craik, F. I. M. (1977). Interaction between encoding and retrieval operations in cued recall. *Journal of Experimental Psychology: Human Learning and Memory, 3,* 701–711.

Fisher, R. P., & Geiselman, R. E. (1992). *Memory-enhancing techniques for investigative interviewing: The cognitive interview.* Springfield, IL: Charles Thomas.

Fisher, R. P.; Geiselman, R. E.; & Raymond, D. S. (1987). Critical analysis of police interview techniques. *Journal of Police Science and Administration, 15,* 177–185.

Fiske, D. W., & Maddi, S. R. (1961). *Functions of varied experience.* Homewood, IL: Dorsey.

Flaherty, C. F. (1982). Incentive contrast: A review of behavioral changes following shifts in reward. *Animal Learning & Behavior, 10,* 409–440.

Flaherty, C. F., & Caprio, M. (1976). Dissociation between instrumental and consummatory measures of incentive contrast. *American Journal of Psychology, 89,* 485–498.

Flaherty, C. F.; Riley, E. P.; & Spear, N. E. (1973). Effects of sucrose concentration and goal units on runway behavior in the rat. *Learning and Motivation, 4,* 163–175.

Flavell, J. H. (1979). Metacognition and cognitive monitoring: A new area of cognitive-developmental inquiry. *American Psychologist, 34,* 906–911.

Flexser, A. J., & Tulving, E. (1978). Retrieval independence in recall and recognition. *Psychological Review, 85,* 153–171.

Fowler, H. (1965). *Curiosity and exploratory behavior.* New York: Macmillan.

Fowler, H.; Blond, J.; & Dember, W. N. (1959). Alternation behavior and learning: The influence of reinforcement magnitude, number, and contingency. *Journal of Comparative and Physiological Psychology, 52,* 609–614.

Fowler, H., & Miller, N. E. (1963). Facilitation and inhibition of runway performance by hind and forepaw shock of various intensities. *Journal of Comparative and Physiological Psychology, 56,* 801–806.

Fowler, H., & Trapold, M. A. (1962). Escape performance as a function of delay of reinforcement. *Journal of Experimental Psychology, 63,* 464–467.

Freagon, S. (1990). One educator's perspective on the use of punishment or aversives: Advocating for supportive and protective systems. In A. C. Repp & N. N. Singh (Eds.), *Perspectives on the use of nonaversive and aversive interventions for persons with developmental disabilities.* Sycamore, IL: Sycamore Publishing Company.

Frey, P. W., & Sears, R. J. (1978). Model of conditioning incorporating the Rescorla-Wagner associative axiom, a dynamic attention process, and a catastrophe rule. *Psychological Review, 85,* 321–340.

Friedman, H., & Guttman, N. (1965). Further analysis of the various effects of discrimination training on stimulus generalization gradients. In D. I. Mostofsky (Ed.), *Stimulus generalization.* Stanford: Stanford University Press.

Gallistel, C. R. (1980). *The organization of action: A new synthesis.* Hillsdale, NJ: Erlbaum.

Gammack, J. G., & Young, R. M. (1985). Psychological techniques for eliciting expert knowledge. In M. A. Bramer (Ed.), *Research and development in expert systems.* Cambridge: Cambridge University Press.

Gamzu, E., & Williams, D. R. (1971). Classical conditioning of a complex skeletal response. *Science, 171,* 923–925.

Gantt, W. H. (1966). Conditional or conditioned, reflex or response? *Conditioned Reflex, 1,* 69–74.

Ganz, L., & Riesen, A. H. (1962). Stimulus generalization to hue in the dark-reared macaque. *Journal of Comparative and Physiological Psychology, 55,* 92–99.

Garcia, J.; Ervin, F. R.; & Koelling, R. A. (1966). Learning with prolonged delay of reinforcement. *Psychonomic Science, 5,* 121–122.

Garcia, J., & Koelling, R. A. (1966). Relation of cue to consequence in avoidance learning. *Psychonomic Science, 4,* 123–124.

Gardiner, J. M.; Craik, F. I. M.; & Bleasdale, F. A. (1973). Retrieval difficulty and subsequent recall. *Memory & Cognition, 1,* 213–216.

Gardiner, J. M., & Java, R. I. (1993). Recognising and remembering. In A. F. Collins, S. E. Gathercole, M. A. Conway, & P. E. Morris (Eds.), *Theories of memory* (pp. 163–188). Hillsdale, NJ: Erlbaum.

Gauci, M.; Husband, A. J.; Saxarra, H.; & King, M. G. (1994). Pavlovian conditioning of nasal tryptase release in human subjects with allergic rhinitis. *Physiology and Behavior, 55,* 823–825.

Gazzaniga, M. S. (1995). Principles of human brain organization derived from split-brain studies. *Neuron, 14,* 217–228.

Gazzaniga, M. S.; Ivry, R. B.; & Manjun, G. R. (1998). *Cognitive neuroscience: The biology of the mind.* New York, NY: W. W. Norton & Company.

Geiselman, R. E. (1975). Semantic positive forgetting: Another cocktail party problem. *Journal of Verbal Learning and Verbal Behavior, 14,* 73–81.

Gentry, W. D. (1968). Fixed-ratio schedule-induced aggression. *Journal of the Experimental Analysis of Behavior, 11,* 813–817.

Gerall, A. A., & Obrist, P. A. (1962). Classical conditioning of the pupillary dilation response of normal and curarized cats. *Journal of Comparative and Physiological Psychology, 55,* 486–491.

Gibbs, M. E., & Mark, R. F. (1973). *Inhibition of memory formation.* New York: Plenum Press.

Gillan, D. J. (1981). Reasoning in chimpanzees: II. Transitive inference. *Journal of Experimental Psychology: Animal Behavior Processes, 7,* 150–164.

Gillund, G., & Shiffren, R. M. (1984). A retrieval model for both recognition and recall. *Psychological Review, 91*(l), 1–67.

Glanzer, M., & Clark, W. H. (1962). Accuracy of perceptual recall: An analysis of organization. *Journal of Verbal Learning and Verbal Behavior, 1,* 289–299.

Glanzer, M., & Clark, W. H. (1963). The verbal loop hypothesis: Binary numbers. *Journal of Verbal Learning and Verbal Behavior, 2,* 301–309.

Glanzer, M., & Cunitz, A. R. (1966). Two storage mechanisms in free recall. *Journal of Verbal Learning and Verbal Behavior, 5,* 351–360.

Glanzer, M., & Dolinskey, R. (1965). The anchor for the serial position curve. *Journal of Verbal Learning and Verbal Behavior, 4,* 267–273.

Glass, A. L., & Holyoak, K. J. (1975). Alternative conceptions of semantic memory. *Cognition, 3,* 313–339.

Glaze, J. A. (1918). The association value of nonsense syllables. *Journal of Genetic Psychology, 35,* 255–269.

Gleitman, H. (1971). Forgetting of long-term memories in animals. In W. K. Honig and P. H. R. James (Eds.), *Animal memory.* New York: Academic Press.

Glickman, S. E., & Jensen, G. D. (1961). The effects of hunger and thirst on Y maze exploration. *Journal of Comparative and Physiological Psychology, 54,* 83–85.

Glover, J. A., & Corkhill, A. J. (1987). Influence of paraphrased repetitions on the spacing effect. *Journal of Educational Psychology, 79,* 198–199.

Goddard, M. J., & Jenkins, H. M. (1987). Effect of signaling extra unconditioned stimuli on autoshaping. *Animal Learning & Behavior, 15,* 40–46.

Godden, D. R., & Baddeley, A. D. (1975). Context-dependent memory in two natural environments: On land and under water. *British Journal of Psychology, 66,* 325–331.

Gold, P. E., & King, R. P. (1974). Retrograde amnesia: Storage failure versus retrieval failure. *Psychological Review, 81,* 465–469.

Goldstein, A. G., & Chance, J. E. (1971). Visual recognition memory for complex configurations. *Perception and Psychophysics, 9,* 237–241.

Gonzales, R. C., & Bitterman, M. E. (1964). Resistance to extinction in the rat as a function of percentage and distribution of reinforcement. *Journal of Comparative and Physiological Psychology, 58,* 258–263.

Goodrich, K. P. (1959). Performance in different segments of an instrumental response chain as a function of reinforcement schedule. *Journal of Experimental Psychology, 57,* 57–63.

Goodrich, K. P. (1960). Running speed and drinking rate as a function of sucrose concentration and amount of consummatory activity. *Journal of Comparative and Physiological Psychology, 53,* 245–250.

Goodwin, C. J. (1991). Misportraying Pavlov's apparatus. *American Journal of Psychology, 104,* 135–141.

Goodwin, D. W.; Powell, B.; Bremer, D.; Hoine, H.; & Stern, J. (1969). Alcohol and recall: State-dependent effects in man. *Science, 163,* 1358–1360.

Gordon, W. C. (1981). Mechanisms of cue-induced retention enhancement. In N. E. Spear and R. R. Miller (Eds.), *Information processing in animals: Memory mechanisms.* Hillsdale, NJ: Erlbaum.

Gordon, W. C. (1983). The malleability of memory in animals. In R. L. Mellgren (Ed.), *Animal cognition and behavior.* New York: North Holland.

Gordon, W. C.; Brennan, M. J.; & Schlesinger, J. L. (1976). The interaction of memories in the rat: Effects on short-term retention performance. *Learning and Motivation, 7,* 406–417.

Gordon, W. C.; Flaherty, C. F.; & Riley, E. P. (1973). Negative contrast as a function of the interval between preshift and postshift training. *Bulletin of the Psychonomic Society, 1*(1a), 25–27.

Gordon, W. C.; McCracken, K. M.; Dess-Beech, N.; & Mowrer, R. R. (1981). Mechanisms for the cueing phenomenon: The addition of the cueing context to the training memory. *Learning and Motivation, 12,* 196–211.

Gordon, W. C.; McGinnis, C. M.; & Weaver, M. S. (1985). The effect of cueing after backward conditioning trials. *Learning and Motivation, 16,* 444–463.

Gordon, W. C., & Mowrer, R. R. (1980). The use of an extinction trial as a reminder treatment following ECS. *Animal Learning & Behavior, 8*(3), 363–367.

Gordon, W. C.; Mowrer, R. R.; McGinnis, C. P.; & McDermott, M. J. (1985). Cue-induced memory interference in the rat. *Bulletin of the Psychonomic Society, 23*(3), 233–236.

Gordon, W. C.; Smith, G. J.; & Katz, D. S. (1979). Dual effects of response blocking following avoidance learning. *Behavior Research and Therapy, 17*, 479–487.

Gordon, W. C., & Spear, N. E. (1973). The effect of reactivation of a previously acquired memory on the interaction between memories in the rat. *Journal of Experimental Psychology, 99*, 349–355.

Gormezano, I. (1965). Yoked comparisons of classical and instrumental conditioning of the eyelid response, and an addendum on "voluntary responders." In W. F. Prokasy (Ed.), *Classical conditioning: A symposium*. New York: Appleton-Century-Crofts.

Gormezano, I. (1966). Classical conditioning. In J. B. Sidowski (Ed.), *Experimental methods and instrumentation in psychology*. New York: McGraw-Hill.

Graf, P. (1982). The memorial consequences of generation and transformation. *Journal of Verbal Learning and Verbal Behavior, 21*, 539–548.

Graf, P., & Schacter, D. L. (1985). Implicit and explicit memory for novel associations in normal and amnesic subjects. *Journal of Experimental Psychology: Learning, Memory, & Cognition, 11*, 501–518.

Grant, D. A. (1973). Cognitive factors in eyelid conditioning. *Psychophysiology, 10*, 75–81.

Grant, D. S. (1976). Effect of sample presentation time on long-delay matching in the pigeon. *Learning and Motivation, 7*, 580–590.

Grant, D. S. (1981). Short-term memory in the pigeon. In N. E. Spear and R. R. Miller (Eds.), *Information processing in animals: Memory mechanisms*. Hillsdale, NJ: Erlbaum.

Grant, D. S., & Roberts, W. A. (1973). Trace interaction in pigeon short-term memory. *Journal of Experimental Psychology, 101*, 21–29.

Grant, D. S., & Roberts, W. A. (1976). Sources of retroactive inhibition in pigeon short-term memory. *Journal of Experimental Psychology: Animal Behavior Processes, 2*, 1–16.

Greene, E.; Flynn, M. S.; & Loftus, E. F. (1982). Inducing resistance of misleading information. *Journal of Verbal Learning and Verbal Behavior, 21*, 207–219.

Greene, R. L. (1990). Spacing effects on implicit memory tests. *Journal of Experimental Psychology: Learning, Memory, and Cognition, 16*, 1004–1011.

Greenspoon, J., & Ranyard, R. (1957). Stimulus conditions and retroactive inhibition. *Journal of Experimental Psychology, 53*, 55–59.

Grings, W. W.; Lockhart, R. A.; & Dameron, L. E. (1962). Conditioning autonomic responses of mentally subnormal individuals. *Psychological Monographs, 76*, No. 558.

Groninger, L. D. (1971). Mnemonic imagery and forgetting. *Psychonomic Science, 23*, 161–163.

Grossen, N. E., & Bolles, R. C. (1968). Effects of a classically conditioned "fear signal" and "safety signal" on nondiscriminated avoidance behavior. *Psychonomic Science, 11*, 321–322.

Groves, P. M., & Thompson, R. F. (1970). Habituation: A dual-process theory. *Psychology Review, 77*(5), 419–450

Gruppuso, V.; Lindsay, D. S.; & Kelley, C. M. (1997). The process-dissociation procedure and similarity: Defining and estimating recollection and familiarity in recognition memory. *Journal of Experimental Psychology: Learning, Memory, & Cognition, 23*, 259–279.

Gustafson, C. R.; Garcia, J.; Hankins, W. G.; & Rusiniak, K. W. (1974). Coyote predation control by aversive conditioning. *Science, 184*, 581–583.

Guttman, N. (1965). Effects of discrimination formation on generalization measured from a positive-rate baseline. In D. I. Mostofsky (Ed.), *Stimulus Generalization* (pp. 210–217). San Francisco, CA: Stanford University Press.

Guttman, N., & Kalish, H. I. (1956). Discriminability and stimulus generalization. *Journal of Experimental Psychology, 51*, 79–88.

Haber, A., & Kalish, H. I. (1963). Prediction of discrimination from generalization after variation in schedule of reinforcement. *Science, 142*, 412–413.

Haber, R. N. (1983). The impending demise of the icon: A critique of the concept of iconic storage in visual information processing. *The Behavioral and Brain Sciences, 6*, 1–11.

Haber, R. N., & Standing, L. G. (1969). Direct measures of short-term visual storage. *Quarterly Journal of Experimental Psychology, 21*, 43–54.

Haggbloom, S. J.; Lovelace, L.; Brewer, V. R.; Levins, S. M.; & Owens, J. D. (1990). Replacement of event-generated memories of nonreinforcement with signal-generated memories of reinforcement during partial reinforcement training: Effects on resistance to extinction. *Animal Learning & Behavior, 18*, 315–322.

Hake, D. F., & Powell, T. (1970). Positive reinforcement and suppression from the same occurrence of the unconditioned stimulus in a positive conditioned suppression procedure. *Journal of the Experimental Analysis of Behavior, 14,* 247–257.

Hall, G. (1974). Transfer effects produced by overtraining in the rat. *Journal of Comparative and Physiological Psychology, 87,* 938–944.

Hall, J. F. (1954). Learning as a function of word frequency. *American Journal of Psychology, 67,* 138–140.

Hall, J. F. (1984). Backward conditioning in Pavlovian-type studies. *Pavlovian Journal of Biological Science, 19,* 163–170.

Hallam, S. C.; Grahame, N. J.; Harris, K.; & Miller, R. R. (1992). Associative structures underlying enhanced negative summation following operational extinction of a Pavlovian inhibitor. *Learning and Motivation, 23,* 43–62.

Hammond, L. J. (1967). A traditional demonstration of the active properties of Pavlovian inhibition using differential CER. *Psychonomic Science, 9,* 65–66.

Hammond, L. J. (1968). Retardation of fear acquisition by a previously inhibitory CS. *Journal of Comparative and Physiological Psychology, 66,* 756–759.

Hanson, H. M. (1959). Effects of discrimination training on stimulus generalization. *Journal of Experimental Psychology, 58,* 321–334.

Harley, T. A., & Bown, H. E. (1998). What causes the tip-of-the-tongue state? Evidence for lexical neighbourhood effects in speech production. *British Journal of Psychology, 89,* 151–174.

Harrison, J. M. (1979). The control of responding by sounds: Unusual effect of reinforcement. *Journal of Experimental Analysis of Behavior, 32,* 167–181.

Hart, J. T. (1965). Memory and the feeling-of-knowing experience. *Journal of Educational Psychology, 56,* 208–216.

Hart, J. T. (1967). Memory and the memory-monitoring process. *Journal of Verbal Learning and Verbal Behavior, 6,* 685–691.

Hartman, T. F., & Grant, D. A. (1960). Effect of intermittent reinforcement on acquisition, extinction, and spontaneous recovery of the conditioned eyelid response. *Journal of Experimental Psychology, 60,* 89–96.

Hasher, L., & Zachs, R. T. (1979). Automatic and effortful processes in memory. *Journal of Experimental Psychology: General, 108,* 356–388.

Hayes, J. R. M. (1952). Memory span for several vocabularies as a function of vocabulary size. In *Quarterly Progress Report.* Cambridge, MA: Acoustics Laboratory, Massachusetts Institute of Technology.

Hearst, E. (1978). Stimulus relationships and feature selection in learning and behavior. In S. H. Hulse, H. Fowler, and W. K. Honig (Eds.), *Cognitive processes in animal behavior.* Hillsdale, NJ: Erlbaum.

Hearst, E., & Jenkins, H. M. (1974). *Sign-tracking: The stimulus-reinforcer relation and directed action.* Austin, TX: Psychonomic Society.

Hearst, E., & Koresko, M. B. (1968). Stimulus generalization and amount of prior training on variable-interval reinforcement. *Journal of Comparative and Physiological Psychology, 66,* 133–138.

Hearst, E.; Koresko, M. B.; & Popper, R. (1964). Stimulus generalization and the response-reinforcer contingency. *Journal of the Experimental Analysis of Behavior, 7,* 369–380.

Hebb, D. O. (1949). *The organization of behavior.* New York: Wiley.

Hebb, D. O. (1955). Drives and the CNS (conceptual nervous system). *Psychological Review, 62,* 243–254.

Hendry, D. P. (1969). Introduction. In D. P. Hendry (Ed.), *Conditioned reinforcement* (pp. 1–33). Homewood, IL: Dorsey Press.

Herrnstein, R. J. (1961). Relative and absolute strength of response as a function of frequency of reinforcement. *Journal of the Experimental Analysis of Behavior, 4,* 267–272.

Herrnstein, R. J. (1969). Method and theory in the study of avoidance. *Psychological Review, 76,* 49–69.

Herrnstein, R. J. (1979). Acquisition, generalization, and discrimination reversal of a natural concept. *Journal of Experimental Psychology: Animal Behavior Processes, 5,* 116–129.

Herrnstein, R. J. (1985). Riddles of natural categorization. *Philosophical Transactions of the Royal Society, B 308,* 129–144.

Herrnstein, R. J. (1990). Levels of stimulus control: A functional approach. *Cognition Special Issue: Animal Cognition, 37*(1–2), 133–166.

Herrnstein, R. J., & de Villiers, P. A. (1980). Fish as a natural category for people and pigeons. In G. H. Bower (Ed.), *The psychology of learning and motivation: Advances in research and theory,* Vol. 14 (pp. 60–97). New York: Academic Press.

Herrnstein, R. J., & Hineline, P. N. (1966). Negative reinforcement as shock-frequency reduction. *Journal of the Experimental Analysis of Behavior, 9,* 421–430.

Herrnstein, R. J.; Loveland, D. H.; & Cable, C. (1976). Natural concepts in pigeons. *Journal of Experimental Psychology: Animal Behavior Processes, 2,* 285–302.

Hess, E. N. (1965). Excerpt from: Ethology: An approach toward the complete analysis of behavior. In T. E. McGill (Ed.), *Readings in animal behavior.* New York: Holt, Rinehart & Winston.

Heth, D. C., & Rescorla, R. A. (1973). Simultaneous and backward fear conditioning in the rat. *Journal of Comparative and Physiological Psychology, 82,* 434–443.

Heth, C. D., & Warren, A. C. (1978). Response deprivation and satiation as determinants of instrumental performances: Some data and theory. *Animal Learning & Behavior, 6,* 299–300.

Higbee, K. L. (1977). *Your memory: How it works and how to improve it.* Englewood Cliffs, NJ: Prentice-Hall.

Hilgard, E. R., & Marquis, D. G. (1940). *Conditioning and learning.* New York: Appleton-Century-Crofts.

Hill, W. F., & Spear, N. E. (1962). Resistance to extinction as a joint function of reward magnitude and the spacing of extinction trials. *Journal of Experimental Psychology, 64,* 636–639.

Hineline, P. N. (1977). Negative reinforcement and avoidance. In W. K. Honig & J. E. R. Staddon (Eds.), *Handbook of operant behavior* (pp. 364–414). Englewood Cliffs, NJ: Prentice-Hall.

Hinson, R. E. (1982). Effects of UCS pre-exposure on excitatory and inhibitory rabbit eyelid conditioning: An associative effect of conditioned contextual stimuli. *Journal of Experimental Psychology: Animal Behavior Processes, 8*(l), 49–61.

Hinson, R. E., & Siegel, S. (1980). Trace conditioning as an inhibitory procedure. *Animal Learning & Behavior, 8,* 60–66.

Hintzman, D. L. (1974). Theoretical implications of the spacing effect. In R. L. Solso (Ed.), *Theories in cognitive psychology: The Loyola Symposium.* Hillsdale, NJ: Erlbaum.

Hintzman, D. L. (1976). Repetition and memory. In G. H. Bower (Ed.), *The psychology of learning and motivation,* Vol. 10. New York: Academic Press.

Hintzman, D. L. (1986). "Schema abstraction" in a multiple-trace memory model. *Psychological Review, 93*(4), 411–428.

Hintzman, D. L. (1993). On variability, Simpson's paradox, and the relation between recognition and recall: A reply to Tulving and Flexser. *Psychological Review, 100,* 143–148.

Hintzman, D. L., & Block, R. A. (1971). Repetition and memory: Evidence for a multiple-trace hypothesis. *Journal of Experimental Psychology, 88,* 297–306.

Hintzman, D. L.; Block, R. A.; & Inskeep, N. R. (1972). Memory for mode of input. *Journal of Verbal Learning and Verbal Behavior, 11,* 741–749.

Hintzman, D. L.; Block, R. A.; & Summers, J. J. (1973). Modality tags and memory for repetitions: Locus of the spacing effect. *Journal of Verbal Learning and Verbal Behavior, 12,* 229–239.

Hintzman, D. L.; Summers, J. J.; & Block, R. A. (1975). Spacing judgments as an index of study-phase retrieval. *Journal of Experimental Psychology: Human Learning and Memory, 1,* 31–40.

Hintzman, D. L.; Summers, J. J.; Eki, N. T.; & Moore, M. O. (1975). Voluntary attention and the spacing effect. *Memory and Cognition, 3,* 576–580.

Hoffeld, D. R.; Kendall, S. B.; Thompson, R. F.; & Brogden, W. J. (1960). Effect of amount of preconditioning training upon the magnitude of sensory preconditioning. *Journal of Experimental Psychology, 59,* 198–204.

Hoffman, J. W., & Fitzgerald, R. D. (1982). Bidirectional heart-rate response in rats associated with excitatory and inhibitory stimuli. *Animal Learning & Behavior, 10,* 77–82.

Holland, P. C. (1977). Conditioned stimulus as a determinant of the form for the Pavlovian conditioned response. *Journal of Experimental Psychology: Animal Behavior Processes, 3,* 77–104.

Holland, P. C. (1980). CS-US interval as a determinant of the form of Pavlovian appetitive conditioned responses. *Journal of Experimental Psychology: Animal Behavior Processes, 6,* 155–174.

Holland, P. C. (1983). "Occasion-setting" in conditional discriminations. In B. L. Commons, R. J. Hernstein, & A. R. Wagner (Eds.), *Quantitative analyses of behavior: Discrimination processes,* Vol. 4 (pp. 183–206). New York: Ballinger.

Holland, P. C. (1983). Occasion-setting in Pavlovian feature positive discriminations. In M. L. Commons, R. J. Herrnstein, and A. R. Wagner (Eds.), *Quantitative analyses of behavior: Discriminative processes,* Vol. 4. New York: Ballinger.

Holland, P. C. (1985). The nature of conditioned inhibition in serial and simultaneous feature negative discriminations. In R. R. Miller & N. E. Spear (Eds.), *Information processing in animals: Conditioned inhibition* (pp. 267–297). Hillsdale, NJ: Erlbaum.

Holland, P. C. (1989). Occasion setting with simultaneous compounds in rats. *Journal of Experimental Psychology: Animal Behavior Processes, 15,* 183–193.

Hollis, K. L. (1982). Pavlovian conditioning of signal-centered action patterns and autonomic behavior: A biological analysis of function. In J. S. Rosenblatt, R. A. Hinde, C. Beer, and M. Busnel (Eds.), *Advances of the study of behavior, 12,* 1–64.

Hollis, K. L.; Cadieux, E. L.; & Colbert, M. M. (1989). The biological function of Pavlovian conditioning: A mechanism for mating success in the blue gourami (*Trichogaster trichopterus*). *Journal of Comparative Psychology, 103,* 115–121.

Hollis, K. L.; Martin, K. A.; Cadieux, E. L.; & Colbert, M. M. (1984). The biological function of aggressive behavior in territorial fish. *Learning and Motivation, 15,* 459–478.

Hollis, K. L.; Pharr, V. L.; Dumas, M. J.; Britton, G. B.; & Field, J. (1997). Classical conditioning provides paternity advantage for territorial male bule gouramis (*Trichogaster trichopterus*). *Journal of Comparative Psychology, 111,* 219–225.

Holloway, F. A., & Wansley, R. (1973). Multiphasic retention deficits at periodic intervals after passive-avoidance learning. *Science, 180,* 208–210.

Homme, L. E.; Debaca, P. C.; Devine, J. V.; Steinhorst, R.; & Rickert, E. J. (1963). Use of the Premack principle in controlling the behavior of nursery school children. *Journal of the Experimental Analysis of Behavior, 6,* 544.

Honig, W. K. (1970). Attention and the modulation of stimulus control. In D. I. Mostofsky (Ed.), *Attention: Contemporary theory and analysis.* New York: Appleton-Century-Crofts.

Honig, W. K. (1978). Studies of working memory in the pigeon. In S. H. Hulse, H. Fowler, and W. K. Honig (Eds.), *Cognitive processes in animal behavior.* Hillsdale, NJ: Erlbaum.

Horowitz, L. M. (1961). Free recall and ordering of trigrams. *Journal of Experimental Psychology, 62,* 51–57.

Houston, J. P. (1966). First-list retention and time and method of recall. *Journal of Experimental Psychology, 71,* 839–843.

Howell, W. C. (1973). Representation of frequency in memory. *Psychological Bulletin, 80,* 44–53.

Huchinson, R. R.; Azrin N. H.; & Hunt, G. M. (1968). Attack produced by intermittent reinforcement of a concurrent response. *Journal of the Experimental Analysis of Behavior, 11,* 489–495.

Hug, J. J. (1970). Number of food pellets and the development of the frustration effect. *Psychonomic Science, 21,* 59–60.

Hull, C. L. (1920). Quantitative aspects of the evolution of concepts. *Psychological Monographs, 28,* (123).

Hull, C. L. (1929). A functional interpretation of the conditioned reflex. *Psychological Review, 36,* 495–511.

Hull, C. L. (1935). The conflicting psychologies of learning: A way out. *Psychological Review, 42,* 491–516.

Hull, C. L. (1943). *Principles of behavior.* New York: Appleton-Century-Crofts.

Hull, C. L. (1952). *A behavior system.* New Haven: Yale University Press.

Hull, C. L.; Hovland, C. I.; Ross, R. T.; Hall, M.; Perkins, D. T.; & Fitch, F. B. (1940). *Mathematico-deductive theory of rote learning.* New Haven: Yale University Press.

Hull, C. L.; Livingston, J. R.; Rouse, R. O.; & Barker, A. N. (1951). True, sham and esophageal feeding as reinforcements. *Journal of Comparative and Physiological Psychology, 44,* 236–245.

Hulse, S. H., Jr. (1958). Amount and percentage of reinforcement and duration of goal confinement in conditioning and extinction. *Journal of Experimental Psychology, 56,* 48–57.

Hunt, G. M., & Azrin, N. H. (1973). A community-reinforcement approach to alcoholism. *Behaviour Research and Therapy, 11,* 91–104.

Hunt, R. R. (1995). The subtlety of distinctiveness: What von Restorff really did. *Psychonomic Bulletin & Review, 2,* 105–112.

Hyde, T. S., & Jenkins, J. J. (1969). Differential effects of incidental tasks on the organization of recall of a list of highly associated words. *Journal of Experimental Psychology, 82,* 472–481.

Hyman, I. E.; Husband, T. H.; & Billings, F. J. (1995). False memories of childhood experiences. *Applied Cognitive Psychology, 9,* 181–197.

Intraub, H. (1979). The role of implicit naming in pictorial encoding. *Journal of Experimental Psychology: Human Learning and Memory, 5,* 78–87.

Ison, J. R. (1962). Experimental extinction as a function of number of reinforcements. *Journal of Experimental Psychology, 64,* 314–317.

Jacoby, L. L. (1978). On interpreting the effects of repetition: Solving a problem versus remembering a solution. *Journal of Verbal Learning and Verbal Behavior, 17,* 649–667.

Jacoby, L. L. (1991). A process dissociation framework: Separating automatic and intentional uses of memory. *Journal of Memory and Language, 30,* 513–541.

Jacoby, L. L., & Dallas, M. (1981). On the relationship between autobiographical memory and perceptual learning. *Journal of Experimental Psychology: General, 110,* 306–340.

Jacoby, L. L., & Kelley, C. M. (1992). A process-dissociation framework for investigating unconscious influences: Freudian slips, projective tests, subliminal perception, and signal detection theory. *Current Directions in Psychological Science, 1,* 174–179.

Jacoby, L. L.; Kelley, C. M.; & Dywan, J. (1989). Memory attributions. In H. L. Roediger & F. I. M. Craik (Eds.), *Varieties of memory and consciousness: Essays in honour of Endel Tulving* (pp. 391–422). Hillsdale, NJ: Erlbaum.

Jacoby, L. L., & Whitehouse, K. (1989). An illusion of memory: False recognition influenced by unconscious perception. *Journal of Experimental Psychology: General, 118,* 126–135.

Jacoby, L. L., & Witherspoon, D. (1982). Remembering without awareness. *Canadian Journal of Psychology, 36,* 300–324.

Jacoby, L. L.; Yonelinas, A. P.; & Jennings, J. (1996). The relation between conscious and unconscious (automatic) influences: A declaration of independence. In J. Cohen & J. W. Schooler (Eds.), *Scientific approaches to the question of consciousness* (pp. 13–48). Hillsdale, NJ: Erlbaum.

James, C. T., & Abrahamson, A. A. (1977). Recognition memory for active and passive sentences. *Journal of Psycholinguistic Research, 6,* 37–47.

James, W. (1890). *Principles of Psychology.* New York: Holt.

Jenkins, H. M. (1973). Effects of the stimulus-reinforcer relation on selected and unselected responses. In R. A. Hinde & J. Stevenson-Hinde (Eds.), *Constraints on learning.* New York: Academic Press.

Jenkins, H. M., & Harrison, R. H. (1962). Generalization gradients of inhibition following auditory discrimination learning. *Journal of the Experimental Analysis of Behavior, 5,* 435–441.

Jenkins, H. M., & Moore, B. R. (1973). The form of the auto-shaped response with food or water reinforcers. *Journal of the Experimental Analysis of Behavior, 20,* 163–181.

Jenkins, J. J. (1963). Mediated associations: Paradigms and situations. In C. N. Cofer and B. S. Musgrave (Eds.), *Verbal behavior and learning.* New York: McGraw-Hill.

Jenkins, J. J., & Russell, W. A. (1952). Associative clustering during recall. *Journal of Abnormal and Social Psychology, 47,* 818–821.

Jenkins, P. E.; Chadwick, R. A.; & Nevin, J. A. (1993). Classically conditioned enhancement of antibody production. *Bulletin of the Psychonomic Society, 21,* 485–487.

Jenkins, W. O.; Pascal, G. R.; & Walker, R. W. (1958). Deprivation and generalization. *Journal of Experimental Psychology, 56,* 274–277.

Jensen, A. R. (1962). Transfer between paired associate and serial learning. *Journal of Verbal Learning and Verbal Behavior, 1,* 269–280.

Jensen, A. R., & Rohwer, W. D., Jr. (1965). What is learned in serial learning? *Journal of Verbal Learning and Verbal Behavior, 4,* 62–72.

John, E. R. (1967). *Mechanisms of memory.* New York: Academic Press.

Johnson, M. K.; Hashtroudi, S.; & Lindsay, D. S. (1993). Source monitoring. *Psychological Bulletin, 114,* 3–28.

Joinson, P. A., & Runquist, W. N. (1968). Effects of intra-list similarity and degree of learning on forgetting. *Journal of Verbal Learning and Verbal Behavior, 7,* 554–559.

Jonides, J. (1995). Working memory and thinking. In E. E. Smith & D. N. Osherson (Eds.), *An invitation to cognitive science: Thinking,* Vol. 3 (pp. 215–265). Cambridge, MA: MIT Press.

Jonides, J.; Kahn, R.; & Rozin, P. (1975). Imagery improves memory for blind subjects. *Bulletin of the Psychonomic Society, 5,* 424–426.

Joordens, S., & Merikle, P. M. (1993). Independence or redundancy? Two models of conscious and unconscious influences. *Journal of Experimental Psychology: General, 122,* 462–467.

Jung, J. (1963). Effects of response meaningfulness (in) on transfer of training under two different paradigms. *Journal of Experimental Psychology, 65,* 377–384.

Kahneman, D. (1973). *Attention and effort.* Englewood Cliffs, NJ: Prentice-Hall.

Kalish, H. I., & Haber, A. (1965). Prediction of discrimination from generalization following variations in deprivation level. *Journal of Comparative and Physiological Psychology, 60,* 125–128.

Kamil, A. C.; Krebs, J. R.; & Pullium, H. R. (Eds.) (1987). *Foraging behavior.* New York: Plenum.

Kamil, A. C., & Sargent, T. D. (Eds.) (1981). *Foraging behavior: Ecological, ethological, and psychological approaches.* New York: Garland STPM.

Kamin, L. J. (1954). Traumatic avoidance learning: The effects of CS-US interval with a trace conditioning procedure. *Journal of Comparative and Physiological Psychology, 47,* 65–72.

Kamin, L. J. (1957a). The effects of termination of the CS and avoidance of the US on avoidance learning: An extension. *Canadian Journal of Psychology, 11,* 48–56.

Kamin, L. J. (1957b). The gradient of delay of secondary reward in avoidance learning tested on avoidance trials only. *Journal of Comparative and Physiological Psychology, 50,* 450–456.

Kamin, L. J. (1957c). The retention of an incompletely learned avoidance response. *Journal of Comparative and Physiological Psychology, 50,* 457–460.

Kamin, L. J. (1959). The delay-of-punishment gradient. *Journal of Comparative and Physiological Psychology, 52*, 434–437.

Kamin, L. J. (1965). Temporal and intensity characteristics of the conditioned stimulus. In W. F. Prokasy (Ed.), *Classical conditioning: A symposium.* New York: Appleton-Century-Crofts.

Kamin, L. J. (1968). "Attention-like" processes in classical conditioning. In M. R. Jones (Ed.), *Miami symposium on the prediction of behavior: Aversive stimulation.* Oxford, OH: University of Miami Press.

Kamin, L. J. (1969). Predictability, surprise, attention, and conditioning. In B. A. Campbell and R. M. Church (Eds.), *Punishment and aversive behavior.* New York: Appleton-Century-Crofts.

Kamin, L. J.; Brimer, C. J.; & Black, A. H. (1963). Conditioned suppression as a monitor of fear of the CS in the course of avoidance training. *Journal of Comparative and Physiological Psychology, 56*, 497–501.

Kasper, L. F., & Glass, A. L. (1988). An extension of the keyword method facilitates the acquisition of simple Spanish sentences. *Applied Cognitive Psychology, 2*(2), 137–146.

Kasprow, W. J.; Cacheiro, H.; Balaz, M. A.; & Miller, R. R. (1982). Reminder-induced recovery of associations to an overshadowed stimulus. *Learning and Motivation, 13*, 155–166.

Kazdin, A. L. (1980). *Behavior modification in applied settings.* Homewood, IL: Dorsey Press.

Keil, F. C. (1989). *Concepts, kinds, and cognitive development.* Cambridge, MA.: MIT Press.

Keller, F. S., & Schoenfeld, W. N. (1950). *Principles of psychology.* New York: Appleton-Century-Crofts.

Kelley, C. M., & Lindsay, D. S. (1996). Conscious and unconscious forms of memory. In E. L. Bjork & R. A. Bjork (Eds.), *Memory* (pp. 33–67). San Diego: Academic Press.

Kellogg, R. T. (1982). Hypothesis recognition failure in conjunctive and disjunctive concept identification tasks. *Memory and Cognition, 19*, 327–330.

Kellogg, R. T.; Robbins, D. W.; & Bourne, L. E. (1978). Memory for intratrial events in feature identification. *Journal of Experimental Psychology: Human Learning and Memory, 4*, 256–265.

Kemenes, G., & Benjamin, P. R. (1989). Goal-tracking behavior in the pond snail, *Lymnaea stagnalis. Behavioral and Neural Biology, 52*, 260–270.

Kendler, H. H., & Kendler, T. S. (1962). Vertical and horizontal processes in problem solving. *Psychological Review, 69*, 1–16.

Kendler, T. (1950). An experimental investigation of transposition as a function of the difference between training and test stimuli. *Journal of Experimental Psychology, 40*, 552–562.

Keppel, G., & Underwood, B. J. (1962). Proactive inhibition in short-term retention of single items. *Journal of Verbal Learning and Verbal Behavior, 1*, 153–161.

Kerr, N. H. (1983). The role of vision in "visual imagery" experiments: Evidence from the congenitally blind. *Journal of Experimental Psychology, 112*, 265–277.

Kimble, G. A. (1961). *Hilgard and Marquis' conditioning and learning, 2nd ed.* New York: Appleton-Century-Crofts.

Kincaid, J. P., & Wickens, D. D. (1970). Temporal gradient of release from proactive inhibition. *Journal of Experimental Psychology, 86*, 313–316.

King, D. L. (1979). *Conditioning: An image approach.* New York: Gardner Press.

Kinoshita, S. (1995). The word frequency effect in recognition: Memory versus repetition priming. *Memory & Cognition, 23*, 569–580.

Kintsch, W. (1962). Runway performance as a function of drive strength and magnitude of reinforcement. *Journal of Comparative and Physiological Psychology, 55*, 882–887.

Kintsch, W. (1968). Recognition and free recall of organized lists. *Journal of Experimental Psychology, 78*, 481–487.

Kintsch, W. (1970). Models for free recall and recognition. In D. A. Norman (Ed.), *Models of human memory.* New York: Academic Press.

Kintsch, W. (1974). *The representation of meaning in memory.* Hillsdale, NJ: Erlbaum.

Kintsch, W. (1976). Memory for prose. In C. N. Cofer (Ed.), *The structure of human memory.* San Francisco: Freeman.

Kintsch, W., & Glass, G. (1974). Effects of propositional structure upon sentence recall. In W. Kintsch (Ed.), *The representation of meaning in memory.* Hillsdale, NJ: Erlbaum.

Kintsch, W., & Keenan, J. M. (1973). Reading rate and retention as a function of the number of propositions in the base structure of sentences. *Cognitive Psychology, 5*, 257–274.

Kintsch, W., & Van Duk, T. A. (1978). Toward a model of text comprehension and production. *Psychological Review, 85*, 363–394.

Kintsch, W., & Witte, R. S. (1962). Concurrent conditioning of bar press and salivation responses. *Journal of Comparative and Physiological Psychology, 55,* 963–968.

Kish, G. B. (1966). Studies of sensory reinforcement. In W. K. Honig (Ed.), *Operant behavior: Areas of research and application.* New York: Appleton-Century-Crofts.

Kish, G. B., & Antonitis, J. J. (1956). Unconditioned operant behavior in two homozygous strains of mice. *Journal of Genetic Psychology, 88,* 121–124.

Klein, M., & Rilling, M. (1974). Generalization of free operant avoidance behavior in pigeons. *Journal of the Experimental Analysis of Behavior, 21,* 75–88.

Knouse, S. B., & Campbell, P. E. (1971). Partially delayed reward in the rat: A parametric study of delay duration. *Journal of Comparative and Physiological Psychology, 75,* 116–119.

Knowlton, B. J., & Thompson, R. F. (1992). Conditioning using a cerebral cortical conditioned stimulus is dependent on the cerebellum and brain stem circuitry. *Behavioral Neuroscience, 106,* 509–517.

Koehler, D. J. (1994). Hypothesis generation and confidence in judgment. *Journal of Experimental Psychology: Learning, Memory, and Cognition, 20,* 461–479.

Köhler, W. (1939). Simple structural functions in the chimpanzee and in the chicken. In W. E. Ellis (Ed.), *A source book of Gestalt psychology* (pp. 217–227). New York: Harcourt Brace Jovanovich.

Kolers, P. A. (1979). A pattern-analyzing basis of recognition. In L. S. Cermak and F. I. M. Craik (Eds.), *Levels of processing in human memory.* Hillsdale, NJ: Erlbaum.

Kolers, P. A., & Ostry, D. J. (1974). Time course of loss of information regarding pattern analyzing operations. *Journal of Verbal Learning and Verbal Behavior, 13,* 599–612.

Konarski, E. A.; Johnson, M. R.; Crowell, C. R.; & Whitman, T. L. (1980). Response deprivation and reinforcement in applied settings: A preliminary analysis. *Journal of Applied Behavior Analysis, 13,* 595–609.

Konorski, J., & Szwejkowska, G. (1950). Chronic extinction and restoration of conditioned reflexes. 1. Extinction against the excitatory background. *Acta Biological Experimentation, 15,* 155–170.

Koriat, A. (1993). How do we know that we know? The accessibility account of the feeling of knowing. *Psychological Review, 100,* 609–639.

Koriat, A. (1995). Dissociating knowing and the feeling of knowing: Further evidence for the accessibility model. *Journal of Experimental Psychology: General, 124,* 311–333.

Koriat, A., & Goldsmith, M. (1996). Monitoring and control processes in the strategic regulation of memory accuracy. *Psychological Review, 103,* 490–517.

Kosslyn, S. M.; Ball, T. M.; & Reiser, B. J. (1978). Visual images preserve metric spatial information: Evidence from studies of image scanning. *Journal of Experimental Psychology: Human Perception and Performance, 4,* 47–60.

Krane, R. V., & Ison, J. R. (1971). Positive induction in differential instrumental conditioning: Effect of the interstimulus interval. *Journal of Comparative and Physiological Psychology, 75,* 129–135.

Krane, R. V., & Wagner, A. R. (1975). Taste aversion learning with a delayed shock US: Implications for the "generality of the laws of learning." *Journal of Comparative and Physiological Psychology, 88,* 882–889.

Krechevsky, I. (1932). "Hypotheses" in rats. *Psychological Review, 39,* 516–532.

Krechevsky, I. (1938). A study of the continuity of the problem-solving process. *Psychological Review, 45,* 107-133.

Kremer, E. F. (1971). Truly random and traditional control procedures in CER conditioning in the rat. *Journal of Comparative and Physiological Psychology, 76,* 441–448.

Krupa, D. J.; Thompson, J. K.; & Thompson, R. F. (1993). Localization of a memory trace in the mammalian brain. *Science, 260,* 989–991.

Kucharskil, D., & Spear, N. E. (1984). Potentiation of a conditioned taste aversion in pre-weanling and adult rats. *Behavioral and Neural Biology, 40,* 44–57.

Kuo, Z. Y. (1932). Ontogeny of embryonic behavior in aves. *Journal of Experimental Biology, 61,* 395–430.

Kupfermann, I.; Castellucci, V. F.; Pinsker, H.; & Kandel, E. R. (1970). Neuronal correlates of habituation and dishabituation of the gill withdrawal reflex in Aplysia. *Science, 167,* 1743–1745.

Kvavilashvili, L. (1987). Remembering intentions as a distinct form of memory. *British Journal of Psychology, 78,* 507–518.

Lacey, J. I., & Smith, R. L. (1954). Conditioning and generalization of unconscious anxiety. *Science, 120,* 1045–1052.

Lachnit, H., & Kimmel, H. D. (1993). Positive and negative patterning in human classical skin conductance conditioning. *Animal Learning & Behavior, 21,* 314–326.

Lashley, K. S. (1942). An examination of the "continuity theory" as applied to discrimination learning. *Journal of General Psychology, 26,* 241–265.

Lashley, K. S. (1951). The problem of serial order in behavior. In L. A. Jeffries (Ed.), *Cerebral mechanisms in behavior*. New York: Wiley.

Lashley, K. S., & Wade, M. (1946). The Pavlovian theory of generalization. *Psychological Review, 53*, 72–87.

Lattal, K. A. (1969). Contingency management of toothbrushing behavior in a summer camp for children. *Journal of Applied Behavior Analysis, 2*, 195–198.

Lawrence, D. H. (1949). Acquired distinctiveness of cues. I. Transfer between discriminations on the basis of familiarity with the stimulus. *Journal of Experimental Psychology, 39*, 770–784.

Lawrence, D. H. (1950). Acquired distinctiveness of cues. II. Selective association in a constant stimulus situation. *Journal of Experimental Psychology, 40*, 175–188.

Lawrence, D. H. (1952). The transfer of a discrimination along a continuum. *Journal of Comparative and Physiological Psychology, 46*, 511–516.

Lawrence, D. H., & DeRivera, J. (1954). Evidence of relational transposition. *Journal of Comparative and Physiological Psychology, 47*, 465–471.

Leonesio, R. J., & Nelson, T. O. (1990). Do different metamemory judgments tap the same underlying aspects of memory? *Journal of Experimental Psychology: Learning, Memory, & Cognition, 16*, 464–470.

Lepley, W. M. (1934). Serial reactions considered as conditioned reactions. *Psychological Monographs, 46* (Whole No. 205).

Leuba, C. (1955). Toward some integration of learning theories: The concept of optimal stimulation. *Psychological Reports, 1*, 27–33.

Levine, M. (1966). Hypothesis behavior by humans during discrimination learning. *Journal of Experimental Psychology, 71*, 331–338.

Levine, M. (1975). *A cognitive theory of learning*. Hillsdale, NJ: Erlbaum.

Lewis, D. J. (1979). Psychobiology of active and inactive memory. *Psychological Bulletin, 86*, 1054–1083.

Lewis, D. J.; Miller, R. R.; & Misanin, J. R. (1968). Control of retrograde amnesia. *Journal of Comparative and Physiological Psychology, 66*, 48–52.

Lieberman, D. A. (1972). Secondary reinforcement and information as determinants of observing behavior in monkeys (*Macaca mulatta*). *Learning and Motivation, 3*, 341–358.

Lieberman, D. A.; McIntosh, D. C.; & Thomas, G. V. (1979). Learning when reward is delayed: A marking hypothesis. *Journal of Experimental Psychology: Animal Behavior Processes, 5*, 224–242.

Light, J. S., & Gantt, W. H. (1936). Essential part of reflex arc for establishment of conditioned reflex. Formation of conditioned reflex after exclusion of motor peripheral end. *Journal of Comparative Psychology, 21*, 19–36.

Likely, D., & Schnitzer, S. B. (1968). Dependence of the overtraining extinction effect on attention to runway cues. *Quarterly Journal of Experimental Psychology, 20*, 193–196.

Lindsay, D. S. (1990). Misleading suggestions can impair eyewitness' ability to remember event details. *Journal of Experimental Psychology: Learning, Memory, and Cognition, 16*, 1077–1083.

Lindsay, D. S. (1993). Eyewitness suggestibility. *Current Directions in Psychological Science, 2*, 86–89.

Lindsay, D. S., & Read, J. D. (1994). Psychotherapy and memories of child sexual abuse: A cognitive perspective. *Applied Cognitive Psychology, 8*, 281–338.

Lockhart, R. S., & Craik, F. I. M. (1978). Levels of processing: A reply to Eysenck. *British Journal of Psychology, 69*, 171–175.

Locurto, C.; Terrace, H. S.; & Gibbon, J. (1976). Autoshaping, random control, and omission training in the rat. *Journal of the Experimental Analysis of Behavior, 26*, 451–462.

Loess, H. (1964). Proactive inhibition in short-term memory. *Journal of Verbal Learning and Verbal Behavior, 3*, 362–368.

Loftus, E. F. (1979). *Eyewitness testimony*. Cambridge, MA: Harvard University Press.

Loftus, E. F. (1992). When a lie becomes a memory's truth: Memory distortion after exposure to misinformation. *Current Directions in Psychological Science, 1*, 121–123.

Loftus, E. F. (1993). The reality of repressed memories. *American Psychologist, 48*, 518–537.

Loftus, E. F., & Coan, J. A. (1994). The construction of childhood memories. In D. Peters (Ed.), *The child witness in context: Cognitive, social, and legal perspectives*. New York: Kluwer.

Loftus, E. F.; Donders, K.; Hoffman, H.; & Schooler, J. W. (1989). Creating new memories that are quickly accessed and confidently held. *Memory & Cognition, 17*, 607–616.

Loftus, E. F., & Hoffman, H. (1989). Misinformation and memory: The creation of new memories. *Journal of Experimental Psychology: General, 118*, 100–104.

Loftus, E. F.; Miller, D. G.; & Burns, H. J. (1978). Semantic integration of verbal information into a visual memory. *Journal of Experimental Psychology: Human Learning and Memory, 4*, 19–31.

Loftus, E. F., & Palmer, J. C. (1974). Reconstruction of automobile destruction: An example of the interaction between language and memory. *Journal of Verbal Learning and Verbal Behavior, 13*(5), 585–589.

Loftus, G. R.; Johnson, C. A.; & Shimamura, A. P. (1985). How much is an icon worth? *Journal of Experimental Psychology: Human Perception and Performance, 11*, 1–13.

Logan, F. A. (1954). A note on stimulus intensity dynamism (V). *Psychological Review, 61*, 77–80.

Logie, R. H. (1986). Visuo-spatial processing in working memory. *Quarterly Journal of Experimental Psychology, 38A*, 229–247.

Loop, M. S. (1976). Auto-shaping—A simple technique for teaching a lizard to perform a visual discrimination task. *Copeia, 3*, 574–576.

Lorenz, K. Z. (1965). *Evolution and modification of behavior.* Chicago: University of Chicago Press.

Lovaas, O. I. (1967). A behavior therapy approach to the treatment of childhood schizophrenia. In J. P. Hill (Ed.), *Minnesota symposium of child psychology.* Minneapolis: University of Minnesota Press.

Lovaas, O. I. (1987). Behavioral treatment and normal educational and intellectual functioning in young autistic children. *Journal of Consulting and Clinical Psychology, 55*, 3–9.

Lovejoy, E. (1968). *Attention in discrimination learning.* San Francisco: Holden-Day.

Lovibond, P. F.; Preston, G. C.; & Mackintosh, N. J. (1984). Context specificity of conditioning, extinction and latent inhibition. *Journal of Experimental Psychology: Animal Behavior Processes, 10*, 360–375.

Low, L. A., & Low, H. I. (1962). Effects of CS-US interval length upon avoidance responding. *Journal of Comparative and Physiological Psychology, 55*, 1059–1061.

Lubow, R. E., & Moore, A. U. (1959). Latent inhibition: The effect of nonreinforced exposure to the conditioned stimulus. *Journal of Comparative and Physiological Psychology, 52*, 415–419.

MacCorquodale, K., & Meehl, P. E. (1951). On the elimination of cue entries without obvious reinforcement. *Journal of Comparative and Physiological Psychology, 44*, 367–371.

MacDonald, W. S.; Gallimore, R.; & MacDonald, G. (1970). Contingency counseling by school personnel: An economical model of intervention. *Journal of Applied Behavior Analysis, 3*, 175–182.

Mackintosh, N. J. (1971). An analysis of overshadowing and blocking. *Quarterly Journal of Experimental Psychology, 23*, 118–125.

Mackintosh, N. J. (1974). *The psychology of animal learning.* London, England: Academic Press.

Mackintosh, N. J. (1983). *Conditioning and associative learning.* Oxford, England: Oxford University Press.

Mackintosh, N. J., & Holgate, V. (1967). Effects of several pretraining procedures on brightness probability learning. *Perception & Motor Skills, 25*, 629–637.

Mackintosh, N. J., & Honig, W. K. (1970). Blocking and attentional enhancement in pigeons. *Journal of Comparative and Physiological Psychology, 73*, 78–85.

Mackintosh, N. J., & Little, L. (1969). Intradimensional and extradimensional shift learning by pigeons. *Psychonomic Science, 14*, 5–6.

Maddock, L., & Young, J. Z. (1987). Quantitative differences among the brains of cephalopods. *Journal of Zoology (London), 212*, 739–767.

Madison, H. L. (1964). Experimental extinction as a function of number of reinforcements. *Psychological Reports, 14*, 647–650.

Mahoney, W. J., & Ayres, J. J. B. (1976). One-trial simultaneous and backward fear conditioning as reflected in conditioned suppression of licking in rats. *Animal Learning & Behavior, 4*, 357–362.

Maier, S. F., & Jackson, R. L. (1979). Learned helplessness: All of us were right (and wrong): Inescapable shock has multiple effects. In G. H. Bower (Ed.), *The psychology of learning and motivation.* New York: Academic Press.

Maier, S. F., & Seligman, M. E. P. (1976). Learned helplessness: Theory and evidence. *Journal of Experimental Psychology: General, 105*, 3–46.

Maki, W. S. (1981). Directed forgetting in animals. In N. E. Spear & R. R. Miller (Eds.), *Information processing in animals: Memory mechanisms.* Hillsdale, NJ: Erlbaum.

Maki, W. S.; Moe, J. C.; & Bierley, C. M. (1977). Short-term memory for stimuli, responses, and reinforcers. *Journal of Experimental Psychology: Animal Behavior Processes, 3*, 156–177.

Maltzman, I. (1977). Orienting in classical conditioning and generalization of the galvanic skin response to words: An overview. *Journal of Experimental Psychology, 106*, 111–119.

Mandler, G. (1972). Organization and recognition. In E. Tulving & W. Donaldson (Eds.), *Organization of memory.* New York: Academic Press.

Mandler, G. (1980). Recognizing: The judgment of previous occurrence. *Psychological Review, 87*, 252–271.

Margolius, G. (1955). Stimulus generalization of an instrumental response as a function of the number of reinforced trials. *Journal of Experimental Psychology, 49,* 105–111.

Marler, P., & Mundinger, P. (1971). Vocal learning in birds. In H. Moltz (Ed.), *The ontogeny of vertebrate behavior.* New York: Academic Press.

Martin, E. (1972). Stimulus encoding in learning and transfer. In A. W. Melton & E. Martin (Eds.), *Coding processes in human memory.* Washington, DC: Winston.

Martin, E. (1975). Generation-recognition theory and the encoding specificity principle. *Psychological Review, 82,* 150–153.

Massero, D. W., & Loftus, G. R. (1996). Sensory and perceptual storage: Data and theory. In E. L. Bjork & R. A. Bjork (Eds.), *Memory.* San Diego, CA: Academic Press.

Matlin, M. W. (1998). *Cognition,* 4th ed. Orlando, FL: Harcourt Brace.

Matzel, L. D.; Brown, A. M.; & Miller, R. R. (1987). Associative effects of US preexposure: Modulation of conditioned responding by an excitatory training context. *Journal of Experimental Psychology: Animal Behavior Processes, 13,* 65–72.

Mayhew, A. J. (1967). Interlist changes in subjective organization during free recall learning. *Journal of Experimental Psychology, 74,* 425–430.

Mazur, J. E. (1975). The matching law and quantifications related to Premack's principle. *Journal of Experimental Psychology: Animal Behavior Processes, 1,* 374–386.

Mazzoni, G., & Cornoldi, C. (1993). Strategies in study time allocation: Why is study time sometimes not effective? *Journal of Experimental Psychology: General, 122,* 47–60.

McAllister, D. E.; McAllister, W. R.; & Dieter, S. E. (1976). Reward magnitude and shock variables (continuity and intensity) in shuttlebox avoidance learning. *Animal Learning & Behavior, 4,* 204–209.

McAllister, W. R., & McAllister, D. E. (1963). Increase over time in the stimulus generalization of acquired fear. *Journal of Experimental Psychology, 65,* 576–582.

McAndrews, M. P.; Glisky, E. L.; & Schacter, D.L. (1987). When priming persists: Long-lasting implicit memory for a single episode in amnesic patients. *Neuropsychologia, 25,* 497–506.

McCain, G. (1969). The partial reinforcement effect following a small number of acquisition trials. *Psychonomic Science, 15,* 146.

McCloskey, M., & Zaragoza, M. S. (1985). Misleading postevent information and memory for events: Arguments and evidence against the memory impairment hypothesis. *Journal of Experimental Psychology: General, 114,* 1–16.

McDaniel, M. A.; Pressley, M.; & Dunay, P. K. (1987). Long-term retention of vocabulary after keyword and context learning. *Journal of Educational Psychology, 79,* 87–89.

McDaniel, M. A.; Waddill, P. J.; & Einstein, G. O. (1998). A contextual account of the generalization effect: A three-factor theory. *Journal of Memory & Language, 27*(5), 521–536.

McDowell, J. J. (1981). On the validity and utility of Herrnstein's hyperbola in applied behavioral analysis. In C. M. Bradshaw, E. Szabadi, & C. F. Lowe (Eds.), *Quantification of steady state operant behaviour.* Amsterdam: Elsevier/North-Holland.

McDowell, J. J. (1982). The importance of Herrnstein's mathematical statement of the law of effect for behavior therapy. *American Psychologist, 37,* 771–779.

McFarland, C. E.; Frey, T. J.; & Rhodes, D. D. (1980). Retrieval of internally versus externally generated words in episodic memory. *Journal of Verbal Learning and Verbal Behavior, 19,* 210–225.

McGaugh, J. L. (1966). Time-dependent processes in memory storage. *Science, 153,* 1351–1358.

McGaugh, J. L., & Dawson, R. G. (1971). Modification of memory storage processes. In W. K. Honig & P. H. R. James (Eds.), *Animal memory.* New York: Academic Press.

McGeoch, J. A. (1932). Forgetting and the law of disuse. *Psychological Review, 39,* 352–370.

McGeoch, J. A. (1942). *The psychology of human learning: An introduction.* New York: Longmans, Green, & Co.

McGeoch, J. A., & Underwood, B. J. (1943). Tests of the two-factor theory of retroactive inhibition. *Journal of Experimental Psychology, 32,* 1–16.

McGonigle, B. O., & Chalmers, M. (1977). Are monkeys logical? *Nature, 267,* 694–696.

McHose, J. H. (1963). Effect of continued nonreinforcement on the frustration effect. *Journal of Experimental Psychology, 65,* 444–450.

McHose, J. H., & Tauber, L. (1972). Changes in delay of reinforcement in simple instrumental conditioning. *Psychonomic Science, 27,* 291–292.

McKay, D. C. (1973). Aspects of the theory of·comprehension, memory, and attention. *Quarterly Journal of Experimental Psychology, 25,* 22–40.

McSweeney, F. K.; Melville, C. L.; Buck, M. A.; & Whipple, J. E. (1983). Local rates of responding and reinforcement during concurrent schedules. *Journal of the Experimental Analysis of Behavior, 40,* 79–98.

Medin, D. L. (1975). A theory of context in discrimination learning. In G. H. Bower (Ed.), *The psychology of learning and motivation,* Vol. 9. New York: Academic Press.

Meirkle, P. M. (1968). Paired-associate transfer as a function of stimulus and response meaningfulness. *Psychological Reports, 22,* 131–138.

Melton, A. W. (1963). Implications of short-term memory for a general theory of memory. *Journal of Verbal Learning and Verbal Behavior, 2,* 1–21.

Melton, A. W. (1970). The situation with respect to the spacing of repetitions and memory. *Journal of Verbal Learning and Verbal Behavior, 9,* 596–606.

Melton, A. W., & Irwin, J. M. (1940). The influence of degree of interpolated learning on retroactive inhibition and overt transfer of specific responses. *American Journal of Psychology, 53,* 173–203.

Mensink, G. & Raaijmakers, J. G. W. (1988). A model for interference and forgetting. *Psychological Review, 95,* 434–455.

Mervis, C. B. (1980). Category structure and the development of categorization. In R. J. Spiro, B. C. Bruce, & W. E. Brewer (Eds.), *Theoretical issues in reading comprehension: Perspectives from cognitive psychology, linguistics, artificial intelligence, and education.* Hillsdale, NJ: Erlbaum.

Metcalfe, J. (1990). Composite holograph associative recall model (CHARM) and blended memories in eyewitness testimony. *Journal of Experimental Psychology: General, 120,* 145–160.

Metcalfe, J. (1996). Metacognitive processes. In E. L. Bjork & R. A. Bjork (Eds.), *Memory* (pp. 383–411). San Diego: Academic Press.

Metcalfe, J.; Funnell, M.; & Gazzaniga, M. S. (1995). Right-hemisphere memory superiority: Studies of a split-brain patient. *Psychological Science, 6,* 157–164.

Meyer, D. E., & Schvaneveldt, R. W. (1971). Facilitation in recognizing pairs of words: Evidence of a dependence between retrieval operations. *Journal of Experimental Psychology, 90,* 227–234.

Meyer, D. E., & Schvaneveldt, R. W. (1976). Meaning, memory structure, and mental processes. *Science, 192,* 27–33.

Meyers, R. J., & Smith, J. E. (1995). *Clinical guide to alcohol treatment: The community reinforcement approach.* New York: Guilford.

Miczek, K. A., & Grossman, S. (1971). Positive conditioned suppression: Effects of CS duration. *Journal of the Experimental Analysis of Behavior, 15,* 243–247.

Mikulka, P. J., & Pavlik, W. B. (1966). Deprivation level, competing responses, and the PREE. *Psychological Reports, 18,* 95–102.

Miller, D. J., & Kotses, H. (1995). Classical conditioning of total respiratory resistance in humans. *Psychosomatic Medicine, 57,* 148–153.

Miller, G. A. (1956). The magical number seven, plus or minus two: Some limits on our capacity for processing information. *Psychological Review, 63,* 81–97.

Miller, G. A.; Galanter, E.; & Pribram, K. (1960). *Plans and the structure of behavior.* New York: Holt, Rinehart & Winston.

Miller, N. E. (1948). Studies of fear as an acquirable drive. *Journal of Experimental Psychology, 38,* 89–101.

Miller, N. E., & DeBold, R. C. (1965). Classically conditioned tongue-licking and operant bar pressing recorded simultaneously in the rat. *Journal of Comparative and Physiological Psychology, 59,* 109–111.

Miller, N. E., & Kessen, M. C. (1952). Reward effects of food via stomach fistula compared with those of food via mouth. *Journal of Comparative and Physiological Psychology, 45,* 555–564.

Miller, R. R. (1970). Effects of environmental complexity on amnesia induced by electroconvulsive shock in rats. *Journal of Comparative and Physiological Psychology, 71,* 267–275.

Miller, R. R.; Barnet, R. C.; & Grahame, N. J. (1995). Assessment of the Rescorla-Wagner Model. *Psychological Bulletin, 117,* 363–386.

Miller, R. R., & Schachtman, T. R. (1985a). The several roles of context at the time of retrieval. In P. D. Balsam & A. Tomie (Eds.), *Context and learning.* Hillsdale, NJ: Erlbaum.

Miller, R. R., & Schachtman, T. R. (1985b). Conditioning context as an associative baseline: Implications for the content of associations and the epiphenomenal nature of conditioned inhibition. In R. R. Miller & N. E. Spear (Eds.), *Information processing in animals: Conditioned inhibition.* Hillsdale, NJ: Erlbaum.

Miller, R. R., & Spear, N. E. (Eds.) (1985). *Information processing in animals: Conditioned inhibition.* Hillsdale, NJ: Erlbaum.

Miller, R. R., & Springer, A. D. (1972). Induced recovery of memory in rats following electroconvulsive shock. *Physiology and Behavior, 8,* 645–651.

Milner, B. (1966). Amnesia following operation on the temporal lobes. In C. W. M. Whitty & O. L. Zangwill (Eds.), *Amnesia.* London, England: Butterworths.

Milner, B.; Corkin, S.; & Teuber, H. L. (1968). Further analysis of the hippocampal amnesic syndrome: 14-year follow-up study of H.M. *Neuropsychologia, 6,* 215–234.

Mineka, S., & Gino, A. (1979). Dissociative effects of different types and amounts of nonreinforced CS exposure on avoidance extinction and the CER. *Learning and Motivation, 10,* 141–160.

Moeser, S. D. (1983). Levels of processing: Qualitative differences or task-demand differences. *Memory and Cognition, 11,* 316–323.

Montague, W. E.; Adams, J. A.; & Kiess, H. O. (1966). Forgetting and natural language mediation. *Journal of Experimental Psychology, 72,* 829–833.

Moon, L. E., & Lodahl, T. M. (1956). The reinforcing effect of changes in illumination on lever pressing in the monkey. *American Journal of Psychology, 69,* 288–290.

Moore, B. R. (1973). The role of directed Pavlovian reactions in simple instrumental learning in the pigeon. In R. A. Hinde & J. Stevenson (Eds.), *Constraints on learning.* New York: Academic Press.

Moray, N. (1959). Attention in dichotic listening: Affective cues and the influence of instructions. *Quarterly Journal of Experimental Psychology, 11,* 56–60.

Morgan, M. J. (1969). Book review of animal discrimination learning. In R. M. Gilbert & N. S. Sutherland (Eds.), *Quarterly Journal of Experimental Psychology, 21,* 291–292.

Morris, C. D. (1978). Acquisition-test interactions between different dimensions of encoding. *Memory and Cognition, 6*(4), 354–363.

Morton, J.; Crowder, R. G.; & Prussin, H. A. (1971). Experiments with the stimulus suffix effect. *Journal of Experimental Psychology Monographs, 91,* 169–190.

Moscovitch, M. (1989). Confabulation and the frontal system: Strategic vs. associative retrieval in neuropsychological theories of memory. In H. L. Roediger & F. I. M. Craik (Eds.), *Varieties of memory and consciousness: Essays in honour of Endel Tulving* (pp. 133–160). Hillsdale, NJ: Erlbaum.

Moscovitch, M. (1994). Memory and working with memory: Evaluation of a component process model and comparisons with other models. In D. L. Schacter & E. Tulving (Eds.), *Memory systems* (pp. 269–310). Cambridge, MA: MIT Press.

Moscovitch, A., & LoLordo, V. M. (1968). Role of safety in the Pavlovian backward fear conditioning procedure. *Journal of Comparative and Physiological Psychology, 66,* 673–678.

Mowrer, O. H. (1947). On the dual nature of learning: A reinterpretation of "conditioning" and "problem-solving." *Harvard Educational Review, 17,* 102–150.

Mowrer, O. H., & Jones, H. (1945). Habit strength as a function of the pattern of reinforcement. *Journal of Experimental Psychology, 35,* 293–311.

Mulligan, N. W., & Hirshman, E. (1997). Measuring the basis of recognition memory: An investigation of the process-dissociation framework. *Journal of Experimental Psychology: Learning, Memory, & Cognition, 23,* 280–304.

Mulvaney, D. E.; Dinsmoor, J. A.; Jwaideh, A. R.; & Hughes, L. H. (1974). Punishment of observing by the negative discriminative stimulus. *Journal of the Experimental Analysis of Behavior, 21,* 37–44.

Mumma, R., & Warren, J. M. (1968). Two-cue discrimination learning by cats. *Journal of Comparative and Physiological Psychology, 66,* 116–122.

Murdock, B. B., Jr. (1962). The serial position effect of free recall. *Journal of Experimental Psychology, 64,* 482–488.

Murdock, B. B., Jr. (1971). A parallel-processing model for scanning. *Perception and Psychophysics, 10,* 289–291.

Nadel, L., & Willner, J. (1980). Context and conditioning. A place for space. *Journal of Comparative and Physiological Psychology, 8,* 218–228.

Naus, M. J. (1974). Memory search for categorized lists: A consideration of alternative self-terminating search strategies. *Journal of Experimental Psychology, 102,* 992–1000.

Naveh-Benjamin, M., & Ayres, T. J. (1986). Digit span, reading rate, and linguistic relativity. *Quarterly Journal of Experimental Psychology, 38,* 739–751.

Neisser, U. (1967). *Cognitive psychology.* Englewood Cliffs, NJ: Prentice-Hall.

Neisser, U. (1969). *Selective reading: A method for the study of visual attention.* London, England: Nineteenth International Congress of Psychology.

Nelson, D. L. (1979). Remembering pictures and words: Appearance, significance and name. In L. S. Cermak & F. I. M. Craik (Eds.), *Levels of processing in human memory.* Hillsdale, NJ: Erlbaum.

Nelson, T. O. (1977). Repetition and depth of processing. *Journal of Verbal Learning and Verbal Behavior, 16,* 151–171.

Nelson, T. O. (1988). Predictive accuracy of feeling of knowing across different criterion tasks and across different subject populations and individuals. In M. Gruneberg, P. Morris, & R. Sykes (Eds.), *Practical aspects of memory: Current research and issues,* Vol. 1 (pp. 190–196). New York: Wiley.

Nelson, T. O. (1993). Judgments of learning and the allocation of study time. *Journal of Experimental Psychology: General, 122,* 269–273.

Nelson, T. O. (1996). Consciousness and metacognition. *American Psychologist, 51,* 102–116.

Nelson, T. O., & Dunlosky, J. (1991). When people's judgments of learning (JOLs) are extremely accurate at predicting subsequent recall: "The delayed-JOL effect." *Psychological Science, 2,* 267–270.

Nelson, T. O., & Dunlosky, J. (1992). How shall we explain the delayed-judgment-of-learning effect? *Psychological Science, 3,* 317–318.

Nelson, T. O.; Gerler, D.; & Narens, L. (1984). Accuracy of feeling of knowing judgments for predicting perceptual identification and relearning. *Journal of Experimental Psychology: General, 113,* 282–300.

Nelson, T. O., & Leonesio, R. J. (1988). Allocation of self-paced study time and the "labor-in-vain effect." *Journal of Experimental Psychology: Learning, Memory, & Cognition, 14,* 476–486.

Nelson, T. O.; Leonesio, R. J.; Shimamura, A. P.; Landwehr, R. S.; & Narens, L. (1982). Overlearning and the feeling of knowing. *Journal of Experimental Psychology: Learning, Memory, and Cognition, 8,* 279–288.

Nelson, T. O., & Narens, L. (1980a). A new technique for investigating the feeling of knowing. *Acta Psychologica, 46,* 69–90.

Nelson, T. O., & Narens, L. (1980b). Norms of 300 general-information questions: Accuracy of recall, latency of recall, and feeling-of-knowing ratings. *Journal of Verbal Learning and Verbal Behavior, 19,* 338–368.

Nelson, T. O., & Narens, L. (1990). Metamemory: A theoretical framework and new findings. In G. Bower (Ed.), *The psychology of learning and motivation,* Vol. 26 (pp.125–141). San Diego, CA: Academic Press.

Neumann, P. G. (1974). An attribute frequency model for the abstraction of prototypes. *Memory and Cognition, 2,* 241–248.

Newman, J. R., & Grice, G. R. (1965). Stimulus generalization as a function of drive level, and the relationship between two measures of response strength. *Journal of Experimental Psychology, 69,* 357–362.

Nickerson, R. S. (1965). Short-term memory for complex meaningful visual configurations: A demonstration of capacity. *Canadian Journal of Psychology, 19,* 155–160.

Nickerson, R. S. (1984). Retrieval inhibition from part-set cueing: A persisting enigma in memory research. *Memory & Cognition, 12,* 531–552.

Nickerson, R. S., & Adams, M. J. (1979). Long-term memory for a common object. *Cognitive Psychology, 11*(3), 287–307.

Noble, C. E. (1952). An analysis of meaning. *Psychological Review, 59,* 421–430.

Norman, D. A. (1968). Toward a theory of memory and attention. *Psychological Review, 75,* 522–536.

Norman, D. A. (1973). Memory, knowledge, and the answering of questions. In R. L. Solso (Ed.), *Contemporary issues in cognitive psychology: The Loyola Symposium.* Washington, DC: Winston.

Norman, D. A.; Rumelhart , D. E.; & The LNR Research Group. (1975). *Explorations in cognition.* San Francisco: Freeman.

North, A. J., & Stimmel, D. T. (1960). Extinction of an instrumental response following a large number of reinforcements. *Psychological Reports, 6,* 227–234.

Northmore, D. P. M.; Skeen, L. C.; & Pindzola, J. M. (1981). Visuomotor perimetry in fish: A new approach to the functional analysis of altered visual pathways. *Vision Research, 21,* 843–853.

O'Keefe, J. (1983). Spatial memory within and without the hippocampal system. In W. Seifert (Ed.), *Neurobiology of the hippocampus* (pp. 375–403). London, England: Academic Press.

Olds, J. (1958). Satiation effects in self-stimulation of the brain. *Journal of Comparative and Physiological Psychology, 51,* 675–678.

Olds, J. (1962). Hypothalamic substrates of reward. *Physiological Reviews, 42,* 554–604.

Olds, J., & Milner, P. (1954). Positive reinforcement produced by electrical stimulation of septal area and other regions of the rat brain. *Journal of Comparative and Physiological Psychology, 47,* 419–428.

Olton, D. S., & Samuelson, R. J. (1976). Remembrance of places passed: Spatial memory in rats. *Journal of Experimental Psychology: Animal Behavior Processes, 2,* 97–116.

Osgood, C. E. (1949). The similarity paradox in human learning: A resolution. *Psychological Review, 56,* 132–143.

Overmeir, J. B., & Seligman, M. E. P. (1967). Effects of inescapable shock upon subsequent escape and avoidance learning. *Journal of Comparative and Physiological Psychology, 63,* 22–33.

Overton, D. A. (1966). State-dependent learning produced by depressant and atropine-like drugs. *Psychopharmacologia, 10,* 6–31.

Overton, D. A. (1972). State-dependent learning produced by alcohol and its relevance to alcoholism. In B. Kissin & H. Begleiter (Eds.), *The biology of alcoholism, Vol. II, Physiology and behavior.* New York: Plenum Press.

Packard, A. (1972). Cephalopods and fish: The limits of convergence. *Biological Reviews, 47,* 241–307.

Packman, J. L., & Battig, W. F. (1978). Effects of different kinds of semantic processing on memory for words. *Memory and Cognition, 6,* 502–508.

Paivio, A. (1969). Mental imagery in associative learning and memory. *Psychological Review, 76,* 241–263.

Paivio, A. (1971). *Imagery and verbal processes.* New York: Holt, Rinehart & Winston.

Paivio, A.; Smythe, P. C.; & Yuille, J. C. (1968). Imagery versus meaningfulness of nouns in paired-associate learning. *Canadian Journal of Psychology, 22,* 427–441.

Palmerino, C. C.; Rusiniak, K. W.; & Garcia, J. (1980). Flavor-illness aversions: The peculiar roles of odor and taste in memory for poison. *Science, 208,* 753–755.

Papini, M. R., & Bitterman, M. E. (1990). The role of contingency in classical conditioning. *Psychological Review, 97,* 396–403.

Parker, J. F.; Bahrick, L.; Fivush, R.; & Levitt, M. (1998). Effects of stress on children's memory for a natural disaster. In C. P. Thompson, D. J. Herrmann, J. D. Read, D. Bruce, D. G. Payne, & M. P. Toglia (Eds.), *Eyewitness memory: Theoretical and applied perspectives.* New Jersey: LEA.

Parkin, A. J. (1987). *Memory and amnesia.* Cambridge, MA: Blackwell.

Parkin, A. J. (1996). *Explorations in cognitive neuropsychology.* Cambridge, MA: Blackwell.

Paul, G. L. (1969). Outcome of systematic desensitization: II. Controlled investigations of individual treatment, technique variations, and current status. In C. M. Franks (Ed.), *Behavior therapy: Appraisal and status.* New York: McGraw-Hill.

Paul, J. H. (1959). Studies in remembering: The reproduction of connected and extended verbal material. *Psychological Issues, 1,* 1–152.

Pavlov, I. P. (1927). *Conditioned reflexes.* Oxford: Oxford University Press.

Pearce, J. M., & Hall, G. (1978). Overshadowing the instrumental conditioning of a lever-press response by a more valid predictor of the reinforcer. *Journal of Experimental Psychology: Animal Behavior Processes, 4,* 356–367.

Pearce, J. M., & Hall, G. (1980). A model for Pavlovian learning: Variations in the effectiveness of conditioned but not unconditioned stimuli. *Psychological Review, 87,* 532–552.

Peckham, R. H., & Amsel, A. (1967). Within subject demonstration of a relationship between frustration and magnitude of reward in a differential magnitude of reward discrimination. *Journal of Experimental Psychology, 73,* 187–195.

Peden, B. F.; Browne, M. P.; & Hearst, E. (1977). Persistent approaches to a signal for food despite food omission for approaching. *Journal of Experimental Psychology: Animal Behavior Processes, 3,* 377–399.

Perin, C. T. (1942). Behavior potentiality as a joint function of the amount of training and degree of hunger at the time of extinction. *Journal of Experimental Psychology, 30,* 93–113.

Perkins, C. C., Jr. (1955). The stimulus conditions which follow learned responses. *Psychological Review, 62,* 341–348.

Perkins, C. C., & Weyant, R. G. (1958). The interval between training and test trials as a determiner of the slope of generalization gradients. *Journal of Comparative and Physiological Psychology, 51,* 596–600.

Perone, M., & Baron, A. (1980). Reinforcement of human observing behavior by a stimulus correlated with extinction or increased effort. *Journal of the Experimental Analysis of Behavior, 34,* 239–261.

Peterson, R. (1974). Isolation of processes involved in state-dependent recall in man. Paper presented at Federation of American Society for Experimental Biology meetings, Atlantic City, NJ.

Peterson, D. A., & Levis, D. J. (1985). The assessment of bodily injury fears via the Behavioral Avoidance Slide-Test. *Behavioral Assessment, 7*(2), 173–184.

Peterson, L. R., & Peterson, M. J. (1959). Short-term retention of individual verbal items. *Journal of Experimental Psychology, 58,* 193–198.

Peterson, N. (1962). Effect of monochromatic rearing on the control of responding by wavelength. *Science, 136,* 774–775.

Peterson, N. (1963). Effect of monochromatic rearing on the control of responding by wavelengths. *Science, 136,* 774–775.

Pinsker, H.; Kupferman, I.; Castelluci, V.; & Kandel, E. (1970). Habituation and dishabituation of the gill-withdrawal reflex in Aplysia. *Science, 167,* 1740–1742.

Pollack, I. (1953). The information of elementary auditory displays. II. *Journal of the Acoustical Society of America, 25,* 765–769.

Polson, M. C.; Restle, F.; & Polson, P. G. (1965). Association and discrimination in paired associates learning. *Journal of Experimental Psychology, 69,* 47–55.

Posner, M. I. (1967). Characteristics of visual and kinesthetic memory codes. *Journal of Experimental Psychology, 75,* 103–107.

Posner, M. I. (1969). Abstraction and the process of recognition. In J. T. Spence & G. H. Bower (Eds.), *Advances in learning and motivation,* Vol. 3. New York: Academic Press.

Posner, M. I.; Boies, S. J.; Eichelman, W. H.; & Taylor, R. L. (1969). Retention of visual and name codes of single letters. *Journal of Experimental Psychology, 79,* 1–16.

Posner, M. I.; Goldsmith, R.; & Welton, K. E., Jr. (1967). Perceived distance and the classification of distorted patterns. *Journal of Experimental Psychology, 73,* 28–38.

Posner, M. I., & Keele, S. (1968). On the genesis of abstract ideas. *Journal of Experimental Psychology, 77,* 353–363.

Posner, M. I., & Keele, S. W. (1970). Retention of abstract ideas. *Journal of Experimental Psychology, 83,* 304–308.

Posner, M. I., & Konick, A. F. (1966). Short-term retention of visual and kinesthetic information. *Organizational Behavior and Human Performance, 1,* 71–86.

Posner, M. I., & Mitchell, R. F. (1967). Chronometric analysis of classification. *Psychological Review, 74,* 392–409.

Postman, L. (1961). Extra-experimental interference and the retention of words. *Journal of Experimental Psychology, 61,* 97–110.

Postman, L. (1962a). Repetition and paired associate learning. *American Journal of Psychology, 75,* 372–389.

Postman, L. (1962b). The effects of language habits on the acquisition and retention of verbal associations. *Journal of Experimental Psychology, 64,* 7–19.

Postman, L. (1962c). Transfer of training as a function of experimental paradigm and degree of first list learning. *Journal of Verbal Learning and Verbal Behavior, 1,* 109–118.

Postman, L. (1972). Transfer, interference, and forgetting. In J. W. Kling & L. A. Riggs (Eds.), *Woodworth and Schlosberg's experimental psychology.* New York: Holt, Rinehart & Winston.

Postman, L., & Stark, K. (1969). Role of response availability in transfer and interference. *Journal of Experimental Psychology, 79,* 168–177.

Postman, L.; Stark, K.; & Fraser, J. (1968). Temporal changes in interference. *Journal of Verbal Learning and Verbal Behavior, 7,* 672–694.

Postman, L.; Stark, K.; & Henschel, D. (1969). Conditions of recovery after unlearning. *Journal of Experimental Psychology Monograph, 82.*

Powell, R. W., & Kelly, W. (1976). Responding under positive and negative response contingencies in pigeons and crows. *Journal of the Experimental Analysis of Behavior, 25,* 219–225.

Premack, D. (1959). Toward empirical behavior laws: 1. Positive reinforcement. *Psychological Review, 66,* 219–233.

Premack, D. (1963). Prediction of the comparative reinforcement values of running and drinking. *Science, 139,* 1062–1063.

Premack, D. (1965). Reinforcement theory. In D. Levine (Ed.), *Nebraska symposium on motivation,* Vol. 13. Lincoln: University of Nebraska Press.

Premack, D. (1971). Catching up with common sense, or two sides of generalization: Reinforcement and punishment. In R. Glaser (Ed.), *The nature of reinforcement.* New York: Academic Press.

Prokasy, W. F. (1956). The acquisition of observing responses in the absence of differential external reinforcement. *Journal of Comparative and Physiological Psychology, 49,* 131–134.

Prokasy, W. F. (1958). Extinction and spontaneous recovery of conditioned eyelid responses as a function of the amount of acquisition and extinction training. *Journal of Experimental Psychology, 56,* 319–324.

Purdy, J. E.; Bales, S. L.; Burns, M.; & Wiegand, N. (1994). Assessing the rewarding aspects of a stimulus associated with extinction through the observing response paradigm. *International Journal of Comparative Psychology, 7,* 101–116.

Purdy, J. E., & Cross, H. A. (1979). The role of R–S expectancy in discrimination and discrimination reversal learning. *Learning and Motivation, 10,* 211–227.

Purdy, J. E.; Ferguson, A.; & Sieve, A. (1998). Sign tracking in goldfish. Paper presented at the annual meeting of the Southwestern Psychological Association, New Orleans.

Purdy, J. E., & Peel, J. L. (1988). Observing response in goldfish (*Carassius auratus*). *Journal of Comparative Psychology, 102,* 160–168.

Purdy, J. E.; Roberts, A. C.; Garcia, C. (1999). Sign tracking in cuttlefish (*Sepia officinalis*). *Journal of Comparative Psychology, 113,* 443–449.

Purtle, R. B. (1973). Peak shift: A review. *Psychological Bulletin, 80,* 408–421.

Pylyshyn, Z. W. (1973). What the mind's eye tells the mind's brain: A critique of mental imagery. *Psychological Bulletin, 80,* 1–24.

Quillian, M. R. (1967). A theory and simulation of some basic semantic capabilities. *Behavioral Science, 12,* 410–430.

Rand, G., & Wapner, S. (1967). Postural status as a factor in memory. *Journal of Verbal Learning and Verbal Behavior, 6,* 268–271.

Randall, P. K., & Riccio, D. C. (1969). Fear and punishment as determinants of passive avoidance responding. *Journal of Comparative and Physiological Psychology, 69,* 550–553.

Randich, A. (1981). The US pre-exposure phenomenon in the conditioned suppression paradigm: A role for conditioned situational stimuli. *Learning and Motivation, 12,* 321–341.

Randich, A., & LoLordo, V. M. (1979). Preconditioning exposure to the unconditioned stimulus affects the acquisition of a conditioned emotional response. *Learning and Motivation, 10,* 245–277.

Randich, A., & Ross, R. T. (1985). The role of contextual stimuli in mediating the effects of pre- and postexposure to the unconditioned stimulus alone on acquisition and retention of conditioned suppression. In P. Balsam & A. Tomie (Eds.), *Context and learning.* Hillsdale, NJ: Erlbaum.

Rea, C. P., & Modigliani, V. (1988). Educational implications of the spacing effect. In M. M. Gruneberg, P. E. Morris, & R. N. Sykes (Eds.), *Practical aspects of memory: Current research and issues, Vol. 1: Memory in everyday life* (pp. 402–406). Chichester, England: John Wiley.

Read, J. D. (1996). From a passing thought to a false memory in two minutes: Confusing real and illusory events. *Psychonomic Bulletin and Review, 3,* 105–111.

Read, J. D., & Lindsay, D. S. (1994). Moving toward a middle ground on the "false memory debate": Reply to commentaries on Lindsay and Read. *Applied Cognitive Psychology, 8,* 407–435.

Reason, J., & Mycielska, K. (1982). *Absent-minded? The psychology of mental lapses and everyday errors.* Englewood Cliffs, NJ: Prentice-Hall.

Reber, A. A., & Allen, R. (1978). Analogical and abstraction strategies in synthetic grammar learning: A functionalist interpretation. *Cognition, 6,* 189–221.

Reed, S. K. (1972). Pattern recognition and categorization. *Cognitive Psychology, 3,* 383–407.

Reese, H. W. (1965). Imagery in paired-associate learning in children. *Journal of Experimental Child Psychology, 2,* 290–296.

Reid, L. S. (1953). The development of noncontinuity behavior through continuity learning. *Journal of Experimental Psychology, 46,* 107–112.

Reiss, S., & Wagner, A. R. (1972). CS habituation produces a "latent inhibition effect" but no active "conditioned inhibition." *Learning and Motivation, 3,* 237–245.

Reitman, J. S. (1971). Mechanisms of forgetting in short-term memory. *Cognitive Psychology, 2,* 185–195.

Reitman, J. S. (1974). Without surreptitious rehearsal, information in short-term memory decays. *Journal of Verbal Learning and Verbal Behavior, 13,* 365–367.

Renner, K. E. (1963). Influence of deprivation and availability of goal box cues on the temporal gradient of reinforcement. *Journal of Comparative and Physiological Psychology, 56,* 101–104.

Rescorla, R. A. (1966). Predictability and number of pairings in Pavlovian fear conditioning. *Psychonomic Science, 4,* 383–384.

Rescorla, R. A. (1967a). Inhibition of delay in Pavlovian fear conditioning. *Journal of Comparative and Physiological Psychology, 64,* 114–120.

Rescorla, R. A. (1967b). Pavlovian conditioning and its proper control procedures. *Psychological Review, 74,* 71–80.

Rescorla, R. A. (1968). Probability of shock in the presence and absence of CS in fear conditioning. *Journal of Comparative and Physiological Psychology, 66,* 1–5.

Rescorla, R. A. (1969a). Conditioned inhibition of fear resulting from negative CS-US contingencies. *Journal of Comparative and Physiological Psychology, 67,* 504–509.

Rescorla, R. A. (1969b). Conditioned inhibition of fear. In W. K. Honig & N. J. Mackintosh (Eds.), *Fundamental issues in associative learning.* Halifax: Dalhousie University Press.

Rescorla, R. A. (1974). Effect of inflation on the unconditioned stimulus value following conditioning. *Journal of Comparative and Physiological Psychology, 86,* 101–106.

Rescorla, R. A. (1980). *Pavlovian second-order conditioning: Studies in associative learning.* Hillsdale, NJ: Erlbaum.

Rescorla, R. A. (1984). Signaling intertrial shocks attenuates their negative effect on conditioned supression. *Bulletin of the Psychonomic Society, 22,* 225–228.

Rescorla, R. A. (1985). Conditioned inhibition and facilitation. In R. R. Miller & N. E. Spear (Eds.), *Information processing in animals: Conditioned inhibition* (pp. 299–326). Hillsdale, NJ: Erlbaum.

Rescorla, R. A. (1986). Excitation of facilitation. *Journal of Experimental Psychology: Animal Behavior Processes, 12,* 16–24.

Rescorla, R. A. (1988). Pavlovian conditioning: It's not what you think it is. *American Psychologist, 43,* 151-160.

Rescorla, R. A.; Durlach, P. J.; & Grau, J. W. (1985). Contextual learning in Pavlovian conditioning. In P. D. Balsam & A. Tomie (Eds.), *Context and learning.* Hillsdale, NJ: Erlbaum.

Rescorla, R. A., & Holland, P. C. (1977). Associations in Pavlovian conditioned inhibition. *Learning and Motivation, 8,* 429–447.

Rescorla, R. A., & LoLordo, V. M. (1965). Inhibition of avoidance behavior. *Journal of Comparative and Physiological Psychology, 59,* 406–412.

Rescorla, R. A., & Skucy, J. C. (1969). Effect of response-independent reinforcers during extinction. *Journal of Comparative and Physiological Psychology, 67,* 381–389.

Rescorla, R. A., & Solomon, R. L. (1967). Two process learning theory: Relationships between Pavlovian conditioning and instrumental learning. *Psychological Review, 74,* 151–182.

Rescorla, R. A., & Wagner, A. R. (1972). A theory of Pavlovian conditioning: Variations in the effectiveness of reinforcement and nonreinforcement. In A. H. Black & W. F. Prokasy (Eds.), *Classical conditioning, Vol. II: Current theory and research.* New York: Appleton-Century-Crofts.

Reynierse, J. H., & Rizley, R. C. (1970). Stimulus and response contingencies in extinction of avoidance by rats. *Journal of Comparative and Physiological Psychology, 73,* 86–92.

Reynolds, G. S. (1961). Behavioral contrast. *Journal of the Experimental Analysis of Behavior, 4,* 57–71.

Richards, W. J., & Leslie, G. R. (1961). Food and water deprivation as influences on exploration. *Journal of Comparative and Physiological Psychology, 55,* 834–837.

Richardson, J., & Brown, B. L. (1966). Mediated transfer in paired-associative learning as a function of presentation rate and stimulus meaningfulness. *Journal of Experimental Psychology, 72,* 820–828.

Richarson-Klavehn, A., & Bjork, R. A. (1988). Measures of memory. *Annual Review of Psychology, 39,* 475–543.

Rips, L. J.; Shoben, E. J.; & Smith, E. E. (1973). Semantic distance and the verification of semantic relations. *Journal of Verbal Learning and Verbal Behavior, 12,* 1–20.

Riley, D. A., & Levin, T. C. (1971). Stimulus generalization gradients in chickens reared in monochromatic light and tested with a single wavelength value. *Journal of Comparative and Physiological Psychology, 75,* 399–402.

Robbins, S. J. (1990). Mechanisms underlying spontaneous recovery in autoshaping. *Journal of Experimental Psychology: Animal Behavior Processes, 16,* 413–424.

Roberts, W. A. (1969). Resistance to extinction following partial and consistent reinforcement with varying magnitudes of reward. *Journal of Comparative and Physiological Psychology, 67,* 395–400.

Roberts, W. A., & Grant, D. S. (1976). Studies in short-term memory in the pigeon using the delayed matching-to-sample procedure. In D. L. Medin, W. A. Roberts, & R. T. Davis (Eds.), *Processes of animal memory.* Hillsdale, NJ: Erlbaum.

Rock, L. (1957). The role of repetition in associative learning. *American Journal of Psychology, 70,* 186–193.

Roe, E. J., & Rose, R. J. (1974). Instructional and spacing effects in judgment of frequency. Paper presented at the annual meeting of the Canadian Psychological Association.

Roediger, H. L. (1974). Inhibiting effects of recall. *Memory & Cognition, 2,* 261–279.

Roediger, H. L. (1996). Memory illusions. *Journal of Memory and Language, 35,* 76–100.

Roediger, H. L., & McDermott, K. B. (1995). Creating false memories: Remembering words not presented in lists. *Journal of Experimental Psychology: Learning, Memory, and Cognition, 21,* 803–814.

Roediger, H. L.; Weldon, M. S.; & Challis, B. H. (1989). Explaining dissociation between implicit and explicit measures of retention: A processing account. In H. L. Roediger & F. I. M. Craik (Eds.), *Varieties of memory and consciousness: Essays in honor of Endel Tulving* (pp. 3–41). Hillsdale, NJ: Erlbaum.

Roitblat, H. L. (1980). Codes and coding processes in pigeon short-term memory. *Animal Learning & Behavior, 8,* 341–351.

Roper, K. L., & Zentall, T. R. (1999). Observing behavior in pigeons: The effect of reinforcement probability and response cost using a symmetrical choice procedure. *Learning and Motivation, 30,* 201–220.

Rosch, E. (1973). On the internal structure of perceptual and semantic categories. In T. E. Moore (Ed.), *Cognitive development and the acquisition of language.* New York: Academic Press.

Rosch, E. H. (1973). Natural categories. *Cognitive Psychology, 4,* 328–350.

Rosch, E. H. (1975). Cognitive representations of semantic categories. *Journal of Experimental Psychology: General, 104,* 192–233.

Rosch, E. H. (1977). Human categorization. In N. Warren (Ed.), *Advances in cross-cultural psychology,* Vol. 1. London, England: Academic Press.

Rosch, E. H., & Mervis, C. B. (1975). Family resemblances: Studies in the internal structure of categories. *Cognitive Psychology, 7,* 573–605.

Rosch, E.; Mervis, C. B.; Gray, W. D.; Johnson, D. M.; & Boyes-Braem, P. (1976). Basic objects in natural categories. *Cognitive Psychology, 8,* 382–439.

Rosch, E.; Simpson, C.; & Miller, R. S. (1976). Structural bases of typicality effects. *Journal of Experimental Psychology: Human Perception and Performance, 1,* 491–502.

Rose, R. J. (1980). Encoding variability, levels of processing, and the effects of spacing of repetitions upon judgments of frequency. *Memory and Cognition, 8*(l), 84–93.

Ross (1959). The decremental effects of partial reinforcement during acquisition of the conditioned eyelid response. *Journal of Experimental Psychology, 57,* 74–82.

Ross, J., & Lawrence, K. A. (1968). Some observations on memory artifice. *Psychonomic Science, 13,* 107–108.

Ross, L. E. (1959). The decremental effects of partial reinforcement during acquisition of the conditioned eyelid response. *Journal of Experimental Psychology, 57,* 74–82.

Ross, R. T., & Holland, P. C. (1981). Conditioning of simultaneous and serial feature-positive discriminations. *Animal Learning & Behavior, 9,* 293–303.

Roth, E. M., & Shoben, E. E. (1983). The effect of context on the structure of categories. *Cognitive Psychology, 15,* 346–379.

Rothkopf, E. Z. (1971). Incidental memory for location of information in text. *Journal of Verbal Learning and Verbal Behavior, 10,* 608–613.

Royer, J. M.; Hambleton, R. K.; & Cadorette, L. (1978). Individual differences in memory: Theory, data, and educational implications. *Contemporary Educational Psychology, 3,* 182–203.

Rudolph, R. L., & Honig, W. K. (1972). Effects of monochromatic rearing on the spectral discrimination learning and the peak shift in chicks. *Journal of the Experimental Analysis of Behavior, 17,* 107–111.

Rudy, J. W., & Sutherland, R. J. (1989). The hippocampal formation is necessary for rats to learn and remember configural discriminations. *Behavioral Brain Research, 34,* 97–109.

Rundus, D. (1971). Analysis of rehearsal processes in free recall. *Journal of Experimental Psychology, 89,* 63–77.

Rundus, D. (1977). Maintenance rehearsal and single-level processing. *Journal of Verbal Learning and Verbal Behavior, 16,* 665–681.

Rusiniak, K. W.; Hankins, W. G.; Garcia, J.; & Brett, L. P. (1979). Flavor-illness aversions: Potentiation of odor by taste in rats. *Behavioral and Neural Biology, 25,* 1–17.

Sachs, J. S. (1967). Recognition memory for syntactic and semantic aspects of connected discourse. *Perception and Psychophysics, 2,* 437–442.

Sacks, O. (1985). *The man who mistook his wife for a hat and other clinical tales.* New York, Harper.

St. Claire-Smith, R. (1979). The overshadowing of instrumental conditioning by a stimulus that predicts reinforcement better than the response. *Animal Learning & Behavior, 7,* 224–228.

Salame, P., & Baddeley, A. D. (1982). Disruption of short-term memory by unattended speech: Implications for the structure of short-term memory. *Journal of Verbal Learning and Verbal Behavior, 21,* 150–164.

Saltzman, I. J. (1949). Maze learning in the absence of primary reinforcement: A study of secondary reinforcement. *Journal of Comparative and Physiological Psychology, 42,* 161–173.

Sanders, F. K., & Young, J. Z. (1940). Learning and other functions of the higher nervous centres of sepia. *Journal of Neurophysiology, 3,* 501–526.

Sanders, G. S., & Simmons, W. L. (1983). Use of hypnosis to enhance eyewitness accuracy: Does it work? *Journal of Applied Psychology, 68,* 70–77.

Santa, J. L., & Lamwers, L. L. (1976). Where does the confusion lie? Comments on the Wiseman and Tulving paper. *Journal of Verbal Learning and Verbal Behavior, 15,* 53–57.

Savage-Rumbaugh, E. S.; Sevcik, R. A.; Brakke, K. E.; & Rumbaugh, D. M. (1990). Symbols: Their communicative use, comprehension, and combination by bonobos (*Pan paniscus*). In C. Rovee-Collier & L. P. Lipsitt (Eds.), *Advances in infancy research,* Vol. 6 (pp. 221–278). Norwood, NJ: Ablex.

Schacter, D. L. (1987). Implicit memory: History and current status. *Journal of Experimental Psychology: Learning, Memory, and Cognition, 13,* 501–518.

Schacter, D. L. (1992). Priming and multiple memory systems: Perceptual mechanisms of implicit memory. *Journal of Cognitive Neuroscience, 4,* 244–256.

Schacter, D. L. (1996). *Searching for memory: The brain, the mind, and the past.* New York: Basic Books.

Schacter, D. L. (1999). The seven sins of memory: Insights from psychology and cognitive neuroscience. *American Psychologist, 54,* 182–203.

Schacter, D. L.; Buckner, R. L.; Koutstaal, W.; Dale, A. M.; & Rosen, B. R. (1997). Late onset of anterior prefrontal activity during retrieval of veridical and illusory memories: An event-related fMRI study. *Neuroimage, 6*, 259–269.

Schacter, D. L.; Cooper, L. A.; & Delaney, S. M. (1990). Implicit memory for unfamiliar objects depends on access to structural descriptions. *Journal of Experimental Psychology: General, 119*, 5–24.

Schacter, D. L.; Eich, J. E.; & Tulving, E. (1978). Richard Semon's theory of memory. *Journal of Verbal Learning and Verbal Behavior, 17*, 721–743.

Schacter, D. L., & Tulving, E. (1994). What are the memory systems of 1994? In D. L. Schacter & E. Tulving (Eds.), *Memory systems 1994* (pp. 1–38). Cambridge, MA: MIT Press.

Schiff, R.; Smith, N.; & Prochaska, J. (1972). Extinction of avoidance in rats as a function of duration and number of blocked trials. *Journal of Comparative and Physiological Psychology, 81*, 356–359.

Schneiderman, N. (1966). Interstimulus interval function of the nictitating membrane response of the rabbit under delay versus trace conditioning. *Journal of Comparative and Physiological Psychology, 62*, 397–402.

Schoenfeld, W. N. (1950). An experimental approach to anxiety, escape and avoidance behavior. In P. H. Hock & J. Zubin (Eds.), *Anxiety.* New York: Grune & Stratton.

Schuster, R., & Rachlin, H. (1968). Indifference between punishment and free shock: Evidence for the negative law of effect. *Journal of the Experimental Analysis of Behavior, 11*, 777–786.

Schvaneveldt, R. W.; Durso, F. T.; Goldsmith, T. E.; Breen, T. J.; Cooke, N. M.; Tucker, R. G.; & Demaio, J. C. (1985). Measuring the structure of expertise. *International Journal of Man-Machine Studies, 23*, 699–728.

Schwartz, B. L. (1994). Sources of information in metamemory: Judgments of learning and feelings of knowing. *Psychonomic Bulletin and Review, 1*, 357–375.

Schwartz, B. L., & Metcalfe, J. (1992). Cue familiarity but not target retrievability enhances feeling-of-knowing judgments. *Journal of Experimental Psychology: Learning, Memory, and Cognition, 18*(5), 1074–1083.

Schwartz, B.L., & Smith, S. M. (1997). The retrieval of related information influences tip-of-the-tongue states. *Journal of Memory and Language, 36*, 68–86.

Schweickert, R., & Boruff, B. (1986). Short-term memory capacity: Magic number or magic spell? *Journal of Experimental Psychology: Learning, Memory, and Cognition, 12*, 419–425.

Scoville, W. N. B., & Milner, B. (1957). Loss of recent memory after bilateral hippocampal lesions. *Journal of Neurology, Neurosurgery, and Psychiatry, 20*, 11–21.

Seligman, M. E. P. (1969). Control group and conditioning: A comment on operationism. *Psychological Review, 76*, 484–491.

Seligman, M. E. P. (1970). On the generality of the laws of learning. *Psychological Review, 77*(5), 406–418.

Seligman, M. E. P. (1975). *Helplessness: On depression, development, and death.* San Francisco: Freeman.

Seligman, M. E. P., & Campbell, B. A. (1965). Effect of intensity and duration of punishment on extinction of an avoidance response. *Journal of Comparative and Physiological Psychology, 59*, 295–297.

Seligman, M. E. P., & Hager, J. L. (Eds.) (1972). *Biological boundaries of learning.* Englewood Cliffs, NJ: Prentice-Hall.

Seligman, M. E. P., & Johnston, J. C. (1973). A cognitive theory of avoidance learning. In F. J. McGuigan & D. B. Lumsden (Eds.), *Contemporary approaches to conditioning and learning* (pp. 69–110). Washington DC: Winston.

Seward, J. P. (1949). An experimental analysis of latent learning. *Journal of Experimental Psychology, 39*, 177–186.

Seyfarth, R. M., & Cheney, D. L. (1986). Vocal development in vervet monkeys. *Animal Behaviour, 34*, 1640–1658.

Seyfarth, R. M., & Cheney, D. L. (1997). Behavioral mechanisms underlying vocal communication in nonhuman primates. *Animal Learning & Behavior, 25*, 249–267.

Seyfarth, R. M.; Cheney, D. L.; & Marler, P. (1980). Monkey responses to three different alarm calls: Evidence for predator classification and semantic communication. *Science, 210*, 801–803.

Shallice, T., & Warrington, E. K. (1970). Independent functioning of verbal memory stores: A neuropsychological study. *Quarterly Journal of Experimental Psychology, 22*, 261–273.

Shaughnessy, J. J. (1976). Persistence of the spacing effect in free recall under varying incidental learning conditions. *Memory and Cognition, 4*, 369–377.

Shaw, J. S., III; Bjork, R. A.; & Handal, A. (1995). Retrieval-induced forgetting in an eyewitness paradigm. *Psychonomic Bulletin & Review, 2*, 249–253.

Sheffield, F. D. (1966). A drive-induction theory of reinforcement. In R. N. Haber (Ed.), *Current research and theory in motivation* (pp. 98–111). New York: Rinehart & Winston.

Sheffield, F. D., & Roby, T. B. (1950). Reward value of a nonnutritive sweet taste. *Journal of Comparative and Physiological Psychology, 43,* 471–481.

Sheffield, F. D.; Roby, T. B.; & Campbell, B. A. (1954). Drive-reduction versus consummatory behavior as determinants of reinforcement. *Journal of Comparative and Physiological Psychology, 47,* 349–354.

Sheffield, F. D.; Wulff, J. J.; & Backer, R. (1951). Reward value of copulation without sex-drive reduction. *Journal of Comparative and Physiological Psychology, 44,* 3–8.

Shepard, R. N. (1967). Recognition memory for words, sentences, and pictures. *Journal of Verbal Learning and Verbal Behavior, 6,* 156–163.

Shepard, R. N. (1978). The mental image. *American Psychologist, 33,* 125–137.

Shepard, R. N., & Metzler, J. (1971). Mental rotation of three-dimensional objects. *Science, 171,* 701–703.

Shepp, B. E., & Eimas, P. D. (1964). Intradimensional and extradimensional shifts in the rat. *Journal of Comparative and Physiological Psychology, 57,* 357–361.

Shepp, B. E., & Schrier, A. M. (1969). Consecutive intradimensional and extradimensional shifts in monkeys. *Journal of Comparative and Physiological Psychology, 67,* 199–203.

Sherry, D. F.; Krebs, J. R.; & Cowie, R. J. (1981). Memory for the location of stored food in marsh tits. *Animal Behavior, 29,* 1260–1266.

Shettleworth, S. (1988). Foraging as operant behavior and operant behavior as foraging: What have we learned? In G. H. Bower (Ed.), *The psychology of learning and motivation: Advances in research and theory,* (1–49). New York: Academic Press.

Shiffren, R. N. (1973). Information persistence in short-term memory. *Journal of Experimental Psychology, 100,* 39–49.

Shimamura, A. P., & Squire, L. R. (1986). Memory and metamemory: A study of the feeling-of-knowing phenomenon in amnesic patients. *Journal of Experimental Psychology: Learning, Memory, and Cognition, 12,* 452–460.

Shulman, H. G. (1972). Semantic confusion errors in short-term memory. *Journal of Verbal Learning and Verbal Behavior, 11,* 221–227.

Sidman, M. (1953). Avoidance conditioning with brief shock and no exteroceptive warning signal. *Science, 118,* 157–158.

Sidman, M. (1962). Classical avoidance without a warning stimulus. *Journal of the Experimental Analysis of Behavior, 5,* 97–104.

Siegel, S.; (1989). Pharmacological conditioning and drug effects. In A. J. Goudie & M. W. Emmett-Oglesby (Eds.), *Psychoactive drugs: Tolerance and sensitization.* Clifton, NJ: Humana Press.

Siegel, S., & Allan, L. G. (1996). The widespread influence of the Rescorla-Wagner model. *Psychonomic Bulletin and Review, 3,* 314–321.

Siegel, S., & Domjan, M. (1971). Backward conditioning as an inhibitory procedure. *Learning and Motivation, 2,* 1–11.

Siegel, S.; Hinson, R. E.,; Krank, M. D.; & McCully, J. (1982). Heroin "overdose" death: Contribution of drug-associated environmental cues. *Science, 216,* 436–437.

Silva, F. J.; Silva, K. M.; & Pear, J. J. (1992). Sign-versus goal-tracking: Effects of conditioned-stimulus-to-unconditioned-stimulus distance. *Journal of the Experimental Analysis of Behavior, 57,* 17–31.

Silva, F. J.; Timberlake, W.; & Gont, R. S. (1998). Spatiotemporal characteristics of serial CSs and their relation to search modes and response form. *Animal Learning & Behavior, 26,* 299–312.

Silva, K., & Timberlake, W. (1998). A behavior systems view of responding to probe stimuli during an inter-food clock. *Animal Learning & Behavior, 26,* 313–325.

Singer, M., & Rosenberg, S. T. (1973). The role of grammatical relations in the abstraction of linguistic ideas. *Journal of Verbal Learning and Verbal Behavior, 12,* 273–284.

Skinner, B. F. (1938). *The behavior of organisms.* New York: Appleton-Century-Crofts.

Skinner, B. F. (1948). Superstition in the pigeon. *Journal of Experimental Psychology, 38,* 168–172.

Skinner, B. F. (1966). The phylogeny and ontogeny of behavior. *Science, 11,* 159–166.

Slamecka, N. J. (1964). An inquiry into the doctrine of remote associations. *Psychological Review, 71,* 61–77.

Slamecka, N. J., & Graf, P. (1978). The generation effect: Delineation of a phenomenon. *Journal of Experimental Psychology: Human Learning and Memory, 4,* 592–604.

Smith, E. E.; Shoben, E. J.; & Rips, L. J. (1974). Structure and process in semantic memory: A feature model for semantic decisions. *Psychological Review, 81,* 214–241.

Smith, J. W. (1991). Counterconditioning methods. In J. A. Cocores (Ed.), *The clinical management of nicotine dependence.* New York: Springer.

Smith, M. C.; Coleman, S. R.; & Gormezano, I. (1969). Classical conditioning of the rabbit's nictitating membrane response at backward, simultaneous and forward CS–US intervals. *Journal of Comparative and Physiological Psychology, 69,* 226–231.

Smith, S. M.; Glenberg, A. M.; & Bjork, R. A. (1978). Environmental context and human memory. *Memory and Cognition, 6,* 342–353.

Snyder, H. L., & Hulse, S. H. (1961). Effects of volume of reinforcement and number of consummatory responses on licking and running behavior. *Journal of Experimental Psychology, 61,* 474–479.

Solomon, R. L.; Kamin, L. J.; & Wynne, L. C. (1953). Traumatic avoidance learning: The outcomes of several extinction procedures with dogs. *Journal of Abnormal and Social Psychology, 48,* 291–302.

Solomon, R. L., & Turner, L. H. (1962). Discriminative classical conditioning in dogs paralyzed by curare can later control discriminative avoidance responses in normal states. *Psychological Review, 69,* 202–219.

Solomon, R. L., & Wynne, L. C. (1953). Traumatic avoidance learning: Acquisition in normal dogs. *Psychological Monographs, 67* (Whole No. 354).

Solomon, R. L., & Wynne, L. C. (1954). Traumatic avoidance learning: The principles of anxiety conservation and partial irreversibility. *Psychological Review, 61,* 353–385.

Soltysik, S. (1971). The effect of satiation upon conditioned and unconditioned salivary responses. *Acta Biological Experimentation, 31,* 59–63.

Spear, N. E. (1970). Verbal learning and retention. In M. R. D'Amato (Ed.), *Experimental psychology: Methodology, psychophysics, and learning.* New York: McGraw-Hill.

Spear, N. E. (1971). Forgetting as retrieval failure. In W. K. Honig & P. N. R. James (Eds.), *Animal memory.* New York: Academic Press.

Spear, N. E. (1973). Retrieval of memory in animals. *Psychological Review, 80,* 163–194.

Spear, N. E. (1976). Retrieval of memories. In W. K. Estes (Ed.), *Handbook of learning and cognitive processes, Vol. IV, Attention and memory.* Hillsdale, NJ: Erlbaum.

Spear, N. E. (1978). *The processing of memories: Forgetting and retention.* Hillsdale, NJ: Erlbaum.

Spear, N. E. (1981). Extending the domain of memory retrieval. In N. E. Spear & R. R. Miller (Eds.), *Information processing in animals: Memory mechanisms.* Hillsdale, NJ: Erlbaum.

Spear, N. E.; Gordon, W. C.; & Martin, P. A. (1973). Warm-up decrement as failure in memory retrieval in the rat. *Journal of Comparative and Physiological Psychology, 85,* 601–614.

Spence, K. W. (1936). The nature of discrimination learning in animals. *Psychological Review, 43,* 427–449.

Spence, K. W. (1937). The differential response in animals to stimuli varying within a single dimension. *Psychological Review, 44,* 430–444.

Spence, K. W. (1945). An experimental test of the continuity and non-continuity theories of discrimination learning. *Journal of Experimental Psychology, 35,* 253–266.

Spence, K. W. (1956). *Behavior theory and conditioning.* New Haven: Yale University Press.

Spence, K. W., & Ross, L. E. (1959). A methodological study of the form and latency of eyelid responses in conditioning. *Journal of Experimental Psychology, 58,* 376–385.

Sperling, G. (1960). The information available in brief visual presentations. *Psychological Monographs, 74* (Whole No. 11).

Sperling, G., & Speelman, R. G. (1970). Acoustic similarity and auditory short-term memory: Experiments and a model. In D. A. Norman (Ed.), *Models of human memory.* New York: Academic Press.

Sperling, S. E., & Perkins, M. L. (1979). Autoshaping with common and distinctive stimulus elements, compact and dispersed arrays. *Journal of the Experimental Analysis of Behavior, 31,* 383–394.

Spetch, M. L.; Wilkie, D. M.; & Pinel, P. J. P. (1981). Backward conditioning: A reevaluation of the empirical evidence. *Psychological Bulletin, 89,* 163–175.

Spivey, J. E., & Hess, D. T. (1968). Effect of partial reinforcement trial sequences on extinction performance. *Psychonomic Science, 10,* 375–376.

Squier, L. H. (1969). Autoshaping key responses with fish. *Psychonomic Science, 17,* 177–178.

Squire, L. R. (1987). *Memory and brain.* New York: Oxford University Press.

Squire, L. R. (1992). Memory and the hippocampus: A synthesis from findings with rats, monkeys, and humans. *Psychological Review, 99,* 195–231.

Staats, A. W.; Staats, C. K.; & Heard, W. G. (1959). Language conditioning of meaning to meaning using semantic generalization paradigm. *Journal of Experimental Psychology, 57,* 187–192.

Stabler, J. R. (1962). Performance in instrumental conditioning as a joint function of time of deprivation and sucrose concentration. *Journal of Experimental Psychology, 63,* 248–253.

Staddon, J. E. R. (1979). Operant behavior as adaptation to constraint. *Journal of Experimental Psychology: General, 108,* 48–67.

Standing, L.; Conezio, J.; & Haber, R. N. (1970). Perception and memory for pictures: Single trial learning of 2560 visual stimuli. *Psychonomic Science, 19,* 73–74.

Stein, B. S. (1978). Depth of processing reexamined: The effects of the precision of encoding and test appropriateness. *Journal of Verbal Learning and Verbal Behavior, 17,* 165–174.

Stein, L.; Xue, B. G.; & Belluzzi, J. D. (1993). A cellular analogue of operant conditioning. *Journal of the Experimental Analysis of Behavior, 60,* 41–53.

Steiner, J. (1967). Observing responses and uncertainty reduction. *Quarterly Journal of Experimental Psychology, 19,* 18–29.

Sternberg, S. (1966). High speed scanning in human memory. *Science, 153,* 652–654.

Sternberg, S. (1967). Retrieval of contextual information from memory. *Psychonomic Science, 8,* 55–56.

Sternberg, S. (1969). Memory scanning: Mental processes revealed by reaction-time experiments. *American Scientist, 57,* 421–457.

Sternberg, S. (1975). Memory scanning: New findings and current controversies. *Quarterly Journal of Experimental Psychology, 27,* 1–32.

Strobel, C. F. (1967). Behavioral aspects of circathan rhythms. In J. Zubin & H. F. Hunt (Eds.), *Comparative psychopathology.* New York: Grune & Stratton.

Struhsaker, T. T. (1967). Auditory communication among vervet monkeys (*Cercopithecus aethiops*). In S. A. Altmann (Ed.), *Social communication among primates* (pp. 281–324). Chicago: University of Chicago Press.

Sulzer-Azaroff, B., & Mayer, R. (1977). *Applying behavior-analysis procedures with children and adults.* New York: Rinehart & Winston.

Sutherland, N. S., & Mackintosh, N. J. (1971). *Mechanisms of animal discrimination learning.* New York: Academic Press.

Suzuki, S.; Aucerinos, G.; & Black, A. H. (1980). Stimulus control of spatial behavior on the eight arm maze in rats. *Learning and Motivation, 11,* 1–18.

Swartzentruber, D. (1995). Modulatory mechanisms in Pavlovian conditioning. *Animal Learning & Behavior, 23,* 123–143.

Teichner, W. H. (1952). Experimental extinction as a function of the intertrial intervals during conditioning and extinction. *Journal of Experimental Psychology, 44,* 170–178.

Terrace, H. S. (1973). Classical conditioning. In J. A. Nevin & G. S. Reynolds (Eds.), *The study of behavior: Learning, motivation, emotion and instinct.* Glenview, IL: Scott Foresman.

Terry, W. S., & Wagner, A. R. (1975). Short-term memory for "surprising" versus "expected" unconditioned stimuli in Pavlovian conditioning. *Journal of Experimental Psychology: Animal Behavior Processes, 1,* 122–133.

Theios, J.; Smith, P. G.; Haviland, S. E.; Traupmann, J.; & Moy, M. C. (1973). Memory scanning as a serial self-terminating process. *Journal of Experimental Psychology, 97,* 323–336.

Thomas, D. R. (1962). The effects of drive and discrimination training on stimulus generalization. *Journal of Experimental Psychology, 64,* 24–28.

Thomas, D. R.; Freeman, F.; Svinicki, J. G.; Burr, D. E. S.; & Lyons, J. (1970). Effects of extradimensional training on stimulus generalization. *Journal of Experimental Psychology Monograph, 83,* 1–21.

Thomas, D. R., & King, R. A. (1959). Stimulus generalization as function of level of motivation. *Journal of Experimental Psychology, 57,* 323–328.

Thomas, D. R., & Lopez, L. J. (1962). The effects of delayed testing on generalization slope. *Journal of Comparative and Physiological Psychology, 55,* 541–544.

Thomas, D. R., & Switalski, R. W. (1966). Comparison of stimulus generalization following variable-ratio and variable-interval training. *Journal of Experimental Psychology, 71,* 236–240.

Thomas, D. R.; Windell, B. T.; Bakke, I.; Kreye, J.; Kimose, E.; & Aposhyan, H. (1985). Long-term memory in pigeons: I. The role of discrimination difficulty assessed by reacquisition measures. II. The role of stimulus modality assessed by generalization slope. *Learning and Motivation, 16,* 464–477.

Thomas, M. H., & Wang, A. Y. (1996). Learning by the keyword mnemonic: Looking for long-term benefits. *Journal of Experimental Psychology: Applied, 2,* 330–342.

Thompson, C. P.; Hamlin, V. J.; & Roenker, D. L. (1972). A comment on the role of clustering in free recall. *Journal of Experimental Psychology, 94,* 108–109.

Thompson, R. F. (1986). The neurobiology of learning and memory. *Science, 233,* 941–947.

Thompson, R. F. (1990). Neural mechanisms of classical conditioning in mammals. *Philosophical Transactions of the Royal Society (London), Series B, 329,* 161–170.

Thompson, R. F.; Hicks, L. H.; & Shvyrok, U. B. (1980). *Neural mechanisms of goal directed behavior and learning.* New York: Academic Press.

Thomson, D. M., & Tulving, E. (1970). Associative encoding and retrieval: Weak and strong cues. *Journal of Experimental Psychology, 86,* 255–262.

Thorndike, E. L. (1898). Animal intelligence: An experimental study of the associative process in animals. *Psychological Review Monograph Supplement, 2,* 8.

Thorndike, E. L. (1911). *Animal intelligence.* New York: Macmillan.

Thorndike, E. L. (1913). *Educational psychology, Vol. II: The psychology of learning.* New York: Teachers College, Columbia University.

Thorndike, E. L., & Lorge, I. (1944). *The teacher's word book of 30,000 words.* New York: Columbia University Press.

Thune, L. E. (1950). The effect of different types of preliminary activities on subsequent learning of paired associates material. *Journal of Experimental Psychology, 40,* 423–438.

Timberlake, W. (1980). A molar equilibrium theory of learned performance. In G. H. Bower (Ed.), *The psychology of learning and motivation,* Vol. 14. New York: Academic Press.

Timberlake, W. (1983). Rats' responses to a moving object related to food or water: A behavior-systems analysis. *Animal Learning & Behavior, 11,* 309–320.

Timberlake, W. (1984). Behavior regulation and learned performance: Some misapprehensions and disagreements. *Journal of the Experimental Analysis of Behavior, 41,* 355–375.

Timberlake, W. (1993). Behavior systems and reinforcement: An integrative approach. *Journal of the Experimental Analysis of Behavior, 41,* 355–375.

Timberlake, W. (1994). Behavior systems, associationism, and Pavlovian conditioning. *Psychonomic Bulletin and Review, 1,* 405–420.

Timberlake, W., & Allison, J. (1974). Response deprivation: An empirical approach to instrumental performance. *Psychological Review, 81,* 146–164.

Timberlake, W., & Farmer-Dougan, V. A. (1991). Reinforcement in applied settings: Figuring out ahead of time what will work. *Psychological Bulletin, 110,* 379–391.

Timberlake, W., & Lucas, G. A. (1989). Behavior systems and learning: From misbehavior to general principles. In S. B. Klein & R. R. Mowrer (Eds.), *Contemporary learning theories: Instrumental conditioning theory and the impact of biological constraints on learning* (pp. 191–223). Hillsdale, NJ: Erlbaum.

Timberlake, W.; Wahl, G.; & King, D. (1982). Stimulus and response contingencies in the misbehavior of rats. *Journal of Experimental Psychology: Animal Behavior Processes, 8,* 62–85.

Tinbergen, N. (1951). *The study of instinct.* Oxford: Clarendon Press.

Tinbergen, N. (1952). The curious behavior of the stickleback. *Scientific American, 187,* 22–60.

Tolman, E. C., & Honzik, C. H. (1930). Introduction and removal of reward, and maze performance in rats. *University of California Publications in Psychology, 4,* 257–275.

Tomback, D. F. (1983). Nutcrackers and pines: Coevolution or coadaptation? In H. Nitecki (Ed.), *Coevolution.* Chicago: University of Chicago Press.

Tombaugh, T. N. (1966). Resistance to extinction as a function of the interaction between training and extinction delays. *Psychological Reports, 19,* 791–798.

Tombaugh, T. N. (1970). A comparison of the effects of immediate reinforcement, constant delay of reinforcement, and partial delay of reinforcement on performance. *Canadian Journal of Psychology, 24,* 276–288.

Tomie, A. (1976). Interference with autoshaping by prior context conditioning. *Journal of Experimental Psychology: Animal Behavior Processes, 2,* 232–234.

Trabasso, T.; Deutsch, J. A.; & Gelman, R. (1966). Attention and discrimination learning of young children. *Journal of Experimental Child Psychology, 4,* 9.

Tracy, W. K. (1970). Wavelength generalization and preference in monochromatically reared ducklings. *Journal of the Experimental Analysis of Behavior, 13,* 163–178.

Tranberg, D. K., & Rilling, M. (1980). Delay interval illumination changes interfere with pigeon short-term memory. *Journal of the Experimental Analysis of Behavior, 33,* 33–49.

Trapold, M. A., & Fowler, H. (1960). Instrumental escape performance as a function of the intensity of noxious stimulation. *Journal of Experimental Psychology, 60,* 323–326.

Trapold, M. A., & Spence, K. W. (1960). Performance changes in eyelid conditioning as related to the motivational and reinforcing properties of the UCS. *Journal of Experimental Psychology, 59,* 209–213.

Treisman, A. M. (1960). Contextual cues in selective listening. *Quarterly Journal of Experimental Psychology, 12,* 242–248.

Treisman, A. M. (1964). Verbal cues, language, and meaning in selective attention. *American Journal of Psychology, 77,* 206–219.

Treisman, A. M. (1969). Strategies and models for selective attention. *Psychological Review, 76,* 282–299.

Treisman, A. M., & Geffen, G. (1967). Selective attention: Perception or response? *Quarterly Journal of Experimental Psychology, 19,* 1–17.

Tulving, E. (1962). Subjective organization in free recall of "unrelated words." *Psychological Review, 69,* 344–354.

Tulving, E. (1968). When is recall higher than recognition? *Psychonomic Science, 10,* 53–54.

Tulving, E. (1972). Episodic and semantic memory. In E. Tulving & W. Donaldson (Eds.), *Organization and memory.* New York: Academic Press.

Tulving, E. (1983). *Elements of episodic memory.* Oxford: Clarendon Press/Oxford University Press.

Tulving, E., & Osler, S. (1968). Effectiveness of retrieval cues in memory for words. *Journal of Experimental Psychology, 77,* 593–601.

Tulving, E., & Pearlstone, Z. (1966). Availability versus accessibility of information in memory for words. *Journal of Verbal Learning and Verbal Behavior, 5,* 381–391.

Tulving, E., & Schacter, D. L. (1990). Priming and human memory systems. *Science, 247,* 301–306.

Tulving, E.; Schacter, D. L.; & Stark, H. A. (1982). Priming effects in word-fragment completion are independent of recognition memory. *Journal of Experimental Psychology: Learning, Memory, and Cognition, 8,* 336–342.

Tulving, E.; Schacter, D. L.; McLachlan, D. R.; & Moscovitch, M. (1988). Priming of semantic-autobiographical knowledge: A case study of retrograde amnesia. *Brain and Cognition, 8,* 3–20.

Tulving, E., & Thomson, D. M. (1973). Encoding specificity and retrieval processes in episodic memory. *Psychological Review, 80,* 352–373.

Tulving, E., & Watkins, O. C. (1977). Recognition failure of words with a single meaning. *Memory and Cognition, 5,* 513–522.

Twedt, H. M., & Underwood, B. J. (1959). Mixed vs. unmixed lists in transfer studies. *Journal of Experimental Psychology, 58,* 111–116.

Twitmyer, E. B. (1905). Knee-jerks without stimulation of the patellar tendon. *Psychological Bulletin, 2,* 43–44.

Uhl, C. N., & Garcia, E. E. (1969). Comparison of omission with extinction in response elimination in rats. *Journal of Comparative and Physiological Psychology, 69,* 554–562.

Uhl, C. N., & Young, A. G. (1967). Resistance to extinction as a function of incentive, percentage of reinforcement, and number of reinforced trials. *Journal of Experimental Psychology, 73,* 556–564.

Uhl, N. P. (1966). Intradimensional and extradimensional shifts as a function of amount of training and similarity between training and shift stimuli. *Journal of Experimental Psychology, 72,* 429–433.

Ulrich, R. E., & Azrin, N. H. (1962). Reflexive fighting in response to aversive stimulation. *Journal of the Experimental Analysis of Behavior, 5,* 511–520.

Underwood, B. J. (1945). The effect of successive interpolations on retroactive and proactive inhibition. *Psychological Monographs, 59* (Whole No. 273).

Underwood, B. J. (1952). Studies of distributed practice. VII. Learning and retention of serial nonsense lists as a function of intralist similarity. *Journal of Experimental Psychology, 44,* 80–87.

Underwood, B. J. (1957). Interference and forgetting. *Psychological Review, 64,* 49–59.

Underwood, B. J. (1961). Ten years of massed practice on distributed practice. *Psychological Review, 68,* 229–247.

Underwood, B. J. (1964). The representativeness of rote verbal learning. In A. W. Melton (Ed.), *Categories of human learning.* New York: Academic Press.

Underwood, B. J. (1966). Individual and group predictions of item difficulty for free learning. *Journal of Experimental Psychology, 71,* 673–679.

Underwood, B. J. (1969). Attributes of memory. *Psychological Review, 76,* 559–573.

Underwood, B. J.; Ekstrand, B. R.; & Keppel G. (1964). Studies of distributed practice. XXIII. Variations in response-term interference. *Journal of Experimental Psychology, 68,* 201–212.

Underwood, B. J.; Ekstrand, B. R.; & Keppel, G. (1965). An analysis of intralist similarity in verbal learning with experiments on conceptual similarity. *Journal of Verbal Learning and Verbal Behavior, 4,* 447–462.

Underwood, B. J., & Erlebacher, A. H. (1965). Studies of coding in verbal learning. *Psychological Monographs, 79* (Whole No. 606).

Underwood, B. J., & Goad, D. (1951). Studies of distributed practice. I. The influence of intralist similarity in serial learning. *Journal of Experimental Psychology, 42,* 125–134.

Underwood, B. J., & Keppel, G. (1962). One-trial learning? *Journal of Verbal Learning and Verbal Behavior, 1,* 1–13.

Underwood, B. J., & Keppel, G. (1963a). Coding processes in verbal learning. *Journal of Verbal Learning and Verbal Behavior, 1,* 250–257.

Underwood, B. J., & Keppel, G. (1963b). Retention as a function of degree of learning and letter sequence interference. *Psychological Monographs, 77* (Whole No. 567).

Underwood, B. J.; Runquist, W. N.; & Schulz, R. W. (1959). Response learning in paired associates lists as a function of intralist similarity. *Journal of Experimental Psychology, 58,* 70–78.

Underwood, B. J., & Schulz, R. W. (1960). *Meaningfulness and verbal learning.* Philadelphia: Lippincott.

Vallar, G., & Baddeley, A. D. (1984). Fractionation of working memory: Neuropsychological evidence for a phonological short-term store. *Journal of Verbal Learning and Verbal Behavior, 23,* 151–161.

Van Dijk, T. A., & Kintsch, W. (1983). *Strategies of discourse comprehension.* New York: Academic Press.

Von Fersen; Wynne, C. D. L.; Delius, J. D.; & Staddon, J. E. R. (1991).Transitive inference in pigeons. *Journal of Experimental Psychology: Animal Behavior Processes, 17,* 334–341.

Von Restorff, H. (1933). Über die Wirkung von Bereichsbildungen im Spurenfeld. *Psychologische Forschung, 18,* 299–342.

Von Wright, J. M. (1959). The effect of systematic changes of context stimuli on repeated recall. *Acta Psychologia, 16,* 59–68.

Wagner, A. R. (1959). The role of reinforcement and nonreinforcement in an "apparent frustration effect." *Journal of Experimental Psychology, 57,* 130–136.

Wagner, A. R. (1961). Effects of amount and percentage of reinforcement and number of acquisition trials on conditioning and extinction. *Journal of Experimental Psychology, 62,* 234–242.

Wagner, A. R. (1969). Stimulus validity and stimulus selection in associative learning. In W. K. Honig & N. J. Mackintosh (Eds.), *Fundamental issues in associative learning.* Halifax: Dalhousie University Press.

Wagner, A. R. (1976). Priming in STM: An information processing mechanism for self-generated or retrieval-generated depression in performance. In T. J. Tighe & R. N. Leaton (Eds.), *Habituation: Perspectives from child development, animal behavior, and neurophysiology.* Hillsdale, NJ: Erlbaum.

Wagner, A. R. (1978). Expectancies and priming in STM. In S. H. Hulse; H. Fowler; & W. K. Honig (Eds.), *Cognitive processes in animal behavior.* Hillsdale, NJ: Erlbaum.

Wagner, A. R. (1981). S.O.P.: A model of automatic memory processing in animal behavior. In N. E. Spear & R. R. Miller (Eds.), *Information processing in animals: Memory mechanisms.* Hillsdale, NJ: Erlbaum.

Wagner, A. R., & Brandon, S. E. (1989). Evolution of a structured connectionist model of Pavlovian conditioning (AESOP). In S. B. Klein & R. R. Mowrer (Eds.), *Contemporary learning theories: Pavlovian conditioning and the status of traditional learning theory* (pp. 233–265). Hillsdale, NJ: Erlbaum.

Wagner, A. R., & Larew, M. B. (1985). Opponent processes and Pavlovian inhibition. In R. R. Miller & N. E. Spear (Eds.), *Information processing in animals: Conditioned inhibition* (pp. 233–265). Hillsdale, NJ: Erlbaum.

Wagner, A. R.; Logan, F. A.; Haberlandt, K.; & Price, T. (1968). Stimulus selection in animal discrimination learning. *Journal of Experimental Psychology, 76,* 171–180.

Wagner, A. R.; Rudy, J. W.; & Whitlow, J. W. (1973). Rehearsal in animal conditioning. *Journal of Experimental Psychology, 97,* 407–426 (monograph).

Wagner, A. R., & Terry, W. S. (1975). Backward conditioning to a CS following an expected vs. a surprising UCS. *Animal Learning & Behavior, 3,* 370–374.

Walk, R. D., & Walters, C. P. (1973). Effect of visual deprivation on depth discrimination of hooded rats. *Journal of Comparative and Physiological Psychology, 85,* 559–563.

Wang, A. Y., & Thomas, M. H. (1992). The effect of imagery-based mnemonics on the long-term retention of Chinese characters. *Language Learning, 42,* 359–376.

Wang, A. Y., & Thomas, M. H. (1995). The effect of keywords on long-term retention: Help or hindrance? *Journal of Educational Psychology, 87,* 468–475.

Ward, L. B. (1937). Reminiscence and rote learning. *Psychological Monographs, 49* (Whole No. 220).

Warner, L. H. (1932). The association span of the white rat. *Journal of Genetic Psychology, 41,* 57–90.

Warrington, E. K., & Shallice, T. (1969). The selective impairment of auditory short-term memory. *Brain, 92,* 885–896.

Warrington, E. K., & Weisenkrantz, L. (1973). An analysis of short-term and long-term memory deficits in man. In J. A. Deutsch (Ed.), *The physiological basis of memory* (pp. 365–395). New York: Academic Press.

Warrington, E. K., & Weisenkrantz, L. (1982). Amnesia: A disconnection syndrome? *Neuropsychologia, 20,* 233–247.

Wasserman, E. A. (1973). The effect of redundant contextual stimuli on autoshaping the pigeon's keypeck. *Animal Learning & Behavior, 1,* 198–206.

Wasserman, E. A., & Astley, S. L. (1994). A behavioral analysis of concepts: Its application to pigeons and children. In D. L. Medin (Ed.), *The psychology of learning and motivation: Advances in research and theory,* Vol. 31 (pp. 73–132). New York: Academic.

Wasserman, E. A.; DeVolder, C. L.; & Coppage, D. L. (1992). Non-similarity-based conceptualization in pigeons via secondary or mediated generalization. *Psychological Science, 3,* 374–379.

Watkins, M. J. (1974). When is recall spectacularly higher than recognition? *Journal of Experimental Psychology, 102,* 161–163.

Watkins, M. J., & Tulving, E. (1975). Episodic memory: When recognition fails. *Journal of Experimental Psychology: General, 1,* 5–29.

Waugh, N. C. (1970). On the effective duration of a repeated word. *Journal of Verbal Learning and Verbal Behavior, 9,* 587–595.

Waugh, N. C., & Norman, D. A. (1965). Primary memory. *Psychological Review, 72,* 89–104.

Weaver, C. A. III (1993). Do you need a "flash" to form a flashbulb memory? *Journal of Experimental Psychology: General, 122,* 39–46.

Weinberg, H. I.; Wadsworth, J.; & Baron, R. S. (1983). Demand and the impact of leading questions on eyewitness testimony. *Memory and Cognition, 11,* 101–104.

Weingardt, K. R.; Loftus, E. F.; & Lindsay, D. S. (1995). Misinformation revisited: New evidence on the suggestibility of memory. *Memory & Cognition, 23,* 72–82.

Weingartner, H.; Miller, H.; & Murphy, D. L. (1977). Mood-state-dependent retrieval of verbal associations. *Journal of Abnormal Psychology, 86*(3), 276–284.

Weisman, R. G., & Litner, J. S. (1969). Positive conditioned reinforcement of Sidman avoidance behavior in rats. *Journal of Comparative and Physiological Psychology, 68,* 597–603.

Weiss, R. F. (1960). Deprivation and reward magnitude effects on speed throughout the goal gradient. *Journal of Experimental Psychology, 60,* 384–390.

Welsh, D. H.; Bernstein, D. J.; & Luthans, F. (1992). Application of the Premack principle of reinforcement to the quality performance of service employees. *Journal of Organizational Behavior Management, 13,* 9–32.

Wheeler, M. A. (1995). Improvement in recall over time without repeated testing: Spontaneous recovery revisited. *Journal of Experimental Psychology: Learning, Memory, and Cognition, 21,* 173–184.

Whitlow, J. W. (1976). The dynamics of episodic processing in Pavlovian conditioning. In D. L. Medin, W. A. Roberts, & R. T. Davis (Eds.), *Processes of animal memory.* Hillsdale, NJ: Erlbaum.

Whitlow, J. W., & Estes, W. K. (1979). Judgments of relative frequency in relation to shifts of event frequencies: Evidence for a limited-capacity model. *Journal of Experimental Psychology: Human Learning and Memory, 5,* 395–408.

Whitlow, J. W., & Skaar, E. (1979). The role of numerosity in judgments of overall frequency. *Journal of Experimental Psychology: Human Learning and Memory, 5,* 409–421.

Wickelgren, W. A. (1966). Distinctive features and errors in short-term memory for English consonants. *Journal of the Acoustical Society of America, 39,* 388–398.

Wickelgren, W. A. (1977). *Learning and memory.* Englewood Cliffs, NJ: Prentice-Hall.

Wickelgren, W. A. (1979). *Cognitive psychology.* Englewood Cliffs, NJ: Prentice-Hall.

Wickens, D. D. (1970). Encoding categories of words: An empirical approach to meaning. *Psychological Review, 77,* 1–15.

Wickens, D. D. (1972). Characteristics of word encoding. In A. W. Melton & E. Martin (Eds.), *Coding processes in human memory.* Washington, DC: Winston.

Wiesel, T. N., & Hubel, D. H. (1965). Comparison of the effects of unilateral and bilateral eye closure on cortical unit responses in kittens. *Journal of Neurophysiology, 28,* 1029–1040.

Wiesel, T. N., & Hubel, D. H. (1965). Extent of recovery from the effects of visual deprivation in kittens. *Journal of Neurophysiology, 28,* 1060–1072.

Wike, E. L.; Mellgren, R. L.; & Wike, S. S. (1968). Runway performance as a function of delayed reinforcement and delayed box confinement. *Psychological Record, 18,* 9–18.

Wilcoxon, H. C.; Dragoin, W. B.; and Kral, P. A. (1971). Illness-induced aversions in rats and quail: Relative salience of visual and gustatory cues. *Science, 171,* 826–828.

Williams, B. A. (1974). The role of local interactions in behavioral contrast. *Bulletin of the Psychonomic Society, 4,* 543–545.

Williams, B. A. (1976). Behavioral contrast as a function of the temporal location of reinforcement. *Journal of the Experimental Analysis of Behavior, 26,* 57–64.

Williams, D. R. (1965). Classical conditioning and incentive motivation. In W. F. Prokasy (Ed.), *Classical conditioning: A symposium* (pp. 340–357). New York: Appleton-Century-Crofts.

Williams, D. R., & Williams, H. (1969). Automaintenance in the pigeon: Sustained pecking despite contingent non-reinforcement. *Journal of the Experimental Analysis of Behavior, 12,* 511–520.

Williams, S. B. (1938). Resistance to extinction as a function of the number of reinforcements. *Journal of Experimental Psychology, 23,* 506–521.

Wills, S., & Mackintosh, N. J. (1998). Peak shift on an artificial dimension. *The Quarterly Journal of Experimental Psychology, 51B,* (1), 1–31.

Wingfield, A. (1973). Effects of serial position and set size in auditory recognition memory. *Memory and Cognition, 1,* 53–55.

Wingfield, A., & Bolt, R. A. (1970). Memory search for multiple targets. *Journal of Experimental Psychology, 85,* 45–50.

Winograd, E., & Neisser, U. (1992). *Affect and accuracy in recall: Studies of flashbulb memories.* New York: Cambridge University Press.

Wiseman, S., & Tulving, E. (1976). Encoding specificity: Relation between recall superiority and recognition failure. *Journal of Experimental Psychology: Human Learning and Memory, 2,* 349–361.

Wittgenstein, L. (1953). *Philosophical investigations.* New York: Macmillan.

Wollen, K. A.; Weber, A.; & Lowry, D. (1972). Bizarreness versus interaction of mental images as determinants of learning. *Cognitive Psychology, 3,* 518–523.

Wolpe, J. (1958). *Psychotherapy by reciprocal inhibition.* Stanford, CA: Stanford University Press.

Wolpe, J. (1990). *The practice of behavior therapy.* Elmsford, NY: Pergamon Press.

Woodard, W. T., & Bitterman, M. E. (1974). Autoshaping in the goldfish. *Behavior Research Methods & Instrumentation, 6,* 409–410.

Wyckoff, L. B., Jr. (1952). The role of observing responses in discrimination learning: Part 1. *Psychological Review, 59,* 431–442.

Wyckoff, L. B., Jr. (1969). The role of observing responses in discrimination learning. In D. P. Hendry (Ed.), *Conditioned reinforcement* (pp. 237–260). Homewood, IL: Dorsey Press.

Wynne, J. D., & Brogden, W. J. (1962). Effect upon sensory preconditioning of backward, forward, and trace preconditioning training. *Journal of Experimental Psychology, 64,* 422–423.

Yates, F. A. (1966). *The art of memory.* London: Routledge & Kegan Paul.

Yerkes, R. M., & Morgulis, S. (1909). The method of Pavlov in animal psychology. *Psychological Bulletin, 6,* 257–273.

Young, R. K. (1962). Tests of three hypotheses about the effective stimulus in serial learning. *Journal of Experimental Psychology, 63,* 307–313.

Young, R. K., & Casey, M. (1964). Transfer from serial to paired-associate learning. *Journal of Experimental Psychology, 67,* 594–595.

Zeaman, D., & House, B. J. (1963). The role of attention in retardate discrimination learning. In N. R. Ellis (Ed.), *Handbook of mental deficiency: Psychological theory and research.* New York: McGraw-Hill.

Zelniker, T. (1971). Perceptual attenuation of an irrelevant auditory verbal input as measured by an involuntary verbal response in a selective-attention task. *Journal of Experimental Psychology, 87,* 52–56.

Zentall, T. R. (1973). Memory in the pigeon: Retroactive inhibition in a delayed matching task. *Bulletin of the Psychonomic Society, 1,* 126–128.

Zentall, T. R.; Collins, W.; & Hearst, E. (1971). Generalization gradients around a formerly positive S−. *Psychonomic Science, 22,* 257–259.

Zentall, T. R., & Sherburne, L. M. (1994). Transfer of value from S+ to S− in a simultaneous discrimination. *Journal of Experimental Psychology: Animal Behavior Processes, 20,* 176–183.

Ziff, D. R., & Capaldi, E. J. (1971). Amytal and the small trial, partial reinforcement effect: Stimulus properties of early trial nonrewards. *Journal of Experimental Psychology, 87,* 263–269.

Name Index

Adams, C., 153, 155
Adams, M. J., 295, 296
Ader, R., 2, 27
Akins, C. A., 36, 80
Allan, L. G., 74
Allison, J., 143–146, 147
Alptekin, S., 159
Amsel, A., 156–157, 159–160
Anderson, J. R., 223, 275, 302
Anderson, M. C., 310–311
Anderson, S. J., 310
Anger, D., 171–172
Antonitis, J. J., 139
Aposhyan, H., 202
Archer, E. J., 277
Ardrey, R., 10
Armus, H. L., 127
Asratyan, E. A., 87
Astley, S. L., 228, 229
Atkinson, R. C., 235–238, 244, 246, 249, 251, 256, 257, 308
Averbach, I., 240–241, 243
Axelrod, S., 163
Ayres, J. J. B., 35, 53, 66, 76, 185
Ayres, T. J., 245–246
Azrin, N. H., 99, 112, 153, 160–161, 162, 163

Backer, R., 138–139
Baddeley, A. D., 5, 237, 256–259, 260, 271, 279, 303, 305, 341
Bahrick, L., 317
Bahrick, H. P., 264–265, 266, 280–281
Baker, A. G., 53, 54

Bakke, I., 202
Balaz, M. A., 43, 89
Bales, S. L., 176, 177
Balsam, P. D., 89
Barker, A. N., 142
Barnet, R. C., 74, 75
Baron, A., 104, 176, 177
Baron, M. R., 120
Barsalou, L., 227
Batsche, C. J., 108
Batsche, G. M., 108
Battig, W. F., 271
Bauermeister, J. J., 142
Beach, F., 282
Beauchamp, R. D., 119–120
Beecroft, R. S., 30
Beery, R. G., 110
Begg, I., 274, 284
Bellezza, F. S., 271, 284
Belli, R. F., 314–315
Belluzzi, J. D., 124–125
Benjamin, A. S., 338
Benjamin, P. R., 182, 185
Berlyne, D. E., 140, 176, 191
Bernstein, D. J., 141–142
Bevan, P., 104
Bexton, W. H., 139
Bhatt, R. S., 228
Billings, F. J., 316, 317
Birch, D., 129
Birmingham, K. M., 159
Bitterman, M. E., 35, 68, 69, 70, 179, 188
Bjork, E. L., 5, 280, 301–302, 308, 310

Bjork, R. A., 5, 235, 246–247, 269, 279–281, 287, 294, 301–302, 306, 308, 310, 311, 338
Blanchard, R., 176, 177
Bleasdale, F. A., 338
Blesbois, E., 79
Blodgett, H. C., 148
Blond, J., 140
Blough, D. S., 205–206, 229
Boakes, R. A., 182
Boe, E. E., 121
Boies, S. J., 248
Bolles, R. C., 17, 41, 52, 122–123, 153
Boruff, B., 245
Bouton, M. E., 55, 69, 202, 206–207, 230
Bowe, C. A., 176
Bowen, J. N., 127
Bower, G. H., 110, 307
Boyes-Braem, P., 228–229
Bradshaw, C. M., 104
Brakke, K. E., 19
Brandon, S. E., 75, 188
Bransford, J. D., 275
Breitmeyer, B. G., 241
Breland, K., 123, 173–174, 174–175
Breland, M., 123, 173–174, 174–175
Bremer, D., 306
Brennan, M. J., 101
Brewer, V. R., 159
Britton, G. B., 79
Broadbent, D. E., 235
Brogden, W. J., 48, 84
Brooks, D. C., 55
Brown, A. S., 335

Subject Index